MODERN
MACROECONOMICS

MODERN MACROECONOMICS

Michael Parkin
& Robin Bade
University of Western Ontario

SECOND EDITION

Philip Allan

First published 1982 by
PHILIP ALLAN PUBLISHERS LIMITED
MARKET PLACE
DEDDINGTON
OXFORD OX5 4SE

Reprinted 1983, 1985, 1986

Second edition published 1988 by
PHILIP ALLAN PUBLISHERS LIMITED

British Library Cataloguing in Publication Data

Parkin, Michael, *1939–*
  Modern macroeconomics. — 2nd ed.
  1. Macroeconomics. Theories
  I. Title   II. Bade, Robin
  339.3'01

  ISBN 0-86003-077-6
  ISBN 0-86003-180-2 Pbk

Set by MHL Typesetting Ltd, Coventry
Printed and bound in Great Britain by the Camelot Press, Southampton

Contents

PART IV: Understanding the Facts

Preface to the First Edition

This book presents a comprehensive and up-to-date account of macroeconomics — that branch of economics which seeks to explain inflation, unemployment, interest rates, foreign exchange rates, the balance of payments and other related phenomena. Unlike any other book currently available at this level, a considerable amount of space and attention is devoted to developments that have taken place in the subject in the past ten years. The chief of these is the incorporation into macroeconomics of the rational expectations hypothesis. The rational expectations hypothesis is explained in simple, intuitive terms, and its implications for the determination of inflation, unemployment and economic stabilization policy are explained and analysed. The book does not only deal with the developments in macroeconomics that have taken place in the past decade. It also provides an account of the mainstream neoclassical synthesis which grew out of Keynesian and pre-Keynesian theories. In addition, it shows how the new macroeconomics relates to these earlier approaches. The book pays careful attention to the interrelations between the domestic economy and the rest of the world — open economy macroeconomics — and to the design and conduct of macroeconomic policy.

In presenting an account of modern macroeconomics, we have attempted to avoid the extremes of dry theory and passionate policy advocacy. Theory is presented in such a way that the reader may quickly and easily see its predictive content. Those predictions are checked against the facts, revealing in the process the extent to which a theory is capable of explaining the facts as well as its main shortcomings. Policy is handled by analysing the implications of pursuing the policy recommendations of different schools of thought in such a way that the reader may clearly see why it is that different economists reach different conclusions on these important questions.

The central purpose of the book is to make modern macroeconomics accessible to beginning and intermediate students. To this end, we have used the simplest available analytical techniques, intuitive explanations and, wherever possible, illustrations drawn directly from United Kingdom macroeconomic experience. The book is pitched for the most part at a level which we hope is appropriate for university students who are in their second undergraduate year, although large parts of the book will be easily understood by beginnning students; and other parts will be found useful by more advanced students who are looking for a simplified and intuitive explanation of material which is only otherwise available in journal articles. Indeed, in view of the lack of any alternative exposition (other than original research articles in learned journals) of much of the material that is presented here, the book will be found useful even by beginning graduate students who are looking for a broad overview of material which they will study in greater depth in their postgraduate courses, as well as by those whose formal study of economics was completed before the rational expectations revolution hit macroeconomics and who are now professional economists in government, industry and commerce and wish to be given a quick guided tour of this material.

The book is organized around three main themes — facts, theories and policies. The two introductory sections set out the facts that macroeconomics seeks to explain and also give an account of the ways in which macroeconomic phenomena are observed and measured. The core of the book deals with theory. It is organized around a series of progressively more comprehensive models of the economy, each of which has some merits in explaining a limited set of facts, but each of which also has some shortcomings which are highlighted. Following the development of alternative theories, macroeconomic policy — the problem of stabilizing output, employment and prices — is discussed at considerable length.

Macroeconomics is a controversial subject and economists often disagree vehemently on policy issues. Despite this, there is a considerable measure of agreement on most matters. There do, however, remain crucial issues that divide economists and, although it is a slight oversimplification, it seems resonably accurate to divide macroeconomists into two camps — Keynesians and Monetarists. One of us is widely regarded as being a Monetarist and, as a descriptive matter, neither of us can seriously quarrel about being so labelled. We have, nevertheless, tried to write a book which avoids falling into the trap of being a Monetarist tract. Some, no doubt, will conclude that we have failed. We have certainly not shied away from presenting alternative views on macroeconomic policy in the sharpest possible focus. We have attempted to do justice to the positions of each view and explain precisely what it is that each believes and why. Acceptance of the hypothesis that expectations are formed rationally is often regarded as being synonymous with Monetarism. The fact that this book, unlike any other at this level, presents an account of rational expectations (and a sympathetic one at that) will no doubt lead some to conclude that for that reason alone this book is a Monetarist tract. Such a view will be seen, on careful reflection, to be incorrect. There are rational expectations Keynesians (usually referred to as new Keynesians) as well as rational expectations Monetarists (usually referred to as New Classicals). Both of these strands in the literature are presented and explained.

This book would not have been completed without the help of a large number of people. Michael Cox (of the Virginia Polytechnic Institute) has been involved in the project from which the book has resulted since its inception and has read and commented upon substantial parts of the manuscript and provided many of the review questions. Bob Nobay (of the University of Liverpool) and our colleagues David Laidler and Stephen Margolis have provided extensive comments on various parts of the manuscript. We also benefited from the comments on some earlier drafts of what were, at the time, anonymous referees, but whom we now know to have been Brian Scarfe of the University of Alberta and James Pesando of the University of Toronto. Several generations of undergraduate students and graduate teaching assistants at the University of Western Ontario have been of considerable help in providing comments and criticisms upon various parts of the book at different stages of its development. We are expecially grateful to Rosalind Wong, Monica van Huystee and David Abramson. Jane McAndrew provided expert library and clerical assistance and research assistance was provided by Kevin Dowd and Eddie McDonnell. The many drafts and revisions of this book have been typed with great skill by Marg Gower, Yvonne Adams, Leslie Farrant and Brenda Campbell. Ann Hirst has provided the speediest and most thorough copy and production editing that we have ever seen. We are immensely indebted to them all.

Although out debts to all the people named above are considerable, we owe a special debt to Michael Sumner of the University of Salford. The contribution which he has made to this book is enormous. He read the complete penultimate and final drafts with meticulous care and supplied us with the most extensive comments on both style and substance, helping us to remove both blemishes and outright errors. Whatever merit this final product has is in no small measure to be credited to him. We do, of course, absolve him, and all our other helpers, from responsibility for the errors that remain.

Michael Parkin and Robin Bade
London, Ontario
March, 1982

Preface to the Second Edition

This second edition is a substantially revised version of *Modern Macroeconomics*. All the chapters have been revised and rethought to reflect new data, new research, readers' comments and suggestions, as well as out own ideas and efforts to improve the exposition and content of the book.

The single most important change in this edition is one of structure. In the first edition the body of macroeconomic theory was organized around the historical development of the subject — the classical, Keynesian, and modern rational expectations approaches. This revision organizes its presentation of theory around the three great concepts of aggregate demand, aggregate supply, and macroeconomic equilibrium. This broad way of thinking about the functioning economy in aggregate is itself relatively uncontroversial. Also, the theory of aggregate demand is in a relatively settled state. As a consequence, we are able to move quickly through the uncontroversial parts of macroeconomics and also present the alternative and competing theories of aggregate supply and macroeconomic equilibrium. Thus we can present a more streamlined and less taxonomic development of macroeconomic theory than was possible in the first edition. We can also focus more clearly on areas that are controversial and bring the nature of the controversies to the attention of the reader. This organization, however, permits us to cover the entire body of macroeconomic theory all the way through to the new rational expectations models, and can be completed in a half-year course.

In addition to organizing our presentation of macroeconomic theory in a more streamlined way, we have provided a more unified and coherent series of chapters that seek to use macroeconomic theory to understand the key facts about macroeconomic performance. Four chapters dealing with inflation, unemployment, output growth, and cycles, draw out the implications of economic theories and show how they account for the facts. The output growth chapter is new. The other chapters represent substantial reworkings and reorganizations and updating of material that was scattered throughout the first edition. The chapter on unemployment has been updated to reflect some interesting and potentially important new ideas.

The policy chapters have been expanded and there is an additional chapter on supply-side policies.

In developing this second edition we have been greatly helped by the many readers of both the first edition and the Canadian and United States versions. We are expecially grateful to Ben Benanke (Stanford University); Ronald Bodkin (University of Ottawa); Paul Boothe (University of Alberta); Laura Finestone (University of Rochester); David Gordon (University of Rochester); Gary Grant (Acadia University); Jeremy Greenwood (University of Western Ontario); Herschel Grossman (Brown University); Joseph Guerin (St. Joseph's University); Geoffrey Kingston (University of Queensland); John Lapp (North Carolina State University); David Laidler (University of Western Ontario); Glenn MacDonald (University of Western Ontario); Andrea Maneschi (Vanderbilt University); Stephen Margolis (North Carolina State University); Patrick Minford and Bob Nobay (University of Liverpool); Andrew Policano (University of Iowa); Nicholas Rowe (Carleton University); Michael Sumner (University of Sussex); Randall Wigle (University of Western Ontario); Ian Wooton (University of Western Ontario).

We have prepared a totally revised version of the Instructor's Manual which is available on request from the publisher. Also, a Study Guide has been prepared by Robin Bade to accompany this edition, which provides a wide range of questions of progressively increasing difficulty. It also provides worked examples to sample problems, as well as answers to all questions.

In preparing this second edition we have been greatly assisted by Catherine Parkin and Laura Noble. The numerous drafts of revisions have been handled with cheerfulness and skill by Yvonne Adams, Leslie Farrant, and Nancy Joslin. We are deeply indebted to them all.

Robin Bade
Michael Parkin
London, Ontario
January, 1988

Part I

INTRODUCTION

1

Macroeconomic Questions

This book is going to help you to get abreast of the current state of knowledge in macroeconomics. By the time that you have completed this introductory chapter you will be able to:

(a) State the questions which macroeconomics seeks to answer.
(b) Explain the macroeconomic problems facing the UK in the late 1980s.
(c) Distinguish between macroeconomic science, policy and popular debate.
(d) State the macroeconomic policy issues on which economists disagree.
(e) Describe the views of the leading schools of thought.

A. Macroeconomic Questions

Macroeconomic questions have changed over the years and have usually been motivated by a concern to understand the economic problems of the day.

(i) Inflation

The oldest macroeconomic question is, what determines the general level of prices? Or the very closely related question, what determines the rate of inflation (or the rate of deflation)? Concern over this issue goes back at least to the late Roman Empire, when rampant inflation was exper- 引得和此
ienced. In more modern times the world has had a chequered inflationary history. Following the period of European (particularly Spanish) coloniza-

3

tion of the Americas and the influx into Europe of vast quantities of gold, there was a substantial rise in the general level of prices in Europe and North America. This inflation went on well into the early seventeenth century. There then followed a period of price stability, which in turn was followed (from about 1750 to the early nineteenth century) by further very strong inflation. In the early part of the nineteenth century, following the Napoleonic wars, there was a period of falling prices. The next hundred years saw alternating periods of rising and falling prices but, over the century as a whole, there was remarkable price stability. Since the 1930s, prices have persistently risen and especially strongly so between the late 1960s and the early 1980s.[1] By the middle 1980s, more moderate inflation rates have returned to most of the developed countries.

The questions for macroeconomics are, why have there been periods of prolonged inflation and deflation? What has caused these major movements in the general level of prices? Can we predict future price level movements? How can we control inflation?

(ii) Unemployment

The second major question for macroeconomics is, what determines the percentage of the labour force that is unemployed? This problem became particularly acute in the late 1920s and 1930s when high and persistent unemployment dominated the entire world economy. In many countries unemployment hardly fell below 20 per cent for almost fifteen years. In the period immediately following the Second World War unemployment was, throughout the whole world, remarkably low. Its rate began to rise, however, during the 1960s and, in the 1970s and especially in the 1980s unemployment has again emerged as a major concern.

The questions for macroeconomics are, what determines the level of unemployment? Why does its rate fluctuate and why, at certain times, does unemployment remain persistently high? What actions, if any, can the government take to smooth out fluctuations in unemployment and lower its average rate?

(iii) Aggregate Output — GDP

What determines a country's level of aggregate output — or level of Gross Domestic Product — or GDP? The precise meaning of GDP will be given in Chapter 3. For now, and loosely speaking, you may think of GDP as a measure of the volume of the goods and services that can be bought with the income of all the individuals in the economy. Fluctuations in GDP give rise to fluctuations in the standard of living, and differences

---

1 An excellent account of the long-term movements in prices may be found in Anna J. Schwartz, 'Secular Price Change in Historical Perspective,' *Journal of Money, Credit and Banking*, Vol. V, No. 1, pt II (February 1973) pp. 243–69.

in average growth rates of GDP between countries produce large inter-country differences in living standards. Macroeconomics seeks to understand the reasons why there are persistent differences in GDP growth rates between countries and why there are fluctuations in GDP around its trend growth rate. Macroeconomics also seeks to understand how policy actions that governments might take may influence the growth and fluctuations in GDP.

(iv) Interest Rates

A fourth question which macroeconomics addresses is, what determines the level of interest rates? In a modern economy there are many rates of interest. In the study of macroeconomics it is customary to study average levels of interest rates but also to distinguish between short-term and long-term rates of interest. *Short-term* rates (or more simply, *short rates*) are the rates of interest paid and received on loans of a short-term or temporary nature — up to five years. *Long-term rates* are those on loans of more than five years — and could be on loans that run indefinitely. There is a tendency for all interest rates to move up and down together, but for short rates to fluctuate more strongly than long rates. An essential problem for macroeconomics is to understand what determines the general ups and downs in interest rates and why short-term rates fluctuate more than long-term rates. Macroeconomics also seeks to understand how actions of the government — such as, for example, financing government spending by borrowing — by creating a large deficit — affects interest rates.

(v) Balance of Payments and Foreign Exchange Rate

A fifth question is, what determines a country's balance of payments with the rest of the world? and a sixth, related question is, what determines the value of one country's currency in relation to that of another country? — that is, what determines the foreign exchange rate? These questions have a long history. Countries have been concerned with their balance of payments for as long as there has been international trade. In recent years fluctuations in foreign exchange rates have become a major issue.

Macroeconomics seeks to understand why foreign exchange rates and balance of payments fluctuate and also to determine the influence of government policy actions on these variables.

B. UK Macroeconomic Problems in the 1980s

It is evident that although some of the macroeconomic questions posed above have been more important at certain stages in history than at others, in recent years they have all taken on a considerable importance — not least in the UK.

(i) Inflation

As the 1980s opened the UK inflation rate was running at close to 20 per cent a year. The average rate of inflation for the 1970s had been in the double-digit region and it was widely expected that inflation in excess of 10 per cent would persist into the indefinite future. Double-digit inflation had come to be regarded as 'normal'. To almost everyone's surprise, by the middle-1980s inflation had been dramatically lowered.

This unexpected and large drop in the rate of inflation, though welcomed by many, presented problems for some. These were the people who had borrowed and locked themselves into loans with high rates of interest. Many businesses that borrowed money at interest rates in the high teens of per cents a year expected to be able to repay their loans and pay the interest on them with a rise in revenue from the sale of products whose prices were expected to rise at more than 10 per cent a year. When inflation collapsed and revenue growth also collapsed a large number of businesses found themselves in serious trouble and laid off their workers at an unprecedented rate.

(ii) Unemployment

Unemployment is *the* macroeconomic problem of the decade for the UK economy. Having opened the decade at a post-war historical high level of 6.8 per cent, inflation relentlessly climbed throughout the decade to almost 13 per cent. Not only is the average rate of unemployment historically very high, its regional distribution is very uneven. Unemployment rates in Scotland and Northern England, as well as Wales vastly exceed those in the South-east. It is this tremendous disparity of unemployment that has created the 'two-nation' description of the UK economy.

(iii) Aggregate Output — GDP

Aggregate output — GDP — fell for the first two years of the 1980s by a total of almost 3 per cent. By 1982 growth had begun to pick up again and there were two years of above-average growth, 1983 and 1985. The overall growth performance of the UK economy in the 1980s has been below its long-term historical trend. This state of affairs, though far from a disaster, stands in marked contrast to the one that we have become accustomed to — a situation in which income and consumption per head grow persistently year after year.

(iv) Interest Rates

The 1980s, like the 1970s before them, have been years of double-digit interest rates. Such high interest rates have been welcome, of course, by those doing the lending, but have been greeted with alarm by borrowers. Businessmen and farmers, as well as homeowners with mortgages, have experienced serious financial hardship as a result of the interest rate fluctuations that we have seen. Also, the UK's largest borrower, the government, has found its own deficit seriously worsened as a consequence of having to meet ever-increasing interest payments on its outstanding debt.

(v) Balance of Payments and (vi) Exchange Rate

Overall the UK balance of payments has not been a serious problem during the decade of the 1970s. There has been a slight deficit but, when expressed as a fraction of Gross Domestic Product, that deficit has been small.

What has been a problem is the movement in the foreign exchange rate of the pound. When the decade opened a pound was worth about 2 1/3 US dollars. At its low point the pound was worth less than 1.30.

Movements in foreign exchange rates, like movements in inflation rates and interest rates, have important effects on individuals and firms. Exporters, and those competing with foreign imports, usually make short-term gains when there is an unexpected drop in the value of the pound but those consuming imported goods, including consumers and those taking foreign holidays, suffer a short-term loss in such a situation.

We have now reviewed the major UK macroeconomic problems in the 1980s. We have reviewed seven years in which inflation dramatically collapsed; unemployment increased to levels unseen in more than half a century; real income growth was negative for two years and, for the decade as a whole, it was below the long-term average; and the foreign currency value of the pound declined dramatically. Thus as we approach the end of the 1980s, the macroeconomic questions for the UK are, why did we have so much inflation at the beginning of the decade and why did its rate collapse after 1983? Why has unemployment increased to and persisted at such historically high levels? Why has aggregate output grown at such a slow rate? Why have interest rates been so high and volatile* and why has the value of the pound declined so sharply against the dollar?

A related and more important set of questions, which are nonetheless harder to answer, are, what are the effects on inflation, unemployment, aggregate output growth, interest rates and the foreign exchange rate of the policies which the British government — and the Bank of England — might adopt, and how might policy be arranged so as to achieve steadier and more predictable inflation, lower unemployment, higher output growth, lower interest rates and a more stable and predictable value of the pound sterling? To what extent must the UK live with the market forces that influence and drive these variables, and to what extent can policy enable the UK to steer an independent and steadier course?

The questions set out in Section A, and the manifestation of those questions in the recent UK economic experience, provide the subject matter of macroeconomics.

C. Macroeconomic Science, Policy and the Popular Debate

We have seen, in the two previous sections of this chapter, that macroeconomics deals with things that people care about and that affect their well-being. As a result a great deal of macroeconomics features in the contemporary policy debate. Politicians offer their favoured solutions to the whole range of macroeconomic policy problems. Journalists — both in print and on the airwaves — add their voice to the chorus. Trade union leaders, prominent businessmen, public servants, and academics (whether trained in economics or not) all provide an endless stream of views on current macroeconomic problems. The contemporary macroeconomic policy debate is so important and, at times, so exciting that it becomes difficult for students of economics — whether they are just embarking on the subject or are seasoned professionals — to pursue their science with objectivity and untrammelled logic.

It is also difficult, at times, especially when discussing policy issues that are of major contemporary importance, to keep firmly in mind the fact that the science of macroeconomics is a very young one whose body of theory, though extensive, is not sufficiently reliable to deliver solutions to all of the perceived macroeconomic problems of the day. The purpose of this book is to give an account of the *science* of macroeconomics. That is, the book presents an account of the current state of knowledge on macroeconomic *theory*. In order to help you to see the relevance of particular pieces of theory, examples drawn from the UK's macroeconomic experience will be presented. These examples are intended as nothing more than illustrations of a particular piece of theory in action. They are emphatically not offered as a commentary on, or as a contribution to, the UK's contemporary macroeconomic policy debate. We find it helpful to try to keep three activities clearly distinguished. They are:

(a) macroeconomic science
(b) macroeconomic policy recommendations, and
(c) macroeconomic policy debates

Macroeconomic science is the body of knowledge — incomplete and imperfect — that seeks to *understand* the macroeconomic phenomena that we have set out above.

Macroeconomic policy proposals are recommendations concerning how government policy should be pursued and are usually accompanied by predictions as to what the effects of those policies on macroeconomic performance will be. Macroeconomic policy proposals may or may not make use of macroeconomic science. Clearly, policy proposals that achieve their desired objectives will be based on macroeconomic science (assuming that the science has developed to an appropriate level of reliability). There is no logical reason, however, why someone should not make macroeconomic policy recommendations even in the absence of a reliable body of economic science capable of generating predictions concerning the effects of pursuing the recommended policies.

Macroeconomic policy debates are attempts to persuade a sufficient number of people that a particular policy should be pursued. Macroeconomic science clearly can be one ingredient in that debate. The argument that some particular policy should be pursued because a particular body of science predicts that the policy will have certain well-defined and desired effects is often a compelling one. There is, however, no restriction on the rules of debate requiring that some underlying science be invoked to legitimize the proposed policy. Debaters, even those who are macroeconomic specialists, often stray outside the limits of their science in order to score a point!

This book tries very hard to stay within the confines of the science of macroeconomics — to pursue the activity of seeking to understand macroeconomic phenomena and to make statements about macroeconomic policy that are implied by — that are in line with — the current state of macroeconomic theory.

Although it appears to aid clear thinking to make a sharp distinction between the three activities of science, policy advice, and policy debate there are, of course, important connections between them. These connections were identified and reflected on in a manner that we believe is particularly relevant and illuminating for our present purposes by Professor George J. Stigler of the University of Chicago in his Nobel Lecture.[2] In that lecture Stigler remarked that:

> The central task of an empirical science such as economics is to provide general understanding of events in the real world, and ultimately all of its theories and techniques must be instrumental to that task. That is very different from saying, however, that it must be responsive to the contemporanious conditions and problems of the society in which it is situated. The responsiveness of economics to environmental problems will naturally be more complete and more prompt the more urgent the problems of the day. The response will also be more complete, the less developed the rele-

---

2 George J. Stigler, Nobel Lecture: 'The Process and Progress of Economics', *Journal of Political Economy*, Vol. 91, No. 4 (1983) pp. 529–44. The quotation came from pp. 534–5.

vant body of economic analysis. The responsiveness of macroeconomics to contemporary events is notorious. Keynes's conquest in the 1930s was due to the fact that the neoclassical theory could not account for the persistent employment of that decade. A generation later, persistent inflation even with less than full employment was equally decisive in ending Keynes's supremacy. If and when macroecnomics produces a good theory of the business cycle, its responsiveness to environmental changes will diminish sharply.

A viable and healthy science requires both the persistent and almost timeless theories that naturally ignore the changing conditions of their society and the unsettled theories that encounter much difficulty in attempting to explain current events. Without the base of persistent theory, there would be no body of slowly evolving knowledge to constitute the science. Without the challenge of unsolved, important problems, the science would become sterile.

Macroeconomics is, we believe, 'a viable and healthy science'. It is, however, one that has very little danger of running out of 'challenges of unsolved, important problems, [likely to make] the science . . . become sterile'. The policy problem and the policy debate that fuels macroeconomic science is too important, exciting, and durable for that to happen.

Let us now turn our attention more fully to some macroeconomic policy issues.

D. Macroeconomic Policy Issues

There is, as you know, a widespread belief that the government can and should take actions designed to influence key economic variables such as inflation and unemployment. Economists do not agree amongst themselves, however, on what measures will achieve the desired results. The main reason why there is disagreement is that we still lack a deep enough understanding of macroeconomic phenomena. Another way of saying the same thing is that we lack good theories; that is, no one particular theory fits the facts so exactly that it is compelling. As a result each of us tends to subscribe to that theory that best supports our predisposition (or perhaps even our prejudices). This should not be taken to mean that macroeconomics is just a matter of opinion. On the contrary, there exists a solid 'core' of theory that commands widespread support among economists regardless of the policy view that they adopt. There are, however, some areas where agreement on the relevant theoretical approach is still lacking. Even in these cases, there is general agreement among economists on the way to proceed to resolve conflicts of view.

There is also virtually complete agreement among economists that many of the popular explanations for macroeconomic problems are simply too shallow to be useful. The most common source of such explanations are the media and politicians. Pay attention the next time the BBC or ITN is telling you about the latest figures on inflation or unemployment or interest rates. You will usually hear something like:

Inflation has risen this month *because* of sharp rises in the prices of oil and food.

or

Unemployment rose in April *because* of massive layoffs in the car industry.

or

Interest rates have eased *because* of a return of investor confidence. You are going to discover that the answers to these questions are too superficial or shallow to be of any value. In effect they are simply descriptions of the phenomenon that needs to be understood or explained.

Although we know that many popular so-called explanations of macroeconomic phenomena are not really explanations at all and provide no basis for the conduct of macroeconomic policy we are not able to provide a satisfactory explanation using what Stigler called 'almost timeless theories' that are sufficiently reliable to provide unambiguous and uncontroversial direction to the design and conduct of macroeconomic policy. This means that, as macroeconomic scientists, we have to maintain a due humility when asked for advice on contemporary policy problems. It does not mean, however, that we have nothing to say. Although we do not know all of the answers we certainly *do* know that some of the proposed answers are wrong. A fine story that will give you the flavour of what I mean by this was told recently by Robert E. Lucas, Jr.[3]

> The archaeologist Heinrich Schliemann, the discoverer of Troy, became convinced, we are told, that a particular skull unearthed in a later excavation was the head of Agamemnon. To the frustration of this creative and productive scientist, his associates confronted him with one devastating argument after another to the effect that this could not possibly be the case. Exhausted, Schliemann took up the skull and thrust it in the faces of his unconstructive critics: 'All right then, if he is not Agamemnon, who is he?'.

Just as the science of archaeology is incapable of answering Schliemann's question, so the science of macroeconomics is incapable of answering equivalent questions such as, for example, why is the UK unemployment rate in the mid-1980s so much higher than it was in the 1970s? Just as the science of archaeology *is* capable of saying whose skull Schliemann had *not* found so the science of macroeconomics is capable of demonstrating that some of the alleged explanations for the rise in unemployment (and the policy implications of such an explanation) simply cannot be correct.

The lack of complete agreement and the lack of a close enough correspondence between the currently available theories and the facts will

---

3 Robert E. Lucas Jr, 'Tobin and Monetarism: A Review Article', *Journal of Economic Literature*, Vol. 19, No. 2 (June 1981) pp. 558–67.

be highlighted and emphasized throughout this book. You will come to know and understand the existing theories; you will also learn the facts — both those that the theories 'fit' or explain and those that they do not. It is the as yet unexplained facts that provide much of the agenda for future research.

This book, unlike any of the others that are currently available, is not going to shortchange you by neglecting to bring to your attention some of the new theories in macroeconomics. On the contrary, it is going to present a comprehensive account of *all* the alternative theories that have been advanced to explain macroeconomic phenomena. It is going to be bold in showing where particular theories fail. The most recently advanced theories have not yet been shown to fail. Because of that, you may gain the false impression that we are asserting that all the 'old' theories of macroeconomics are wrong and the 'new' theories are right. We are indeed going to assert, and as far as we can in the confines of a book of this level, we are going to demonstrate, that some features of the 'old' theories are indeed failing. We are not, however, going to assert that the new theories are correct. It is still too soon to tell. They are, for the moment, the best that are available. It would be surprising, however, if they were to survive unscathed when subjected to the test of fitting all future circumstances.

Let us turn now to the final task of this introductory chapter and examine some of the leading alternative views of economists concerning macroeconomic policy questions.

E. Leading Schools of Thought

There are almost as many alternative positions on macroeconomic policy questions as there are macroeconomists. (There might even be more opinions than economists since one of the occupational hazards of this business is indecisiveness — you have probably heard of the three-handed economist: 'on the one hand ..., on the other hand ..., and ...'!)

Despite this tremendous diversity of opinion some classification and grouping can be illuminating. We find it useful to focus on two broad macroeconomic policy questions on which economists disagree among themselves. They are: (i) should macroeconomic policy be global or should it be detailed? And (ii) should policy be governed by a set of rules or be active and responsive to the current economic situation?

(i) Should Macroeconomic Policy be Global or Detailed?

Global policies are those which are directed at influencing the values of a small number of aggregate variables such as the money supply, the foreign exchange rate, the overall level of government expenditures, the overall level of taxes, and the size of the government's budget deficit.

Those who take the view that a small number of aggregate policy instruments should be the central concern of macroeconomic policy generally believe that it is desirable to leave as much scope as possible for individual initiative to be coordinated through the market mechanism.

Detailed policies are directed at controlling the prices or other terms concerning the exchange of a large number of specific goods and services. Such policies are too numerous to list in full. Some examples are: prices and incomes policies that regulate the wages and prices of a large number of types of worker and individual products; interest rate ceilings or other regulations on banks, building societies, and insurance companies; regional policies in the form of special subsidies to particular regions; investment incentives; regulation and control of private manufacturing industry; regulation of international trade by the use of tariffs and quotas; and regulation of international capital flows. Those economists (and others) who favour detailed policies generally take the view that there are a large number of important areas in which markets fail to achieve a desirable economic outcome. They believe that detailed government intervention is needed to modify the outcome of the market process.

Often the disagreement between those advocating detailed intervention and those arguing against it is not so much a disagreement about the existence of a problem which the free market is having trouble solving, but rather about whether or not the government can solve the problem better than the market can.

(ii) Should Macroeconomic Policy be Governed by a Set of Rules or
be Active and Responsive to the Current Economic Situation?

Those economists favouring rules are not unanimously agreed on what the rules should be. They are agreed, however, on one crucial point — that controlling an economy is fundamentally different from controlling a mechanical (or electrical, or electronic) system, such as, for example, the heating/cooling system in a building. What makes controlling the economy different is the fact that it is people who are being controlled, and unlike machines, people know that they are being controlled and are capable of learning the procedures that are being employed by the controllers — the government — and of organizing their affairs so as to take best advantage of the situation created by policy. A policy based on fixed rules minimizes the uncertainty that people have to face and thus enables a better economic performance.

Those who favour active intervention argue that if new information becomes available, it is foolish not to use it. By committing itself to a set of rules, the government ties its hands and bars itself from being in a position to exploit the new information.

The key difference between the advocates of rules and activism is a judgment as to whether individuals acting in their own interests, coordinated by markets, are capable of reacting to, and taking account of, new information without the need for government assistance in the matter.

In view of the major source of the disagreement on global versus detailed policies and rules versus discretion, you will not be surprised to be told that, on the whole, those economists who favour global policies also favour rules, while those who favour detailed policies also favour active intervention.

Broadly speaking, economists fall into two schools of thought on macroeconomic policy. There are no widely accepted, neat labels for identifying these two schools; however, the term *monetarist* is often applied to one group, and the term *Keynesian* to the other. Monetarists advocate fixed rules whereas Keynesians favour active intervention. These labels give flavour to, but sometimes fail to do full justice to, some of the subtleties of the distinctions between the two broad schools of thought. Neyertheless, in this book, the terms will be used to identify the two schools.[4]

(iii) The Monetarist View

Monetarists advocate that the government have policies towards a limited number of global macroeconomic variables such as money supply growth, government expenditure, taxes, and/or the government deficit. They advocate the adoption of fixed rules for the behaviour of these variables. A well-known example is the rule that the money supply should grow at a certain fixed percentage rate year in and year out. Another proposed rule is that the government budget should be balanced, on the average, over a period of four to five years. More strongly, some monetarists urge the introduction of a constitutional amendment mandating the government to balance its budget and limiting the fraction of people's incomes that the government may take in taxes. In any event, monetarists argue, the policy interventions that do occur should be announced as far ahead as possible so as to enable people to take account of them in planning and ordering their own economic affairs.

The intellectual leaders of this school are Milton Friedman (formerly of the University of Chicago and now working at the Hoover Institution at Stanford University), Karl Brunner (University of Rochester) who is credited with coining the term 'monetarist', and Robert E. Lucas Jr. (University of Chicago). Leading British monetarists are Professor Patrick Minford of the University of Liverpool and Alan Walters, recently Economic Adviser to Mrs Thatcher. Indeed, most of the economists associated in some official capacity with the Thatcher government have leanings in the monetarist direction.

---

4   An excellent, though demanding, discussion of the identifying characteristics of the different schools may be found in Douglas D. Purvis, 'Monetarism: A Review,' *Canadian Journal of Economics*, Vol. 13, no. 1 (February 1980) pp. 96–122. The two-fold classification suggested here is qualified in many subtle ways by Purvis.

(iv) The Keynesian View

Keynesians advocate detailed intervention to 'fine tune' the economy in the neighbourhood of full employment and low inflation. They would, if necessary, attempt to control inflation directly by controlling prices and incomes and to control unemployment by stimulating demand, using monetary and fiscal policy. They would use discretion in seeking to stimulate the economy in a depression and holding it back in a boom, modifying their policy in the light of the current situation. In their view, policy changes are best not pre-announced so as to deter speculation.

The intellectual leaders of this group of macroeconomists are Franco Modigliani (Massachusetts Institute of Technology) and James Tobin (Yale University). Most British academic economists identify themselves with the Keynesian tradition. Perhaps the most vocal in recent years has been Professor Frank Hahn of Cambridge who organized what became a famous academic economist's revolt against the Thatcher government's 'monetarist' policies.

An Analogy

Imagine that you are listening to an FM radio station in a crowded part of the wave band. The signals are repeatedly and randomly drifting, so that, from time to time, your station drifts out of hearing and a neighbouring station in which you have no interest comes through loud and clear. What should you do to get a stronger and more persistent signal from the station you want to hear?

The Keynesian says, 'Hang on to the tuning knob and whenever the signal begins to fade, fiddle with the knob attempting, as best you can, to stay with the signal.'

The monetarist says, 'Get yourself an AFC (Automatic Frequency Control) tuner; set it on the station you wish to hear; sit back; relax and enjoy your music. Do not fiddle with the tuner knob; your reception will not be perfect; but on the average, you will not be able to do any better than the AFC.'

Although we have identified two groups — monetarists and Keynesians — these labels are becoming increasingly inadequate to describe the divisions of opinion among economists. They also neglect to emphasize the fact that many macroeconomists have very little interest in policy and very little to say about it. They see their job as getting on with the business of understanding macroeconomic phenomena and not of applying the fruits of that understanding directly to designing macroeconomic policy. This kind of division of labour is much like that that occurs in the natural sciences and engineering. Some people specialize in better understanding the properties of materials, for example, while others get on with the business of applying that understanding in a variety of practical situations. This specialization and division of labour within macroeconomics seems to be on the increase and is a natural consequence of the increasing technical requirements of macroeconomic research.

Summary

A. Macroeconomic Questions

There are six main questions in macroeconomics; they are, what determines:

  (i) the rate of *inflation*?
  (ii) the *unemployment* rate?
  (iii) the level of *aggregate output*?
  (iv) the *rate of interest*?
  (v) the *balance of payments*?
  (vi) the *foreign exchange rate*?

B. UK Macroeconomic Problems in the 1980s

The decade opened with inflation running at almost 20 per cent. By mid-decade inflation had collapsed to less than 5 per cent, catching most people by surprise. Unemployment has been *the* problem of the decade starting out at the historically high 7 per cent and then almost doubling as the decade progressed. Output growth has been slow and was negative for the first two years of the 1980s. Interest rates have been high and volatile. The pound has lost value against the American dollar.

C. Macroeconomic Science, Policy and the Popular Debate

Macroeconomic science is the body of knowledge that seeks to *understand* macroeconomic phenomena. Macroeconomic policy proposals or recommendations concern how government policy should be pursued to achieve particular objectives. Macroeconomic policy debates are attempts to persuade a sufficient number of people that a particular policy should be pursued. This book is about macroeconomic science. It also analyses macroeconomic policy, evaluating alternative policies in the light of the current state of macroeconomic theory.

D. Macroeconomic Policy Issues

Economists do not agree among themselves concerning all macroeconomic policy issues. A major reason for disagreement arises from a lack of good theories.

  There are two major disagreements among economists concerning macroeconomic policy. One concerns whether policy should use *global* instruments or whether it should involve *detailed* intervention in individual markets. The second concerns whether policy should be governed by fixed *rules* or whether it should be varied from time to time at the *discretion* of the government in the light of current economic conditions.

E. Leading Schools of Thought

There are two major schools of thought: (1) *monetarists* who advocate *global* instrument setting under fixed *rules,* and (2) *Keynesians,* who advocate *detailed* intervention in a large number of individual markets with *discretion* to vary that intervention from time to time.

Review Questions

The following statements from the *Bank of England Quarterly Bulletin (BEQB),* and the *National Institute Economic Review (NIER)* all concern some aspect or other of British economic policy or economic problems. Read the statements carefully and then classify them according to whether:

(i) they deal with *macro*economic issues or not
(ii) they deal with *detailed* or *global* policy
(iii) they are talking about *rules* or *discretion* in the conduct of policy.

1. 'The essential aim of monetary policy ... [is] ... maintaining confidence in the future value of money.' (*BEQB*, August 1987, p. 365)
2. 'During the year the monetary policy operators have to take the fiscal stance, like so many other economic factors, as given.' (*BEQB*, August 1987, p. 366)
3. 'The broad aims of economic policy ... are the creation of a strong and growing economy ... higher levels of employment, higher living standards and higher standards of social care.' (*BEQB*, December 1986, p. 499)
4. 'The deviations of monetary growth from target have not provided a simple automatic rule. A whole range of indicators need to be taken into account in forming a judgement on the appropriateness of current financial conditions.' (*BEQB*, December 1986, p. 506)
5. 'The substance of [monetary] policy ... is quite clear. We will persist in bearing down on inflation.' (*BEQB*, December 1986, p. 507)
6. 'Monetary policy cannot directly reduce the rise in labour costs; nor, more generally, can it bring about improvements in industrial innovation and efficiency which are needed to take advantage of the opportunities now available to British producers in world markets.' (*BEQB*, December 1986, p. 508)
7. 'The continuing fall in unemployment is partly due to the recovery

of manufacturing output [and] partly to the increase in the effects of special unemployment and training measures.' (*NIER*, May 1987, p. 3)

8. 'Wage settlements remain high this year but we expect a gradual deceleration beginning from the next wage round.' (*NIER*, May 1987, p. 3)

9. 'Exchange market intervention as well as interest-rate changes is now being used very actively to influence the value of sterling.' (*NIER*, May 1987, p. 7)

10. 'The growth in nominal earnings failed to reflect the fall in the rate of inflation. Other personal income also grew faster, with self-employed income especially buoyant.' (*NIER*, May 1987, p. 8)

11. 'Investment by distribution and services . . . is now almost twice as large as investment by manufacturing.' (*NIER*, May 1987, p. 9)

12. 'A variety of special measures have been introduced which, taken together, probably account for the whole of the change [in unemployment last year].' (*NIER*, February 1987, p. 4)

13. 'We assume that income tax cuts are made in each Budget as opportunities arise.' (*NIER*, February 1987, p. 5)

14. 'National insurance contributions paid by employers, the tax on jobs, should be cut.' (*NIER*, February 1987, p. 5)

15. 'No attempt has been made to staunch the flow of consumer credit.' (*NIER*, February 1987, p. 7)

2

UK Macroeconomic History Since 1900

Too often in the past economists have disagreed with each other about theory while paying little or no attention to the basic questions, what are the facts? Which, if any, of the theories being advanced are capable of explaining the facts? All useful theories begin with *some* facts in need of explanation. Theories are, in effect, 'rigged' to explain a limited set of facts. They are subsequently tested by checking their ability to explain other facts, either not known or not explicitly taken into account, when 'rigging' the theory. The theories of macroeconomics that are presented in this book have been designed to explain some aspect or other of the facts about inflation, unemployment, real income, interest rates, the foreign exchange rate and the balance of payments. The evolution of these variables over time is a country's macroeconomic history. This chapter is designed to give you a 'broad brush' picture of the macroeconomic history of the UK. It should be thought of as a first quick look at some of the facts which macroeconomics seeks to explain. It presents the facts in the most direct, uncluttered manner possible, but in no way tries to begin the task of explaining the facts. The chapter will serve two main purposes. First it will provide you with some basic equipment that will enable you to reject some of the more obviously incorrect theories that you may come across. Second it will provide you with a quick reference source — especially the Appendix to this chapter and the data sources listed there — in case you want to pursue a more systematic testing of macroeconomic theories.

By the time you have completed this chapter you will be able to:

(a) **Describe the main features in the evolution of the key macroeconomic variables since 1900: (i) inflation, (ii) unemployment, (iii) real income, (iv) interest rates, (v) the balance of payments, and (vi) the exchange rate.**

(b) **Describe the main macroeconomic characteristics of each decade since 1900.**

A. Evolution of Macroeconomic Variables

(i) Inflation

Figure 2.1 shows two measures of UK inflation. One is the annual rate of change of an Index of Retail Prices. The other is known as the GDP Deflator. Chapter 5 will explain precisely how these inflation rates are calculated and measured. For now, it is sufficient if you think of inflation as being simply the rate at which prices, on average, are rising. Notice that although the two measures of inflation are not identical, they do, nevertheless, tend to move up and down together. What do they tell us about UK inflation?

The first rather striking thing that they suggest is that UK inflation has been on a *rising trend* in the period since the early 1920s. In both the 1920s and 1930s there were several years in which prices were falling (inflation measured negatively). Since 1934, however, there has not been a single year in which prices fell. Further, from the early 1960s to 1981, the rate at which prices rose became progressively more severe.

irregular The second thing that we learn from the figure about UK inflation is that it has been erratic. There are some distinct *cycles* in the inflation rate, but the up and down movements could not be described as following a regular cycle. Before the First World War there were two distinct cycles with inflation reaching a peak in 1907 and 1912. There then followed a much longer swing with strongly rising prices during the First World War and falling prices in the years of the early 1920s. A more regular cyclical pattern is clear in the 1930s and again in the post-Second World War period.

immense The range of UK inflation experience in the twentieth century is enormous. As measured by the Retail Price Index it goes from a maximum of almost 22 per cent (in 1975) to a minimum of minus 21 per cent (in 1922). As measured by the GDP Deflator, the range is from 24 per cent (1975) down to a minimum of minus 17 per cent (1921). These extreme values are uncommon as you can see from the figure.

With the exception of the late 1970s and early 1980s, the biggest bursts

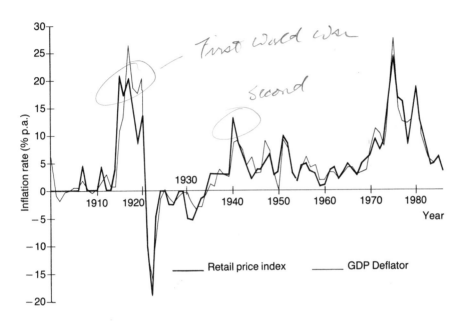

**Figure 2.1
Inflation:
1900–1986**

Two measures of inflation (the Retail Price Index and the Gross Domestic Product Deflator) tell broadly the same story. Prices rose at a rapid rate during the First World War, again (though slightly less so) in the Second World War and very strongly at the end of the 1970s. Prices were falling in the years between the two World Wars. The inflation rate has cycled in a periodic fashion over the entire period since 1900, but most noticeably so in the post-war years. In the last few years inflation has returned to its longer-term average level.
Source: Appendix to this chapter.

of inflation occurred during the war years, with the First World War displaying more severe inflation than the Second World War. There was also a burst of inflation in the early 1950s associated with the Korean War. The years of strongest deflation are those immediately after the First World War and during the 1930s.

Aside from these extreme experiences of strongly rising or strongly falling prices, UK inflation rate for the most part has been moderate, though by no means zero. In fact, the average inflation rate over the 87 years chosen in the figure has been 4.3 per cent per annum. Maintained over 87 years, this rate of inflation has increased the price level almost forty-fold.

Let us now turn to look at the second macroeconomic variable — the unemployment rate.

(ii) Unemployment

Figure 2.2 shows the UK unemployment rate since 1900. As with inflation, the precise definition of, and method of measuring, unemployment
will be dealt with in Chapter 5. For the present you may think of
unemployment as measuring the extent to which people who have
indicated that they wish to work, are not able to find a job.

The most striking features of unemployment in the UK in this century
are its persistently very high level all the way from the early 1920s to the
early 1940s and its dramatic rise in recent years.

The second half of this period, from 1929 to the end of the 1930s, was
the period known as the Great Depression — a period when the whole
world economy was in a state of high unemployment. As you can see
from the figure, however, the UK suffered from high unemployment
before the world depression of the 1930s set in.

In addition to the massive unemployment experienced during the 1920s
and 1930s, you will also be struck, perhaps, by the rather clear long cycles
in unemployment. There is a tendency for unemployment to move
downwards from the beginning of the century to 1916. It then rises persistently to 1932, falls continuously until 1944, and then tends to rise in
the period after 1944. Although one may describe these long swings as
a long cycle, there are less than two such complete cycles and, of course,
no guarantee that this long swing pattern will repeat.

Superimposed upon the long cycles in unemployment are some very
distinct shorter cycles. There are many of these and it would not be instructive simply to catalogue them. You may, by carefully inspecting
Figure 2.2, observe some of these shorter up-and-down movements that
are distinctly present in the data.

The range of UK unemployment goes all the way from a peak of 22.1
per cent in 1932, down to a trough of less than 1 per cent during the war
years of 1916 and 1944. The average unemployment rate over the entire
century has been 6.0 per cent.

(iii) Real Income

There are two ways in which the evolution of real income can be examined. One fairly natural thing to do is to look at the behaviour of its *growth
rate*. Another is to look at the percentage deviations of its level from trend.
Let us do both of these things.

Figure 2.3 sets out the behaviour of the growth rate of real income in
Britain since 1900. Chapter 3 will describe exactly how the level of real
income is calculated. For now you can think of it as a measure of the value
of the goods and services produced in the economy each year.

The first thing that immediately strikes the eye when inspecting Figure
2.3 is the erratic nature of the path of real income growth. It seems to

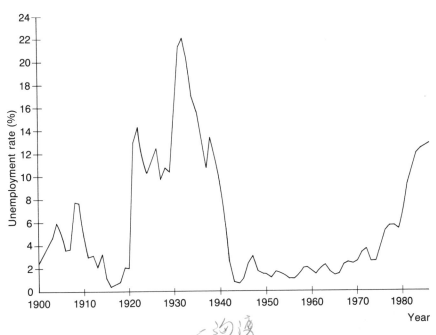

The dominant features of UK unemployment are its massive rate from the early 1920s to the late 1930s and its strong upsurge in the 1980s. A second noteworthy feature is the periodic cycle. Since the early 1950s unemployment has trended upwards and strongly so in the late 1970s.
Source: Appendix to this chapter.

**Figure 2.2
Unemployment:
1900–1986**

bounce around all over the place and, to a large degree, at random. The range of the apparently random fluctuations in real income growth seem to have narrowed slightly in the period after the Second World War as compared with the first four decades of the century. To some extent that is probably an illusion that arises from the fact that we are able to measure real income more accurately in recent years than we were in earlier years. It is probably not, however, entirely illusory. Certainly there were some big reductions in real income in the Great Depression years of the 1930s. Also, real income growth did become very strong in the recovery from the Great Depression as we moved towards the Second World War. There were some fairly strong swings in real income growth in the first decade of the century. In the period since the Second World War the swings seem to have been less violent and have been remarkably frequent in their occurrence. There has been a tendency since the Second World War for real income to grow (though not by very much) every year. Exceptions were 1947, 1958, 1974–75 and 1980–81.

Figure 2.3. The growth rate of output: 1900—1986

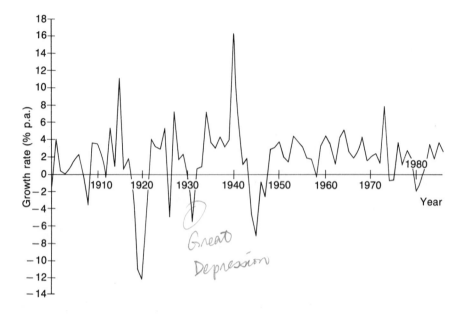

Output growth has been quite erratic. It averaged just under 2 per cent per annum. The growth rate was much more variable in the early part of this century than after the Second World War.
Source: Appendix to this chapter.

The range of real income growth has been substantial. The maximum positive growth rate was rather more than 9 per cent and occurred in the recovery from the Great Depression in 1934. The biggest fall in real income occurred at the onset of the Great Depression in 1931 when it fell by more than 7 per cent. The trend real income growth rate over the entire period since 1900 has only been 1.7 per cent per annum which implies that aggregate income has increased only some 4 1/3 fold this century.

Before examining the deviations of real income from its trend level, it will be instructive to look at the actual level of real income graphed on a logarithmic scale in the period since 1900. This is done in Figure 2.4.

It is immediately obvious from inspecting Figure 2.4 that there is no single constant trend growth rate that adequately describes the path of real income in the UK over this entire 87-year period. From the beginning of the century to the end of the Second World War, the average growth rate was almost exactly 1 per cent per annum. From 1947 to 1970 the average growth rate was 2.5 per cent per annum. During the 1970s and 1980s the trend growth rate has slowed down again and has averaged about 1.8 per cent. We have calculated a trend line of real GDP that

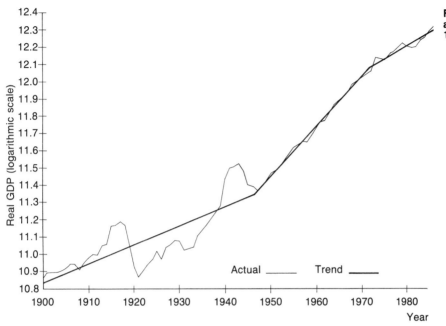

Figure 2.4 Actual and trend output: 1900–1986

Output is plotted on a logarithmic scale so that its growth trends are evident. No single trend describes the growth of output through this century. From the beginning of the century to 1946 the growth trend was about 1 per cent a year. In the 1950s and 1960s the trend was 2.5 per cent a year. In the 1970s and 1980s the trend growth rate has been 1.8 per cent a year. The trend line shown with three segments describes these three separate trends.
Source: Appendix to this chapter.

reflects these three growth rates for the three subperiods and that line is shown, alongside actual output, in Figure 2.4.

The deviations of actual real income from the trend line (with a different growth trend for the three sub-periods), expressed as a percentage, are shown in Figure 2.5. The deviations from trend, like the growth rate, are much more erratic in the first half of the century than after the Second World War. The biggest deviation below trend occurred in 1921 when real income was 20 per cent below trend. The biggest positive deviation occurred in 1943 when real income was almost 22 per cent above trend. In the post-war years there has been a series of rather short cyclical movements. In interpreting the deviations from trend it is important to remember that the trend growth rate for the 1950s and 1960s is much higher than that for the 1970s and 1980s. If we measured real income in the 1970s and 1980s as deviations from the 1960s growth trend there would

Figure 2.5 Deviations of output from trend, 1900–1986

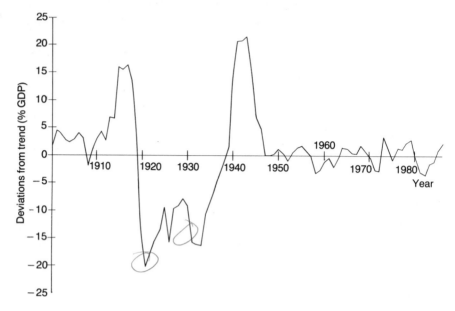

Fluctuations of output about trend were much more volatile in the first half of this century than the second half. The most important positive deviations occur in the years of the two major wars (1914–18) and (1939–45). The biggest negative deviations from trend occurred during the Great Depression years of the 1930s and also in the depressed years of the 1920s.
Source: Appendix to this chapter.

be serious negative deviations as large almost as those of the depression years of the 1930s.

(iv) Interest Rates

Figure 2.6 sets out the behaviour of two rates of interest. One of them is the rate on long-term government bonds and the other the rate on three-month Treasury bills. It is evident that the long-term rate of interest is less volatile than the short-term rate and than the other macroeconomic variables that we have examined. Both rates display the same long-term movements. There is a tendency for rates to rise slightly from the beginning of the century up to 1920. They then fall until the end of the Second World War and, after that, display a strongly rising trend. There are shorter cycles in the movement of both rates with the short-term rate and with the other macroeconomic variables that we have examined. Both rates display the same long-term movements. There is a tendency for rates to rise slightly from the beginning of the century up to 1920. They then fall until the end of the Second World War and, after that, display a strongly rising trend. There are shorter cycles in the movement of both rates with the short-term rate fluctuating much more markedly than the long-term rate.

The range in interest rates is quite considerable. Long-term rates were at their lowest at the beginning of the century (2.5 per cent) and at their highest in 1974 (14.6 per cent). Short-term rates were at their lowest during the Second World War, when they averaged 0.5 per cent a year, and were at their highest in 1979, when they reached 16.5 per cent. Interest rates remained at a high level throughout the 1980s.

(v) Balance of Payments

Let us now turn our attention to the UK balance of payments. The precise way in which the balance of payments is measured will be dealt with in

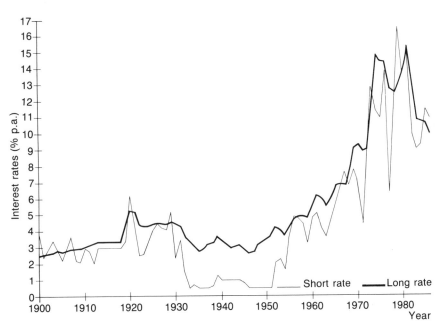

Figure 2.6 Interest rates: 1900–1986

Interest rates have followed a similar path to inflation (Figure 2.1) but long-term rates have been much less volatile than inflation. Short-term rates fluctuate with greater amplitude than long-term rates. Interest rates have remained historically high throughout the 1980s.
Source: Appendix to this chapter.

Chapter 6. For now you may think of it as a measure of the net payments to, or receipts from, the rest of the world by residents of the UK taken in aggregate. If, in their economic relations with the rest of the world, aggregate British sales of goods and services plus borrowing exceed British purchases of goods and services plus lending, then the balance of payments will be in surplus. The reverse situation, in which British residents sell less than they buy and borrow less than they lend, is referred to as a deficit.

Figure 2.7 shows the post-war history of the UK balance of payments (the history since 1946). Earlier figures are not shown because the ones that are readily available refer not to the UK alone but to the entire sterling area of which, in the period before the Second World War, the UK was the centre. The balance of payments figures are expressed as a percentage of aggregate income.

Several features of the balance of payments are striking. First, there is a clear tendency for the balance of payments to have followed a negative trend from around 1950 to 1968. After 1968 the balance of payments became highly volatile for a few years. In the most recent years the balance

**Figure 2.7
Balance of
payments:
1946–1986**

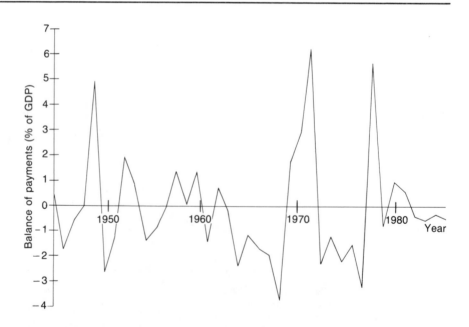

Balance of payments fluctuations followed a negative trend from 1950 into the late 1960s. The balance of payments became very volatile during the 1970s but have been close to zero in the middle to late 1980s.
Source: Appendix to this chapter.

of payments has been close to zero. There are some fairly clear cyclical swings in the balance of payments. The range of fluctuation is between a surplus of 6.25 per cent of income in 1971 and a deficit of 3.7 per cent of income in 1968.

(vi) Exchange Rate

The exchange rate is the value of the pound in terms of other currencies. The particular other currency chosen here to represent the foreign exchange value of the pound is the United States dollar. The history of the value of the pound measured as the number of United States dollars that would have to be paid for one pound sterling is set out in Figure 2.8. During some parts of this history, the value of the pound was *flexible*

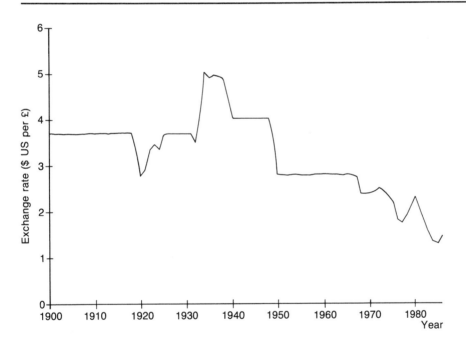

**Figure 2.8
Exchange rate:
1900–1986**

The foreign exchange value of the pound was pegged at $3.79 US per pound up to 1918. After the First World War the pound floated and depreciated. The pre-war fixed value was restored when the pound returned to the gold standard in 1925. In 1931 the pound was floated again and its value dipped at first, but then appreciated strongly to exceed $5 US briefly in 1934. Throughout the Second World War the value of the pound was pegged again at $4.03 US. A devaluation to $2.80 US occurred in 1949, but that new value was maintained until 1967 when a further devaluation took place. The exchange value of the pound floated again after 1972. During the period of floating exchange rates the pound has trended downwards in value and reached an all-time low of $1.30 US in 1985.
Source: Appendix to this chapter.

— the exchange rate was free to fluctuate, much like the prices of ordinary goods, and during other parts of the history, the pound was *fixed* — a situation in which the government pegs the exchange rate. The fixed exchange rate periods have been the most common ones. From 1900 all the way up to the end of the First World War the pound was pegged at $3.70 US. During the early 1920s the pound sank in value to hit $2.78 US in 1920. From 1926 to 1931 the pre-war value of $3.70 US was restored. Then, in the 1930s the pound rose in value to exceed $5 US in 1934. By the beginning of the Second World War, the foreign exchange value of the pound was pegged again, this time at $4.03 US. The pound was devalued in 1949 to $2.80 US at which it was pegged by the British government until 1967 when it was devalued again, this time to $2.40 US. This rate was maintained until 1971 when the foreign exchange value of the pound was allowed to find its own level. In the period since then, the pound has fluctuated, reaching a trough value of $1.74 US in 1977. From 1977 to 1980, the exchange value of the pound rose again to $2.32 US by 1980. Since 1980 the pound has again fallen in value, reaching an all time low of $1.30 US in 1985.

B. Decade Summaries

In order to present the UK macroeconomic history in a slightly more compact manner, this section focuses on the decade averages of the variables since 1900. Those averages are set out in Table 2.1. Also, for purposes of comparison, the averages for the 87 years from 1900 to 1986 are presented in the last row of that table.

The first decade of the century is somewhat unremarkable. Prices were almost exactly stable, though unemployment was fairly high (slightly below the average for the entire 80-year period). Output growth was very sluggish at only 0.9 per cent per annum. Interest rates were steady at below 3 per cent and the foreign exchange value of the pound was held steady at $3.70 US.

The period 1910–20 was dominated by the First World War. This was a decade of substantial inflation — almost 10 per cent per annum on the average — but also a decade of lower unemployment. It was another decade in which output grew by less than 1 per cent a year. Interest rates moved up slightly but the foreign exchange value of the pound remained constant.

The 1920s was a period of great economic hardship in the UK. Prices fell substantially during that decade and the unemployment rate moved up to average more than 10 per cent. Interest rates also moved up and the foreign exchange value of the pound sagged a little. Although the

Table 2.1   The decade averages

| Decade | Inflation | | Unemployment rate (%) | Real income (GDP) | | Interest rates | | Balance of payments (% GDP) | Exchange rate ($US per £) |
	RPI (% p.a.)	GDP Deflator (% p.a.)		Growth (% p.a.)	Deviations from trend (%)	Long-term (% p.a.)	Short-term (% p.a.)		
1900s	0.5	0.0	4.8	0.9	2.4	2.7	2.9		3.70
1910s	8.8	9.0	2.1	0.8	8.6	3.4	2.9		3.67
1920s	−3.9	−4.2	10.6	1.6	−13.1	4.6	4.1		3.43
1930s	0.3	0.2	16.1	2.1	−8.5	3.5	1.2		4.43
1940s	4.3	5.2	3.0	−0.1	10.6	3.0	0.8	−0.4	4.00
1950s	4.0	4.2	1.5	2.2	−0.2	4.5	3.2	0.7	2.80
1960s	3.4	2.9	1.9	2.8	0.1	6.6	5.7	0.1	2.71
1970s	11.8	12.3	4.1	2.0	0.6	12.0	10.3	−0.1	2.20
1980s	5.6	5.2	11.0	1.7	−0.9	11.9	11.4	0.1	1.68
Average 1900–86	4.3	4.3	6.0	1.7	0.0	5.6	4.4	0.1	3.2

Source: Appendix to this chapter.

decade was one of severe depression, it was a decade of a somewhat higher average output growth than the previous 20 years. This happened because the decade both opened and closed with roughly equally severe depression, but these depressions were superimposed upon a reasonably strong rising output trend.

The 1930s saw a continuation of the problems of the 1920s. Prices stopped falling and were roughly constant. Unemployment rose even further, however, to average 16 per cent for the decade as a whole. Through this decade, the output growth trend of a little over 2 per cent per annum was maintained.

Like the 1920s, the 1940s were dominated by war. In the Second World War, inflation was less severe than it had been in the First World War (of the order of a half the severity). As in the previous war, unemployment fell to a very low average level. For the decade as a whole, output growth was modest compared with the more severely depressed 1920s and 1930s.

The 1950s was a decade of macroeconomic calm and solid progress. Prices rose, but only by 4 per cent per annum (practically the same as the 80-year average). Unemployment was modest and averaged even less than it had done in the two war decades of the 1910s and 1940s. Output growth moved up to more than 2 per cent per annum. After being lowered in 1949, the foreign exchange value of the pound was maintained

throughout the decade at its new fixed level of $2.80 US. Through this
period the balance of payments behaved in an unremarkable way, fluctuating from year to year, but averaging a surplus of just over £40 million
per annum.

The 1960s was another decade of solid progress and looked very much
like the 1950s. Inflation averaged less than 4 per cent per annum,
unemployment remained low and output growth hit almost 3 per cent
on average. Some signs of problems were beginning to emerge, however,
with interest rates and the external aspect of the economy. In contrast
to the previous decade, the balance of payments had now moved into
a deficit of almost £300 million a year. The foreign exchange value of the
pound was maintained until 1967 but, in that year, was lowered to $2.40
US. Interest rates began to move up quite significantly during this decade.

The 1970s was a decade of inflation, rising unemployment and strongly
rising interest rates. The average inflation rate turned out to be in the
middle teens, with unemployment almost double what it had been in the
1960s. Interest rates also almost doubled from their previous decade
average level.

The 1980s has been a decade of macroeconomic upheaval and change.
The decade opened with the high inflation of the 1970s and with historically high unemployment. As the decade unfolded, inflation collapsed,
but unemployment climbed to almost 13 per cent. The output growth rate
was less than it had been in the previous 30 years but remained higher
than that for the first part of this century. Interest rates remained high
and the external value of the pound continued to fall.

We have now reviewed the behaviour of the six key macroeconomic
variables in the UK and have looked at the main macroeconomic
characteristics of each decade during the twentieth century. Many questions will no doubt be occurring to you.

C. Questions

(i) On Inflation

Why are there some periods when the inflation rate is very high, others
when it is moderate, and yet others when prices are falling? Can the ups
and downs in inflation be controlled and perhaps eliminated, or do we
have to live with them? What caused the strong trend rise in the UK inflation rate from the 1920s to the late 1970s? Was the very high inflation
of the 1970s and early 1980s a temporary aberration or is inflation going
to rise again to those levels? What has to be done to moderate the fluctuations in the rate of inflation and to keep its rate low?

We do not know the full answers to any of these questions. We know substantial parts of the answers to all of them, however, and explaining what we know constitutes one of the primary tasks of this book.

(ii) On Unemployment

Why was there such an enormous and prolonged burst of unemployment during the 1920s and 1930s? Why has unemployment increased so dramatically in the past five years? You will discover that important though these questions are, a satisfactory answer eludes us. Part III of the book deals with the most comprehensive and systematic attempt to answer this question and explains why we are still searching for a fully satisfactory answer. Why have there been such marked fluctuations in unemployment?

(iii) On Real Income

Why does real income grow in a cyclical but erratic fashion? Why was income so severely depressed in the 1920s and early 1930s? Why has real income deviated from its trend in the post-war period? What can be done to eradicate the fluctuations in real income?

(iv) On Interest Rates

Why are long-term interest rate movements relatively smooth? Why did interest rates gradually trend downwards through the 1920s and then gradually rise again — not so gradually in recent years? Why are the fluctuations in short-term interest rates more pronounced than those in long-terms rates?

(v) On the Balance of Payments and the Exchange Rate

Why has the UK balance of payments fluctuated so much? Why was there a tendency for the balance of payments to follow a falling trend during the 1950s and 1960s? Why were the balance of payments so erratic in the 1970s? What has caused the more moderate fluctuations in recent years?

Why is it that sometimes the foreign exchange value of the pound has been fixed and at other times it has been allowed to fluctuate? Why has the value of the pound fallen successively in the period since the Second World War?

These questions concerning the UK's external macroeconomic relations will also be given prominence in what follows in this book.

It would not be sensible or useful to attempt a detailed mapping out of the specific parts of the book that deal with each of these questions. Many of the questions turn out to be intimately related to each other in a way that you will find hard to appreciate if you have little or no knowledge of macroeconomics, but that will seem obvious and natural once you have made some progress with your study of the subject. To help you see some of the connections between the questions, after explaining in more detail how the macroeconomic variables are defined, observed and measured, but before embarking upon the tasks of *explanation* of macroeconomic phenomena, Chapter 7 will explore some of the connections among the variables by defining and describing the business cycle. In the final section of that chapter you will have a further opportunity to return to the features of the six variables described here and to gain some further insights into the way that they behave.

Summary

A. Evolution of Macroeconomic Variables

Inflation's main feature has been a distinctly rising trend. There have also been clear but irregular cycles. The range of inflation (as measured by retail prices) runs from falling prices of 21 per cent per annum (in 1922) to rising prices of 22 per cent per annum in 1975. The average rate of inflation between 1900 and 1987 has been 4.3 per cent per annum.

Unemployment has displayed a long cyclical swing with clear shorter cycles superimposed upon it. The worst unemployment occurred during the 20 years from 1920 to 1940, with 1932 being the single worst year when unemployment was 22.1 per cent, but the past five years have also been very severe. Unemployment reached its lowest levels during the two World Wars when it was below 1 per cent.

Real income growth has average just over 1.5 per cent per annum during this century. There has been a marked amount of random fluctuations in the growth rate, however, about that average. The highest growth rate ever achieved was 9.2 per cent (in 1934) as the economy was coming out of the worst of the Great Depression. The biggest drop in output occurred in 1931 when output fell by 7.5 per cent.

Interest rates were remarkably steady through the first half of the century, but trended upwards strongly after the middle 1950s. Long-term interest rates have a smooth pattern, while short-term rates fluctuate more markedly.

The balance of payments has followed a series of cycles and, between

1950 and the late 1960s, was on a falling trend. The balance of payments was most volatile in the early 1970s and, in recent years, has been very close to zero.

The exchange rate has been fixed in value against the US dollar with the exception of the years between the start of the First and the Second World War and in the period since 1971. During the period of fixed exchange rates the pound was devalued in 1949 and again in 1967. Since 1971 the pound has been free to find its own level on the foreign exchange market and has tended to decline in value. It reached an all-time low against the US dollar in 1985.

B. Decade Summaries

The averages of the macroeconomic variables in each decade since 1900 are set out in Table 2.1 and should be studied carefully. The first decade was an unremarkable one with virtually stable prices, slow output growth and moderately high unemployment. The second decade was dominated by the First World War and saw an average inflation rate of 10 per cent, lower unemployment, but a poor output growth rate. Through both of these decades the pound was held at a constant level against the US dollar and interest rates were close to 3 per cent. The 1920s and 1930s were decades of severe depression with unemployment climbing to the teens, and prices either steady or falling. An output growth rate in excess of 2 per cent per annum, nevertheless, was maintained throughout this period. Interest rates also remained fairly steady at between 3 and 5 per cent.

Like the 1920s, the 1940s were dominated by war and saw the inflation rate rise and unemployment fall. The 1950s was a decade of macroeconomic calm and steady progress with inflation around 4 per cent, output growing strongly above its long-term average level, and unemployment being very low. Interest rates remained steady and the external payments were in surplus. The 1960s was much like the 1950s, except that interest rates started to move up and the balance of payments began to show an increasing deficit. The 1970s was a decade of inflation and high unemployment, high interest rates and volatile external payments. The 1980s opened with all the problems of the 1970s. As that decade unfolded, inflation moderated dramatically, but unemployment became an extremely serious problem. Real output growth slackened off but only slightly so. Interest rates remained high and the pound continued to lose value on the foreign exchange markets.

C. *Questions*

Why is there such variation in our inflation experience? Can we control inflation?

Why was unemployment so high in the 1920s and 1930s and why has unemployment increased so much in the last five years?

Why does real income grow in a cyclical but erratic fashion?

Why are long-term interest rate movements relatively smooth? Why do short-term interest rates fluctuate more markedly than long-term rates?

Why has the UK balance of payments fluctuated so much? Why has the foreign exchange value of the pound fallen since the Second World War?

Review Questions

1. Briefly describe the history of each of the following macroeconomic variables in the UK since 1945: (i) inflation; (ii) unemployment; (iii) real income; (iv) interest rates; (v) the balance of payments; and (vi) the exchange rate.
2. Briefly describe the history of each of the above macroeconomic variables in the UK in the 'inter-war years' — 1920 to 1940.
3. Using later editions of the sources given at the foot of the table in the Appendix to Chapter 2, update the table for each of the variables. Describe how each of these variables has evolved so far in the 1980s.
4. One of these six macroeconomic variables has at some time been fixed by the government. Which variable is this, and for what periods has it been fixed?
5. In which decade was inflation the major macroeconomic problem in the UK? Was it associated with any other major macroeconomic problems?
6. What were the major macroeconomic problems in the UK of the 1930s?
7. In which decade since 1900 has the UK suffered the highest average unemployment rate? Compare this average with that so far in the 1980s.
8. In which decade of UK history since 1900 has the average long-term interest rate been highest? Compare this with the average long-term interest rate so far for the 1980s.
9. Has the UK balance of payments on average been in deficit in any decade since 1900? Would you deduce from this that the UK has had balance of payment problems?
10. Looking at decade averages of the history of the exchange rate and the balance of payments, does there appear to be a relationship between them? If so, what is the relationship?
11. What are the major economic problems of the UK in the 1980s?

12. Assume that you are employed as an economic speech writer by Mrs Thatcher. Write a short speech which argues as strongly as possible that UK macroeconomic performance in the 1980s compares favourably with that of earlier decades and is a credit to the economic management of the government.

13. Assume that you are employed as an economic speech writer by Mr Kinnock. Write a short speech which argues as strongly as possible that UK macroeconomic performance in the 1980s compares unfavourably with that of earlier decades and discredits the government's economic management.

Appendix: Macroeconomic Variables, 1900−1986

| | Inflation | | | Real income (GDP) | | Interest rates | | | |
| | RPI | GDP Deflator | Unemployment rate | Growth | Deviations from trend | Long-term | Short-term | Balance of payments | Exchange rate |
Year	(% p.a.)	(% p.a.)	(%)	(% p.a.)	(%)	(% p.a.)	(% p.a.)	(% GDP)	($US per £)
1900		6.6	2.5	−1.74	1.61	2.5	3.9	—	3.70
1901	0.0	−0.7	3.3	4.10	4.50	2.6	2.4	—	3.70
1902	0.0	−1.9	4.0	0.43	3.81	2.6	2.9	—	3.70
1903	0.0	−0.3	4.7	0.05	2.74	2.7	3.4	—	3.69
1904	0.0	0.0	6.0	0.69	2.31	2.8	2.9	—	3.70
1905	0.0	0.6	5.0	1.68	2.86	2.7	2.2	—	3.69
1906	0.0	0.5	3.6	2.33	4.04	2.8	3.0	—	3.69
1907	4.8	1.9	3.7	0.10	3.02	2.9	3.7	—	3.69
1908	0.0	0.0	7.8	−3.63	−1.80	2.9	2.2	—	3.69
1909	0.0	−0.4	7.7	3.67	0.69	2.9	2.1	—	3.70
1910	0.0	0.3	4.7	3.59	3.09	3.0	3.0	—	3.69
1911	4.5	1.5	3.0	2.29	4.24	3.1	2.8	—	3.69
1912	0.0	3.0	3.2	−0.38	2.74	3.2	2.0	—	3.70
1913	0.0	0.8	2.1	5.36	6.84	3.3	3.0	—	3.69
1914	4.3	0.7	3.3	0.69	6.68	3.3	3.0	—	3.71
1915	20.8	10.8	1.1	11.05	16.04	3.3	3.0	—	3.71
1916	17.2	14.1	0.4	0.66	15.57	3.3	3.0	—	3.71
1917	20.6	26.4	0.6	1.95	16.39	3.3	3.0	—	3.71
1918	14.6	18.7	0.8	−1.73	13.53	3.3	3.0	—	3.71
1919	8.5	17.7	2.1	−10.99	0.77	4.6	3.4	—	3.36
1920	13.7	20.5	2.0	−12.15	−13.31	5.3	6.2	—	2.78
1921	−8.6	−10.6	12.9	−5.68	−20.28	5.2	4.5	—	2.92
1922	−18.9	−16.0	14.3	4.12	−17.36	4.4	2.5	—	3.36
1923	−4.7	−8.0	11.7	3.25	−15.29	4.3	2.6	—	3.47
1924	0.0	−1.4	10.3	2.95	−13.50	4.3	3.3	—	3.35
1925	0.0	0.3	11.3	5.34	−9.41	4.4	4.0	—	3.67
1926	−2.4	−1.5	12.5	−4.97	−15.63	4.5	4.5	—	3.69
1927	−2.5	−2.4	9.7	7.32	−9.68	4.5	4.2	—	3.69
1928	0.0	−1.0	10.8	1.78	−9.03	4.4	4.1	—	3.69
1929	0.0	−0.4	10.4	2.40	−7.78	4.6	5.2	—	3.69

Appendix (Contd)

	Inflation			Real income (GDP)		Interest rates			
Year	RPI (% p.a.)	GDP Deflator (% p.a.)	Unemployment rate (%)	Growth (% p.a.)	Deviations from trend (%)	Long- term (% p.a.)	Short- term (% p.a.)	Balance of payments (% GDP)	Exchange rate ($US per £)
1930	−5.1	−0.4	16.0	−0.14	−9.04	4.4	2.4	—	3.69
1931	−5.4	−2.4	21.3	−5.46	−15.77	4.3	3.5	—	3.69
1932	−2.9	−3.6	22.1	0.70	−16.19	3.7	1.4	—	3.50
1933	−2.9	−1.3	19.9	0.95	−16.37	3.3	0.5	—	4.21
1934	0.0	−0.9	16.7	7.12	−10.61	3.1	0.7	—	5.04
1935	3.0	1.0	15.5	3.74	−8.06	2.8	0.5	—	4.90
1936	2.9	0.5	13.1	3.05	−6.17	2.9	0.5	—	4.97
1937	2.9	3.8	10.8	4.34	−3.05	3.2	0.5	—	4.94
1938	2.8	2.7	13.5	3.12	−1.09	3.3	0.6	—	4.89
1939	2.7	2.5	11.6	4.11	1.82	3.7	1.3	—	4.46
1940	13.2	8.6	9.7	16.30	15.81	3.4	1.0	—	4.03
1941	9.3	9.0	6.6	6.26	20.76	3.1	1.0	—	4.03
1942	6.4	7.2	2.4	1.14	20.77	3.0	1.0	—	4.03
1943	4.0	4.5	0.8	1.93	21.56	3.1	1.0	—	4.03
1944	1.9	6.0	0.7	−4.96	15.36	3.1	1.0	—	4.03
1945	3.8	3.0	1.2	−7.07	6.91	2.9	0.8	—	4.03
1946	3.6	3.2	2.5	−0.86	4.93	2.6	0.5	0.62	4.03
1947	5.3	9.0	3.1	−2.57	−0.03	2.7	0.5	−1.69	4.03
1948	6.7	7.1	1.8	2.93	0.00	3.2	0.5	−0.62	4.03
1949	2.6	2.9	1.6	3.17	0.28	3.3	0.5	−0.03	3.68
1950	3.4	0.2	1.5	3.82	1.18	3.5	0.5	5.01	2.80
1951	9.8	9.1	1.2	2.04	0.35	3.7	0.5	−2.61	2.80
1952	8.6	7.6	1.7	1.45	−1.06	4.2	2.1	−1.25	2.79
1953	3.1	3.3	1.6	4.50	0.49	4.0	2.3	1.97	2.81
1954	1.7	1.8	1.4	3.83	1.41	3.7	1.7	0.79	2.81
1955	4.6	3.9	1.1	3.29	1.80	4.1	3.7	−1.34	2.79
1956	5.0	6.1	1.1	1.93	0.87	4.7	4.9	−0.86	2.79
1957	3.6	4.1	1.4	1.88	−0.12	4.9	4.8	0.07	2.79
1958	3.2	4.6	2.0	−0.27	−3.23	4.9	4.5	1.42	2.81
1959	0.6	1.7	2.1	3.44	−2.70	4.8	3.3	0.08	2.81
1960	0.8	1.8	1.7	4.56	−1.08	5.4	4.8	1.42	2.81
1961	3.6	3.3	1.5	3.53	−0.46	6.2	5.1	−1.39	2.80
1962	4.2	3.2	2.0	1.18	−2.13	5.9	4.1	0.75	2.81
1963	2.0	2.0	2.3	4.32	−0.74	5.5	3.6	−0.21	2.80
1964	3.2	3.1	1.7	5.13	1.41	6.0	4.6	−2.36	2.79
1965	4.8	4.1	1.4	2.72	1.25	6.7	5.6	−1.12	2.80
1966	3.9	4.1	1.5	1.95	0.33	6.9	6.6	−1.64	2.79
1967	2.4	2.8	2.3	2.80	0.25	6.8	7.6	−1.90	2.75
1968	4.5	3.2	2.5	4.46	1.77	7.6	6.8	−3.70	2.39
1969	5.6	3.6	2.4	1.58	0.49	9.1	7.8	1.71	2.39

Appendix (Contd)

	Inflation		Unemployment	Real income (GDP)		Interest rates		Balance of	Exchange
		GDP			Deviations	Long-	Short-		
	RPI	Deflator	rate	Growth	from trend	term	term	payments	rate
Year	(% p.a.)	(% p.a.)	(%)	(% p.a.)	(%)	(% p.a.)	(% p.a.)	(% GDP)	($US per £)
1970	6.3	7.7	2.6	2.06	−0.32	9.3	6.9	2.92	2.40
1971	9.4	11.0	3.4	2.54	−2.59	8.9	4.4	6.27	2.44
1972	7.3	10.2	3.7	1.40	−2.69	9.0	8.4	−2.26	2.50
1973	9.1	7.9	2.6	7.95	3.47	10.8	12.8	−1.18	2.45
1974	16.0	16.8	2.6	−0.69	1.29	14.8	11.3	−2.18	2.34
1975	24.2	27.4	3.9	−0.60	−0.81	14.4	10.9	−1.53	2.22
1976	16.5	14.4	5.3	3.77	1.40	14.4	14.0	−3.19	1.81
1977	15.9	12.3	5.7	1.13	1.04	12.7	6.3	5.70	1.75
1978	8.3	12.1	5.7	2.91	2.42	12.5	11.9	−0.76	1.92
1979	13.4	12.8	5.4	1.97	2.88	13.0	16.5	1.11	2.12
1980	18.0	18.8	6.8	−1.95	−0.58	13.8	13.6	0.69	2.33
1981	11.9	10.1	9.4	−0.96	−3.03	14.7	15.4	−0.32	2.03
1982	8.6	7.1	10.9	1.07	−3.45	12.9	10.0	−0.55	1.75
1983	4.6	5.7	12.0	3.55	−1.45	10.8	9.0	−0.32	1.52
1984	4.9	4.8	12.4	1.78	−1.18	10.7	9.3	−0.48	1.34
1985	6.1	5.9	12.6	3.81	1.07	10.6	11.5	0.57	1.30
1986	3.4	2.8	12.8	2.66	2.21	9.9	10.9	0.91	1.47

Sources and Methods:
British Economy Key Statistics 1900–1964, Time Publishing Company Ltd. (KS below).
United Kingdom National Accounts, 1987 edition, HMSO, London, August, 1987 (BB below).
Feinstein, C.H., *Statistical Tables of National Income*, Cambridge University Press, Cambridge, 1976 (F below).
Economic Trends Annual Supplement, 1981 edition, HMSO, London, 1981 (TAS81 below).
Economic Trends Annual Supplement, 1986 edition, HMSO, London, 1986 (TAS86 below).
Economic Trends Annual Supplement, 1987 edition, HMSO, London, 1987 (TAS87 below).
Economic Trends, August 1987 edition, HMSO, London, 1987 (ET below).
(1) Inflation:
  (a) Retail Price Index
    The General Index of Retail Prices (all items 1900–47, KS p.8: 1948–85, TAS87 p.114: 1986, ET p.42. The figures in the table are percentage changes in the index over the previous year.
  (b) GDP Deflator
    The GDP Deflator is GDP at factor cost divided by real GDP at factor cost, 1900–45, F pp.T10, T11, T15 and T16: 1946–64, TAS87 p.8: 1965–86, BB pp.10, 11, 14 and 15. The figures in the table are percentage changes in the index over the previous year.
(2) Unemployment:
  1900–48, KS p.8: 1949–80, TAS87 p.97: 1981–86, ET p.36.
  The figures for 1949 to 1986 are the ratio of

unemployed, excluding school leavers, to the sum of employees in employment and the unemployed excluding school leavers. The figures for other years are as published.
(3) Real Income:
  Real Income is Real GDP at factor cost. 1900–45, F pp.T15 and T16: 1946–64, TAS86 p.8: 1965–86, BB pp.14–15.
  (a) Deviations from Trend are calculated as the percentage deviations from trend lines fitted separately to the subperiods 1900–45, 1946–70, 1971–86.
(4) Interest rates:
  (a) Long-term rates:
    1900–63 is the rate on 2.5 per cent Consols and 1964–86 is the rate on 20-year Government Bonds. 1900–54, KS p.16: 1955–63, TAS81 p.194: 1964–85, TAS87 p.196: 1986, ET p.66.
  (b) Short-term rates:
    Treasury bill yield. 1900–54, KS p.16: 1955–85, TAS p.196: 1986, ET p.66.
(5) Balance of payments:
  1946–84, TAS86, p.124.
  The figure in the table is the negative of the official financing figure expressed as a percentage of GDP 1985–86, *United Kingdom Balance of Payments*, 1987 Edition, p.11..
(6) Exchange rate:
  Annual average exchange rate between the pound sterling and the US dollar expressed as dollars per pound. 1900–44, KS p.15: 1955–85, TAS87 p.142: 1986, ET p.50.

Part II

MEASURING
MACROECONOMIC
ACTIVITY

3

Aggregate Income Accounting

Aggregate income accounting provides one of the major sources of data that are needed in order to do macroeconomic analysis. The other major data needs are met by aggregate balance sheet accounting – which provides a statement of what people in the economy owe and own – and the measurement of inflation and unemployment. This chapter deals with aggregate income accounting; Chapter 4 with aggregate balance sheet accounting; Chapter 5 with the measurement of inflation and unemployment; and Chapter 6 with international transactions. As a preliminary to examining aggregate income and balance sheet accounts, this chapter also deals with the distinction between flows and stocks.

By the time you have completed this chapter you will be able to:

(a) **Distinguish between flows and stocks.**

(b) **Define output (or product), income, and expenditure; domestic and national; gross and net; market price and factor cost; nominal and real.**

(c) **Explain the concepts of aggregate output, income (or product), and expenditure.**

(d) **Explain how aggregate income is measured, using the expenditure approach; the factor incomes approach; and the output approach.**

(e) **Explain how aggregate income in constant (real) pounds is measured.**

(f) **Read the UK national income accounts.**

A. Flows and Stocks

A macroeconomic variable that measures a *flow* measures a rate per unit of time. In contrast, a *stock* is a value at a point in time. Examples of flows are income and expenditure. The dimension of these variables is pounds per unit of time — for example, pounds per month or pounds per year. Examples of stocks are: money in the bank, the value of a car or a house, the value of the railway carriages, trains, and track owned by British Rail, and the value of the telephone lines and exchange switching equipment owned by British Telecom. All these variables are measured in pounds on a given day.

Although such items as cars, houses, and physical plant and equipment are stocks, the purchase of additional equipment and the physical wearing out of plant and equipment are flows. Stocks of physical plant and equipment are called *capital*. Additions to capital are called *investment*. The reduction in the value of equipment as a result of wear and tear and/or the passage of time is known as *depreciation*.

Let us illustrate investment and depreciation with a concrete example. Imagine that on the 1st of June 1986, you had a car that had a current market value of £1000. In the year from the 1st of June 1986 to the 1st of June 1987, the market value of the car fell to £800. The value of the car on the 1st of June each year is a stock. That stock has fallen from £1000 in 1986 to £800 in 1987. The depreciation (the loss in the value of the car) is a flow. That flow is £200 per year (or, equivalently, £16.67 per month). If, in May 1987, you sold your car and replaced it with a better car, the value of which is £1500, your capital stock in June of 1987 would be the same £1500. In that case you would have *invested* a total of £700. (The £700 is the difference between the £1500 that your newer car is worth and the £800 that your old car would have been worth, had you kept it.) The change in your capital stock from June 1986 to June 1987 is not £700 but £500. This change is made up of an investment in a new car known as a *gross* investment of £700, minus the depreciation of the old car of £200. The difference between your gross investment and the depreciation of your capital is known as *net* investment.

A useful analogy to illustrate the distinction between flows and stocks is a physical one involving a bathtub, a tap, and a drain. Suppose a bathtub has some water in it, the tap is turned on, and there is no plug in the drain, so that water is flowing into the bathtub and flowing out of it. The water in the tub is a stock, the water entering the tub through the tap and the water leaving the tub through the drain are flows. If the flow through the tap is greater than the flow through the drain, the stock will be rising. If, conversely, the flow through the drain is greater than the flow through the tap, the stock will be falling. In this example there are two flows and one stock, and the stock is determined by the flows. Suppose that the rate of outflow through the drain is a constant which cannot be controlled. The stock can be increased by opening the tap so that the inflow exceeds the outflow, and the stock can be decreased by closing the tap so that the outflow exceeds the inflow.

In terms of the capital stock, investment, and depreciation concepts illustrated earlier with reference to transactions in used cars, you can think of the water in the bathtub as the capital stock, the outflow through the drain as depreciation, and the inflow through the tap as gross investment. The difference between the outflow and inflow is net investment, which may be positive (if the water level is rising) or negative (if the water level is falling).

Suppose that we introduce a human element into the story. Imagine that someone wants to maintain the water level in the tub at a particular depth. That is, they have a desired stock of water. If the actual stock exceeds the desired stock, the corrective action would be to slow down the rate of inflow. If the actual stock was less than the desired stock, the corrective action would be to speed up the rate of inflow. You can see that in this extended story, the stock determines the flow in the sense that individual actions that adjust the flow are triggered by the level of the stock. In the economic analysis that you will be doing shortly, flows (such as national income and expenditure) will be determined by stocks (such as the supply of money).

The remaining tasks in this and the next chapter are a necessary prelude to conducting such economic analyses. The rest of this chapter explains how the national income and expenditure flows are measured and Chapter 4 deals with the measurement of the stocks of assets and liabilities in the economy. Let us begin by reviewing some of the definitions of the main aggregate income and expenditure flows.

B. Some Frequently Used Terms

You have almost certainly encountered in newspapers or on television current affairs programmes, terms like *gross domestic product* or *gross national income*, or, perhaps *gross national product in constant pounds*. This section will enable you to know what these and a few other important terms mean. Following are five groups of words between which you need to be able to distinguish.

(i) Output (or Product), Income and Expenditure

Three concepts of aggregate economic activity are commonly used. These are dealt with in some detail in the next section. For now, all that you need to know are the definitions of these terms. *Output* (or *product*) means the value of the output of the economy. *Income* means the sum of the incomes of all the factors of production (labour, capital and land) employed in the economy. *Expenditure* means the sum of all the expenditures in the economy on final goods and services. (*Note*: see below for the distinction between expenditure on *final* goods and services and expenditure on *intermediate* goods and services.)

(ii) Domestic and National

In the preceding paragraph the term *the economy* is used as if it is unambiguous. There is ambiguity, however, as to what is meant by 'the economy'. What is the 'UK economy'? There are two possible answers. One involves the *domestic economy*, which is all economic activity taking place in the geographical domain of the UK. The other involves the *national* economy, which is all economic activity of the residents of the UK wherever in the world that activity happens to be performed.

Thus, *domestic* output (or product), income, and expenditure refers to the aggregate of output, income, and expenditure in the geographical domain of the UK. And the concept of *national* output (or product), income, and expenditure refers to the output produced by, the income earned by, or expenditure made on goods produced by residents of the UK, no matter where in the world that economic activity takes place. The difference between these two aggregates is known as 'net property income from (or paid) abroad'. It is not large for most countries and is very small for the UK. Thus, since no special purpose is served by the distinction between the two concepts, this book will use the term *aggregate product, income,* and *expenditure* to refer to either or both the national and domestic concepts.

(iii) Gross and Net

Gross national (or domestic) product (or income or expenditure) means that the aggregate is measured *before* deducting the value of the assets of the economy which have been used up or depreciated in the production process during the year.

Net national (or domestic) product (or income or expenditure) means that the aggregate is measured *after* deducting the value of the assets of the economy which have been used up or depreciated in the production process during the year. Macroeconomics is concerned with explaining the overall scale of economic activity and uses the gross concept. The net concept is of use in measuring the standard of living, a topic outside the scope of macroeconomics.

(iv) Market Price and Factor Cost

In most modern economies (and certainly in the UK) the government taxes expenditure on some goods and subsidizes expenditure on others. An example of an expenditure tax is value added tax (VAT). An example of a subsidy is the sale of milk at less than cost. There are two ways of measuring the value of a good or service. One is based on the prices paid by the final user (consumer) and is known as the *market price* valuation. The other is based on the cost of all the factors of production, including the profits made. This measure is known as the *factor cost* valuation. Market prices include taxes on expenditure and are net of subsidies. Factor costs exclude taxes on expenditure, but do not have subsidies netted out.

The various aggregates defined above can be measured on either the market price or factor cost basis. If value added taxes were increased and income taxes cut by equal amounts, nothing (as a first approximation) would happen to the level of aggregate economic activity. The market price concept of national income, however, would rise. The factor cost concept would not change. Macroeconomics is concerned with measuring the scale of economic activity and, ideally, would use the factor cost concept. In practice, provided care is taken to interpret any large changes in indirect taxes and subsidies, the market price concept is used.

(v) Nominal and Real

The various aggregates defined above can be measured either in current pounds (nominal) or in constant pounds (real). The *nominal* valuation uses prices of goods or factors of production prevailing in the *current* period to value the current period's output or expenditure. The *real* valuation uses prices of goods or factors that prevailed in an earlier period, called the *base* period, to value the current period's output or expenditure. Real values are the appropriate ones for measuring the level of economic activity. Since macroeconomics is concerned with both the scale of activity and prices (and inflation), both of these concepts are of importance and will appear again later in this chapter and in Chapter 5.

It is now time to go beyond learning definitions and to develop a deeper understanding of the central concepts of output (or product), income, and expenditure.

C. Aggregate Output (or Product), Income and Expenditure

In order to help you *understand* the central concepts of aggregate output (or product), income, and expenditure, it will be conveninent to begin by considering an economy that is much simpler than the one in which you live. We will then successively add various features of the economy until we have a picture which corresponds quite closely to the world that we inhabit.

(i) The Simplest Economy

Let us suppose that the economy is one which has no transactions with the rest of the world; that is, no one exports anything to foreigners or imports anything from them. Also no borrowing or lending takes place across the national borders. Indeed, no communications of any kind occur between the domestic economy and the rest of the world.

Next, suppose that there is no government; that is, no one pays taxes; all expenditures by households are voluntary; and all the goods and services that firms produce are bought by households, rather than some of them being bought by the government or its agencies.

The economy consists of just two kinds of economic institutions or agents: households and firms. A *household* is an agent that:

(1) Owns factors of production.
(2) Buys all final consumer goods.

A firm is an agent which:

(1) Owns nothing.
(2) Hires factors of production from households.
(3) Sells the goods which it produces to households.
(4) Pays any profits that it makes on its activities to households.

This economy can be visualized more clearly by considering Figure 3.1. The households in this economy are represented by the circle labelled *H*, and the firms are represented by the circle labelled *F*. Two kinds of flows take place between households and firms. First, real things are supplied by households to firms and by firms to households. Second, money passes between households and firms in exchange for these real things. The real flows are shown with the dashed lines, and the money flows

Figure 3.1
Real flows and money flows in the simplest economy

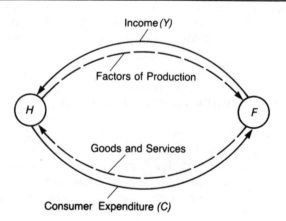

The flow of factors of production from households (*H*) to firms (*F*) and the flow of goods and services from firms to households (clockwise dashed lines) are matched by equivalent flows of money — firms paying income to households (*Y*) and households paying firms (*C*) for consumer goods and services (anti-clockwise continuous lines).

are shown with the continuous lines. Households are shown as supplying factors of production to firms, and firms are shown as supplying goods and services to households. Moving in the opposite direction to these real flows are the money flows. Firms pay income to households, and households spend their income on consumer goods. The aggregate income payment is denoted by Y and aggregate consumer expenditure by C.

It is evident that in this economy the income that households receive from firms must be equal to the expenditure which households make on consumer goods. If this were not so, firms would be making either gains or losses that they would not be passing on to the households, who are the ultimate suppliers of factor services. It will also be evident that the *value* of the goods and services produced by the firms — the value of output of the firms — is also equal to the expenditure on those goods and services by the households. In other words,

$$\text{expenditure} = \text{income} = \text{value of output} \tag{3.1}$$

This very simple economy, which abstracts from much of the detail of the actual world in which we live, has enabled us to establish the equality of income, expenditure, and output, which follows purely from the definitions of the terms involved. We now want to go on to see that this equality also applies to the more complicated world in which we live.

(ii) Some More Realistic Economies

There are three features of the 'real world' which are not captured in the story above and in Figure 3.1. They are:

(1) Households typically do not spend all their income on consumer goods — they also save some of their income.
(2) Governments are large (and indeed growing) institutions in the modern world that tax individual incomes and use their tax proceeds to buy large quantities of goods and services from firms.
(3) Economic activity is not restricted to trading with other domestic residents. International trade, travel, and capital movements are commonplace.

These three characteristics of the world in which we live will be introduced one by one, rather than all at once.

(iii) Savings by Households

Since households typically do not spend all their income on consumer goods, but also do some saving, it looks as if Figure 3.1 has a serious defect. If households save some of their income, then consumer expenditure must be less than income, and, therefore, the flow of expenditure from households to firms shown in Figure 3.1 must be smaller than the flow of income received by households from firms. This would mean that firms are continually short of cash because they are paying out more than they are receiving. How does this complicating factor affect the concepts of national income, expenditure, and output and their equality?

The easiest way of dealing with this complication is to consider a still slightly fictitious (but less fictitious than previously) representation of the economy in which we think of there being two kinds of firms — those that produce consumer goods and those that produce capital goods. Denote consumer goods firms by the letters F_c and capital goods firms by the letters F_k. You can think of F_c firms as being, for example, those that produce food, clothing, and the thousands of commodities that households typically consume; and you can think of F_k firms as those that produce, for example, steel mills, highways, generating stations, and the like. (Of course, in the real world there isn't a clear-cut, hard-and-fast division.)

Figure 3.2 illustrates the real flows and the money flows between the various kinds of firms and households. Households supply factors of production to both consumer goods producers and capital goods producers.

**Figure 3.2
Real flows and
money flows in an
economy with sav-
ings and investment**

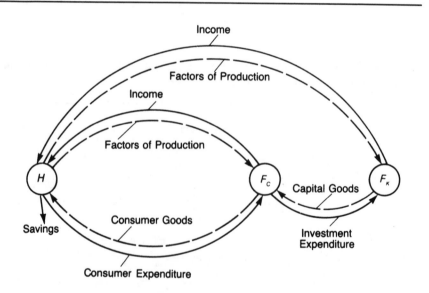

Households (H) supply factor services to producers of consumer goods (F_c) and capital goods (F_k). Consumer goods producers supply households, and capital goods producers supply consumer good producers with new equipment. These real flows (clockwise dashed lines) are matched by equivalent money flows (anti-clockwise continuous lines). Income is paid to households equal in value to the production of both consumer and capital goods. Households pay firms for the purchase of consumer goods. Consumer goods producers pay capital goods producers for their purchases of new equipment. These payments are known as investment expenditure.

These are shown as the two continuous lines representing flows from households to the two kinds of firm. The consumer goods producers, F_c, supply consumer goods to households, and the capital goods producers, F_k, supply capital goods to the producers of consumer goods. (Two further fictions that we will maintain are first, that capital goods firms do not themselves buy capital goods and second, that households do not buy capital goods. We could easily relax these assumptions, although it would make the pictorial representation of what is going on more complicated.)

To summarize: the real flows in the economy are the two sets of factor services flowing from households to the two kinds of firms and goods flowing in the opposite directions – capital goods flowing from capital goods producers to consumer goods producers, and consumer goods flowing from consumer goods producers to households.

Financial flows move in a direction opposite to the goods and factor flows. Two kinds of firms pay income to households. Households make consumer expenditure, which represent the flow of money from households to consumer goods producers, and consumer goods producers make investment expenditure by paying money to capital goods producers in exchange for the capital goods supplied. In addition, households save some of their income. This saving is shown as the flow going *from* households (H). Households' savings are not a payment to either capital goods or consumer goods producers directly and therefore are not shown as a flow into either of these two institutions, but simply as a flow out of households.

In order to make the picture of the economy simpler, let us now add

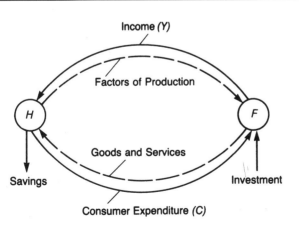

Income (Y)

Factors of Production

H   F

Goods and Services

Savings   Investment

Consumer Expenditure (C)

**Figure 3.3
Real flows and
money flows in an
economy with savings and
investment simplified**

Consumer and capital goods producers are consolidated into an aggregate firm sector (F). Firms in total buy factor services from households (H) in exchange for income. Households buy consumer goods and services in exchange for the money flow of consumer expenditure. What households do not spend on consumer goods they save. Households' savings are equal in value to firms' investment expenditure.

together the two kinds of firms (F_c and F_k) into a single, aggregate firms sector (F). This is done in Figure 3.3. Now, instead of having two income flows from firms to households, there is one, which represents the sum of the two flows in Figure 3.2. Also, instead of there being two flows of factor services to firms, there is one, which also represents the sum of the two flows shown in Figure 3.2. The expenditure by households on goods and services to firms is exactly the same as before, namely, the expenditure on consumer goods. Also, the flow of goods and services from firms to households is the same as the flow from the consumer goods firms to households. By aggregating all the firms in the economy into a single sector, the flow of capital goods from one kind of firm to another and the flow of investment expenditure on those goods have been lost, so to speak, in the aggregation. That is, by only looking at the aggregate of firms and the transactions that they have with households, we are not able to 'see' in the picture the flow of investment expenditure and the flow of capital goods between firms. As a substitute, and so that we do not forget the flow of investment expenditure, Figure 3.3 shows it as a net receipt by firms.

To simplify things further and to make it easier to move on to the next two stages of complexity, Figure 3.4 reproduces Figure 3.3, but leaves out the real flows of factors of production and goods and services, show-ing only the financial flows. Also, this figure uses only the symbolic names for the flows rather than their full names. Let us now focus on Figure 3.4. What this figure shows us is that income (Y) is paid by firms to households; households' consumption expenditure (C) is received by firms; households also save (S). This latter activity simply represents the

Figure 3.4
The money flows in an economy with savings and invest-ment — a more abstract representation

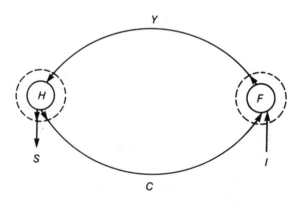

The money flows only are shown, with symbols denoting: income (Y), consumer expen-diture (C), savings (S), and investment (I). The broken circles around the households (H) and firms (F) contain arrows going to or from households and firms. An arrow leading into a sector represents a receipt. An arrow leaving a sector represents a payment. Total receipts by a sector equal total payments. Thus, for households, $Y = C + S$. For firms, $Y = C + I$. It follows directly that $S = I$.

non-spending of income by households and does not represent *direct* transfers of resources to firms. In addition, firms make investment (I) expenditure on new capital goods.

The savings which households make out of their income and the investment that firms make in new capital goods clearly are in some sense related to each other. It is capital markets — markets in which people borrow and lend — that provide the mechanism whereby these two variables are linked. Households place their savings in various kinds of financial assets, and firms borrow in a variety of ways from households in order to undertake their investment activity. Thus, it is the capital markets that provide the financial flow linkage between savings and investment.

Let us now return to Figure 3.4 and look again at the concepts of income, output, and expenditure embodied in this more complicated representation of the world. To highlight matters, focus first of all upon the firms (the circle labelled F). We have put an extra circle (dotted) around F that contains three arrows — two leading into the F, and one going from the F. Recall that everything a firm receives it also has to pay out. Firms do not own anything, and the profits they make are paid out to households as factor income. Given this fact, it is clear that the income paid out by firms must be equal to the expenditure by households on consumer goods and the expenditure by firms on investment goods; that is

$$Y = C + I \qquad (3.2)$$

Next, focus on households (H) and on the dotted circle surrounding H in Figure 3.4. This circle also has three arrows, one leading to H and two leading from H. Since households must, in some way, dispose of their income, either by consuming or saving, it is evident that consumption plus savings (the outflows from households) must be equal to household income, i.e.

$$Y = C + S \qquad (3.3)$$

Equation (3.2) above tells us that the value of all income in the economy is equal to the value of all expenditure. The expenditure is now broader than it was in the first example and includes investment expenditure as well as consumer expenditure.

Further, just as it was in the simpler example, the value of output in the economy is also equal to income or expenditure. To see this equality, all you have to do is to recognize that the value of the goods and services produced is equal to the value placed upon them by the final demanders of those goods and services. That value is consumer expenditure plus investment expenditure. Thus, income, expenditure, and output are equal again in this more 'realistic' representation of the world.

You must be careful to distinguish between expenditure on final goods and services, payment to factors of production, and expenditure on intermediate goods and services. These distinctions are easier to see in this simplified economy, but apply to all the more complicated economies described later.

The distinction between expenditure on final goods and services, payment to factors of production, and expenditure on intermediate goods and services is most easily understood with the aid of an example. Suppose you buy a chocolate bar from the local university store for 50p. The university store bought that chocolate bar from its wholesale supplier for 40p; the wholesaler bought it from the manufacturer for 36p; the manufacturer bought milk for 2p, cocoa beans for 4p, sugar for 4p and, electricity for 6p; it paid wages to its workers of 14p and made a 6p profit which it paid to its stockholders. The total expenditure in the story of the chocolate bar is 50 + 40 + 36 + 2 + 4 + 4 + 6 + 14 + 6 = £1.62. Of this £1.62, only 50p represents expenditure on final goods and services. The rest is expenditure on intermediate goods and services or payment to factors of production. The expenditure can be classified as shown in Table 3.1.

Table 3.1   Intermediate and final expenditures and factor incomes

Item	Expenditure on final goods and services	Factor incomes	Expenditure on intermediate goods and services
Purchase price of chocolate bar	50p	—	—
Wholesaler's selling price	—	—	40p
Manufacturer's selling price	—	—	36p
Farmer's income (milk)	—	2p	—
Farmer's income (cocoa beans)	—	4p	—
Farmer's income (sugar)	—	4p	—
Electricity producer's income	—	6p	—
Chocolate producer's wages	—	14p	—
Chocolate producer's profits	—	6p	—
Wholesaler's profit	—	4p	—
Retailer's profit	—	10p	—
Total	50p	50p	

Notice that the first column gives the expenditure (expenditure on final goods and services) on a chocolate bar, the second column total gives the incomes earned by all those who had a hand in producing the chocolate bar, and the final column simply records some intermediate transactions. From the viewpoint of macroeconomics, these last items are irrelevant. They arise from a particular form of industrial structure and would change if the industrial structure changed. For example, if the manufacturer sold directly to the retailer (for the 40p charged by the wholesaler in the above example), the expenditure on intermediate goods and services would fall by 36p. Nothing important, however, would have changed. Total expenditure on final goods and services would still be 50p. Also, factor incomes would still be 50p; the profit of the wholesaler would have been eliminated and transferred to the manufacturer (by assumption in the above story). To count the expenditure on intermediate goods and services as well as the expenditure on final goods and services involves counting the same thing twice (or more than twice if there are several intermediate stages) and is known as 'double counting'.

(iv) Government Expenditure and Taxes

Now let us consider a yet more complicated world — one in which government economic activity plays a role. Figure 3.5 illustrates this type of economy. In addition to households (H) and firms (F), we also have government (denoted as GOV). Figure 3.5, which shows the relationship between households, firms, and government is drawn on the simplified basis introduced in Figure 3.4. That is, we do not show both the real flows and the money flows. We show only the money flows. Also, we only label the various flows with their symbolic rather than their full names. There are two new symbols: T stands for taxes and G stands for government expenditure on goods and services.

In this more complicated world, households receive incomes (Y) from firms. They dispose of that income either by buying consumer goods (C), paying taxes (T), or saving (S). Firms, as before, receive households' consumption expenditure (C) as well as investment expenditure (I) (financed by various capital market operations). Firms also have receipts from the

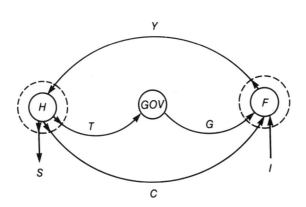

Figure 3.5
Money flows in an economy with savings, investment, and government economic activity

Government (GOV) taxes households (H) and buys goods and services produced by firms (F) — government expenditure on goods and services are shown by (G), and government revenue — taxes — are shown by T. When these flows are added to those shown (and defined) in the previous figures, the households' income and expenditure account is modified to become $Y = C + S + T$. The firms' income and expenditure account is modified to become $Y = C + I + G$. It follows directly from these last two statements that $S + T = I + G$. There is no reason why government expenditure should equal taxes. The government may run a surplus ($T > G$) or a deficit ($T < G$).

government in exchange for its purchase of goods and services (G). The government itself simply receives taxes (net of any transfers that it makes to households) and makes expenditure on goods and services.

Now, to see the national income accounts that emerge from this more complex world, focus again, first of all, on firms (F) and on the arrows in the broken circle surrounding (F). Notice that now firms pay out income (Y) and receive consumer expenditure (C), government expenditure (G), and investment expenditure (I). Since, as before, they have no ultimate ownership of resources, everything that they receive is paid out to households. Hence

$$Y = C + I + G \tag{3.4}$$

Next, focus on households (H). They receive income and dispose of that income in the activities of consuming (C), saving (S) and paying taxes (T). Hence

$$Y = C + S + T \tag{3.5}$$

In this economy, expenditure is still equal to income, but expenditure now incorporates consumer expenditure, firms' investment expenditure, and in addition, government expenditure on goods and services.

It is important that you understand that government payments to households such as, for example, unemployment benefits, are *not* government expenditure on goods and services; they are the transfer of money from the government to households and are called *transfer payments*. You can think of these as negative taxes, so that total tax payments (denoted as T), need to be thought of as being *net taxes* equal to the gross taxes paid by households minus the transfers from government to households.

As in the two simpler economies considered above, not only are income and expenditure equal to each other, but output is also equal to income and expenditure. The value of the goods and services bought by households (C), firms (I), and government (G) represent the value of the goods and services produced in the economy — the output of the economy. Hence, even in this more complex economy, aggregate income, expenditure, and output are one and the same.

(v) The Rest of the World

Now consider the final complication arising from the fact that economic agents do business with their counterparts in the rest of the world. Figure 3.6 illustrates the story here. Now we have households (H), firms (F), government (GOV), and the rest of the world (R). All the flows are as before, except for some additional flows between the rest of the world and the domestic economy. The left-hand part of Figure 3.6 is identical to Figure 3.5. and does not need to be described again. The additional activities in Figure 3.6 are imports and exports of goods and services.

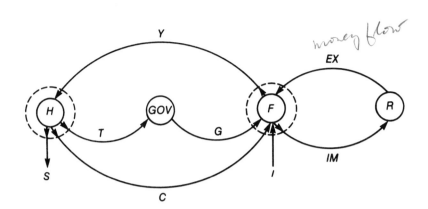

**Figure 3.6
Money flows in an
economy with sav-
ings, investment,
government
economic activity,
and transactions with
the rest of the world**

The flow transactions with the rest of the world are exports that give rise to a receipt by the firms doing the exporting (*EX*) and imports that give rise to payments by firms doing the importing (*IM*). These receipts and payments run between firms (*F*) and the rest of the world (*R*). Extending the flows to include those with the rest of world leaves the households' income and expenditure unchanged. They remain $Y = C + S + T$. The firms' accounts now become $Y = C + I + G + EX$. There is no requirement that exports (*EX*) equal imports (*IM*). There may be a trade surplus (*EX* > *IM*) or a trade deficit (*EX* < *IM*) with the rest of the world.

Foreigners buy goods from domestic firms and, therefore, there is a flow of money from the rest of the world to those firms for exports (*EX*). In addition, domestic firms buy goods from the rest of the world, transferring money to foreigners in exchange for those goods – imports (*IM*). From the way the figure has been drawn, it looks as if only firms do the importing. We know that sometimes households import goods directly. This could easily be shown in the picture, but it would not add anything of substance.

Let us see how the national income accounts now look in this economy. There is no change in the flows into and out of households. It is true that households now buy consumer goods, some of which have been imported from the rest of the world by the firms from whom they buy them. That, however, will not show up directly in the households' accounts. Their accounts still say that income (*Y*) is equal to consumption (*C*) plus savings (*S*) plus taxes (*T*).

We get a slightly different picture, however, when we look at firms. We now have two arrows leading out of the *F* circle – flows of money from firms to other agents – and four arrows flowing into *F*. Firms pay factor incomes to households (*Y*) and pay foreigners for the value of goods and services that have been imported from them (*IM*). They receive from foreigners the value of exports (*EX*), from government the value of goods and services purchased by government (*G*), and from households the value of consumer goods purchased (C). There is also a net inflow of funds to finance the firms' investment expenditures (I). Thus, considering all the arrows showing flows into and out from the firms, it is clear that

$$Y = C + I + G + EX - IM \tag{3.6}$$

The items on the right-hand side of Equation (3.6) are total *net* expenditures on domestic output. Hence, the equality between income and expenditure is retained in the world pictured in Figure 3.6. Income is the flow of money from firms to households, and it represents the value of the factor services supplied by households to firms. Expenditure is equal to the consumption expenditure of households (C), the value of purchases of capital equipment by firms (I), government expenditures of goods and services (G), and the net value of foreigners' expenditure on domestic output. By *net* value we mean the difference between the gross purchases by foreigners (exports) and the purchase of foreign goods by domestic citizens (imports). Also, the value of output is equal to income (and expenditure).

There is an additional interesting implication in the national income accounts in this more 'realistic' picture of the world. It follows immediately from the equality between income and expenditure and the fact that income is allocated by households to consumption, savings and taxes. If you begin by considering Equations (3.5) and (3.6), it will be immediately apparent to you that

$$I + G + EX = S + T + IM \tag{3.7}$$

If we deduct savings, taxes, and imports from both sides of this equation and rearrange the order of the terms we obtain

$$(I - S) + (G - T) + (EX - IM) = 0 \tag{3.8}$$

The three terms in brackets in Equation (3.8) have a very natural interpretation. The first term $(I - S)$, is the excess of investment over savings by the private sector of the economy. The second term, $(G - T)$, is the government's budget deficit. The third term, $(EX - IM)$, is the surplus on the balance of trade with the rest of the world.

What Equation (3.8) says is that the sum of these three items must always be zero. There are various alternative ways in which this equation could be satisfied. One way, which is perhaps helpful, is to notice that Equation (3.8) implies that if firms are investing more than households are saving, then either it is necessary for there to be a balance of trade deficit — that is, for imports to exceed exports — so that the extra investment goods may indeed be acquired by firms; or it is necessary for government expenditure to be less than taxes, so that, in effect, the government is doing some of the saving that is enabling capital goods to be accumulated by firms. Another way of putting the same thing would be to say that if the government insists on spending more than it generates in taxes — if there is a government budget deficit — then there must either be a shortfall of investment as compared with savings or there must be a balance of trade deficit with the rest of the world to enable the government to acquire the value of the resources in excess of the taxes that it is levying.

偽矣.

D. Measuring Aggregate Income

(i) *The Expenditure Approach*

In order to measure national income (or expenditure or output), it is necessary to record and add together the appropriate flows that are taking place in the economy. There are three common methods of measuring national income. The first is the *expenditure approach*. You can think of the expenditure approach as an attempt by the national income statisticians to measure the total value of consumer expenditure on goods and services (C), firms' investment expenditure (I), government expenditure on goods and services (G), as well as exports (EX), and imports (IM). When they combine these flows in accordance with Equation (3.6), they provide one estimate of the value of national income, expenditure, or output.

These items can be measured with varying degrees of accuracy. Consumer expenditure is measured partly by taking surveys of what households are spending and partly by observing the value of the sales of consumer goods by producers. Government expenditure is measured directly from the accounts of government itself. Investment expenditure is measured by surveying firms' capital spending programmes and inventories. Finally, foreign trade is monitored through the official documentation required to conduct that trade. Most countries have some form of control over international movements of goods and services, and· in some cases, these items are subject either to quotas or tariffs. In order to implement these arrangements, governments automatically collect data on the volume of international trade flows.

Thus, by measuring these items, C, I, G, EX and IM, it is possible to obtain a measure of aggregate income, expenditure or output by using the previous formula

$$Y = C + I + G + EX - IM \qquad (3.6)$$

By adding these expenditures, the aggregate that results is based on market prices and includes expenditure taxes less subsidies. To convert this valuation to the factor cost measure needed for macroeconomic analysis, it is necessary to deduct the expenditure taxes and add the subsidies to give aggregate income (output or expenditure) at factor cost.

(ii) The Factor Incomes Approach

A second method of measuring national income is to measure factor incomes directly. The major sources of such measurements are the returns which individuals and firms make to the tax-collecting branch of government — in the UK, Inland Revenue. Since most taxes are collected as a levy on incomes earned, the reporting of those incomes for the purpose of tax calculations provides the major input for the *factor incomes approach* to the measurement of aggregate income. By using these sources, it is possible to arrive at an estimate of aggregate income. This measure of aggregate income (output or expenditure) is automatically on a factor cost basis and needs no further adjustment.

The two measures of aggregate income — the expenditure approach (adjusted to the factor cost basis) and the factor incomes approach — never quite agree with each other. There is always a statistical discrepancy since it is simply too costly to devote the necessary resources to obtain precise values of these flows.

(iii) The Output Approach

A third method of measuring national income is to measure the value of output of each industry and then aggregate those output measures to arrive at an estimate of aggregate output. The major sources of direct output measurement are surveys of production and sales by firms. By using data collected from such surveys, it is possible to arrive at estimates of aggregate output by what is known as the *output approach*. In addition to providing a third way of arriving at an estimate of aggregate economic activity, this approach also provides estimates of the output of each major sector of the economy.

E. Measuring Aggregate Income in Constant Pounds (Real)

The *expenditure approach* to measuring aggregate income provides the basis for the measurement of aggregate income (output or expenditure) in constant pounds, or real terms. A base period is chosen. At the moment, in the UK, that base period is 1980. The average level of prices prevailing in the base period is defined to be equal to 100. The expenditures of a particular year are revalued using the prices prevailing in the base year. They are then aggregated using the formula in Equation (3.6) above to arrive at real income, output, or expenditure.

F. Reading National Income and Expenditure Accounts

The UK aggregate income accounts are assembled by the Central Statistical Office. The annual accounts are published in the *United Kingdom National Accounts* (known as the *Blue Book*) each year. The detailed definitions, concepts, sources, and methods are described, with immense attention being paid to the intricacies involved in national accounts statistics; see *National Accounts Statistics: Sources and Methods, Third Edition*, Studies in Official Statistics, No. 37 (HMSO, 1985). A useful but brief summary entitled 'An Introduction to the U.K. National Accounts', is also provided in the first section of the *Blue Book*.

Reading the National Income Accounts and translating them into the aggregate concepts that you have become familiar with in the preceding parts of this chapter is a relatively straightforward business. You may, nevertheless, need some guidance in the task.

If you look at the National Income *Blue Book* (you will find a copy in any university library and in the business/economics section of many public libraries), the first thing that will strike you (probably with mild alarm) is the immense detail presented. The 1987 edition of the *Blue Book* has a new format. Its Table of Contents provides the conversion formula so that, where tables have changed their number or order of appearance, you can find the comparable table in earlier years. The *Blue Book* contains no fewer than 117 tables spread over almost 130 pages. Fortunately, for our present purposes, a small number of summary tables in Chapter 1 contain most of what is needed. Table 1.2 provides an estimate of the gross national product classified according to the expenditure approach and using both market prices and factor costs as the basis of valuation. Table 1.3 provides an estimate by the income approach, aggregating incomes over various categories. That table provides an estimate of gross national product from the income approach and shows the discrepancy (residual error) between the income and expenditure methods of measuring aggregate activity. Table 1.5 provides an estimate of gross domestic product by industry from the output approach measured in constant 1980 pounds. Table 1.6 provides comparable figures to those supplied in Table 1.2, but revalues all the items in constant 1980 prices.

Some of the more important items in the National Income *Blue Book* tables are brought together, in Table 3.2 below, in a form that will enable you to see the relationships between the variables, using the concepts developed earlier in this chapter. The name (or names) of the items given in parentheses beneath each major item refers to the details contained in the *Blue Book* tables. There is little to be gained from committing this table to memory. You may, however, find it a useful reference in the event that you want to construct your own accounts for a year, or years, other than 1986 (the example used here).

Looking at the major items in Table 3.2 you will see that consumption

Table 3.2   UK aggregate income, expenditure and product in 1986

	Item	£ million
	Consumption (*C*)	
	(Consumer expenditure)	234,167
add	Investment (*I*)	
	(Gross domestic fixed capital formation 64,227	
	plus value of physical increase in stocks and	
	work in progress 551)	64,778
add	Government expenditure (*G*)	
	(General government final consumption)	79,423
add	Exports (*EX*)	
	(Exports of goods and services)	97,835
deduct	Imports (*IM*)	
	(Imports of goods and services)	−101,308
equals	Gross domestic product at market prices	374,895
deduct	Taxes on expenditure less subsidies	−55,806
equals	Gross domestic product at factor cost	319,089
add	Net property income from abroad	4,686
equals	Gross national product at factor cost	323,775
	(Capital consumption)	(46,004)

Source: *United Kingdom National Accounts*, Table 1.2 (HMSO, 1987)

(*C*) plus investment (*I*) plus government expenditure (*G*) plus exports (*EX*) less imports (*IM*) add up to gross domestic product at market prices. By deducting indirect taxes less subsidies, an estimate of gross domestic product at factor cost is arrived at. Adding the net property income from abroad provides an estimate of gross national product at factor cost. The bottom of the table notes the amount of capital consumption — that is, depreciation of fixed capital — which has accrued in the year. By subtracting that amount from any of the other gross figures you may arrive at the corresponding net national or domestic product estimate either at factor cost or market price.

Summary

A. Flows and Stocks

A flow is a rate per unit of time such as income per year or expenditure per month. A stock is the value of a variable at a point in time such as the amount of money you have in the bank on a particular day.

B. Some Frequently Used Terms

(1) Output (or product), income and expenditure:
Output (or *product*) is the value of the goods and services produced in the economy.
Income is the sum of all the incomes earned in producing the output of the economy.
Expenditure is the sum of all expenditures on final goods and services in the economy.

(2) Domestic and national:
Domestic refers to an aggregation of economic activity taking place in a particular country.
National refers to an aggregation of the economic activity of all residents no matter in which country the activity takes place.

(3) Gross and net:
Gross is before deducting the depreciation of assets.
Net is after deducting the depreciation of assets.

(4) Market price and factor cost:
Market price valuations are based on the prices paid by consumers and include expenditure taxes on and are net of subsidies.
Factor cost valuations are based on the amounts paid to the factors of production, including profits, and exclude expenditure taxes and are gross of subsidies.

(5) Nominal and real:
Nominal valuation uses prices prevailing in the current period.
Real valuation uses prices that prevailed in a base period.

C. Aggregate Output (or Product), Income and Expenditure

Aggregate output is the value of all the goods and services produced in the economy. Aggregate income is the sum of all the incomes of all the individuals in the economy. Aggregate expenditure is the sum of all the expenditures on *final* goods and services produced by the economy. The value of aggregate output, income, and expenditure are equal to each other.

D. Measuring Aggregate Income

The *expenditure approach* to aggregate income measurement samples the expenditures of households, firms, government, and foreigners and makes an estimate of the sum of those expenditures. From the fact that income, expenditure, and output are equal to each other, this estimate of expenditure is also an estimate of income and output.

The *factor incomes approach* samples the incomes of individuals and forms an estimate of aggregate income. From the conceptual equality of income, expenditure, and output, this approach provides an alternative estimate of aggregate expenditure and output as well as income.

The *output approach* samples the production of individual firms and forms an estimate of the value of output in each sector of the economy and in aggregate.

The three approaches never produce identically the same estimate, but provide a good approximation to the value of aggregate output, income and expenditure.

E. Measuring Aggregate Income in Constant Pounds (Real)

To measure real income (output and expenditure), the expenditure approach is used. The final goods and services bought in each year are valued at the prices which prevailed in the base year.

F. Reading National Income and Expenditure Accounts

The UK national income and expenditure accounts (annual data) are published in August of each year by the Central Statistical Office in *United Kingdom National Accounts* known more commonly as the *Blue Book*). The key tables in that publication are Table 1.2 (National product by category of expenditure), Table 1.3 (Gross domestic product by category of income), Table 1.5 (Gross domestic product: output based measure at constant factor cost) and Table 1.6 (Gross national product by category of expenditure at 1980 prices). The way in which the detailed items supplied by the Central Statistical Office aggregate into the concepts employed in macroeconomics is set out in Table 3.2, and that table may be used as a reference guide.

Review Questions

1. Indicate which of the following are flows and which are stocks:

    (a) The amount of water that flows under the Tower Bridge in a day
    (b) The amount of oil under the North Sea
    (c) Gross domestic product
    (d) Real national income
    (e) The value of the airplanes owned by British Airways

2. Review the definition of each of the following terms:

    (a) Gross domestic product
    (b) Gross domestic product at market price
    (c) Gross national product at factor cost
    (d) Real national income

3. Give examples which illustrate the differences between the following terms:

    (a) Nominal and real
    (b) Gross and net
    (c) National and domestic
    (d) Factor cost and market price

4. What are the units of measurement of (a) a nominal variable and (b) a real variable?

5. Using the latest available data from the *United Kingdom National Accounts*, calculate the latest year values of (a) aggregate income, (b) aggregate expenditure, and (c) aggregate output.

6. Using the latest *United Kingdom National Accounts*, calculate aggregate income for 1987 using (a) the expenditure approach, and (b) the factor incomes approach. Is your measure of aggregate income a gross or a net measure? What is the difference between gross aggregate income and net aggregate income in 1987?

7. Using gross aggregate income for 1987 (calculated in Question 6) and other relevant data from the *United Kingdom National Accounts*, calculate 1987 aggregate income in constant 1980 prices.

8. Suppose that you want to describe the pattern of aggregate output in the UK during the last decade. Which of the following would be the best series to use, and why?

    (a) Aggregate expenditure at market prices
    (b) Aggregate output at factor cost
    (c) Gross domestic product in constant pounds
    (d) Gross domestic product

    Say exactly what *all* the faults are with *all* the series that you would *not* use.

9. A troupe of Russian dancers tours the UK. The dancers fly to London on an *Aeroflot* (Soviet airline) flight at a total round trip cost of £200,000. They travel inside the UK on British Rail at a total cost of £185,000. Their hotel and food bills in the UK amount to £150,000. The receipts from ticket sales for performances of the troupe amount to £1,000,000. The cost of renting theatres, hiring British musicians is £200,000, and advertising is £350,000. The Russian dancers' wages amounted to £75,000 for the period of the visit. The dancers bought British-made souvenirs worth a total of £2500. Any profit or loss on the visit accrued to or was borne by the Soviet government. Show

where each of the economic activities described here appears in the national income accounts of the United Kingdom.

10. The following activities took place in an imaginary economy last year:

Item	£ millions
Wages paid to labour	700,000
Consumer expenditure	650,000
Taxes paid on wages	200,000
Government payments to support the unemployed, sick and aged	50,000
Firms' profits	200,000
Investment	250,000
Taxes paid on profits	50,000
Government purchases of goods and services	200,000
Exports	250,000
Interest and rent	100,000

Note: There was no property income paid to or received from non-residents.

(a) Calculate:
   gross domestic income
   gross national expenditure
   savings
   imports
   the government budget surplus/deficit
(b) What extra information do you need in order to calculate net national income?

4

Aggregate Balance Sheet Accounting

This is an unusual topic to appear in an introductory macroeconomics text, and it reflects the unusual nature of the book with which you are working. Keynesian macroeconomics places a great deal of emphasis on the national income accounts and on aggregate income and expenditure flows, and the last chapter dealt with the concepts that lie behind that accounting framework. If you were working with a conventional Keynesian-oriented macroeconomics book you would now be reading the first 'theory' chapter. That chapter would present a theory about how national income is determined, and the theory would be based purely on the items from national income flow accounts. It would postulate hypothetical relationships between various flows — hypotheses that one flow depends in some behavioural way on another flow — and from that it would develop a predictive theory of the determination of national income.

That route is not taken here. The kind of macroeconomics that you are studying in this book is built on the presumption that the most important behavioural relationships are not only those between various flows, but also those between flows and stocks. Accordingly, as a prelude to studying macroeconomic theory, this chapter explains the connections between the main stocks (the assets and liabilities in the economy) and also explains how those stocks are measured.

By the time you have completed your study of this chapter you will be able to:

(a) **Explain the meaning of 'asset', 'liability', and 'balance sheet'.**
(b) **Define money.**
(c) **Describe the main items in the balance sheets of households, firms, commercial banks, the central bank, government, and the rest of the world.**
(d) **Describe the main sources of information about the UK aggregate balance sheets.**

A. Asset, Liability and Balance Sheet

(i) Asset and Liability

An *asset* is simply something which someone owns. A *liability* is what someone owes.

There are two types of assets: financial and real. A *real asset* is concrete, tangible, a real piece of nuts and bolts. Examples of real assets are the desks and tables at which you sit and study; your stereo and records; your car, motorcycle, skis, books, etc. Other examples are highways, steel mills, coal mines, power stations, and trains.

There is one special real asset which you probably do not ordinarily think of as an asset — that is yourself (and everyone else). The value of that asset in the economy as a whole is the value of all the work that human beings are capable of doing now and in the future. This asset is called human capital. Of course, in societies such as our own where slavery is prohibited, it is not possible to buy and sell human capital. It is possible, however, to borrow from a bank against a promise to commit future income (i.e. human capital) to the repayment of the loan.

Financial assets are different from real assets. They are pieces of paper which constitute an asset to one economic agent and a liability to another. That is, they *define a debt relationship* between two agents. Examples of financial assets (which are also someone else's financial liabilities) are: (a) your savings account at the local bank — from your point of view that is a financial asset (you *own* the deposit) while from the point of view of your bank it is a liability (the bank *owes* you the deposit); (b) an ICI bond — it is an asset to the person who owns it, but a liability to stockholders of ICI; (c) a Bank of England £5 note — it is an asset to you, but is it anyone's liability? Yes it is. It is a liability of the Bank of England — this country's central bank. The Bank of England owes you five pound's worth of goods and services in exchange for that note and has to hold assets (government securities) that it could sell in order to meet its commitment. In reality, since just about everyone is willing to accept your £5 note in exchange for goods and services, the Bank of England never has to!

All financial assets are like the three examples in the above paragraph. Each financial asset has a financial liability that goes with it. It is a piece of paper that specifies that someone X has a claim on someone else Y; that is, a financial asset is an asset to X and a liability to Y.

(ii) Balance Sheet

A balance sheet is a statement about what is owned by (is an asset of) and what is owed by (is a liability of) a particular individual or agency. It could be an individual like yourself, or it could be an agency like the Bank of England, a commercial bank like Barclays Bank, the British government, or ICI. The best way to get a feel for a balance sheet is to consider the balance sheet of an individual like yourself.

Table 4.1 sets out an example of what an individual student's balance sheet might look like. The balance sheet shown in Table 4.1 lists the assets in the first column and the liabilities in the second column. The assets are divided between financial items (in the top part of the balance sheet) and real items (in the bottom part of the balance sheet). The person whose balance sheet is shown here has some bank notes and coins, £25 (item 1); a deposit account, £150 (item 2); and a National Savings certificate, £100 (item 3). These are the person's financial assets. The individual has two financial liabilities: a bank loan, £500 (item 4); and an outstanding balance of £100 with a credit card company — Access (item 5). Item 6 totals the financial assets and liabilities. You will see that this person owes more (has bigger liabilities) than he or she owns (has assets).

The next items are real assets. The individual has a car worth £1000 and a stereo and records worth £500 giving a total of real assets (item 9) of £1500. The total assets and liabilities are shown in item 10. This individual has assets of £1775 and liabilities of £600.

Table 4.1   An individual's balance sheet

	Assets £	Liabilities £
Item		
1. Bank notes and coins	25	
2. Deposit account	150	
3. National Savings certificate	100	
4. Bank loan		500
5. Access account		100
6. *Total financial assets and* *liabilities*	275	600
7. Car	1000	
8. Stereo and records	500	
9. *Total real assets*	1500	
10. *Total assets and liabilities*	1775	600
11. Wealth		1175
12. Totals	1775	1775

It is a feature of a balance sheet that it must balance. Clearly, as depicted in item 10, the assets of this individual exceed the liabilities. The amount by which the assets exceed the liabilities is £1175. This amount of money is the wealth of the individual. *Wealth* is defined as a 'fictitious' liability (yes, liability) and is shown in item 11 as a liability of £1175. If you add the wealth of the individual to the other liabilities you see that total liabilities (item 12) equal the total assets, £1775. In order to feel more comfortable with the idea of wealth as a liability, you may like to think of it as the amount which is owed by an individual to himself. Another equivalent way of defining wealth, which is perhaps more appealing, is simply: wealth equals total assets less total liabilities. In the example:

	Total assets	= £1775
less	Total liabilities	= £ 600
equals	Wealth	= £1175

Wealth is commonly referred to by the alternative name *net worth*.

B. Definition and Nature of Money

Money is anything which is generally acceptable as a medium of exchange. A medium of exchange is anything which is acceptable in exchange for goods and services. Which precise assets constitute the medium of exchange varies from one society to another and has varied over the years. Gold has commonly served as a medium of exchange; so has silver and so have other metals. In some prisoner-of-war camps in the Second World War, cigarettes circulated as a medium of exchange. These are all examples of the commodity money.

In modern societies, money is a financial asset that is the financial liability either of the central bank or of other banks. There are two widely used alternative measures of the money supply in the UK today. One is sometimes called 'narrow money' or M1, and the other is referred to as 'broad money' or M3.

Narrow money (M1) consists of currency (Bank of England notes and coins) in circulation with the public plus sterling sight deposits held by domestic households and firms at commercial banks.

Broad money (M3) is M1 plus sterling time deposits held by the households and firms at commercial banks. The private sector accounts that are included in the M3 definition of money but excluded from the M1 measure, are not directly transferable from one person to another by writing a cheque, and although it is customary to think of such deposits as 'money in the bank', it is important to recognize that only M1 is money in the strict sense that it is a means of payment.

In recent years, innovations in the banking sector made possible in part by the advance of computer technology and in part by financial deregulation have begun to blur the distinction between M1 and M3 and between

M3 and some even broader aggregates that include, for example, building society deposits. Some of the accounts which banks make available to their customers have the properties of a means of payment and, therefore, ought to be regarded as M1, although in other respects they have the properties of savings accounts — which would put them in the M3 category. A good example of such arrangements are interest bearing sight deposits. Bank customers operating with such accounts are able to earn interest while at the same time keeping their deposits available for active transactions use. These forms of bank deposits are in effect, identical to regular sight deposits from the point of view of the holder and are counted as part of M1. The Bank of England constantly monitors the definition of the aggregate that serves as the means of payment and, from time to time, revises the aggregate so as to take account of innovations that occur in the financial sector to ensure that the measured aggregate is as close as possible to the total stock of the means of payment in the economy.

Although there are some imprecise borderline cases between money and non-money, there is no doubt at all that money does not include credit cards, such as a Visa or Access card. These cards are convenient identification tags that enable you to create two debts simultaneously. One debt is between yourself and the credit card company and the other is between the credit card company and the seller. These debts are settled when you pay the credit card company and the credit card company pays the seller.

Money in the modern world stands in sharp contrast to commodity money in that it is a financial asset not backed by any commodity and not exchangeable by the issuer for anything other than another unit of itself. Its value arises from the fact that it is universally accepted in exchange for goods and services.

C. Main Balance Sheet Items

We are going to look at the balance sheets of six agents:

Households	H
Firms	F
Commercial banks	B
Bank of England	CB
Government (central and local)	GOV
Rest of world	R

You will identify this list as an extension of the agents whose flow activities we analysed when dealing with the aggregate income accounts in the previous chapter. There we examined households, firms, government, and the rest of the world. We did not deal with commercial banks or the Bank of England. The reason for that is that these institutions are not major actors in the flow of goods and services. They are, however, major actors in the monetary and balance sheet structure of the economy.

(i) Financial Assets and Liabilities

Table 4.2 records the main financial items in the balance sheets of these six agents (or sectors). A '+' denotes an asset and a '−' denotes a liability. Additional explanations for the items and diagrams in Table 4.2 are given below.

Table 4.2   The structure of financial indebtedness

Item	H	F	B	CB	GOV	R
Commercial bank deposits with the Bank of England			+	−		
Currency (notes and coins)	+	+	+	−	−	
Sterling sight deposits	+	+	−		+	
Sterling time deposits	+	+	−			
Other deposits	+	−	−		+	+
Government securities	+	+	+	+	−	+
Bank loans	−	−	+			
Debentures	+	−				+
Equities	+	−				+
Foreign securities	+	+	+			−
Foreign exchange				+	+	−
Net financial assets	+	−	0	0	−	±

Notes:(+) denotes assets; (−) denotes liabilities. The sectors are: Households (*H*); Firms (*F*); Commercial banks (*B*); Bank of England (*CB*); Government (*GOV*); Rest of the world (*R*). The boxes show the items included in the alternative definitions of the money supply: *M1* is the solid box and *M3* is the dashed box. The triangle shows the items included in the monetary base *M0*.

(a) *Commercial bank deposits with the Bank of England.*   Commercial banks maintain cheque accounts just as individuals do. The banker to the commercial banks is the central bank—the Bank of England. As far as the banks are concerned, their deposits with the Bank of England are like money and are part of their assets. These deposits are a liability of the Bank of England. A bank can convert its deposits with the Bank of England into notes and coins, or vice versa, as it chooses.

(b) *Currency.*   Currency consists of all Bank of England notes and coins held by (and therefore assets of) households, firms, and banks. The notes are a liability of the Bank of England, but the coins are issued by the Royal Mint, a government agency and are therefore shown (in Table 4.2) as a liability of the government.

(c) Monetary base (M0). All the liabilities of the Bank of England added together, plus the coin liabilities of the government, make up what is known as the *monetary base.* It is shown by the rectangle in Table 4.2.

(d) Sterling sight deposits. Current accounts are bank accounts from which funds may be withdrawn on demand, typically by writing a cheque. They are liabilities of banks and assets of households, firms, and the government.

(e) Narrow money (M1). The total of currency held by households and firms and sterling sight deposits held by households and firms is 'narrow money' or M1. The solid box in Table 4.2 shows the total of M1. Notice that M1 does *not* include the currency held inside the banking system, nor does it include commercial bank deposits with the Bank of England. Further, M1 does not include the sterling sight deposits at the commercial banks owned by government or by non-residents.

(f) Sterling time deposits. These are all the deposits held at commercial banks by households and firms and typically may only be withdrawn on demand by incurring an interest penalty. Thus, they are not quite as useful as current accounts as a means of payment.

(g) Other deposits. These are all the other deposits of households, firms, government and foreigners with the bank sector. They include foreign currency deposits. Notice that for the firms sector other deposits are negative. This happens because some of the firms are financial institutions such as building societies and such firms are deposit-taking institutions.

(h) Broad money (M3). If we add the sterling time deposits above to M1, we obtain M3, which is shown as the dashed box in Table 4.2.

(i) Government securities. Next there is a whole class of financial assets called government securities. Very many different types of assets are in this category. Examples are: National Savings certificates, marketable securities and Treasury bills. These items are a liability of the British government and are held by (are assets of) all of the other sectors. The government securities held by the Bank of England are the assets that provide the backing for the monetary base. In order to raise the size of the monetary base, the Bank of England buys government securities with newly created money.

(j) Bank loans. The next major item to consider in the sectoral balance sheets is banks loans. These include the personal and business loans that are assets as far as the commercial banks are concerned and are liabilities of the households and firms that have borrowed the money.

(k) Debentures.   Companies raise money to buy capital equipment by selling bonds or debentures. They also finance shorter term activities such as trade, credit and inventory holding by discounting commercial bills of exchange.

(l) Equities.   In addition to raising funds to buy capital equipment by selling bonds, companies also issue equities. An equity holder in a firm is in fact a part owner of the firm. That is, the households and foreigners that own equities really own a share of the firm's physical capital stock. In legal terms the owner of a share in a firm can only sell the share. The owner of a share cannot decide to sell the whole of (or even that individual's share of) the physical plant itself. Thus, in legal terms there is an indebtedness between households and foreigners who own firms and the firm itself. The firm has a liability, and the households and foreigners own the corresponding asset.

(m) Foreign securities.   There are various securities issued by foreign governments and foreign companies which are held by British households, firms and banks.

(n) Foreign exchange reserves.   The final item in Table 4.2 is the foreign exchange reserves of the country. These constitute an asset to the Bank of England and to the government, which hold (and own) the country's foreign exchange reserves. These reserves are in the form of deposits and other short-term securities issued by foreign governments, central banks, and commercial banks. You can think of this item as representing the UK bank account with the rest of the world.

(ii) Net Financial Assets

If we add up all ten items in Table 4.2, we arrive at the net financial assets of each of the major sectors in the economy. The net assets for the commercial banks and for the Bank of England will approximately add up to zero, reflecting the fact that these institutions have comparatively small holdings of real assets. (They do, of course, have large *absolute* holdings of real assets. For example, they own quite a large amount of real estate and office space. However, compared with their financial assets and liabilities, such items are relatively insignificant and, for our purposes, can be ignored.)

Typically, households and firms, which together constitute what is called the *non-bank private sector*, have positive net financial assets. That is, they own financial assets in excess of the liabilities which they have issued. The government, on the other hand, typically has a net financial liability. That liability is sometimes referred to as the *national debt*. The net financial asset position of the country *vis-à-vis* the rest of the world may be positive or negative. That is, the rest of the world may have a net financial claim on the UK (if the UK has a net liability, in which case it is referred to as a *net debtor*) or the UK may have a net financial claim on the rest of the world (if the UK has a net financial asset, in which case it is referred to as a *net creditor*). As a matter of fact, the UK is a fairly sizable net creditor.

(iii) Real and Financial Assets

Table 4.3 shows the net financial assets of the six sectors. It also shows some additional (non-financial) items that will be described below. Further, this table contains an extra column which shows the British economy-wide total value of its five sectors' holdings of the various items.

Table 4.3 Financial assets and liabilities and real assets

	Sector						
Item	*H*	*F*	*B*	*CB*	*GOV*	*R*	*Economy*
Net financial assets	+	−	0	0	−	+	Net claims on the rest of the world
− Real assets	+	+			+	§	Non-human wealth
− Future tax liabilities	−	−			+		Monetary base
− Undistributed profits	+	−					0
− Human wealth	+						Human wealth
Wealth	+	0	0	0	0	+	Wealth

Notes: (+) denotes an asset, (−) denotes a liability and (§) denotes item excluded. The sectors are: Households (*H*); Firms (*F*); Commercial banks (*B*); Bank of England (*CB*); Government (*GOV*); Rest of the world (*R*). The column headed Economy refers to the economy as a whole and is the sum of the first five sectors. A zero in the table denotes that the item in question *sums* to zero. A blank in the table denotes that the item in question does not appear (or appears negligibly) in a particular sector's balance sheet.

For the world as a whole (not shown in Table 4.3), net financial assets are zero — someone's financial asset is someone else's liability. For the UK, however, net financial assets are positive since foreigners, not counted as part of the British economy, hold the corresponding liability. Thus in the final 'economy' column of Table 4.3 the entry 'net claims on the rest-of-world' appears.

(a) Real assets. Real assets — plant, equipment, buildings, etc. — are owned by households, firms, and the government. (As discussed earlier, the banks' holdings are very small in relation to the total and are ignored.) The 'rest-of-world' holding of real assets is excluded from the table since these do not constitute part of the British economy.

The total of all the real assets held by households, firms, and government constitute the *non-human wealth* of the economy.

(b) *Future tax liabilities.* If the government has liabilities that exceed its real assets — which it typically does — then it is the households and firms that pay taxes that will be responsible for meeting those liabilities. The goverment will have to levy taxes on households and firms that equal in value the excess of its liabilities over its assets. These future taxes may be thought of as an *implicit* financial asset. It is implicit because no explicit paper claim exists to represent this item. It is an asset to the government and a liability to households and firms.

 There is one important government sector liability that never has to be repaid and that does not even involve the government in having to raise taxes to make interest payments. This liability is the coin that the government has issued, together with the value of the government bonds that are held by the Bank of England as backing for its liabilities — deposits held by commercial banks and Bank of England bank notes. That the currency never has to be redeemed by the government and the Bank of England is obvious. That the government securities held by the Bank of England are in the same category is perhaps less obvious and needs explaining. The reasoning is as follows. First, the Bank of England is under no obligation to redeem its liabilities, and it does not have to pay any interest on them. Second, the income made by the Bank of England on its holdings of government securities is, except for having to cover some relatively small expenses, a profit which the Bank of England pays to the government. In effect, the government does not have to pay interest on that part of its debt held by the Bank of England because, although it pays the interest, it gets nearly all of it back as the profit of the Bank of England. Since the Bank of England does not have to redeem its liabilities and since the government gets a free loan that never has to be repaid equal to the value of the Bank of England's liabilities, those liabilities are exactly like currency in the sense that they do not attract any future tax liability.

The future tax liabilities of households and firms is less than the value of the corresponding asset of the government by the amount of coin and Bank of England liabilities that never have to be redeemed by the government. The sum of coin and the Bank of England's liabilities is the monetary base (see Table 4.2). Therefore, in Table 4.3, the sum of future tax liabilities for the economy as a whole is shown as being equal to the value of the monetary base.[1]

---

1   You may be thinking that the government is under no obligation to redeem (buy back) any of its debt and could go on issuing additional debt for ever, and further, could issue debt to pay interest on debt. This policy is certainly possible. Nevertheless, each time the government sells a bond that it has no intention of redeeming (except for another like bond), it commits itself to the payment of an interest stream that has the same value as the funds raised by the bond rate and so may be thought of as establishing a *future* liability on households and firms. Chapter 29 will provide a more precise and thorough explanation of this.

(c) Undistributed profits. The government and firms are fundamentally different legal entities from households. Households (and the individuals which constitute them) are the ultimate wealth holders. Firms can be regarded as owing to households the net undistributed profits from their activities. These profits (or losses) are exactly equal to the difference between the firms' real assets and net financial liabilities and are shown as an asset to households and as a liability to firms. In the case of firms that have issued equity, undistributed profits are already taken into account (provided that the equity has been valued correctly).

   As an example, consider two firms that are identical in all respects except that one of the firms has purchased some plant and equipment with undistributed profits, whereas another has purchased the equivalent amount of plant and equipment with the proceeds from a bond sale. The stock market value of the equity of the firm with undistributed profits will clearly be higher than that of the firm that has financed some of its planned acquisitions with the proceeds of a bond sale. For firms that do not issue equity, however, for example partnerships and other private firms, the undistributed profits need to be counted as a liability to the firm and as an asset to the owner or owners of the firm, even though there is no explicit marketable security representing that asset and liability.

(d) Human wealth. The value of the future income of the individuals in the economy constitutes the economy's human wealth (or human capital). You will probably understand the concept of human wealth most thoroughly if you consider the example of your own human wealth. Your human wealth is the sum of money which, if used here and now to buy an annuity would provide an income each year for the rest of your life equal in value to the income that you will earn each year. It is an *implicit* asset (rather than an *actual* asset) in the sense that (at least since the abolition of slavery) human capital is not traded directly in markets. It is possible, however, for people to borrow using part of their human capital as collateral. This happens whenever an individual borrows purely for consumption purposes and promises to repay the debt out of *future labour income*. Another, and more precise, definition of human capital is the present value of future labour income.

(e) Wealth. The sum of all the net claims on the rest of the world, the non-human wealth, the monetary base, and human wealth is the economy's wealth. The household sector owns all the wealth because of the implicit asset/liability items that take account of future tax liabilities and undistributed profits. Government has no wealth on its own account. It owes any excess of assets over liabilities to the households, and the households are liable for its net debts. Similarly, firms have no net wealth because they owe (are liable to) households any undistributed profits (and households have to stand any losses).

(iv) National Balance Sheets and National Income Accounts

Changes in the net financial asset position of the various sectors are related to flows in the national income accounts which we examined in Chapter 3. The change in the net financial assets of households and firms taken together represents the difference between savings (S) and investment (I) (shown in Table 4.4 as $S - I$). The reason for this is very natural. Savings constitute the difference between what is earned (the economy's income) and what is spent on consumer goods and paid in taxes. Some of that saving is used to buy physical capital goods. That is, it is invested in real assets. That which is not invested (i.e. not used to buy real assets) is used to buy financial assets. Therefore, the change in the net financial assets of households and firms is the same thing as savings minus investment.

Table 4.4 Change in financial assets and the national income flows

Item	Sectors					
	H	F	B	CB	GOV	R
Change in net financial assets	$S - I$		0	0	$T - G$	$IM - EX$

Note: The sectors are: Households (H); Firms (F); Commercial banks (B); Bank of England (CB); Government (GOV); Rest of the world (R). S is savings; I is investment; T is total taxes net of transfer payments; G is government expenditure on goods and services; IM is imports; and EX is exports.

Commercial banks and the Bank of England having zero net financial assets also, of course, have zero change in net financial assets.

The change in the government's financial assets is exactly equal to the difference between its current tax receipts (T) and its current expenditure (G). Thus, in Table 4.4 we show $T - G$ as the change in net financial assets of the government.

The change in the net financial assets of the rest of the world is measured by the difference between the flow of expenditures by domestic residents on foreign goods (imports, IM) and the flow of foreign expenditures on domestic goods (exports, EX). We show the change in net financial assets of the rest of the world as being the difference between imports and exports ($IM - EX$).

It is evident that if we aggregate net financial assets across all the sectors then we get zero. That is, what is issued as a liability by one sector is held as an asset by another sector, or sectors. If we add up the net financial asset changes, that is, savings minus investment ($S - I$), plus taxes minus government expenditure ($T - G$), plus imports minus exports ($IM - EX$), then we also always come out with zero, reflecting a fact which we discovered when examining the national income accounts, namely, that savings plus taxes plus imports are equal to investment plus government expenditure plus exports.

$$S + T + IM = I + G + EX$$

(v) The Sectoral Balance Sheets

If you look at each column of Table 4.2 separately, you will see the financial aspects of the balance sheets of each of the six sectors. Usually in macroeconomics we do not separately analyse the balance sheets of households and firms but rather aggregate them together. If we aggregate the two items – currency and sterling sight deposits – across both households and firms (solid box), the total of those items equals the narrow money supply, M1. If we aggregate the three items – currency, sterling sight deposits, and sterling time deposits – across both households and firms, then the total (the dashed box) equals the broad measure of the money supply, M3. These magnitudes are of crucial importance in macroeconomic analysis.

Consider next the third column (B) of Table 4.2, which shows the balance sheet of the commercial banks. It is clear that the liabilities of this sector are the deposits that the commercial banks issue in the form of sight and time deposits. Their assets consist of deposits at the Bank of England, currency, government securities, loans to households and firms, and foreign securities.

The Bank of England's balance sheet has a very simple structure. The liability of the Bank of England consists of all the Bank of England notes outstanding, plus the commercial banks' deposits at the Bank of England. This aggregate, plus the coin issued by the Royal Mint, is the monetary base (M0). The assets of the Bank of England that back that monetary base are government securities and foreign exchange reserves. The Bank of England can change the volume of the monetary base either by buying and selling government securities or by trading in the foreign exchange market. If the Bank of England wants to increase the monetary base, it will simply buy government securities, paying for the securities with newly created money. It could equivalently buy foreign exchange, that is buy, say, US dollars using newly created pounds sterling. It could reduce the monetary base with the opposite operation.

The balance sheets of the government sector and the rest of the world do not in and of themselves have any intrinsic interest for our present purposes and have been presented here so that you can have a complete picture of the structure of indebtedness in the economy and the connection between changes in net financial assets and the flows in the national income accounts.

D. Measuring Aggregate Balance Sheets

Two agencies collect information about aggregate balance sheets in the UK – the Bank of England and the Central Statistical Office.[2]

---

2 National balance sheet accounts are relatively new in the UK. Only in the 1987 edition of the *United Kingdom National Accounts*, the *Blue Book*, did these balance sheets first appear.

The Bank of England collects and publishes balance sheet data for itself (the Central Bank balance sheet) and for the UK banking and monetary sectors. These data are published regularly in the *Bank of England Quarterly Bulletin* statistical annex.

The Central Statistical Office collects and regularly publishes as part of the system of national accounts, two types of data: flow of funds accounts and sectoral and national balance sheets. The financial flows and balance sheets are arranged by eight sectors: personal, industrial and commercial companies, monetary, other financial institutions, public corporations, central government, local government and the rest of the world. The eight sectors of the national balance sheets are related to the six sectors of Table 4.2 in the following way: first, the Bank of England which appears as a separate sector in the above table is aggregated with the rest of the central government sector in the official balance sheet accounts. Next, the firms sector is divided into three subgroups: industrial and commercial companies, other financial institutions, and public corporations. The remaining sectors in the official national balance sheet correspond to those used in Section C above: the personal sector of the official accounts corresponds to households; the monetary sector corresponds with banks; and the national balance sheet shows the nation's aggregate financial relations with the rest of the world.

The official financial accounts and balance sheets report more than 50 different asset and liability categories rather than the 11 into which we have grouped items in the previous section.

Data for the national balance sheets arranged to conform with Tables 4.2 and 4.3 have been constructed from the official data and are brought together in Table 4.5. All the data in this table are in billions of pounds. The items that add up to net financial assets as well as the next item, real assets, correspond to the official figures in the national balance sheet accounts. The remaining items in the table, future tax liabilities, undistributed profits, and human wealth have been supplied by us and their calculation will be described below.

Let us look at the financial assets and liabilities. First, you can see the magnitudes of the monetary base (M0), narrow money (M1) and broad money (M3) highlighted in the three boxes. At the end of 1986 the monetary base was £16 billion, narrow money was £76 billion, and broad money was more than twice as large as narrow money at £153 billion.

Other deposits are a large item and consist partly of foreign currency deposits with banks which is the bulk of the £481 billion item shown in the table. Other deposits of the firms sector are negative, indicating a liability. As noted above, this liability arises from the fact that some firms are deposit-taking financial institutions like insurance companies and building societies. Loans and equities are very large and important items as are foreign securities.

Net financial assets are positive for households and banks and negative for the other sectors. The final items in the table have been constructed

Table 4.5 The national balance sheets in 1986 (£ bn)

Item	H	F	B	CB	GOV	R	Economy
				Sector			
Commercial bank deposits with the Bank of England			1	−1			0
Currency (notes and coins)	11	3	2	−16		0	0
Sterling sight deposits (current accounts)	27	35	−72		2	8	0
Sterling time deposits	33	44	−110		3	30	0
Other deposits	161	−108	−481		−34	462	0
Government securities	24	86	11	2	−138	16	0
Loans	−198	−26	638		38	−452	0
Equities	435	−474	−5		23	21	0
Bonds and other securities	2	−13	−1	14	−9	7	0
Foreign securities	6	146	36		−1	−187	0
Foreign exchange					16	−16	0
Net financial assets	501	−307	16	0	−99	−111	0
Real assets	848	615	9		227		1699
Future tax liabilities	128				−128		0
Undistributed profits	333	−307	−26				0
Human wealth	5029						5029
Wealth	6839	0	0	0	0	−111	6728

Notes: M1 M3 M0

Source: United Kingdom National Accounts, 1987 edition, HMSO, London 1987, Tables 11.1 to 11.8 pp.78–85; *Bank of England Quarterly Bulletin* (27, 1, February 1987) Statistical Annex. Data shown in the table for the Bank of England (CB) and for sterling sight deposits and sterling time deposits are from the *Bank of England Quarterly Bulletin*. All the other data are from the national balance sheet accounts. The data shown in the table for the Central Bank have been subtracted from those in the official accounts for the central government. The data for other deposits in the table are the deposit aggregates from the national balance sheet accounts minus the sterling items that comprise *M1* and *M3* that are separately identified in the table.

according to their theoretical definitions earlier in the chapter. There we argued that government and firms (and banks are firms) have no net worth because, whatever net assets they have, their assets belong to their ultimate owners, the households. In the case of firms and banks any net assets consist of undistributed profits that are the property of the households that own the equity in the firms and banks. These two items (£307 billion and £26 billion) appear in the table of the net assets of those two sectors.

In the case of the government sector any outstanding debt constitutes a future tax liability for the households and any net assets constitute a reduction in future taxes. As it turns out the government sector owns real assets considerably in excess of its financial liabilities so that the net worth of the government sector consitutes a negative future tax liability.

The final item, human wealth, has been inserted to give an example of the order of magnitude involved. We do not have a market measure of human wealth, but we know the value of labour income. If we suppose that the rate of return on human wealth is the same as the rate of return on non-human wealth then we can calculate the capital value of human wealth. The figure in the table has been constructed to make the ratio of labour income to human wealth equal to the ratio of non-labour income to non-human wealth.

Summary

A. Asset, Liability and Balance Sheet

An asset is what someone owns. A liability is what someone owes. There are two types of assets, financial and real. A financial asset is always someone else's liability. An individual's wealth equals total financial and real assets less total liabilities. A balance sheet is a statement of assets and liabilities.

B. Definition and Nature of Money

Money is anything which is generally acceptable as a medium of exchange. In the UK today, money is narrowly defined (M1) as the sum of notes and coins in circulation with the public plus sterling sight deposits held by households and firms. Money is defined more broadly (M3) as M1 plus sterling time deposits held by households and firms.

The monetary base is defined as the total liabilities of the Bank of England — notes outstanding plus commercial banks deposits with the Bank of England — together with the stock of coins in circulation.

C. Main Balance Sheet Items

Main balance sheet items are summarized in Tables 4.2 and 4.3 above. The net value of financial assets in an economy is its net claims on the rest of the world. The change in net financial assets of the economy equals savings minus investment $(S - I)$, plus taxes minus government expenditure $(T - G)$, plus imports minus exports $(IM - EX)$, which is always zero.

The aggregate of net claims on the rest of the world, non-human wealth, monetary base, and human wealth is the wealth of the economy.

A major part of the macroeconomic analysis that we will be doing centres on the relationships between stocks and flows. In particular, it centres on the connection between the stock of money and the flows of expenditure. The theory of aggregate demand which we will be developing shortly builds on the concepts that have been defined and on the accounting frameworks that are dealt with in this and in the previous chapter.

D. Measuring Aggregate Balance Sheets

The Bank of England and the Central Statistical Office are the two insitutions responsible for coordinating and publishing information about aggregate balance sheets in the UK.

The *Bank of England's Quarterly Bulletin* statistical annex contains monthly balance sheets for the monetary and financial sectors of the economy.

The complete national balance sheet and sectoral balance sheets appear as part of the UK national accounts. This balance sheet is arranged in eight sectors and covers a large number of individual asset and liability categories.

The numerical magnitudes of items in the national and sectoral balance sheets at the end of 1986 are shown in Table 4.4.

Review Questions

1. Which of the following are *stocks* and which are *flows*?

    (a) a pocket calculator worth £20
    (b) a bank deposit of £25
    (c) the *purchase* of pocket calculator for £20
    (d) a car
    (e) the labour used to make a car
    (f) the consumption of petrol by a car
    (g) the labour used to serve petrol
    (h) an outstanding bank loan
    (i) the interest paid on a bank loan

2. Which items in a balance sheet are stocks and which are flows?
3. What is the difference between an asset and a liability?
4. Construct your own personal balance sheet. What are your total financial assets and liabilities? What are your real assets? What is your wealth?
5. Using the *Bank of England Quarterly Bulletin*, set out, for a recent date, the balance sheets of the Bank of England and of the commercial bank sector.

6. Indicate how you would set about calculating the British national debt.
7. How would you set about calculating the future tax liabilities of the British government? Whose liabilities are these, and why?
8. Which of the following are 'money' in the UK today?

    (i) Visa card
    (ii) Building society deposits
    (iii) Bank of France FFr.10 notes
    (iv) Bank of England £5 notes
    (v) Federal Reserve System (US) $1 notes
    (vi) Sight deposits at commercial banks
    (vii) Time deposits at commercial banks
    (viii) Cheques
    (ix) Bank loans
    (x) Bank overdrafts

9. Using data that you will find in the *Bank of England Quarterly Bulletin*, draw a time-series graph from 1970 to the present of: (a) M1 growth rate, and (b) M3 growth rate. Describe these two series. Highlight when each grew the fastest and the slowest. Compare and contrast the magnitude and the direction of change of each.
10. What are the links between aggregate balance sheets and aggregate income accounts? In describing the links, be explicit about flows and stocks.
11. Trace the effects on the balance sheets of the seven sectors of Table 4.2 of the following:

    You take a bank loan of £1000 from a commercial bank with which you buy a new computer costing £1500 from Radio Shack in Houston, Texas. You use your deposit account to make up the difference between the bank loan and the purchase price. The Radio Shack computer is made in the United States with US-made component parts.

12. Show the effect of the above transaction on the aggregate income accounts. What are the effects on savings and investment? Show the effects also on the net changes in financial assets and show that these are consistent with the aggregate income accounts.

5

Measuring Inflation and Unemployment

Inflation and unemployment are two of the central variables which macroeconomic theory is designed to explain and that macroeconomic policy seeks to control. By the time you have completed this chapter you will be able to:

(a) **Define inflation.**
(b) **Explain the concept of a price index and its percentage rate of change.**
(c) **Describe how inflation is measured in the United Kingdom.**
(d) **Define unemployment.**
(e) **Describe how unemployment is measured in the United Kingdom.**

A. Definition of Inflation

Inflation may be defined, if somewhat loosely, as the percentage rate at which the general level of prices is changing. We refer to the general level of prices' as the *price level*. You will notice that the dimension of inflation is the percentage rate of change per unit of time. The concept of the general level of prices is a little bit vague, but we will make it precise below.

First of all, it is important to notice that inflation is an *on-going process* – that is, a process of prices rising on a more or less continuous basis rather than on a once-and-for-all basis. Figure 5.1 illustrates this distinction. The price level is measured on the vertical axis, and time is measured in years on the horizontal axis.

Looking at Figure 5.1, suppose that the economy started out in year 0 with a price level equal to 100. If, over the four-year period shown, the price level rose gradually and continuously to 200 (as indicated by the continuous, upward-sloping straight line), then we would want to describe that four-year period as a period of inflation. In contrast, suppose that the economy started out at the price level 100 and had stable prices, that is, with the price level remaining at 100 all the way through the first two years. Then suppose that at the beginning of year 2, there was a sudden jump in the price level, from 100 to 200. Suppose thereafter that the price level remained at 200 and was stable at that level for the remaining two years. We would not normally want to describe this second economy as having had an inflationary four years. Indeed, the price level would have been stable in that economy for the first two years at 100 and stable for the second two years at 200.

It is true that the price level starts out at 100 and finishes up at 200 in both cases. However, in the first case, inflation was present in the economy throughout the four-year period. In the second case, we could think of there having been a single instant of inflation when the price level doubled (from 100 to 200) at the beginning of year 2, whereas for the rest of the four-year period the economy was characterized by stable prices. That is, there was a once-and-for-all rise in the price level at the beginning of year 2. In practice, the distinction between a once-and-for-

**Figure 5.1
The distinction be-
tween inflation and a
once-and-for-all rise
in the price level**

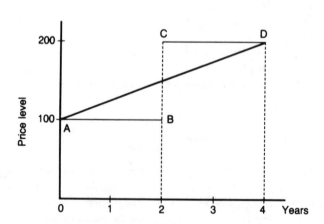

The economy that moves directly along the line AD is one that experiences inflation. The economy that moves along the line ABCD experiences a once-and-for-all rise in the price level in year 2.

all rise in the price level and inflation may be somewhat blurred because it is possible that a shock to the economy that produces a once-and-for-all rise in prices may have effects that are somewhat drawn out. Thus, although the distinction between inflation and a once-and-for-all rise in the price level is an important one in principle, it may in practice often be hard to distinguish one from the other.

The second feature of the phenomenon of inflation that is worth emphasizing at this stage is that it is a rise in the *general* level of prices and not the rise in some particular price or group of prices. The economy may, for example, be experiencing rapid increases in the prices of food and yet not be undergoing an inflation. The rapid increases in food prices may be offset by rapid decreases in prices of some other commodities such as, for example, electronic data processing equipment, video-games, fuel-efficient cars, and the like. Such price movements, even though they may be very rapid and of great social consequence, are not inflation. They are changes in relative prices.

In order to give more precision to the meaning of inflation, it is now necessary to give more precision to the meaning of the term *the general level of prices* or *price level*.

B. Price Index and its Percentage Rate of Change

There can be no unique measure of the price level. The prices of some commodities rise faster than others, and the prices of some things even fall. Movements in the price level can only be calculated once we have fixed *the basket of goods* to which the price level refers.

A price index measures the amount that would have to be paid for a specific basket of goods in the current period compared with what would have had to have been paid for that same basket in some previous period, known as the *base period*. The basket of goods used may be representative of typical consumption patterns in the base period or in the current period. The value of the index in the base period is defined to be 100. Percentage changes in the value of a price index from one year to the next measure the rate of inflation according to the particular index being used.

In order to gain a more concrete understanding of the ideas just set out in summary form, it will be best if we move straight to the next task and illustrate the above propositions.

C. Measuring UK Inflation

There are two widely used price indexes for measuring inflation in the UK today. One is known as the General Index of Retail Prices (RPI), and the other is known as the Gross Domestic Product (GDP) Deflator.

(i) The General Index of Retail Prices

The General Index of Retail Prices (which is calculated and published by the Central Statistical Office each month) is an index which attempts to measure movements in the prices of goods and services which are typically consumed by all types of households in the UK.

This index is a weighted average of price movements of approximately 600 representative items. The weight attached to each item is revised each January on the basis of the most recent Family Expenditure Survey.

Each month, price statistics are collected by the local offices of the Department of Employment in more than 180 local office areas, selected so as to secure an adequate representation of different localities through the country. The prices used are the prices actually charged in retail shops. As far as possible the prices collected relate to goods of unchanged quality at successive dates; when the quality changes an appropriate adjustment is made. An index is calculated using the following formula:

$$\frac{P_1^t Q_1^0 + P_2^t Q_2^0 + \ldots + P_{600}^t Q_{600}^0}{P_1^0 Q_1^0 + P_2^0 Q_2^0 + \ldots + P_{600}^0 Q_{600}^0} \times 100$$

Although this formula looks formidable, it is in fact very simple. Let us take it piece by piece. The numerator

$$P_1^t Q_1^0 + P_2^t Q_2^0 + \ldots + P_{600}^t Q_{600}^0$$

represents the total amount of money that it would cost in month t at the prices ruling in month t to buy the bundle of commodities which is being used to weight the prices. The term P_1^t is simply the price of commodity 1 in a month t, and the number Q_1^0 is the number of units of commodity 1 in the basket of goods that is being valued. If we simply add up the total outlay on each of the 600 commodities in the index, then we arrive at the number of pounds that would have to be spent to buy the basket of commodities at the prices prevailing in month t. (The dots in the middle of the expression stand for commodities 3 to 599.)

The denominator of the index number calculation

$$P_1^0 Q_1^0 + P_2^0 Q_2^0 + \ldots + P_{600}^0 Q_{600}^0$$

is the amount of money that would have had to have been spent in the base period to purchase the index basket of commodities valued at the prices ruling in the base period. The term P_1^0 is the price of commodity 1 in the base period, period 0. So, $P_1^0 Q_1^0$ is the outlay on commodity 1 in the base period. Adding the outlays on all commodities that make up the basket gives the amount of money that would have had to have been spent purchasing the index bundle of commodities in the base period.

The ratio of the outlay in month t to the base period outlay multiplied by 100 gives the index number for the General Index of Retail Prices in month t. If that index number is 100, then prices are the same as in the base period. If the index is greater than 100, prices are higher than in the base period; and if less than 100, prices are less than in the base period.

Various subsidiary index numbers are available for 12 main groups and 87 subgroups, including food; all non-food items; housing; clothing and footwear; transport and vehicles; fuel and light; durable household goods; services; tobacco; meals bought outside and consumed outside the home; and alcoholic drink. In addition, separate RPIs are published for 15 urban centres, as well as for pensioner households.

A detailed description of the calculation of the General Index of Retail Prices is given in the *Method of Construction and Calculation of the General Index of Retail Prices* (HMSO, 1967).

(ii) Gross Domestic Product (GDP) Deflator

The General Index of Retail Prices seeks to measure movements in the prices of a basket of goods which would typically be consumed by all households in the UK. In contrast, the GDP Deflator measures movements in the general level of prices of the entire basket of goods and services produced in the British economy.

If you think of gross domestic product, measured by the income approach, as being equal to the sum of the values of all the goods and services produced, then you have the starting point for the GDP Deflator. In order to calculate that total, it is necessary to take the quantity of each good, Q_i, and multiply by its factor cost, P_i. We then have to add up the resulting values over all the goods and services in the economy which gives gross domestic product in current pounds. That is, gross domestic product at current factor cost equals

$$P_1^t Q_1^t + P_2^t Q_2^t + \ldots + P_n^t Q_n^t$$

The Ps and Qs in this formula stand for the factor costs and quantities of the entire production of final goods and services in the economy, and not simply for that typical consumer basket that was referred to in the preceding section on the General Index of Retail Prices. It includes the typical consumer expenditure of all households as well as expenditure on all other consumer goods, capital goods (investment), government purchases of goods and services, exports and imports.

Now, instead of valuing gross domestic product by multiplying the quantity of each good produced in a given year by the factor cost of the good in that year, we could multiply output in a given year by the factor costs that prevailed in some base year — for example, year 0. If we performed such a calculation, we would calculate gross domestic product at constant factor cost, which equals

$$P_1^0 Q_1^t + P_2^0 Q_2^t + \ldots + P_n^0 Q_n^t$$

This measure of gross domestic product in year t is valued at the factor costs prevailing in the base year, year 0.

If we divide GDP at constant factor cost into GDP at current factor cost, we obtain the GDP Deflator:

$$\text{GDP Deflator} = \frac{\text{GDP at current factor cost}}{\text{GDP at constant factor cost}} \times 100$$

The GDP Deflator is sometimes called the GDP *implicit* Deflator. The Deflator is implicit because we arrive at it from the evaluation of the gross domestic product on the basis of two alternative sets of factor costs.

(iii) The Percentage Rate of Change in the Price Index as a Measure of Inflation

We can now define British inflation precisely: British inflation is the percentage rate of change over a specified unit of time (usually a year) in either the General Index of Retail prices or GDP Deflator.

For example, in June 1987, the General Index of Retail Prices was 298.3. In June of the year earlier, 1986, the index was 286.2. To calculate the rate of inflation as measured by the General Index of Retail Prices for the year from June 1986 to June 1987, perform the following calculation:

$$\text{Inflation} = \frac{(298.3 - 286.2)}{286.2} \times 100$$

$$= 4.2 \text{ per cent per annum}$$

We could perform a similar calculation using the GDP Deflator.

The General Index of Retail Prices is available monthly and gives continuous monitoring of the economy's inflation rate. The GDP Deflator is available quarterly. Movements in these indexes do not coincide, but they are not excessively divergent. The table in the Appendix to Chapter 2 lists the rate of inflation in the UK each year from 1900 to 1986 as measured by these indexes and Figure 2.1 of Chapter 2 shows how they behave.

For convenience, the inflation rates as measured by the two price indexes over the last ten years are reproduced here as Table 5.1. The broad picture presented by each of these two index numbers is the same. Inflation was at its strongest in 1976–7 and again in 1979–81. Inflation was lower in 1983–6 than earlier. The detailed picture given by each index is, however, different. In particular, the General Index of Retail Prices seems to suggest a higher inflation rate than the GDP Deflator. There are several reasons for this, two of which are worth highlighting.

The first reason for the different measured inflation rates arises from the weights used to compile the index numbers. The General Index of Retail Prices uses fixed weights, which means that the attempts by consumers to substitute away from relatively more expensive items towards relatively less expensive items are not captured in the RPI. Perhaps an example will make this clearer. Suppose that oranges and apples were consumed in equal quantities in the base year. Suppose that between the

Table 5.1   A comparison of inflation rates as measured by the General Index of Retail Prices (RPI) and Gross Domestic Product (GDP) Deflator

	Inflation		Inflation Differential
Year	(RPI)	(GDP Deflator)	(RPI less GDP Deflator)
1976	16.5	14.4	2.1
1977	15.9	12.3	3.6
1978	8.3	12.1	−3.8
1979	13.4	12.8	0.6
1980	18.0	18.8	−0.8
1981	11.9	10.1	1.8
1982	8.6	7.1	1.5
1983	4.6	5.7	−1.1
1984	4.9	4.8	0.1
1985	6.1	5.9	0.2
1986	3.4	2.8	0.6

Source: Appendix to Chapter 2.

base year and the current year, the prices of oranges have doubled, but the prices of apples have increased by only 20 per cent. It would be expected that these price changes would lead people to substitute away from oranges and towards apples so that, in the current year, more apples and fewer oranges are consumed compared with the base year. If an index was calculated of the price of fruit, which assumed that equal quantities of apples and oranges were consumed in both the base year and the current year, then the index would tend to overstate the rise in expenditure on fruit (the rise in the average price of fruit). If the weights attaching to oranges and apples were changed, however, in accordance with the changed spending patterns in the current year, then the substitution away from the now more expensive oranges towards the now less expensive apples would be captured. The RPI presumes unchanged weights, whereas the GDP Deflator allows for substitutions to take advantage of relatively less expensive items.

The second reason for the differences in the two indexes reflects difficulties that the General Index of Retail Prices has in coping with quality changes and with the introduction of new products. Again, an example will perhaps make this clear. Suppose that between 1983 and 1984 the price of cars rose by 10 per cent. Suppose also, however, that improvements took place in the fuel efficiency of their engines so that their gas consumption was down by 5 per cent on the average between the two years. How much have car prices really increased during that year? The answer is that they have increased by less than 10 per cent. But how much less? How can one allow adequately for quality improvements of that type? With sufficient ingenuity we could presumably figure out the exact answer to the question and allow for quality improvements in this case.

There will be other cases, however, where allowance for quality improvements will be virtually impossible. For example, over the years the quality of the picture and sound delivered by a television set has improved dramatically. How should that be allowed for in calculating the true rate of inflation of television prices? This question (and similar ones in connection with many thousands of other products) are hard to answer and, as a result, there is a general presumption that the General Index of Retail Prices does not adequately allow for gradual improvements in product quality.

The difference in the inflation rates of the RPI and the GDP Deflator is shown in column 3 of Table 5.1. Since 1976, this difference has ranged from −3.8 in 1978 to 3.6 percentage points in 1977. The reason why the GDP Deflator inflation rate differs from that of the RPI lies mainly in the fact that it measures the prices of a much broader basket of goods, one that includes capital goods as well as those goods bought by government and net exports. The difference in the GDP Deflator and the General Index of Retail Prices, then, can be seen as reflecting changes in the relative price of consumer goods to all other goods.

We will be analysing the determination of the rate of inflation as measured by the GDP Deflator in our theoretical analysis later in this book. However, since movements in the two index numbers are broadly in line with each other, you can, for most purposes, think of the analysis as relating to the General Index of Retail Prices as well, although there may be some specific exercises for which such a presumption would not be warranted.

Let us now turn our attention to the definition and measurement of unemployment.

D. Definition of Unemployment

A person is said to be unemployed when he or she is able and willing to work and is available for work (that is, the person is actively searching for employment) but does not have work. The number of people unemployed in an economy is the number of people whom that description fits. The unemployment rate in an economy is the number of people unemployed expressed as a percentage of the total labour force. The total labour force is defined as the number of people employed plus the number of people unemployed.

You will notice that the definition of unemployment says nothing at all about the reasons for unemployment. It simply defines an aggregate or a percentage rate based on an explicit and objective criterion for classifying individuals. Much economic analysis of the causes of unemployment and fluctuations in its rate uses terms such as *voluntary* and *involuntary* to describe different types of unemployment.

We will not have any reason to use such definitions. It may be very interesting for some purposes to know whether a person is voluntarily or involuntarily unemployed. From our point of view, however, it is irrelevant. We are going to be concerned with an objective analysis of the factors that lead to variations in unemployment and to develop theories which will enable us to predict the consequences for unemployment of certain well-defined policies. It will not be necessary for us to enquire into the state of mind of the unemployed person concerning the voluntary or involuntary nature of the unemployment being experienced.

E. Measuring UK Unemployment

Unemployment figures are calculated by the Department of Employment and are published in the *Department of Employment Gazette*. Figures are provided for unemployment by region, by sex and age, by industry and by duration.

   As already indicated, the unemployment rate represents the number of unemployed persons as a percentage of the labour force. All the unemployment figures published in the UK are based on information generated by the Department of Employment through the operation of the unemployment benefits available under the National Insurance Acts. The measured unemployment series records the number of persons registered at employment exchanges and youth employment service offices who were unemployed and capable of and available for work on a particular day on which the monthly count took place. A distinction is made in the published figures between those with no work (wholly unemployed) and those who are working shorter than normal hours, or who have been temporarily laid-off from work with a clear understanding that they will shortly be returning to their previous employment (known as temporarily stopped).

   No information is available concerning the wages at which a person who is capable of and available for work would be willing to work. Thus, although the measured unemployment rate shows the number of persons registered at an employment exchange who are capable of and available for work, there is no indication as to whether or not they are willing to work at wages that are currently available. What we would really like to know is the total number of people who are capable of, available for, and willing to work on terms and conditions currently available. There can be no presumption that the way in which unemployment is measured in the UK captures that concept.

   The fact that the unemployment rate is measured on the basis of the number of persons registered at employment exchanges provides a further source of bias in the measurement. Many people, especially older people and married women who have opted for a more limited national insurance coverage plan, will typically enter and leave the labour force without passing through the ranks of the measured unemployed, even though, from an economic point of view, their position may be identical to an equivalent, say, prime age male who appears on the unemployment register.

It may well be that, although the absolute measurement of unemployment is distorted by both a failure to account for the wages at which unemployed persons would be willing to work and by the failure to measure non-registered unemployed, the general cyclical movements in the unemployment rate may nevertheless provide a good indication of the direction of change in unemployment if not its precisely measured magnitude.

Summary

A. Definition of Inflation

Inflation is defined as the percentage rate of change in a price index.

B. Price Index and its Percentage Rate of Change

A price index is calculated by valuing a specific basket of goods at the prices prevailing in a base period and at the prices prevailing in a subsequent period. The price index is the ratio of the values of these two baskets multiplied by 100. The rate of inflation between the base period and the subsequent period is measured by the percentage rate of change of the index.

C. Measuring UK Inflation

There are two commonly used price indexes in the UK: the General Index of Retail Prices (RPI), and the Gross Domestic Product (GDP) Deflator. The RPI is based on a fixed basket of goods and services typical of the consumption patterns of all types of households. The GDP Deflator is calculated on the basis of a current basket of goods and services, with the GDP Deflator covering all consumption and investment purchases, government purchases, and net exports.

D. Definition of Unemployment

Unemployment is defined as the number of people able and willing to work and available for work, but not having work.

E. Measuring UK Unemployment

Unemployment is measured in the UK by counting the number of people who have registered at job centres, who are capable of work, but who do not have work. This overestimates unemployment to the extent that some people are registered as being unemployed but are not willing to work on terms and conditions currently available, and underestimates unemployment to the extent that others are available and willing to work on current terms and conditions but are not registered at a job centre.

Review Questions

1. What is inflation?
2. What are the two commonly used measures of inflation?
3. How is the General Index of Retail Prices calculated? What is the General Index of Retail Prices designed to measure?
4. Using the latest *Economic Trends*, find the General Index of Retail Prices (RPI) for the period from 1970 to the present. Be sure you are consistent and collect either mid-year (June) or end-of-year (December) figures.

   (a) What is the base year of the RPI that you have collected?
   (b) Calculate the percentage rate of change of the RPI each year since 1970 and explain exactly what it measures.

5. What does the GDP Deflator measure and how is it calculated? Why is it called an *implicit* Deflator?
6. From the latest *United Kingdom National Accounts*, calculated the GDP Deflator for the period from 1970 to the present. Calculate the percentage rate of change of the GDP Deflator. Explain exactly what this series measures.
7. The table in the Appendix to Chapter 2 gives a comparison of inflation rates as measured by RPI and GDP Deflator. Plot these time-series graphs for the period since 1966. Describe these series. Highlight the highest and lowest measures of inflation. Compare and contrast inflation as measured by these series.
8. What is unemployment?
9. Exactly how does the Department of Employment define unemployment?
10. How is unemployment measured?
11. The unemployment rate in the UK varies from region to region. Use the *Department of Employment Gazette* to collect time-series data starting

in 1970 on the unemployment rate of the region in which you live and for the UK as a whole. Plot these two time-series as graphs. Describe, compare and contrast them. Does your region have higher or lower unemployment than the UK on the average? Try to think of reasons why your region differs in the way that it does from the national average.

12. What are the main problems with the way unemployment is measured in the UK?

6

Economic Transactions with the Rest of the World

The British economy has extensive economic links with the rest of the world. In 1985, of every pound spent in the UK on final goods and services, almost 32 pence represented expenditure on goods imported from other countries. Similarly, of every pound's worth of goods produced, 29 pence worth was sent abroad as exports. In the 5-year period 1981–85, the UK had an overall deficit in its trading and capital transactions with the rest of the world of close to £4000 million. During that same 5-year period, the value of the pound sterling in terms of the US dollar fell by almost 36 per cent to $1.30.

This chapter is going to explain the concepts of the balance of payments and foreign exchange rate, how these magnitudes are measured, and how you can obtain more detailed information on them. By the time you have completed this chapter you will be able to:

(a) Define the current account, the capital account, the official settlements account, and the balance of payments.
(b) Describe how the UK balance of payments accounts are measured.
(c) Define a foreign exchange rate, a fixed exchange rate, a flexible exchange rate, a managed floating exchange rate, an effective exchange rate, and a real exchange rate.
(d) Describe how the exchange rate is measured.

A. Definitions of the Balance of Payments

(i) The Current Account

The *current account of the balance of payments* is the account in which the values of the flows of goods and services and other *current* receipts and payments between residents of the UK and residents of the rest of the world are recorded. Specifically, the current account contains the items shown in Table 6.1 (The values of the items for 1986 are given so that you may have a feel for the orders of magnitude involved.) The items recorded in the current account refer to three types of transaction. The first concerns the import and export of goods and services. The export of goods and services is the sum of the value of all the goods and services purchased by non-residents from residents of the UK in a given period. Examples include the export of North Sea oil, Scotch whisky, and Rolls-Royce cars. It would also include the export of services such as banking, insurance and general financial services as well as shipping services. It also includes, in principle, the spending by non-residents on holidays in the UK.

Table 6.1   The current account, 1986

	Item	£ million
	1. Exports of goods and services	97,835
less	2. Imports of goods and services	101,308
	3. Dividends and interest received from abroad (net)	4,686
	4. Unilateral transfers paid abroad (net)	−2,193
equals	Current account balance	−980

Source: United Kingdom Balance of Payments, 1987 Edition, p.9.

Imports of goods and services consist of purchases by UK residents of goods and services made in the rest of the world. Examples include oranges from Israel, cars and television sets from Japan, and cotton goods from Hong Kong and Taiwan. It also includes the purchase of insurance, shipping and other general services by UK residents from residents of the rest of the world. In principle, it also includes the expenditure by UK residents when visiting other countries.

The difference between the value of exports of goods and services and imports of goods and services is usually referred to as the *trade balance*. Often, the trade balance itself is subdivided into two balances, one called the visible trade balance which refers to the difference between the values of the exports of goods and the imports of goods and the invisible balance which refers to the difference between the value of the export and import of services. No operational significance attaches to the visible/invisible distinction.

The second class of items that appears in the current account of the balance of payments is the dividends and interest payments made between residents and non-residents. This item is shown in Table 6.1 as a net item and, in 1986, represented net payments by residents to non-residents. The dividends and interest received from abroad are payments on investments made by residents of the UK in the rest of the world. Examples would include the dividends paid by IBM to UK stockholders and interest paid by the United States government on United States Treasury bills held by banks and other financial institutions in London. Dividends and interest paid abroad are the payments made in respect of UK securities that have been bought by non-residents. Examples would include payments to American oil companies in connection with their investments in the North Sea oil programme, or payments by the UK government of interest on Treasury bills and other government securities held by non-residents.

The final class of items is unilateral transfers and this item, like the previous one, is shown simply as a net figure. Unilateral transfers are payments received from or made to non-residents by residents, in effect as gifts. The biggest single item in this category is the aid given by the UK government and private organizations to less developed countries.

The difference between the total receipts on the current account and the total outlays on the current account is called the *current account balance*. The current account is said to be in surplus when the receipts exceed outlays, and in deficit when the expenses exceed the receipts.

It is useful to think of an individual analogy to the country's current account balance. The exports of goods and services of a country can be thought of as being analogous to an individual's labour income. That is, from the viewpoint of the country as a whole, exports of goods and services are similar to the receipt of wages and salaries and other fees for labour services from the viewpoint of an individual. Dividends and interest received are analogous to income from investments made by an individual, and unilateral transfers are analogous to gifts. On the outgoing side, imports of goods and services are analogous to an individuals's expenditures on consumption goods and capital goods. Dividends and interest paid abroad are analogous to an individual's payment of interest on loans made to him by, for example, banks and mortgage companies; unilateral transfers are the equivalent of gifts made by the individual to others.

A moment's reflection will reveal that for an individual, the current account balance just described represents the net addition to (surplus) or subtraction from (deficit) his wealth. If an individual has a current account surplus, he/she is becoming wealthier in the sense that assets are being acquired and/or liabilities are being paid off. It is exactly the same for a country. If a country has a current account surplus, its residents in aggregate have become wealthier in the sense that their assets have increased (and/or their liabilities have decreased). Conversely, if a country has a current account deficit, it has become poorer in the sense that it now has fewer assets or more liabilities than previously.

(ii) The Capital Account

The capital account records the receipts from non-residents and payments made to non-residents arising from the issuing of new debt or the repayment of old debt. For example, the purchase by American residents of shares in British Petroleum appears as an import of capital. Such a transaction would be recorded as a receipt in the UK capital account. Conversely, if a foreign corporation or government issues new debt, some of which is bought by UK residents, then the payment to this foreign corporation or government will appear as an export of capital from the UK. Equivalently, if a UK resident buys a villa in Spain for £50,000, using (say) a British bank deposit when the villa is paid for, there will be a capital outflow of £50,000 from the UK and that too will be recorded in the capital account as a capital export.

The difference between capital imports and capital exports represents a country's *capital account balance*. In 1986, the capital account of the UK showed a deficit of almost £7.9 million. That is, in 1986, the capital imports of the UK exceeded capital exports by almost £7.9 million.

Another individual analogy may be helpful. The capital account of an individual is a statement of the receipts of that individual arising from the negotiation of new loans minus the outlays for paying off old loans. Thus, for example, if an individual negotiated a bank loan for £3,000 and a mortgage for £15,000 and repaid a credit card account outstanding of £500, that individual would have a capital account surplus of £17,500.

(iii) The Official Settlements Account

The official settlements account records the net receipts and payments of gold and foreign currency that result from the current account and capital account transactions just described. The balance on the official settlements account, known more simply as the *official settlements balance*, is the change in the foreign exchange reserves less the change in official borrowing of the country. It is, if everything is accurately measured, exactly equal to the sum of the current account balance and the capital account balance. By accounting convention, the official settlements balance is defined as the negative of the sum of the current account and capital account balance, so that when the balances on all three accounts are added together, the resulting sum is always zero.

Another individual analogy might be helpful here. Suppose an individual had a current account deficit of, say, £20,000 in some particular year in which perhaps a house and some furnishing and other durable goods had been bought. That is, in the particular year, the individual received from his/her labour services and in interest and dividends and gifts £20,000 less than was spent on goods and services. Suppose further that the individual negotiated loans such that there was a net capital account surplus of £15,000. If the individual spent £20,000 in excess of income and received £15,000 from new loans, where did the difference of £5000 come from? It must be the case that the individual used £5000 of the cash balances that were previously being held. If this were not so, the individual's expenditure could not have exceeded total receipts by the £5000, which according to the example, that they did. Thus, the individual analogy of the official settlements balance is simply the change in the individual's cash balances — bank account and currency holdings.

Although the individual's cash holdings have fallen, in this example by £5000, this would be recorded (using the accounting convention noted above) as a positive balance on the individual's equivalent of the official settlements account.

(iv) The Balance of Payments

When studying the theory of the balance of payments, it will be convenient and more natural if you think of the balance of payments simply as the sum of the balances on the current and capital accounts and not as the official settlements balance. The magnitude of the balance of payments, so defined, will be the same as the official settlements balance but its algebraic sign will be reversed. Thus, when the sum of the current and capital accounts is positive we will call that a balance of payments surplus, even though, as measured by the balance of payments accountants, the official settlements balance is negative.

Now that the concepts lying behind the balance of payments accounts have been described, let us turn to an examination of the UK's balance of payments accounts and see how these concepts are put into practice.

B. Measuring the UK Balance of Payments Accounts

The UK balance of payments are published in an annual Central Statistical Office publication called The *United Kingdom Balance of Payments* and often referred to simply as the *Pink Book*. The accounts are also published on a quarterly basis in *Economic Trends* and *Financial Statistics*. The accounts for the years 1976—86 are set out in Table 6.2. The first two columns show the current account and capital account balances and the fourth column shows the official settlements balance. Although the theoretical concepts of the current account, capital account, and official settlements account add up to zero, there are problems measuring international transactions.

Table 6.2   UK balance of payments, 1974–84 (£ million)

Year	Current account	Capital account	Errors and omissions	Official settlements
1976	− 920	− 235	+ 302	+ 853
1977	− 136	+ 6337	+ 3387	− 9588
1978	+ 966	− 5410	+ 2115	+ 2329
1979	− 661	+ 1170	+ 550	− 1059
1980	+ 2916	− 2415	− 210	− 291
1981	+ 6312	− 8665	− 66	+ 2419
1982	+ 4035	− 3683	− 1773	+ 1421
1983	+ 3338	− 5349	+ 1404	+ 607
1984	+ 1474	− 7824	+ 5442	+ 908
1985	+ 2919	− 5663	4502	− 1758
1986	− 980	− 7856	11727	− 2891

Source: United Kingdom Balance of Payments, 1987 Edition, p.9, p.11.

In the period since 1977 those measurement problems have become quite serious. The third column of Table 6.2, headed 'Errors and omissions', shows the extent to which the measured capital account and current account and official settlements account fail to reconcile with each other. In the published UK balance of payments accounts this item is referred to as the 'balancing item'. It is suspected that a high level of unrecorded capital flows associated with the deregulation of London financial markets (the 'Big Bang') are responsible for the exceptionally large 'balancing item' in 1986.

The transactions which appear in the current account are recorded mainly for the purpose of administering the customs and excise service. This activity provides the primary raw material for estimating the total volume and value of exports and imports. It is not unlikely that this item is the main source of the increase in the errors and omissions in recent years. Such errors and omissions arise mainly from valuation problems. Foreign transactions may be invoiced either in sterling or in some other currency. When they are invoiced in some other currency, the precise date on which the payment is made will determine the exchange rate relevant to the transaction. When exchange rates are moving around considerably, such as they have done in recent years, imprecise knowledge of the precise timing of the transactions makes the valuation of exports and imports in sterling an approximate rather than an exact activity.

C. Exchange Rate Definitions

(i) Foreign Exchange Rate

A foreign exchange rate is the relative price of two national monies. It expresses the number of units of one currency that must be paid in order to acquire a unit of some other currency. There are two ways in which a relative price may be defined. It may be expressed as so many units of *a* per unit of *b*, or as so many units of *b* per unit of *a*. For example, the average exchange rate between the pound sterling (£) and the United States dollar ($US) in 1986 was $1.47 per £. This exchange rate may be expressed equivalently as 68 pence per US dollar.

It is always necessary to be precise as to which way around the exchange rate is being defined. When the value of a currency *rises* (called *appreciation*), the exchange rate, expressed as units of domestic currency per unit of foreign currency, *falls*; but expressed the other way as units of foreign currency per unit of domestic currency, the exchange rate *rises*. Conversely, when the value of a currency *falls* (called *depreciation*), the exchange rate, expressed in units of domestic currency per unit of foreign currency, *rises*; but expressed the other way as units of foreign currency per unit of domestic currency, the exchange rate *falls*. It is common in the UK to express the exchange rate as units of foreign currency per pound. It is very common (indeed probably more common) in theoretical analysis to define the exchange rate the other way around as the number of units of domestic currency per unit of foreign currency.

(ii) A Fixed Exchange Rate

A fixed exchange rate regime is one in which the Bank of England declares a central or par value at which it will act to maintain the value of its currency. It also usually involves declaring what is known as an *intervention band*. That is, in declaring a fixed exchange rate, the central bank announces that if the exchange rate rises above the par value by more than a certain percentage amount, then it will intervene in the foreign exchange market to prevent the rate from moving any further away from the par value. Likewise, if the rate falls below the par value by a certain percentage amount, the central bank declares that it will intervene to prevent the rate from falling any further.

In order to maintain a fixed exchange rate, a central bank stands ready to use its stock of foreign exchange reserves to raise or lower the quantity of money outstanding so as to maintain its price relative to the price of some other money.

From 1945 to 1972 the Western world operated on a fixed exchange rate system sometimes called the Bretton Woods system. That name derives from the fact that the plan for the world monetary system, which survived for 30 years after the war, was negotiated at Bretton Woods, near Washington, DC by John Maynard Keynes and Harry D. White. This system pegged the world's monetary system to gold by the United States agreement to declare that one fine ounce of gold was worth $US 35. Each country then defined its own currency value in terms of the US dollar. Under the Bretton Woods fixed exchange rate system, the United States took no responsibility for maintaining the exchange rates between the US dollar and other currencies. Its job was to maintain the price of gold at $US 35 per ounce. Each of the other countries was then left to worry about its own exchange rate against the US dollar. Thus, for example, if the pound began to fall in value to the lower limit or rise in value to the upper limit of the exchange rate band, the Bank of England would intervene in the foreign exchange market, exchanging US dollars from its foreign exchange reserves for pounds, or exchanging pounds for US dollars, in order to keep the value of the pound inside the target band.

(iii) A Flexible Exchange Rate

A flexible exchange rate — sometimes also called a floating exchange rate — is one which is determined by market forces. The central bank declares no target value for the exchange rate and has no direct interest in the value of the exchange rate. The central bank holds a constant stock of foreign exchange reserves — or even a zero stock — and does not intervene in the foreign exchange market to manipulate the price of its currency.

(iv) A Managed Floating Exchange Rate

A managed floating exchange rate is one in which the exchange rate is manipulated by the central bank, but is not necessarily being held constant. Usually, a managed floating regime is one in which the central bank announces that it is floating, but the bank does not give any indication to the market concerning the course that it would like to see the exchange rate follow. It does, however, have a view about the appropriate behaviour of the exchange rate, and it intervenes in order to achieve its desires. This method of operating the foreign exchange market is one that gives most difficulty to speculators. They not only have to speculate on what other private individuals on average will be doing, but they also have to make predictions about central bank intervention behaviour.

(v) An Effective Exchange Rate

There is not, of course, only one foreign exchange rate. Rather, there are as many foreign exchange rates as there are foreign currencies. The more commonly encountered exchange rates are those between the pound sterling and the currencies of the major trading partners of the UK such as the US dollar, the French franc, the German mark, and the Japanese yen. So as to be able to measure the value of one currency in relation to an average of other currencies the concept of the *effective exchange rate* is used.

The effective exchange rate is an index number — just like the Retail Price Index, for example. This index number is calculated as a weighted average of the value of one currency in terms of all other currencies where the weights reflect the importance of each currency in the exports and imports of the country in question.

If we denote the effective exchange rate in some period, t, by EER_t, the formula with which EER_t may be calculated is

$$EER_t = \frac{a_1 E_{1_0} + a_2 E_{2_0} + \ldots + a_n E_{n_0}}{a_1 E_{1_t} + a_2 E_{2_t} + \ldots + a_n E_{n_t}} \times 100 \qquad (6.1)$$

In this formula, the as represent weights — the fraction of UK trade with country 1 is a_1, the fraction with country 2, a_2, and so on. The Es represent exchange rates between the pound and each other currency — E_1 being the number of pounds per unit of the currency of country 1, E_2 being the number of pounds per unit of the currency of country 2, and so on. The subscript t denotes the current period and the subscript 0 denotes the base period — the period for which the effective exchange rate is, by definition, 100.

The effective exchange rate of the pound is calculated by the International Monetary Fund using this type of formula. You should be careful to note that the effective exchange rate will behave in the same way as a measure of a single exchange rate expressed as the number of units of foreign currency per unit of domestic currency. That is, when the effective exchange rate falls in value, the domestic currency depreciates. Conversely, when the effective exchange rate rises in value, the domestic currency appreciates.

Instead of calculating an effective exchange rate using Equation (6.1) — the type of calculation performed by the International Monetary Fund — we could alternatively calculate an effective exchange rate which represents the number of units of domestic currency per unit of foreign currency. Such a calculation would be performed by using Equation (6.2).

$$E_t = \frac{a_1 E_{1_t} + a_2 E_{2_t} + \ldots + a_n E_{n_t}}{a_1 E_{1_0} + a_2 E_{2_0} + \ldots + a_n E_{n_0}} \qquad (6.2)$$

As you will see by comparing Equation (6.2) with Equation (6.1) the effective exchange rate E is equal to 100 divided by EER. The effective exchange rate measured by E behaves in the opposite way to EER. When the value of E rises the domestic currency depreciates and when the value of E falls the domestic currency appreciates. When EER is equal to 100, E is equal to 1.

The effective exchange rate expressed as E is a more natural definition to use for the purposes of conducting macroeconomic analysis. If a foreign price index is multiplied by the effective exchange rate E it becomes, in effect, a domestic price index. That is, a price expressed in foreign currency units is converted into a price expressed in domestic currency units by multiplying that price by E. It is the definition of the exchange rate based on Equation (6.2) that we will use in subsequent chapters when analysing the behaviour of an open economy.

(v) Real Exchange Rate

The foreign exchange rate as it has been described in the preceding sections is a relative price. It is the relative price of two monies. There is another concept of the exchange rate which is useful in macroeconomic analysis and that is the real exchange rate. The real exchange rate is also a relative price. It is not, however, the relative price of two monies; rather it is the relative price of two baskets of goods, a domestic basket and a rest of the world basket. A concept of a basket of goods is simply a list of goods combined together with specified weights. The real exchange rate represents the number of baskets of domestic goods that will exchange for one basket of foreign goods. To calculate the real exchange rate it is necessary to take a specific basket of goods, value them in the prices prevailing in the rest of the world, convert those prices into domestic currency, and then compare the result with the price of that same basket of goods in the domestic economy. Clearly, there are many different examples of a real exchange rate. Attention may focus on the real exchange rate between only the goods that feature in international trade or the entire gross domestic product.

D. Measuring Exchange Rates

Foreign exchange rates are continuously varying even from minute to minute and the foreign exchange market is open, taking account of time zone differences, for practically 24 hours a day. Thus, in principle, an enormous amount of continuous information is generated on this particular set of prices — the relative prices of the different national monies. In effect, the recorded and reported exchange rate figures that are available to us constitute a sampling of this continuous process at a particular point in time. The Bank of England records and reports the foreign exchange value of the pound by recording the rate 'during the late afternoon' each day. The Bank of England reports in the *Bank of England Quarterly Bulletin* figures expressed as values on particular days, as well as annual averages of the exchange rate. It gives the value of the pound sterling on this basis in terms of US dollars, Belgian francs, Swiss francs, French francs, Italian lira, Netherlands guilders, German marks, and Japanese yen.

The International Monetary Fund in its monthly publication, *International Financial Statistics*, provides more detail and covers the exchange rates between all currencies.

Effective exchange rates are calculated and published by the Bank of England and the International Monetary Fund. The method used by each of these institutions to calculate the effective exchange rate is essentially the same, although they differ in some details. As the Bank of England comments:

An effective exchange rate index is a measure of the overall value of a currency against a number of other currencies relative to a certain base date. The measure depends upon which other currencies are included in the calculation and the relative importance (weight) attached to each of them. Various effective exchange rate indices can therefore be calculated for any one currency.

The Bank of England calculates and reports effective exchange rates for the eight currencies listed above. The International Monetary Fund does the calculation for all the currencies. The weights used to calculate the effective exchange rate are derived from a statistical model called MERM (Multilateral Exchange Rate Model) developed by the International Monetary Fund. The weights used in the calculation are in principle supposed to be 'such that any combination of changes in other currencies

**Figure 6.1
Exchange rates,
1975–86**

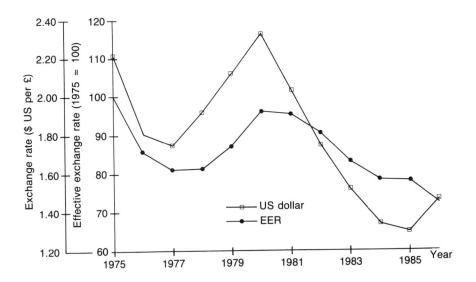

The effective exchange rate of the pound fell steadily from 1975 to 1978. It then rose strongly up to 1980. Since then it has fallen each year to 1986. From 1975 to 1980 movements of the effective exchange rate and the US dollar exchange rate were similar. But since 1980 the effective exchange rate has fallen, but not as strongly as the US dollar exchange rate.
*Sources:*US dollar exchange rate, Appendix to Chapter 2. Effective exchange rate, *Bank of England Quarterly Bulletin*, March 1977, pp. 46–7; March 1981, Table 18; December 1982, Table 18; and August 1987, Table 18.

against sterling which would have the same effect on the United Kingdom trade balance as a one per cent change in sterling against each of the other currencies is reflected as a one per cent change in the index' of the effective sterling exchange rate. 'For example, the US dollar has a weight of approximately one quarter in the present calculation of the sterling effective rate: thus a one per cent depreciation of the US dollar is considered to have the same impact on the UK trade balance as a uniform appreciation of sterling of some one quarter of one per cent against all currencies in the basket' (*Bank of England Quarterly Bulletin*, March 1981, p. 69). What the Bank of England is saying in the above quotation is that it uses weights to calculate the effective exchange rate. These weights are supposed to tell us the effect of the measured change in the effective exchange rate on the country's trade balance, regardless of whether the change occurred because sterling changed its value uniformly against all other currencies or in a non-uniform way.

A good description of the effective exchange rate, sometimes called the Sterling Exchange Rate Index, is given in *Financial Statistics Explanatory Handbook*, 1986 Edition, February 1986, pp.116–17, The Sterling Exchange Rate Index is an index against the currencies of 17 countries. The Bank of England also calculates an index against the eight currencies which participate in the European Monetary System (EMS). This effective exchange rate is called the Sterling Exchange Index Against EMS Exchange Rate Mechanism Currencies.

The effective exchange rate for sterling or the Sterling Exchange Rate Index as calculated by the Bank of England is shown in Figure 6.1. Alongside it is also shown the value of sterling against the US dollar. Clearly these two representations of the value of the pound do not exactly coincide, but they do follow the same broad general pattern.

Summary

A. Definitions of the Balance of Payments

(i) The *current account* is the account which records the values of current goods and services sold abroad, and purchases of goods and services from abroad, debt interest receipts and payments, and unilateral transfers received from and paid abroad.

(ii) The *capital account* records the receipts and payments between residents and non-residents arising from the issue of new debt or the retirement of old debt.

(iii) The *official settlements account* records the movements in gold and foreign currency reserves (adjusted by any official borrowing) resulting from the net of the balances on the current and capital accounts. By accounting convention it is measured as the negative of the sum of the current and capital account balances so that the sum of the balances on all three accounts is always zero.

(iv) The *balance of payments* is defined as the sum of the balances on the current and capital accounts or, equivalently, as the negative of the official settlements balance.

B. Measuring the UK Balance of Payments Accounts

The current account of the balance of payments is measured mainly from documentation required for customs and excise purposes. When exchange rates are fluctuating markedly, the conversion of foreign currency invoice values into sterling is only approximate and gives rise to measurement errors. The capital account transactions are recorded incompletely and also contain errors. The official settlements balance is measured exactly by the Bank of England. The difference between the measured balance on the current and capital accounts and the official settlements balance has grown in recent years.

C. Exchange Rate Definitions

(i) A *foreign exchange rate* is the relative price between currencies.

(ii) A *fixed exchange rate* is one which takes on a value declared by and maintained by the active intervention of the central bank.

(iii) A *flexible exchange rate* is an exchange rate, the value of which is determined purely by market forces, with no direct central bank intervention.

(iv) A *managed floating exchange rate* is one that is manipulated by the central bank but it is not manipulated according to any pre-announced rules.

(v) An *effective exchange rate* is an index representing the relative price between one national currency and an average of other currencies. The weights of other currencies on average reflect the importance of each currency in the international trade of the country in question.

(vi) *Real exchange rate* is the relative price of two baskets of goods, one domestic and one foreign.

D. Measuring Exchange Rates

Exchange rates are continuously varying and are measured at a specific time of the day. They are recorded and reported in the *Bank of England Quarterly Bulletin* and in *International Financial Statistics*.

Review Questions

1. Divide the following items into four categories: those items that belong in (a) the current account, (b) the capital account, (c) the official settlements account, and (d) none of the balance of payments accounts:

    (a) Your summer vacation expenses in Europe.
    (b) The British government's receipts for the sale of bonds to US residents.
    (c) Barclays Bank purchase of US dollar travellers' cheques from the American Express Company in New York.
    (d) The transfer by the Bank of England to the Bank of Canada of 1000 ounces of gold.
    (e) British imports of Japanese cars.
    (f) British exports of Scotch whisky.
    (g) The takeover of a US company by a British company.
    (h) The payment of interest on its bonds by the British government.
    (i) The money taken out of the UK by departing emigrants.
    (j) UK aid to poor countries.

2. Using the following items and numbers, construct the balance of payments accounts of the hypothetical economy:

Item	$m
Capital imports	2000
Debt interest received from abroad	800
Exports of goods and services	1000
Capital exports	1800
Gifts made to foreigners	100
Imports of goods and services	1100
Debt interest paid abroad	700
Rise in gold and foreign exchange reserves	400

    (a) What are the 'errors and omissions'?
    (b) What is the current account balance?
    (c) What is the capital account balance?
    (d) What is the balance on the official settlements account?
    (e) What is the balance of payments?

3. What is a foreign exchange rate?
4. What is an effective exchange rate?
5. What is a fixed exchange rate? How is it kept fixed?
6. What is a flexible exchange rate?
7. What is a managed floating exchange rate? How is it 'managed'?

7

Patterns in the Data

The final chapter of this section is different from the other four. It does not deal with the problem of measuring a single macroeconomic variable (or group of variables). Rather, it is concerned with the problem of observing and discerning patterns in the evolution of the economic aggregates and in the relationships among variables. In short, it is concerned with the business cycle.[1]

Until the mid-1930s, the term *business cycle* was used to describe the phenomenon which students of short-term movements in economic aggregates sought to explain and understand. Scholars saw their task as one of understanding the general recurrent ups and downs in economic activity *viewed as an ongoing process*. In 1936, however, with the publication by John Maynard Keynes of *The General Theory of Employment, Interest, and Money*,[2] there was a fundamental redirection of research effort. What Keynes did was to change the question which students of aggregate economic phenomena tried to answer. Instead of trying to understand the recurrent ups and downs of economic activity viewed as an ongoing process, Keynes redirected our research efforts to an apparently easier question, namely, that of the determination of output, employment, prices, interest rates, etc. viewed *at a point in time*, taking the past history of the economy and expectations about the future as given.

---

1   This chapter draws heavily on, and in places will be recognized as a paraphrase of, parts of the important paper 'Understanding Business Cycles', by Robert E. Lucas, Jr. in *Stabilization of the Domestic and International Economy*, Carnegie-Rochester Conference Series on Public Policy, 5, eds. Karl Brunner and Allan H. Meltzer (Amsterdam: North-Holland, 1977.)
2   John Maynard Keynes, *The General Theory of Employment, Interest and Money* (London: Macmillan, 1936).

At about the same time as Keynes's simplification enabled scholars to direct their attention to the simpler question of the determination of the aggregate economic variables at a point in time, strides were being made in the mathematical formulation and statistical testing of economic theories, notably by the Dutch economist Jan Tinbergen. As a result of the pioneering efforts of Keynes and Tinbergen, subsequent scholars were able to develop a considerable refined body of knowledge which came to be known as *macroeconomics*. In this new macroeconomic analysis, there seemed to be no special place for business cycle theory. Indeed, as far as Keynes himself was concerned, the job of explaining what determined the values of economic variables at a moment in time is almost the same thing as explaining the business cycle (or *trade cycle* as it is known in Europe). Keynes said that

> since we claim to have shown ... what determines the volume of employment at any time, it follows, if we are right, that our theory must be capable of explaining the phenomena of the Trade Cycle.[3]

Further, not only did it appear that there was no need for a special theory of the business cycle; it even seemed as if the earlier attempts to find a theory of the business cycle were hopelessly muddled and confused in comparison with the clarity that had been brought to the task of understanding the determination of the aggregate economic variables at a point in time.

It was not until the early 1970s, with the seminal work of Robert E. Lucas, Jr. of the University of Chicago, that attention was redirected to the problem of understanding more than what determines income, employment, prices, etc. at a point in time, given their past history. Lucas suggested that the bigger question of what determines the evolution of the aggregate economic variables over time, and viewed as a process, had to be tackled head on if we were to develop a deep enough understanding of aggregate economic phenomena for us to be able to design policy arrangements that would stand some chance of improving matters.

As Lucas sees things, and as we will elaborate more fully later in this book, the task of understanding what determines income, employment, and prices at a moment in time, given their past history, cannot be accomplished without *analysing the entire ongoing cyclical process* that determines these aggregate economic variables. The key reason for this is that what people do today depends on their expectations of what is going to happen in the future. To formulate an expectation as to what is going to happen in the future, people have to do the best they can to assess how the economy will evolve in the future. Thus their current action depends on their expectations of future actions by themselves and others. Now it is evident that the only guide that is available concerning what will happen

---

3   *Ibid.*, p.313.

in the future is what has happened in the past, which means that if present actions depend on expectations of the future, they must also depend on what has happened in the past. Only by analysing an entire economic process – past, present and future – will we be able to understand what is happening at any given moment.

The redirection of research effort in macroeconomics by Keynes was not, in our view, a blind alley. Rather, it was a necessary stage in the process of developing a satisfactory theory of the business cycle. Not until we had made a great deal of progress with the simpler question posed by Keynes were we able to go back to the harder question to which Lucas has now redirected us.

To progress through the subject matter of modern macroeconomics all the way to the new theories of the business cycle will take most of the rest of this book. Not until we get to Chapter 27 will it be possible to summarize our current understanding of what determines business cycles.

In order to pave the way, this chapter will take you through five tasks that are designed to enable you to understand what we mean by business cycles. By the time you have completed your study of this chapter you will be able to:

(a) **Define the definition of the business cycle.**
(b) **Explain the concept of autocorrelation.**
(c) **Explain the concept of co-movement.**
(d) **State the properties of the business cycle.**
(e) **State the features of the UK business cycle.**

A. Definition of the Business Cycle

Although business cycles have been studied for well over a hundred years, it was not until the 1940s that a clear definition of business cycles emerged, due to the efforts of a group of outstanding and careful observers of cycles working under the auspices of the National Bureau of Economic Research in New York. Wesley Clare Mitchell and Arthur F. Burns (Burns subsequently became Chairman of the Board of Governors of the Federal Reserve System) defined the business cycle as follows:

> Business cycles are a type of fluctuation found in the aggregate economic activity of nations that organize their work mainly in business enterprises: A cycle consists of expansions occurring at about the same time in many economic activities, followed by similarly general recessions, contractions and revivals which merge into the expansion phase of the next cycle; this sequence of changes is recurrent but not periodic; in duration business cycles vary from more than one year to ten or twelve years; they are not divisible into shorter cycles of similar character with amplitudes approximating their own.[4]

---

4 This definition is from Arthur F. Burns and Wesley Clare Mitchell, *Measuring Business Cycles* (New York: National Bureau of Economic Research, 1946), p.3.

Let us dissect this definition a little bit. Three aspects of the definition are worth highlighting. First, let us ask, what is a business cycle a cycle in? The answer to that is given in the first part of definition: the business cycle is a cycle (or fluctuation) in aggregate economic activity. Although there are several alternative ways in which 'aggregate economic activity' may be measured, the most natural comprehensive measure is the level of real income (output or expenditure) — real GDP. Such a measure summarizes all the many individual producing and spending activities in the economy. Because real GDP, on the average, grows from one year to the next, it is necessary, in defining the cycle, to abstract from that growth trend and define the cycle as 'deviations of real GDP from trend'. By regarding the deviations of real GDP from trend as defining the cycle, it is possible to examine the ups and downs of other aggregate variables in relation to or *with reference to* the cycle in real GDP.[5]

The second thing to notice about the definition of the cycle is that it involves two turning points, an upper turning point and a lower turning point; and two phases, an expansion phase and a contraction phase.

Figure 7.1
A hypothetical
business cycle

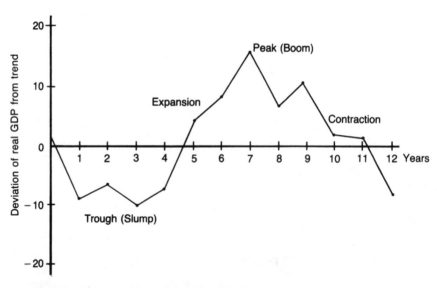

A cycle in the deviation of real GDP from trend begins in the contraction phase, reaches a trough (or slump), moves through an expansion to a peak (or boom) and then turns into a further contraction phase.

5 In their pioneering work on measuring the business cycle, the National Bureau of Economic Research economists (referred to above) developed a concept of the *reference cycle*, which was somewhat more general than simply using deviations of real GDP from trend. Their methods, however, to some degree involve judgment, and to describe them and fully appreciate them would divert us too far.

Figure 7.1 illustrates the hypothetical cycle of Table 7.1. The upper turning point is often referred to as the *cyclical peak* and the lower turning point as the *cyclical trough*. The movement from the peak to the trough is the *contraction*, and the movement from trough back to peak is the *expansion*. If a contraction is particularly severe it is referred to as a *recession*. Technically, a recession is defined as occurring when real GDP falls for two successive quarters. An even more severe contraction and prolonged trough would be known as a *depression* or if particularly severe, the prefix *great* would be attached to it. The picture of the cycle shown in Figure 7.1 gives just one complete up-and-down movement in the deviation of real GDP from trend.

Table 7.1 Calculating deviations of real GDP from trend

	Real GDP		
Year	Actual value	Trend value	Deviation from trend
0	101.2	100.0	+1.2
1	94.9	104.0	−9.1
2	101.4	108.2	−6.8
3	102.4	112.5	−10.1
4	109.4	117.0	−7.6
5	126.0	121.7	+4.3
6	134.7	126.5	+8.2
7	147.8	131.6	+16.2
8	144.0	136.9	+7.1
9	152.7	142.3	+10.4
10	150.8	148.0	+2.8
11	155.9	153.9	+2.0
12	151.7	160.1	−8.4

The third feature of the definition of the business cycle emphasizes the fact that cycles are not regular *periodic* ups and downs but are *irregular* though *recurrent* ups and downs, the duration of which (measured from trough to trough) could run from something slightly more than one year to as long as ten or twelve years. To see how we might characterize this feature in a simple way involves introducing a technical idea which will be developed in the next section of this chapter — the concept of autocorrelation.

The fourth and final feature of the definition of the cycle given above — that 'they are not divisible into shorter cycles of similar character with amplitudes approximating their own' — is simply designed to capture the idea that the cycle is a basic unit of observation and analysis. It is not divisible into smaller similar patterns.

Let us now turn to the first of the two technical tasks that face us in this chapter.

B. Autocorrelation

This section and the next one deal with technical matters. They do so, however, in a non-technical way.[6] It is worthwhile becoming familiar with the concept of autocorrelation because it will give you a more precise, and at the same time very simple, way of viewing a process that may be used to describe the recurrent but non-periodic ups and downs in economic activity that characterize the business cycle.

Two key ideas are combined in the concept of autocorrelation. First, *the present is influenced by the past;* second, *the present is not completely predictable from knowledge of the past.* An alternative way of capturing the same two ideas would be to say that the current value of some variable may be better predicted by knowledge of its past values, but may not be exactly predicted on the basis of such knowledge.

There are many examples in everyday life of autocorrelation. One obvious one is the state of the weather. Wet days and dry days tend to go in runs. If you were to try predicting tomorrow's weather without using refined meterological observations and methods, one possible rule might be to predict that tomorrow will be much like today. If today is wet, you predict that tomorrow will also be wet. If today is dry you predict that tomorrow will be dry. Such a prediction will often be wrong. It turns out, however, that you will be right more often than wrong. You will certainly do better than flipping a coin and calling 'dry' for heads and 'wet' for tails. How much better you will do depends in part on where you live and what the longer-term climatic patterns are. Nevertheless, the basic idea of predicting tomorrow's weather on the basis of today's is a sound one (though not the best available) and one which exploits the autocorrelation in weather patterns.

Another example concerns the movements of waves on the ocean surface. Sitting at the ocean side you can predict the pattern and timing of the wave movements breaking on the shoreline by supposing that the next wave will look much like the one that has just preceded it. You will not be exactly right because the wind patterns and the interaction of the waves ensure that no wave is exactly like its predecessor. There is, however, a strong resemblance.

A third example would be the movement of a child's swing or rocking horse. If you wanted to predict the extent of the movement of the horse or the height attained by the swing on a given movement, predicting an outcome similar to that which occurred on the previous rock or swing would be fairly accurate. It would not be exactly right because you wouldn't know exactly how much work the child was doing to keep the motion of the swing or horse at a constant level. An unpredictable surge of effort on the child's part would send the swing or horse on a more

---

6 If you want a more technical though still simplified treatment of this topic you should work through the Appendix to this chapter.

extreme course, whereas an unpredicted slackening off of effort would cause the horse or swing to come closer to a rest position.

These are all examples of the existence of autocorrelation in the behaviour of variables that we commonly observe in the ordinary course of life. We need to be more precise, however, in specifying how the current value of some variable relates to its previous value or values. The simplest case would be where the value of a variable at a given point in time depends only on its own value at the previous point in time. (The units in which time is measured will vary from case to case and could be as short as an instant or as long as a decade. In economics we typically think of units of time as coming either in calendar quarters or years.) Such a case is given the special name *first-order autocorrelation*. If the current value of a variable depends on its own values at the previous point in time *and* at the time before that, then it is given the special name *second-order autocorrelation*. This idea clearly can be generalized to permit any degree of influence of the past on the present.

The aspect of autocorrelation having to do with imperfect predictability simply reflects the obvious fact that the world is a fairly complicated place and is not capable of prediction by the application of simple (mechanical) rules linking current values of variables to their own past values. A different way of saying the same thing is that, to some extent, the world is *random* (or *stochastic*).

Let us now use the notion of autocorrelation to describe the evolution of real GDP from one year to the next. Real GDP would be autocorrelated if next year's GDP could be better predicted, although not exactly predicted, from knowledge of the current (and perhaps some previous) year's GDP. We can capture this idea by writing an equation that says

$$y_t = 25 + 0.75y_{t-1} + e_t \tag{7.1}$$

The variable y_t represents the value of real GDP in year t. The same variable with the subscript $t - 1$ represents the value of real GDP in the previous year. The variable e_t represents all the random unpredictable influences that affect real GDP that are not predictable on the basis of knowledge of previous values of GDP. What this equation says (and it is of course just an example) is that real GDP in a given year will be equal to three quarters of its previous year's value, plus 25, plus some unpredictable random amounts.

Such an equation, as we will see in the final section of this chapter, fairly well describes the movements not in GDP itself but in the deviations of GDP from its trend values.

You have now discovered what autocorrelation is. Autocorrelation simply means that the value of some particular variable at some particular date is related to its own value at some earlier date. In the above example, income at date t is related to income at date $t - 1$. The relationship is not perfect. There is a randomness that loosens the link between income at date t and at date $t - 1$. In rough terms, an autocorrelated series is one that shows systematic recurrent up-and-down movements.

It is important to realize that *describing* the path of GDP by a low-order stochastic difference equation is not the same thing as *understanding* what *causes* GDP movements — that is, what causes the business cycle. The description is simply a neat and convenient way of thinking about the process. It also directs our attention to potential explanations in the sense that it alerts us to the idea that we will have to find, in any theory of the business cycle, two things:

(1) A source of or, more generally, sources of random disturbance to the economy.
(2) Systematic sources of inertia causing movements of GDP (and other aggregates) from one period to another to be gradual — that is, to display autocorrelation.

Although you are now able to describe the recurrent ups and downs in real income in very simple terms, you need to be aware of some other technical language that will help you talk about the broader aspects of the business cycle.

C. Co-Movement

In fully characterizing business cycles, it is going to be necessary to talk about the way in which different variables move in relation to each other. That is, we will want to be able to say how employment and unemployment, prices and wages, money and interest rates all move in relationship to the movements in real income. In other words, we want to be able to characterize the co-movements of various pairwise combinations of variables.

There are four features of co-movements among variables that may be identified. First, co-movements may be *procyclical* or *counter-cyclical*. A procyclical co-movement is a movement in a variable that has broadly the same cyclical pattern as the variable with which it is being compared. It tends to rise when the reference variable rises and to fall when the reference variable falls. Since the reference variable for the business cycle is deviations of GDP from trend, procyclical variables are those that rise as GDP rises above trend and fall as GDP falls below trend.

A counter-cyclical co-movement is a movement in one variable that is in the opposite direction to the movement in the reference variable. Thus, a counter-cyclical variable is one that falls as real GDP rises above its trend and that rises as real GDP falls below its trend.

Usually, variables do not exactly move in a procyclical or counter-cyclical manner. They tend to either *lead* or *lag* the reference variable. This second feature of co-movement can be seen in Figure 7.2, which illustrates leading and lagging procyclical variables.

**Figure 7.2
Leading and lagging
procyclical
co-movements**

(b) (a) (c)

Time

Deviation from trend

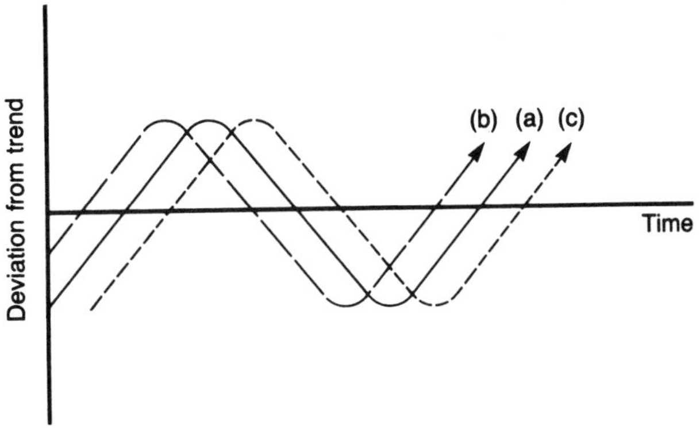

The three variables plotted here have procyclical co-movements. If (a) describes the
reference cycle of real income deviation from trend, then the variable (b) leads the cycle
in income and the variable (c) lags that cycle.

Suppose that the curve labelled (a) represents the cycle in deviations
of real GDP from trend. Then the line (b) would represent a variable that
leads the cycle, and (c) would represent a variable that lags the cycle.
Both variables are generally procyclical. That is, they generally move up
with income and down with income, but they don't move at exactly the
same time. Figure 7.3 illustrates a counter-cyclical co-movement. If (a)
again is the path of deviations of real GDP from trend then (d) would
be the path of a variable which moves counter-cyclically.

You will recognize that there is a potential element of ambiguity as to
whether a variable is counter-cylical or procyclical if it leads or lags the

**Figure 7.3
Counter-cyclical
co-movements**

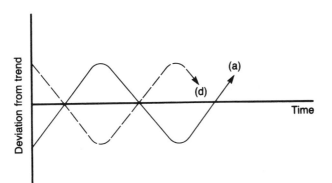

(a)

(d)

Time

Deviation from trend

The variable marked (d) displays perfect counter-cyclical co-movement with the variable
marked (a).

reference variable by 'too much'. You could, as a matter of description, regard a variable that is exactly counter-cyclical as one that is procyclical but lagged by half a cycle. However, that would seem to be using language in an awkward way. We don't think of leads and lags as being as big as half a cycle.

A third feature of co-movement has to do with the *amplitude* of fluctuation in one variable relative to another. Roughly speaking, the amplitude of fluctuation in a variable is the distance from the average value to its peak value, or average value to trough value. Figure 7.4 illustrates.

Figure 7.4
Amplitude

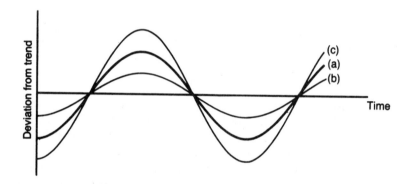

The cycle (b) has smaller amplitude than the reference cycle (a), and the cycle (c) has larger amplitude than the reference cycle.

Suppose that the line labelled (a) measures the deviation of real GDP from trend. The thin lines marked (b) and (c) are examples of variables that display smaller amplitude (b), and larger amplitude (c) than the fluctuations in real GDP (a). Of course, there has to be a unit-free method of comparing different variables. It would not do to measure GDP in billions of dollars and interest rates in percentages, for example. The most natural unit-free measure is the percentage deviation of each variable from its trend.

The fourth and final feature of a co-movement which we need to identify is the *conformity* between the two variables. We will say that co-movement has a high degree of conformity if two series 'look the same'. For example, all the series graphed in Figures 7.2 and 7.3 have a high degree of conformity. A low degree of conformity occurs if one variable sometimes appeared to follow the same cyclical pattern as the reference variable, but did not always do so. Figure 7.5 illustrates.

Suppose that (a) is the reference variable. We would describe the variable plotted with the broken line marked (b) as displaying a lower degree of conformity. There is obviously some rough procyclical relationship between (a) and (b), but it is by no means exact.

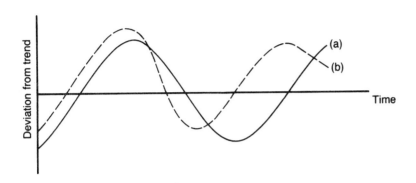

Figure 7.5
Conformity

The variables (a) and (b) display only a moderate degree of conformity. Variable (b) follows the same general pattern as the reference cycle (a) in the first up- and down-swing, but begins to lead the reference cycle in the second up-swing.

We may thus speak about the co-movements (joint movements, if you like) between two variables as being either procyclical or counter-cyclical, as involving a lead or a lag of one variable in relation to the other, as displaying greater or less amplitude of fluctuation, and as having a high- or low-degree of conformity. This language merely describes a business cycle. It is now possible to go on and use this language to address the more substantive tasks of this chapter. The first of these is to characterize the business cycle more fully.

D. Properties of the Business Cycle

The properties of the business cycle may now be set out more precisely, using the language that has been introduced to you in the previous two sections.

The first feature of business cycles has to do with the movements in the deviations of real GDP from trend.

> Technically, movements about trend in Gross [Domestic] Product in any country can be well described by [a low order autocorrelation]. These movements do not exhibit uniformity of either period or amplitude, which is to say, they do not resemble the deterministic wave motions which sometimes arise in the natural sciences.[7]

The second feature of business cycles has to do with the co-movements among the various aggregates. The chief regularities observed are in the co-movements among different aggregate time-series.

The principal among these are the following:[8]

7 Lucas, Jr., 'Understanding Business Cycles', p.9.
8 *Ibid.*, with slight adjustments from the original.

(1) Output movements across broadly defined sectors of the economy move together.
(2) Production of durable goods exhibits much greater amplitude than production of non-durables.
(3) Production and prices of agricultural goods and natural resources have lower than average conformity.
(4) Business profits show high conformity and much greater amplitude than other series.
(5) Prices generally are procyclical.
(6) Short-term interest rates are procyclical; long-term rates slightly so.
(7) Monetary aggregates and velocity measures are procyclical.

For the purpose of what will follow in this book, where the primary emphasis is on economic aggregates, we will be concerned with five features of the cycle selected from those set out above. First, we will want to understand why it is that movements in deviations of real GDP from trend can be described by a low-order autocorrelation process; second, we will want to understand why fluctuation in output of durable goods exhibits greater amplitude than that of non-durables; third, why prices are generally procyclical; fourth, why interest rates are procyclical; and fifth, why the monetary aggregates and velocity measures of money are procyclical.

These are the central features of the business cycle which macro-economics seeks to understand. In addition, implicit in the characterization but needing to be made explicit, we will be concerned to explain why unemployment is counter-cyclical and employment procyclical. If unemployment is counter-cyclical and prices (inflation) procyclical, in general, there will be a negative relationship between inflation and unemployment.

Before moving on to begin these tasks, let us look at some of the broad facts about the UK business cycle.

E. The UK Business Cycle

(i) The Movements in Real GDP about Trend

As you have already discovered in Chapter 2, real GDP (real income) in the UK has grown at an average rate of 1.7 per cent over the period 1900 to 1986. The deviations of real GDP from its growth trend were set out in Figure 2.4 (Chapter 2). Recall that the most dominant feature of those deviations was the large negative deviation during the 1920s and the Great Depression years of the 1930s and the large positive deviation during the Second World War (1942–5). There were also distinct but irregular smaller cycles visible in the data. Can this history of deviations of real GDP from trend in the UK be described by a low-order autocorrelation process? You are about to discover that, as a matter of fact, it can.

The fluctuations around trend in real GDP since 1900 are well described by the following equation:[9]

$$(y_t - y_t^*) = 0.89(y_{t-1} - y_{t-1}^*) + e_t \qquad (7.2)$$

The way to read this is as follows: y_t represents real GDP in year t, and y_t represents the trend real GDP in year t. Thus $(y_t - y_t^*)$ represents the deviation of real GDP from trend in year t. The same variable with the subscript $t - 1$ represents the deviation from trend in the previous year. As before, e_t represents a random disturbance. Notice that in Equation (7.2) the magnitude of the coefficient is very similar to the one that we used as an example in the section on autocorrelation above (and in the Appendix to this chapter). It says that real GDP will deviate from its trend value by 0.88 of its previous deviation plus a random disturbance.

In interpreting Equation (7.2) recall that you discovered that this way of looking at the movements in the deviations of GDP from trend simply involves breaking the actual movement into two components: (1) a source of (or, more generally, sources of) random disturbance to the economy, and (2) systematic sources of inertia. In the above equation, the inertia is represented by the term $0.89(y_{t-1} - y_t^*)$ and the sources of random disturbance in any one year are represented by the term e_t.

To give you a better feel for what has been going on, Figure 7.6 plots the deviations of real GDP from trend and its two components – the systematic source of inertia and the random component. Frame (a) of the figure shows the deviations of real GDP from trend. [These are exactly the same as those shown in frame (b) of Figure 2.4 Chapter 2.] This cycle in deviations of real GDP from trend is decomposed into a purely random element[10] and an inertia element in frames (c) and (b) of Figure 7.6.

---

9 Equation (7.2) and Figure 7.6 were constructed in the following way. First, deviations of real GDP from trend were calculated by fitting a trend line to real GDP from 1900 to 1986. The deviations were then analysed to determine their degree of autocorrelation and it was discovered that although not quite a perfectly satisfactory relationship, that shown as Equation (7.2) in the text could be regarded as a useful approximate description of the data. The random shock charted in frame (c) of the Figure 7.6 is the calculated residual movements in real GDP about its trend not accounted for by the previous year's value of that variable multiplied by the coefficient 0.89. As a matter of fact, a *second*-order difference equation – one that says that the deviation of real GDP from trend in year t depends on the deviations in year $t - 1$ and year $t - 2$ as well as a random disturbance – describes the data best. The improvement in the description is not, however, so enormous as to render the first-order description misleading.

10 What we are calling a 'purely random element' is, in fact, only approximately so. The movements in deviations of real GDP from trend not accounted for by a second-order difference equation are indistinguishable from purely random disturbances. The disturbances in Figure 7.5 could be reduced slightly and made 'more random' by taking account of this. The broad picture would not, however, be changed by adding this complication.

**Figure 7.6
Random and
systematic com-
ponents of deviation
of GDP from trend
1950-86**

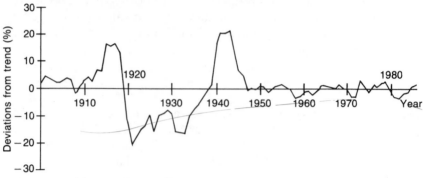

(a) Actual deviations from trend

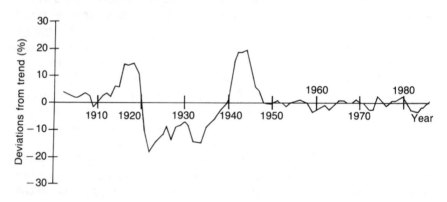

(b) Systematic sources of inertia

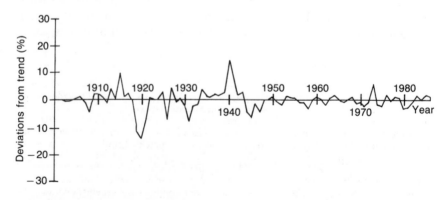

(c) Purely random shocks

The actual deviations of real GDP from trend [frame (a)] are decomposed into a
systematic source of inertia [frame (b)] and purely random shocks [frame (c)].

Source: Appendix to Chapter 2.

Frame (c) of the figure shows the purely random disturbances that have hit the British economy over this time period. Those disturbances add up to zero over the entire period. Sometimes they have been as large as a negative shock of 14.0 and a positive shock of 14.2 (per cent of GDP). Most of the time, however, the shocks have been small, 61 per cent of them lying between +2 and −2, a further 27 per cent lying between +5 and −5, a further 7 per cent lying between +10 and −10 and only 5 per cent being greater than +10 or less than −10 (per cent of GDP). These shocks impact on the economy to produce the cycle in deviations of real GDP from trend described by Equation (7.2) and plotted as frame (a) of Figure 7.6.

Frame (b) of Figure 7.6 represents the contribution of inertia to the deviations of GDP from trend. The line in frame (a) of Figure 7.6 represents nothing other than the summation of the lines in frames (b) and (c).

To get a feel for how this decomposition works, consider a particular year. The year 1940 will illustrate the story well. According to this description of events, in 1940 there was a positive random shock of 14.2 per cent of GDP − the biggest of the positive shocks recorded. The shocks from 1934 to 1939 had also been positive, and had accumulated over those years to produce a positive deviation of GDP from trend in 1939 of 1.8 per cent, which can be read off in frame (a) of Figure 7.6. This positive deviation in 1941, when multiplied by the coefficient 0.89 gave positive inertia to GDP in 1942 of 1.6 per cent as shown in frame (b) of Figure 7.6. This inertia, other things remaining the same, would have put real GDP above trend by that same 1.6 per cent in 1940. Other things, however, were not the same. In 1940 a large positive shock (14.2 per cent of GDP) occurred. Adding this random shock to the positive inertia moves the actual value of GDP to 15.8 per cent above trend. Thus, the 15.8 per cent deviation of GDP from trend in 1940 represents the sum of a large positive shock (14.2 per cent) and inertia (1.6 per cent) coming from the accumulation of previous positive shocks.

It cannot be emphasized sufficiently that this decomposition is merely *a way* of *describing* the movement of deviations of GDP from trend. It does, however, provide us with a valuable way of thinking about what has been happening to GDP. The economy is bombarded by shocks as described in frame (c) of Figure 7.6, and those shocks affect the level of output (and other variables as well) in a manner which looks much less random than the shocks themselves. We can translate the random shocks into a more systematic up-and-down movement of output by the device of describing output as following a first-order difference equation which is stochastically (randomly) disturbed. The task for explanation is to figure out: (1) what causes the shocks shown in frame (c) of Figure 7.6; (2) what gives rise to the translation of those shocks into movements of output and other variables; and (3) what are the sources giving rise to inertia as described in frame (b).

(ii) The Production of Durables and Non-durables

The second feature of the business cycle that was identified above was the tendency for the production of durables (investment goods and consumer durables) to fluctuate with greater amplitude than the production of non-durables (consumer goods and services). This general feature of the business cycle is very evident in the the British data, as Figure 7.7 shows. Data for the post-war years only have been used in this figure because the division of output into durables and non-durables was severely distorted in the war years (1942-45) and obscures the basic peace-time pattern.

Frame (a), which illustrates the movements in durables, shows fluctuations commonly ranging from as much as 25 per cent above or below trend. In contrast, the production of non-durables [frame (b)] never gets even 5 per cent away from its trend. The ups and downs in durable production also occur with greater frequency than those in non-durable production.

(iii) Output and Unemployment

A further general feature of the business cycle that was identified above was the tendency for output and employment to move together or, equivalently, for output and unemployment to move opposite each other. A useful way of exploring the co-movements among variables is to plot one variable against another in the same diagram. That is, to construct what is called a *scatter diagram*. Figure 7.8 does this for unemployment and deviations of real GDP from trend. Each mark in Figure 7.8 represents a year and shows the levels of unemployment and the deviation of real GDP from trend in a particular year. To be sure that you know how to read Figure 7.8, consider the mark labelled 32 — in the bottom right-hand corner of the figure. This mark represents the observation for the year 1932. In 1932, unemployment was 22 per cent (which you can read off on the horizontal axis of the diagram) and real GDP was 16 per cent below trend (which you can read off on the vertical axis of the diagram).

Evidently, there is a clear tendency for unemployment to move in the opposite direction to deviations of real GDP from trend. The relationship is by no means perfect, but is nevertheless very distinct. It is evident from the figure that there has been a tendency for the relationship to drift to the right over the post-war years. Abstracting from this rightward drift, it is evident that there is a clear systematic tendency for unemployment to move counter-cyclically with reference to deviations of real GDP from trend.

(iv) Price Movements

A general feature of the business cycle is that the price level moves pro-cyclically. Thus, inflation rates are higher when output deviates above

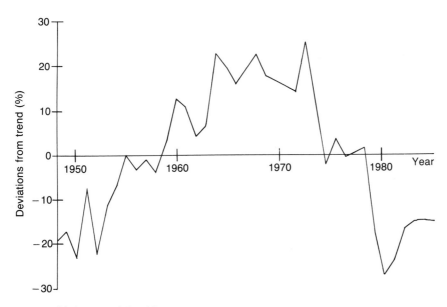

Figure 7.7
The production of durables and non-durables: 1950–86

(a) Output of non-durables

(b) Output of durables

The production of durables [frame (a)] fluctuates with much greater amplitude than the production of non-durables [frame (b)].

Source: Household durables: 1948–83, *Economic Trends Annual Supplement*, 1986 Edition, p.26; 1984–86, *Economic Trends*, August 1987, p.10. Gross Investment, Inventories and GDP: 1948–81, *Economic Trends Annual Supplement*, 1987 Edition, p.13; 1982–86, *Economic Trends*, August 1987, p.8. Durables is the sum of household durables, investment and inventories and non-durables is GDP minus durables.

**Figure 7.8
Unemployment and
the deviation of real
GDP from trend**

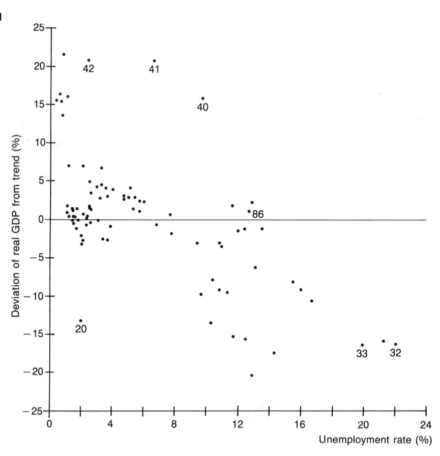

Each point shows the deviation of real GDP from trend and the unemployment rate occurring in a particular year. Some years are identified by their last two digits (e.g. 1932 is
labelled as 32). There is a clear tendency for unemployment to be highest when real GDP
is furthest below trend and lowest when real GDP is furthest above trend.

Source: Appendix to Chapter 2.

trend and lower when output deviates below trend. Equivalently, we
could expect to find a negative association between inflation and
unemployment movements. That is, inflation is generally higher when
unemployment is lower. Viewing the procyclical nature of inflation as
a counter-cyclical relation between inflation and unemployment enables
us to focus on a relationship known as the Phillips relation (named after

**Figure 7.9
Co-movements of
inflation and
unemployment:
1900–86**

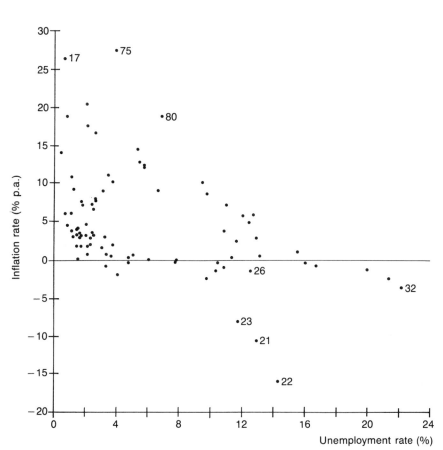

Each point shows the inflation rate and the unemployment rate that occurred in a given year. Some years are identified by their last two digits (e.g. 1932 is shown as 32). There have been long periods when inflation and unemployment move in opposite directions and other periods when there is considerable independence in the movements of the two series.

Source: Appendix to Chapter 2.

the New Zealand economist A.W. Phillips who popularized this relationship).[11]

11 Phillips' original contribution is A.W. Phillips, 'The Relation between Unemployment and the Rate of Change of Money Wage Rates in the United Kingdom, 1861-1957', *Economica*, 25 November 1958, pp.283–99.

Figure 7.9 shows the co-movements of inflation and unemployment in the UK between 1900 and 1986.

Notice that there is, from time to time, a tendency for inflation and unemployment to move in opposite directions. Notice, however, that there is no single relationship that characterizes all the co-movements between inflation and unemployment. Two-thirds of the movements are *inverse* (i.e. when inflation rises, unemployment falls or when inflation falls, unemployment rises) but there are significant occasions on which both variables move in the same direction. Consideration of the Phillips relation in the UK data raises as many questions having to do with these

**Figure 7.10
Co-movements of
inflation and interest
rates**

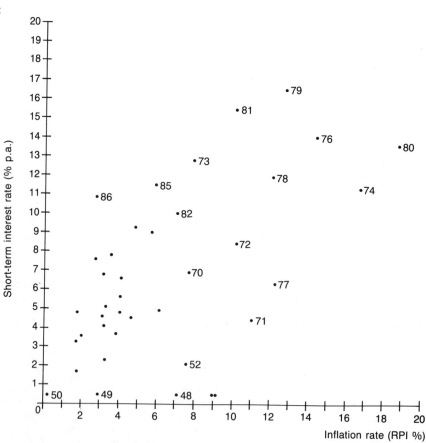

The trends in these two variables are similar, but the movements in interest rates sometimes lag behind those in inflation.

Source: Appendix to Chapter 2.

simultaneous increases in inflation and unemployment (or simultaneous decreases) as it does concerning their negative co-movement. All of these stylized facts will have to be coped with by any viable theory concerning the causes of inflation and unemployment. It will be necessary to understand why, most of the time, the two variables move in opposite directions and why there are other periods when they move in the same direction as each other.

(v) Interest Rates

The general description of the business cycle is that short-term interest rates are procyclical and long-term rates only slightly so. A useful way of looking at the cyclical nature of short-term interest rates is to examine how they move with inflation. Since we know that inflation is generally procyclical, then if interest rates and inflation move together we know that interest rates also are procyclical.

Figure 7.10 shows the relationship between short-term interest rates and inflation in the UK. The generally procyclical nature of short-term interest rates is visible in this figure. You can see that, although there is no perfect relationship between interest rates and inflation, there is nevertheless a tendency for these two variables to move in the same direction. This feature of interest rates and inflation rates to move together is also something for which our theories are necessarily going to have to be able to account.

There is no need to examine separately the movements of long-term interest rates. You know from Figure 2.4 that long-term interest rates are much smoother than short-term rates. You also know that there is a general tendency for long-term rates to move in the same broad direction as short rates. It immediately follows that long-term interest rates do have the general characteristic that they are procyclical, but only slightly so.

These, then, are the major features of the UK's business cycle that macroeconomic theory needs to be able to explain. The rest of this book is concerned with the task of explanation.

Summary

A. Definition of the Business Cycle

Business cycles are recurrent but non-periodic fluctuations in aggregate economic activity as measured by fluctuations in real GDP about its trend.

B. Autocorrelation

Autocorrelation is a technical term which means that the value of some variable is related to itself at some earlier date (or dates). An auto-correlated variable is described by a difference equation which is stochastically or randomly disturbed.

C. Co-Movement

The term *co-movement* is used in the description of the movement of one variable in relation to another. Co-movements may be pro-cyclical, in which case two variables move up and down together; or counter-cyclical, in which case two variables move in the opposite direction to each other. The cycle in one variable may lead or lag the cycle in another. The cycle in one variable may display a greater or smaller amplitude than the cycle in the other. Co-movements may display high conformity, in which case, the two variables move in a similar manner; or low conformity, in which case they do not move in close sympathy with each other.

D. Properties of the Business Cycle

Movements in real GDP about trend are well described by a simple difference equation which is stochastically disturbed. In general, employment, prices, and interest rates are procyclical. Unemployment is counter-cyclical.

E. The UK Business Cycle

The general features of the business cycle set out above apply precisely to the UK case, with the important observation that movements in inflation, while generally procyclical, are not univer-sally so. There are important co-movements of inflation and unemployment which do not fit a simple pattern.

Review Questions

1. What are business cycles cycles *in*?
2. Describe the different phases of a cycle.
3. What is a 'recession'?
4. Are all business cycles the same length? If not, why do we use the term *cycle* to describe the phenomenon of non-periodic economic fluctuations?

5. What is a difference equation? Can a difference equation describe the path followed by deviations of real GDP from trend?
6. Explain how random shocks combine with inertia to describe recurrent but non-periodic up and down movements in economic activity.
7. What is meant by the term *co-movement*?
8. What is meant by the term *conformity*?
9. Try to think of examples (not necessarily economic) of:

   (a) Procyclical co-movements which have high conformity or low conformity.
   (b) Counter-cyclical co-movements which have high conformity or low conformity.

10. Describe the general character of business cycles.
11. How might the deviation of real GDP from trend in the UK be described in the period since 1900?
12. What have been the co-movements between deviations of real GDP from trend and inflation, unemployment and interest rates in the period since 1960?
13. (You will only want to tackle this question if you have worked through the appendix to this chapter.) Reinforce your understanding of the concept of autocorrelation by conducting the following experiments

    (a) Using the same 'economic shocks' as set out in Table 7A.2 (in the Appendix), generate a path for real income if it is described by the processes

    $$y_t = 90 + 0.1y_{t-1} + e_t$$

    and

    $$y_t = 1 + 0.99y_{t-1} + e_t$$

    (b) compare the paths of y_t in the above two equations with each other and with that derived in the Appendix using Equation (7A.2). How do the paths differ? What do you learn from this experiment?

Appendix: Autocorrelation

This Appendix deals with the concept of autocorrelation in a slightly more technical way than was done in the preceding text. The Appendix contains no fundamentally new ideas that are not treated in any intuitive way in the body of the chapter. It may, however, provide you with a better understanding of the concept of autocorrelation, and certainly the numerical example will provide you with an opportunity to review your understanding of the concept.

It is useful to approach the concept of autocorrelation in two steps. The first is to understand what is meant by a *difference equation*. A difference equation is nothing other than a statement that tells us how some variable evolves over time. We will only deal with the simplest kind of difference equation and even then only with an example. Let us suppose that we want to describe the evolution of real GDP over time. Let us call real GDP, y. So that we are clear about the date that attaches to the variable, let us denote the value of real GDP in some particular year, the tth year, as y_t. Let us suppose that real GDP in year t is always related in some way to its own value in the previous year. Never mind why for the present. Specifically, let us suppose that the following equation describes the evolution of real GDP from one year to the next:

$$y_t = 25 + 0.75y_{t-1} \tag{7A.1}$$

Let us first of all satisfy ourselves that we can read this equation. What it says in words is that real GDP in year t (y_t) will be equal to 25, plus three quarters (0.75) of the level of real GDP in the previous year (year $t - 1$), that is, (y_{t-1}). To get a feel for this equation, imagine that real GDP in year $t - 1$ was equal to 100. You can calculate 3/4 of 100 (equals 75), add 25 to that, and the result is the value of real GDP in year t. The answer that you have obtained is that real GDP in year t will be 100. Now imagine going forward to year $t + 1$. At year $t + 1$ the previous year becomes year t. Since real GDP in year t is 100, in year $t + 1$, by the same calculation, it will also be 100. You can quickly convince yourself that real GDP will be 100 in each and every year if the above equation describes the evolution of real GDP and if real GDP in year $t - 1$ was equal to 100.

Now suppose that real GDP in the previous year (y_{t-1}) was not 100 but 110. What then would the value of real GDP be in year t? You can calculate that answer by finding 3/4 of 110 and adding 25 to that to give you the value of GDP in year t. You should get an answer of 107.5. In the next year, year $t + 1$, GDP will be 25 plus 3/4 of l07.5, which is 105.6. By repeating the calculation, you will obtain for the next successive years values of 104.2, 103.2, 102.4, 101.8, 101.3, 101.0, 100.8 ... Thus, in the indefinite future, GDP converges to the level of 100. The value of 100 is known as the steady-state value of GDP. It is that value towards which the above equation always tends.

You are probably now saying to yourself, 'Well that's all very simple but so what?' Clearly, real GDP doesn't behave like either of these paths that have just been calculated. According to the first exercise that we did, if GDP starts out at 100, it always stays at 100; and according to the second exercise, if it starts out at something other than 100, it monotonically converges towards 100. How does this help us understand the movements of real GDP such as those which occur in an actual economy like that of the UK? The answer is that, on its own, it is of no help at all. With one tiny addition, however, the first-order difference Equation (7A.1) (*first order* means that real GDP today depends *only* on real GDP yesterday) can be capable of producing patterns in the evolution of real GDP which are similar in character to the pattern that we observe in the data.

That simple addition is to make the difference equation above a *stochastic difference equation*. A stochastic difference equation is very similar to a difference equation. That is, it has all the properties of the equation that you have just looked at and become familiar with. In addition, however, it adds on to the above equation a *random* shock. In other words, instead of real GDP in one year being uniquely determined, given knowledge of real GDP in the previous year, there is an additional random element that will allow real GDP in the current year to deviate from the prediction of the above equation by a random amount. We could write a stochastic difference equation comparable to the above equation as follows:

$$y_t = 25 + 0.75y_{t-1} + e_t \tag{7A.2}$$

The term e_t at the end of the equation represents a random shock. On the average it will take on the value of 0. From time to time, however, it will take on different values than 0, sometimes positive and sometimes negative.

To keep things simple and concrete, let us generate an example of a random shock (or a series of random shocks) and then see how GDP evolves when the difference equation that describes its path is stochastically disturbed.

We have created a set of random shocks by conducting a simple experiment which you can conduct for yourself. The experiment involves rolling a die and assigning an economic shock depending on the score of the die roll. Table 7A.1 sets out the way that we have converted die scores into economic shocks. You will see that if the die came up 3 or 4, we scored an economic shock of 0, so that there is a 1 in 3 chance that there is no random disturbance to the economy. If the die came up 2, we scored a negative shock of 5 (think of that as a shock that is depressing the economy), and if the die scored 1, then we gave a bigger weight to the depressing effect on the economy (-10). If the die came up 5 or 6, we scored a positive shock to the economy (a boom) assigning a shock of 5 for a die score of 5 and 10 for a die score of 6. Thus you can see that there is a 1 in 6 chance that the economy will be hit with any of the shocks $+10$, $+5$, -5, -10, and a 1 in 3 chance of no shock. The shocks, then, that will hit the economy are symmetrical and have an average value of 0 and a range of 20, ranging from $+10$ to -10.

We rolled the die 30 times, and Table 7A.2 records the scores of our 30 die rolls together with the value of the economic shock implied by the scoring scheme set out in Table 7A.1. You will notice that our 30 rolls turned out to have an average value that was greater than 0 (in fact our average was $+1$), indicating that we rolled rather more 5s and 6s than we did 1s and 2s. Nevertheless, if we had rolled, say, 1000 times, then it is certain that our average would have been very close to 0.

With the series of economic shocks shown in Table 7A.2, it is now possible to see how the economy would evolve if the above stochastic

Table 7A.1   Converting die scores into economic shocks

Die score	Economic shock
1	− 10
2	− 5
3	0
4	0
5	+ 5
6	+ 10

difference equation describes the evolution of real GDP. The calculation for the first ten values of real GDP are set out in Table 7A.2. The first column shows the level of real GDP in year t and the second column in year $t − 1$. The third column records the value of the shock, $e t$. The values of the shocks listed there are the first ten shocks from Table 7A.2.

Table 7A.2   Thirty random shocks in an imaginary economy

Die roll	Die score	Economic shock
1	5	+ 5
2	1	− 10
3	6	+ 10
4	6	+ 10
5	4	0
6	4	0
7	6	+ 10
8	4	0
9	2	− 5
10	3	0
11	3	0
12	4	0
13	4	0
14	6	+ 10
15	5	+ 5
16	5	+ 5
17	1	− 10
18	1	− 10
19	3	0
20	2	− 5
21	3	0
22	6	+ 10
23	5	+ 5
24	6	+ 10
25	2	− 5
26	5	+ 5
27	2	− 5
28	4	0
29	1	− 10
30	5	+ 5

Imagine that in year 0, the economy started out in its steady state with real GDP equal to 100 and with real GDP in the previous year equal to 100 and with no random shock. The shocks then begin. In year 1 we need to take 3/4 of the previous real GDP (75) and add 25 which gives 100 and then add the shock of 5 to get the value shown for real GDP of 105. In year 2, real GDP in years 1 (105) becomes the previous year's real GDP level. To calculate real GDP in year 2, we take 3/4 of 105 and add 25 to that; we then subtract 10, the current year's shock of −10, to give a value of 94 for real GDP. This process is repeated throughout the table. Check that you can reproduce the figures listed in column 1 of Table 7A.3 by applying the above-described formula. (The figures given in the table are rounded. To calculate the correct values you should carry the unrounded figures in the memory of your calculator.)

Table 7A.3 Calculation of evolution of GDP in an imaginary economy (periods 0 to 10 only)

Year	$y_t = 25 + 0.75y_{t-1} + shock$ y_t	y_{t-1}	Shock
0	100	100	0
1	105	100	+ 5
2	94	105	− 10
3	105	94	+ 10
4	114	105	+ 10
5	111	114	0
6	108	111	0
7	116	108	+ 10
8	112	116	0
9	104	112	− 5
10	103	104	0

Figure 7A.1 illustrates the values of real GDP over the full 30-year experiment that is described in Tables 7A.2 and 7A.3. The graph of the ups and downs of GDP in this imaginary economy looks remarkably as if it could have been generated from plotting actual figures for the deviation of real GDP from trend, such as those shown in Chapter 2. Notice that there is certainly a recurrent up-and-down movement, but there is no exact periodicity. The timing from the trough of observation 2 to the next trough (year 13) is eleven years. The next trough occurs at year 20 − a seven-year cycle. The next trough occurs at year 29 − a nine-year cycle. Thus, the cycle lengths in this example, as measured from trough to trough, vary from a short cycle of seven years to a long cycle of eleven years. Notice too that the severity of the down phase varies. The downturn that begins in year 8 continues throughout year 13 but never gets very deep. The next downturn that begins in year 17 only runs for four years, but it goes all the way to 10 points below the steady-state value.

**Figure 7A.1
A hypothetical cycle
generated by a first-
order autoregressive
process**

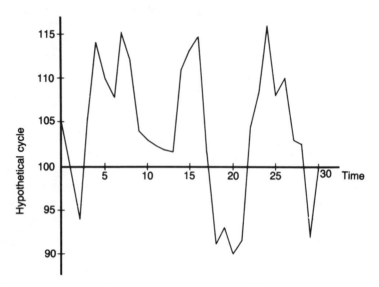

The simple stochastic difference equation $y_t = 25 + 0.75y_{t-1} + e_t$ generates non-periodic but recurrent fluctuations that could easily be taken to be real-world deviations of real GDP from trend.

The particular path of real GDP generated by a stochastic difference equation depends in an important way on the degree of the inertia in the process — that is, on the magnitude of the effect of previous income on current income. In our example, that effect is 3/4. If, instead of current income depending on previous income with a weight of 3/4, we were to lower that weight, almost to zero, then real GDP would no longer display much systematic movement but would be purely random (completely unpredictable) like the random shocks, e_t, that are bombarding the economy. At the other extreme, if we were to raise the weight on previous income from 3/4 to almost 1, then the cyclical swings in real GDP would be much longer (the time from the peak of one cycle to the peak of the next one would be longer).

The key thing to take careful note of is that a very simple process — a stochastically disturbed, first-order difference equation — is capable of generating a path for a variable that is very similar in its characteristics to the recurrent but non-periodic ups and downs of real GDP (and other variables) over the course of the business cycle. Of course, the specific path of actual GDP movements about trend will only be capable of description by specific shocks and a specific difference equation.

Part III

MACROECONOMIC THEORY

8

Aggregate Demand and Supply: An Overview

You have now reviewed: the questions that macroeconomics seeks to answer; the main facts about the evolution of the key macroeconomic variables in the UK since 1900; the way in which the macroeconomic variables are measured; and how to characterize the ups and downs of aggregate economic activity and the co-movements among the variables as business cycles.

It is now time to move on to the more challenging — and more interesting and exciting — problem of *explanation* of macroeconomic phenomena. Macroeconomic phenomena are explained — or understood — by using *macroeconomic theory*. Unlike many areas of the natural sciences, and indeed unlike some areas of economics, macroeconomic theory is still in a state of controversy and rapid development. As a consequence, there is no single, universally accepted, theory capable of explaining macroeconomic phenomena. Instead there is a variety of competing and conflicting theories. In such a state of affairs it is necessary to become familiar with *all* the alternative theories and to develop procedures for choosing among the alternatives ultimately, hopefully, rejecting all of them except one.

Although macroeconomic theory is not in a settled and uncontroversial state, there are some basic tools of analysis that are common to all theories. This chapter introduces these tools. Central among them are the tools of aggregate demand, aggregate supply, and macroeconomic equilibrium.

By the time you have completed this chapter you will be able to:

(a) **Explain the concept of aggregate demand.**
(b) **Explain the concept of aggregate supply.**
(c) **Explain the concept of macroeconomic equilibrium.**
(d) **Explain how shifts in aggregate demand and aggregate supply generate movements in aggregate output and the price level.**

A. Aggregate Demand

Aggregate demand is the demand for goods and services in total. It is the demand for aggregate output. The *aggregate demand curve* is defined as the relationship between the aggregate quantity of goods and services which people want to buy in a given period of time and the price level.

The questions that we will be interested in concerning the aggregate demand curve, are:

(1) What is the shape of the aggregate demand curve? Does it slope downwards? That is, would the level of aggregate demand rise if the price level fell?

(2) What variables cause the aggregate demand curve to shift? That is, what variables, other than the price level, cause aggregate demand to vary?

Before we tackle these questions directly, it will be useful to recall some familiar ideas about *demand* in the *micro* economic study of demand for particular goods and services.

You are familiar, from your study of microeconomics, with the concept of *demand* when it is applied to individual goods or services — the demand for orange juice, the demand for fish and chips, etc. You are also familiar, in such a context, with the notion of a *demand curve* — the relationship between the quantity of orange juice demanded and the price of orange juice. You are also familiar with the idea of the *elasticity of demand* — that is, with the responsiveness of the quantity demanded to a change in its price. You are accustomed to talking about demand being *elastic* if a 1 per cent change in price leads to a more than 1 per cent change in the quantity demanded; *inelastic* if a 1 per cent change in price leads to a less than 1 per cent change in quantity demanded; and *unit elastic* in the case where a 1 per cent change in price leads to a 1 per cent change in the quantity demanded. Finally, you are accustomed to thinking about *shifts* in the *demand* curve for a particular good (such as orange juice) as arising from changes in all those factors that influence the quantity demanded — other than the price of the good itself.

When we talk about the *demand* for orange juice, we do not mean the same thing as the quantity of orange juice that people *actually purchased*. Rather, we mean the quantity of orange juice that would be purchased at a particular price of orange juice and at particular prices for grapefruit juice, apple juice, etc., and at a given level of income.

It is a good idea to think of statements about demand (and about supply that we will be getting to in the next section) as statements about *decision rules*. That is, in effect, we pretend that people calculate their best response in all conceivable situations — they decide upon rules of behaviour for all conceivable circumstances — and then, in any given situation, implement the previously chosen rule.

Decision rules can be stated in a variety of alternative, but equivalent, ways. For example, a decision rule could be represented as a table that lists the alternative prices of orange juice and opposite each price states the quantity of orange juice that an individual would choose to consume. An equivalent way of representing a decision rule is in the form of a diagram in which the quantity that would be purchased is shown on one axis and the price on the other. Such a representation is the standard way in which we represent decision rules about quantities to purchase in economics. It is called the demand curve.

The decision rule concerning how much orange juice to consume is not completely described by the two variables — the quantity of orange juice consumed and its price. Many things other than price affect the quantity demanded and a complete statement of the decision rule about how much to buy requires that all those other factors be taken into account. We represent changes in those other factors — factors other than the price of the good — as shifts in the demand curve. Thus, for example, if an individual's income was to rise that would trigger a rise in the demand for orange juice at each different level of orange juice prices.

We can apply these same ideas that are familiar from the study of microeconomics to the macroeconomic analysis of *aggregate* demand. In doing so, however, we need to exercise some care.

As noted at the beginning of this section, aggregate demand is the demand for goods and services in total — the demand for the real gross domestic product. No one individual, of course, demands in equal proportions, the many different goods and services that comprise the gross domestic product. The variety of items in the gross domestic product is immense — orange juice, haircuts, video shows, train rides, new orange juice production plants, new TV studios, new aeroplanes, tanks, submarines, satellites, etc. Some of these things are demanded by households, some by firms, some by governments and some by foreigners. Aggregate demand is the total of the demands for goods and services of all these different agents — of households, firms, government, and the rest of the world.

Just as we are careful to distinguish between the quantity demanded and the quantity actually purchased when talking about an individual good so we must also be careful when dealing with aggregate demand. *Aggregate demand* is *not* the same thing as the *total volume of goods and services actually purchased*. Rather, it is the aggregate quantity of goods and services that would be bought at a particular price level and in a particular set of circumstances.

Just as it is helpful to think of an individual's demand for orange juice as a decision rule, so it is also helpful to think of aggregate demand as the aggregate of the decision rules of all the individual agents in the economy concerning expenditures on all goods and services. Just as the demand curve for orange juice tells us the quantity of orange juice that will be demanded as the price of orange juice changes, so the aggregate demand curve tells us the quantity of goods and services in total that will be demanded as the general price level varies. Figure 8.1 illustrates an aggregate demand curve.

Figure 8.1
Aggregate demand

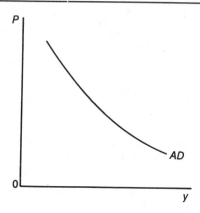

The aggregate demand curve slopes downwards. At lower price levels there is substitution away from rest-of-world goods to domestic goods and also wealth rises because the real value of the financial assets in the economy rise, thereby generating additional demand for goods and services.

Why is the aggregate demand curve shown as a downward-sloping curve? We will explore the precise reasons why this is so later in the book. For now we will content ourselves with some intuition on why the demand curve may be presumed to slope downwards.

We know that the demand curve for an individual good slopes downwards primarily because of the so-called substitution effect. As the price of one good falls *relative to the prices of other goods,* people reallocate their expenditures substituting the good that has become relatively inexpensive for goods that have become relatively more expensive. This factor is part of the reason why the aggregate demand curve slopes downwards. If the average price of goods and services produced in a single economy decline while the prices in other countries remain constant there will be a tendency for people both in the domestic economy and in the rest of the world to substitute in favour of the output of the domestic economy. This international substitution of demand is, then, one reason why the aggregate demand curve slopes downwards.

A second reason why the aggregate demand curve may be presumed to slope downwards has to do with what are called *wealth effects*. At any given moment, there is a certain stock of real and financial assets that constitute the wealth of all the agents in the economy. As the price level varies nothing happens to the real value of the stock of real assets. There is, though, a change in the real value of the stock of financial assets. The higher the price level, the smaller is the real value of the stock of financial assets. Thus, at a higher price level, people would feel less well-off than at a low price level and may be presumed to demand a smaller quantity of goods and services.

This loose intuitive reasoning that suggests a downward-sloping aggregate demand curve does not provide us with any insights into the elasticity of aggregate demand. Aggregate demand could be highly elastic or highly inelastic. A deeper study of the factors influencing aggregate demand, later in this book, will shed some light on the elasticity of aggregate demand.

One of the key ingredients in the theory of demand for an individual good concerns an analysis of the factors that shift the demand curve. That is also an important matter for macroeconomics. Many things can, in principle, change the level of aggregate demand, thereby shifting the aggregate demand curve. Some examples are the total population, the wealth of the economy, the level of output and wealth in the rest of the world (which would influence the demand by foreigners for domestic output), the level of government demand for goods and services (which in turn is determined by a large number of social and political considerations), and the rate at which firms are seeking to add to their stock of capital equipment (which in turn depends on the pace of technical change, business confidence, and a variety of other factors).

The above list of things that can make the aggregate demand curve shift should be seen at this point as purely illustrative. Our subsequent, more detailed study of the theory of aggregate demand will make much more precise and sharp statements about how these potential influences on aggregate demand have their effects. We will also discover that in certain cases some of the factors which we have listed above as having a possible effect on aggregate demand have, in fact, no effect at all.

You now have a fairly clear idea of the concept of aggregate demand and the aggregate demand curve, and have some rough notion as to why the aggregate demand curve is downward sloping. You also have some idea as to what sorts of things might make the aggregate demand curve move over time.

Let us now turn our attention to aggregate supply.

B. Aggregate Supply

Aggregate supply is the quantity of output that all the producers in the economy would wish to supply at each given price level.

You will probably find it helpful to begin considering aggregate supply in the same way as we began our consideration of aggregate demand, by considering the case of an individual commodity. You are already familiar with the concept of the supply curve of, say, orange juice. In general, the quantity of orange juice supplied rises as the price of orange juice rises relative to the prices of other things.

The concept of aggregate supply applies these same considerations to the supply of aggregate output or real GDP. Aggregate supply is the total quantity of goods and services that all producers would like to supply in any given circumstances. To use the same language as we used before, it is the aggregation of the *decision rules* of all the individual producers in the economy. We know that the quantity of orange juice supplied rises when the price of orange juice rises. Is the same true of the supply of goods and services in total? That is, does the level of aggregate supply rise as the general price level rises? There seems to be two interesting possibilities that can be explored. The orange juice example will help to get things straight.

Imagine that a competitive producer of orange juice experiences a 10 per cent rise in the price of orange juice. Further imagine that nothing else happens to the orange juice producer's costs and technology. The firm is using the same production techniques, hiring the same labour and paying out the same wages. In that case, the firm will slide up its marginal cost (supply) curve, thereby increasing the total supply of orange juice.

Consider a second case. This time, when the price of orange juice rises by 10 per cent so too do the wages of the orange juice workers and so also do all the other costs of production. In this situation the firm's cost curves will rise by 10 per cent. The combination of a 10 per cent rise in price with a 10 per cent rise in all costs will leave the profit-maximizing quantity of supply exactly the same as it was before.

Now extend the reasoning from the case of the orange juice producer to that of the producers of all goods and services. If the prices of all final outputs were to rise but the prices of all factors of production were to remain constant, then the producers of all goods and services would seek to raise their output so that the amount of aggregate output would rise. In this case the level of aggregate supply would rise as the price level rises.

Consider the second case. This time the prices of all final outputs rise and the prices of all inputs — labour, capital, and all other factors of production — rise by the same percentage amount. In such a situation there would be no incentive for producers to change their output so that, as the price level rises, the level of aggregate supply remains constant.

Figure 8.2 illustrates these two cases. The curve labelled AS_1 illustrates the first case where, as the price level rises, the costs of production — wage rates and other input costs — do not rise. In this case, a higher price level induces a higher level of aggregate supply. The curve labelled AS_2 illustrates the second case in which, as the price level varies, so the prices of all inputs to the production process also vary by the same percentage amount. In that case there is no change in the level of aggregate supply as the price level varies.

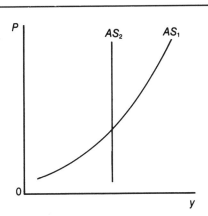

Figure 8.2
Aggregate supply

If, as the price level rises, the prices of factors of production remain constant (or do not rise as quickly as the price level), producers will raise output and aggregate output will rise. The aggregate supply curve is AS_1. If, as the price level rises the prices of all inputs rise by the same percentage amount, producers will not change their output and aggregate output will be constant. The aggregate supply curve is AS_2.

Many factors can shift the supply curve of orange juice. Favourable growing conditions will produce a rise in supply; unseasonal frost will produce a fall in supply. Improvements in orange tree varieties can generate higher yields. The application of improved fertilizers can also increase supply. Further, the application of capital in the form of irrigation schemes could increase supply.

Similar considerations apply to aggregate supply. Aggregate supply can be affected by major climatic factors; by improved technologies; and by increased investment in productivity-increasing capital equipment and also by investment in human capital — by education and training of the labour force. Each or any of these types of factors can produce shifts in the aggregate supply curve.

Let us now go on to consider the interaction between supply and demand at the level of the economy as a whole.

C. Macroeconomic Equilibrium

Macroeconomic equilibrium is a situation in which aggregate demand equals aggregate supply. Figure 8.3 illustrates a state of macroeconomic equilibrium. When the price level is P_0, the level of aggregate demand is y_0 and the aggregate supply is also y_0. The price level P_0 and the output level y_0 are equilibrium values.

Figure 8.3
Macroeconomic
equilibrium

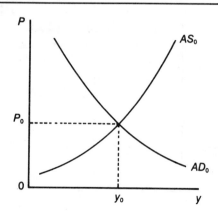

Macroeconomic equilibrium occurs where aggregate demand equals aggregate supply. The price and output levels (P_0,y_0) represent an equilibrium if aggregate supply is AS_0 and aggregate demand is AD_0.

It is a feature of macroeconomic equilibrium that the plans of individual agents in the economy are compatible with each other. People are implementing their decision rules — that is, they are doing what they said they would do in a given set of circumstances. There is nothing particularly 'good' about an equilibrium. The equilibrium output level could be a very low one and the equilibrium price level could be a very high one. The equilibrium output and price levels are simply the values of those variables determined by a particular theory.

Notice that an important implication of this is that every actual state of affairs that has any predictive content is an equilibrium *by definition*. Equilibrium and disequilibrium are not states of affairs in the actual world. They are propositions about a model. We can talk about disequilibrium and we can hypothesize disequilibrium states within a model. That is, we can conjecture about what would happen if the conditions of equilibrium were not satisfied. In effect, we can conduct *thought experiments* about what would happen out of equilibrium. These thought experiments do not, however, say anything about the world. When we conduct such thought experiments we are imagining how some particular agents would adjust their behaviour in a situation in which their plans — their decision rules — could not be implemented. Thus, only equilibrium statements have empirical content. That is, only points of equilibrium are statements about the world.

These points can be made more vividly by considering Figure 8.4, which shows an equilibrium level of output at y_0 and price level of P_0. What would happen if the price level was, for some reason, stuck at P_0? The answer is that we cannot say. The model does not tell us what happens in such a situation. It only tells us what happens when agents' decision rules can be implemented. If those decision rules are correctly summarized in the supply curve AS_0 and the demand curve AD_0 then, at the price level P_0, plans are incompatible and cannot be carried out. Either the price level cannot be P_0 or the aggregate demand and aggregate supply curves cannot be correct representations of agents' decision rules. If the aggregate demand and aggregate supply curves are in fact correct representations of decision rules, then the price level has to be P_0 and the output level y_0.

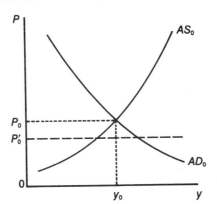

Figure 8.4
Disequilibrium?

Disequilibrium cannot be a state predicted by a model. It can only be a state that can be conjectured about in a thought experiment. If agents' decision rules are correctly summarized in the supply curve AS_0 and demand curve $\overline{AD_0}$ then, at the price level P_0, agents plans are incompatible and cannot be carried out. Either the price level cannot be P_0 or the decision rules cannot be correct. If the decision rules are correct, the price level has to be P_0 and the output level y_0.

D. Price and Output Changes

Your final task in this chapter is to see how you can put the basic framework of aggregate supply, aggregate demand, and macroeconomic equilibrium to work in understanding movements of output and the price level. Figure 8.5 provides the vehicle for the analysis. Focus first on the aggregate demand curve AD_0 and the aggregate supply curve AS_0. Where those curves intersect a macroeconomic equilibrium is determined at the price level P_0 and the output level y_0.

If the level of aggregate demand rises for some reason to AD_1, what

Figure 8.5
Shifts in aggregate demand

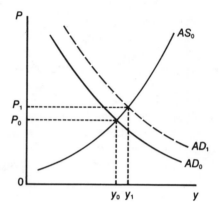

Shifts in the aggregate demand curve generate changes in both output and price level in the same direction. A rise in aggregate demand raises both output and the price level; a drop in aggregate demand lowers both output and the price level.

happens? The answer is that output rises to y_1 and the price level rises to P_1. Thus, a rise in aggregate demand raises both the output level and the price level. You can easily conduct the reverse experiment of considering what happens when there is a drop in aggregate demand. To do this, imagine that the economy starts out at P_1,y_1 where the aggregate demand curve AD_1 cuts the aggregate supply curve AS_0. Then imagine that there is a drop in aggregate demand to AD_0. In this case the price level falls to P_0 and output falls to y_0. Thus, a drop in aggregate demand lowers both the output level and the price level.

Next consider the case of a shift in the aggregate supply curve. Figure 8.6 illustrates this case. Suppose, again, that the economy starts out at P_0,y_0 where the curves AD_0 and AS_0 intersect. Then suppose that aggregate supply shifts from AS_0 to AS_1 with aggregate demand remaining at AD_0. In this case the price level rises to P_1 but output would now falls to y_1. As you can see a backward shift in the aggregate supply curve raises the price level and lowers output. Again you can consider the reverse experiment. Imagine that the economy starts out at P_1,y_1 — the intersection of the curves AD_0 and AS_1. Now imagine that aggregate supply increases to AS_1. In this event output rises to y_0 and the price level falls to P_0.

You can now see that a change in aggregate demand changes both output and the price level in the same direction. If aggregate demand rises both output and the price level rise; if aggregate demand falls both output and the price level fall. In contrast, a shift in the aggregate supply curve generates movements in output and the price level in opposite directions. A fall in aggregate supply lowers output and raises the price level and a rise in aggregate supply raises output and lowers the price level.

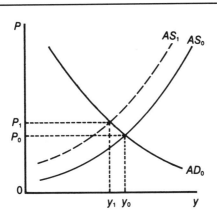

Figure 8.6
Shifts in aggregate supply

Shifts in the aggregate supply curve generate movements in output and the price level in opposite directions to each other. A drop in aggregate supply lowers the level of output and raises the price level. A rise in aggregate supply raises output and lowers the price level.

It will be evident to you that this basic framework is capable of tracking macroeconomic events both when output and the price level move in the same direction as each other and when they move in opposite directions.

You have now studied the basic framework of aggregate demand and aggregate supply analysis and have a general understanding of the concepts of aggregate supply and aggregate demand and, more importantly, a clear view of the nature of macroeconomic equilibrium and the place of equilibrium analysis in making predictions. You are now going on to explore in greater depth and detail some particular theories of aggregate demand and aggregate supply that place stronger restrictions on the supply and demand curves and that enable us to make predictions about movements in output and the price level (and other variables as well).

The general framework of aggregate supply and demand analysis presented in this chapter is, in effect, devoid of any predictive content. We have not actually said what determines the positions of the curves (and, implicitly, the things that make them move) or what determines their slopes. Clearly, both of these factors are important in generating predictions about the actual movements of output and the price level that might occur in the world.

The next seven chapters will take you through a detailed development of the theory of aggregate demand both in the closed economy and in the open economy. This theory is relatively uncontroversial. After that, there will be three chapters on the theory of aggregate supply. There is less agreement in this area, and three alternative theories of aggregate supply will be presented. We will then go on to consider macroeconomic equilibrium and the crucial role of expectations about the price level in determining that equilibrium. After we have completed this block of thirteen chapters we will return to the facts and see how the theories of macroeconomics help us to understand the macroeconomic facts that are described in Chapters 2 and 7.

Summary

A. Aggregate Demand

Aggregate demand is the demand for all goods and services — the demand for aggregate output. The aggregate demand curve is the relationship between the price level and the demand for output. It summarizes the aggregate of the expenditure decision rules of all the agents in the economy.

B. Aggregate Supply

Aggregate supply is the supply of all goods and services — the supply of aggregate output. The aggregate supply curve is the relationship between the price level and the total quantity of goods and services supplied — it is the aggregate of the output decision rules of all agents in the economy.

C. Macroeconomic Equilibrium

Macroeconomic equilibrium occurs when aggregate demand equals aggregate supply. The equilibrium point is the only point that has empirical content. Disequilibrium points can be conjectured about and be the subject of thought experiments but not the subject of predictions about the world. This is not an empirical matter. It is an axiom — a matter of principle.

D. Price and Output Changes

Shifts in aggregate demand produce positive co-movements of output and the price level. Shifts in aggregate supply produce negative co-movements between output and the price level.

Review Questions

1. What is meant by aggregate demand?
2. What is the difference between aggregate demand and the quantity of goods and services bought?

*3. Why would we expect the aggregate demand curve to be downward sloping?

4. List some of the things that might shift the aggregate demand curve.

5. What is the key difference between the theory of demand for orange juice and the theory of aggregate demand? (*Hint*: What kind of a price is the price of orange juice and what kind of a price is the price level?)

6. What do we mean by aggregate supply?

7. Why might the aggregate supply curve slope upwards?

8. In what circumstances would it make sense to suppose that the aggregate supply curve is vertical?

9. List some of the things that might shift the aggregate supply curve.

10. What is meant by macroeconomic equilibrium?

11. Why is disequilibrium only a state of mind and not the prediction of a theory?

12. Suppose there was a rise in aggregate demand and a fall (backward shift) in aggregate supply. What would happen to (a) the price level and (b) the level of output?

9

Aggregate Demand and Consumption

The subject matter of this and the next four chapters was, for the 20 years from the late 1950s through to the late 1970s, the heart of macroeconomics. Several generations of intermediate textbooks on the subject, many important research monographs, and literally thousands of important articles in learned journals deal with various aspects of the material presented here. It is the theory of aggregate demand that has grown out of the work of John Maynard Keynes. You should be aware that the material presented here covers only the essential features of that theory. As a result of the developments in macroeconomics in the past 10 to 15 years — developments that will be explained in some detail in Chapters 17 to 21 — we now have a much better perspective than ever before on the Keynesian theory of aggregate demand. It no longer stands as the whole of macroeconomics. It does not even provide the centrepiece of the explanation for macroeconomic fluctuations. That is not to say, however, that the Keynesian theory of aggregate demand is wrong. There is nothing wrong with an analysis that is but one part of the complete story. The part of the story that Keynesian analysis contains is the determination of aggregate demand at a given price level.

By the time you have completed this chapter you will be able to:

(a) State the components of aggregate demand.
(b) Explain the theories of the consumption function proposed by Keynes, Friedman, and Modigliani.
(c) Explain the connection between wealth and income and why current income is a major determinant of consumption.

(d) **Represent the consumption and savings functions in simple equations and diagrams.**

(e) **State the main features of the UK consumption function.**

(f) **Explain the Keynesian cross model.**

First, it will be useful to know the components into which aggregate demand is divided.

A. Components of Aggregate Demand

Just as a matter of arithmetic, aggregate demand could be divided up in an infinite number of different ways. It would be possible to distinguish between the demand for beer, for peanuts, for steak, for HP sauce, for power stations, for nuclear submarines, and so on. For some purposes, such a detailed disaggregation of the total volume of demand in the economy is essential. For the purpose of the questions addressed in macroeconomics, however, such a detailed classification of the components of aggregate demand appears to be unnecessary. It is useful, nevertheless, to divide aggregate demand into a small number of key components, the determination of each of which involves different considerations. Specifically, for the purpose of doing macroeconomic analysis, aggregate demand is divided into four components. They are:

(1) Consumption demand
(2) Investment demand
(3) Government demand
(4) Net foreign demand

These four components of aggregate demand are closely related to the components of aggregate expenditure dealt with in Chapter 3. (For example, see Equation (3.6).) There are, however, two important distinctions between the components of aggregate expenditure and the components of aggregate demand. One of these distinctions will be explained now and the other reserved until we have examined the components of aggregate demand.

One distinction between the components of aggregate expenditure and those of aggregate demand turns on the distinction between the terms *expenditure* and *demand*. *Expenditure* refers to what people have actually spent. *Demand* refers to what people are *planning* to spend — to their decision rules. Expenditure is an actual *quantity*. Demand is a *schedule* — a statement about how much would be spent under certain specified conditions. Keep this distinction in mind when dealing with the theories that you will meet in this chapter and later in the book.

Let us now go on to describe briefly the four components of aggregate demand. When we have completed our description of consumption and investment demand, it will be possible to come back and emphasize another distinction between the components of aggregate demand and those of aggregate expenditure.

(i) Consumption Demand

Consumption demand is the aggregate demand by households for goods and services to be used up for current consumption purposes. Examples of consumption demand would be the demand for beer and peanuts and for steak and HP sauce. Other examples would be expenditures on vacations, travel, movies and entertainment; rent of houses and flats; the purchase of electricty, gas or oil; the purchase of haircuts, skiing lessons, etc. — indeed, any of the many thousands and thousands of activities on which we spend our income.

(ii) Investment Demand

Investment demand is distinguished from consumption demand by the fact that an *investment is the purchase of a capital good* — defined as a new piece of equipment that is durable and that provides services over a number of years. Sometimes the services will be in the form of consumption services, and sometimes they will be production services. Both households and firms make investment expenditures. Examples of investment expenditures made by households are the purchase of a new house, a new car, a new refrigerator, or any of the other many thousands of new consumer durable goods. Examples of investment expenditures by firms are the purchase of a new steel mill, an electricity generating plant, a car assembly line, a computer, or again, any of the many thousands of different types of new capital goods used in the production process.

It is important that you clearly understand the distinction between consumption and investment. *Consumption* is the purchase of goods and services for current use. *Investment* is the purchase of goods and services for current and future use. When you buy a consumption good, you buy a current flow of services. When you invest, you buy a capital good that is a stock of equipment that gives rise to a current and future flow of either production or consumption services.

It is also important to distinguish clearly between the term investment in the sense in which economists use it when doing macroeconomic analysis and the way in which the term is used in everyday speech. In everyday usage, investment often means the purchase of a stock, a share, or a bond. That is not investment in macroeconomic analysis. Such an activity is a portfolio reallocation and has very different causes and consequences from the purchase of newly produced capital equipment.

Before going on to deal with the other components of aggregate demand, let us also notice a further distinction between the components of aggregate demand and the components of aggregate expenditure set out in Chapter 3. We are here distinguishing between consumption and investment in terms of the *durability* of the goods purchased. Consumption is the purchase of goods and services that are going to be used up in the current period. Investment is the purchase of goods that are more durable than a single period and that will provide either productive or consumption services into the future.

In Chapter 3, we did not make that distinction. Rather, we talked of consumer expenditure as being the purchase of all goods and services by households regardless of whether they were durable or not, and we refer to investment as the purchase of capital equipment by firms only. There are two reasons why Chapter 3 used the definitions that it did. First, that is the way the National Accounts are put together. Second, the flow diagrams used in that chapter would have been more cumbersome if we had allowed both households and firms to invest in capital equipment. (You may find it beneficial to go back to Chapter 3 and develop for yourself some flow charts that take into account this additional investment activity.) Now that we are about to embark upon an analysis of the determination of the demand for consumption and capital goods, it becomes necessary to be more careful in distinguishing between the demand for consumption services and the demand for capital goods.

Let us now go on to consider the remaining two components of aggregate demand.

(iii) Government Demand

The third component of aggregate demand is government expenditure on goods and services. Much of government expenditure represents the demands by the government for goods and services produced by the private sector of the economy. Examples of the demand by the government for goods and services produced by the private sector are the demand for nuclear submarines, for highways, for new administrative buildings, or for paper clips and paper. Notice that the examples just given include both capital and consumption goods. No distinction is made between what might be termed government investment demand (nuclear submarines, highways, and buildings) and what might be termed government consumption demand (paper clips and paper).

For the purpose of macroeconomic analysis, there is no advantage to be gained from dividing government expenditure into its investment and consumption components. Indeed, such a decision is, to a large extent, arbitrary. For example, two of the big items of expenditure by the government, health and education expenditure, could be regarded as either consumption or investment. They are consumption in the sense that they provide an immediate flow of services — of good health and knowledge. They are also interpretable as investment expenditure because a healthy and educated person has an asset — human capital — which is capable of generating an income stream not just at the present but in the future as well. For some purposes it is crucial to be able to distinguish correctly the investment from the consumption component of government expenditure. For present purposes, however, there is no gain from pursuing that distinction.

In addition to buying goods and services produced by the private sector, the government also demands goods and services that it supplies itself. Examples are administrative services, police and law enforcement services, and military services. In its undertaking of these activities, you may think of the government as being like a firm. It hires labour from households (soldiers, sailors, public servants, judges, and so on) and produces goods and services — goods and services that it uses itself. Government expenditure on goods and services is treated as being exogenous. That is, the quantity of government expenditure on goods and services is treated as something that it is not our task to explain and that can be determined by the government at whatever level the government so chooses, independently of the values of any of the other variables in our macroeconomic model.[1]

Much of government expenditure in the modern world is excluded from the above definition of government demand. For example, government social security expenditures on pensions and welfare programmes and subsidies to various industries, although vast in volume, do not represent government expenditures on goods and services. Rather, they are transfers of money — of purchasing power — from the government to private individuals and firms. These expenditures are called *transfer payments*. Their effects on aggregate demand are analysed by examining their effects on private consumption and investment demand. They are not ignored, therefore, but they are not treated as direct demands for goods and services by the government.

(iv) Net Foreign Demand

Net foreign demand for goods and services is the difference between exports and imports. Foreigners place demands on the domestic economy by demanding those goods and services that are exported from the domestic economy. Residents of the domestic economy place demands on the rest of the world, and these are measured by the quantity of imports of goods and services. The difference between these two magnitudes represents net foreign demand. For the purposes of what follows, it will be assumed that net foreign demand is always exactly zero. This assumption does not correspond with the facts, but making the assumption, it turns out to be possible to simplify considerably the task of understanding the main elements of the theory of aggregate demand. In Chapter 16, the theory of aggregate demand is modified to take explicit account of international trade and investment.

---

1 As a matter of fact, in some very elaborate statistical models of the economy, government expenditure on goods and services is broken into two parts, that which is exogenous and that which responds to the state of the economy. Such a dichotomization of government expenditure is important for some purposes, but not essential to the task on which you are currently embarked.

Aggregate demand has been divided into four components — consumption, investment, government, and net foreign demand for goods and services. The last item is being ignored for the present, and government demand is being treated as exogneous and, therefore, does not have to be explained. The other two items, however, do need explanation. The rest of this chapter deals with the determinants of consumption demand, and the next chapter with investment.

B. Theories of the Consumption Function Proposed by Keynes, Friedman and Modigliani

In his analysis of the determination of aggregate demand, Keynes regarded the so-called theory of the consumption function as the centrepiece of his new theory of income and employment. We now suspect that Keynes had an exaggerated opinion of the importance of this innovation. It is, nevertheless, an important ingredient in the theory of aggregate demand.

(i) Keynes's Theory of the Consumption Function

Keynes's theory of the determinants of consumption was that of the many possible factors that influence the level of consumption demand, the most important is the level of real disposable income.[2] By real disposable income is meant real income (real GDP) minus the real value of taxes levied by the government. The way in which consumption demand is influenced by real disposable income is, according to Keynes, based on what he called 'the fundamental psychological law upon which we are entitled to depend with great confidence'. That law, Keynes went on to outline, is the proposition 'that men are disposed, as a rule and on the average, to increase their consumption as their income increases, but not by as much as the increase in their income'. What Keynes is saying is that consumption depends on income such that, for a given rise in income, consumption will rise by some fraction of the rise in income.

Following the first statement of Keynes's consumption function hypothesis, a great deal of statistical work was undertaken that sought to test Keynes's theory with the newly available national income accounting data. It was discovered, as a result of this work, that although Keynes's basic ideas seemed well founded, there was an important difference in the relationship between consumption and income in the short run (year by year) as compared with the long run (decade by decade). The long-run data revealed that consumption was proportional to income. The short-run

---

2   Keynes set out his theory of the consumption function in Chapters 8 and 9 of the *General Theory of Employment, Interest and Money* (London: Macmillan, 1936). The two quotations in this paragraph are taken from p.96 of this source.

data revealed that although consumption and income move in the same direction, the relationship between the two is not proportional. Furthermore, when individual consumption and income data were examined, it was discovered that although people with higher incomes consumed more, variations in consumption were much smaller, in proportionate terms, than variations in income. Also, these individual variations in income and consumption were less than those observed for variations in aggregate income and consumption over time.

These puzzles and problems revealed by the data led to a more refined formulation of the theory of the consumption function. The two leading architects of the refining were Milton Friedman, who developed the permanent income hypothesis[3] and Franco Modigliani, who developed the life-cycle hypothesis[4]. These two contributions have more similarities than differences and hark back to the work of one of the greatest pre-Keynesian economists, Irving Fisher. They can be conveniently summarized by treating them as if they are a single theory.

(ii) Friedman's and Modigliani's Theory of the Consumption Function

Friedman and Modigliani reasoned as follows: if people can borrow and lend freely through financial institutions, then their consumption in any one particular period will not be constrained by their income in that particular period. If for some reason income is *temporarily* high, it will be possible to save a larger than normal fraction of that temporarily high income, so that consumption would be a low fraction of income. If, in some other year, income was temporarily low, it would be possible to consume the whole of income and perhaps also to consume some previous savings (or, if previous savings were inadequate, to borrow against future income).

Recognizing the possibility of breaking the direct link between income and consumption through borrowing and lending, Modigliani and Friedman suggested that the ultimate constraint on how much consumption an individual can undertake is the amount of that individual's wealth. They proposed the hypothesis that the wealthier an individual is, on the average, the more will that individual consume. In the Modigliani's version of the theory (called the *life-cycle* hypothesis), the individual attempts to smooth out the path of consumption over the life span, even

3   Milton Friedman, *A Theory of the Consumption Function* (Princeton, NJ: Princeton University Press, 1957).
4   Franco Modigliani gave a useful and comprehensive appraisal of his work in his paper 'The Life-Cycle Hypothesis of Saving Twenty-five Years Later', in Michael Parkin and A.R. Nobay, eds, *Contemporary Issues in Economics* (Manchester, England: Manchester University Press, 1975) pp.2–36. This paper also contains a fairly comprehensive bibliography on the consumption function.

though income received would vary from year to year. In Friedman's version of the theory (called the *permanent income* hypothesis), families are assumed to live forever and seek to smooth consumption both over lifetimes of individual family members and across generations.

Upon careful investigation of the data, it turns out that both the *permanent income* hypothesis and *life-cycle* hypothesis, which say that consumption depends on wealth, are theories that fit the facts better than the Keynesian hypothesis that consumption depends primarily on disposable income.

C. Connection Between Wealth and Income and Why Current Income is a Major Determinant of Consumption

Wealth and income are related to each other in a simple way. As we already know, wealth is a stock and income is a flow. The relationship between income and wealth can be put in terms of stocks and flows. Income is the flow that is generated by the stock of wealth.

You have already seen in Chapters 3 and 4 how the main macroeconomic flows and stocks are defined and measured. You are now able to deepen your understanding of the relationship between these stocks and flows. The easiest way to see the connection is in the case of a financial asset. Suppose that you own a deposit account in a bank that has a value of £100 and pays interest at the rate of 15 per cent per annum. Evidently, if you have a deposit of £100 yielding a rate of return of 15 per cent per annum, you will receive an income from that deposit of £10 per annum. The deposit of £100 is a *stock* and is part of your *wealth*. The income of £10 per annum is a *flow* and is part of your *income*. The rate of interest is what converts the stock of wealth into the flow of income. We could write an equation to describe this connection, which would read:

Wealth × Interest Rate = Income

This same type of relationship holds between *all* forms of wealth and all forms of income. For example, the stocks of physical assets held − plant and equipment − and their rate of return generate an income. Also, the stock of human capital (see Chapter 4) and its rate of return generate labour income. That is:

Human Wealth × Interest Rate = Labour Income

Of course, financial assets are traded in markets and pay an explicit rate of interest. Human wealth is unlike other forms of wealth in that it is not (at least in societies that do not have slavery) traded directly in markets. Nevertheless, conceptually the relationship between human wealth and labour income is identical to that between other forms of wealth and the income stream that they generate.

If we were to add up all the forms of wealth owned by an individual, we obtain the individual's total wealth. The rate of return on that total wealth generates the individual's total income.

The concept of *permanent income*, which gives the name to Milton Friedman's theory of the consumption function, can now be understood. It is the level of income that would be sustained on the average through the infinite future, while maintaining a constant stock of wealth. Permanent income can be thought of as the stock of wealth multiplied by the normal long-run average real rate of return. Actual income fluctuates about permanent income from year to year as a result of random fluctuations in the actual rate of return.

So far we have talked about how to convert wealth into income — by multiplying the relevant wealth stock by a rate of return. We could equivalently convert a future stream of income into its equivalent current stock of wealth. In performing such a calculation it is important to notice that the value today (today's wealth) of £1 of income earned in the future depends on how far in the future that income is earned. One pound earned in the next 5 minutes is worth much more than £1 earned in the last 5 minutes of your life. The reason for this is easy to see. One pound earned in the next 5 minutes could be used to buy an interest-bearing security that would lead to the accumulation of more pounds in the future from interest receipts. One pound earned 50 years in the future would be worth less than £1 earned in the next 5 minutes simply because it would be incapable of earning interest for you over the next 50 years. To calculate the wealth equivalent of future income, the future income stream has to be converted to a common valuation basis.

The most useful common valuation basis is known as the *present value*. The present value of a future sum of money is simply that sum of money that, if you were to receive it today, would, when invested at the average rate of interest, accumulate to the prestated future value. For example, if the rate of interest is 10 per cent, £100 invested today would accumulate in 1 year to £110. It would be said, therefore, that the present value of £110 to be received 1 year hence, at a 10 per cent rate of interest, is equal to £100. The sum of £100 invested today at a rate of interest of 10 per cent for 2 years would, at the end of that period, accumulate to £121 — £10 interest in the first year accumulating to £110, plus £11 in the second year (£10 interest on the principal and £1 interest on the £10 of interest earned in the first year). It would be said, therefore, that the present value of £121 to be received 2 years hence, at a 10 per cent rate of interest is equal to £100.

It is important that you recognize the distinction between real and nominal or market interest rates when performing present value calculations. The purpose in calculating a present value is not simply to cancel out the effects of inflation. It would be necessary to calculate a present value even in a world in which there was no inflation.

The arithmetic example given in the preceding paragraph, where the rate of interest is 10 per cent, could be thought of as applying to a world in which there is no inflation (although in such a case the rate of interest used is unrealistically high). What is being said in that example is that £110 received 1 year hence would be worth less to someone today than would £110 received today, even though one year from now it would have the same purchasing power in terms of goods as £110 would today. The reason for this is that if the individual had £110 today, it would be possible to use that money and earn a real rate of interest so that in 1 year from now more goods than £110 worth could be bought. With constant prices and a real rate of interest of 10 per cent, £100 today is the equivalent of (would be regarded by anyone as being just as good as) £110 to be delivered 1 year from today. The calculation of a present value, therefore, is a *real* calculation. It is the conversion of a real stream of future income into a present value.

If we add up the present values of the incomes that an individual will (or expects to) receive each year in the future, we arrive at a total that is the individual's wealth. That is, we arrive at a sum of money that is a present stock and that has an equivalent value to the future (discounted) income flow.

Now that you understand the connection between income and wealth, you will be aware that the life-cycle and permanent income hypotheses of consumption are, in effect, generalizations of the Keynesian theory of consumption. They both say that consumption depends on today's disposable income and on all future (discounted) disposable income. Other things being equal, the larger that today's disposable income is, the larger wealth is, and the greater will be the level of consumption. The larger that future disposable income is, other things being equal, the larger wealth is, and the greater will be today's consumption.

There are two lines of reasoning that lead to the proposition that the most important factor determining current consumption is current disposable income. The first follows directly from the discussion above concerning the relationship between wealth and income. Although it is true that if borrowing and lending in free capital markets is possible, then it is wealth rather than income that is the ultimate constraint on consumption. There is nevertheless good reason for elevating the level of current disposable income to a more important status than wealth.

As you saw above, wealth can be equivalently thought of as current disposable income plus all future disposable income converted to a present value. There is an important distinction, however, between the present and future that arises from the information that we have about them. The present is known and certain, whereas the future is unknown and probabilistic. It is very likely that what is happening in the present to an individual's disposable income is a signal concerning what is likely to happen in the future. It seems sensible to hypothesize, therefore, that wealth, as perceived by an individual, is positively related to current disposable income. If that is so, it is current disposable income rather than wealth that is, from an operational or observational point of view, the major determinant of current consumption.

Another way of putting this result is to say that to a large extent, wealth is not a directly observable and measurable variable. It contains, in part, future expected income flows that are not yet known. Those future expected income flows must be forecasted on the basis of things that are known, one important ingredient of which is current disposable income.

There is a second reason why current disposable income is an important determinant of consumption. The permanent income and life-cycle hypotheses both reach the conclusion that consumption depends on wealth by assuming that individuals may borrow and lend unlimited amounts in order to smooth out consumption over their lifetime. However, there are good reasons why this may not, in general, be possible. It is difficult to borrow unlimited funds against future labour income. It may be possible, therefore that an individual is constrained in the amount of consumption that can be undertaken by the amount of current disposable income, since that amount will be used as an indication to a potential lender concerning the individual's ability to repay the loan and pay the interest on it.

For two reasons, then, (1) because current income provides good information to an individual about future income and therefore about wealth and (2) because current disposable income provides good information to potential lenders, it seems reasonable to suppose that it is current disposable income that is the most important single factor determining current consumption demand.[5]

---

5 The account of the theory of the consumption function given in this chapter has been highly condensed and selective. The best, lengthy textbook treatment of the subject that will fill in a lot of the detail for you is David F. Heathfield (ed.), *Topics in Applied Macroeconomics* (London: Macmillan, 1976). An up-to-date survey of the empirical issues (from a US perspective, though) is Walter Dolde, 'Issues and Models in Empirical Research on Aggregate Consumer Expenditure', in Karl Brunner and Allan H. Meltzer, (eds.), *On the State of Macro-Economics*, Carnegie-Rochester Conference Series on Public Policy, Vol. 12 (Spring 1980) pp.161–206. There is an enormous body of published literature on the UK consumption function. All of this literature is technically much more demanding that the level of material presented in this book. Some examples are: R. P. Byron, 'Initial Attempts in Econometric Model Building at NIESR', in K. Hilton and D. F. Heathfield (eds.), *The Econometric Study of the United Kingdom* (London: Macmillan, 1970) Ch. 1; Angus S. Deaton, 'Wealth Effects on Consumption in a Modified Life-Cycle Model', *Review of Economic Studies*, Vol. 39 (1972) pp.443–54; David F. Hendry, 'Stochastic Specification in an Aggregate Demand Model of the United Kingdom', *Econometrica*, Vol. 42 (1974) pp.559–78; R. J. Ball et al., 'The London Business School Quarterly Econometric Model of the UK Economy', in G. A. Renton (ed.), *Modelling the Economy* (London: Heinemann, 1975) Ch. 1 (The Renton book also includes papers by John Bispham and James Shepherd and others which explain the National Institute's and Treasury's consumption functions.) The most comprehensive and up-to-date treament of the UK consumption function is that by James Davidson, David Hendry, Frank Srba, and Stephen Yeo, 'Econometric Modelling of the Aggregate Time Series Relationship Between Consumers' Expenditure and Income in the United Kingdom', *Economic Journal*, Vol. 88 (December 1978) pp.661–92. The most recent survey is by E. P. Davies in 'The Consumption Function in Macroeconomic Models: A Comparative Study', Bank of England Discussion Paper, Technical Series 1. Unfortunately, this study is now available only in photocopy form from University Microfilms International, 30–32 Mortimer St., London W1N 7RA.

D. Consumption and Savings Functions in Simple Equations and Diagrams

The discussion and analysis that has been conducted above may now be summarized in a very compact form by writing a simple equation to describe the determination of consumption demand. Such an equation is

$$c = a + b(y - t) \qquad a > 0, 1 > b > 0 \qquad (9.1)$$

The value of aggregate real consumption demand is represented by c, real income (real gross national product) is represented by y, the total collection of taxes by the government net of transfer payments is represented by t, and a and b are *constants* or *parameters*. According to Keynes's 'fundamental psychological law', the parameter b is a positive fraction, an example, say, 3/4. The parameter a captures the effects of all these things that influence consumption other than disposable income. These other factors include such things as demographic trends and tastes. There are, of course, many such things. The assumption being made, however, is that all the other influences on consumption have effects that may be ignored either because their effects are slight or because they are factors which are themselves changing slowly. The parameter a is presumably positive, indicating that if people had very low current income, they would seek to consume more than their income, thereby using up part of their past accumulated savings.

The consumption function written as an equation above may be shown in a simple diagram. Figure 9.1 illustrates the consumption function. The vertical axis measures real consumption demand, and the horizontal axis measures real income. In order to show the relationship between consumption demand and income on a diagram, it is necessary to be precise about how taxes vary as income varies. For present purposes, it will be assumed that taxes are set by the government to yield a certain total amount of revenue, t, independently of what the level of income is. In other words, taxes will be treated as a constant. This assumption is not the only one that could have been made, nor is it necessarily the most natural one. Permitting taxes to vary with income would be more natural, but it makes the presentation of the analysis slightly more cumbersome and does not modify the results that we will get in any qualitative way.

Proceeding then with the assumption that taxes are constant, we can now illustrate the relationship between real consumption demand and real income in Figure 9.1. The dashed line labelled $c = a + by$ represents the consumption function in an economy in which taxes and transfer payments sum to zero. The continuous line labelled $c = a + by - bt$ represents the consumption function in an economy that has net taxes at the level t. The other line in the diagram is a 45° line and can be read as telling you that at each point on that line, consumption would be exactly equal to income. You may use this line as a reference therefore, to figure

Figure 9.1
The consumption
function

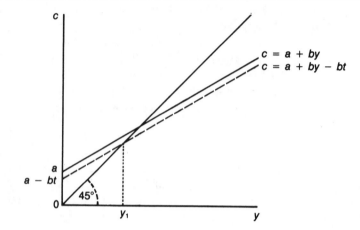

Consumption is a function of disposable income. When consumption (c) is graphed against income (y), the consumption function slopes upwards at the rate of the marginal propensity to consume (the parameter b). If the level of taxes (t) is zero, the intercept of the consumption function on the vertical axis is equal to a. If the level of taxes is not zero, the intercept of the consumption function on the vertical axis is equal to a minus the product of the marginal propensity to consume (b) and the level of taxes (t).

out whether consumption demand exceeds, equals, or falls short of current income. For example, at the income level y_1 and the level of net taxes t, consumption demand exactly equals income. At income levels above y_1, consumption is less than income, and at income levels below y_1, consumption exceeds income.

This equation and diagram summarize the theory of the determinants of consumption demand. The slope of this line (represented by the parameter b) is given a name, and that name is the *marginal propensity to consume*. If the marginal propensity to consume is high (close to 1), the consumption function will be steep (almost as steep as the 45° line). The lower the marginal propensity to consume, the flatter is the consumption function.

Notice that the consumption function as drawn in Figure 9.1 will shift if there is a change in the level of taxes. You can see this effect directly in Figure 9.1 by comparing the dashed line drawn for zero taxes with the continuous line drawn for a tax level of t. This figure shows that the higher the level of taxes, the further the consumption function shifts downwards. What this shift means is that the higher the tax level, the lower is the level of disposable income, and therefore, the lower is the level of consumption associated with each level of gross domestic product. The amount by which the consumption function shifts down for a £1 rise in taxes is the fraction b of a pound. The reason why the consumption function shifts down by only the fraction b and not by the whole amount of the increase in taxes is that some of the increase in taxes comes from a reduction in savings, and only fraction b of the increase in taxes comes from a reduction in consumption. You will be able to see this more clearly by considering the relationship between consumption, savings, and taxes, which is the next and final task in what has been a long section of this chapter.

A household can do only three things with its income: it can consume, save, or pay taxes. This allocation of income can be written as an equation, namely

$$y = c + s + t \tag{9.2}$$

Savings are what are left over after meeting consumption expenditures and paying taxes. Clearly, in planning its consumption, the household is also implicitly planning how much saving to undertake. If consumption is determined by Equation (9.1) above, that is, if $c = a + b(y - t)$, it must be the case that the household is planning to save an amount given by another equation, namely

$$s = -a + (1 - b)(y - t) \tag{9.3}$$

How do we know that Equation (9.3) tells us about the household's savings plans? The answer is simply that if we add together the household's consumption plan Equation (9.1) and its savings plan Equation (9.3), we get the proposition that

$$c + s = y - t \tag{9.4}$$

namely, that consumption plus saving is equal to disposable income. You will recognize this equation as simply a rearrangement of Equation (9.2) above. Equation (9.3) is usually referred to as the *savings function*, and the slope of the savings function $(1 - b)$ as the *marginal propensity to save*. The marginal propensity to save plus the marginal propensity to consume always add up to unity.

You may find it helpful to represent the consumption function and the savings function in a diagram that shows how the two are related. Figure 9.2 illustrates this connection. Frame (a) shows consumption plotted against income, and frame (b) shows savings plotted against income. Indeed, frame (a) is nothing other than Figure 9.1. The two frames are related to each other in the following way. Look first at the dashed lines that represent an economy with no taxes, so that disposable income and aggregate income are the same number. In this case, the vertical distance between the consumption function and the 45° line in frame (a) is equal to the vertical distance between the horizontal axis and the savings function in frame (b). As an example, at the income level y_2, consumption exactly equals income, and savings exactly equals zero. At an income level above y_2, for example, y_h, savings can be represented in frame (a) by the vertical line marked h and equivalently in frame (b) by the vertical distance h.

Next, consider the economy in which taxes are not zero. In this case

**Figure 9.2
The consumption
and savings
functions**

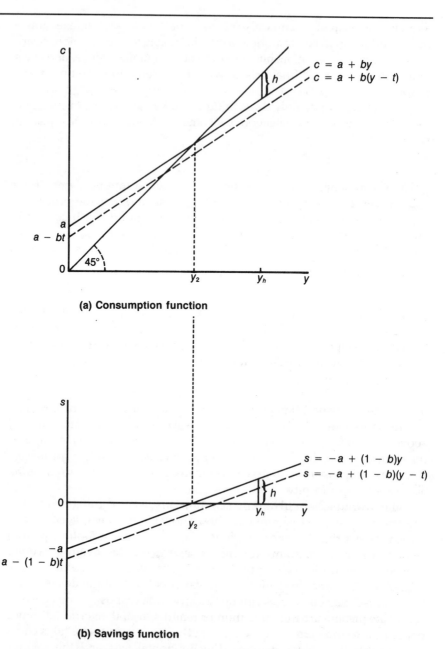

(a) Consumption function

(b) Savings function

Since income must be disposed of either by consuming, saving, or paying taxes, the
consumption function implies a savings function. When saving and consumption plans are
added together they exactly exhaust disposable income. For example, if taxes are zero
(the continuous lines) and if income is y_h, then the amount saved, h, may be read off
directly from the savings function in frame (b) or as the distance marked h in frame (a).
When taxes are t the consumption function is lower by bt [frame (a)] and the savings function is lower by $(1 - b)t$ [frame (b)].

the consumption function shifts downwards by an amount equal to b times taxes. The savings function also shifts down, but by an amount equal to $1 - b$ times taxes. What do these shifts mean? It means simply that for a £1 rise in taxes, consumption drops by fraction b of a pound, and savings drop by fraction $1 - b$ of a pound – the drop in savings and consumption taken together being enough to make up the £1 of taxes. The after-tax consumption and savings functions are parallel to the pre-tax functions.

Adding the consumption function and the savings function together gives a number equal to disposable income; that is, a number equal to income minus taxes.

You have now covered the major aspects of the theory of consumption demand and the related theory of savings. Let us now turn to the task of examining the actual UK data on consumption and discover the properties of the British consumption function.

E. The UK Consumption Function

What does the UK consumption function look like? We cannot answer this question precisely because we do not have a precise measure of the *consumption* of durables. We know how much people spend on durables each year. We do not, however, have a good measure of the rate at which the stock of durables is being used up – is being depreciated – and therefore, consumed. There are two ways that we can proceed in taking a look at the actual consumption function. One is to pretend that expenditure on durable goods gives us a good indication as to the actual consumption of the stock of durable goods. In other words we could treat total consumer expenditure as a proxy measure for actual consumption. An alternative would be to look only at expenditure on non-durables. This alternative would understate total consumption, for it would ignore the consumption services yielded by the stock of durable goods. The first method of attempting to approximate the value of consumption seems to be the more desirable one.

Using total consumers' expenditure as a measure of consumption, Figure 9.3 plots the UK consumption function. Each year (point) in that diagram represents the combination of real disposable income and real consumer expenditure.

Notice that the UK consumption function shown in Figure 9.3 looks remarkably like the theoretical consumption function shown in Figure 9.1. Consumption rises as income rises, but by a smaller amount than the rise in income. As a matter of fact the marginal propensity to consume implied by these data is 0.828.

Notice that, like the theoretical consumption function in Figure 9.1, the actual consumption function shows that when income is very low,

Figure 9.3
The UK consumption function

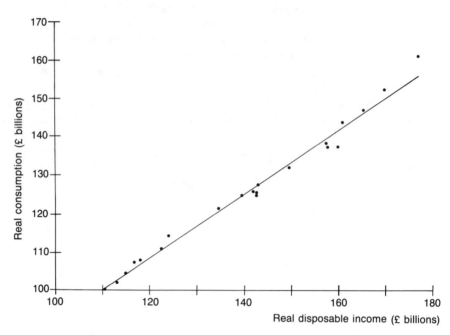

The relationship between real consumer expenditure and real disposable income in the UK is a close one and is similar to the theoretical consumption function proposed by Keynes. The marginal propensity to consume is 0.828 and the equation describing real consumption expenditure is $c = 9124 + 0.828y_d$.
Source: United Kingdom National Accounts, (HMSO, 1987)

consumption exceeds income. In this situation people would be running down the values of their assets by temporarily spending more than they are earning.

If, instead of measuring consumption as total consumers' expenditure we focused only on expenditure on non-durables, the consumption function would look similar to that shown in Figure 9.3 but it would have a flatter slope and would be lower down. The marginal propensity to consume on non-durables only in the data is about 2/3.

We have now covered not only the major aspects of the theory of consumption demand and the related theory of savings, but also have examined the UK consumption function. It is now possible to move on to explore the simplest theory of income determination, the Keynesian cross model.

F. Keynesian Cross Model

The essence of the Keynesian theory of aggregate demand — what has come to be called the *Keynesian cross model* — may now be understood.

This simplest theory of income determination applies to an economy in which there is a considerable amount of underutilization of labour and capital resources so that output can fluctuate independently of the capacity of the economy to produce goods and services. It also applies only in the special circumstances in which the aggregate supply curve (introduced in Chapter 8) is perfectly elastic — that is, is horizontal. You should be suspicious that these are pretty unusual and not very likely circumstances. To fit the real world such circumstances would require that all producers face a technology that enables them to produce output at a constant cost regardless of the scale of output and would also require a situation in which the costs of all factors of production remain constant as output (and employment of factors of production) vary. Such circumstances (unlikely though they are) would, were they to occur in the world, give rise to a horizontal aggregate supply curve.

If the aggregate supply curve did happen to be horizontal then the quantity of output demanded would determine the actual level of output. That is the situation visualized in this simplest Keynesian cross theory of the determination of output. Let us now proceed to see how the theory works.

In Figure 9.2, you have already become familiar with a diagram in which output is measured on the horizontal axis (recalling that output and real income are equal to each other) and consumption demand (one of the major components of aggregate demand) is measured on the vertical axis. We don't have to move very far from the content of Figure 9.2 to determine aggregate demand and aggregate output (real income) in the simplest Keynesian cross framework. We can, by broadening our view slightly as we do in Figure 9.4, measure on the vertical axis of the diagram not just consumption demand but all the components of aggregate demand added together; that is, y^d. We continue to measure actual output, y, on the horizontal axis.

The first thing to understand about the diagram in this slightly modified form is the meaning of the 45° line. That line has been labelled $y = y^d$. You may interpret the 45° line as saying that actual output, y will be determined as the quantity of output that is actually demanded, y^d. There is a sense in which this line might be thought of as the aggregate supply curve, although you must be careful not to confuse it with the aggregate supply curve defined in Chapter 8.

The consumption function, the line labelled $c = a + b(y - t)$, already introduced in Figure 9.2, is reproduced in Figure 9.3. Consumption demand is only part of total demand. The other elements of aggregate demand (ignoring net foreign demand) are investment and government expenditure on goods and services. We have already agreed to treat

Figure 9.4
The Keynesian cross
model

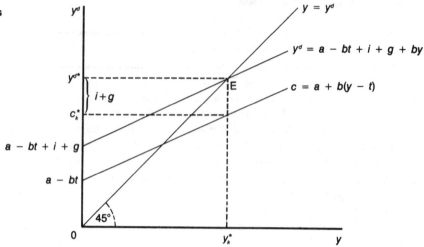

The Keynesian cross model is the essence of the Keynesian theory of output determination. Actual output (y) is equal to aggregate demand (along the 45° line). Aggregate
demand is the sum of consumption demand (c) and autonomous expenditure ($i + g$).
The point where the aggregate demand line ($y^d = a - bt + i + g + by$) cuts the 45°
line determines the equilibrium level of real income (y_k^*).

government expenditure as exogenous. Let us, for the moment, treat
investment in the same way. That is, let us suppose that the level of
investment is fixed. (The next chapter actually goes on to discuss the
factors that determine investment.) Aggregate demand, then, can be
written

$$y^d = c + i + g \qquad\qquad (9.5)$$

where i and g are real investment and real government expenditure on
goods and services, respectively. In order to graph aggregate demand
y^d in Figure 9.3, all that we have to do is to add the fixed amount of
investment and government expenditure to the consumption function.
That is, we need to displace the consumption function upwards by an
amount equal to investment plus government expenditure. In the diagram
aggregate demand is represented by the line labelled

$$y^d = a - bt + i + g + by$$

This curve tells us what the total level of demand will be at each level
of income. Total demand rises as income rises, but it will not, however,
rise by as much as income since the consumption function itself has a
slope of less than 1. At low income levels, total demand exceeds income,
and at high income levels, total demand falls short of income. There is
only one income level, y_k^*, that generates a level of aggregate demand
equal to itself. This is the equilibrium level of aggregate demand in the
Keynesian cross model.

Income, rather than the price level, is the variable that adjusts to achieve the equilibrium. To see this adjustment, consider hypothetically what would happen if income was greater than y_k^*. This experiment is a purely hypothetical and could not actually happen in the world described in Figure 9.3. In such a case, the level of demand would be less than the level of income. You can see this is true because the curve labelled y^d is lower than the 45° line at all points to the right of y_k^*, which means that total spending (gross domestic product) was less than income. However, you know this to be impossible. Hence, the conjectured income level greater than y_k^* could not occur. Similarly, income levels below y_k^* could not occur. There is one, and only one, income level that is compatible with the relationships hypothesized here, and that is the income level y_k^*, or the point E at which the aggregate demand curve cuts the 45° line.

The analysis that you have just gone through is the essence of Keynes's general theory.[6] (Keynes himself was explicit about this on p.29 of the *General Theory of Employment, Interest and Money*.)

An important and interesting implication of this analysis is the simple so-called autonomous expenditure multiplier. Investment and government expenditure (and taxes) are all variables whose values change autonomously with respect to (independently of) real income. Only consumption changes as income changes. If there is a change in the value of taxes, investment, or government expenditure, there will be induced changes in consumption and income, and the change in income will be larger than the initial change in autonomous expenditure.

To see this, consider, by way of an example, the effects of a rise in investment. Suppose that taxes and government spending are held constant, but investment rises. We know that any change in income that occurs will be equal to the change in investment plus any induced change in consumption. That is, using the symbol 'Δ' to denote 'change in', we have

$$\Delta y = \Delta c + \Delta i \tag{9.6}$$

But we know from the theory of the consumption function that the change in consumption will be equal to the change in income multiplied by b, the marginal propensity to consume; that is,

$$\Delta c = b\Delta y \tag{9.7}$$

Substituting this equation into the previous one tells us that the change in income will be equal to b times the change in income plus the change in investment. That is,

$$\Delta y = b\Delta y + \Delta i \tag{9.8}$$

---

6 The presentation of this model on pp. 28 and 29 of the *General Theory* is slightly disguised by the fact that Keynes uses the level of employment rather than the level of output (income) as the variable determined by the analysis, but if you work carefully through these two pages of Keynes's book, you will find the above model there.

Rearranging this equation by taking the term $b\Delta y$ to the left-hand side and then dividing through by $(1 - b)$ gives

$$\Delta y = \frac{1}{1 - b}\,\Delta i \qquad\qquad (9.9)$$

You have just worked out the famous Keynesian multiplier. The change in income that is induced by a change in autonomous expenditure (investment in this case) is equal to 1, divided by the marginal propensity to save, times the initial change in autonomous expenditure. If the propensity to consume was, for example, 0.828 (the value obtained from the UK data in Section E above), then the multiplier would be 7.

Figure 9.5
The multiplier in the Keynesian cross model

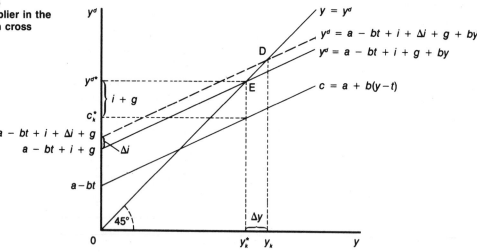

A rise in autonomous expenditure (for example, a rise in investment by Δi) raises aggregate demand and raises equilibrium income (output) by Δy, an amount equal to $[1/(1 - b)]\Delta i$.

Figure 9.5 illustrates the multiplier. It is possible to mark the rise in investment (Δi) on the vertical axis of the figure, thereby generating a new aggregate demand curve — the curve labelled

$$y^d = a - bt + i + \Delta i + g + by$$

The new equilibrium level of income is at point D at an income level y_k. The rise in income is marked in the figure as Δy, and the initial rise in investment is Δi. A change in government expenditure induces a change in income that is identical to that induced by a change in investment expenditure and shown in Equation (9.9).

A change in taxes, however, induces a change in income that has a different multiplier from that on investment and government spending.

Why is that? It is for two reasons: first, a rise in taxes will lower income, whereas a rise in investment and a rise in government spending will raise income. This occurs because when taxes rise, disposable income and, therefore, consumption, fall. However, a rise in taxes of £1 will in part be paid out of lower savings. Savings will be cut by £1 times the marginal propensity to save by $(1 - b)$, and consumption will only be cut by b. Thus, a £1 rise in taxes leads to a fraction b of £1 cut in consumption. It is this number that has to be scaled up by the standard multiplier so that the change in income induced by a tax change is

$$\Delta y = \frac{-b}{1 - b} \Delta t \qquad (9.10)$$

Continuing with the example of a marginal propensity to consume of 0.8, the multiplier for a tax change would be -4. Thus a £1 rise in taxes would cut income by £4.

   You have now discovered that in the simplest version of the Keynesian theory of aggregate demand, the level of demand (which equals the level of actual income and output) is determined by the level of autonomous expenditure. Change taxes, government spending, or investment and there will be a change in income that is bigger than the initial change in autonomous expenditure.

Summary

A. Components of Aggregate Demand

The components of aggregate demand are consumption, investment, government purchases of goods and services, and net exports.

B. Theories of the Consumption Function Proposed by Keynes, Friedman and Modigliani

Keynes hypothesized that the major determinant of consumption was current disposable income. Keynes supposed that the level of consumption would rise as income rose, but the fraction of income consumed would decline. Friedman and Modigliani developed the permanent income and life-cycle hypotheses, which emphasized the role of wealth as the ultimate constraint upon consumption.

C. Connection Between Wealth and Income and Why Current Income is a Major Determinant of Consumption

Wealth is the present value of current and future income. By borrowing and lending, it is possible to break the direct connection between current income and current consumption. Nevertheless, current income is an important indicator of potential future income and therefore will influence the extent to which an individual can borrow against future labour income and will influence the individual's own assessment of what represents a desirable, sustainable consumption and savings plan. Therefore, current income is a major determinant of consumption.

D. Consumption and Savings Functions in Simple Equations and Diagrams

The consumption function may be written as

$$c = a + b(y - t)$$

Since savings plus consumption must equal disposable income, it follows that the savings function must be

$$s = -a + (1 - b)(y - t)$$

If savings and consumption are added together, they always add up to disposable income $(y - t)$.

E. The UK Consumption Function

The UK consumption function looks almost identical to the theoretical consumption function set out in Figure 9.1. The marginal propensity to consume (defining consumption as total consumers' expenditure) is 0.828. There is a close and linear relationship between real consumers' expenditure and real disposable income.

F. Keynesian Cross Model

The essence of the simple Keynesian theory of aggregate demand can be summarized in the Keynesian cross diagram. Aggregate demand is measured on the vertical axis and actual output on the horizontal axis. The 45° line says that the level of actual output will equal the quantity demanded. The aggregate demand curve plotted in the diagram shows the consumption function plus the assumed fixed level of investment and government expenditure. The point where the aggregate demand line cuts the 45° line determines the equilibrium level of income. It is an equilibrium in the sense that it is the only income level that generates a level of consumption that, when added to investment and government spending, equals that same level of income.

  A rise in investment or government spending will shift the aggregate demand curve upwards and produce a higher equilibrium income level. The rise in income will be equal to the rise in investment or government expenditure multiplied by $1/(1-b)$, where b is the marginal propensity to consume. A rise in taxes will change income by $-b/(1-b)$ times the rise in taxes (i.e. a tax rise will lower income).

Review Questions

1. What are the components into which aggregate demand is separated in order to study the determination of aggregate demand?
2. Classify the following items according to whether they are consumption (c), investment (i), government expenditure (g), none of these and not part of aggregate demand (n), or, there is not enough information to say:

    (a) your purchase of lunch today.
    (b) the purchase of a new car.
    (c) the purchase of a used car.
    (d) the purchase of a new office block by the government.
    (e) the payment of unemployment benefits by the government.
    (f) the purchase by British Airways of a Boeing 747 aeroplane.
    (g) the purchase by British Airways of food for in-flight service. (*Hint:* Be careful — look at Chapter 3 on the distinction between final and intermediate expenditure.)
    (h) your purchase of a ticket on a British Airways flight.
    (i) the purchase of a computer by Barclays Bank.
    (j) your income tax payments to the government.

3. What is Keynes's theory of the consumption function?
4. What, according to the permanent income and life-cycle hypotheses, is the fundamental constraint on consumption?
5. What is the connection between income and wealth?
6. If a person's income was to rise next year by £1000, but thereafter to return to its original path, and if the rate of interest was 10 per cent a year, by how much would that person's wealth rise today?
7. Why is it that despite the fact that wealth is the fundamental constraint on consumption, disposable income is regarded as the major determinant of consumption?
8. What is the meaning of the term *marginal propensity to consume* (b)? Why is the parameter b less than one?
9. What is the savings function? What is the relationship between the savings function and the consumption function?
10. If the marginal propensity to consume is 0.75, income is 1000 and taxes are 200, what is consumption? What is savings? If income rises to 1200, what now are consumption and savings? But if income rises

to 1200 and taxes also rise to 400, what is the change in consumption?

11. You are given the following information about a hypothetical economy:

$$c = 100 + 0.8(y - t)$$
$$i = 500$$
$$g = 400$$
$$t = 400$$

(c = consumption, i = investment, g = government expenditure on goods and services, y = real income, t = taxes).

(a) Calculate the equilibrium level of output and consumption.

(b) If government expenditure is cut to 300, what is the *change* in income and the *change* in consumption?

(c) What is the size of the multiplier effect of government expenditure on output?

10

Investment Demand

You already know from the definitions given at the beginning of the last chapter that investment demand is the purchase of durable goods by both households and firms. You also know from your examination of the characteristics of the business cycle in Chapter 7 that the fluctuations in the output of durables have much greater amplitude than those in nondurables. Understanding what determines investment is, therefore, of crucial importance in understanding some of the major sources of fluctuations in aggregate demand. What determines investment, and why does it fluctuate so much? These are the principal questions for this chapter.[1] Answering these questions is a fairly big task and one that is going to be more easily approached by breaking it up into a series of specific subtasks.

By the time you have completed this chapter you will be able to:

(a) **State the distinction between investment and the capital stock.**
(b) **Explain what determines the demand for capital.**
(c) **Explain what is meant by the rental rate of capital.**
(d) **Explain how investment demand is related to the demand for capital.**
(e) **Represent the investment demand function in a simple equation and diagram.**
(f) **State the properties of the UK investment demand function.**

---

1 The development of the theory of investment presented in this chapter is based very closely on Dale W. Jorgensen, 'Capital Theory and Investment Behavior', *American Economic Review Papers and Proceedings*, 53 (1963), pp.247–59.

A. Distinction Between Investment and Capital Stock

Investment demand is the demand for capital goods for use in production or consumption-yielding activities. Investment may be undertaken for two purposes:

(1) To add to the existing stock of capital.
(2) To replace capital equipment that has depreciated.

You already know that investment is a flow. It is the flow of additions to the capital stock or replacements for worn-out capital. In any one year, the amount of investment is small relative to the size of the capital stock. For example, in 1986, gross investment in the UK is 21 per cent of GDP. Of this amount 70 per cent is replacement investment, so that the rate of net investment (addition to the capital stock) is 6 per cent of GDP. The capital stock is estimated to be slightly more than five times GDP, which means that net investment is of the order of 1 per cent of the capital stock.

To summarize: the capital stock is the total value of the capital equipment located in the economy at a particular point in time. The level of investment is the rate of flow of additions to that capital stock, plus the rate of flow of expenditure on capital goods to replace worn out capital equipment.

What determines the rate of investment? This question is best answered in a slightly roundabout manner. Rather than answering it directly, we are going to approach it by asking first of all, what determines the amount of capital stock that, in the aggregate, the agents in the economy want to hold. Let us now examine that question.

B. Demand for Capital

In any productive or consumption-yielding activity, there is a range of choice of techniques available. For example, it will be possible to undertake almost any imaginable task by using only labour as the resource and using no capital at all. At the other extreme, it would be possible to undertake almost any imaginable task by using a very capital intensive technology, that is, a technology that involves very little labour and large amounts of capital. (It is true that there are some tasks that one could not imagine doing in any way other than by using large amounts of capital — for example, putting a satellite into earth orbit.) Nevertheless, over a very large range of economic activities, it is possible to visualize differing degrees of intensity of use of capital. A classical example would be the building of a dam, which could be undertaken with massive earth-moving equipment and a small amount of labour or by masses of labour workng by hand or using small wooden shovels, themselves made by hand. A technology that uses a lot of capital and a small amount of labour is called a *capital-intensive technology*. The opposite, which uses large amounts of labour and very little capital is called a *labour-intensive technology*.

What determines the extent to which a capital-intensive technology will be used rather than a labour-intensive technology? A moment's reflection suggests that the choice depends on the relative costs of the alternative techniques of production, which in turn depends on the relative costs of capital and labour. If capital is cheap relative to labour, then it would seem efficient to use a capital-intensive technology. If, on the other hand, labour is cheap relative to capital, then a labour-intensive technology would seem to be indicated.

All this seems obvious enough until one reflects a little further and begins to wonder how to calculate whether or not capital was cheap relative to labour. After all, buying a piece of equipment is buying something that is durable and that is going to be usable over a long period of time, whereas hiring labour is something that is more in the nature of a consumption activity. How can we compare the price of capital and the price of labour in order to know whether capital is cheap or not? The answer lies in a concept called the *rental rate* of capital. By comparing the rental rate of capital with the wage rate of labour we can establish the relative price of capital and labour.

The term rental rate of capital suggests the notion of a price that has to be paid for the *use* of a piece of capital and not the price that has to be paid to *buy* a piece of capital. Most capital equipment is not, however, rented at all; it is bought and used, as needed. It is convenient to think of the owner of a piece of capital equipment as wearing two hats; one hat is that of the owner, the other is the hat of the user. Put differently, the owner rents the equipment and is the renter of the equipment. We call the rent *implicit* because no actual rent is explicitly paid.

There are many examples of explicit renting — when the owner and user of a piece of capital are different people. Examples include the rental of a car at an airport, or more commonly, the rental of a flat or a house. Firms often rent equipment, for example, the rental of heavy earth-moving and other specialized equipment by civil engineering contractors.

Whether capital equipment is explicitly rented by its user from its owner or implicitly rented by its owner from himself for his own use makes no difference to the general concept of the rental rate of capital.

C. Rental Rate of Capital

The best way of understanding what is meant by the rental rate of capital is to proceed by example. How much would you be willing to pay each year to rent a house that you could otherwise buy for £60,000? To answer that question, you need to know a little bit more information than you have just been given. Let's supply some more pieces of information.

The house will last for 50 years, so that if you bought the house, it would wear out at a rate of 2 per cent a year.[2] The interest rate that you would face is 15 per cent per annum. That means that you would have to pay 15 per cent per annum for any money that you borrowed (any mortgage money) to buy the house. Equivalently, if you sold some existing securities to buy the house, you would have to forgo a 15 per cent rate of interest on those securities. Either way, the opportunity cost of funds that you used to buy the house is going to be 15 per cent. House prices are rising and are expected to rise indefinitely through the future at a rate of 10 per cent per annum.

You now have enough information with which to answer the question. How much would you pay each year to rent a house that you could otherwise buy for £60,000? The answer is you wouldn't pay any more rent than the amount that you would implicitly have to pay to yourself if you were to buy the house and live in it for as long as you needed it and thereafter sell the house. How much is that amount? To figure it out, consider the following three costs of owning the house and renting it to yourself. First, there is a cost in the form of physical depreciation on the house; second, there is a cost in the form of the interest that you would have to pay in order to acquire the £60,000 needed to buy the house; and third, there is a negative cost, the gain, that arises from the fact that the value of the house on the housing market will rise at a rate at which house prices are expected to rise (in the example, 10 per cent per annum).

If you are going to buy a £60,000 house, the depreciation of 2 per cent per annum would cost you £1200 a year. The interest payment at 15 per cent would cost a further £9000 a year. Thus your total cost so far is £10,200. However, offset against this is the fact that the house value will appreciate by 10 per cent a year, which will give you a capital gain of £6000. This has to be offset against the £10,200 to give a net annual cost of £4200. Ignoring tax considerations and ignoring the costs of searching for a house and of transacting to buy and sell a house — abstracting from all those things — £4200 per annum is the implicit rental rate that you would have to pay to yourself if you were to buy the house. If houses actually rented for less than £4200 a year, it would pay you to rent rather than buy. If houses of this type rented for more than £4200 a year, it would pay you to buy rather than rent.

Since everyone is capable of doing the kind of calculations that you have just performed, it might be expected that there would be some equilibrating forces at work in the marketplace ensuring that the actual

---

2 Actually, to say that a house will last 50 years and that it will wear out at the rate of 2 per cent a year is slightly contradictory. The two statements are approximately equivalent, however. If a house wore out in 50 years at exactly a rate of 1/50 of the initial house each year, then the depreciation expressed as a percentage of the remaining value of the house would rise. If we express the depreciation rate as a constant per cent each year, what we are really saying is that the asset will never finally wear out. This is known as radioactive depreciation. It makes the arithmetic easier and is approximately the same as a constant absolute amount of depreciation.

rental rates on houses did not stray too far away from the implicit rental rate that we have just calculated. That is, if the implicit rental rate was less than the actual market rent, there would be a rise in the demand for houses to buy and a fall in the demand for houses to rent. This would tend to raise the purchase price of houses and lower house rental rates. The process would continue until people were indifferent between owning and renting. The same considerations apply in the opposite case. If the implicit rental rate was greater than the market rental rate on houses, then there would be a drop in the demand for houses to buy and a rise in the demand for houses to rent. This would have the reverse effect on rents and purchase prices and, again, would bring about an equality between the actual and implicit rental rates. Thus, the actual rent of capital goods (a house in this example) and the implicit rent may be regarded as the same.

You have now calculated a formula that can be stated in general terms; namely, the rental rate of a piece of capital equipment is equal to the price of the capital multiplied by the sum of the rate of depreciation plus the market rate of interest minus the expected rate of change of the price of the piece of capital equipment. Let us write that as an equation, defining P_k as the price of capital, δ as the depreciation rate, r_m as the market rate of interest, and $\Delta P_k^e/P_k$ as the rate at which the price of capital is expected to rise. The formula for the rental rate becomes:

$$P_k[(\delta + r_m) - (\Delta P_k^e/P_k)] \tag{10.1}$$

Let us check that this formula gives us the right answer for the annual rental rate of a house. Using the numbers introduced above, P_k equals £60,000, and δ is 2 per cent per annum, expressed in proportionate terms as 0.02. The interest rate, r_m (again expressed as a proportion), is 0.15, and the expected rate of increase of house prices, $\Delta P_k^e/P_k$ (also expressed as a proportion), is 0.10. Putting these numbers into the formula, we have:

$$
\begin{aligned}
\text{Rent} &= \text{£60,000 } (0.02 + 0.15 - 0.10) \\
&= \text{£60,000} \times 0.07 \\
&= \text{£4200 per annum.}
\end{aligned}
$$

Evidently the formula works.

Now that you have the basic idea of how to calculate the rental rate on a piece of capital equipment, let us return to the task of figuring out how a producer will choose how much capital and labour to employ in the production process. You already know that, in order to maximize profits, a producer will set the marginal product of a factor of production equal to its real price. In the case of labour, this involves setting the marginal product of labour equal to the real wage. For capital, the producer has to set the marginal product of capital equal to the real rental rate. What we have just calculated above is the nominal rental rate. The real rental rate (RR) is obtained by dividing the nominal rental rate by the price level (P) to give:

$$RR = \frac{P_k}{P} [(\delta + r_m) - (\Delta P_k^e/P_k)] \tag{10.2}$$

Since we are interested in aggregate economic phenomena we are interested in the economy average real rental rate. In terms of the above equation, this means that we want to interpret P_k/P as the relative price of capital goods to goods and services in general. It is a reasonable approximation to regard that ratio as constant. (During the period between 1960 and 1979 capital goods prices in the United Kingdom decreased by 0.03 of 1 per cent per annum relative to consumer good prices.) By calculating a price index for capital goods (P_k) and for consumer goods in general (P) with the same base, we can regard the relative price as being equal to one. Further, since capital goods prices inflate at approximately the same rate as prices in general, we can replace the term $\Delta P_k^e/P_k$ with the expected rate of inflation, π^e. This enables us to write the formula for the rental rate of capital in a simpler way as:

$$RR = (\delta + r_m - \pi^e) \tag{10.3}$$

Notice that the expected change in the price of capital now becomes π^e, the expected rate of inflation.

The term $r_m - \pi^e$ is very important and is given a special name. It is the *expected real rate of interest*. In what follows, we will suppose that the expected rate of inflation, π^e, and the actual rate of inflation, π, are equal so that the expected real rate of interest is equal to the actual real rate of interest. Let us denote the real rate of interest as r. Using this we may simplify the formula for the real capital rental rate as:

$$RR = \delta + r \tag{10.4}$$

If the rate of depreciation is a technologically given constant, it is clear that the only *variable* that affects the real capital rental rate is the real rate of interest. Thus, the higher the real rate of interest, the higher is the real capital rental rate.

If producers utilize capital and labour resources in an efficient way, at a lower real rate of interest they will seek to use a more capital-intensive technology. Figure 10.1 illustrates the relationship between the desired capital stock (K) and the real rate of interest (r), the demand for capital. If the real rate of interest was the level r_0, then the capital stock that producers would wish to have is shown as K_0. If the interest rate was lower, at r_1, then the higher capital stock K_1 would be desired.

Now that you understand the relationship between the real rate of interest and the rental rate of capital and also the relationship between the real rate of interest and the demand for capital stock, it is possible to take the next step and see how the rate of investment is determined.

**Figure 10.1
The demand for
capital stock**

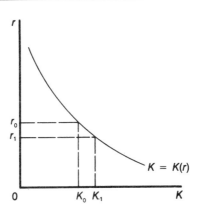

The demand for capital stock (K) depends inversely on the rental rate of capital. The rental rate is equal to the technologically given rate of depreciation plus the difference between the money rate of interest and the rate of inflation of asset prices. The difference between the money rate of interest and the rate of inflation of asset prices is the real rate of interest (r). The demand for capital (K) therefore depends inversely on the real rate of interest (r). If the real rate of interest falls from r_0 to r_1 the demand for capital would rise from K_0 to K_1.

D. Investment and the Demand for Capital

As already stated earlier in this chapter, investment demand is the demand for capital goods for use in productive (or consumption-yielding) activities. Investment is a flow that represents either additions to the existing stock of capital or replacement of worn-out (depreciated) pieces of capital equipment. Capital equipment that is wearing out will be proportional to the stock of capital in existence, and from the discussion that we had above concerning the rental rate of capital, the depreciation rate, denoted there as δ, implies that the rate at which capital stock is being worn out is equal to δK. The rate at which the capital stock is changing is equal to ΔK. Therefore, investment, i, is the sum of these two things; that is,

$$i = \delta K + \Delta K \tag{10.5}$$

There are some very elaborate theories that explain the speed with which firms will seek to add to their capital stock. For our purposes, it seems sufficient to remark that if firms added to their capital stock too quickly, they would incur a variety of high costs in the form of organizational problems and planning bottlenecks. If, on the other hand, they added to their capital stock too slowly, then they would have to put up with having too little equipment for too long. There would seem to be some optimum rate at which to add to the capital stock, which might be thought of as depending on the extent to which the capital stock currently in place falls short of (or exceeds) the desired capital stock.

We know what the preferred capital stock is. It is shown in Figure 10.1 and depends on the real rate of interest. If the change in the capital stock proceeds at some rate that depends on the gap between this preferred capital stock and the actual capital stock, then the rate of investment will depend on two things: first, the rate of interest, since this determines the desired capital stock; and second, the existing capital stock, since this affects how much capital shortage or surplus there is. How do these two variables, the real rate of interest and the stock of capital, affect the investment rate? A moment's reflection will reveal, other things being constant, that they each have a negative effect on investment. We have already seen that the higher the real rate of interest, the smaller will be the desired capital stock. The bigger the actual capital stock, the smaller, other things being equal, will be the gap between the desired and the actual capital stock that firms seek to close. Both of these forces, then, would work to reduce the rate of investment.

To summarize, then, the rate of investment will depend on the real rate of interest and the capital stock. The higher is either of those two variables, the lower will be the rate of investment.

There is one final simplification that will be useful to introduce into the analysis, and this concerns the approximation arising from the fact that investment is a small number relative to the capital stock, so that even though positive investment is being undertaken at all times, the capital stock is a very slowly changing variable and may be regarded as approximately constant. This being so, it is possible to simplify the theory of investment still further by ignoring, at least for short-run purposes, the effect of the capital stock on the rate of investment. Thus, the theory of investment used in short-run macroeconomic models is one that supposes that investment depends only on the real rate of interest.

In developing the proposition that investment depends only on the real rate of interest, a great deal has been set aside. Indeed, it would not be an exaggeration to say that the major sources of fluctuation in investment are ignored by focussing exclusively on the real rate of interest as a determinant of investment. There are obviously many things other than the real rate of interest that will influence the pace of investment. Such things as taxes; changes in technology that make some types of equipment outmoded and stimulate massive demand for new, previously unknown types of capital; changes in population (both in terms of its size, age, and sex distribution); and changes in entrepreneurs' perceptions of profit opportunities as well, as the slowly changing capital stock itself, are all examples of things that undoubtedly exert a major influence upon investment.

Furthermore, because investment is the *flow* by means of which the *stock* of capital is changed, anything that changes the desired stock of capital will have a magnified effect on the flow of investment. When the demand for capital (a stock demand) rises, the flow of investment will jump. When the stock of capital reaches its desired level, the pace of investment will slacken off to a rate consistent with replacing worn-out capital.

The bathtub analogy that we have used before illustrates this pheno-menon well. The desire to soak in a tub leads to a rise in the demand for a *stock* of water. This results in opening the tap to maximum pressure — a *flow* — for as long as necessary to achieve the desired water level. Then the tap is closed and the flow stops — although the stock remains. Thus, a flow rises from zero to its maximum rate and back to zero very quickly. The flow displays large fluctuations. It is exactly the same with the variables that lead to changes in the desired capital stock. These variables result in large fluctuations in investment. This, indeed, is the reason why the cycles in durables have greater amplitude than in non-durables.

The key to understanding the theory of investment as used in macro-economic analysis is the realization that all the factors that influence investment, other than the real rate of interest may, as a reasonable approximation, be taken to be independent of all the other variables that a macroeconomic model determines. This means that when such factors change, a shift occurs in the investment demand curve, and this sets up repercussions for income, prices, interest rates, and other macroeconomic variables. It is assumed, however, that there are no significant feedbacks onto the rate of investment itself other than those that go through the real rate of interest.

E. Investment Demand Function

The entire discussion in this chapter can now be summarized very compactly. The investment demand function implied by the previous discussion may be written as a simple equation, which is

$$i = i_0 - hr \qquad i_0, h > 0 \tag{10.6}$$

This equation says that the level of investment will be equal to some amount that is independent of all the other variables in our macro-economic model, i_0, and, over and above that, will vary inversely with the real rate of interest. The way that the equation is specified makes the relationship linear. A one percentage point rise in the real rate of interest would produce an h-million pound drop in the rate of investment. The same relationship as appears in Equation (10.6) is shown in Figure 10.2. You should think of the volatility of investment as being reflected in shifts in the investment function as shown in Figure 10.2, or equivalently, in exogenous changes in the intercept of the investment function, i_0. These changes would arise from the many factors, such as changes in taxes, technology, population size and composition, entrepreneur's perceptions of profit opportunities, and the (slowly evolving) capital stock itself.[3]

Figure 10.2
The investment
function

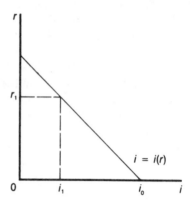

Investment (i) will be undertaken to replace existing capital and to close the gap between the desired and actual capital stock. Since the desired capital stock depends inversely on the real rate of interest (r), and since the actual capital stock changes only slowly over time, investment (i) is itself a function, [$i(r)$], of the real rate of interest (r). Many other factors, summarized in the intercept i_0, influence investment. None of the variables that influence the position of the investment demand function, i_0, is determined in the macroeconomic model. Rather, shifts in the investment demand function may be important exogenous sources of fluctuation in aggregate demand. At the real rate of interest r_1 investment demand is i_1

F. The UK Investment Demand Function

Let us now turn from the theory of investment to an examination of the facts about investment in the UK. Does UK investment vary inversely with the real rate of interest as predicted by the theory of investment? Is investment volatile? That is, are there massive fluctuations in invest-

3   As in the case of the consumption function, the theory of investment presented here is highly condensed and selective. A superb treatment of the subject at a more advanced level, however, may be found in Frank Brechling, *Investment and Employment Decisions* (Manchester: Manchester University Press, 1975). Another even more up-to-date but technically yet more demanding study is that by Stephen J. Nickell, *The Investment Decisions of Firms* (James Nisbet and Cambridge University Press, 1978). A good, up-to-date, though again fairly demanding survey is Andrew B. Abel 'Empirical Investment Equations: An Integrative Framework', in Karl Brunner and Allan H. Melzer (eds), *On the State of Macro-Economics*, Carnegie-Rochester Conference Series, Vol. 12 (Spring 1980), pp.39–92. Empirical studies of investment behaviour in the UK can be found in the reports of the content of the large-scale econometric models of the National Institute of Economic and Social Research, the London Business School, the Treasury, and the University of Southampton, in G.A. Renton (ed.), *Modelling the Economy* (London: Heinemann, 1975) Part I. A more straightforward though somewhat dated study is that by A.R. Nobay, 'Forecasting Manufacturing Investment — Some Preliminary Results', *National Institute Economic Review*, No. 52 (1970) pp.58–66.

ment that are independent of movements in the rate of interest? Another way of asking this same question is, Does the intercept in the investment equation, i_0 fluctuate as the theory of investment would predict?

To answer these questions we need to examine the facts about investment and about the real rate of interest. We know, from our study of the UK macroeconomic history in Chapter 2, that interest rates fluctuate and that trends in interest rates are quite similar to trends in inflation. The timing of the ups and downs in interest rates is not quite the same, however, as the timing of the ups and downs in inflation. Since the real rate of interest is the difference between the market rate of interest and the expected rate of inflation we might expect that the real rate of interest would fluctuate fairly markedly but that it would not display any major trends.

We also know, from our study of the UK macroeconomic history, that aggregate income has been dominated by its trend growth path. The same is true of investment. That is, although investment fluctuates as a fraction of gross domestic product it is dominated by an upward trend over the long term.

If we wish to study the relationship between investment and the real rate of interest we are, inevitably, looking at the relationship between a variable that is dominated by its upward trend (investment) and one that fluctuates and does not show any major trend (the real rate of interest). In order to take the trend out of investment, it is convenient to look not at the level of investment but at the fraction of GDP represented by investment; that is the ratio i/y.

One further preliminary matter has to be mentioned. The real rate of interest is the difference between the market rate of interest and the *expected* rate of inflation. We know what the market rate of interest is. It is a number that is recorded on a regular basis and we have shown some of its history in Chapter 2. We know what the actual rate of inflation is. We have also examined its behaviour in Chapter 2. We do not, however, know what the *expected* rate of inflation is. When we get to Chapter 21 we shall have a great deal to say about expectations, how they are formed, and how they fluctuate. For present purposes we are going to suppose that we can measure the expected rate of inflation by making it equal to the actual rate of inflation. In other words, to calculate the real rate of interest we are going to calculate what is sometimes called the *ex post* real rate of interest − the difference between the market rate of interest and the actual rate of inflation.

Figure 10.3 provides a summary statement of the facts about the relationship between the real rate of interest (*ex post*) and the fraction of GDP invested (i/y). Each date (point) in that figure represents the combination of the real rate of interest and real investment (as a fraction of GDP) in that year.

The first thing that immediately becomes apparent from the data shown in Figure 10.3 is that both the real rate of interest and the fraction of GDP

Figure 10.3
UK investment
demand function

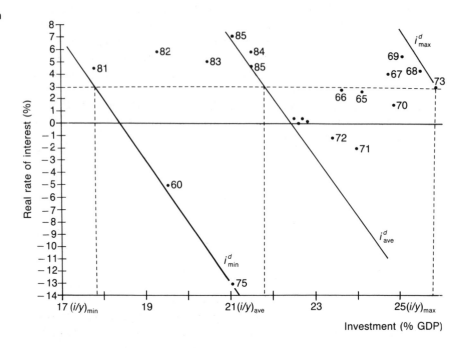

The vertical axis shows the *ex post* real rate of interest. The horizontal axis shows investment as a percentage of GDP. Evidently there are large fluctuations in the fraction of GDP
invested and in the real rate of interest. The data may be interpreted (as just one possibility) as being generated by an investment demand curve that has a slope of $(-1/5)$ and
that fluctuates between i^d_{max} and i^d_{min}.
Source: United Kingdom National Accounts, (HMSO, 1987).

invested vary enormously. Real rates of interest range from a high of
almost 8 per cent to a low of almost −14 per cent. Investment fluctuates
from almost 26 per cent of GDP down to about 17 per cent. Real rates
of interest between 0 and 5 per cent are the most common and investment
rates in the range 21 to 25 per cent are the most common.

In addition to the points in Figure 10.3, you will observe three
downward-sloping lines. The particular slope of those lines has no
scientific status. They are arbitrarily determined such that the parameter
h in Equation (10.6) is equal to one fifth. In other words, the lines represent a particular example of an investment demand function in which
a 5 per cent point drop in the real rate of interest produces a rise in
investment of 1 per cent of GDP. It is certainly possible to imagine that
these data were generated by such an equation. The intercept of the

equation, i_0, will fluctuate between a low level as shown in the case of the curve labelled i^d_{min} and a high level as shown in the case of the curve labelled i^d_{max}. On the average investment demand is as indicated by the line labelled i^d_{ave}. Thus, at a real rate of interest of 3 per cent marked $\bar{r}$ investment is almost 22 per cent of GDP. At that interest rate however, investment fluctuates between just below 18 per cent of GDP and almost 6 per cent of GDP (marked $(i/y)_{min}$, and $(i/y)_{max}$).

It is evident from this review of the UK data on investment that the data may be interpreted using the simple theory of investment developed earlier in this chapter.

Summary

A. Distinction Between Investment and Capital Stock

Investment demand is the demand for capital goods for use in production or consumption-yielding activities. It represents additions to the stock of capital or replacement of depreciated capital. Thus investment is the *flow* that augments or maintains the *stock* of capital.

B. Demand for Capital

The demand for capital is determined by cost-minimizing or profit-maximizing considerations. Capital will be demanded up to the point at which its marginal product equals its rental rate.

C. Rental Rate of Capital

Where capital equipment is explicitly rented, as is often the case with houses, and occasionally with cars, TV sets, and industrial equipment, the rental rate of capital is simply the rate per hour that has to be paid for the use of a particular type of equipment. Most capital is not rented explicitly, but is owned by the individual or firm that uses it. In such a case, the rental rate on capital is *implicit*. The individual implicitly rents the equipment from him/herself. That implicit rental rate will be equal to the price of capital multiplied by the sum of the rate of depreciation plus the market rate of interest (nominal rate of interest) minus the rate of appreciation of the asset in question.

D. Investment and the Demand for Capital

The rate of investment will be determined by the size of the capital stock relative to the profit-maximizing capital stock. The bigger the stock of capital relative to the desired stock, the slower will be the rate of investment. Since the capital stock is a slowly changing variable, as an approximation, the rate of investment may be presumed to depend only upon the rental rate of capital. The rental rate will in turn depend primarily upon the real rate of interest. Thus, the simple macroeconomic theory of investment is that it depends on the real rate of interest. A higher real rate of interest will induce a lower rate of investment. This theory leaves out more than it includes. What is left out, however, may be presumed to be independent of (exogenous with respect to) the other variables that macroeconomics seeks to understand. It is fluctuations in those other variables, however, that are responsible for some of the major swings in investment activity.

E. Investment Demand Function

The investment demand function can be written in a simple equation

$$i = i_0 - hr$$

This equation states that as the real rate of interest, r, rises, the level of investment, i, falls. The constant, h, is the degree of responsiveness of investment to interest rate changes. Volatility of investment is reflected in changes in i_0 that shift the investment demand function.

F. The UK Investment Demand Function

The UK data on investment and real interest rates can be readily interpreted using the theory of investment demand developed in this chapter. Figure 10.3 shows the relationship between investment (as a fraction of GDP) and the real rate of interest (*ex post*). The data may be interpreted by imagining large swings in an investment demand function that has a slope of $-(1/5)$.

Review Questions

1. What is the difference between investment and the capital stock?
2. What is the difference between a change in investment and a change in the capital stock?
3. How do firms decide on the size of the desired capital stock?

4. What is the rental rate of capital? How does it relate to the price of capital goods?

5. A car that you are thinking of buying costs £3000 and will, after one year, have a resale value of £2500. The rate of interest on the bank loan that you would take if you did buy the car is 15 per cent. A friend who already owns an identical car offers to lease you that car for one year for £600 (you buy the petrol and pay for maintenance). Should you accept the offer from your friend or should you buy the car? What is the rental rate that your friend is asking? What is the implicit rental rate if you buy?

6. What determines the rate of investment?

7. What is the investment demand function? What is being held constant, and what is varying as we move along the investment demand function?

8. What causes shifts in the investment demand function?

9. Use the *United Kingdom National Accounts* (*Blue Book*), HMSO, London and obtain data on investment expenditure over the last 10 years. (Refer back to Chapter 3 if you are not sure how to do this.) Draw a time-series graph of investment. Describe the main movements. What relationship, if any, can you find between investment and the difference between the long-term rate of interest and the actual rate of inflation? (Use the Appendix to Chapter 2 for data on interest rates and inflation rates.) Is the difference between the long-term rate of interest and the rate of inflation the real rate of interest?

11

The *IS* Curve

There are various stages in the process of learning economics that involve mastering certain steps of analysis that seem, at the time, completely pointless. It is as if analysis is being mastered for its own sake, rather than to achieve some objective in terms of having greater insights or better understanding of how the economy works. It is not until a later stage in the learning process that the point of a particular piece of analysis becomes fully apparent. You are about to embark on such a piece of analysis in this chapter. The objective toward which you are working is to have an understanding of what determines aggregate demand and how aggregate demand is affected by such things as government expenditure, taxes, and the money supply.

Achieving a level of expertise and understanding that is worthwhile involves mastering a body of analysis that, in its entirety, is hard to grasp the first time through (and even the second or third time for some of us). It is easier to grasp and understand if it is broken down into a series of individual easy-to-manage steps. This makes the process of comprehension and understanding easier. At the same time, it does give rise to the problem that we describe above; namely, that while a series of small intermediate steps are being taken, the final objective, the point to where it is all leading, may be lost from sight.

Try to keep in mind where you are going. You are going to end up, by the time you get to Chapter 14, with a clear understanding of the theory of aggregate demand. You are going to see how the various bits and pieces, one of which is now going to be developed in this chapter, all fit together.

The part of the aggregate demand story that you are going to master in this chapter involves a relationship called the *IS* curve. *I* stands for investment and S for savings. By the time you have completed this chapter you will be able to:

(a) **Define the *IS* curve.**
(b) **Derive the *IS* curve.**
(c) **Explain what determines the slope of the *IS* curve.**
(d) **Explain what makes the *IS* curve shift and by how much.**

A. Definition of the *IS* Curve

The *IS* curve is a relationship between the level of output and the real rate of interest. It is the relationship that links the level of income and the real rate of interest such that investment demand plus government demand equals savings plus taxes.[1] Equivalently, it is the relationship between the level of real income and the real rate of interest that ensures that aggregate demand (consumption demand plus investment demand plus government demand) is equal to the level of real income.

It might be helpful to put this slightly differently and in a more long-winded way. Since consumption depends on income, different levels of income will bring forth different levels of consumption. When consumption is added to investment and government spending, the result is a particular level of total demand for output (real income). The *IS* curve traces the relationship between the level of output (real income) and the real rate of interest when the level of aggregate demand is equal to the level of real income that generates that level of aggregate demand.

The *IS* curve is not a description of the desires or decisions of any single agent or group of agents. Rather, it is the same kind of relationship as the aggregate demand curve that you have already met. It is an equilibrium locus. It traces the locus of points that give an equality between the aggregate demand for goods and services and the level of output of goods and services. Indeed, you can think of the *IS* curve as a kind of aggregate demand curve. The aggregate demand curve as we defined it in Chapter 8 is a relationship between the total demand for goods and services and the price level. That meaning of the term aggregate demand curve is a useful one, and we shall reserve it for something other than the *IS* curve. Nevertheless, the *IS* curve tells us what the total demand for goods and services is as we vary, not the price level, but the real rate of interest.

It is important not to interpret the *IS* curve as implying anything about

---

1 You may think that the *IS* curve is peculiarly named since it is a curve that describes the equality of investment (I) plus government spending (G), and savings (S) plus taxes (T). Aside from *IGST* being a clumsy name, when the analysis presented here was first invented by Sir John Hicks in 1936, he illustrated the analysis for an economy in which government spending and taxes were assumed to be zero; hence the name *IS*.

causality. The *IS* curve emphatically does not say that different levels of aggregate demand are caused by different levels of the real rate of interest. All that it is telling us is that the real rate of interest and the level of real income cannot be just any values that they like. They must be restricted to lie on the *IS* curve. The two variables will be determined simultaneously (by a procedure that we will get to in Chapter 14).

What you are going to be looking at next, then, is the way in which the *IS* curve is derived.

B. Derivation of the *IS* Curve

The easiest way to learn how to derive the *IS* curve is to begin by refreshing your memory about the components of aggregate demand for goods and services and the ways in which aggregate income may be allocated by households. Recall that aggregate income may be allocated in three ways. It may be spent on consumption, saved, or paid in taxes; that is,

$$y = c + s + t \tag{11.1}$$

(Recall that c is consumption demand, s is savings, t is taxes, and y is real income (output).) Also recall that aggregate demand is decomposed into three components — consumption demand, investment demand, and government demand for goods and services. That is,

$$y^d = c + i + g \tag{11.2}$$

You subtract c from both sides of Equation (11.1) to obtain

$$y - c = s + t \tag{11.3}$$

This equation simply says that income minus consumption demand must be equal to savings-plus-taxes. It does not say anything about behaviour, of course. It is simply a statement about the necessary relationship between income and expenditure. It is nothing other than the household sector's budget constraint.

Next, subtract c from both sides of Equation (11.2) to obtain

$$y^d - c = i + g \tag{11.4}$$

What this equation says is that the difference between aggregate demand and consumption demand is equal to investment-plus-government spending. Equation (11.1) says exactly the same thing as Equation (11.3), and Equation (11.2) says the same thing as Equation (11.4). They are simply different ways of looking at the same thing.

The *IS* curve, the derivation of which you are now embarking upon, traces the relationship between the level of aggregate demand and the real rate of interest when the level of aggregate demand is equal to the level of real income. In other words, the *IS* curve has to be derived satisfying the condition

$$y = y^d \tag{11.5}$$

This says that points on the *IS* curve are points such that aggregate demand is equal to aggregate real income (output).

You will notice, if you replace y with y^d in Equation (11.3), that the left-hand side of Equation (11.3) is exactly the same as the left-hand side of Equation (11.4). It follows, therefore, that the right-hand side of Equation (11.3) must be equal to the right-hand side of Equation (11.4) when we are on the *IS* curve. That is,

$$s + t = i + g \tag{11.6}$$

Equation (11.6) says that planned savings-plus-taxes must equal investment-plus-government spending at all points on the *IS* curve. It is Equation (11.6) that gives the name to the *IS* curve. If there was no government, so that t and g were equal to zero, it would simply say that to be on the *IS* curve, savings plans must equal investment demand. With government spending and taxes not being zero, these have to be added to private savings and investment to obtain the equivalent flow equilibrium condition in the goods market that underlies the *IS* curve.

With this background it is now possible to proceed to derive the *IS* curve. It will be helpful to proceed in easy stages, however, and first to examine the right-hand side of Equation (11.6) — investment-plus-government spending. Figure 11.1 illustrates this aspect of the demand for goods. The real interest rate is measured on the vertical axis, and investment is measured on the horizontal axis. The thin curve labelled $i = i_0 - hr$ is the investment demand function, the derivation of which was discussed in Chapter 10. It shows that the level of investment demand increases as the real rate of interest falls. For example, at the interest rate

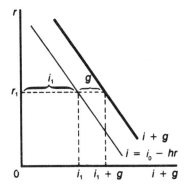

Figure 11.1
Investment-plus-government spending

Investment (the thin line) varies inversely with the real rate of interest. Government spending is fixed independently of the rate of interest. Investment-plus-government spending (the thick line) has the same slope as the investment line but is shifted to the right by the amount of government spending (g). For example, at the real interest rate r_1, investment is i_1 and investment-plus-government spending is $i_1 + g$.

r_1, the level of investment demand will be i_1. At higher interest rates, the level of investment demand will be less than i_1.

The thicker line in the figure, which is drawn parallel to the investment demand curve, is the level of investment demand plus the level of government demand for goods and services. You will recall that the level of government demand is assumed to be exogenous. It is determined independently of the level of the interest rate or of any other of the variables in the model. The horizontal distance between the investment demand curve and the curve labelled $i + g$ is the fixed level of government expenditure. It is illustrated by the horizontal line g at the interest rate r_1. You can see, however, that the distance between i and $i + g$ is the same at all rates of interest. The thick line $i + g$ represents the total amount of investment demand and the total demand for goods and services by the government added together — investment-plus-government spending. We will return to this diagram later.

Next, consider the other side of Equation (11.6), savings-plus-taxes. This is slightly trickier than the previous analysis. The reason that it is trickier is that savings depend on *disposable* income. Disposable income, in turn, depends in part on taxes, so taxes have a double influence on the volume of savings-plus-taxes. That is, higher taxes mean lower savings, but higher taxes also mean bigger savings-*plus*-taxes all taken together. You need to be careful, therefore, in sorting out the relationships involved here. Figure 11.2 illustrates what goes on. Looking at Figure 11.2, first focus

**Figure 11.2
Savings-plus-taxes**

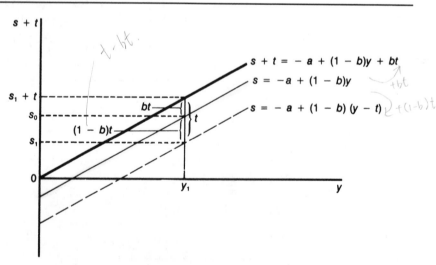

In the absence of taxes, the savings function would be s, the centre thin line. With taxes at level t, the savings function is the lower dashed line. It is displaced downwards by the propensity to save $(1 - b)$ times taxes. Taxes are treated as constant. The savings-plus-taxes function therefore is displaced upwards above the savings function by the amount of taxes and is shown as the thick line. If taxes rise, the savings-plus-taxes line rises by the marginal propensity to consume (b) times the rise in taxes.

on the middle line. This line shows the level of savings that would be forthcoming at each level of income if taxes were equal to zero. It is simply describing the equation $s = -a + (1 - b)y$. This savings relation is implied by the consumption function that was discussed in Chapter 9. Now, focus on the income level y_1 and notice that if taxes were indeed zero, savings would be equal to s_0 at the income level y_1.

Now, drop the assumption that taxes are zero and allow taxes to be some positive number, t. You will recall, from the discussion in Chapter 9, that with taxes at level t, the savings function shifts downwards by an amount equal to $(1 - b)$ times the level of taxes. When taxes go up, both consumption and savings must fall such that the sum of their shifts equals the tax rise. Fraction b of the taxes is paid for by reducing consumption, and fraction $1 - b$ is paid for by reducing savings. The bottom line in Figure 11.2 illustrates the savings function, allowing for taxes at level t. With taxes at level t and income at y_1, savings will be equal to s_1. The vertical distance between the line labelled $s = -a + (1 - b)y$ and the line $s = -a + (1 - b)(y - t)$ is equal to $(1 - b)t$.

Now, according to Equation (11.6), it is savings-plus-taxes that must be equal to investment-plus-government spending, and it is therefore the total of savings-plus-taxes that we are interested in. The top line of Figure 11.2 is a graph of savings-plus-taxes. It is nothing other than the level of taxes, t, added (vertically) to the lowest of the three lines in the diagram. This is illustrated at the income level y_1 by the distance indicated by t.

You are now in a position to understand the nature of the relationship between savings-plus-taxes and income. This relationship is similar to the relationship between savings and income. If you start from the curve describing the relationship between savings and income when taxes are zero, the savings-plus-taxes curve is equal to that original savings curve, plus taxes times the marginal propensity to consume. What this equation says is that a rise in taxes does not raise savings-plus-taxes one-for-one. A rise in taxes raises savings-plus-taxes by less than the rise in taxes because there is going to be a drop in savings in order to meet part of the tax payments.

You are now in a position to derive the *IS* curve graphically. Figure 11.3 is the source of the derivation. It looks much more formidable than it is, so try not to be put off by your first glance at that figure. Just follow the text carefully and slowly as it leads you through what, as you will soon see, is a straightforward derivation.

Frame (a) is nothing other than Figure 11.1 — investment-plus-government spending. The interest rate r_1, the investment level i_1, and the government spending level g shown in that frame are the same as the values shown in Figure 11.1. Frame (c) is exactly the same as Figure 11.2 — savings-plus-taxes. Again, the income level y_1, the savings level s_1, and the tax level t are the same in frame (c) as those shown and already discussed in Figure 11.2. The new frames of Figure 11.3 are frames (b) and (d). Frame (b) of the figure is just a graphical representation of the equilibrium condition that defines the IS curve. It is a 45° line. You will readily verify that measuring investment-plus-government spending on the horizontal axis in the same units as savings-plus-taxes are measured on the vertical axis implies that at each point on that 45° line, savings-plus-taxes are equal to investment-plus-government spending.

You can think of the IS curve now as being a relationship between the level of real income and the real rate of interest such that the economy is located on each of the three curves depicted in frames (a), (b), and (c). One point on the IS curve is the point A depicted in frame (d). Notice that the axes of frame (d) measure the real rate of interest and real income. Opposite this real interest rate axis, in frame (a), the real interest rate is also measured. Transferring the real interest rate r_1 across from frame (a) to frame (d) takes us horizontally across to point A. You will also notice that the level of real income on the horizontal axis of frame (d) is the same as the horizontal axis of frame (c) immediately above it. Transferring the income level y_1 down from frame (c) to frame (d), we shall reach the same point A. Notice that the level of savings-plus-taxes generated by income level y_1 is exactly equal to the level of investment-plus-government spending generated by the interest rate r_1. You can verify this by tracking up vertically from frame (a) to frame (b) and across horizontally from frame (c) to frame (b). Point A, then, is a point on the IS curve.

Let us complete the derivation of the IS curve in a slightly less cluttered-up diagram but one that is in every respect identical to Figure 11.3 except that it has some of the lines removed for clarity. Figure 11.4 reproduces the curves $i + g$ and $s + t$ from Figure 11.3. First of all, familiarize yourself with Figure 11.4 and satisfy yourself it is identical to Figure 11.3 except that some lines have been left off to give the diagram a fresher and clearer appearance.

Now choose a higher interest rate than r_1, such as r_2. Notice that at r_2, the level of investment-plus-government spending is $i_2 + g$, which is less than $i_1 + g$. Then track up from frame (a) to frame (b) and record the level of investment-plus-government spending $i_2 + g$ on the horizontal axis of frame (b). Notice that if investment-plus-government spending is equal to savings-plus-taxes (if we are going to be at a point on the IS curve), the level of savings-plus-taxes must equal $s_2 + t$ as shown on the vertical axis of frame (b). Now transfer that amount of savings-plus-taxes horizontally across to frame (c). You may now read off from frame (c) the level of real income that is necessary to ensure that the volume of savings-plus-taxes equals $s_2 + t$. That level of income is given by y_2. Now transfer the income level y_2 down to the horizontal axis of frame (d) and transfer the interest rate level r_2 horizontally across from frame (a) to frame (d). Where these two lines join, labelled B, is another point on the IS curve. Joining together points A and B with other intermediate points traces out the IS curve.

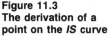

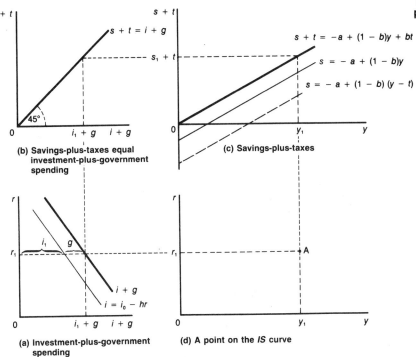

Figure 11.3
The derivation of a
point on the IS curve

The *IS* curve traces the relationship between the real rate of interest and the level of real income at which investment-plus-government spending equals savings-plus-taxes. Point A is a point on the *IS* curve. At point A, real income is y_1 [horizontal axis of frames (d) and (c)], so that savings-plus-taxes are $s_1 + t$. At A, the interest rate is r_1 [vertical axis of frames (d) and (a)], so that investment-plus-government spending is $i_1 + g$. Looking at frame (b), you see that $s_1 + t$ equals $i_1 + g$, so that point A satisfies the definition of the *IS* curve.

You will probably find it helpful to derive an IS curve for yourself by setting up the diagrams shown as frames (a), (b) and (c) and then deriving explicitly points on the IS curve for a series of interest rates such as r_1, r_2 and other intermediate rates. Be sure that you are thoroughly conversant with the way in which the IS curve is derived before moving on to the next two sections of this chapter.

C. Determinants of the *IS* Curve Slope

You already know that the IS curve slopes downwards. You can see this simply from frame (d) of Figure 11.4 in which you have derived an IS

Figure 11.4
The derivation of the
***IS* curve**

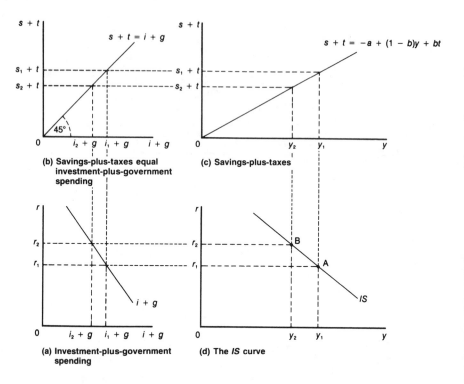

(b) Savings-plus-taxes equal investment-plus-government spending

(c) Savings-plus-taxes

(a) Investment-plus-government spending

(d) The *IS* curve

This figure is exactly like Figure 11.3 except that in frames (a) and (c), only the $i + g$ and $s + t$ curves are plotted. Point A in this figure is the same as point A in Figure 11.3. Point B [in frame (d)] is equivalent to point A but relates to the income level y_2 and the interest rate r_2. At point B the income level is y_2 and savings-plus-taxes are $s_2 + t$. The interest rate at point B is r_2, so that investment-plus-government spending is $i_2 + g$. By looking at frame (b), you can see that $i_2 + g$ equals $s_2 + t$, so that B is also a point on an *IS* curve. Joining up A and B and extending the line beyond those points traces out the *IS* curve.

curve. You can also see from inspecting Figure 11.4 and comparing frame (d) with frame (a) that the *IS* curve is flatter than the slope of the investment demand curve. What does this mean? It means that as the interest rate falls from, say, r_2 to r_1, the investment rise from i_2 to i_1 is less than the amount by which income rises from y_2 to y_1. Call the change in investment Δi and call the change in income Δy. What is the relationship between the change in income and the change in investment when the interest rate is (hypothetically) allowed to drop from r_2 to r_1? Figure 11.5 illustrates this relationship.

Figure 11.5
The slope of the *IS* curve

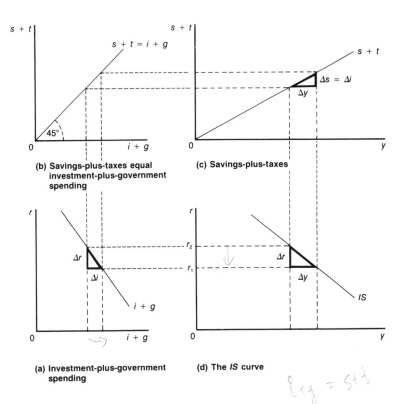

(b) Savings-plus-taxes equal investment-plus-government spending

(c) Savings-plus-taxes

(a) Investment-plus-government spending

(d) The *IS* curve

$i + g = s + t$

The *IS* curve slopes downwards. The lower the real rate of interest, the higher is the level of investment, and since investment-plus-government spending must equal savings-plus-taxes, the higher too is the level of savings. Since savings depend on income, higher savings will require higher income levels. Hence, to be on the *IS* curve, the lower rate of interest has to be associated with a higher level of income. For a given drop in the rate of interest, the rise in income is equal to the rise in investment divided by the marginal propensity to save or, $\Delta i/(1 - b)$.

You can figure this out by using a small amount of geometry. A thickened triangle is shown in frame (c). What are the properties of that triangle? Its base clearly has length Δy, and its height has length Δi. You also know that the hypotenuse of that triangle has a slope equal to $1 - b$, the marginal propensity to save or, equivalently, one minus the marginal propensity to consume. Now recall your geometry. The proposition that you need is the one that goes 'slope equals rise over run'. The 'slope' in this case is $1 - b$, the 'rise' is Δi, and the 'run' is Δy. Translating 'slope equals rise over run' into the numbers that represent the 'slope', 'rise', and 'run' of the triangle in frame (c), we have:

$$\text{'slope'} = 1 - b$$
$$\text{'rise'} = \Delta i$$
$$\text{'run'} = \Delta y$$

so that

$$1 - b = \frac{\Delta i}{\Delta y}$$

Now multiply both sides of this equation by the change in income (Δy) to give

$$\Delta y(1 - b) = \Delta i$$

Then divide both sides of the equation by the marginal propensity to save, $(1 - b)$, to give

$$\Delta y = \frac{1}{1 - b}(\Delta i)$$

This is the famous Keynesian multiplier that you have already met in Chapter 9. It says that the change in income will be related to the change in investment by the amount $1/(1 - b)$. Clearly, since b is a fraction, $1 - b$ is also a fraction, and $1/(1 - b)$ is a number bigger than one, a multiple giving rise to the name *multiplier*.

You have now discovered that the slope of the *IS* curve is negative and that it is flatter than the slope of the investment demand curve. The slope of the investment demand curve is $-1/h$ (the ratio of the change in the interest rate to a one percentage change in investment). The slope of the *IS* curve is equal to the slope of the investment demand curve multiplied by the marginal propensity to save, or one minus the marginal propensity to consume.

D. Shifts in the *IS* Curve

The *IS* curve will shift if government spending changes, if taxes change, and if autonomous expenditure, i_0 or a, changes. Notice that this implies that the *IS* curve will shift due to a change in any of its determinants that is not itself induced by a change in either real income or the rate of interest. We shall focus only on changes in government spending and taxes. Changes in i_0 and a have identical effects on the *IS* curve to changes in government spending, as you will be readily able to verify for yourself once you are familiar with the analysis.

First, let us look at the effects of a change in government spending.

Figure 11.6 will illustrate the analysis. The thickened curves simply reproduce the curves already introduced here and used in Figures 11.4 and 11.5. Now suppose that there is a rise in government spending by an amount that will be called Δg. What does that do to this diagram? The answer is shown in frame (a). The curve labelled $i + g$, which shows investment-plus-government spending, shifts to the right by an amount equal to the rise in government spending. This is illustrated by the thinner line in frame (a) that is displaced horizontally to the right from the original $i + g$ line by an amount indicated as Δg.

Holding taxes constant for the moment, there are no changes to be recorded in frame (c). All that remains is to work out the implications of the shift in the curve $i + g$ for the IS curve. You can do that by deriving a new IS curve, using the new $i + g + \Delta g$ line in frame (a). Applying the method that you have learned in the previous section on derivation

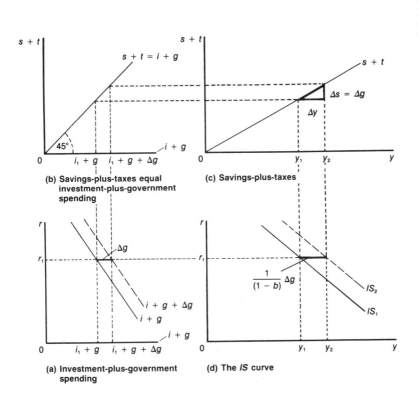

**Figure 11.6
A change in govern-
ment spending shifts
the IS curve**

A rise in government spending of Δg shifts the investment-plus-government spending function to the right by the amount Δg. As a result the IS curve shifts to the right by an amount equal to $\Delta g/(1 - b)$.

of the *IS* curve, you will discover that the new *IS* curve is the one labelled IS_2 in frame (d). (If you are not sure how to derive the *IS* curve, you should go back to that section and reinforce your understanding of how to derive the *IS* curve.)

What is the effect on the *IS* curve of the rise in Δg? Suppose that g rises by an amount that will be called Δg. You can see by inspecting Figure 11.6 what happens to the *IS* curve. It shifts to the right. Further, it shifts to the right by more than the rise in government spending (Δg). You can see this by visual inspection of frames (a) and (d).

By how much more to the right has the *IS* curve shifted than the rise in government spending? The answer to this question turns out to be identical to the answer that you have already derived concerning the relationship between the slope of the $i + g$ curve and the slope of the *IS* curve. You can see this directly because of a visual trick that we have used in selecting the amount by which to raise government spending, Δg. Notice that we chose the rise in government spending, Δg, to be an amount such that when the interest rate is r_2 with the new higher level of government spending, the total level of investment-plus-government spending is identical to what had been previously at the interest rate r_1. You have already established that a fall in the rate of interest from r_2 to r_1 (a movement along the *IS* curve) raises income by $1/(1 - b)$ times the induced rise in investment. In Figure 11.5, this rise in income is labelled Δy [frame (d)]. In Figure 11.6, you can see this same amount shown as $y_2 - y_1$ (moving along the curve IS_2). You can see by further inspecting Figure 11.6 that the rise in income induced by a fall in the rate of interest from r_2 to r_1 along IS_2 is exactly the same as the rise in income, at the constant interest rate r_1, induced by a rise in government expenditure of Δg. Thus, you have established that the rise in income at a given rate of interest — the shift in the *IS* curve — induced by a rise in g is the rise in g multiplied by $1/(1 - b)$.

Now let us turn to an analysis of the effects of a rise in taxes on the *IS* curve. This is slightly more complicated, and the extra complexity arises from the fact that the savings-plus-taxes schedule is a slightly more tricky relationship than the investment-plus-government spending schedule. Figure 11.7 illustrates the analysis. Let us again familiarize ourselves with the set-up by noting that the thick curves in Figure 11.7 are identical to those used in Figure 11.4. The *IS* curve labelled IS_1 is the *IS* curve that would be derived under the conditions prevailing in Figure 11.4.

We now want to ask what happens to the *IS* curve if taxes rise by an amount that will be called Δt. The impact effect of the rise in taxes is to be seen in frame (c). You know that if taxes rise, the savings-plus-taxes schedule shifts up but not by the full amount of the tax rise. This arises because savings themselves fall somewhat. If taxes rise by Δt, the savings-plus-taxes schedule moves to become the schedule labelled $s' + t + \Delta t$.

Figure 11.7
A change in taxes
shifts the *IS* curve

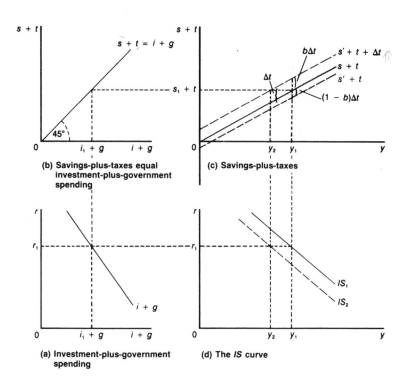

A rise in taxes of Δt raises the savings-plus-taxes curve by $b\Delta t$ and shifts the *IS* curve to the *left*.

You should satisfy yourself that this new schedule is higher than the original schedule by an amount equal to $b\Delta t$. Savings will have dropped to s', which is $(1 - b)\Delta t$ lower than originally. The total rise in taxes is the distance between the top line and the bottom line in frame (c).

Now let us figure out what this change in taxes has done to the *IS* curve. Derive a new *IS* curve, using exactly the same technique as before but using the curve labelled $s' + t + \Delta t$, the new savings-plus-taxes curve in frame (c). This *IS* curve, you will discover, is the one labelled IS_2 in frame (d).

How does this *IS* curve compare with the curve IS_1? First, you will notice that a rise in taxes leads to a shift in the *IS* curve but in the opposite direction to the shift resulting from an increase in government spending. By how much does the *IS* curve shift leftwards when the level of taxes is increased? You can answer this question with another piece of high-school geometry illustrated in Figure 11.8.

Figure 11.8
The size of the shift
in the IS curve
resulting from a
change in taxes

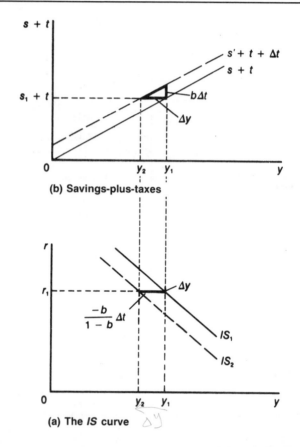

(b) Savings-plus-taxes

(a) The IS curve

A tax rise of Δt raises the savings-plus-taxes curve by $b\Delta t$ and shifts the IS curve to the left by $b\Delta t/(1 - b)$. The effect of a tax change on the IS curve is less than the (opposite) effect of an equivalent change in government spending. Government spending affects aggregate demand directly, whereas taxes affect aggregate demand indirectly through their effect on consumption. A £1 change in taxes produces a £b change in spending. Thus, the tax multiplier is $-b/(1 - b)$, whereas the government spending multiplier is $1/(1 - b)$.

Figure 11.8 reproduces frames (c) and (d) of Figure 11.7. Focus on the interest rate at r_1 with the income level at y_1. Notice that at the interest rate r_1, the tax rise shifts the IS curve such that, if the interest rate was to remain constant at r_1, income would fall to y_2. Call the change in income from y_1 to y_2, Δy. That income change is labelled Δy in frame (a). Transferring that income change up to frame (b), you see that it forms the base of a triangle whose height is given by b times the change in taxes. Again, use the formula 'slope equals rise over run' to figure out what the change in income is in this case. You know that the 'slope' of the hypotenuse of that triangle is $1 - b$, the 'rise' is $b\Delta t$, and the 'run' is $(-\Delta y)$, so you may establish that 'slope equals rise over run' becomes

$$1 - b = \frac{b\Delta t}{(-\Delta y)}$$

(Why have we put a minus sign in front of Δy? Because income *falls* as taxes *rise*, so they move in opposite directions.) Now multiply both sides of this equation by the change in income (Δy) to give

$$\Delta y(1 - b) = -b\Delta t$$

Then divide both sides of this equation by $1 - b$, the marginal propensity to save, and obtain

$$\Delta y = \left(\frac{-b}{1 - b}\right)\Delta t$$

What does this say? It says that a change in taxes changes income in the opposite direction and by an amount that is equal to the marginal propensity to consume divided by the marginal propensity to save times the change in taxes.

Summary

A. Definition of the IS Curve

The IS curve is the relationship between the aggregate demand for goods and services and the real rate of interest when flow equilibrium prevails in the goods market, that is, when investment-plus-government spending is equal to planned savings-plus-taxes.

B. Derivation of the IS Curve

The IS curve is derived from the investment-plus-government spending curve, the planned savings-plus-taxes curve, and the equality of investment-plus-government spending and savings-plus-taxes. Figure 11.1 to 11.4 illustrate the derivation and should be thoroughly understood.

C. Determinants of the IS Curve Slope

The IS curve slopes downwards. That is, at lower real interest rates, higher levels of real income are required to maintain flow equilibrium in the goods market. This arises because at lower interest rates there is more investment spending, and with higher investment there needs to be higher savings to maintain equilibrium. Higher savings require a higher level of income, so that lower interest rates require higher income levels. More precisely, the slope of the IS curve is equal to the slope of the investment demand curve multiplied by $1/(1 - b)$, where b is the marginal propensity to consume.

D. Shifts in the IS Curve

The IS curve shifts when government spending and taxes change. A rise in government spending leads to a rightward shift in the IS curve by an amount equal to $1/(1 - b)$ times the change in government spending. A rise in taxes causes the IS curve to shift leftwards. The amount of the shift is equal to the rise in taxes times $b/(1 - b)$.

Review Questions

1. What is the IS curve?
2. Which markets are in equilibrium along the IS curve?
3. Why does the IS curve slope downwards?
4. Why is the IS curve flatter than the investment demand curve?
5. What happens to the position of the IS curve if there is a £1 million rise in government expenditure on goods and services?
6. What happens to the position of the IS curve if there is a £1 million rise in government transfers to individuals in the form of increased pensions and unemployment benefits?
7. What happens to the position of the IS curve if the government cuts pensions and raises defence spending by £1 million?
8. You are given the following information about a hypothetical economy:

$$c = 100 + 0.8(y - t)$$
$$i = 500 - 50r$$
$$g = 400$$
$$t = 400$$

(c = consumption; i = investment; g = government expenditure on goods and services; t = taxes; y = real rate of interest)

(a) Find the equation for the IS curve.
(b) Show that the slope of the IS curve is the same as the slope of the investment demand curve multiplied by one minus the marginal propensity to consume.
(c) Show that a rise in g shifts the IS curve to the right by five times the rise in g.
(d) Show that a rise in t shifts the IS curve to the left by four times the rise in t.

Appendix: The Algebra of the *IS* Curve

This appendix sets out the algebra of the *IS* curve. The material presented here is simply another way of looking at the derivation given in the body of the chapter. For those who prefer an algebraic treatment, this may be found to be more compact and straightforward. It does not, however, contain anything of substance that is not stated in words and diagrams in the chapter.

Aggregate demand for goods and services is shown by

$$y^d = c + i + g \tag{11A.1}$$

Consumption demand is determined by

$$c = a + b(y - t) \qquad a < 0, 0 < b < 1 \tag{11A.2}$$

and investment demand is determined by

$$i = i_0 - hr \qquad i_0, h > 0 \tag{11A.3}$$

Substituting c and i from Equations (11A.2) and (11A.3) into Equation (11A.1) gives

$$y^d = a + b(y - t) + i_0 - hr + g \tag{11A.4}$$

To be on the *IS* curve,

$$y = y^d \tag{11A.5}$$

so replacing y^d with y in Equation (11A.4) gives

$$y = a + b(y - t) + i_0 - hr + g \tag{11A.6}$$

which may be rearranged as

$$(1 - b)y = a + i_0 + g - bt - hr \tag{11A.7}$$

and dividing both sides by $1 - b$, we have

$$y = \frac{1}{1 - b}(a + i_0 + g - bt - hr) \tag{11A.8}$$

or, equivalently,

$$y' = \frac{a + i_0}{1 - b} + \frac{1}{1 - b}(g) - \frac{b}{1 - b}(t) - \frac{h}{1 - b}(r) \tag{11A.9}$$

Equations (11A.8) and (11A.9) are alternative ways of writing the equation for the *IS* curve. The second of these is perhaps the clearest way of writing the *IS* curve and the one that makes interpretation of it most straightforward.

The variables that enter the *IS* curve are government spending (g), taxes (t), and the rate of interest (r). The parameters that affect the *IS* curve are the constant in the consumption function (a), the constant in the investment demand function (i_0), the responsiveness of investment to a change in the rate of interest ($-h$), and the marginal propensity to consume (b). The way in which these various parameters enter the *IS* curve is made very precise in Equation (11A.9).

First, the level of output that would obtain, even if government spending, taxes, and the rate of interest were all zero, is the first term in Equation (11A.9); that is,

$$\frac{a + i_0}{1 - b}$$

The slope of the *IS* curve (the change in the rate of interest that occurs when income changes) is given by the inverse of the coefficient in front of the rate of interest, namely,

$$\frac{-(1 - b)}{h}$$

Since $-1/h$ is the slope of the investment curve, you can immediately verify the proposition derived in the text that the slope of the *IS* curve is equal to the slope of the investment curve multiplied by $1 - b$.

A change in government spending shifts the *IS* curve by an amount indicated by the coefficient that multiplies g in Equation (11A.9). That coefficient is $1/(1 - b)$ and agrees with the derivation in the text.

A rise in taxes lowers the level of income (shifts the *IS* curve leftwards) since the coefficient in front of taxes has a minus sign attached to it. The size of the change in income that results from a rise in taxes is equal to $b/(1 - b)$ times the change in taxes. This also agrees with the derivation in the text.

12

The Demand for Money

The three preceding chapters have taken you through an analysis of the determination of equilibrium between the *flows* of consumption, savings, investment and income. That analysis is built on the flow accounts — the aggregate income and expenditure accounts — that you studied in Chapter 3.

The next part of the story of the determination of aggregate demand concerns equilibrium in the markets for money and the *stocks* of assets. The accounts for these markets are the ones that you studied in Chapter 4.

In that chapter, we set out a fairly elaborate set of interrelated balance sheets so that you would have a clear picture of the indebtedness between the various sectors of the economy. Here we will aggregate those sectors and consider a single aggregate private sector. We will also aggregate assets and distinguish between just two classes of them — money on the one hand and everything else on the other.

We study equilibrium in the asset markets by considering how the equilibrium allocation of wealth between money and all other non-money forms of holding wealth is determined. It is interesting to note, however, that we have already studied one aspect of the way in which people will want to allocate their wealth — our study of the demand for capital. We are now going to go on to apply a similar line of reasoning to investigate the way in which people allocate their wealth between money and all other forms of wealth holding.

By the time you have completed this chapter you will be able to:

(a) **Explain what is meant by the demand for money.**
(b) **Explain what determines the demand for money.**
(c) **Explain why the market rate of interest is the opportunity cost of holding money.**

(d) **Represent the demand for money function in a simple equation and diagram.**

(e) **Explain the other factors influencing the demand for money function.**

(f) **State the properties of the UK demand for money function.**

A. Demand for Money

Money[1] is the *stock* of currency and demand deposits[2] in existence at a given point in time. <u>Most of us acquire money as a *flow* of income which, typically, is received at either weekly or monthly intervals.</u> At the beginning of payday, the amount of money that we are holding is at a minimum, and just after we have been paid, it is at a maximum. In the period between the moment that we have been paid through to the next payday, we typically spend our income gradually, thereby running down our money balances.

Figure 12.1 illustrates the pattern of money holdings for an individual who receives an income of £1000 per month at monthly intervals and who spends that £1000 in equal daily amounts through the month. The saw-tooth line shows the actual money holdings of that individual. Those money holdings are £1000 at the beginning of each month and zero at the end of each month. The broken line through the middle of the diagram shows the average money holding of this individual, which, in this case, is £500.

Figure 12.1
Money balances

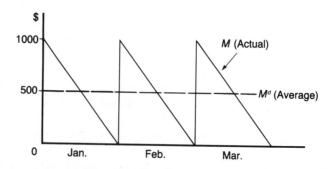

Actual money balances are at their peak at the beginning of each month and are gradually run down to their minimum as expenditure takes place throughout the month. The demand for money refers to the average money holdings (indicated in the diagram by the dashed line).

---

1   The analysis of the demand for money presented here is highly simplified. A comprehensive treatment of this topic may be found in David Laidler, *The Demand for Money: Theories and Evidence*, 2nd edn (New York: Harper and Row, 1978).
2   This definition of money is known as M1 (see Chapter 4).

It is the average money holding that we refer to as the individual's *demand* for money. The amount of money demanded is an average *stock*, and the income is a *flow*. Call the quantity of money demanded M^d (the superscript d on the M is to remind you that M^d is the *demand* for money), and call money income Py – the price level, (P), multiplied by real income, (y). Then let us define the ratio of money demanded (M^d) to money income (Py) as k. That is,

$$k = \frac{M^d}{Py} \text{ money income}$$

(12.1)

The individual in the above example has an annual income of £12,000 (£1000 each month) and a demand for money £500. For this individual therefore, the ratio of average money holdings to annual money income is

$$k = \frac{£500}{£12,000} = \frac{1}{24}$$

An alternative way of writing Equation (12.1) would be (by multiplying both sides of the equation by Py) as

$$M^d = kPy$$

(12.2)

This equation says that the demand for money is some fraction k of money income equation. Let us give a name to k: we will call it the *propensity to hold money*.

B. Determinants of the Demand for Money

The next question to be dealt with is, what determines the propensity to hold money? Will it be constant or will it vary in some systematic way? Put slightly differently, would it make sense for individuals mechanically to hold money balances equal, on the average, to one-half of their periodic income? That is, would it make sense for an individual paid weekly to hold money balances equal, on the average, to one-half a week's income; a person paid monthly to hold money balances equal, on the average, to one-half a month's income; and so on? The answer, in general, is that it would not. Rather it would be sensible to attempt to *economize* on money holdings.

Consider the example of a person who receives £12,000 a year, paid at quarterly intervals. Specifically, suppose a person receives £3000 on the 1st of January, April, July, and October. Would it make sense for such a person to run down his money balances at an even rate over each quarter? Notice that if such a person did spread his outlays evenly, the propensity to hold money would be one-eighth. That is, on the average, one-eighth of a year's income would be held in the form of money. The average money holding of such a person would be £1500. What could such a person do to economize on his money holdings? There are two possibilities: (1) he could make a loan by buying and holding some financial asset other than money, an asset that unlike money, pays interest; or (2) he could bunch the purchase of goods towards the beginning of the income period, thereby holding less money, on the average, and having a higher average inventory of goods.

Under what circumstances would an individual attempt to use one or both of these devices for economizing on money holdings? Obviously, the higher the rate of interest, the more will an individual lose by holding money rather than buying interest-earning financial assets. Equally obviously, the higher is the rate of inflation, the more will an individual lose by holding money rather than buying and holding inventories of goods. It seems reasonable to suppose, therefore, that the higher the rate of interest, the more will individuals seek to switch out of money holdings and into the holdings of financial assets that earn a return. This action will lower an individual's propensity to hold money.

It also seems reasonable to suppose that the faster prices are rising or, equivalently, the higher is the rate of inflation, the more it would pay an individual to bunch purchases of goods so that most goods are bought soon after payday. There is, however, an important difference between the interest rate that an individual can earn on a financial asset and the consequences of inflation that can be avoided by buying goods earlier rather than later. When an individual buys a financial asset, the interest rate that will be paid on that financial asset is known at the time of the purchase. But when an individual seeks to avoid losses from inflation by buying goods early, he does not know with any certainty what the inflation rate will in fact turn out to be over some relevant future period. Thus, what will determine the decision to economize on money holdings and buy bigger inventories of goods, is not the actual but the *expected* rate of inflation.

In the example that we have just worked through, we dealt with an individual whose income was received at quarterly intervals. This meant that the individual received a fairly sizeable amount of money on each payday and therefore would be able to earn a substantial amount of interest income (or avoid losses from inflation) by taking economizing actions of the type discussed. However, the more frequently a person is paid, the less is the incentive to take advantage of these economizing actions. In fact, for people paid at very frequent intervals, such as a week, it may well be that the best they can do is to hold money balances that roughly equal one-half a week's income. This is because the interest that could be earned on a half a week's income would not be sufficient to justify the costs of moving between money and interest-earning securities and back again into money all within a week. For these individuals, the propensity to hold money (k) would be 1/104. For such individuals then, the propensity to hold money would indeed be a constant.

There is another factor working in the direction of reducing the incentive to economize on money holdings and that is the increasing tendency for

certain types of monetary assets themselves to bear interest. If all forms
of money received interest at a rate that moved up and down in line with
movements in other interest rates, then there would be no tendency for
the incentive to economize on money holdings to vary with the level of
interest rates. In a situation, however, in which not all monetary assets
bear interest (such as in today's world), there remains an incentive to
economize on money holdings as interest rates and inflation fluctuate.

Let us now summarize the above: there are two ways of economizing
on money holdings — (1) by buying financial assets, and (2) by buying
real goods. Buying financial assets is a way of earning interest, and buying
goods is a way of avoiding some of the loss in the value of money resulting
from inflation. The higher interest rates and the higher the expected rate
of inflation, the more will people seek to economize on money holdings
and the lower will be the propensity to hold money.

↑r ↑inflation

C. Opportunity Cost of Holding Money

The next step in developing the theory of the demand for money is to
show that the opportunity cost of holding money is nothing other than
the market rate of interest. At first this seems surprising because we have,
in the previous section, discovered that there are *two* ways of economizing
on money holdings. One of these ways, buying financial assets, results
in a rate of return equal to the market rate of interest. The other method
of economizing, buying real goods, avoids money balances losing value
as a result of inflation. Thus, it appears as if there should be two distinct
opportunity costs of holding money — the rate of inflation and the market
rate of interest. There is, however, a connection between these two that
we are now going to explore.

Let us begin by refreshing our understanding (briefly introduced in
Chapter 9) of the link between the market rate of interest and the real
rate of interest.

The rate of interest actually paid and received is the *money* (or, equivalently, *nominal*) rate of interest — to emphasize its distinction from the
real rate of interest. The distinction between real and money (or nominal)
interest is a vital and natural one. In an economy in which prices are expected to rise by, say, 10 per cent a year, money that is borrowed and
lent will be expected to lose value at the rate of 10 per cent a year. Thus
someone who lends money for a year will expect to be repaid at the end
of the year in dollars that are worth 10 per cent less than the dollars that
were lent. Similarly, the borrower will expect to repay the loan with
cheaper dollars. This expected fall in the value of money — *expected
inflation* — must be subtracted from the rate of interest — the *money rate
of interest* — in order to calculate the interest rate that people expect they
will *really* pay and receive.

We can summarize this relationship in a simple equation. Call the money rate of interest r_m and the real rate of interest r. Then the real rate of interest is the difference between the money rate of interest and the expected rate of inflation; i.e.

$$r = r_m - \pi^e \tag{12.3}$$

Equation 12.3 tells us the rate of return that people will *really* obtain if they place their wealth in interest-earning assets. What will they *really* earn if, instead of placing their wealth in interest-earning assets they hang on to their money balances? A moment's reflection will lead you to the conclusion that the real rate of return from holding money is equal to minus the rate of inflation, that is $(-\pi)$. Holding money delivers a rate of return equal to minus the rate of inflation because the quantity of goods and services that can be purchased in the future will be smaller than what can be purchased today when inflation is positive. Also the quantity of goods and services that can be purchased in the future relative to today will be smaller by a percentage amount that is related one to one with the rate of inflation.

You can think of the opportunity cost of holding money as being the difference between the real rate of return on holding money and the real rate of return on placing wealth in the form of interest-bearing assets. What is that opportunity cost? Define opportunity cost as the difference between the real rate of return on assets and the real rate of return on money holding (minus the rate of inflation). Thus we would have:

Opportunity Cost of Holding Money $= r - (-\pi)$

When people make decisions about how much money to hold they do not know what the future rate of inflation is going to be and have to base their decisions on expectations of its rate. That is, they base their decision on the expected opportunity cost of holding money. The expected opportunity cost of holding money is given by:

Expected Opportunity Cost of Holding Money $= r - (-\pi^e)$

We already know from Equation 12.3 that the real rate of interest is equal to the market rate of interest minus the expected rate of inflation. Substituting for r in the above equation gives:

Expected Opportunity Cost of Holding Money $=$
$r_m - \pi^e - (-\pi^e)$

Remembering that the negative of a negative number is positive you will immediately see that the above equation implies that:

Expected Opportunity Cost of Holding Money $= r_m$

In effect, what you have discovered is that movements in the market rate of interest, r_m, capture movements in the real rate of interest and movements in the expected rate of inflation. The higher the market rate of interest, the more will people seek to economize on their money holdings — the lower will be their marginal propensity to hold money.

Let us now go on to summarize these ideas in a simple representation of the demand for money function.

D. The Demand for Money Function

The entire discussion of the previous sections can now be summarized in some very simple propositions. We have discovered that the propensity to hold money varies inversely with the market (or nominal) rate of interest.

We can write this relationship as an equation, which says

$$M^d/Py = k(r_m) \qquad (12.4)$$
$$(-)$$

where $k(r_m)$ stands for 'k is a function of, or depends on, r_m, the rate of interest'. The minus sign $(-)$ below the equation is there to remind you that as the rate of interest *rises*, the propensity to hold money *falls*.

We can also illustrate the proposition with Figure 12.2.

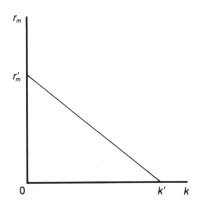

Figure 12.2
The propensity to hold money

The opportunity cost of holding money is the market rate of interest. It is the difference between the real rate of return on other assets and the real rate of return on money (the negative of the rate of inflation). The higher the market rate of interest, the lower the propensity to hold money.

↑ r_m ↓ propensity to hold money.

The downward-sloping line shows how k rises as r_m falls. If the rate of interest was as high as r_m, people would no longer want to use money, and trade would be undertaken with barter or some commodity means of exchange. If the rate of interest was zero, then k would equal k'.

Equivalently, we can write Equation (12.4) in the form of Equation (12.2), as

$$M^d = k(r_m)Py \qquad (12.5)$$
$$(-)$$

Recalling that the market rate of interest is the sum of the real rate of interest and the expected rate of inflation enables us to write the demand for money function equivalently as

$$M^d = k(r + \pi^e)Py \tag{12.6}$$

This equation states that the demand for money (M^d) depends on the level of money income (Py), the *real* rate of interest, and the expected rate of inflation (π^e). Writing the demand for money function in this way enables us to focus on a crucial distinction between the effects on the demand for money of *inflation* and of the *price level*.

If the price level doubled overnight, and if everything else (including the rate of inflation) remained the same,[3] then the amount of money that people would want to hold would also double. Thus, the demand for money is proportional to the level of prices. This idea, that the amount of money demanded is proportional to the price level, enables us to make use of a simpler statement about the demand for money based on a definition of real money. Real money is the quantity of money (M) divided by the price level (P). That is,

Real money = M/P

In contrast, if the rate of inflation was to rise, raising with it the market rate of interest, the demand for money — the demand for real money — would decline.

We may, therefore, express the demand for money function as a demand for real money. The demand for real money depends on the level of real income and on the rate of interest. The higher the level of real income, the more real money will be demanded; and the higher the rate of interest, the less real money will be demanded.

We can derive a simple equation for the demand for real money from Equation (12.5), which says:

$$M^d/P = k(r_m)y \tag{12.7}$$
$$(-)$$

E. Other Influences on the Demand for Money

So far, in our discussion of the things that determine the demand for money, we focused only on the level of income and the money rate of interest. If these two variables were the only ones that affected the demand for money that demand would be highly predictable.

There are, of course, many other things that influence the demand for money. One of them we have already implicitly discussed — the

---

3   If the idea of the price level doubling overnight and the rate of inflation remaining constant seems puzzling, recall the distinction between a once-and-for-all change in the price level and inflation — Figure 5.1.

frequency with which people are paid and make payments. If people were paid every month and spent their income at a uniform rate across the month their average money holdings would equal 1/2 of a month's income. In such an economy the demand for money would equal 1/24 of annual income. If people were paid every three months and spent their money at a uniform rate across the three month period, average money holdings would equal 1/8 of annual income (or 1/2 of 1/4).

Even when the frequency of income payments is fixed, the pattern of expenditures out of income affect the demand for money. For example, if spending is not spread uniformly over the income interval but concentrated at the beginning of the income period, the demand for money is reduced. If spending is delayed until the end of the income period the demand for money is increased. Variation in transactions timing is a potentially important source of influence on the demand for money.

We have emphasized the importance of the opportunity cost of holding money as a factor influencing the demand for money. That opportunity cost has been characterized as the rate of interest on alternative assets. In reality there is more than one rate of interest. For example substitutes for money are building society shares and deposits, national savings certificates, bank deposits and currencies other than sterling, government bonds and Treasury bills, and real assets such as land and houses. All of these different assets have rates of return which, though linked in competitive asset markets, do, to some degree, have independent fluctuations. Identifying the oppportunity cost of holding money as *the* rate of interest, usually a rate on some short-term three months security, represents a substantial abstraction from reality.

The third influence on the demand for money is the environment of financial regulation. A financial system in which it is not possible to pay interest on cheque accounts will result in a different demand for money from that in which daily interest payments are permissible. Further, regulations on the scale of interest and the conditions that must be satisfied in order to build or pay interest will affect the amount of money that people demand.

All these other influences on the demand for money will change the propensity to hold money independently of the average level of the money rate of interest. Whether or not these other factors are important is essentially an empirical matter and not one on which it is possible to make strong *a priori* statements.

F. The UK Demand for Money Function

What does the UK demand for money function[4] look like? Is the theoretical formulation shown in Figure 12.2 anything like a representa-

---

4 There are several excellent discussions of the theory of, and empirical evidence on, the demand for money function. In our view you can do no better than study David Laidler's

tion of the facts about the demand *for* money in the UK? Or do the other influences on the demand for money that we have just discussed produce important shifts in the demand function?

Figures 12.3 and 12.4 contain the answers to these questions. In Figure 12.3 we have plotted, on the vertical axis, the short-term rate of interest (from Chapter 2) and on the horizontal axis we have plotted k – the ratio of M1 to nominal GDP (expressed as a percentage). The data shown are

**Figure 12.3
The demand for
money (M1) in the
UK**

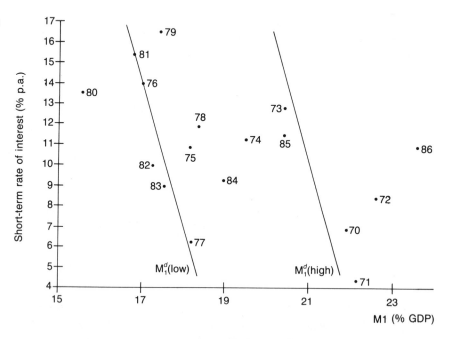

The relationship between the short-term rate of interest and M1 as a percent of GDP is shown in the figure. The two downward-sloping lines are possible demand for money functions. No simple stable demand for money function describes these data. The demand for money fluctuates between 15.5 and 24 per cent of GDP. There is a tendency for there to be an inverse relationship between the demand for money and the rate of interest, but that relationship is not strong and the demand function shifts as a result of other influences.
Source: Bank of England Quarterly Bulletin, various issues.

The Demand for Money: Theories and Evidence, 3rd edn (New York: Harper and Row, 1985); and M.J. Artis and M.K. Lewis's *Monetary Control in the United Kingdom* (Deddington, Oxford: Philip Allan, 1981). A very good, but dated, survey of studies of the demand for money in the United Kingdom may be found in C.A.E. Goodhart and A.D. Crockett, 'The Importance of Money', *Bank of England Quarterly Bulletin*, Vol. 10, No. 2 (June 1970) pp.159–98. A more up-to-date survey of the evidence is presented by Alan Budd, Sean Holly, Andrew Longbottom and David Smith 'Does Monetarism Fit the U.K. Facts?' in Brian Griffiths and Geoffrey E. Wood, (eds) *Monetarism in the United Kingdom*, 1984, London and Basingstoke: Macmillan, pp. 75–119.

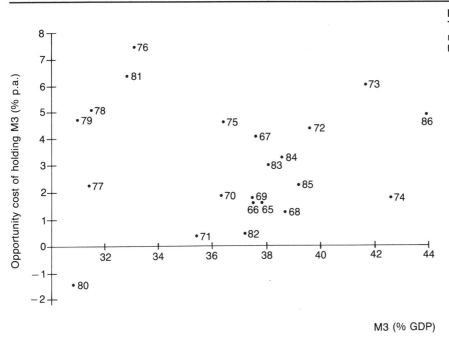

Figure 12.4
The demand for
money (M3) in the
UK

The demand for M3 is much more volatile than that for M1. M3 fluctuates from between 30 and 44 per cent of GDP. There is no simple relationship between the demand for M3 and the opportunity cost of holding that broad money aggregate.
Source: Bank of England Quarterly Bulletin, various issues.

for the period between 1970 and 1986. Each point represents a year identified by the last two digits. The two downward-sloping lines represent two possible demands for money functions. That labelled M_1^d(low) roughly fits the data for the years 1976–7 and 1981–3. The other line labelled M_1^d(high) roughly fits the data for the years 1970–1, 1973 and 1985. The years 1974–5, 1978–9, and 1984 lie between these two lines. In 1980 the demand for money function lies substantially to the left of the lower line and in 1972 and 1986 it lies to the right of the upper line.

The downward-sloping lines are possible demand for money functions. It is evident, though, that there is no simple stable demand for money function that describes these data. The demand for money fluctuates between a low of about 15.5 per cent of GDP and a high of almost 24 per cent of GDP. Most of the observations are concentrated in the region 18–22 per cent. There is a slight apparent tendency for there to be an inverse relationship between the demand for money and the rate of interest, but that relationship is not strong.

Figure 12.4 plots M3/GDP as a percentage against the difference between the rate of interest on time deposits and the short-term rate of interest — a measure of the opportunity cost of holding interest-bearing M3 deposits. It is evident that the demand for M3 is even more volatile than the demand for M1. Notice the range of variation on the quantity axis. In the case of M1 that range runs from 15 per cent to 24 per cent of GDP (a range of 9 percentage points). In the case of M3 the range is from 30 per cent to 44 per cent (a range of 14 percentage points).

By taking careful account of the rates of interest on the many alternative assets to money and by taking careful account of the short-run fluctuations in income, interest rates, and the price level, all of which separately influence the demand for money, it is possible to find a statistical model that fits the quantity of money demanded much more closely than is apparent from the pictures in Figures 12.3 and 12.4. Nevertheless it is evident that the simple theory of the demand for money presented in this chapter has to be qualified heavily in order to provide an adequate characterization of the actual data.

Like the investment demand function, the demand for money function is not a highly stable function of one or two variables. It is a demand function that is subject to sizable and important shifts.

Summary

A. Demand for Money

The demand for money is a demand for an average stock of money to hold.

B. Determinants of the Demand for Money

The demand for money depends on the level of real income and (inversely) on the market rate of interest. The demand for money is the demand for real money.

C. Opportunity Cost of Holding Money

The market rate of interest is the difference between the real rate of return on earning assets and the real rate of return on money. The real rate of return on money is the negative of the expected rate of inflation.

D. The Demand for Money Function

The demand for money function may be represented as a simple equation such as Equation (12.7) or in the form of a simple diagram such as Figure 12.2.

E. *Other Influences on the Demand for Money*

Other influences on the demand for money are the frequency of income receipts and the timing of payments as well as the rates of interest on the many alternative assets to money.

F. *The UK Demand for Money Function*

The theory of the demand for money fits the UK facts only when allowance is made for the other influences on the demand for money. Figures 12.3 and 12.4 show the relationship between the demand for M1 (12.3) and M3 (12.4) and a measure of the opportunity cost of holding money. There is no visible demand for money function in these data. It is possible to interpret the demand for M1 and arising from a steep demand function that fluctuates substantially as a result of changes in the other influences on the demand for money.

Review Questions

1. What does the term *demand for money* mean?
2. Calculate your own average holding of money. What are the units of this quantity? Is it a stock or a flow?
3. Calculate your own demand for money.
4. Calculate your own propensity to hold money. What are the units of this quantity?
5. If the interval between the days on which you are paid is lengthened (i.e. multiplied by 2 or 4) would your demand for money change? Explain why or why not.
6. Some people 'economize' on their money holdings. What does this term mean? Explain why they would 'economize'.
7. If the inflation rate dropped to zero tomorrow and remained there, would your demand for money change? Explain why or why not.
8. If the inflation rate doubled tomorrow and remained at that level, would you 'economize' on your money holdings? Explain why or why not.
9. The propensity to hold money is related to the inflation rate. What is this relationship? Draw a diagram to illustrate this relationship.
10. What is the relationship between the demand for money and money income?
11. What is the relationship between the demand for money and the price level?
12. What is the relationship between the demand for money and real income?

13. What is the relationship between the demand for money and the market rate of interest?

14. Why do you think the demand for both M1 and M3 was so low in 1980 compared with other years? (To see that it was low take a look at Figures 12.3 and 12.4.)

15. Why do you think the demand for both M1 and M3 was so high in 1986 compared with other years? (To see that it was high take a look at Figures 12.3 and 12.4.)

13

The *LM* Curve

The subject matter of this chapter is very similar to that of Chapter 11. In that chapter we studied the way in which the *IS* curve summarizes *flow equilibrium* in the market for goods and services. *Stock equilibrium* in the markets for money (and assets) may be similarly summarized by an equivalent relation called the *LM* curve. This chapter deals with the *LM* curve. When you have completed your study of this chapter you will be able to:

(a) **Define the *LM* curve.**
(b) **Derive the *LM* curve.**
(c) **Understand what determines the slope of the *LM* curve.**
(d) **Understand what makes the *LM* curve shift and by how much.**

A. Definition of the *LM* Curve

Like the *IS* curve that you studied in Chapter 11, the *LM* curve is also a relationship between the rate of interest and the level of real income. Specifically, the *LM* curve is the relationship between the rate of interest and the level of real income that makes the demand for money equal to the supply of money.[1] Thus, like the *IS* curve, the *LM* curve is an equilibrium locus. It is worth emphasizing again that the *LM* curve does

---

1   You may be wondering why the *LM* curve is so called. The name was first used by Sir John Hicks who invented the *IS–LM* analysis. The letter *L* stands for 'Liquidity Preference', the name that Keynes gave to the demand for money (what we are calling M^d). The letter *M* stands for the supply of money. Thus, the label *LM* reminds us that this curve depicts values of the rate of interest and the level of income at which the demand for money (L) equals the supply of money (M).

not imply any causal relationship from the rate of interest to the level of income or in the reverse direction. Like the *IS* curve, it places further restrictions on the values that these two variables may take on. Let us now proceed to see how the *LM* curve is derived.

B.   Derivation of the *LM* Curve

The starting point for the derivation of the *LM* curve is to recall the theory of the demand for money. This theory, set out in the previous chapter, says that the amount of real money balances that people want to hold in the aggregate varies directly with the level of real income and inversely with the level of the market or *money* rate of interest.

Purely for convenience, the demand for money function will be treated as *linear* in real income and the rate of interest.[2] Specifically, we will suppose that the demand for money is determined by the equation

$$M^d/P = ky + m_0 - lr_m \qquad (13.1)$$

where M^d stands for the quantity of nominal money balances demanded, P is the price level, y is real income, r_m is the market rate of interest, and k, m_0 and l are constants. This equation says that the demand for real balances (M^d/P) depends on the level of real income and the market rate of interest. For each extra pound of real income in the economy, k real pounds of extra money balances are demanded. For every 1 percentage point rise in the market rate of interest on bonds, the demand for bonds rises and the demand for money balances drops by l pounds. Even at a zero level of income and a zero rate of interest, there would be some rock-bottom level of money balances demanded equal to m_0.

The market rate of interest equals the real rate of interest plus the inflation rate. That is,

$$r_m = r + \pi \qquad (13.2)$$

The *LM* curve depicts a relationship between the level of income and the rate of interest when the supply of money is equal to the demand for money. Evidently the demand for money depends on the level of

---

2   The precise functional form of the demand for money that best fits the facts is a logarithmic function that says that the logarithm of real money demanded is a linear function of the logarithm of real income and the level (not logarithm) of the rate of interest. The different forms of the function used in Chapter 12 and here are selected for analytical convenience and may be regarded as holding approximately for small enough movements in the variables.

income, the real rate of interest, the rate of inflation and the price level. To define the *LM* curve we treat the price level as being given at some fixed number, P_0, and the rate of inflation, π, as zero. We can write the demand for real money as follows:

$$M^d/P_0 = ky + m_0 - lr \qquad (13.3)$$

This equation incorporates the fact that the amount of nominal money demanded is deflated by a particular fixed price level, P_0, and the market rate of interest, r_m, is exactly the same as r, the real rate of interest, because with a fixed price level the inflation rate, π, is equal to zero.

Equilibrium in the money market requires the demand for money to be equal to the supply of money. Calling the supply of money that is determined by the actions of the monetary authorities M, the equilibrium condition in the money market is:

$$M^d = M \qquad (13.4)$$

Just as in Chapter 11 government spending and taxes were regarded as exogenous, so in this chapter, M is treated as being exogenous. That is, the money supply, M, does not respond directly to the values of any of the variables in the model, but rather is determined externally to the model and influences the values of those variables. In fact, the supply of money is determined by the actions of the central bank and the banking system and this process will be analysed in some detail in Chapter 30. In treating the supply of money as being determined exogenously we are bypassing that process.[3]

Making the assumption that the supply of money (M) is exogenous enables us to move on to examine how money market equilibrium determines the level of aggregate demand for goods and services.

If M^d is replaced in Equation (13.3) by M, we obtain

$$M/P_0 = ky + m_0 - lr \qquad (13.5)$$

---

3 When proper account is taken of the linkages between the domestic economy and the rest of the world, it is not always possible to regard the supply of money as being determined exogenously. If the economy has a floating exchange rate, such an assumption may be in order. In the case of an economy with a fixed exchange rate, however, it is inappropriate to regard the money supply as being determined exogenously. For present purposes, therefore, you should regard the exercise that is being conducted as one that applies to an economy that does not have any trading links with the rest of the world, or as applying to an economy that has a floating exchange rate. (The world as a whole is the only interesting example of an economy that does not have trading links with the rest of the world.) Chapter 15 will introduce the explicit modifications that have to be made to this analysis in order to allow for international transactions.

which is the equation for the *LM* curve. Notice that there are two variables in this equation, y and r. All the others terms in the equation are constants. The money supply, M, is a constant determined by the monetary authorities; P_0 is being treated as a constant (because we are studying the determinants of aggregate demand at a given price level); and m_0, l, and k are constants, being parameters of the demand for money function.

Figure 13.1 illustrates the derivation of the *LM* curve. First break the demand for real balances into two parts. Define the first part, ky, as m_A^d

Figure 13.1 The derivation of the *LM* curve

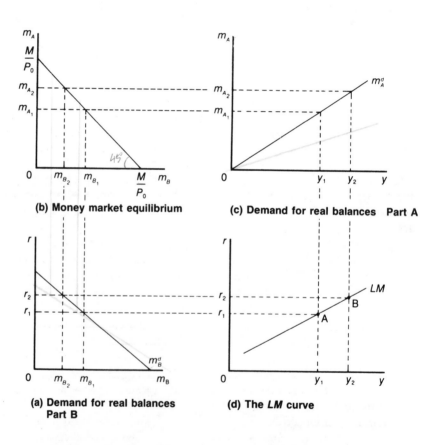

(b) Money market equilibrium

(c) Demand for real balances   Part A

(a) Demand for real balances Part B

(d) The *LM* curve

The *LM* curve traces the relationship between the rate of interest and the level of income which ensures that the demand for real balances equals the supply of real balances. The *LM* curve slopes upwards. For a given supply of real balances, a higher income level (which gives rise to a higher demand for real balances) can only be sustained if there is more economizing on real balances. A higher rate of interest is needed to induce such economizing.

and the second part, $(m_0 - lr)$, as m_B^d. The demand for real balances may be written as:

$$M^d/P_0 = m_A^d + m_B^d$$

Now turn to Figure 13.1. The figure has four parts. Frame (c) contains a graph of the part of the demand for real balances m_A^d. Frame (a) contains the other part of the demand for real balances m_B^d. Notice that frame (a) is very similar to Figure 12.2 in Chapter 12. Frame (b) measures m_B^d on the horizontal axis and m_A^d on the vertical axis. The line drawn in frame (b) slopes at 'minus one' and is located in the following way. Measure on the horizontal axis the exogenously given amount of money divided M by the price level P_0; then measure the same distance on the vertical axis, and join together the two points. This line tells us that the amount of real money that is in existence must be 'allocated' to either m_A^d or m_B^d. In effect, this line is the supply of real balances. The *LM* curve, derived in frame (d), is a relationship such that the supply of real balances depicted in frame (b) is held and is demanded in accordance with the two-part demand function plotted in frames (a) and (c).

To derive the *LM* curve proceed as follows. First, pick an interest rate — say, r_1. Focus on frame (a) and notice that at the interest rate r_1 the amount of real balances demanded under the B part of the demand for real balances is m_{B_1}. Transfer that amount of real balances demanded up to frame (b) and notice that if m_{B_1} is demanded under part B, then under part A, m_{A_1} real balances must be demanded ($m_{B_1} + m_{A_1}$ exactly equals the supply of real balances available). Then transfer m_{A_1} across to the vertical axis of frame (c) and using the curve drawn in that figure, work out the level of income that is necessary to ensure that m_{A_1} is demanded. That level of income is y_1. Now transfer the initially selected interest rate r_1 rightwards across to frame (d) and transfer the income level y_1 vertically downwards from frame (c) to frame (d). These two lines meet at point A indicating that with the interest rate r_1 the income level y_1 will generate a sufficient demand for real balances to ensure that the quantity of money in existence is willingly held.

Now repeat the above experiment with the interest rate r_2. At interest rate r_2, m_B real balances are demanded in part B. That leaves m_A real balances to be demanded in part A of the demand for real balances. According to frame (c), in order that M_{A_2} real balances be demanded, the income level would have to be y_2. Thus, the interest rate r_2 and the income level y_2, taken together, would lead to a demand for real balances equal to the supply of real balances, point B in frame (d). The points A and B are both points on the *LM* curve as defined above. Joining those points together and extending the curve beyond those points plots the *LM* curve.

The *LM* curve that you have just derived graphically can be derived by a simple piece of algebra that involves nothing more than a slight re-arrangement of Equation (13.5). By dividing through Equation (13.5) by k, the equation for the *LM* curve can be written with real income, y, on the left-hand side as

$$y = \frac{1}{k}\frac{M}{P_0} - \frac{m_0}{k} + \frac{l}{k}r \qquad (13.6)$$

Alternatively by dividing Equation (13.5) through by l and rearranging things slightly, the equation for the *LM* curve can be written as

$$r = -\frac{1}{l}\frac{M}{P_0} + \frac{m_0}{l} + \frac{k}{l}y \qquad (13.7)$$

which is an equation relating y to r. Equations (13.6) and (13.7) are identical and, indeed, are identical to Equation (13.5).

You have now seen how the *LM* curve may be derived graphically and you have seen how it can be represented in a simple equation. Equation (13.7) is a direct representation of the *LM* curve shown in frame (d) of Figure 13.1. Let us now go on to explore more thoroughly the properties of the *LM* curve.

C. Determinants of the *LM* Curve Slope

The slope of the *LM* curve has considerable importance for the relative effectiveness of changes in the money supply and changes in government spending and taxes on the level of aggregate demand. You will see this in the next chapter. For now, let us focus on the factors that determine the slope of the *LM* curve. You can see from inspecting frame (d) in Figure 13.1 that the *LM* curve slopes upwards. What determines how steep or flat the *LM* curves will be? There are only two things that underlie the slope of the *LM* curve — the parameters k and l. These determine the sensitivity of the demand for real balances with respect to changes in the level of real income and the rate of interest.

Figure 13.2 illustrates the effects on the *LM* curve of changing the sensitivity of the demand for real balances to changes in the rate of interest, by changing the parameter l.

The curve LM_2 is derived from the steeper demand for real balances plotted in frame (a). Notice that the steeper demand for real balances makes the *LM* curve steeper. That is, the less sensitive the demand for real balances to changes in the interest rate, the steeper will be the *LM* curve. In the limit, if the demand for real balances became perfectly elastic with respect to the rate of interest, the *LM* curve would become horizontal; and if the demand for real balances became completely inelastic with respect to the rate of interest, the *LM* curve would become vertical. Check that you can derive those two extreme cases.

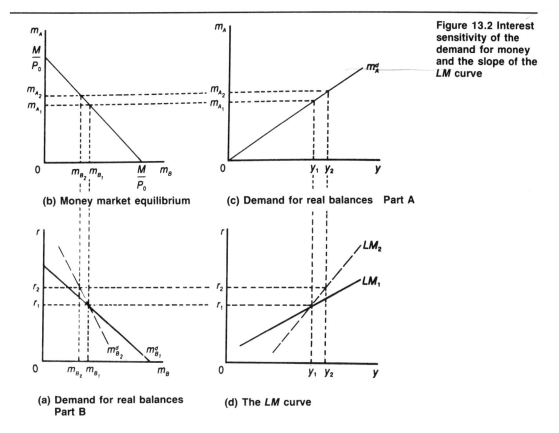

Figure 13.2 Interest sensitivity of the demand for money and the slope of the LM curve

(b) Money market equilibrium

(c) Demand for real balances Part A

(a) Demand for real balances Part B

(d) The LM curve

The less sensitive the demand for money to interest rate changes, the steeper will be the slope of the *LM* curve. As the demand for real balances becomes steeper [frame (a)], the *LM* curve rotates to become steeper [frame (d)]. In the extreme, if the demand for real balances was completely elastic [horizontal demand in frame (a)], the *LM* curve would be horizontal; whereas if the demand for real balances was totally inelastic [vertical in frame (a)], then the *LM* curve would become vertical.

Figure 13.3 illustrates the effects of changing the sensitivity of the demand for real balances to changes in income, by changing the parameter k. Again, LM_1 is identical to the *LM* curve in Figure 13.1. The curve LM_2 is derived for the steeper m_A^d curve in frame (c). Notice that the more sensitive the demand for real balances to changes in income (the bigger the value of k), the steeper is the *LM* curve.

You can obtain these results that we have just derived directly from Equation (13.7), the equation to the *LM* curve. Notice that the *LM* curve equation says that the rate of interest is equal to some constants that involve only the money supply, the price level, and the parameters l and m_0, plus a term equal to $(k/l)y$. Clearly, the ratio k/l measures the slope of the *LM* curve. The bigger that k is, the steeper the *LM* curve; and the bigger that l is, the flatter the *LM* curve.

Figure 13.3 Real income sensitivity of the demand for money and the slope of the *LM* curve

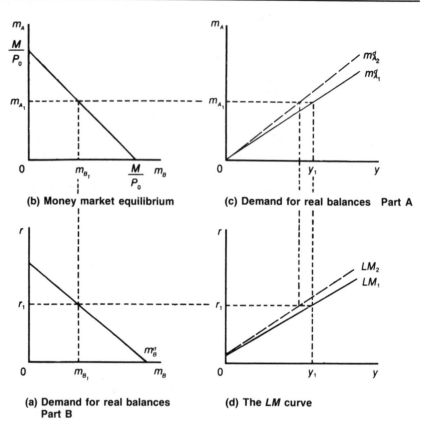

(b) Money market equilibrium

(c) Demand for real balances   Part A

(a) Demand for real balances
Part B

(d) The *LM* curve

The bigger the effect of a change in income on the demand for real balances, the steeper will be the slope of the *LM* curve. As the demand for money becomes more sensitive to the level of income [frame (c)], the *LM* curve becomes steeper [frame (d)].

What all this means is very simple. If money is a poor substitute for other assets, so that the demand for money is inelastic with respect to the rate of interest (*l* is very small), then the *LM* curve will be very steep. Thus small changes in income will require big changes in the rate of interest in order to preserve money market equilibrium. Conversely, if money and other assets are very close substitutes for each other so that the demand for money is elastic with respect to the rate of interest, big variations in income will be possible with only small variations in the rate of interest, while maintaining money market equilibrium.

D.   Shifts in the *LM* Curve

There are three things that can make the *LM* curve shift. One is a shift in the demand for money (a change in one of the parameters, m_0, *l*, or *k*), another is a change in the money supply, and the third is a change in the price level. We shall focus attention on the second and third factors. Notice that in the equation that defines the *LM* curve, the money supply is divided by the price level. In other words, the position of the *LM* curve depends upon the real money supply. It follows immediately that a 1 per cent rise in the money supply will have exactly the same effect on the position of the *LM* curve as a 1 per cent cut in the price level. It is possible, therefore, to discuss both the factors that shift the *LM* curve by considering what would happen to the *LM* curve if the money supply changed. Once you know how the *LM* curve shifts when the money supply changes, you also know, by implication, how the *LM* curve shifts in response to price level changes.

Figure 13.4 illustrates the effects on the *LM* curve of a rise in the money supply. The thick curves in Figure 13.4 are identical to those in Figure

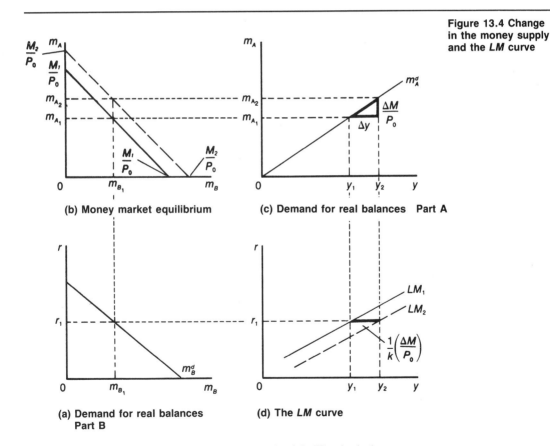

Figure 13.4 Change in the money supply and the LM curve

A rise in the supply of money shifts the *LM* curve to the right. The rise in the money supply ($\Delta M/P_0$) shifts the *LM* curve from LM_1 to LM_2 in frame (d). The *LM* curve shifts by an amount curve equal to $(1/k)$ times the rise in the real money supply ($\Delta M/P_0$), as shown in frame (c).

13.1. Now suppose that there is a rise in the money stock of an amount ΔM. This is shown in the diagram in frame (b) by the parallel shift of the money supply curve. Notice that it is shifted horizontally by an amount $\Delta M/P_0$, indicating that at all interest rates and income levels there is an extra $\Delta M/P_0$ of real balances to be held. You can derive the new LM curve for this new higher quantity of real balances in exactly the same manner as the original LM curve, LM_1, was derived. You will notice that this new LM curve LM_2, is to the right of LM_1. Thus, a rise in the quantity of money shifts the LM curve to the right. The amount by which the LM curve shifts to the right is evidently equal to $(1/k)$ times the rise in the quantity of real balances. How do we know that? We know it by exactly the same line of reasoning that led us to work out the size of the shift in the IS curve in the previous chapter. Notice that the thickened triangle in frame (c) provides the detailed calculation of the amount of the shift in the LM curve. The rise in the money stock $\Delta M/P_0$ measures the height of that triangle. We know that its slope is equal to k, and we know that its base is the change in income that would occur at a given interest rate. Using the formula 'slope equals rise over run', we can see that

$$k = \frac{\Delta M/P_0}{\Delta y}$$

Dividing both sides of that equation by k and multiplying both sides by Δy gives

$$\Delta y = \frac{1}{k}\left(\frac{\Delta M}{P_0}\right)$$

That is, the size of the shift of the LM curve to the right, Δy, equals $(1/y)$ times the rise in real money supply, $\Delta M/P_0$.

A percentage fall in the price level equal to the rise in the money stock just considered would shift the LM curve in exactly the same way.

Summary

A. Definition of the LM Curve

The LM curve is defined as an equilibrium locus that traces out the relationship between the rate of interest and the level of real income when the money supply is equal to the amount of money demanded.

B. Derivation of the LM Curve

The LM curve is derived graphically in Figure 13.1. This derivation should be thoroughly understood.

C. *Determinants of the* LM *Curve Slope*

The *LM* curve slopes upwards. This is due to the fact that as the interest rate rises, people economize on their holdings of money. With a given quantity of money in existence the only way that monetary equilibrium can be maintained at higher interest rates is for there to be a higher level of real income to induce a rise in the demand for real balances to offset the economizing on money holdings. The less elastic the demand for real balances with respect to the rate of interest, the steeper will be the *LM* curve. Also, the more responsive the demand for real balances to income changes, the steeper will be the *LM* curve. The slope of the *LM* curve is (k/l).

D. *Shifts in the* LM *Curve*

The *LM* curve will shift if the money supply changes or if the price level changes. A rise in the quantity of money will make the *LM* curve shift to the right by an amount equal to $(1/k)$ times the rise in the real money supply. A rise in the price level will have an equivalent but opposite effect on the *LM* curve to that of a rise in the money supply.

Review Questions

1. What is the *LM* curve?
2. Which markets are in equilibrium along the *LM* curve?
3. Why does the *LM* curve slope upwards?
4. If money was a perfect substitute for bonds, what would be the slope of the *LM* curve?
5. If money and bonds were completely non-substitutable, what would be the slope of the *LM* curve?
6. What happens to the position of the *LM* curve when the money supply rises?
7. What happens to the position of the *LM* curve when the price level rises?
8. What happens to the position of the *LM* curve if the money supply grows at a constant rate?
9. Why does the demand for money depend on the money rate of interest rather than on the real rate of interest?

14

Aggregate Demand in the Closed Economy

It is now possible to see the light at the end of the aggregate demand tunnel![1] You may feel that you have been groping in the darkness of that tunnel for the last few chapters. Very soon you should be able to see the light! By the time you have completed this chapter you will be able to:

(a) Understand why the intersection of the *IS* and *LM* curves determines the equilibrium levels of output and the interest rate, at a given price level.
(b) State the properties of the *IS–LM* equilibrium.
(c) Understand the effects of changes in government expenditure and taxes at a given price level.
(d) Understand the effects of a change in the money supply at a given price level.
(e) Understand how the *IS–LM* model represents a theory of aggregate demand.

---

1 This chapter presents the analysis developed by J.R. (now Sir John) Hicks in 'Mr. Keynes and the "Classics": A Suggested Interpretation', *Econometrica*, 5 (April 1937), pp. 147–59. The sheer brilliance of John Hicks is displayed in this paper which managed to cut through the complexities of the *General Theory* so soon after the work appeared.

A. Equilibrium at the *IS–LM* Intersection

You will have noticed in the above list of what you will get out of this chapter the repetitive phrase 'at a given price level'. What does that phrase mean? It means that we are going to study what would happen to real income and the (real) rate of interest, when certain things are changed, *if* the price level was to remain constant. It does not mean that some of the exogenous changes that we shall analyse will not, in fact, lead to a change in the price level. A different way of saying the same thing is that we are going to study *only* aggregate demand. We are not going to study (yet) the interaction of aggregate demand and aggregate supply.

You may, if you wish, think of the analysis that we are conducting as applying to a world in which the aggregate supply curve is horizontal at a given price level P_0.

The basis of the analysis that we are now going to perform has already been established in Chapters 11 and 13. In Chapter 11 the theory of the *IS* curve was set out and it told us what the level of aggregate demand will be at each level of the rate of interest. In Chapter 13 we studied the *LM* curve which tells us the relationship between the level of income and the level of the rate of interest at which the amount of money supplied will equal the amount demanded. In effect, the *IS* curve and the *LM* curve give us two equations in two unknown variables — the level of real income and the rate of interest. When the economy is on both the *IS* curve and the *LM* curve, a unique level of real income and of the rate of interest are determined.

According to the *IS–LM* analysis, we shall never observe the economy 'off' either of these two curves. If the economy was, in an imaginary sense, 'off' the *IS* curve, investment-plus-government spending would not be equal to savings-plus-taxes. Equilibrating forces (which will be described below) would be set up that would produce an equality between these two variables. If the economy was 'off' the *LM* curve, the demand for money would not be equal to the supply of money. Again, equilibrating forces would be set up to bring about this equality. Only when the demand for money and the supply of money are equal, and savings-plus-taxes are equal to investment-plus-government spending, will individuals' plans be compatible with each other, and will the economy be in equilibrium.

An analogy may be useful here. Suppose that Lake Windermere was arbitrarily divided by a straight line running north–south midway along its length. Now ask the question, What would happen if the water level on the left-hand side of this line was 10 feet higher than the water level on the right-hand side? This is a perfectly sensible question to ask. The answer is that the molecular structure of the water is such that the force of gravity would very quickly act upon the higher level to reduce it to equality with that of the lower level. We would never, in the ordinary course of events, observe such an inequality, although the theory that explains why the lake surface is flat involves conceptually letting the level be temporarily and hypothetically perturbed. It is the same in the money market. The very forces that would lead to money market equilibrium will, in the ordinary course of events, prevent the money market from ever straying very far away from such an equilibrium.[2]

Let us now go on to characterize the equilibrium level of output and interest rate in the *IS–LM* model.

B.   Properties of the *IS–LM* Equilibrium

(i)   *Equilibrium*

The *IS* curve derived in Figure 11.4 and the *LM* curve derived in Figure 13.1 are brought together and shown in the same diagram in Figure 14.1.

Since the *IS* curve slopes downwards and the *LM* curve slopes upwards, these two curves cut in just one place. Label this point y_1, r_1. It is a property of the interest rate r_1 and the income level y_1 that two sets of equilibrium conditions are simultaneously satisfied. First, planned savings-plus-taxes are equal to investment- plus-government spending. Second, the stock of money in existence is equal to the stock of money demanded. The point at which the income level is y_1 and interest rate is r_1 is the only point at which these two equilibrium conditions are simultaneously satisfied. This position is the equilibrium level of real income and the interest rate in the *IS–LM* model.

**Figure 14.1 *IS-LM*
Equilibrium**

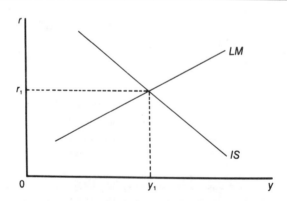

When investment-plus-government spending equals savings-plus-taxes (the economy is on the *IS* curve), and when the demand for money equals the supply of money (the economy is on the *LM* curve), then the economy is in equilibrium. Such an equilibrium is shown as y_1, r_1 in the diagram.

---

2   David Hume first suggested this water-level analogy. See his essay 'Of the Balance of Trade' in *Essays: Moral, Political and Literary* (London: Oxford University Press, 1963), p. 319.

To determine the values of the other variables in the economy — the level of investment and savings — all that is necessary is to use a diagram like Figure 11.4 and work backwards from the quadrant that displays the *IS* and *LM* curves. Figure 14.2 illustrates the values of investment and savings.

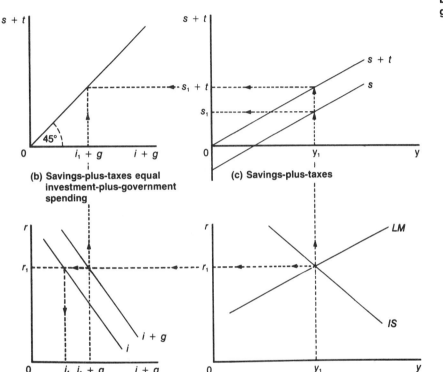

**Figure 14.2
Equilibrium in the
goods market**

(b) Savings-plus-taxes equal
investment-plus-government
spending

(c) Savings-plus-taxes

(a) Investment-plus-government
spending

(d) The *IS* and *LM* curves

Once the equilibrium level of income, y_1, and the rate of interest, r_1, are determined by the intersection of *IS* and *LM* [frame (d)], it is possible to trace backwards to establish the levels of savings, s_1 [frame (c)] and investment, i_1, [frame (a)]. When taxes are added to savings, $s_1 + t_1$, and government spending to investment, $i_1 + g$, as frame (b) shows, investment-plus-government spending is equal to savings-plus-taxes.

In frame (d), the *IS* and *LM* curves from Figure 14.1 are reproduced. The *IS* curve itself is derived from the underlying savings and investment decisions that are shown in frames (a) and (c). By working backwards from frame (d), we can work out the equilibrium levels of savings and investment. Transfer the equilibrium income level y_1 from frame (d) to frame (c), and you can read off immediately the equilibrium level of savings in the economy. Tracking leftwards across to frame (a), you can read off the equilibrium level of investment that is generated by the equilibrium interest rate r_1. By tracking this level of investment-plus-government spending vertically upwards to frame (b) and by tracking the level of savings-plus-taxes horizontally leftwards across from frame (c) to (b) you can see that the position depicted is indeed in equilibrium, for the two lines meet on the 45° line that describes the equality of $i + g$ with $s + t$.

(ii) Convergence to Equilibrium

Just what are the forces that bring about the equilibrium between investment-plus-government spending and savings-plus-taxes on the one hand and the supply of and demand for money on the other? To answer this question it is necessary to perform a conceptual experiment just like the lake water analogy. Suppose, in a hypothetical sense, that the economy was 'off' the *IS* curve. Frame (a) of Figure 14.3 can be used to illustrate the discussion.

If the economy was 'off' the *IS* curve and to its right, investment-plus-government spending would be less than savings-plus-taxes. That is, you could view the interest rate as being too high, thereby depressing investment to too low a level, or income too high, raising savings to too high a level. Either way, savings-plus-taxes would exceed investment-plus-government spending. On the left side of the *IS* curve, the reverse inequality will hold. The interest rate is too low and is stimulating too much investment or conversely, income is too low and is generating too little saving. Either way, investment-plus-government spending exceeds savings-plus-taxes.

Suppose the economy is in this second situation of too much investment-plus-government spending relative to the amount of savings-plus-taxes. What would happen? According to this model this would be a situation in which income would not be stationary, but would be rising. The reason why income would be rising is that the total amount of spending that individuals are attempting to undertake exceeds the level of income out of which they are attempting to undertake that spending. To see this, recall that consumption is simply income minus savings minus taxes; this means that if savings-plus-taxes are less than investment-plus-government spending, the sum of consumption and investment-plus-government spending must be a bigger number than income. Such a situation clearly cannot be because we know that, as a matter of fact, income is equal to consumption plus investment-plus-government spending. We can illustrate this point with a story (analogous to the story told above about different levels of water in Lake Windermere). The story would go like this. As people *tried* to spend more than current income, income would rise and keep on rising until it had reached a high enough level to be equal to the total level of spending that individuals were under-

Figure 14.3
Equilibrating forces

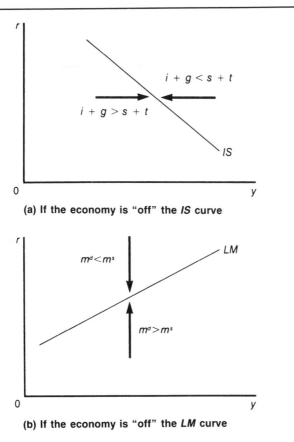

(a) If the economy is "off" the *IS* curve

(b) If the economy is "off" the *LM* curve

If the economy is 'off' the *IS* curve, planned expenditures will differ from income. In such a case, income would have to rise ($i + g > s + t$) or fall ($i + g < s + t$). The movement in income would be rapid, and the economy quickly would be brought to a point on the *IS* curve. If the demand for money was not equal to the supply of money, the economy would be 'off' the *LM* curve. This would lead to the buying or selling of securities, which would produce a rise or fall in the interest rate, so that money market equilibrium was achieved. These equilibrating forces are assumed to operate quickly, so that the economy is not, in the normal course of events, observed to be 'off' either the *IS* or the *LM* curves.

taking. We know where that point is. For any given interest rate, it is the point at which income is read off from the *IS* curve.

To reinforce your understanding, consider the reverse situation. Suppose the economy was to the right of the *IS* curve, with savings-plus-taxes bigger than investment-plus-government spending. In that case, total spending plans would add up to a number less than income, and would be falling and would continue to fall until it had reached a low enough level for spending plans to have reached equality with income. Again, that is a point on the *IS* curve.

Thus, one part of the equilibrating force is a change in income that ensures that investment-plus-government spending is equal to savings-plus-taxes. In other words, income adjusts to put the economy on its *IS* curve. Income, not the price level or the interest rate, is the equilibrating variable at work in this case.[3]

Next, consider a conceptual experiment in the money market. Suppose the economy is 'off' the *LM* curve, as shown in frame (b) of Figure 14.3. If it was below the *LM* curve, then the demand for money would exceed the supply of money. That is, the interest rate would be too low or income would be too high, generating a larger demand for money than the amount of money available. If the economy was above the *LM* curve, the demand for money would be less than the supply of money. That is, the interest rate would be too high and/or the income level too low, making the amount of money demanded fall short of the amount available to be held.

What would happen if the economy was in one of these situations? Imagine that it is in a situation in which the demand for money was less than the supply of money. Obviously, since the supply of money is physically present in the economy, even though the amount demanded is less than the amount supplied, the amount supplied would have to be the same as the amount being held. In other words, individuals would have in their pockets, purses and bank accounts more money than they would want to be holding in current conditions. What would they do in such a situation? The answer is they would try to get rid of the excess money.

This model assumes that in order to lower their money holdings, people would buy bonds and other kinds of financial assets. Of course, each individual can get rid of unwanted excess money holdings by buying bonds. Individuals in aggregate, however, cannot do this because there is a certain fixed amount of money in existence in the economy. One individual's purchase of bonds is another individual's sale of bonds. The reduction in one individual's holdings of money will be matched by an increase in someone else's. For the economy as a whole then, the attempts by individuals to rid themselves of excess money balances cannot result in a drop in the amount of money being held. Something else has to do

---

3   Don Patinkin (of the Hebrew University in Jerusalem), the world's leading Keynes scholar, believes that the essential originality in Keynes *General Theory* was this idea — that income rather than prices plays the equilibrating role in the economy. If you wish to pursue this matter in greater depth and also get some experience of how a first-rate historian of economic thought works, you can do no better than read two of Don Patinkin's pieces on this subject. They are: 'A Study of Keynes' Theory of Effective Demand', *Economic Inquiry*, 17 (April 1979), pp. 155–76; and 'The Process of Writing the *General Theory*, A Critical Survey', pp. 3–24, in *Keynes, Cambridge, and the General Theory*, D. Patinkin and J. C. Leith (eds) (London: Macmillan, 1977).

the adjusting. What is it that adjusts? The answer is the rate of interest. The effect of buying bonds is to raise the demand for bonds and bid up their prices. Bidding up the price of a bond has the effect of bidding down its rate of return — the rate of interest.

You might find it helpful to have this spelled out. Suppose a bond pays £5 a year in interest in perpetuity, and suppose that the bond has a current market price of £50. The rate of interest clearly, then, is 10 per cent a year — £5 divided by £50 expressed as a per cent. Now suppose that instead of being £50, the bond price is £25. The interest payment is still £5 a year, but now the interest rate has increased to 20 per cent a year (£5 divided by £25). Yet again, suppose that instead of being £50, the bond price is £100. In this case, with an interest payment of £5 a year, the interest rate would be 5 per cent a year (£5 divided by £100). You see, then, that the rate of interest on a bond (the market rate of interest in the economy) is inversely related to the price of a bond.

Continuing now with the story — as people tried to get rid of their unwanted excess money balances by buying bonds, they would bid up the price of bonds and bid down the rate of interest. This process would continue until a situation arose in which the excess supply of money was eliminated. The interest rate would fall far enough to eliminate the excess supply of money because people would continue to buy bonds, bidding up their price and bidding down the interest rate, until they were satisfied that the money they were holding was equal to the amount that they wanted to hold.

The same mechanism could work in the opposite direction. If the demand for money exceeded the amount of money in existence, individuals would seek to add to their money balances. They would do this by selling bonds. As they sold bonds, the price of bonds would fall, and the interest rate on them would rise. This process would continue until the interest rate had risen sufficiently to make the amount of money in existence enough to satisfy people's demand for money. Either way, then, an excess demand or excess supply in the money market would lead to a movement in the rate of interest by an amount sufficient to place the economy on the *LM* curve.

Now bring these two stories together. If the economy was 'off' the *IS* curve, income would adjust to bring about an equality between savings-plus-taxes and investment-plus-government spending. If the economy was 'off' the *LM* curve, the interest rate would adjust to bring about an equality between the demand for money and the supply of money. These two forces, operating simultaneously, ensure that both the stock equilibrium in the money market and the flow equilibrium between investment-plus-government spending and savings-plus-taxes are simultaneously achieved. It is an assumption of the *IS–LM* model that these forces are sufficiently strong that the economy is observed only at points of intersection of the *IS* and *LM* curves.

C. Changes in Government Expenditure and Taxes

You have now studied all the key ingredients of the *IS–LM* model and are in the position to analyse, in a fairly straightforward manner, the effects of changes in government spending and taxes on the level of real income and the rate of interest. You should not confuse such an exercise with an analysis of macroeconomic policy. Properly understood, it is just one ingredient in a full policy analysis — the ingredient that tells us how changes in the government's monetary and fiscal policies influence the level of aggregate demand. A comprehensive analysis of macroeconomic policy cannot be performed using only the aggregate demand side of the economy. We shall conduct a thorough analysis of macroeconomic policy in Part V of this book. Nevertheless, this is a useful stage of your study at which to analyse the effects of changes in government macroeconomic policy variables on the level of aggregate demand. Let us now turn to that task.

(i) Changes in Government Expenditure

First, let us analyse the effects of a change in government spending. You already know that a change in government spending leads to a shift in the *IS* curve. Specifically, you know that a rise in government spending leads to a rightward shift of the *IS* curve by an amount equal to the change in government spending multiplied by one over one minus the marginal propensity to consume. What is the effect of the change in government spending, not on the shift in the *IS* curve but on the equilibrium level of income and the rate of interest? Figure 14.4 provides the basis for answering this question.

Figure 14.4 The effect of government spending on the interest rates and real income

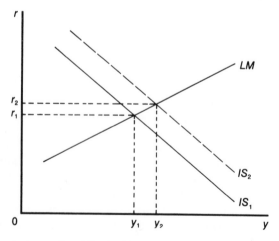

A rise in government spending shifts the *IS* curve from IS_1 to IS_2. The result is a higher income level (y_1 to y_2) and a higher interest rate (r_1 to r_2).

Assume that initially the level of government spending is such that the *IS* curve is represented by IS_1. This intersects the *LM* curve at the interest rate r_1 and the income level y_1. Now imagine that there is a rise in government spending by an amount sufficient to shift the *IS* curve from IS_1 to IS_2. Recall that the horizontal distance of the shift in the *IS* curve is equal to the change in government spending multiplied by one over one minus the marginal propensity to consume. You can discover, by inspecting Figure 14.4, that the effect on the equilibrium levels of income and the rate of interest of this shift in the *IS* curve is to raise the interest rate from r_1 to r_2 and to raise income from y_1 to y_2. This result, depicted in Figure 14.4, is a general result. A rise in government spending raises both real income and the rate of interest.

The amounts by which income and the interest rate rise depend on the slopes of both the *LM* and *IS* curves. To see how the slope of the *LM* curve affects the outcome, consider Figure 14.5.

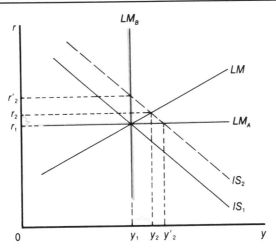

Figure 14.5 Government spending and the steepness of the LM curve

The flatter is the *LM* curve, the bigger the effect of a change in government spending on real income, and the smaller its effect on the interest rate. A rise in government spending shifts the *IS* curve from IS_1 to IS_2, raising real income to y_2 and interest rates to r_2. In the extremes, with a horizontal *LM* curve (LM_A) real income will rise from y_1 to y'_2, and the interest rate stays constant; and with a vertical *LM* curve (LM_B), the interest rate will rise from r_1 to r'_2, and real income will remain unchanged at y_1.

In this figure two extreme slopes for the *LM* curve are shown. The curve labelled LM_A is horizontal. This would be one limiting case of the slope of the *LM* curve — the case in which money and non-money assets are such perfect substitutes for each other that people really don't care how much money they are holding, relative to other assets. If the interest rate was slightly above r_1, they would want to hold entirely non-money assets. If the interest rate was slightly below r_1, they would want to hold nothing but money. So r_1 represents the interest rate at which people are entirely indifferent as to whether they want to hold money or other assets. This is a pretty unlikely case, but one that serves to illustrate one of the extreme outcomes of the effects of a change in government spending. In this particular case, you can see that the effect of a change in government spending would be to raise income and leave the interest rate unchanged. The rise in income would be equal to the full amount of the horizontal shift of the *IS* curve. That is, it would be equal to the rise in government spending multiplied by one over one minus the marginal propensity to consume.

The other extreme case illustrated in Figure 14.5 is that of the *LM* curve labelled LM_B. The *LM* curve would be vertical if the demand for money did not depend on the interest rate at all. This would be the case if people regarded non-money assets as completely useless as substitutes for money, so that regardless of the opportunity cost of holding money, there would be a certain amount of money that they felt it absolutely necessary to hold. In that not so unlikely but nevertheless exaggerated case, the rise in government spending that shifts the *IS* curve to IS_2 would raise the interest rate to r_2' but would leave the level of real income unaffected. What is going on here is that the amount of money which people want to hold is, in effect, a rigid fraction of the level of income. Since the amount of money in the economy has not been changed, then neither can the level of income change. Any change in government spending is fully 'crowded out' by a rise in the interest rate choking off an equal amount of private investment demand.

The analysis in Figure 14.5 serves to illustrate the propositions that the effect of a change in government spending on real income is smaller when the interest elasticity of the demand for money is smaller, and the effect of a change in government spending on the rate of interest is larger when the interest elasticity of the demand for money is smaller.

The size of the government spending multiplier is also affected by the slope of the *IS* curve. This is illustrated in Figure 14.6.

Consider first the *IS* curve labelled IS_1, and the equilibrium r_1, y_1. Now imagine that government spending increases, shifting the *IS* curve to IS_2. This produces a change in income to y_2 and a change in the interest rate to r_2. Now imagine that the *IS* curve is flatter than those depicted as IS_1 and IS_2. In particular, let the initial *IS* curve be IS_1'. Now conduct the same experiment of raising government spending. Raise it by exactly the same amount as before. We know that the new *IS* curve will be parallel to the original one and will shift to the right by the same absolute amount, so that at the interest rate r_1 the curve IS_2' intersects the curve IS_2. Now the new equilibrium income level is y_2' and the interest rate level is r_2'. Notice that y_2' is lower than y_2 and r_2' is lower than r_2.

The analysis in Figure 14.6 shows that the flatter the *IS* curve, the smaller will be the effect of a change in government spending on income and on the rate of interest.

The consequences of the slopes of the *LM* and *IS* curves may now be

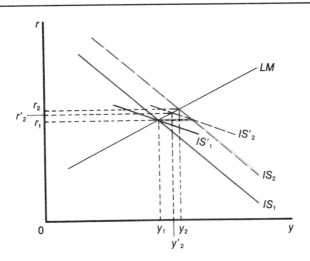

Figure 14.6 Government spending and the steepness of the *IS* curve

The flatter the *IS* curve, the smaller is the effect of fiscal policy on both interest rates and real income. When the *IS* curve is IS_1, the rise in government spending shifts the *IS* curve to IS_2, raising real income from y_1 to y_2 and interest rates from r_1 to r_2. If the *IS* curve is flatter, IS'_1, a rise in government spending shifts the *IS* curve to IS'_2 raising real income and interest rates to y'_2 and r'_2.

summarized succinctly. The smaller the interest elasticity of the demand for money and the greater the interest elasticity of investment demand, the smaller will be the effect of a change in government spending on the level of real income. The smaller the interest elasticity of demand for money and the smaller the interest elasticity of investment demand, the larger will be the effect of a change in government spending on the interest rate.

(ii) Changes in Taxes

Considering the effects of tax changes is a straightforward extension of the exercise that you have just conducted. You already know from Chapter 11 that a rise in taxes shifts the IS curve in the *opposite* direction to that of a rise in government spending. That is, a rise in taxes will shift the IS curve to the left, whereas a rise in government spending will shift the IS curve to the right. You also know that the distance of the shift is fraction b (marginal propensity to consume) of the shift for an equivalent change in government spending. The differences between the effects of changes in government spending and taxes end here. The other effects of each of the two changes are identical in this IS–LM setup. All the remarks made above concerning the effects of the slopes of the LM and IS curves on the size of the government expenditure multipliers apply identically to the tax multipliers. The effects of a tax rise on income and the rate of interest are opposite in direction and fraction b of the magnitude of the effects of changes in government spending.

D. Change in the Money Supply

You already know that a change in the money supply will shift the *LM* curve. The effects of an *LM* curve shift on the equilibrium level of real income and the interest rate will, like the effects of the *IS* curve shift just analysed, depend on the slopes of both the *IS* and *LM* curves. Let us consider first the general case. Figure 14.7 illustrates the effects of a change in money supply on the equilibrium level of real income and the rate of interest.

Figure 14.7 The effects of monetary policy on real income and the rate of interest

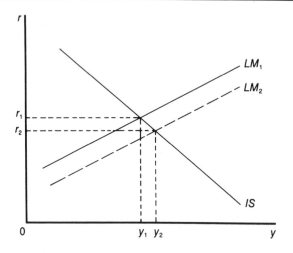

A rise in the money supply shifts the *LM* curve to the right — from LM_1 to LM_2. This lowers the rate of interest from r_1 to r_2 and raises the level of real income from y_1 to y_2.

The economy is initially in equilibrium, with the *IS* curve intersecting LM_1 at the interest rate r_1 and the output level y_1. Now imagine the money supply is increased, so that the *LM* curve moves to LM_2. The new intersection of the *IS* and *LM* curves is at the income level y_2 and the interest rate r_2. You can see by inspection of Figure 14.7 that the rise in the money supply leads to a rise in real income and a fall in the rate of interest. This is the general prediction of the *IS–LM* model.

Now consider what happens to these effects when the slope of the *IS* curve is allowed to vary. The relationship between the effects of a change in monetary policy and the slope of the *IS* curve is illustrated in Figure 14.8.

Just as in the previous case, two extreme slopes for the *IS* curve are shown. If the *IS* curve is the horizontal curve IS_A, the effect of a change in the money stock is to raise real income by the full amount of the horizontal shift of the *LM* curve. The interest rate remains unchanged.

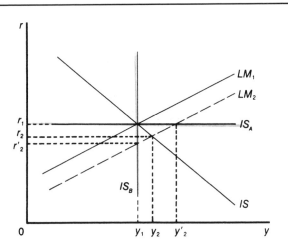

Figure 14.8 Monetary policy and the steepness of the IS curve

The flatter the *IS* curve, the bigger the effect of a change in the money stock on the level of real income and the smaller its effect on the rate of interest. If the *IS* curve were horizontal (IS_A) the shift in the *LM* curve from LM_1 to LM_2 raises real income from y_1 to y_2' and leaves the interest rate unchanged. If the *IS* curve was vertical (IS_B), a rise in the money supply that shifts the *LM* curve from LM_1 to LM_2 lowers the interest rate from r_1 to r_2' and leaves real income unchanged.

This result would arise if the marginal productivity of capital was completely constant, independent of the size of the capital stock. The opposite case, depicted as the vertical curve IS_B, leads to the predicition that the interest rate would drop to r_2', and income would remain unchanged at y_1. This would arise if, no matter how much the rate of interest changed, firms saw no reason to change their capital stock.

What is going on in these two cases is straightforward to interpret. With a horizontal IS curve (with a fixed rate of interest), the level of aggregate demand moves one-for-one with the level of the money stock. In the case of a vertical IS curve, the change in the money supply merely changes the rate of interest, leaving the level of aggregate demand unaffected. This arises because, with investment being completely insensitive to interest rates, the level of investment will remain unchanged no matter what the interest rate is. Since the level of government spending is also constant (by assumption), and since consumption demand depends only on income, there is nothing being altered on the expenditure side of the economy to produce any change in the quantity of output demanded. All the adjustment, therefore, has to come out in a lower interest rate.

What Figure 14.8 illustrates is the general proposition that the more elastic the demand for investment with respect to the rate of interest, the bigger is the effect of a change in the money stock on income, and the smaller is the effect of a change in the money stock on the rate of interest.

Next, consider the effect of the slope of the LM curve on the size of the change in the real income and the rate of interest resulting from a change in the money stock. This is illustrated in Figure 14.9.

Again, let the economy initially be in an equilibrium where the *IS* curve intersects the curve LM_1 at the interest rate r_1 and the income level y_1.

Figure 14.9 Monetary policy and the steepness of the *LM* curve

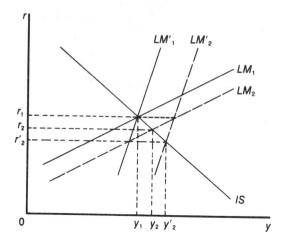

The steeper the *LM* curve, the bigger the effects of a change in the money supply on both the level of income and the rate of interest. If the *LM* curve is *LM′*, then the changes in income and the rate of interest are from y_1 to y'_2 and r_1 to r'_2. These are larger than the shifts arising in the case of the increased money supply shifting the flatter *LM* curve from LM_1 to LM_2.

Now let the money stock increase, so that the *LM* curve shifts to LM_2. As in the case of Figure 14.7, this produces a rise in income to y_2 and a drop in the interest rate to r_2. Now imagine that instead of the *LM* curve being $LM_1(LM_2)$, it is steeper than that, indicating a less elastic demand for money with respect to the rate of interest. Specifically, suppose the *LM* curve initially is LM'_1. When the money stock rises, the *LM* curve will shift to LM'_2. (Remember that the horizontal shift at a given interest rate, in this case r_1, is independent of the steepness of the *LM* curve.) What is the effect of an equivalent change in the money stock in this case? It is to raise income to y'_2 and lower the interest rate to r'_2. Notice that the change in both income and interest rate is bigger in this case than it was in the previous case. This serves to illustrate the general propostion that the smaller is the interest elasticity of the demand for money, the bigger will be the effect of a change in the money supply on both the rate of interest and the level of income.

You have now completed your investigation of the properties of the *IS–LM* model. The final section of this chapter is designed to help you see how the *IS–LM* model may be seen as a theory of aggregate demand.

E.   Theory of Aggregate Demand

Just as there are various stages in the process of learning economics that
involve mastering some steps of analysis that seem, at the time, completely pointless, so also there are times when everything seems to be
falling into place. You have now reached one such point. It is as if a major
section of a complicated jigsaw puzzle is just about to have the final piece
put in, and a single pattern connecting previously seemingly distinct sections is revealed. Specifically, you are now going to be able to see not
only the *IS*–*LM* model in its entirety but also how that model generates
the theory of aggregate demand.

Begin by recalling the concept of the aggregate demand curve. As set
out in Chapter 8, the aggregate demand curve is defined as the relationship between the aggregate quantity of goods and services that people
want to buy in a given period of time and the general price level. This
definition (and concept) is sufficiently general to embrace all conceivable
theoretical frameworks and certainly that of the *IS*–*LM* model.

It is easy to derive the *IS*–*LM* model aggregate demand curve in a two-
part diagram, as set out in Figure 14.10. Frame (a) has the rate of interest
on the vertical axis and real income on the horizontal axis. Frame (b) has
the price level on the vertical axis and real income on the horizontal axis.
Frame (a) shows an *IS* curve and an *LM* curve labelled $LM(P_0)$. These
two curves intersect at the income level y_0 and interest rate r_0. This is
exactly the solution that we have been working with throughout this
chapter. That solution point can also be characterized in frame (b). It is
point A. We know that it is point A because we know that we have been
treating the price level as predetermined at P_0. Also we know that the
model has determined for us an output level of y_0.

It is possible, to ask, hypothetically, what the level of aggregate demand
would be in the *IS*–*LM* framework if the price level was different from
P_0. Suppose the price level was higher than P_0, say at P_1. What then
would be the quantity of goods and services demanded if everything else
was the same? From the analysis of the *IS* curve in Chapter 11 you can
quickly verify that the position of the *IS* curve is independent of the price
level. It is entirely a real curve that relates real income to the rate of interest and depends only on other real variables, namely real taxes and
real government spending. The *LM* curve, in contrast, is not independent of the price level. You can quickly verify from its definition and
derivation that a change in the price level has the same type of effect (but
opposite in direction) on the *LM* curve as does a change in the money
supply. If we *lower* the money supply, we shift the *LM* curve to the left.
If we *raise* the price level to P_1, we know that the *LM* curve will also shift
to the left. Let us suppose that it shifts to become the curve $LM(P_1)$ in
frame (a).

This new *LM* curve intersects the *IS* curve at the interest rate r_1 and
the output level y_1. Since we know the price level that gave rise to that

**Figure 14.10 Deriva-
tion of the aggregate
demand curve**

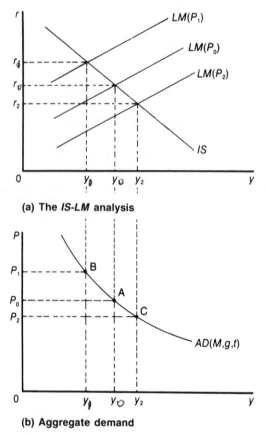

(a) The IS-LM analysis

(b) Aggregate demand

By hypothetically allowing the price level to vary from P_0 to P_1 to P_2, the LM curve shifts
[frame (a)], generating different equilibrium interest rates and income levels. Each
equilibrium income level is also the level of aggregate demand at the relevant price level.
These combinations of the price level and level of aggregate demand give us points A, B
and C on the aggregate demand curve in frame (b). In general, aggregate demand
depends on the money supply, government spending and taxes.

LM curve is P_1, we can read off from frame (b) the point at which the
income level y_1 is associated with the price level P_1. That point is B. Point
B is, like point A, another point on the aggregate demand curve. Next,
imagine that the price level is at some lower level than P_0, say, P_2, as
shown on the vertical axis of frame (b). With a lower price level we know
that the LM curve would shift to the right (equivalent to a rise in the
money stock). Suppose, in fact, that the LM curve shifts to the curve labelled $LM(P_2)$, which generates the income level y_2 and the interest rate r_2.
Dropping that income level y_2 down to frame (b) shows that point C is
also a point on the IS–LM aggregate demand curve. Joining up points
B, A, C and extrapolating to points beyond B and C traces out the aggregate demand curve.

In conducting the *IS–LM* analysis of the determination of output, it was possible to focus only on point A. By looking at what happens to the *IS* and *LM* curve intersections at the given price level, P_0, we are simply examining how the point A travels horizontally. You can now see, however, that the same analysis applies at each and every possible price level and tells us how the aggregate demand curve shifts as the levels of taxes, government spending and the money supply are varied.

This is the key thing to understand about the analysis of aggregate demand that we have conducted in the *IS–LM* framework. The analysis tells us about the factors that cause horizontal shifts in the aggregate demand curve. Anything that shifts point A will also shift point B and point C in the same horizontal direction. Thus, a rise in government spending or a cut in taxes or a rise in the money stock will all produce a rightward shift of the aggregate demand curve.

The *AD* curve in frame (b) in Figure 14.10 is labelled $AD(M,g,t)$ to remind us of this. The size of that shift will depend on the slopes of the *IS* and *LM* curves. Those slopes will in turn depend on the slopes of the demand for money function and the investment demand function. In general, the steeper the demand for money function with respect to the interest rate and/or the flatter the investment demand function with respect to the interest rate, the bigger will be the effect of a change in the money supply on the horizontal shift of the aggregate demand curve, and the smaller will be the effect of a change in government spending or taxes.

In the limiting case where the *IS* curve is horizontal (the interest rate is fixed) or where the *LM* curve is vertical (money is completely non-substitutable for other assets), then only changes in the money supply will lead to changes in the aggregate demand curve, and changes in government spending and taxes will leave the aggregate demand curve unaffected.

At the other extreme, if money is a perfect substitute for other assets so that the *LM* curve is horizontal, or if investment demand is completely unresponsive to interest rate changes so that the *IS* curve is vertical, then only changes in government spending and taxes will lead to shifts in the aggregate demand curve, and changes in the money stock will leave the aggregate demand curve unaffected.

The Keynesian cross model that we examined in Chapter 9 may be seen as another special case of this *IS–LM* set up. That model is the case in which either the *IS* curve is vertical or the *LM* curve is horizontal, so that changes in the rate of interest do not affect the level of investment.

There is one final special case — a vertical *LM* curve. In this case only changes in the money stock will shift the aggregate demand curve. In general, none of these extremes will be a relevant description of an actual economy and the aggregate demand curve will shift both because of changes in the money stock and because of changes in the levels of government spending and taxes.

Summary

A. Equilibrium at the IS—LM Intersection

The IS curve shows at each level of the interest rate, the level of real income that equates savings-plus-taxes with investment-plus-government spending. The LM curve gives another relationship between real income and the interest rate, that equates the supply of and the demand for money. There is just one level of the interest rate and of real income at which both of these relationships are simultaneously satisfied. This point is the equilibrium of the IS—LM model.

B. Properties of the IS—LM Equilibrium

The IS—LM equilibrium occurs when both the demand for money equals the supply of money and savings-plus-taxes equal investment-plus-government spending. It is assumed that the forces making for equality of both these sets of magnitudes are strong enough to ensure that the economy is never observed away from equilibrium. If saving-plus-taxes were to exceed investment-plus-government spending, real income would fall to restore the equality. If the supply of money exceeded the demand for money, the act of attempting to reduce money balances and acquire bonds would put downward pressure on interest rates to the point at which the amount of money in existence was willingly held. Both sets of forces have sufficient strength for the economy never to be observed 'off' either the IS or LM curves. Thus, the intersection point of the IS and LM curves is the point that describes the state of the economy.

C. Changes in Government Expenditure and Taxes

In general, a rise in government spending or a cut in taxes will raise the level of real income and the rate of interest. The steeper the IS curve the greater will be the rise in both variables. The flatter the LM curve the greater will be the rise in real income and the smaller will be the rise in the interest rate.

D. Change in the Money Supply

In general, a rise in the money supply will lead to a rise in real income and a fall in the rate of interest. The steeper the LM curve the larger will be the change in both variables. The flatter the IS curve, the greater will be the change in real income and the smaller will be the change in the interest rate.

E. *Theory of Aggregate Demand*

By solving the *IS–LM* model for a variety of different price levels, an aggregate demand curve may be traced out. That aggregate demand curve will be downward sloping. In general, the aggregate demand curve will shift when the money stock changes, when government spending changes, or when taxes change. There are special extreme cases in which some of the variables under government control have no effect on the aggregate demand curve. If the *IS* curve is vertical or if the *LM* curve is horizontal, only government spending and taxes will shift the aggregate demand curve; changes in the money supply will leave the curve unaffected. (This is the Keynesian cross model of Chapter 9.) At the other extreme, if the *IS* curve is horizontal or if the *LM* curve is vertical, then changes in the money supply will shift the aggregate demand curve, but changes in government spending and taxes will leave it unaffected.

Review Questions

1. Which markets are in equilibrium at the point of intersection of the *IS* and *LM* curves?
2. What would be happening if the economy was 'off' its *IS* curve?
3. What would be happening if the economy was 'off' its *LM* curve?
4. Show the effects in the *IS–LM* model of a rise in government expenditure on the the level of real income and the rate of interest. What conditions would lead to only the rate of interest changing? What conditions would lead to only real income changing?
5. Suppose there was a rise in the government's budget deficit (g rises relative to t). What does the *IS–LM* model predict will happen to the rate of interest?
6. Could your answer to Question 5 be part of the reason for high interest rates in the UK in recent years? (Be careful to distinguish between real and money rates of interest in your answer to this question.)
7. Show the effect in the *IS–LM* model of a rise in the money supply on the rate of interest and the level of real income. What conditions would lead to only the level of real income changing?
8. What is the aggregate demand curve? Which markets are in equilibrium along that aggregate demand curve? What is being held constant along the aggregate demand curve? Why does the curve slope downwards? Are there any conditions that would make the aggregate demand curve vertical?
9. You are given the following information about a hypothetical economy:

$$c = 100 + 0.8(y - t)$$
$$i = 500 - 50r$$

$$g = 400$$
$$t = 400$$
$$M/P = 0.2y + 500 - 25r$$

The price level is fixed at 1.

The money supply is 520.

(c = consumption; i = investment; g = government expenditure; t = taxes; r = rate of interest; M = money supply; P = price level; y = real income)

(a) Find the equilibrium values of real income, consumption, investment, and the rate of interest.

(b) Find the effect on those equilibrium values of a unit rise in M, g and t.

✗ Appendix: The Algebra of the *IS–LM* Model of Aggregate Demand

This Appendix takes you through the algebra of the determination of the equilibrium levels of output and the rate of interest in the *IS–LM* model. Like the Appendix to Chapter 11, it contains nothing of substance that is not explained in words and diagrams in the body of the chapter. It may, nevertheless, provided that you feel comfortable with algebraic formulations, give you a clearer picture of how the *IS–LM* model works. The case analysed in this Appendix is that in which the price level is fixed at P_0, so that output is varying only in ranges up to, but not including, full-employment output.

Aggregate demand is determined by the sum of consumption, investment, and government demand. That is

$$y^d = c + i + g \tag{14A.1}$$

Consumption demand is determined by the consumption function, which is

$$c = a + b(y - t), \quad a > 0, 0 < b < 1 \tag{14A.2}$$

Investment demand is determined by

$$i = i_0 - hr, \quad i_0, h > 0 \tag{14A.3}$$

Flow equilibrium prevails in the goods market when aggregate demand equals actual income. That is

$$y^d = y \tag{14A.4}$$

The above four equations taken together constitute the equation for the *IS* curve. That equation may be derived by using Equations (14A.2), (14A.3), and (14A.4) together with Equation (14A.1) to give

$$y = \overbrace{a + b(y - t)}^{c} + \overbrace{i_0 - hr}^{i} + g \tag{14A.5}$$

This equation may be rearranged or 'solved' for real income as

$$y = \frac{1}{1-b}(a + i_0 + g - bt - hr) \qquad (14A.6)$$

Equation (14A.6) is the equation for the *IS* curve.
The demand for money function is given by

$$\frac{M^d}{P_0} = m_0 + ky - lr, \quad k > 0, l > 0 \qquad (14A.7)$$

Monetary equilibrium requires that the demand for money be equal to the supply of money; that is,

$$M^d = M \qquad (14A.8)$$

Substituting Equation (14A.7) into Equation (14A.8) yields an equation for the *LM* curve which may be 'solved' for income as

$$y = \frac{1}{k}\left[\frac{M}{P_0} - (m_0 + lr)\right] \qquad (14A.9)$$

Equation (14A.9) describes the *LM* relation.

Equations (14A.6) and (14A.9), the equations for the *IS* and *LM* curves, contain two unknowns — real income and the rate of interest. By setting the real income level in Equation (14A.6) equal to the real income level in Equation (14A.9) and solving for the rate of interest, you readily obtain

$$r = \frac{1}{1-b+kh/l}\left[\frac{k}{l}(a + i_0 + g - bt) - \frac{(1-b)}{l}\left(\frac{M}{P_0} - m_0\right)\right] \qquad (14A.10)$$

Equation (14A.10) is an algebraic expression for the equilibrium value of the rate of interest in the *IS−LM* model. By substituting Equation (14A.10) back into Equation (14A.9) to eliminate the rate of interest, you may obtain an expression for the level of real income. It is possible to 'tidy up' the expression to give

$$y = \frac{1}{1-b+(kh/l)}\left[(a + i_0 + g - bt) + \frac{h}{l}\left(\frac{M}{P_0} - m_0\right)\right] \qquad (14A.11)$$

Equation (14A.11) is the solution of the *IS−LM* model for the equilibrium level of real income.

In order to obtain a better understanding of what those equations are saying, let us examine Equations (14A.10) and (14A.11) to see how the interest rate and the level of income vary as we vary the three policy instruments — government spending, taxes, and the money supply. Imagine that each of those three policy variables took on a different value from g, t, and M. Specifically, suppose that g was to increase to g' and *t* to *t'*, and *M* to *M'*. In that case, we know that the solutions for the interest rate and the level of income could be expressed as

$$r' = \frac{1}{1-b+(kh/l)} \left[\frac{k}{l} (a + i_0 + g' - bt') - \frac{(1-b)}{l} \left(\frac{M'}{P_0} - m_0 \right) \right]$$

$$\text{(14A.12)}$$

$$y' = \frac{1}{1-b+(kh/l)} \left[(a + i_0 + g' - bt') + \frac{h}{l} \left(\frac{M'}{P_0} - m_0 \right) \right] \text{(14A.13)}$$

Equations (14A.12) and (14A.13) are identical to Equations (14A.10) and (14A.11) except that the values of the variables (*r* and *y* on the left-hand side and *g*, *t*, and *M* on the right-hand side) have all changed from their original values to their new (primed) values.

Now subtract Equation (14A.10) from Equation (14A.12) to obtain Equation (14A.14). Also subtract Equation (14A.11) from Equation (14A.13) to obtain Equation (14A.15). Notice that in Equations (14A.14) and (14A.15) the terms *a*, i_0 and m_0 have disappeared since they are common to both the original solutions and the new solutions for *y* and *r*. Thus,

$$r' - r = \frac{1}{1-b+(kh/l)} \left[\frac{k}{l} (g' - g) - \frac{bk}{l} (t' - t) \right.$$

$$\left. - \frac{1-b}{l} \left(\frac{M'}{P_0} - \frac{M}{P_0} \right) \right]$$

$$\text{(14A.14)}$$

and

$$y' - y = \frac{1}{1-b+(kh/l)} \left[(g' - g) - b(t' - t) + \frac{h}{l} \left(\frac{M'}{P_0} - \frac{M}{P_0} \right) \right].$$

$$\text{(14A.15)}$$

Now call the gap between *y'* and *y* the change in *y* and label it *Δy*. Similarly, call the gap between *r'* and *r*, *Δr*, and likewise for the policy variables. That is, *g' − g* is *Δg*, *t' − t* is *Δt*, and *M' − M* is *ΔM*. Using this convention, you can write Equations (14A.14) and (14A.15) slightly more compactly as Equations (14A.16) and (14A.17); that is

$$\Delta r = \frac{1}{1-b+(kh/l)} \left[\frac{k}{l} \Delta g - \frac{bk}{l} \Delta t - \frac{(1-b)}{l} \frac{\Delta M}{P_0} \right] \text{(14A.16)}$$

$$\Delta y = \frac{1}{1-b+(kh/l)} \left[\Delta g - b\Delta t + \frac{h}{l} \frac{\Delta M}{P_0} \right] \text{(14A.17)}$$

You can now interpret Equations (14A.16) and (14A.17) very directly. Notice that the expression

$$\frac{1}{1-b+(kh/l)}$$

is a positive coefficient relating the changes in the policy variables to the changes in the rate of interest and the level of real income. (You know that it is positive since b is a positive fraction, $1-b$ is also a positive fraction, and k, h and l are all positive parameters.) You can immediately see that Equation (14A.16) says that, in general, a rise in g will raise the interest rate, whereas a rise in t and a rise in M will cut the interest rate. From Equation (14A.17) you can see that in general, a rise in g or a rise in M will raise income, but a rise in t will cut income. Equations (14A.16) and (14A.17) are nothing other than algebraic expressions for the equivalent propositions obtained in Chapter 14 by direct inspection of the diagrammatic solution for equilibrium output and the interest rate.

In this chapter some extreme cases were presented, and the way in which the policy instrument multipliers are affected by the slopes of the *IS* and *LM* curves was examined. This can now be done fairly precisely with the algebraic solutions in Equations (14A.16) and (14A.17). Let us now look at this.

Some Special Cases

First, suppose that the parameter h became infinitely big. An infinitely big h means that the investment demand curve and hence, the *IS* curve is horizontal; it also means that the rate of interest remains constant. What do the multipliers become when h is infinitely big? By inspecting Equations (14A.16) and (14A.17), you can establish that the multipliers are as follows:

$$\Delta r = 0 \tag{14A.18}$$

$$\Delta y = \frac{1}{kP_0} \Delta M \tag{14A.19}$$

What Equation (14A.19) says is that the aggregate demand curve will shift (y will change by Δy) only as a result of a change in the money stock. The shift will be equal to $1/(kP_0)$ times the change in the money stock. Changes in government spending and taxes will have no effect on aggregate demand in this special case.

Consider as the next special case that in which $l = 0$. This would be where the demand for money is completely insensitive to interest rates. You can think of this situation as arising when money is such a unique asset that it is completely non-substitutable for any other assets. In this case, by inspection of Equations (14A.16) and (134.17), you will discover that the multipliers become

$$\Delta r = \frac{1}{h}\left(\Delta g - b\Delta t - \frac{(1-b)}{kP_0}\Delta M\right) \tag{14A.20}$$

and

$$\Delta y = \frac{1}{kP_0}\Delta M \tag{14A.21}$$

In this case, the interest rate will change when government spending, taxes, and the money stock change. It will rise with a rise in government spending, and it will fall with a rise in taxes or the money supply. The change in y will be exactly the same as in the previous special case.

Now consider the opposite special case to the first one, where instead of h being infinitely big, it becomes infinitely small, specifically, zero. This would be the case where firms' investment plans were completely unresponsive to interest rates. In this case, the changes in the rate of interest and in the real income level will be given by

$$\Delta r = \frac{1}{1-b}\left(\frac{k}{l}\Delta g - \frac{kb}{l}\Delta t - \frac{(1-b)}{l}\frac{\Delta M}{P_0}\right) \tag{14A.22}$$

$$\Delta y = \frac{1}{1-b}(\Delta g - b\Delta t) \tag{14A.23}$$

This tells you that, in this case, a rise in government spending will raise the interest rate, and a rise in taxes or the money supply will cut the interest rate. Unlike the two previous special cases, a rise in government spending or a cut in taxes will raise real income, but a change in the money stock will leave real income unaffected. Equation (14A.23) says that in the special case $h = 0$, the aggregate demand will change only as a result of changes in fiscal policy variables and will remain unchanged when the money stock changes.

Now consider the opposite special case to the second one, in which we let the parameter l become infinitely big. This would be the case where money is regarded as a perfect substitute for other non-money assets. Substituting an infinite value for l in Equations (14A.16) and (14A.17) gives the solutions for the change in interest rate and the change in income as

$$\Delta r = 0 \tag{14A.24}$$

$$\Delta y = \frac{1}{1-b}(\Delta g - b\Delta t) \tag{14A.25}$$

This time the interest rate is entirely unaffected by changes in any of the variables. Real income changes, however, as a result of changing government spending or taxes (rises when government spending rises and falls when taxes rise) but is unaffected by a change in the money stock.

Notice that Equations (14A.23) and (14A.25) are identical, just as Equations (14A.19) and (14A.21) are identical. Equations (14A.19) and (14A.21) say that only money affects aggregate demand, whereas (14A.23) and (14A.25) say that only fiscal policy variables affect aggregate demand.

These two sets of results are the two extreme cases that arise as the parameter values l and h are allowed to vary. The effect of a change in government spending, taxes, and the money supply on real income actually only depends upon the ratio of h to l. As that ratio goes from zero to infinity so the value of the fiscal policy multipliers falls from $1/(1 - b)$ to 0, and that of the money multipliers rise from 0 to $1/k$.

15

The *IS–LM–BP* Model of the Open Economy

It will be convenient to approach aggregate demand in the open economy in two stages. This chapter extends the *IS–LM* model to the open economy case and introduces the open economy extensions of the *IS* and *LM* curves. It also introduces a new relationship known as the *BP* curve.[1] With these basic open economy tools in hand, we will go on in Chapter 16 to study the determination of aggregate demand in the open economy under two alternative exchange rate regimes — fixed exchange rates and flexible exchange rates. We will study the determination of output at a given fixed price level under those two exchange rate regimes.

By the time you have completed this chapter you will be able to:

(a) Derive the *IS* curve for an open economy.
(b) Define the *BP* curve.
(c) Derive the *BP* curve.
(d) Explain what makes the *IS* and *BP* curves shift.
(e) Explain what makes the *LM* curve shift.

---

1 The material presented in this chapter was developed primarily by Robert Mundell and J. Marcus Fleming. The two most important papers by these two outstanding scholars are: Robert A. Mundell, 'The Appropriate Use of Monetary and Fiscal Policy Under Fixed Exchange Rates', *IMF Staff Papers*, 9 (March 1962), pp. 70–7; and J. Marcus Fleming, 'Domestic Financial Policies Under Fixed and Floating Exchange Rates', *IMF Staff Papers*, 9, (March 1962), pp. 369–77. The material in the chapter is often called the Mundell–Fleming analysis.

A. Derivation of the *IS* Curve for an Open Economy

You already know the meaning of the *IS* curve for an economy which has balanced trade or, equivalently, a closed economy. It is the relationship between the rate of interest and level of income at which savings-plus-taxes are equal to investment-plus-government expenditure. In the open economy there are two additional expenditure flows to be taken into account in defining and deriving the *IS* curve. They are exports and imports of goods and services. In a closed economy, aggregate demand is the sum of consumption plus investment plus government spending, whereas in an open economy, aggregate demand is equal to the sum of those three items plus net foreign demand or, equivalently, exports minus imports. That is, defining exports as *ex* and imports as *im*, aggregate demand in an open economy is

$$y = c + i + g + ex - im \qquad (15.1)$$

Subtracting consumption from both sides of Equation (15.1) gives

$$y - c = i + g + ex - im \qquad (15.2)$$

The left-hand side of the above equation $(y - c)$ is simply savings-plus-taxes. We could equivalently, therefore, write this equation as

$$s + t = i + g + ex - im \qquad (15.3)$$

Adding imports to both sides of the above equation gives

$$s + t + im = i + g + ex \qquad (15.4)$$

This is the condition which, for the open economy, must be satisfied at all points on the *IS* curve. That is, savings-plus-taxes-plus-imports must equal investment-plus-government spending-plus-exports.

To derive the open economy *IS* curve, we need some propositions about how imports and exports are determined. Let us now proceed to do that.

First, consider exports. Two key variables determine a country's exports. The first of these is the total level of income of the people who are demanding those exports. That income level is, of course, the aggregate income of the rest of the world. It is the sum of the gross domestic products of all the countries in the world other than the country whose economy we are analysing. The second variable that influences exports is the price of the goods produced in the domestic economy relative to the prices prevailing in the rest of the world. That relative price, expressed as an economy-wide average, could be stated precisely as

$$\theta = \frac{EP_f}{P} \qquad (15.5)$$

The price of foreign goods is P_f, the domestic price level is P, and the effective exchange rate (as defined in Chapter 6) is E. Thus, θ (the Greek letter theta) may be thought of as the price of foreign goods relative to the price of domestic goods. This ratio is called the *real exchange rate*. (You can check this by referring back to the definition of a real exchange rate in Chapter 6, Section B.) The real exchange rate is the effective exchange rate E multiplied by the ratio of foreign to domestic prices (P_f/P). The bigger the value of θ, the bigger will be the volume of exports. That is, the higher is the foreign price level relative to the domestic price level, the bigger will be the rest of the world's demand for domestically produced goods.

We can summarize these propositions about exports as follows: exports will be higher, the higher rest of the world income and the higher the real exchange rate.

Next, consider the factors that determine imports. Again, there are two key variables which may be isolated as having important effects on imports. The first is the level of domestic income (real GNP). The higher the level of domestic real income, the higher will be imports. The other influence is the same real exchange rate variable that influences exports. This time its effect will be opposite in sign. That is, a rise in the rest of world prices relative to domestic prices — a rise in the real exchange rate — will lead to a reduction in imports. To summarize: imports will be higher, the higher is real income, and imports will be lower, the higher is the real exchange rate.

We may now proceed to derive the *IS* curve for an open economy. Figure 15.1 illustrates this derivation. This figure is set up with an *IS* curve labelled *IS*(C)−C standing for closed economy — which is identical to the *IS* curve derived in Figure 11.4. The *IS* curve for the open economy is labelled *IS*(O)−O standing for open economy. To see the differences between the *IS* curve of the closed economy and that of the open economy, begin by considering frame (c) of Figure 15.1. There, on the horizontal axis, we are measuring investment-plus-government spending-plus-exports. For given values of world income and the real exchange rate, exports will be constant. We may therefore add exports to investment-plus-government spending by drawing a line parallel to the *i* + *g* curve, giving the new curve representing *i* + *g* + *ex*. The horizontal distance between *i* + *g* + *ex* and *i* + *g* in frame (c) represents the volume of exports *ex*.

The second change occurs in frame (a) of Figure 15.1. There we are measuring savings-plus-taxes-plus-imports on the vertical axis, and investment-plus government spending-plus-exports on the horizontal axis. The 45° line defines the open economy equilibrium condition for the *IS* curve.

The third change comes in frame (b). In this frame we measure savings-plus-taxes-plus-imports on the vertical axis. It is necessary, therefore, to add imports to the previously derived savings-plus-taxes schedule. To do this, recall that imports are presumed to depend on the level of domestic real income, and the real exchange rate. As in the case of exports, hold the real exchange rate at some fixed value. That done, the level of

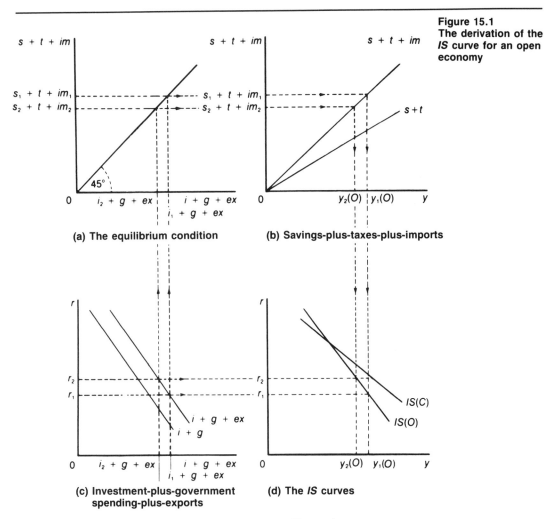

Figure 15.1
The derivation of the *IS* curve for an open economy

Frame (a) shows the equilibrium condition that defines the *IS* curve in an open economy — the equality of savings-plus-taxes-plus-imports with investment-plus-government spending-plus-exports. In frame (c), exports are added to investment-plus-government spending to give the $i + g + ex$ line. In frame (b), imports are added to savings-plus-taxes to give the steeper $s + t + im$ line. In frame (d), the *IS* curve, *IS(C)*, is that for a closed economy (ignoring exports and imports) and that labelled *IS(O)* is for the open economy. The two curves intersect at the real income level that generates a volume of imports equal to the fixed volume of exports. A rise in exports shifts the $i + g + ex$ line and shifts the *IS* curve. The relationship between these two shifts depends on the slope of the $s + t + im$ curve. The steeper the slope of the $s + t + im$ line, the smaller is the shift in *IS* for a given shift in $i + g + ex$.

imports will depend solely on the level of domestic real income. We can show this in frame (b) by drawing the line $s + t + im$ above the savings-plus-taxes line that is steeper than the $s + t$. The vertical distance between the two lines in frame (b) measures the volume of imports.

To derive the *IS* curve for the open economy, we proceed in the same way as for the closed economy but use the $i + g + ex$ and the $s + t + im$ lines. Following exactly the same procedure as in Chapter 11, you can readily verify that the curve $IS(O) - O$ for open — is the open economy IS curve. Notice that it is steeper than that for the closed economy. It cuts the closed economy IS curve at the level of income that generates a volume of imports exactly equal to the fixed volume of exports.

Since, in deriving the IS curve, we hold the real exchange rate fixed, it follows that at each different exchange rate there will be a different IS curve. Precisely how the IS curve shifts as the real exchange rate (and other variables) change will be explored below. Before that, let us go on to define and derive a new curve — the BP curve.

B.   Definition of the *BP* Curve

The BP curve is a relationship between the rate of interest and level of income such that at all points on the BP curve there is a balance of payments equilibrium. Put differently, at all points on the BP curve, the balance of payments is zero — i.e. balanced. Equivalently, there is a capital account surplus that exactly matches the current account deficit (or capital account deficit that exactly matches the current account surplus).

C.   Derivation of the *BP* Curve

The starting point for deriving the BP curve is the balance of payments equilibrium condition that states that the sum of the current account balance and the capital account balance is zero. The prices at which a country exports and imports goods and services is determined by the world price level P_f, converted into domestic money units at the exchange rate E, so that the current account balance is $EP_f ex - EP_f im$. Dividing this by the domestic price level, P, and remembering that EP_f/P equals θ, gives the real current account balance as $\theta(ex - im)$. Adding the real capital account surplus denoted by kas gives the condition for the BP curve as

$$\theta(ex - im) + kas = 0 \qquad (15.6)$$

This says that the balance of payments (BP) is equal to the *value* of exports minus the *value* of imports (of goods and services) plus the capital account surplus (denoted as kas). We have already discussed the determinants of the *volume* of exports and imports and the real exchange rate θ, and need now only concern ourselves with the things that determine the capital account surplus.

The capital account of the balance of payments depends primarily on rates of return on investments that are available in the domestic economy compared with rates of return available in the rest of the world. As a general proposition, the higher the rates of return available in the domestic economy relative to those available in the rest of the world, the greater will be the tendency for domestic capital to stay at home and for foreign capital to be sucked into the domestic economy. Conversely, the lower are domestic rates of return relative to foreign rates of return, the greater will be the tendency for domestic capital to seek the higher returns available in other countries, and the greater will be the tendency for foreign capital to stay at home.

Relevant rates of return that have to be compared in the two countries are the *real* rates. Thus, the basic hypothesis is that the net inflow of capital into a country increases as the differential between the domestic real rate of interest and the rest of world (foreign) real rate of interest increases. The variety of risk factors could make that differential either positive or negative (or zero) in equilibrium. Whatever the equilibrium value of the differential, net capital inflows will rise as that differential rises. We can write this as a simple equation such as

$$kas = f(r - r_f) \tag{15.7}$$

We are now in a position to derive the *BP* curve. Figure 15.2 illustrates the derivation. First, it will be useful to familiarize yourself with what we are measuring on the axes of the different frames: frame (d) is going to show the *BP* curve and measures the rate of interest against the level of income; frame (c) measures the rate of interest against total receipts from the rest of the world — exports-plus-capital account surplus; frame (b) measures imports against the level of income; and frame (a) measures imports on the vertical axis and exports-plus-capital account surplus on the horizontal axis.

The line in frame (a) defines the balance of payments equilibrium condition. It is a 45° line indicating that when imports equal exports-plus-capital account surplus, then there is a zero balance on the balance of payments. In frame (c), the upward-sloping line *kas* denotes the capital account surplus. It slopes up, indicating that the higher the domestic rate of interest, other things equal, the larger will be the capital account surplus. In drawing that line, the foreign rate of interest and the expected change of the exchange rate are being held constant. The second, thicker line in frame (c) results from adding the fixed volume of exports (for constant world real income and real exchange rate) to the capital account surplus to denote the total inflow of money from the rest of the world. In deriving the *BP* curve it will be convenient to assume that the real exchange rate is one. Later in this chapter we will examine what happens to the *BP* curve when the value of θ changes.

Frame (b) shows the import function — the relationship between imports and real income. In drawing the line in frame (b), as in frame (c), the real exchange rate is held constant. To derive the *BP* curve, select a rate of interest r_1 and notice that in frame (c), at the interest rate r_1, there is a capital account surplus of kas_1 and a total inflow of money from the

**Figure 15.2
The derivation of the
BP curve**

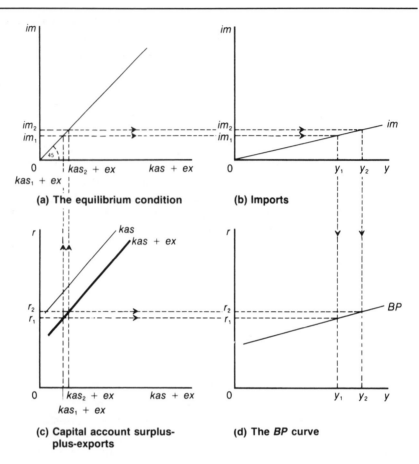

(a) The equilibrium condition

(b) Imports

**(c) Capital account surplus-
plus-exports**

(d) The BP curve

Frame (a) contains the condition that defines the BP curve — the equality of imports, im, with the capital accounts surplus plus exports, kas + ex. Frame (c) shows the capital account surplus rising with the rate of interest. Exports are added to the capital account surplus in frame (a) to give the line kas + ex. Frame (b) shows imports rising with income. Frame (d) shows the BP curve as the relationship between the interest rate and real income that satisfies the three lines in the other frames. The BP curve will shift if there is a rise in exports. The distance of the horizontal shift of the BP curve relative to the shift in kas + ex depends solely on the slope of the import function. The flatter the im curve, the greater will be the shift in the BP curve for any given change in exports, ex, in the kas + ex curve.

rest of the world of $kas_1 + ex$. Tracing up from frame (c) to frame (a), we know that if there is to be a balance of payments equilibrium, the level of imports must equal im_1. Taking that import level across to frame (b), we discover that in order for the import level to equal im_1, it will be necessary for domestic income to be y_1. Transferring that income level into frame (d), and transferring the initially assumed rate of interest r_1 across to frame (d) gives a point on the BP curve. The income level y_1 combined with the interest rate r_1 generates a level of imports and a capital account surplus such that there is a zero balance on the balance of payments. By selecting other interest rates, it is possible to derive other income levels, and by experimenting you will discover that you can generate the entire line labelled *BP*.

The *BP* curve will slope upwards in general, but could, in a particular and important circumstance, be horizontal. That circumstance would be one of perfect capital mobility. Perfect capital mobility means that any interest differential between the domestic economy and the rest of the world would automatically and instantly bring in, or drive out, funds, so that the domestic interest rate is always at a level such that the *real* rate of return on domestic investments equals the *real* rate of return available in the rest of the world. In that case, the domestic real rate of interest would always be equal to the foreign real rate and the *BP* curve would be a horizontal line at that rate of interest. As a general matter, the *BP* curve will slope up, as shown in the figure. It may be presumed, however, that it will not be a very steep relationship since modest interest differentials seem to be sufficient to induce large international movements of capital. (The perfect capital mobility case will feature prominently in the next chapter.)

Let us now go on to consider the things that make the open economy *IS* and *BP* curves shift.

D.   Shifts in the *IS* and *BP* Curves

Recall that when we derived the *IS* curve, we held constant the level of world income, which influences exports, and the real exchange rate, which influences both exports and imports. What happens to the *IS* curve if either of those variables change? If world income rises, exports rise and as a result the *IS* curve shifts to the right. If the real exchange rate rises exports rise and imports fall. This, too, shifts the *IS* curve to the right. The real exchange rate might rise because of a rise in the exchange rate (depreciation), a rise in the foreign price level, or a fall in the domestic price level.

Next, consider the factors that shift the *BP* curve. In drawing the capital account surplus line in Figure 15.2, we held constant the world real rate of interest and the expected rate of change of the exchange rate. A rise in either the world real rate of interest or the expected rate of depreciation of the domestic currency will shift the *kas* line to the left (or upwards). The factors that determine exports and imports have already been discussed in the above discussion of the factors which shift the *IS* curve. Changes in world income or the real exchange rate that shift the *IS* curve will also, necessarily, shift the *BP* curve. Anything that raises exports or lowers imports will shift the *BP* curve to the right. Thus, a devaluation of the currency (a higher value of E), a rise in foreign prices, a rise in world real income, or a fall in the domestic price level will all have the effect of shifting the *BP* curve to the right.

You have now seen that some factors shift the *IS* curve and the *BP* curve simultaneously. It is of some importance to establish which of these two curves shifts more in the event of a change that shifts them both. There is no ambiguity about this when the factor leading to a shift in both curves is a change in world income. In this case, both curves will shift in the same direction, but the *BP* curve will shift by more than the *IS* curve. To see this, all that you need do is to examine Figures 15.1 and 15.2 again. Consider the effect of a rise in world income, which raises exports. In Figure 15.1, this rise in exports shifts the investment-plus-government spending-plus-exports line to the right, and also the *IS* curve to the right. The amount by which the *IS* curve shifts depends solely on the initial change in $i + g + ex$ and on the slope of the savings-plus-taxes-plus-imports line in frame (b). The steeper the $s + t + im$ line, the smaller is the shift in the *IS* curve.

Now consider what happens to the *BP* line. In frame (c) of Figure 15.2, the $kas + ex$ line would shift to the right. Also, the *BP* curve in frame (d) would shift to the right. The amount by which the *BP* curve shifts depends solely on the initial shift in $kas + ex$ and on the slope of the import line in frame (b). The flatter this line, the bigger is the shift in the *BP* curve. The initial change in exports recorded in frame (c) of both figures is identical. Since we know that the slope of the savings-plus-taxes-plus-import line is steeper than the slope of the imports line (convince yourself of this by simply noting that savings also rise as income rises), we also know that the *BP* curve must shift to the right by more than the *IS* curve shifts.

A change in world real income is not the only factor that leads to shifts in both the *IS* and *BP* curves. A change in the real exchange rate (a change in the exchange rate or the domestic or world price level) also shifts both curves. In this case, there is a potential ambiguity as to which of the two curves shifts more. The ambiguity arises from the fact — apparent by comparing Equations 15.4 and 15.6 above — that the definition of real expenditure that underlies the *IS* curve is one based on a constant (base period) real exchange rate whereas the definition of the balance of payments that underlies the *BP* curve is one based on the current real exchange rate. Thus, when analysing a change in the real exchange rate, it is necessary to work out its effects on the *volume* of exports and imports in order to calculate the *IS* curve shift, and its effect on the real *value* of exports and imports in order to calculate the *BP* curve shift. To avoid a lengthy treatment of all possible cases, we will *assume* that a change in the real exchange rate has the same type of effect on the *IS* and *BP* curves as the effect of a change in world real income that we have just analysed. That is, we will assume that a rise in the real exchange rate (a rise in $\theta = EP_f/P$) raises both the volume and value of (net) exports and shift both the *IS* and *BP* curves to the right. The *BP* curve is assumed to shift further to the right than the *IS* curve.

It will be useful for the subsequent analysis to introduce a further curve that summarizes the shifts of the *IS* and *BP* curves. Let us call that curve the *IS–BP* curve. Figure 15.3 illustrates its derivation.

Figure 15.3
The *IS-BP* locus

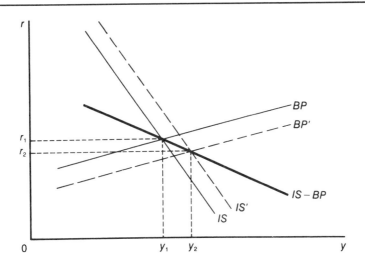

Because a shock that influences both the *IS* and *BP* curves shifts the *BP* curve by more than the *IS* curve, the intersection points of successive *BP* and *IS* curves fall on a downward-sloping line *IS–BP*.

Imagine that the economy starts out on the curves *IS* and *BP* at the interest rate r_1 and income level y_1. There is then some shock that shifts both the *IS* and *BP* curves to *IS'*, *BP'*. The new income level is y_2 and the interest rate is r_2. The line traced by the intersection points of the *IS* and *BP* curves will be called the *IS–BP* curve. It slopes downwards because we know that the *BP* curve shifts by more than the *IS* curve following any shock that shifts both of these curves. The *IS*–BP curve will be useful for analysing the effects of changes in rest of world variables and in the exchange rate, all of which shift both the *IS* and *BP* curves in the manner illustrated in Figure 15.3.

E. The *LM* Curve in the Open Economy

The *LM* curve in the open economy is exactly the same (at least in the presentation given given here) as that of the closed economy. As in the case of the closed economy, the only thing that shifts the *LM* curve is a change in the money supply. There is an important difference between the open and closed economies, however, concerning the sources of variation in the quantity of money. To understand this, it is necessary for us to digress slightly and examine the balance sheet structure of the banking system in an open economy. In doing this we will draw on the broader framework of aggregate balance sheets presented in Chapter 4.

The key thing that you need to understand is the connection between the money supply and a country's stock of foreign exchange reserves. This connection is most readily seen by considering the items in the balance sheets of the Bank of England and the commercial banks and the consolidated balance sheet of the banking sector. The balance sheets of the Bank of England and the commercial banks were first introduced in Chapter 4 (columns 3 and 4 of Table 4.2). The *consolidated banking sector* is the Bank of England and the commercial banks viewed as a whole.

(i) The Banking Sector and the Balance Sheets

Table 15.1 sets out the relevant balance sheets. (You might like to refer back to Chapter 4 on aggregate balance sheet accounting to see how these balance sheets fit in with those in the other sectors of the economy.)

Table 15.1   Banking sector balance sheets

BANK OF ENGLAND

Assets		*Liabilities*	
Gold and foreign exchange reserves	F	Monetary base	MB
Domestic credit	DC_c		

COMMERCIAL BANKS

Assets		*Liabilities*	
Notes and coins plus deposits at the Bank of England	MB_b	Deposits	D

CONSOLIDATED BANKING SECTOR

Assets		*Liabilities*	
Gold and foreign exchange reserves	F	Notes and coins in circulation with public $(MB - MB_b)$	MB_p
Domestic credit $(DC_c + DC_b)$	DC	Deposits	D
Money supply	M	Money supply	M

First consider the balance sheet of the Bank of England — the first part of Table 15.1. Its assets are aggregated into two items: gold and foreign exchange reserves, and domestic credit. The gold represents actual gold in the vaults of the Bank of England. The foreign exchange reserves are either bank accounts that the Bank of England maintains with other central banks (i.e. central banks of other countries) or highly liquid foreign currency denominated securities. From the point of view of the country as a whole, the stock of gold and foreign exchange reserves serves the same purpose as notes and coins and a cheque account do for you as an individual. Denote the stock of gold and foreign exchange reserves as F.

The second item in the Bank of England's balance sheet is the stock of government securities that it has purchased. You will recall that the Bank of England creates monetary base by buying government securities, either from the government directly or from the general public, and makes the purchase with newly created money. The whole collection of securities held by the central bank is called *domestic credit*. Denote the domestic credit of the Bank of England as DC_c.

Apart from miscellaneous items such as real estate, which may be ignored, these two items — gold and foreign exchange reserves, and domestic credit — constitute the entire stock of assets of the Bank of England.

The liability of the Bank of England is the monetary base. This is the stock of notes and coins that have been issued and are held either by the general public or in the tills of commercial banks, together with the stock of bank deposits maintained by the commercial banks at the Bank of England. Denote the monetary base as MB.

The Bank of England's balance sheet balances, so that

$$MB = F + DC_c$$

Next, consider the commercial banks. As in the case of the Bank of England, it is useful to distinguish between two sets of assets. First, the commercial banks hold reserves in the form of notes and coins as well as deposits with the Bank of England. Denote commercial bank reserve assets as MB_b.

Notice that the same letters are being used to denote the commercial banks' reserves as those used to denote monetary base because they are in fact the same thing. Part of the monetary base, MB, which is a liability to the Bank of England, is held as an asset by the commercial banks.

The other assets of the commercial banks have all been grouped into a single item — domestic credit of the commercial banks. This item consists of all the securities held by commercial banks, including any loan obligations that private individuals and firms have to the banks. Denote domestic credit of the commercial banks as DC_b.

Apart from some real estate, which may be neglected, these two items — reserve assets and domestic credit — constitute the entire assets of the commercial banks.

The liabilities of the commercial banks consist of the deposits that have been placed with them by households and firms. (You can think of deposits as sight deposits only, and you can think of domestic credit held by commercial banks as being net of savings deposits.) Denote bank deposits as D.

The balance sheet of the commercial banks balances, so total deposits are equal to the stock of reserves plus the domestic credit. That is,

$$D = MB_b + DC_b$$

Next consider the consolidation of these two balance sheets. A consolidated balance sheet is simply the balance sheet that arises from adding together individual balance sheets and netting out any items that appear as an asset in one balance sheet and as a liability in another. To consolidate the two balance sheets of the Bank of England and the commercial banks, first notice that gold and foreign exchange reserves appear only once in the Bank of England's balance sheet and therefore will appear in the consolidated balance sheet. Domestic credit appears twice, as DC_c and DC_b. If those two items are added together, the domestic credit of the economy as a whole is obtained. Denote domestic credit as DC. So that you are absolutely clear what domestic credit is let us elaborate a little. Domestic credit is the total of all the assets held by the Bank of England and by the commercial banks — other than the gold and foreign exchange reserves held by the Bank of England. These assets include holdings of government securities by the Bank of England and by the commercial banks as well as private securities held by and loans made by the commercial banks.

On the liability side of the consolidated balance sheet, notice that the monetary base, MB, is partly held as the reserve asset of the commercial banks, MB_b. In the consolidated balance sheet, the difference between these two items is recorded. This difference is notes and coins in circulation with the public (denoted MB_p).

Bank deposits appear just once, in the commercial banks' balance sheet, and therefore appear again in the consolidated balance sheet.

The total liabilities of the consolidated banking system now have a familiar look. The total liabilities of the consolidated banking system consist of notes and coins in circulation plus bank deposits. This total, of course, is precisely the definition of money.

Since the two underlying balance sheets balance, so also the consolidated balance sheet will balance. From this fact it will be clear that the money supply can be defined either as notes and coins in circulation plus bank deposits, a definition with which you are already familiar, or alternatively, as gold and foreign exchange reserves plus domestic credit. That is,

$$M = MB_p + D$$

or

$$M = F + DC$$

These are simply definitions. The second definition, however, is a useful one in helping us to organize our thinking about the sources of variation of the money supply in the open economy.

(ii)   Changes in Reserves, the Money Supply, and Domestic Credit

The next step is to recognize that the relationship between the money supply and the stock of foreign exchange reserves and domestic credit holds each and every year, and therefore, the change in the money supply from one year to the next will be equal to the change in foreign exchange reserves plus the change in domestic credit. That is (using Δ to denote change):

$$\Delta M = \Delta F + \Delta DC \tag{15.8}$$

This is a very important equation because ΔF is the balance of payments. That is, the change in the stock of foreign exchange reserves is what we mean by the balance of payments. Thus, the balance of payments is related to the change in the money supply and the change in domestic credit.

This relationship may be used in order to determine how the *LM* curve shifts in the open economy. If domestic credit is held constant, which would be the natural way of interpreting a neutral domestic monetary policy, then unless the economy is on the *BP* curve, the quantity of money will be changing. Specifically, at all points above the *BP* curve, the quantity of money will be rising; and at all points below it, the quantity of money will be falling. This means that if the economy is above the *BP* curve, it is experiencing a balance of payments surplus, and the *LM* curve will be shifting to the right. Conversely, if the economy is below the *BP* curve, it is experiencing a balance of payments deficit, and the *LM* curve will be shifting to the left.

An alternative domestic monetary policy would be to stabilize the quantity of money regardless of the state of the balance of payments. This would involve changing domestic credit by an equal but opposite amount to the change in foreign exchange reserves resulting from the balance of payments deficit or surplus. Such an action is known as *sterilizing* the balance of payments. Such a policy can be undertaken, but only for limited periods of time, since, in general, sterilization actions accentuate the balance of payments problem. Pursuing tighter and tighter domestic monetary policies in the face of the balance of payments surplus tends to make that surplus bigger, and pursuing slacker and slacker monetary policies in the face of the balance of payments deficit tends to make the deficit worse. A situation in which the quantity of money changes by the same amount as the change in foreign exchange reserves is, therefore, an interesting one to analyse since it represents the only policy action that can be sustained over an indefinite period. Sterilization cannot.

These shifts of the *LM* curve arising from a balance of payments deficit and surplus can only occur in a fixed exchange rate world. In a flexible exchange rate regime there is no change in the stock of foreign exchange reserves and thus the balance of payments is always zero. That is, the

LM curve in the flexible exchange rate world is identical to that in the closed economy and shifts in that curve result only from changes in domestic monetary policy.

Summary

A.   Derivation of the IS Curve for an Open Economy

The *IS* curve for an open economy shows the relationship between the rate of interest and level of real income at which savings-plus-taxes-plus-imports equals investment-plus-government spending-plus exports. It is steeper than the *IS* curve for a closed economy and intersects the latter at the real income level and interest rate at which imports equal exports.

B.   Definition of the BP Curve

The *BP* curve shows the relationship between the rate of interest and level of real income at which the sum of the current account and capital account and thus the balance of payments is zero.

C.   Derivation of the BP Curve

For a given real exchange rate (i.e. a given level of domestic and foreign prices and nominal exchange rate) and given level of world real income, exports will be fixed. The capital account surplus depends upon the domestic rate of interest, and imports depend on domestic income. By finding the level of real income that generates an import volume equal to the exports-plus-capital account surplus generated by a given interest rate, it is possible to trace out the *BP* curve. The curve slopes upwards, except in the case of perfect capital mobility, in which case it is horizontal.

D.   Shifts in the IS and BP Curves

In addition to the factors that shift the *IS* curve in a closed economy, a change in world real income, the exchange rate, or the foreign price level shifts the *IS* curve in an open economy. A rise in world real income, a rise in the world price level, or a depreciation of the domestic currency shift the *IS* curve to the right. The *BP* curve shifts as a result of changes in world real income, the exchange rate, the world price level, or the world real rate of interest. A rise in world real income, a rise in the world price level, a fall in the world real rate of interest, or depreciation of the currency all shift the *BP* curve to the right. A change in world income that shifts both the *IS* and the *BP* curves shifts both curves in the same direction but shifts the *BP* curve by more than it shifts the *IS* curve. A change in the real exchange rate also shifts both the *IS* and *BP* curves, and we assume that the *BP* curve shifts by more than the *IS* curve.

E. *The* LM *Curve in the Open Economy*

In the open economy the money supply is, by definition, the sum of foreign exchange reserves and domestic credit. The *LM* curve shifts because of changes in the money supply. In an open economy, if the exchange rate is fixed the money supply changes only if the balance of payments is other than zero. The balance of payments surplus is associated with a rising money supply, the balance of payments deficit with a falling money supply. Thus, if the economy is off the *BP* curve, the *LM* curve is shifting. The economy can only be off the *BP* curve if the exchange rate is fixed.

Review Questions

1. What is the equilibrium condition that an open economy satisfies as it moves along its *IS* curve?
2. How does the *IS* curve of an open economy differ from that of a closed economy?
3. What determines the 'slope' of the open economy *IS* curve?
4. What makes the open economy *IS* curve shift, and in what direction?
5. What is the equilibrium condition that is satisfied as the economy moves along its *BP* curve?
6. What determines the slope of the *BP* curve?
7. What makes the *BP* curve shift, and in what direction?
8. Explain how a rise in world real income shifts the *IS* and *BP* curves. Which shifts by more? Why?
9. Explain what the equation means:

$$\Delta M = \Delta F + \Delta DC$$

10. Illustrate your answer to Question 1 by showing what happens to the UK money supply, the stock of foreign exchange reserves, and domestic credit in the event that:

    (a) The Bank of England buys US government bonds with its reserves.
    (b) The Bank of England buys US dollars with newly created pounds.

(c) The Bank of England buys British government bonds with new pounds.

11. What happens to the *LM* curve if the economy is (a) above, (b) below, and (c) on its *BP* curve?

16

Aggregate Demand in the Open Economy

You are now in a position to discover how the aggregate demand curve of the open economy differs from that of the closed economy. There will be two cases: one for fixed exchange rates and the other for flexible exchange rates. It will be convenient to approach the aggregate demand curve in two steps. First, we will study the determination of output and the rate of interest at a given price level. Once we have understood those matters, we will move on to derive the aggregate demand curve under the two alternative exchange rate regimes but for the particular case in which capital is perfectly mobile.

There are some challenging problems in achieving a completely satisfactory analysis of the open economy. In the open economy, there are more variables to be determined and more sources of shocks than in the closed economy, and this raises the dimensionality of the problem which has to be solved. It makes it harder to arrive at simple, intuitive, easily grasped models. In this chapter we are going to try to give you a feel for how the open economy operates using two alternative assumptions about capital mobility. When we study the determination of output and interest rates at a given price level we will permit capital to be imperfectly mobile (though it could easily be regarded as being perfectly mobile as a special case). When we come to study the derivation of the aggregate demand curve we will only look at the case of perfect capital mobility. Our own judgment is that this assumption is only slightly extreme. It is not quite the way the world is but it is very close. The virtue of making this assumption, aside from the fact that it does not strike us as being wildly at odds with the world, is that it simplifies the theory of aggregate demand considerably — and allows us to gain insights that otherwise we would find hard to understand.

There is an alternative extreme assumption that also yields a much simplified theory of aggregate demand, but that yields very different conclusions. That is the opposite extreme to perfect capital mobility — zero capital mobility. That alternative strikes us as being so violently at odds with the world as to be uninteresting and not worthwhile analysing. Both perfect capital mobility and zero capital mobility simplify the task of analysis. One of them does it in a way that only mildly violates the facts while the other does it in a way that renders the analysis utterly pointless. By way of an analogy, assuming perfect capital mobility seems to us to be quite analogous to assuming there to be no atmosphere (a vacuum) for the purpose of calculating the length of time it would take for a 5 kilogram rock to fall from the top of the Telecom Tower and hit the ground. The atmospheric resistance may be presumed to be negligible and, hence, the calculations simplified considerably by assuming it to be zero. The answer obtained will be wrong, but not misleadingly wrong. The alternative assumption of zero capital mobility strikes us as being analogous to simplifying the calculation of the power required to put a satellite into earth orbit by assuming zero gravity. The assumption would be so wildly at odds with the facts that the rocket would never leave the launch pad!

Let us now, with these preliminary justifications for the underlying assumptions about capital mobility, proceed with the theory of aggregate demand in the open economy. When you have completed your study of this chapter you will be able to:

(a) **Determine the levels of output, interest rates, and the balance of payments in a fixed exchange rate regime at a given price level.**
(b) **Determine the levels of output, interest rate, and the exchange rate in a flexible exchange rate regime at a given price level.**
(c) **Derive the aggregate demand curve when capital is perfectly mobile.**

A. Determination of Output, Interest Rate and the Balance of Payments in a Fixed Exchange Rate Regime at a Given Price Level

Let us now determine the equilibrium values of output, the interest rate, and the balance of payments when the exchange rate is fixed and for a given domestic price level. We will do this for given levels of world income, interest rates, the price level, the given fixed exchange rate, government spending and taxes. The equilibrium levels of output, the rate of interest, and the balance of payments are determined at the triple intersection point of the *BP*, *LM*, and *IS* curves as shown in Figure 16.1. The *IS* and *BP* curves are exactly the same as those derived in Figures 15.1 and 15.2. The *LM* curve is exactly the same as the curve derived in Chapter 13.

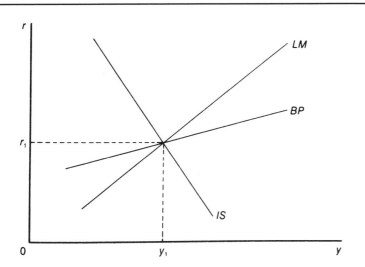

Figure 16.1
Equilibrium with
fixed exchange rates

Equilibrium output and interest rates are determined at the point of intersection of the *IS* and *BP* curves. The *LM* curve also passes through this intersection point because the money supply adjusts to ensure that this happens.

(i) Equilibrium

The way the model works to determine the equilibrium is slightly more complicated than the standard closed economy variant of the *IS–LM* analysis. The idea is that output and the rate of interest are determined at each instant by the intersection of the *IS* and *LM* curves, as they were before in the closed economy analysis. This is not, however, the end of the story. If the intersection of the *IS* and *LM* curves is above the *BP* curve, then there is a balance of payments surplus, and the money supply will be rising. A rising money supply means that the *LM* curve will be shifting to the right, so that income will be rising and the rate of interest falling (the economy will be sliding down the *IS* curve). Such a process would continue until the *LM* curve comes to rest where the *IS* curve intersects the *BP* curve. At such a point, the balance of payments will be zero and the money supply constant, so that the *LM* curve will no longer be shifting.

Conversely, if initially the *IS* and *LM* curves cut each other below the *BP* curve, then there will be a balance of payments deficit. The money supply will be falling, and the *LM* curve will be moving to the left. In the process, the level of income will fall, and the interest rate will rise (the economy will slide up the *IS* curve). This process will continue until the *LM* curve intersects the intersection point of the *IS* and *BP* curves. At that point, the balance of payments deficit will have disappeared and the money supply will be constant.

You will probably get a better feeling for what is going on here by working through a series of experiments that result from the economy being shocked by a variety of domestic and foreign disturbances. We shall now turn to such an exercise.

(ii)   Fiscal Policy

First, consider the effects of an expansionary fiscal policy. Figure 16.2 illustrates. The economy is at an initial equilibrium exactly like that depicted in Figure 16.1, with the interest rate at r_1 and income at y_1. There is then a rise in government spending or a cut in taxes that shifts the *IS* curve to *IS'*. The impact effect of that fiscal policy action is to raise the rate of interest and output to r_2 and y_2 respectively. The economy would now, however, be experiencing a balance of payments surplus since it is operating at a point above the *BP* curve. With a balance of payments surplus, the money supply will be rising, so the *LM* curve will shift to the right. As this happens, the succession of *LM* curves intersect *IS'* at lower and lower interest rates but at higher and higher income levels (along the arrowed path). The economy will finally settle down at the interest rate r_3 and output y_3. The effect, then, of an expansionary fiscal policy in an economy with a given price level and a fixed exchange rate is rising interest rates and rising real income. A balance of payments surplus will bring an inflow of money that will subsequently lower interest rates, but not to their initial level,[1] and will raise output still further.[2]

(ii)   Monetary Policy

Second, consider the effects of an expansionary monetary policy. Again, let the economy start out at the initial equilibrium level (r_1, y_1) depicted in Figure 16.1. Figure 16.3 shows the effect of a monetary disturbance.

Imagine raising the quantity of money (by raising domestic credit) in a once-and-for-all manner, so that the *LM* curve shifts to *LM'*. Initially, the interest rate drops to r_2 and output rises to y_2. Clearly, with a higher

---

1   In the special case of perfect capital mobility, the interest rate will return to its initial level.
2   There is a possible, although most unlikely, case that would arise if the *BP* curve was steeper than the *LM* curve. In this case, the impact effect of the expansionary fiscal policy would be to produce a balance of payments deficit. Money would flow out of the economy, thereby shifting the *LM* curve leftwards, raising the rate of interest, and lowering the level of real income. The new equilibrium would be one in which both interest rates and real income had increased above their initial levels.

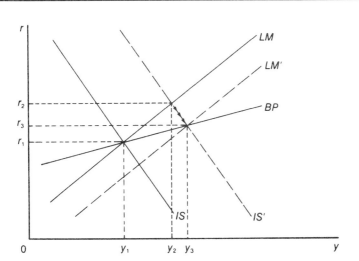

The initial equilibrium at (y_1, r_1) is disturbed by a rise in government spending or tax cut that shifts the *IS* curve to *IS'*. The impact effect is to raise interest rates and income to r_2 and y_2 and to create a balance of payments surplus. The balance of payments surplus raises the money supply, thereby shifting the *LM* curve to the right. The final equilibrium is the interest rate r_3 and real income y_3 where *IS'* intersects the *BP* curve. The *LM* curve will by then have become *LM'*. The adjustment process takes the economy down the *IS* curve.

real income level bringing in more imports and a lower interest rate lowering the capital account surplus, there will be a balance of payments deficit. In that situation, the money supply will fall, and the *LM* curve will move to the left. As it does so, it will intersect the *IS* curve at higher and higher interest rates and lower real income levels (the arrowed path). Eventually, the quantity of money will have returned to its initial level, and the economy will have returned to its initial interest rate and income position. All that will have happened is that the quantity of money will be backed by a higher amount of domestic credit and a smaller amount of foreign exchange reserves in the final situation than initially. This will be the only change between the initial and final situation. Thus, in a fixed exchange rate economy, monetary policy has no permanent effects on aggregate demand.

The analysis that we have just conducted implicitly assumes that the country has a sufficiently large stock of foreign exchange reserves to permit the initially assumed expansion of the domestic money supply. Of course, if the country did not have sufficient foreign exchange reserves, then the experiment could not be conducted. If the country attempted to increase its money supply in a situation in which it had insufficient foreign exchange reserves, it would cease to be a fixed exchange rate country. It would find itself forced off the fixed exchange rate when its foreign exchange reserves fell to such a low level that it was unable to intervene

Figure 16.3
The effects of a rise
in the money supply
under fixed
exchange rates

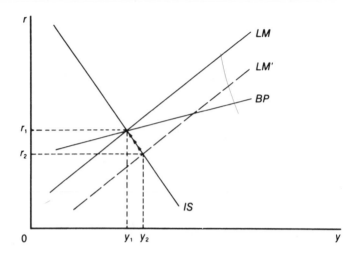

An initial equilibrium at (y_1, r_1) is disturbed by a once-and-for-all rise in domestic credit that shifts the *LM* curve to *LM'*. The impact effect is to lower the interest rate to r_2, raise real income to y_2, and create a balance of payments deficit. The balance of payments deficit leads to an outflow of money. As the money supply falls, the *LM* curve shifts back to the left and settles eventually at the initial equilibrium (y_1, r_1).

in the foreign exchange market to maintain the value of its currency. One possibility in such a situation would be for the country to devalue its currency. Let us now analyse this case along with the effects of foreign shocks.

(iv) Devaluation and Foreign Shocks

Third, consider the effect of a devaluation of the currency. A devaluation is a once-and-for-all rise in the value of the exchange rate, E. Again, suppose the economy starts out at the real income and interest level (y_1, r_1), as depicted in Figure 16.4.

Imagine that there is a once-and-for-all rise in the value of the exchange rate (devaluation). This raises exports and lowers imports, thereby shifting both the *IS* curve and *BP* curve to the right. The new curves are shown as *IS'* and *BP'* and are drawn to reflect the fact that the *BP* curve shifts rightwards by more than does the *IS* curve. The initial impact of the devaluation will be to take the economy to the equilibrium (y_2, r_2), where the original *LM* curve intersects the new *IS* curve. In that situation, there is a balance of payments surplus since the economy is above the new *BP* curve (*BP'*). The balance of payments surplus causes the quantity of money to rise and the *LM* curve to start shifting to the right. As the *LM* curve shifts to the right, it intersects the *IS* curve at lower and lower interest rates and higher and higher real income levels (along the arrowed adjustment path). Eventually real income rises to y_3 and the interest rate

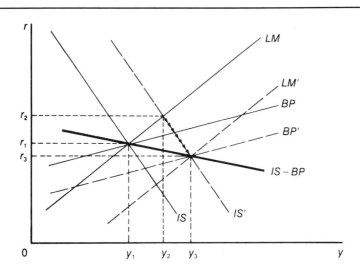

Figure 16.4
The effect of a
devaluation

The initial equilibrium at (y_1, r_1) is disturbed by a devaluation of the currency. This raises exports and lowers imports, shifting the *IS* and *BP* curves to the right. The impact effect of this devaluation is to raise the level of real income to y_2 and interest rate to r_2 and to create a balance of payments surplus. The balance of payments surplus leads to a rising money supply. The *LM* curve shifts to the right producing a falling rate of interest and a continuing increase in real income. The resting point is where the curve *IS'* intersects the curve *BP'*. The *LM* curve will have by then become *LM'*. The adjustment process takes the economy down the curve *IS'*.

falls to r_3. The final effect of a devaluation, therefore, is to raise real income and lower interest rates. The balance of payments moves into surplus during the adjustment process, but is in equilibrium at the end of the process.

It should be emphasized that these responses to a devaluation are all conditional on the price level remaining constant. If the price level was to rise by the same percentage amount as the devaluation, then the real exchange rate would not be affected, and the economy would remain at its initial equilibrium level. Alternatively, if the price level *initially* remained constant, the path described in Figure 16.4 would be set up, and the economy would move from (y_1, r_1), to (y_2, r_2), and then start to proceed towards (y_3, r_3). If, during this process, the price level began to rise and eventually rose all the way to full proportionality with the devaluation, then instead of continuing to travel down the curve *IS'*, both the *IS'* and *BP'* curves would shift leftwards, and the economy would gradually move back to (y_1, r_1).

Shocks emanating from the rest of the world would have effects similar to a devaluation. A rise in world income or a rise in the world price level would have exactly the same effects as a devaluation. Conversely, a fall in the world real rate of interest, which would shift the *BP* line but not the *IS* curve, would have no impact effect on real income and the interest rate. It would, however, set up a process in which the balance of payments was in surplus, and so would start the *LM* curve moving to the right. Real income would rise, and the interest rate would fall until the point of intersection of the original *IS* curve and the new *BP* curve was reached.

This completes our analysis of the effects of domestic policy and foreign shocks on output, interest rates, and the balance of payments in a fixed exchange rate regime at a given price level. Let us now turn to examine a flexible exchange rate economy.

B.   Determination of Output, Interest Rate and the Exchange Rate in a Flexible Exchange Rate Regime at a Given Price Level

Analysing a flexible exchange rate economy is slightly harder than the fixed exchange rate case. The problem arises because the *IS* and *BP* curves have three variables in them — real income, the rate of interest, and the exchange rate — all of which we want to determine, and it is therefore hard to construct diagrams in two dimensions that have the simplicity of those in the fixed exchange rate case. In order to make the analysis of the flexible exchange rate economy as comparable as possible with that of the fixed exchange rate economy, we will use a series of diagrams (Figures 16.5–16.7) drawn in interest rate-real income space, as we did before when analysing the fixed exchange rate case. This means that the exchange rate will not appear explicitly on one of the axes of the picture. It will be possible, nevertheless, to work out directions of change of the exchange rate when various shocks are administered to the economy. This is analogous to the way in which the balance of payments was determined in the previous section.

(i)   Equilibrium

It will be useful, as a starting point, to reinterpret Figure 16.1 as a flexible exchange rate equilibrium rather than as a fixed exchange rate equilibrium. Under flexible exchange rates, the quantity of money (both the stock of foreign exchange reserves and domestic credit) is determined by the central bank. The position of the *LM* curve is therefore bolted down, so to speak, by monetary policy. If the point of intersection of the *IS* and *BP* curves is not on the *LM* curve, something has to adjust. The adjustment that occurs is in the exchange rate. Since domestic and foreign prices are constant, different values of the exchange rate E generate different values of the real exchange rate θ. Different values of θ generate different values of exports and imports and therefore produce different *IS* and *BP* curves.

Since the *IS* curve slopes downwards and the *BP* curve slopes upwards, there is one, and only one, point (a real icome level y, and interest rate r) at which the *IS* and *BP* curves intersect and at the same time falls on the *LM* curve. The value of the exchange rate that underlies the *IS* and *BP* curves when they cut the *LM* curve is the equilibrium exchange rate. Thus, you may interpret Figure 16.1 as a flexible exchange rate equilibrium in the sense that the exchange rate has to be the particular value that causes the *IS* and *BP* curves to intersect each other at a point on the *LM* curve. This contrasts with the fixed exchange rate interpretation of Figure 16.1, which is that the *IS* and *BP* curves are fixed in position, while the *LM* curve takes up the slack — the money supply varying to ensure that the *LM* curve is located at the point of intersection of the fixed *IS* and *BP* curves.

To repeat for emphasis, in a fixed exchange rate world the *IS* and *BP* curves are fixed in position and determine the steady-state equilibrium, while the quantity of money and, therefore, the *LM* curve are dragged along to that fixed intersection point. In the case of the flexible exchange rate economy, the *LM* curve is fixed in position, while the exchange rate is free to move, thereby shifting the *IS* and *BP* curves to an intersection point on the *LM* curve.

(ii) Fiscal Policy

Let us now proceed to analyse the effects of the same set of policy and foreign shocks that were analysed in the preceding section in the flexible exchange rate case. First, consider the effect of an expansionary fiscal policy.

The economy is initially in an equilibrium, such as that shown in Figure 16.5, at (y_1, r_1). There is then expansion of government spending or a tax cut that shifts the *IS* curve from *IS* to *IS'*. The impact effect is to raise the income level to y_2 and the interest rate to r_2. In this situation, if the exchange rate was fixed, there would be a balance of payments surplus. With a flexible exchange rate, however, the balance of payments surplus is not allowed to occur. The central bank simply does not stand ready to take in foreign exchange at a pegged exchange rate. Instead, the exchange rate adjusts. If there is an excess supply of foreign currency, its price falls or, alternatively, the domestic currency appreciates. This depreciation lowers the real exchange rate, thereby raising imports and lowering exports. In this process, the *IS* and *BP* curves shift to the left. Since we are assuming that the *BP* curve shifts by more than the *IS* curve, as they move they intersect along the *IS'−BP* curve. They will eventually come to rest intersecting the *LM* curve at the interest rate r_3 and real income level y_3. The exchange rate at that point is lower than the initial exchange rate (the currency has appreciated). Thus, the effects of an expansionary fiscal policy in a flexible exchange rate economy are to raise real income and the rate of interest and to appreciate the currency.

Domestic manufacturers may be hostile towards such an outcome and may complain about the difficulty of doing profitable business in foreign markets. In effect, what is happening is that because the government is

**Figure 16.5
The effects of an
expansionary fiscal
policy under flexible
exchange rates**

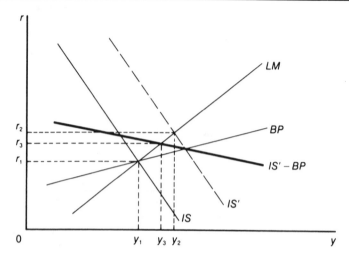

An initial equilibrium at (y_1, r_1) is disturbed by a rise in government spending or a tax cut that shifts the *IS* curve to *IS'*. If there was no change in the exchange rate, real income would move to y_2 and the interest rate to r_2, thereby producing a balance of payments surplus. With a flexible exchange rate, this does not happen. Instead the exchange rate falls (the currency appreciates), thereby lowering exports and raising imports. Both the curve *IS'* and the *BP* curve shift to the left. The equilibrium will be at the point at which the *IS–BP* locus intersects the *LM* curve — at the interest rate r_3 and real income y_3. Thus, the effect of an expansionary fiscal policy is to raise income, raise the rate of interest, and appreciate the currency.

spending more, real resources have to be diverted from the rest of the economy to the government, and this is accomplished by making total world demand for domestic goods decline and domestic demands for rest of world goods increase. The appreciation of the currency is the mechanism whereby this reallocation happens. It is not the *cause* of problems as perceived by domestic manufacturers.

(iii) Monetary Policy

Next, consider the effects of an expansionary monetary policy. Again, start the economy out at the equilibrium (y_1, r_1) shown in Figure 16.6. This is at the triple intersection of *IS*, *BP*, and *LM* curves.

Expansionary monetary policy raises the money supply and shifts the *LM* curve to *LM'*. The new equilibrium clearly has to be somewhere on the curve *LM'*. At the initial exchange rate, the *IS* and *BP* curves intersect on the old *LM* curve. There must be another exchange rate (a higher value) at which the *IS* and *BP* curves intersect on the new *LM* curve, *LM'*. The *IS–BP* curve traces out the intersection points of the *IS* and *BP* curves as the exchange rate changes. The intersection of the *IS–BP* curve and the *LM'* curve determines the new equilibrium level of income y_2 and the interest rate r_2. We know that the exchange rate is higher than the

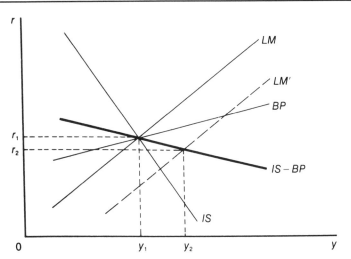

Figure 16.6
The effects of an
expansionary
monetary policy
under flexible
exchange rates

An initial equilibrium at (y_1, r_1) is disturbed by a rise in the money stock that shifts the *LM* curve to *LM'*. This leads to a higher exchange rate (depreciation), which shifts the *IS* and *BP* curves along the *IS–BP* locus until they intersect the new *LM* curve at (y_2, r_2). Thus, the effect of an expansionary monetary policy under flexible exchange rates is to lower the interest rate, raise real income and depreciate the currency.

initial one because we know that it is associated with more exports and fewer imports than prevailed initially. Recall that a higher value of the exchange rate implies a depreciation of the currency.

The effects of an expansionary monetary policy in a flexible exchange rate economy may be summarized as follows: a rise in the money supply leads to a lower rate of interest, a higher level of real income, and a depreciation of the currency.

(iv) Foreign Shocks

Finally, consider the effects of a change in world income. Imagine that the economy is at (y_1, r_1) in Figure 16.7 and that the rise in world real income shifts the *IS* and *BP* curves to *IS'* and *BP'*. These curves necessarily intersect along the *IS–BP* curve. Varying the exchange rate changes exports and imports, thereby shifting the *IS* and *BP* curves. Varying foreign real income (the shock that we are considering here) also changes exports and shifts the *IS* and *BP* curves. Since the *LM* curve has not changed (the domestic money supply being held constant), we know that the final equilibrium must be at a point on the *LM* curve. We further know that it has to involve the intersection of *IS* and *BP* curves — be on the *IS–BP* curve. We can see that there is only one such point, and that is the initial equilibrium income and interest rate level (y_1, r_1). What happens is that the exchange rate has to change (appreciate in this case) so as to return the *IS* and *BP* curves from their shocked positions *IS'*, *BP'* to their initial positions. The initial *IS* and *BP* curves then describe the initial exchange rate and world real income, and also the new higher world real income and lower value of the exchange rate (appreciated currency).

Comparison of Fixed and Flexible Exchange Rate. It is of some interest to compare the responses of the economy in the fixed and flexible exchange rate cases. You can do this by comparing Figure 16.2 with Figure 16.5 (fiscal policy), Figure 16.3 with Figure 16.6 (monetary policy), and Figure 16.4 (interpreted as a foreign shock) with Figure 16.7 (for a rise in world real income). An expansionary fiscal policy has a bigger output effect but smaller interest rate effect under fixed exchange rates than under flexible exchange rates. An expansionary monetary policy raises real income and lowers the interest rate under flexible exchange rates, but in the steady state it has no effect under fixed exchange rates. An expansion of world real income raises domestic real income and lowers domestic interest rates under fixed exchange rates, but in the steady state it has no effect on interest rates and real income in a flexible exchange rate economy.

This completes our analysis of the determination of output and interest rates under both fixed and flexible exchange rates. We will now go on to derive an aggregate demand curve for an open economy under both fixed and flexible exchange rates in the case of perfect capital mobility.

Figure 16.7
The effects of a rise in world income under flexible exchange rates

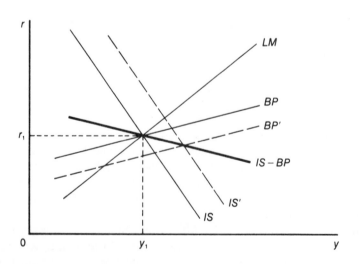

An initial equilibrium at (y_1, r_1) is disturbed by a rise in world real income that shifts the *IS* and *BP* curves to *IS'* and *BP'*. The domestic currency appreciates to produce an equivalent shift of those curves back to their initial positions. The real income level and the interest rate are undisturbed. Thus the effect of a world real income rise under flexible exchange rates comes out entirely as a change in the exchange rate.

C. Aggregate Demand when Capital is Perfectly Mobile

If capital is perfectly mobile, then the domestic real rate of interest, r, is equal to the world real rate of interest, r_f. The *BP* curve will be horizontal at that real rate of interest. The exogeneity of the real rate of interest has powerful simplifying implications for the analysis. In the analysis of the two preceding sections we had to determine the values of three variables — output, the rate of interest, and either the balance of payments (under fixed exchange rates), or the exchange rate (under flexible exchange rates).By assuming perfect capital mobility and, therefore, the exogeneity of the real rate of interest, the problem reduces to that of determining two variables, namely, the level of real income, and either the balance of payments (under fixed exchange rates) or the exchange rate (under flexible exchange rates).

The analysis of those two preceding sections did hold the price level constant. That is a central variable of interest that we will want to determine in our study of macroeconomic equilibrium. That being so, although we have eliminated from consideration the determination of one variable (the real rate of interest), we will want to bring into focus the determination of another variable — the price level. This is a lot easier to do in the case where the real interest rate is fixed than where we simultaneously seek to determine the real interest rate as well as all the other variables of concern.

(i)   Aggregate Demand with a Fixed Exchange Rate

With these preliminary remarks in mind, what we now want to do is to use the *IS–BP–LM* analysis to develop a theory of aggregate demand for the open economy under fixed and flexible exchange rates. The two exchange rate regimes give rise to different propositions about aggregate demand in a rather interesting way. First, recall what the aggregate demand curve is. It is the relationship between the price level and the quantity of output that will be demanded such that the economy is on the *IS* and *LM* curves. Let us derive the aggregate demand curve for an open economy under both fixed and flexible exchange rates in the case where there is perfect capital mobility.

First, consider the fixed exchange rate economy. Figure 16.8 will illustrate the analysis.

Frame (a) contains the *IS*, *BP* and *LM* curves, and frame (b) is where we will generate the aggregate demand curve. The *BP* curve is horizontal at the world rate of interest, r_f. Imagine first that the price level is arbitrarily given as P_0, marked off on the vertical axis of frame (b). With the price level at P_0, the *IS* curve would be the curve labelled $IS(EP_f/P_0)$. We know that under fixed exchange rates, the money supply is endogenous and has to be equal to whatever quantity is demanded at the

Figure 16.8
The aggregate
demand curve under
fixed exchange rates
and perfect capital
mobility

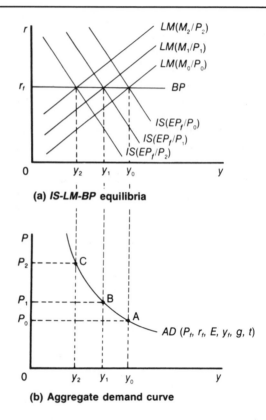

(a) *IS-LM-BP* equilibria

(b) **Aggregate demand curve**

With perfect capital mobility, the *BP* curve is horizontal [frame (a)]. Where the *IS* curve cuts the *BP* curve determines the level of aggregate demand. As the price level rises, the *IS* curve shifts to the left with the level of aggregate demand falling. The curve ABC traces out such an aggregate demand curve. The *LM* curve shifts as a result of a change in the money supply via the balance of payments to ensure money market equilibrium at each point along the aggregate demand curve. Aggregate demand depends only on the factors that underlie the *BP* and *IS* curves, that is, the exchange rate, the world price level, the world rate of interest, world real income, government expenditures and taxes.

level of income generated by the intersection of the IS and BP curves. Thus, the LM curve will automatically pass through the intersection of IS and BP at the world interest rate r_f and the income level y_0. Call the money supply in that case M_0, so that the LM curve is $LM(M_0/P_0)$. Point A in frame (b) at (y_0, P_0) is a point on the aggregate demand curve.

Next, consider raising the price level to P_1. In this case, the IS curve becomes $IS(EP_f/P_1)$ to the left of the original IS curve. Why does this happen? It happens because world prices have fallen relative to the domestic price level, thereby lowering the net demand for domestic output in the rest of the world and raising domestic demand for world output. This leftward shift of the IS curve intersects the BP curve at income level y_1. Again, the money supply will adjust through the balance of payments to ensure that the LM curve passes through this point. Call the new money supply M_1, so that the *LM* curve is that labelled $LM(M_1/P_1)$. Point B in frame (b) at the income level y_1 and price level P_1 is another point on the aggregate demand curve.

Consider a still higher price level, P_2. The *IS* curve is now further to the left to $IS(EP_f/P_2)$, which determines the income level as y_2. The money supply would fall even further now because of the balance of payments deficit, so that the *LM* curve becomes $LM(M_2/P_2)$. Point C at the income level y_2 and price level P_2 is yet another point on the aggregate demand curve. Joining up the points A, B, C generates the aggregate demand curve.

You will notice from the way in which the aggregate demand curve has been derived that the exogenous variables that determine the position of the aggregate demand curve are entirely in the *BP* and *IS* curves. The *LM* curve is a slack relationship that automatically adjusts (via a balance of payments adjustment of the money supply) to ensure an equilibrium money stock to support the interest rate, real income, and price level generated by the *IS–BP* intersection. The position of the aggregate demand curve therefore depends only upon those things that influence the position of *IS* and *BP* curves. These variables are the world price level, real income, and the real rate of interest; government spending and taxes; and the exchange rate. These are shown in parentheses on the label of the aggregate demand curve to remind you that the curve will shift as a result of changes in these variables. The money supply does not in any way determine the position of the aggregate demand curve in the fixed exchange rate, perfect capital mobility, open economy.

To summarize: for a fixed exchange rate open economy with perfect capital mobility, the aggregate demand curve is determined by the intersection of the *IS* and *BP* curves and in no way depends on the *LM* curve. The *LM* curve is not irrelevant in the fixed exchange rate economy; the *LM* curve determines the quantity of money, but not the level of aggregate demand.

(ii) Aggregate Demand with a Flexible Exchange Rate

Let us now go on to consider the derivation of the aggregate demand curve in a flexible exchange rate, perfect capital mobility economy. Figure 16.9 will illustrate this case. For the moment ignore frame (c) of that figure. Frame (a) contains the *IS, BP* and *LM* curves, and frame (b) derives the aggregate demand curve. Again, the *BP* curve is horizontal at the world real rate of interest, r_f. Recall that in the flexible exchange rate case, the exchange rate that underlies the position of the *IS* curve is determined in the analysis, whereas the money supply that underlies the position of the *LM* curve is exogenously determined by the monetary policy actions of the central bank.

To derive the aggregate demand curve, again pick a price level (initially P_0) marked on the vertical axis of frame (b). With a fixed money supply (M_0) and the price level at P_0, the *LM* curve will be $LM(M_0P_0)$.

**Figure 16.9
The aggregate
demand and *RE*
curves in a flexible
exchange rate,
perfect capital
mobility economy**

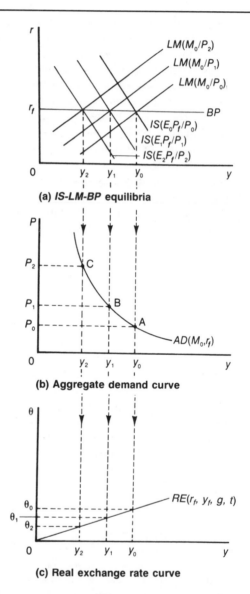

(a) *IS-LM-BP* equilibria

(b) Aggregate demand curve

(c) Real exchange rate curve

Under flexible exchange rates, the intersection of *LM* and *BP* curves determines aggregate demand. As the price level rises from P_0 through P_2, real money balances fall and the level of aggregate demand falls along the line ABC. The real exchange rate is such that the *IS* curve cuts the intersection of *LM* and *BP* curves. The lower the level of real income, the further to the left must the *IS* curve be, and the lower must be the net demand for domestic goods. The real exchange rate must fall, therefore, as real income falls.

The level of aggregate demand y_0 is determined where that curve intersects the *BP* curve. The *IS* curve will pass through the point of intersection of the curves $LM(M_0/P_0)$ and *BP* because the exchange rate will adjust until the change in the real exchange rate generates sufficient domestic demand to ensure that the *IS* curve passes through precisely that point. Indeed, this is how the exchange rate is determined. The output level y_0 determined by the intersection of the *LM* and *BP* curves, along with the price level P_0, marked as point A in frame (b), represent a point on the aggregate demand curve.

Next, consider a higher price level P_1, marked on the vertical axis of frame (b). At this higher price level, while maintaining the money supply at M_0, the *LM* curve will shift to the left to become $LM(M_0/P_1)$. This curve intersects the *BP* curve at the lower income level y_1. The income level y_1 with the price level P_1 [marked as point B in frame (b)] represents another point on the aggregate demand curve. The *IS* curve will pass through this point because the exchange rate will adjust to E_1, giving the *IS* curve, $IS(E_1 P_f/P_1)$.

Finally, suppose the price level was P_2 so that the real money supply was reduced still further, and the *LM* curve shifted yet further to the left to $LM(M_0/P_2)$. This would generate a real income level of y_2, shown as point C in frame (b). Again the *IS* curve would shift to the left with an adjustment in the exchange rate to E_2 to ensure that the real exchange rate moved by exactly the amount required to put the *IS* curve at the point of intersection of *LM* and *BP* curves.

The points A, B, and C in frame (b) trace out the aggregate demand curve for an economy with a flexible exchange rate, when capital is perfectly mobile internationally. Notice that in the derivation of this aggregate demand curve, it was purely the intersection of the *LM* and *BP* curves that determined the level of aggregate demand. This curve is therefore labelled as $AD(M_0, r_f)$ to remind you that it is the variables that underlie the *LM* and *BP* curve, namely, the money supply and the foreign interest rate, that determine the position of the aggregate demand curve in an economy with a flexible exchange rate, when capital is perfectly mobile internationally.

To summarize: under flexible exchange rates with perfect international capital mobility, aggregate demand is determined by the intersection of the *LM* and *BP* curves, and the position of the aggregate demand curve depends only on the world rate of interest and the domestic money supply. Aggregate demand in no way depends on world real income or prices or domestic fiscal policy. The *IS* curve is not irrelevant in the flexible exchange rate economy; it determines the exchange rate but not aggregate demand.

(iii) Aggregate Demand: Summary

Under both the fixed and flexible exchange rates when capital is perfectly mobile internationally, the aggregate demand curves slope downwards, and both curves depend on the world rate of interest. A higher world rate of interest would shift the fixed exchange rate aggregate demand curve to the left and the flexible exchange rate aggregate demand curve to the right. You can easily see why this is so. Under fixed exchange rates, it is the $IS-BP$ intersection that determines aggregate demand, so that a higher world interest rate would mean a lower level of aggregate demand; whereas, under flexible exchange rates, it is the $LM-BP$ intersection that determines aggregate demand, so that a higher world interest rate would give a higher domestic velocity of circulation of money and a higher level of aggregate demand for a given money supply. Aside from the world rate of interest, the two aggregate demand curves have no other variables in common. Under fixed exchange rates, the exchange rate, the world price level, world real income, and domestic fiscal policy variables affect domestic aggregate demand; whereas under flexible exchange rates, the domestic money supply is the only other variable that affects aggregate demand.

(iv)   The Real Exchange Rate

The concept of the real exchange rate was defined in Chapter 6 and met again in Chapter 15. You will recall that the real exchange rate is

$$\theta = EP_f/P$$

In our study of the open economy we will want to discover what determines the real exchange rate and the way in which it interacts with other variables in the economy. One of those other variables is the exchange rate E. Sometimes, for emphasis, or in order to avoid confusion between θ and E the term *nominal exchange rate* will be used to refer to the exchange rate E. Thus, the term 'real exchange rate' will always refer to θ and two alternative terms 'exchange rate' and '*nominal* exchange rate' will be used to refer to E.

It is convenient to begin by examining how the real exchange rate varies with real income. Figure 16.9 [frame (c)] shows this relationship. It plots the real exchange rate (θ) on the vertical axis and real income (y) on the horizontal axis. This curve is called the *real exchange rate curve* and is labelled RE. Why does the RE curve slope upwards? The answer to that question is found in the properties of the IS curve. Indeed, the RE curve in effect shows the value of the real exchange rate that ensures that the IS curve passes through the intersection point of the LM and BP curves. As the price level is raised from P_0 to P_1 and P_2, so the nominal exchange rate moves from E_0 to E_1 to E_2 to ensure that the real exchange rate equals θ_0, θ_1, and θ_2 — the values that make the level of real income read off from the IS curve equal to the level of aggregate demand determined by the $LM-BP$ intersection. That is, as the price level is raised, both real income (y) and the real exchange rate (θ) fall. The RE curve slopes upward.

The variables that make the RE curve shift are the same as those that make the IS curve shift. They are world real income, world interest rates, and domestic fiscal policy variables. The RE curve does not shift as a result of any monetary action. It is, as its name suggests, entirely a real curve. The RE curve will be important in the subsequent analysis of the behaviour of a flexible exchange rate economy.

Summary

A. Determination of Output, Interest Rate and the Balance of Payments in a Fixed Exchange Rate Regime at a Given Price Level

At each instant, the real income level and interest rate are determined at the point of intersection of the *IS* and *LM* curves. If that intersection point is off the *BP* curve, the *LM* curve is shifting. The steady state occurs where the *IS* and *BP* curves intersect. The *LM* curve intersects this point as a result of the money supply adjusting, while the balance of payments is out of equilibrium.

Expansionary fiscal policy raises output and interest rates and leads to a temporary balance of payments surplus. Expansionary monetary policy leads to a temporary balance of payments deficit and no steady-state change in real income or the rate of interest. A devaluation initially raises the rate of interest and real income level, but it eventually lowers the rate of interest below its initial level and raises income still further. In the process, the balance of payments will have been in surplus. A rise in world real income has a similar effect to that of a devaluation.

B. Determination of Output, Interest Rate and the Exchange Rate in a Flexible Exchange Rate Regime at a Given Price Level

Under flexible exchange rates, the *LM* curve is fixed in position. The positions of the *BP* and *IS* curves depend on the value of the exchange rate. As the exchange rate varies, these curves shift to intersect each other along a downward-sloping *IS–BP* locus. The equilibrium exchange rate is the exchange rate that locates the *BP* and *IS* curves at an intersection point along the *LM* curve. In a flexible exchange rate economy, an expansionary fiscal policy raises real income and the rate of interest and appreciates the currency. An expansionary monetary policy lowers the rate of interest, raises the level of real income, and depreciates the currency. An expansion in world income leads to an appreciation of the currency but to no change in real income or the rate of interest.

C. Aggregate Demand when Capital is Perfectly Mobile

If capital is perfectly mobile internationally, the rate of interest is determined exogenously in the rest of the world. In a fixed exchange rate economy, aggregate demand is determined purely by the *IS* curve and the world rate of interest. Shifts in aggregate demand therefore depend on changes in the world price level, world real income, world interest rate, and domestic fiscal policy. In a flexible exchange rate world, aggregate demand is determined solely by the domestic demand for money, supply of money and world interest rate. In that case, therefore, changes in aggregate demand depend only on the world rate of interest and the domestic money supply. In the fixed exchange rate setting, the *LM* curve determines the money supply via the balance of payments; and in the flexible exchange rate setting, the *IS* curve determines the real and the nominal exchange rates.

Review Questions

1. Work out the effects on all the relevant variables, under fixed exchange rates, of the following shocks:

   (a) a rise in government spending
   (b) a rise in domestic credit
   (c) a rise in the exchange rate
   (d) a rise in world real income
   (e) a rise in world prices
   (f) a rise in the world real rate of interest

   How do the effects depend on the degree of capital mobility?

2. Work out the effects on all the relevant variables, in a flexible exchange rate regime, of the six shocks listed in Question 1. How do the effects depend on the degree of capital mobility?

3. On the basis of your answers to Questions 1 and 2, how would you choose between the two alternative exchange rate regimes?

4. What determines aggregate demand in an open economy that faces perfectly mobile international capital flows:

   (a) under fixed exchange rates?
   (b) under flexible exchange rates?

5. Why does the exchange rate regime make a difference to the determinants of aggregate demand?

6. What determines the real exchange rate?

17

Aggregate Supply and the Labour Market

It is now time to embark on the study of aggregate supply. Aggregate supply will be the subject of this and the following two chapters. The theory of aggregate supply, in contrast to the theory of aggregate demand, remains in an unsettled and controversial state. There are three leading theories. The first, *classical*, will be presented in this chapter. A second, *new classical*, will be developed in Chapter 18 and a third, *new Keynesian*, will be presented in Chapter 19.

When you have completed this chapter you will be able to:

(a) **Explain the concept of the short-run aggregate production function.**
(b) **Explain how a competitive aggregate labour market works.**
(c) **Describe the classical theory of aggregate supply.**
(d) **Explain why aggregate supply grows and fluctuates.**

A. Short-Run Aggregate Production Function

A useful starting point in explaining the concept of the short-run *aggregate* production function is with the production function of an individual producer. A production function is simply a statement about the maximum output that can be produced with a given list of inputs, and more than that, a statement of how that maximum level of output will vary as the inputs themselves are varied.

The maximum output of some particular good that can be produced will depend on the amount of capital employed, the state of technology, the amount of land resources used, and the number and skill of the workers employed. Over time, all the inputs used in a production process can be varied. Capital equipment can be purchased, technology can be changed, land use can be modified, and workers can acquire new skills. These ongoing changes are the source of the long-term growth in output.[1] At any given moment, however, these four factors are fixed. The input which can be varied quickly is the quantity of labour employed. The short-run production function shows the relationship between the maximum amount of output that can be produced as the quantity of labour employed is varied while holding constant the other inputs into the production process.

What you have just reviewed is the analysis of the short-run production function that is used in microeconomic theory. It is possible to use this microeconomic analysis to derive an *aggregate* short-run production function. The aggregate short-run production function relates the *aggregate* output to the total number of workers employed. (Recall from Chapter 3 that aggregate output is equal to real expenditure and real income — that is, real GDP.)

Define output as y, and also define number employed as n. Then, the aggregate short-run production function can be written as

$$y = \phi(n) \tag{17.1}$$

The symbol $\phi(\ )$ should be read as 'is a function of' or, more simply, 'is determined by'. Thus, Equation (17.1) states that the maximum value of y that can be produced is determined by the level of n and that it varies as n is varied.

The properties of the short-run production function are most easily described by plotting a specific example. This is done in Figure 17.1.

The label on the curve, $\phi(n)$, is just a shorthand way of saying that output (y) depends on (or is a function of) the amount of labour employed (n). The short-run production function depicted in Figure 17.1 reflects a common technological fact: that as the number employed is increased, the output of the marginal worker — marginal product — declines.

There is a problem concerning the labour input of which you should take note. It concerns the role of 'hours per worker' in the definition of the labour input. Normally, labour is measured in terms of *man-hours*. For example, three people each working for 4 hours a day can produce a similar output to two people working 6 hours a day each. Macroeconomics is more concerned with explaining variation in the

---

1 Chapter 24 deals with the determination of the long-term growth trend.

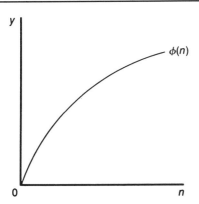

Figure 17.1
The aggregate short-run production function

The production function, $\phi(n)$, shows the maximum attainable output level (y) as the level of labour input (n) is varied. The employment of more units of labour produces more units of output. However, each additional unit of labour produces less additional output than did the previous unit — there is diminishing marginal product.

number of people employed than with explaining the average number of *hours worked per worker*. As the economy goes through a cycle of activity from boom to slump, it may be that output drops by, say, 10 per cent. That output drop could be accommodated by a cut of 10 per cent in the average hours worked by each worker with no one becoming fully unemployed. Typically, however, this does not happen. Average hours per worker employed remains relatively constant, while the number of workers employed declines. It is possible to develop an explanation as to why it is that employment rather than average hours per worker varies with the level of economic activity. Rather than pursue such an explanation, however, we are simply going to assume that each worker works a fairly constant average number of hours, and as economic activity varies, the number of workers employed varies. The variable n will, therefore, throughout this book, be taken to mean the number of workers employed. It will reflect the number of man-hours employed, provided the number of hours per man is constant, which we will assume to be the case.

This completes the definition of the short-run aggregate production function.

B. Competitive Aggregate Labour Market

(i) The Demand for Labour

First consider the demand side of the labour market. Each competitive firm will demand labour and produce output up to the point at which the price of its output is equal to the marginal cost of its production. Let us call the output price of an individual firm P_i and its marginal cost of production MC_i. The subscript i is to remind us that we are dealing with an *individual* firm. Thus,

$$P_i = MC_i \qquad (17.2)$$

If this condition is satisfied, the firm is making maximum profit (provided that the marginal cost curve is rising at this point).

Marginal cost is easy to calculate. Recall that in the short run, the only input which can vary is labour. The cost of hiring one extra worker is equal to the money wage per worker (W). However, the money wage is not the marginal cost. The amount produced by the marginal worker is known as the marginal product (MP_i). The marginal cost is the cost of the marginal worker (W) divided by the output which that marginal worker can produce (MP_i). That is,

$$MC = \frac{W}{MP_i} \qquad (17.3)$$

For example, if the wage rate was £10 an hour and if a worker could produce 100 units of output in an hour, the marginal cost (the cost of the last unit of output) would be £10 ÷ 100 = 10 pence. Now, replacing the marginal cost in Equation (17.3) with the price from Equation (17.2), it is clear that

$$P_i = \frac{W}{MP_i} \qquad (17.4)$$

If we divide both sides of this equation by P_i and multiply both sides by MP_i, we obtain

$$MP_i = \frac{W}{P_i} \qquad (17.5)$$

The Equation (17.5) says that the marginal product of some particular firm will be equal to the money wage (W) divided by the price of the output of that firm (P). To see how this condition leads directly to the demand for labour function, consider Figure 17.2, which plots the marginal product of labour of the ith firm against the number of workers employed in that firm. Call this downward-sloping relation the marginal product curve.

You have seen that a condition for profit maximizing (Equation 17.5) is that the marginal product of labour must equal the ratio of the money wage to the price level. This ratio is the real wage. You can therefore equivalently measure the real wage on the vertical axis of Figure 17.2. The marginal product curve then automatically becomes the demand for labour curve when thought of as being drawn against the real wage.

So far we have talked only about an individual firm's demand for labour. We now want to move on to consider the economy-wide or aggregate demand for labour. We can obtain this by adding the individual demand

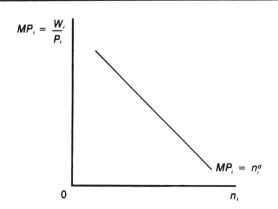

Figure 17.2
The marginal product
curve — the demand
for labour in a com-
petitive industry

Marginal product MP_i declines as labour input (n_i) increases. Profits are maximized when the marginal product is equal to the real wage (W_i/P_i). The marginal product curve and the demand for labour curve of a competitive firm are, therefore, the same curve.

for labour curves across all the firms in the economy. There is no difficulty in adding up the quantities of labour demanded across all the firms. The result is the total quantity of labour demanded in the economy as a whole. We have to be careful, however, in interpreting the aggregate demand for labour curve because, on the vertical axis of the diagram describing an individual firm's demand for labour, the real wage that appears is specific to the individual firm. It is the money wage rate divided by the individual firm's output price. If we take an average of the output prices of all the firms in the economy then what we obtain is simply the economy-wide average price level. In effect, we obtain the GDP deflator. The economy-wide demand for labour curve, therefore, shows the total quantity of labour demanded in the economy plotted against the economy average real wage, which is the same thing as the money wage divided by the average price level. Such a demand for labour curve is shown in Figure 17.3.

(ii) The Supply of Labour

Consider next the supply of labour. The theory of household behaviour predicts that utility-maximizing households will supply more hours of labour as the real wage increases up to some maximum. Thereafter, as the real wage rises, the number of hours supplied will decline since a higher income will lead the household to want to consume more leisure along with other goods. Thus, the supply of hours per individual household would be represented by a supply curve which increases with the real wage up to some maximum and then begins to fall off.

For our purposes we are interested in developing a theory of the aggregate supply, not of hours per worker but of the number of workers. In

Figure 17.3
The demand for
labour

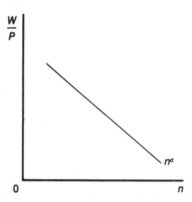

The demand for labour in the economy as a whole n^d is obtained by aggregating the demand for labour in all the individual industries. Like the industry demand curves, the lower the real wage (W/P), the greater the quantity of labour (n) demanded.

effect, we are interested in analysing the outcome of an all-or-nothing choice. That is, the potential worker has to evaluate how much utility would be derived from not working and compare that with the utility that would be derived from working for a fixed number of hours per week. If the utility from working exceeds that from not working, the individual will make the decision to be in the labour force and therefore be part of the labour supply. In general, as the real wage rises, more and more people will evaluate the prospect of working as yielding more utility than the prospect of not working. Let us suppose that this is the case and that

Figure 17.4
The supply of labour

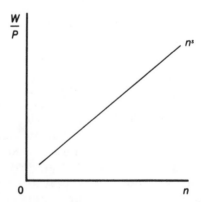

Households choose whether to enter the labour force by comparing the utility they would get from working a fixed number of hours at a certain wage rate with the utility they would derive from taking leisure. The higher the real wage, the larger is the number of households that will regard working as yielding superior utility to consuming leisure. Thus the supply of labour (n^s) rises as the real wage (W/P) rises.

as a consequence, the aggregate supply of labour increases as the real wage increases. Figure 17.4 shows such a relation.

(iii) Competitive Equilibrium

Next, consider the competitive equilibrium in the labour market. Figure 17.5 brings together the demand curve from Figure 17.3 and the supply curve from Figure 17.4. It is supposed that the economy generates sufficient information about supply and demand in the labour market for the real wage to achieve a market-clearing equilibrium value. The economy settles down at the real wage $(W/P)^*$, and at the level of employment n^*. The real wage is the ratio of the *money* wage to the *price level*, and it is the money wage which will adjust in the labour market to ensure that for a given price level, the equilibrium real wage is attained.

We have now determined equilibrium values of the real wage and the level of employment. You can think of the employment level as the aggregate number employed in the economy and the real wage as the economy's average real wage. Individuals' real wages will be highly variable, depending on individual skills and other factors. If relative wages are fairly stable, however, movements in the average real wage in the economy will also reflect movements in each individual's real wage.

The way in which the analysis has been developed has ignored the phenomenon of unemployment. That is not to say that unemployment cannot exist in this model. It is simply to say that at the present time we are not discussing the implications of the model for the rate of unemployment. This will be the subject of Chapter 26. Furthermore, monopolistic elements in the labour market, such as, for example, the operation of trade unions, have been ignored. This, too, will be dealt with in Chapter 26.

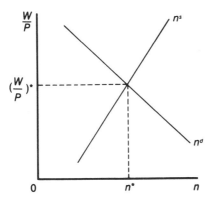

**Figure 17.5
Labour market
equilibrium**

The line labelled n^d is the demand for labour curve and the line labelled n^s is the supply curve of labour. The labour market is in equilibrium when households are maximizing utility (are on their supply curve) and firms are maximizing profits (are on their demand curve). The only such point is where the supply and demand curves cut at the real wage $(W/P)^*$ and the employment level n^*.

C. Aggregate Supply Curve

First, recall the definition of the aggregate supply curve: the aggregate supply curve shows the amount of output that the economy will supply at each different price level. It is a curve which is drawn in a diagram with the price level on one axis and output on the other. In the classical model, the aggregate supply curve shows the amount of output that will be supplied at each price level *given that firms are maximizing profits, households are maximizing utility*, and the *labour market is in equilibrium*.

To derive the aggregate supply curve, it is necessary to bring together the two components of analysis developed above, namely, the short-run production function and the competitive equilibrium in the labour market. Figure 17.6 illustrates the derivation.

First notice that there are four parts to Figure 17.6. Frame (a) is nothing

**Figure 17.6
Derivation of the
aggregate supply
curve**

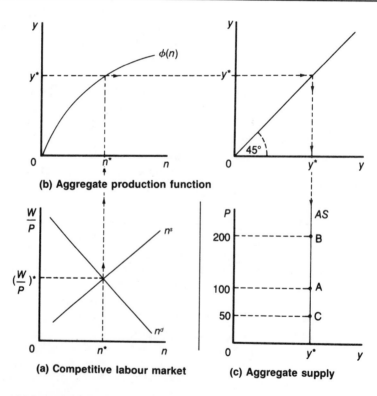

Frame (a) is identical to Figure 17.5 and frame (b) is identical to Figure 17.1. Frame (c) shows the aggregate supply curve (AS). This shows the amount of output which will be supplied as the price level varies when firms are hiring the profit-maximizing quantity of labour and households are supplying the utility-maximizing quantity of labour. There is a unique level of output y^* that will be produced by the equilibrium level of labour input (n^*) at the equilibrium real wage $(W/P)^*$. That level of supply will be independent of the price level, so that the aggregate supply curve is vertical.

other than Figure 17.5, which you have just been studying. It shows a labour market in competitive equilibrium with the real wage equal to $(W/P)^*$ and the level of employment, n^*.

Frame (b), is exactly the same as Figure 17.1, namely, a short-run production function. Notice that the horizontal axes of frames (a) and (b) both measure the same thing — the volume of employment. Adopt the convention that the units of measurement are the same on both horizontal axes. That being the case, you can follow the dotted line and arrow and immediately read off from the horizontal axis of frame (b) the same equilibrium level of employment, n^*, as is determined in frame (a).

With the level of employment equal to n^*, the short-run production function in frame (b) determines the level of output y^* as shown on the vertical axis.

So far, you have used frames (a) and (b) to determine the equilibrium values of the real wage, the level of employment, and the level of output.

To complete the derivation of the aggregate supply curve, the question that has to be answered is: how does the equilibrium level of output vary as the price level varies? The answer to this question (and the aggregate supply curve) will be discovered in frame (c). This part of the figure measures the price level on the vertical axis and the level of output on the horizontal axis. Notice that the vertical axis of frame (b) and the horizontal axis of frame (c) measure the same thing — output. The top right part of the diagram has output on both axes and a 45° line. It is just a pictorial device to enable you to read off from the horizontal axis of frame (c) the same quantity as is shown on the vertical axis of frame (b). Notice, by the way, that the vertical axis of frame (c) *does not* measure the same thing as the vertical axis of frame (a) — there are no arrowed lines going from frame (c) directly to frame (a). The arrows (and the analysis) start in frame (a) and go clockwise to finish in frame (c).

Now go back to the question: how does equilibrium output vary as the price level varies? Suppose that the price level initially is equal to 100. We can arbitrarily define our units so that the initial price level is 100. Then there is a point on an aggregate supply curve, which is identified by the letter A in frame (c), at which the price level is 100 and output is y^*. Suppose now that the price level was doubled from 100 to 200. What would happen to the amount of output which firms would be willing to supply? The answer is quickly seen — nothing would happen to it.

If the price level doubled to 200, then the money wage would also have to double to preserve labour market equilibrium [frame (a)]. To see that this is so, suppose that after the price level had increased, the money wage remained fixed. In such a case, the real wage would have fallen, and the demand for labour would exceed the supply of labour. Such a situation would force the money wage to rise until the labour market was again in equilibrium. The only real wage consistent with equilibrium is the original one. Thus, the money wage must rise by the same percentage amount as does the price level. In this case, following a doubling of the price level, the money wage would also have to double in order to keep the real wage constant. With the labour market remaining at its original equilibrium, the quantity of employment would remain unchanged as would the amount of output supplied. The economy would move, therefore, to the point indentified with the letter B in frame (c).

Next, suppose the price level halved from 100 to 50. The effects of this on the amount of output that the economy would produce are exactly the same as the effects of the doubling of the price level. In this case, the money wage would have to fall to one-half of its previous level in order to maintain the real wage at its market equilibrium value, and employment and output would remain constant at n^* and y^*. The economy would thus move to the point identified with the letter C in frame (c). These three points (and all the other points above, below, and between them) trace an aggregate supply curve for this economy.

The classical aggregate supply curve is perfectly inelastic. The level of output will be equal to y^* no matter what the price level.

D. Growth and Fluctuations in Aggregate Supply

In thinking about the factors that make aggregate supply vary it is convenient to distinguish between those things that generate *long-term growth* of output and those that produce *fluctuations* around the trend increase. Chapter 24 of this book will examine in greater detail the long-term growth process. Most of what you will study in this book abstracts from long-term growth and concentrates on fluctuations in aggregate economic activity around the growth trend.

There are three major sources of long-term growth in the economy — capital accumulation, technical progress, and population growth. Trends in these factors will generate an upward trend in total output.

Fluctuations in output occur for two types of reasons. First, and very importantly, the rate of capital accumulation and the rate of technical progress, although trending upwards, are by no means smooth and steady. There are periods in which there is rapid technical change associated with a very high rate of capital accumulation. There are other periods when technical progress is slow and when hardly any new techniques are being applied to increase output. To some extent the timing of inventions and the application of new techniques is the outcome of rational economic choices. There is always, though, going to be an element of randomness or unpredictability in the timing of such events.

A good example of such randomness concerns the basis of the existing wave of economic growth — the invention and application of the silicon chip. It became obvious in the 1960s that although bigger and more powerful computers could be built simply by stringing together larger and larger circuits of transistors, the labour cost of handling all the connections, ensuring that they were properly made, and checking out the circuits, would be such as to make the cost of very large-scale computers so high that their application would be limited to a small number of activities. The gain from being able to build circuitry that did not involve separately joining together large numbers of individual transistors was obvious to many people working in the field. How to achieve circuits that did not involve that process was, however, far from obvious. Many people worked on the problem from a variety of angles. Then, in the middle 1950s, scientists came up with the idea of introducing impurities into a piece of common sand which, if arranged in appropriate patterns, would replicate the work not just of one transistor but of a whole array of them connected together in a particular way. The basis for very low-cost large-scale computing power was in place. In the period since then, advances on that basic idea and, more importantly, the exploitation of that idea in an incredibly wide array of activities, is leading to a rise in capital accumulation and an increase in output potential.

This modern example also serves to illustrate another very important fact. The invention of something new does not necessarily — indeed does not usually — lead immediately to its rapid deployment or to a rapid increase in the stock of capital equipment — plant and machinery — and a rise in output. At first, a new invention creates a more uncertain environment. People using old techniques to achieve given tasks become aware that a new technique has been discovered. They are not sure how the application of that new technique will affect what they are doing, nor are they sure as to the best time for them to switch from the old to the new ways of doing things. An initial period of uncertainty can lead to a fall in investment. For example, a firm that was just about to replace an old worn out machine with a new version of the same thing might very well delay its investment if a new technique is known to be just around the corner.

The key point to notice is that the invention of new techniques is, to a large degree, a random process over which no one has precise control. As new inventions come along they influence the profitability of existing methods of producing goods and services and influence the pace with which firms will seek to replace their existing plant and machinery with either similar or new technologies. The ebbs and flows in the pace of both the invention and application of new techniques will lead to fluctuations in the total amount of output that the economy can produce.

You can think of these fluctuations using the device that you have studied earlier in this chapter — the short-run production function. At times when the economy is undergoing a rapid expansion because of the application of new productivity increasing technologies the short-run production function will be moving upwards quickly. Thus, any given amount of labour force will produce a rapidly growing amount of total output. At times when there is a low level of activity in the exploiting of new technologies and a low rate of capital accumulation, the production function will be moving upwards but at a pace slower than its overall longer-term growth rate.

There is another set of factors that can lead to fluctuations in aggregate output and that sometimes have been important. These are random shocks either to the natural environment — climate related or to the political environment — war and conflict related. A good example of the latter type of shock occurred in 1973 when the oil producing countries — known as OPEC — imposed a massive oil embargo lowering the shipments of oil to the developed countries and massively raising the price of those shipments. This large cut in the availability of a key input into the production process in effect shifted the aggregate short-run production function in a downward direction making it possible for a given amount of labour to produce a smaller amount of total output than previously.

The first type of shock — climate related — has also been important in recent years. Rainfall is the major variable at work here and has its biggest impact upon economies that have a very large agricultural sector. Low rainfall typically produces low harvests, especially in the grain (and grain related) product classes. Low grain harvests do not only directly lower aggregate output, they have secondary effects. Low grain output raises grain prices and lowers the efficient output rate for grain-eating animals. Thus, food production in total tends to decline. Shocks of this kind can have important impacts upon the aggregate economy.

All of the types of shocks that have just been discussed can be summarized as things that shift the short-run production function. They also, therefore, will shift the aggregate supply curve. The way in which they will shift the aggregate supply curve needs a little analysis. Figure 17.7 is going to provide you with the vehicle for investigating this.

Let us begin to work through Figure 17.7. First of all notice that it is arranged in exactly the same way as Figure 17.6 — frame (a) shows a competitive labour market, (b) an aggregate production function and (c) the aggregate supply curve. Focus first of all on the production function [frame (b)]. Here we have shown two production functions, one labelled $A_0\phi(n)$ and another, higher short-run production function, labelled $A_1\phi(n)$. You can think of these two short-run production functions as representing the range over which the production function might fluctuate as a result of the various shocks that were discussed above.

Next look at frame (a) and first, in that frame, focus on the demand for labour curves. Associated with each production function is a marginal product curve. If the production function is the lower one then the demand for labour curve (the marginal product of labour) will be the line labelled n_0^d. If the production function is the higher of the two then the marginal product curve — and demand for labour curve — will be the higher one, namely, n_1^d. So far we have just looked at the production function and demand for labour curve and summarized the way in which

Figure 17.7
Shifts in the
aggregate supply
curve

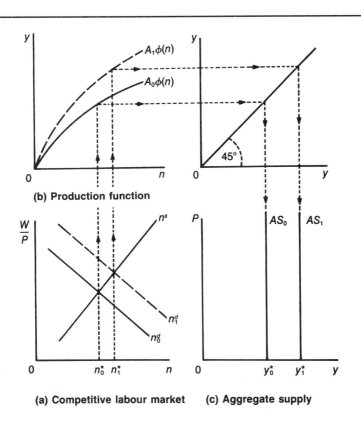

(b) Production function

(a) Competitive labour market   (c) Aggregate supply

A technology shock that shifts the production function from $A_0\phi(n)$ to $A_1\phi(n)$ raises the marginal product of labour curve and raises output. This increases the level of employment from n_0^* to n_1^* and raises output from y_0^* to y_1^*. The aggregate supply curve shifts from AS_0 to AS_1.

shocks to the production function — usually called technology shocks for short — move those curves.

Next, let us consider the supply of labour. We have not studied the factors that underlie the supply of labour curve in any detail. Some considerations might lead us to suppose that the supply of labour would be very unresponsive to real wages — would be inelastic. Casual reasoning would lead us to suppose that this might be the relevant case.

It is conceivable, however, that the supply of labour at any given moment in time is highly elastic. Some lines of reasoning would lead to the presumption that this is the normal case. Taking account of the possibility of working harder at a given point in time and then taking more leisure at a later time — substituting leisure over time — is one of the arguments that would lead to this presumption. The amount by which the aggregate supply curve shifts as a result of technology shocks is influenced by the elasticity of the supply of labour.

Figure 17.8 illustrates the effect of elasticity of the supply of labour on the magnitude of the shift of the aggregate supply curve that result from a technology shock. An inelastic supply of labour curve is the steep curve labelled n_I^s in frame (a); whereas an elastic labour supply is shown by the flat curve n_E^s. We can work out the implications of both alternative cases by deriving the shift in the aggregate supply curve that would occur if the production function moved from its lower to its higher level and for each of the two alternative assumptions about the elasticity of labour supply. First, derive the aggregate supply curve for the original position where the production function is at the lower level. This generates an equilibrium that is identical to that depicted in Figure 17.6. Where the demand for labour curve n_0^d cuts the supply of labour curve (both supply curves are at the same point here) an equilibrium real wage $(W/P)_0^*0$

Figure 17.8
Shifts in the
aggregate supply
curve and the
elasticity of the
supply of labour

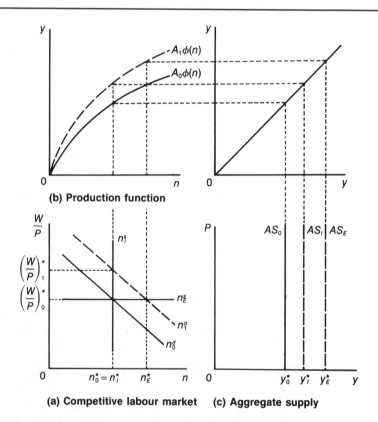

(b) Production function

(a) Competitive labour market   **(c) Aggregate supply**

A technology shock that shifts the production function from $A_0\phi(n)$ to $A_1\phi(n)$ raises the demand for labour from n_0^d to n_1^d. If the supply of labour is inelastic (n_I^s) the real wage rises to $(W/P)_1^*$, unemployment remains constant and the aggregate supply curve shifts from AS_0 to AS_I. If the supply of labour is elastic (n_E^s) the real wage remains constant, employment rises to n_E^* and the aggregate supply of labour curve shifts from AS_0 to AS_E. That is, the more elastic the aggregate supply of labour, the smaller is the rise in real wages and the larger is the rise in both employment ad output.

employment level n_0^* are determined. At that employment level, using the lower production function, the level of output is y_0^*. This level of output will be produced regardless of the price level and so the aggregate supply curve is the vertical line AS_0 in frame (c). Now consider what happens when the production function shifts to $A_1\phi(n)$. The marginal product of labour — the demand for labour — rises to n_1^d. If the supply of labour is inelastic then the real wage rises very sharply to $(W/P)_I^*$. Employment does not change so that n_I^* equals n_0^*. Output rises however, to y_I^* and the aggregate supply curve shifts to become the curve AS_I.

If the supply of labour is very elastic we get a much bigger change in both employment and output. In such a case the real wage does not rise and employment rises very sharply to n_E^*. Output rises to y_E^* and the aggregate supply curve shifts to that labelled AS_E in frame (c). The shift of the aggregate supply curve is larger, the more elasic the supply of labour.

A comparable analysis could be performed for a drop in the production function. You can easily work that case out for yourselves simply by reversing the example that we have just taken you through here.

Summary

A. Short-Run Aggregate Production Function

The short-run aggregate production function shows how the maximum amount of output will vary as the number of workers employed varies, holding constant the stock of capital, the state of technology, and the skills of labour. Its properties are the same as the short-run production function of an individual firm in that it displays diminishing marginal productivity.

B. Competitive Aggregate Labour Market

A competitive aggregate labour market will determine an equilibrium real wage and level of employment where the downward-sloping demand curve (derived from the marginal product curve) cuts an upward-sloping supply curve (derived from utility maximizing decisions of households).

C. Aggregate Supply Curve

The aggregate supply curve shows how output varies as the price level varies when firms are maximizing profits, households are maximizing utility and the labour market is in equilibrium. The classical aggregate supply is perfectly inelastic with respect to the price level.

D. Growth and Fluctuations in Aggregate Supply

Aggregate supply will grow over time as a result of trends in technical progress, population growth and capital accumulation. Aggregate supply will fluctuate around its trend partly because technical change and capital accumulation do not proceed smoothly and partly because of random shocks caused by such things as climate and political instability. Such shocks to the production function — called technology shocks — will shift the aggregate supply curve. The amount by which the aggregate supply curve shifts and the effect of such shocks on the level of employment and real wages depends on the elasticity of aggregate labour supply.

Review Questions

1. A firm produces a good from inputs of labour and capital. Labour is measured by the number of workers employed. Use the following data to draw the firm's short-run production function.

No. of men	1	2	3	4	5	6	7	8	9	10
Output	10	21	33	45	56	66	75	83	90	96

   If the money wage is £18 and the firm sells the good it produces for £2, how many workers will the firm employ?
2. If the economy consisted of 1000 firms, all identical and all exactly like the firm described in Question 1, show in a diagram the shape and position of the *aggregate* short-run production function. Also show the aggregate demand for labour curve. If the aggregate labour supply curve is

   $$n^s = 2000(W/P) - 2000$$

   how many workers will be employed and what will be the economy-wide average real wage?
3. What is an aggregate supply curve?
4. Use your answer to Question 2 to derive the aggregate supply curve for the hypothetical economy described in that question.
5. In drawing the aggregate supply curve, several assumptions have been made. List these assumptions.
6. Labour allocates its time between work and leisure in order to maximize its utility. Along which curve in Figure 17.6 is utility maximized?
7. Firms produce that output which maximizes profit. Along which curve in Figure 17.6 are all firms maximizing profit?
8. Is the aggregate supply curve fixed in position forever, or does it shift from time to time? If it does shift, list some of the things that would cause it to do so.

9. Review the factors that lead to long-term trend increases in aggregate supply.
10. Review the factors that can make the aggregate supply curve shift.
11. Show how the effect of a technology shock on the aggregate supply curve depends on the elasticity of aggregate labour supply.

Appendix A: Monopoly and the Demand for Labour

You may be thinking that the analysis presented in this chapter is fine for a competitive industry but not for a monopoly. You may also have been taught that we simply *know* that there are no competitive industries in the actual world. If so, you will be regarding the preceding analysis as being about as useful for the task in hand as the flat earth theory would be for charting an air route from London to Tokyo! Leaving aside the deep question of whether or not it is possible *simply to know* whether or not competitive industries exist, it is perhaps of some interest to notice that for the task at hand, it simply doesn't matter whether the economy is competitive or monopolistic. To see this, consider how the analysis would go for a monopolist.

Now in order to maximize profits, a monopolist will set marginal cost equal, not to price, but to marginal revenue (MR_i). That is

$$MC_i = MR_i \tag{17A.1}$$

Just as in the case of a competitive firm, the monopolist's marginal cost will be equal to the wage rate divided by the marginal product of labour; that is,

$$MC_i = \frac{W}{MP_i} \tag{17A.2}$$

The monopolist's marginal revenue will be related to price by the formula

$$MR_i = (1 + \eta)P_i, \quad \frac{1}{\eta} < -1 \tag{17A.3}$$

where η is the elasticity of the monopolist's demand curve (see Appendix B to this chapter). To get a feel for how the relationship between marginal revenue and price [Equation (17A.3)] works, notice that if the elasticity of demand (η) was infinite, then MR_i would equal P_i. This, of course, is exactly the case of perfect competition. If η was equal to -1, the demand for the monopolist's output would be unit elastic and the demand curve would be a rectangular hyperbola. In that case, the monopolist's marginal revenue would be zero and the monopolist would not be in business.

In general, the monopolist's marginal revenue will be less than price but a stable fraction of the price.

Using Equations (17A.3) and (17A.2) in (17A.l) enables us to obtain

$$\left(1+\frac{1}{\eta}\right)P_i = \frac{W}{MP_i} \tag{17A.4}$$

Proceeding as we did in the case of the competitive firm, dividing both sides of Equation (17A.4) by P_i, and multiplying both sides by MP_i, we obtain:

$$\left(1+\frac{1}{\eta}\right)MP_i = \frac{W}{P_i} \tag{17A.5}$$

This says that some fraction [the fraction $(1+1/\eta)$] of the marginal product of a monopolistic firm will be equal to the real wage. The monopolist's demand for labour will therefore be *less* than that of a competitive producer (assuming that they have identical production functions) but will still have the crucial property that as the real wage rises, so the demand for labour falls. By aggregating across all producers, whether competitive or monopolistic, we shall still end up with an aggregate demand for labour that looks like that shown in Figure 17.3.

Appendix B: Elasticity of Demand, Marginal Revenue and Price

Elasticity is a measure of responsiveness. The elasticity of demand measures, in a precise way, the responsiveness of the quantity demanded to a change in the price. The higher the elasticity the more responsive is the quantity to a price change. Elasticity is a unit-free measure of responsiveness. To be precise, it is the percentage change in the quantity demanded divided by the percentage change in price or, equivalently, the proportionate change of quantity demanded divided by the proportionate change in price. Calling the elasticity η, the change in quantity ΔQ, the change in price ΔP, the quantity Q, and the price P, the elasticity is measured as

$$\eta = \frac{\Delta Q}{Q} \div \frac{\Delta P}{P} \tag{17A.6}$$

This may equivalently be written as

$$\eta = \frac{\Delta Q}{Q} \times \frac{P}{\Delta P} \tag{17A.7}$$

For future reference it is useful to notice that one over the elasticity (the inverse of the elasticity) is

$$\frac{1}{\eta} = \frac{\Delta P}{\Delta Q} \times \frac{Q}{P} \qquad (17A.8)$$

To obtain the formula used in Appendix A, notice that total revenue (R) is equal to price (P) multiplied by quantity (Q); that is

$$R = PQ \qquad (17A.9)$$

Now suppose that there was a change in price that induced a change in quantity and a change in revenue. Then the new revenue that we could call $R+\Delta R$ will be determined as

$$R+\Delta R = (P+\Delta P)(Q+\Delta Q) \qquad (17A.10)$$

Multiplying out Equation (17A.10) gives

$$R+\Delta R = PQ+P\Delta Q+\Delta PQ+\Delta P\Delta Q \qquad (17A.11)$$

If the change in price (ΔP) is very very small, then Equation (17A.11) is approximately

$$R+\Delta R = PQ+P\Delta Q+Q\Delta P \qquad (17A.12)$$

(You see that we are treating the last term in Equation (17A.12) as if it was zero.) Now subtract Equation (17A.9) from Equation (17A.12) to give

$$\Delta R = P\Delta Q+Q\Delta P \qquad (17A.13)$$

This can be manipulated by multiplying and dividing the second term on the right-hand side by P to give

$$\Delta R = \left[\Delta Q + \frac{Q}{P}(\Delta P)\right]P \qquad (17A.14)$$

Dividing this equation through by ΔQ gives

$$\frac{\Delta R}{\Delta Q} \approx \left[\frac{\Delta Q}{\Delta Q} + \frac{Q}{P}\frac{\Delta P}{\Delta Q}\right]P \qquad (17A.15)$$

The left-hand side of Equation (17A.15) ($\Delta R/\Delta Q$) is what is called *marginal revenue* — the change in revenue induced by a change in the quantity sold. Obviously, the first term in brackets — $\Delta Q/\Delta Q$ — in Equation (17A.15) is equal to one. You can also see, by referring back to Equation (17A.8), that the second term in brackets — $(Q/P)(\Delta P/\Delta Q)$ — in Equation (17A.15) is the inverse of the elasticity of demand. Equation (17A.15) may, therefore, be written more simply as:

$$\frac{\Delta R}{\Delta Q} \approx \left(1+ \frac{1}{\eta}\right)P \qquad (17A.16)$$

This relationship is the one used in Appendix A. In words, it states that marginal revenue equals one plus one over the elasticity of demand multiplied by the price. Clearly if the elasticity of demand is infinitely big (the case of perfect competition), price and marginal revenue are the same as each other.

Another interesting special case is when the elasticity of demand is minus one (the case of a rectangular hyperbola demand curve). In that case, you can verify from Equation (17A.16) that marginal revenue is equal to zero. Notice that, in general, marginal revenue is positive but less than the price since η, in general, is negative and lies between minus infinity (perfect competition) and minus one.

18

The New Classical Theory of Aggregate Supply

This chapter explains the _new classical_ theory of aggregate supply[1] and derives the expectations-augmented aggregate supply curve. When you have completed this chapter you will be able to:

(a) **Describe how incomplete information affects the supply of and demand for labour.**

(b) **Describe how the money wage and level of employment (and unemployment) are affected by wrong expectations.**

(c) **Define the expectations-augmented aggregate supply curve.**

(d) **Derive the expectations-augmented aggregate supply curve.**

A. Incomplete Information and the Labour Market

In the classical model of the labour market presented in the previous chapter the demand for labour, the supply of labour, and the market equilibrating process paid no attention to any special characteristics of labour. We could have been talking about stocks and shares, wheat,

---

1 The theory of aggregate supply presented in this chapter had its origins in Milton Friedman, 'The Role of Monetary Policy', _The American Economic Review_, 58 (March 1968) pp.1–17. It is also similar to that developed by Robert E. Lucas, Jr. in 'Some International Evidence on Output–Inflation Tradeoffs', _American Economic Review_, 63, 3 (1973) pp.326–34.

futures contracts in gold, or just about any competitive market for any commodity at all. There are, however, some features of labour that make it unlike many other commodities. One important feature concerns the scale of the costs that individuals (both suppliers and demanders of labour) have to incur in order to find someone with whom to do business. From the household side, there is a heavy search cost — the cost of finding a job that is attractive enough, well paid enough, and satisfactory in other dimensions. From the point of view of the firm demanding labour, there are recruiting costs — the costs of finding potential employees with the required skills and personal attributes.

The fact that there are heavy search and recruiting costs in the labour market implies that labour will typically be traded in a way that is very different from the way in which stocks and commodities are traded. Instead of being traded on a market that works like a continuous auction, labour generally is traded in markets dominated by medium-term contracts. Individuals enter into arrangements with each other for a specified period of time, often for a year or more ahead.

The contracts that govern labour-trading arrangements could, in principle, be very complex documents that incorporate hundreds (perhaps thousands) of contingency clauses specifying the wages and other employment conditions contingent on a variety of potential future events. The costs of negotiating, writing, monitoring, and enforcing such contracts would, however, be very high. To avoid these costs, most labour market contracts are relatively simple. They specify a *money wage* (and other non-wage terms) that will be paid for a certain type of labour over a specified future period. If the contract is to run for more than a year, it will also typically specify an adjustment in the money wage, either in money terms or as some pre-agreed fraction of the change in the cost of living as measured by the Retail Price Index.

The typical labour market contract is one in which the worker and the employer agree to trade labour services for a certain *money wage*, for a certain period of time into the future, but they make no commitments concerning the quantity of employment. The employer will typically *not* undertake to guarantee employment at the agreed wage and will be free to vary the number of workers hired. Individual workers will also be free to quit their jobs if they can find better ones with other firms.

How will firms decide how much labour to hire, and how will households decide how much labour to supply? Recall that a firm will hire labour up to the point at which the marginal product of that labour equals the real wage paid. In order to calculate the real wage, the firm simply has to divide the money wage by the *price of the firm's own output*. The firm will then hire labour up to the point at which its marginal product equals that firm-specific real wage.

On the other side of the labour market, the amount of labour that a household will want to supply at any particular point in time will depend *not* on the real wage as calculated by the firm for the purpose of figuring out how much labour to demand but rather on the real basket of goods and services that the household can consume with its wage. It will depend on the money wage divided by a general index of prices such as the Retail Price Index.

Thus, there is an asymmetry in the labour market concerning the price level that is relevant for calculating the real wage on the two sides of the market. As far as the firm is concerned, what matters is the ratio of the money wage to the price of the output produced by that firm. What matters on the supply side is the ratio of the money wage to an index of prices of all the goods and services from which households will choose their consumption. This asymmetry is the basis of the new theories of aggregate supply.

Let us consider the information that firms and households need in order to make decisions about how much labour to demand and supply. Firms need to know the money wage rate and the price of their own output. Households need to know the money wage rate and the prices of all the goods and services from which they choose their consumption bundle. A moment's reflection will lead you to a very important conclusion concerning these variables. Nobody has any difficulty in knowing the money wage rate (this is specified when workers and firms are contemplating doing business together). Further, there will be very little problem in figuring out the price of the output of the firm. For some multiproduct firms, this might not be a totally straightforward matter, but it may be presumed that the firm's own accounting procedures are capable of generating accurate up-to-date information on the prices of the firm's output and that that information is readily available both to the firm and its workers.

However, in contrast to these two bits of information, knowledge of the prices of all the goods and services from which individuals choose their consumption bundle will be very imperfect and incomplete. It is true that the Retail Price Index is calculated and published. It is also a fact, however, it is published with a time lag; that is, it refers to the past, and not to the present or the immediate future. Furthermore, it refers to a basket of goods that the mythical average household consumes and that no particular household consumes. From the perspective of any one individual household, what matters is the average level of prices of all the goods and services from which the final consumption bundle is chosen. Actually to know these prices would involve a process of searching and observing prices, a process that is so expensive that by the time the individual had amassed all the relevant information, there would be no time left either for work or consumption!

The implication of all this is that households cannot know everything that they would need to know if they were to make their labour supply decisions on the basis of the ratio of the money wage to the general level of prices. Put more directly, the notion that the supply of labour depends on the real wage cannot be given operational content since no one can know the relevant real wage at the time that a labour supply decision is being made. Thus, in the absence of information about the general level of prices, it becomes necessary for households to make their supply decision on the basis of some other criterion. The most natural criterion is the expected real wage. Since there is no difficulty about knowing the money wage component of the real wage, the only problem remaining is to figure out an expectation of the price level.

We can summarize the discussion so far in the following way: firms decide how much labour to demand by figuring out the real wage on the basis of two known bits of information — the money wage and the price of the firm's own output. Households decide how much labour to supply by calculating the expected real wage based on the known money wage rate and their expectation of the average level of prices prevailing in the markets for all the goods and services from which they choose their consumption bundle. It is worth emphasizing that the price expectation that households have to form in order to make a labour supply decision refers not to past prices but to current and future prices. Any labour supply decision made at a given moment in time, even if it was made on the basis of complete information about prices prevailing at that moment, would still have to be made on the basis of expectations of prices that will prevail at some future point in time when the proceeds from the work are eventually spent.

You may be thinking that it ought to be possible for people to figure out what the general level of prices is simply from knowing the prices in the sector of the economy in which they work, and perhaps knowing the prices of a few goods and services that they are consuming on a regular, almost daily basis. A moment's reflection will convince you, however, that although there is *some* information to be had from such sources, it is not sufficient. The economy is constantly undergoing change that results in constantly changing relative prices. Some relative price changes are predictable, but many and perhaps most are not. They are in the nature of random events that arise from a multitude of forces. That being so, it will be very hard for people to figure out what is happening to the overall general level of prices simply from knowing the prices of one or two things. Therefore, in the rest of this chapter we will make the extreme (and obviously slightly wrong) assumption that people get no help at all in figuring out the general level of prices from knowing the price of the output in their own sector of the economy. This extreme assumption could be modified, but the result of doing so would be to make our analysis a good deal more complicated without producing any change of substance in the conclusions that we reach. We will return to this matter in the next section.

The final thing to notice is that the asymmetry that has been discussed above is not an asymmetry between firms and households concerning the amount of information that each has. Firms are not being supposed, in some sense, to be smarter than households. Rather, the asymmetry arises from the fact that firms sell a small number of goods, so they and their workers are specialized in information concerning the prices of those goods. In contrast, households buy a large number of goods and services and are not specialized in information concerning the prices in all those markets. It is that asymmetry, and not an asymmetry in the amount of information that households and firms have, that provides the basis for a modified theory of aggregate supply that is capable of explaining the observed relationship between output (employment and unemployment) and inflation.

The starting point for developing this theory is an extended analysis of the labour market that builds on the above remarks.

B. Wrong Expectations and the Labour Market

(i) The Labour Market and Money Wages

Recall the classical model of the labour market as shown below in frame (a) of Figure 18.1. This figure shows a competitive labour market in equilibrium at a real wage of $(W/P)^*$ and an employment level n^*. The demand for labour increases as the real wage falls because of profit-maximizing labour demand decisions by firms (marginal product = real wage); the supply of labour increases as real wages rise since more households will enter the labour force, the higher the real bundle of goods that they can buy in exchange for their work.

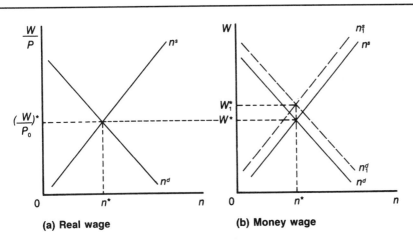

**Figure 18.1
The labour market
and the money wage**

(a) Real wage   (b) Money wage

The supply and demand curves in the labour market that are drawn against the real wage [frame (a)] may equivalently be drawn against the money wage [frame (b)]. In that case, there is a separate supply and demand curve for each price level. Both curves move vertically one-for-one as the price level varies.

Suppose for a moment that the price level is equal to one; i.e. $P_0 = 1$. With the price level equal to one, we may simply rename the vertical axis of Figure 18.1 to measure the money wage. If the price level is fixed at one, and we plot the demand and supply curves against the money wage, which is exactly the same as plotting them against the real wage. Frame (b) reproduces the demand and supply curves, n^d and n^s, and shows the same employment equilibrium, n^*, and the equilibrium money wage, W^*.

Next, notice that the equilibrium real wage $(W/P_0)^*$ [shown in frame (a)] could be attained at *any* money wage. All that is necessary is that the money wage and price level stand in the appropriate relationship to each other: If the price level doubled, the money wage would have to double; if the price level rose by x per cent, the money wage would have to rise by x per cent. In frame (a) where we draw the demand and supply curves against the real wage, changes in the price level are not visible. The equilibrium determined in frame (a) is a real equilibrium and is independent of the price level.

Is the same true of the equilibrium in frame (b)? Is the equilibrium depicted in this figure independent of the price level? The answer is that the *real* equilibrium — real wage and employment level — is independent of the price level, but the money wage, measured on the vertical axis of frame (b), is not. Since in frame (b), the money wage is measured on the vertical axis, it is necessary to be aware that the demand and supply curves can only be drawn for a *given* price level. The demand and supply curves, illustrated as n^d and n^s, are drawn for a price level equal to one.

Suppose the price level increases to P_1, which is higher than P_0 by x per cent, i.e.

$$P_1 = (1 + x)P_0$$

You may find some numbers helpful: if $x = 5$ per cent, then the equation

$$P_1 = (1 + x)P_0 \text{ is } P_1 = (1 + 5/100)P_0 \text{ or } P_1 = 1.05P_0$$

If the price level rises by x per cent, how would the demand and supply curves in frame (b) move? It is clear that the money wages that firms would now be willing to pay for each quantity of labour would be higher by the same x per cent that the price level has increased. Since the firm is only interested in the real wage, an x per cent rise in the price level means that at a money wage x per cent higher, the firm would be willing to hire the same number of workers as it would be at the lower price level and lower money wage. Thus, the demand for labour curve shifts upwards by the same x per cent as the price level has risen by. This is shown as the curve n_1^d in frame (b) of Figure 18.1.

What happens on the supply side? Precisely the same as on the demand side: the quantity of labour that households are willing to supply depends on the real wage. Therefore, if the price level rises by x per cent, the money wage will have to rise by x per cent if the quantity of labour supplied is to remain unchanged. Thus, the curve n_1^s shows the supply of labour at the price level P_1. That is, the supply curve moves upwards by x per cent in exactly the same way as the demand curve does.

It is now a simple matter to see that since the two curves have both moved upwards by the same percentage amounts, they must cut at the same employment level as before and at a money wage that is x per cent higher than before. This new equilibrium *money wage* is shown in frame (b) as W_1^* and is equal to $(1 + x)W^*$. The equilibrium level of employment remains unchanged at n^*.

So far, nothing new has been introduced other than the idea that the labour market can be analysed so as to determine the equilibrium wage and employment in the classical model, with the money wage on the vertical axis of the supply−demand diagram instead of the real wage. With the money wage on the vertical axis, the demand and supply curves shift when the price level changes. With the real wage on the vertical axis, the curves are fixed independently of the price level.

How the labour market works with incomplete information will now be analysed.

(ii) Incomplete Information and Expectations

First, recall the information assumptions that we have made. Firms and households are presumed to know the price at which the firm will be able to sell its output, but neither firms nor households are presumed to have complete knowledge of the prices of all the goods and services from which households will choose their consumption bundles. Labour supply decisions will be made on the basis of the best available estimate or expectation of those prices. Call the price level that consumers expect to have to pay to buy their basket of consumer goods the *expected price level*, and denote it as P^e.

Next, recall the above discussion about the demand for labour by an individual firm. Each firm demands labour up to the point at which the real wage that it faces equals the marginal product of labour. The real wage facing any individual firm is the money wage divided by the price of the individual firm's output. If we add up all the demands of all the individual firms and take an average of the real wages faced by each firm, we obtain the aggregate or economy-wide demand for labour curve. This aggregate demand for labour depends on the *actual* economy-average real wage, W/P.

This may seem puzzling because we have assumed that nobody knows the average price level. A moment's reflection will reveal, however, that nobody needs to know the actual price level for the economy's aggregate demand for labour to depend on the actual real wage. The aggregate demand curve itself is simply arrived at by adding up the individual demands of all the individual firms. Not only does nobody know the average price level, but nobody knows the aggregate demand for labour, and nobody needs to. All that each individual firm needs to know is the price of its own output and its own demand for labour. The aggregate demand for labour and the aggregate price level are constructs of our theory and are not things that are in the minds of the individual firms whose behaviour we are studying.

The supply of labour by each individual household depends, as we have seen, on the expected real wage, that is, on W/P^e. We can obtain the economy-wide aggregate supply of labour by adding all the supply curves of all the households together. Since the supply of each household depends on the expected real wage, so the aggregate supply of labour will also depend on the expected real wage. There is, thus, a crucial difference between the demand and supply curves once we take account of the information that households and firms have concerning price information.

The final thing that we need to do before we can figure out the implications of our assumptions is to make some proposition about the interaction between households and firms in the labour market. We have already noted that, as a descriptive matter, most labour markets work on the basis of there being a pre-commitment to a particular money wage, with households and firms then making decisions about how much labour to supply and demand at that money wage, given actual selling prices of output and expectations of the purchase prices of consumer goods. This seems to suggest that we ought to assume that money wages are rigid and that labour markets do not necessarily achieve equilibrium. This is *not* the assumption of the new classical theory. On the contrary, the theory assumes that there is sufficient flexibility in the money wage rate for the average money wage rate continuously to adjust to maintain labour market equilibrium. This is a crucial assumption of the *new classical* analysis, which distinguishes it from the *new Keynesian* analysis that we will look at in the next chapter.

Although most firms and households do business with each other on the basis of pre-agreed wage schedules there are, in fact, many ways in which you could think of the effective real wage adjusting so as continuously to maintain labour market equilibrium. One possibility is that the contracted wages themselves build in some automatic variation in the average hourly wage rate as a result of overtime schedules. Another possibility is that the intensity of work could be varied so as to vary the wage rate per unit of effort supplied as opposed to per hour supplied. (You probably know from your own labour market experience, and certainly from your experience as a student, that some hours of work are more intense than others. They range all the way from pure leisure to unadulterated drudgery!)

A further source of flexibility in the average wage paid arises from the heterogeneity of labour and the existence of different wages for different types of labour. This makes it possible for firms to change the quality mix of their labour force, perhaps using a higher proportion of higher paid and more highly skilled labour in times of high demand than in times of low demand. As a result there is an automatic variation in the average rates of wages paid, even though the pre-agreed wage schedules remain unchanged.

The key point to take from these 'stories' is not that wages *do in fact* always adjust to achieve labour market equilibrium. Rather, the key point is that the *assumption* that labour markets always achieve equilibrium is not absurd, and is not contradicted by the commonly observed fact that labour is traded on contracts that specify a money wage rate. Let me now summarize the three assumptions that we have made:

(1) The demand for labour depends on the *actual* real wage.
(2) The supply of labour depends on the *expected* real wage.
(3) The *average money wage* rate adjusts continuously to achieve labour market equilibrium.

Let us now see what these assumptions imply.

Figure 18.2 will be the main vehicle for following the analysis. The vertical axis measures the money wage, and the horizontal axis measures the level of employment. The curve $n^d(P_0)$ is the demand for labour curve when the price level is fixed at P_0. The supply of labour curve is plotted for a given *expected* level of prices. The supply curve, marked $n^s(P^e = P_0)$, is for a level of expected prices that equals the actual price level P_0. Thus, the supply curve $n^s(P^e = P_0)$ and the demand curve $n^d(P_0)$ can be thought of as representing the original curves, n^d and n^s, in frame (b) of Figure 18.1. These curves determine an equilibrium money

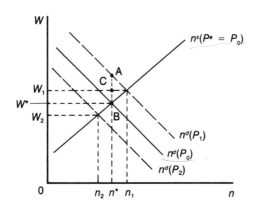

Figure 18.2
Expectations equilibria in the labour market

The demand for labour by each firm depends upon the firm's own output price. This means that the aggregate demand for labour depends on the actual price level. The supply of labour depends on the expected price level. The equilibrium wage rate and employment level will be different at each different price level. At price level P_0 there is full-employment equilibrium; at price level P_1 there is over-full employment (wage rate W_1, employment n_1); and at price level P_2 there is unemployment (wage rate W_2, employment level n_2).

wage W^* and employment level n^*, which we will now call the *full-employment values*. The full-employment values of employment and the real wage are identical to those determined in the classical model.

Now consider what would happen if the price level was higher than P_0, while the expected price level P^e remained at P_0. In particular, consider what would happen if the actual price level increased by x per cent to P_1, where P_1 equals $(1 + x)P_0$. Each firm, knowing that its own selling price had risen by x per cent, would now be willing to pay a higher money wage for its labour. That is, the demand for labour curve would shift upwards. The new demand curve that would result is shown as $n_1^d(P_1)$.

Recall that we are conducting a conceptual experiment in which the general price level *expected* by households does not change. Since the *expected* price level has not changed, the supply curve is not affected by the change in the actual price level and remains in its original position.[2]

The labour market will now attain an equilibrium at the money wage W_1 and the employment level n_1. That is, with the actual price level higher than the expected price level, the money wage will be higher than its full-employment value, and the level of employment will be higher than its full-employment value. The real wage, however, will be lower than its full-employment value – as can be seen in Figure 18.2.

The price level increase is measured by the full vertical shift of the labour demand curve, for example, the distance AB. The money wage, however, rises by a smaller distance, BD. Since the price level rise is greater than the money wage rise, the real wage has fallen. This fall in the real wage has induced firms to hire more labour and has generated the increase in employment from n^* to n_1. Households expect the price level to be P_0, and therefore as the money wage rises, households expect the real wage to be (W_1/P_0). This encourages households to supply the extra amount of labour n^* to n_1. In this situation and while they are doing business with each other, households and firms are in equilibrium. Both households and firms are happy, and there is nothing that either could do to improve their situation. However, as they look backwards to a previous period, households will realize that they have made a mistake.

---

2   Strictly speaking, there is an inconsistency in the treatment here. Everybody knows the price in the market for the commodity that they are concerned with the production of, and yet they do not seem to take this information into account in forming an expectation of the general price level. This is wasting information. A more complete, but more difficult, treatment would extract information from the known price of a particular commodity to obtain a better inference about the general price level. The essence of the new classical theory of aggregate supply is not affected, however, by ignoring this piece of information. For the reader able to follow statistical analysis, the paper by Robert E. Lucas, Jr., 'Some International Evidence on Output–Inflation Tradeoffs', *American Economic Review*, 63, 3 (1973) pp.326–34, and the Appendix to Chapter 21 deal with this problem. The Lucas paper is probably the most important, accessible, original presentation of the new classical theory of aggregate supply.

They will realize that they did too much work and at too low a real wage. Of course, bygones are bygones. All that households can do the next time around is again to use all the information that is available to them and make the best deal that they can. The situation just analysed is called one of *over-full employment*.

Next, consider the opposite experiment — that of a fall in the price level below P_0, while the expected price level P^e remains constant at P_0. In particular, let us suppose that the price level falls by x per cent from P_0 to P_2, but that the expected price level remains at P_0. The demand for labour curve will now shift downwards and is illustrated by the new demand curve, $n_2^d(P_2)$. The supply curve does not shift because the expected price level has not changed. What happens in this event? Again, the answer is clear and is contained in the diagram (Figure 18.2). This time the labour market will come to what is called an *unemployment equilibrium*. The equilibrium wage rate will be W_2 and the employment level n_2. Thus, with a lower price level than that expected, employment and the money wage will fall below their full-employment levels. The real wage, in this case, will rise above its full-employment level. The real wage rises because the price level falls by more than the fall in the money wage. The demand curve falls by the full percentage amount of the fall in the price level; but, as you can see, the money wage falls by only a fraction of that. It is the higher real wage that creates the fall in employment, inducing firms to hire fewer workers. The expected real wage falls, however, because households do not expect the fall in the price level; and when they see a fall in the money wage, they read this as being a fall in the real wage.

There is, therefore, no inconsistency between the behaviour of households and firms concerning the drop in employment and the change in the money wage. Households willingly reduce their employment to n_2 in the face of an expected fall in the real wage, while firms willingly cut their hiring to n_2 since they are facing a higher real wage.

While households and firms are trading labour, everyone is happy; both firms and households are doing the best they can for themselves. The workers $n^* - n_2$ will choose not to be employed, and their decision to be unemployed is correct in the light of their expectation of a low real wage. They expect a low real wage because, although the money wage has fallen, their expectation is that the price level will remain constant. Each firm, on the other hand, knowing its own output price, regards the drop in the money wage as insufficient to compensate for the drop in its own price, and so the resulting higher actual real wage induces them to hire less labour.

You see, then, that if the price level that is expected actually comes about, the economy will settle down at an equilibrium that is the same as the classical labour market equilibrium. That equilibrium is called *full employment*. If the price level is higher than expected, the labour market will equilibrate at a higher level of employment and a lower level of the real wage than the full-employment levels. In this case there will be *over-full employment*. If the price level turns out to be lower than that which is expected, then there will be a cut in the employment level and a higher real wage − there will be *unemployment*.

In the institutional setting of the UK, such a cut in unemployment will usually be recorded as a rise in unemployment since the individuals involved will be 'available for', 'able and willing to' work and usually register with the Department of Employment. They are not, however, willing to work at the wage that is available. The Department of Employment does not distinguish between people who are willing to work at the wage levels currently prevailing but cannot find such work and those who are unwilling to work at the prevailing wage rates but would like to work for a higher wage than is available.

Once expectations are introduced, there is no single unique equilibrium in the labour market The equilibrium level of employment and the real wage is influenced by the actual price level relative to its expected level. The higher the actual price level relative to its expected level, the higher is the level of employment and the money wage, and the lower is the level of unemployment and the real wage.

Higher employment & money wage
Lower unemployment & real wage.

C. Definition of the Expectations-Augmented Aggregate Supply Curve

The expectations-augmented aggregate supply curve shows the maximum amount of output that the economy will supply at each different price level but with a fixed expected price level.

This is an extension of the concept of the aggregate supply curve that was introduced earlier in the classical labour market. The classical aggregate supply curve can be thought of as showing the maximum amount of output that the economy will supply when there is no difference between the actual and the expected price levels. That is, the classical aggregate supply curve is the same as the expectations-augmented aggregate supply curve when everyone has full information and everyone knows the actual price level.

D. Derivation of the Expectations-Augmented Aggregate Supply Curve

It is a straightforward matter to derive the expectations-augmented aggregate supply curve from the analysis that you have already conducted. Figure 18.3 illustrates how this is done.

Frame (a) simply reproduces Figure 18.2. If you have understood Figure 18.2, you will understand frame (a) because it contains nothing new. The demand for labour curve n_1^d is drawn for the price level P_1, the curve n_0^d

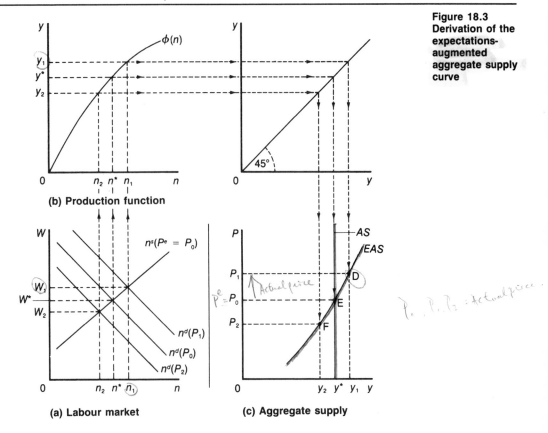

Figure 18.3
Derivation of the
expectations-
augmented
aggregate supply
curve

(b) Production function

(a) Labour market

(c) Aggregate supply

Frame (a) is the same as Figure 18.2. At each different price level there is a different
labour market equilibrium. The employment levels associated with these different equilibria
translate into different output levels [frame (b)]. By associating each of the initially assumed
price levels with the output levels they generate [frame (c)] the expectations-augmented
aggregate supply curve is derived. Position E is the same full-employment equilibrium as
in the classical theory. The expectations-augmented aggregate supply curve cuts the
classical aggregate supply curve at the expected price level.

for the price level P_0, and the curve n_2^d for the price level P_2. The supply
curve is drawn for a fixed expected price level P^e equal to P_0.

Figure 18.3 is used to do something with which you are already familiar.
It is used to derive the classical aggregate supply curve. This is done by
reading off the equilibrium level of output for which the expected price
level equals the actual price level. In this case, everyone has full information — no one is fooled. The equilibrium in the labour market is where
the demand curve n_0^d cuts the supply curve $n^s(P^e = P_0)$. At this point,
employment is n^* and the money wage is W^*.

Transferring this employment level up to frame (b), you can read off
from the production function the equilibrium level of output that will be
supplied at full-employment equilibrium. This is y^*. Transfer that level

of output (following the dotted line) around to frame (c), and plot the level of output that will be produced in full employment equilibrium against the price level P_0, point E. Now, as the price level is varied, *and provided we also vary the expected price level* — so that actual and expected prices are always equal to each other (recall frame (b) of Figure 18.1) — nothing would happen to the equilibrium level of employment or the real wage. The money wage would change proportionately with the price level, and the real equilibrium in the labour market would be undisturbed. This is essentially the exercise we performed when deriving the classical aggregate supply curve: as the price level is varied and as the expected price level is varied so as to always equal the actual price level, the equilibrium level of employment remains constant, and from frame (b), the equilibrium level of output also remains constant. This traces out the classical aggregate supply curve, *AS*, in frame (c).

Next consider what happens when the expected price level is held constant, but the actual price level changes. First, suppose the actual price level rises from P_0 to P_1, while the expected price level stays at P_0. This higher price level is shown on the vertical axis of frame (c) as P_1, which is equal to $P_0(1 + x)$. What is the level of output that profit-maximizing producers would want to supply at that price level? The answer is obtained by starting in the labour market. You know that the demand for labour curve will shift upwards to n_1^d. You also know that the supply curve of labour will not move because its position depends on the expected price level, which has not changed. The labour market will clear at a higher money wage W_1 and a higher level of employment n_1. At this higher level of employment, firms will produce a higher level of output y_1, which is read off from the production function in frame (b). If we translate this level of output (by following the dotted line) to frame (c), we generate the new point D in frame (c). Point D shows the output level y_1 which profit-maximizing firms are willing to supply if the price level is P_1 and the expected price level is P_0.

Next, consider what would happen if the price level fell to x per cent below P_0. Such a price level is shown on the vertical axis of frame (c) as P_2 which equals $P_0(1 - x)$. What is the profit-maximizing supply of output in this case? The answer is again obtained by starting in the labour market. You know that the demand for labour curve falls to n_2^d, so that the equilibrium level of employment and money wage will now move to n_2 and W_2, respectively. At this lower level of employment, firms will produce the lower level of output y_2, read off from frame (b). Now transferring this output level y_2 (following the dotted line) to frame (c) shows that profit-maximizing firms will supply the level of output y_2 at the price level P_2. That is, the economy would operate at point F. Point F says that if the price level is P_2 but the expected price level is P_0, firms will choose to supply y_2 as their profit-maximizing output.

If we join together the points D, E, and F and all other points in between and beyond these, we will generate the expectations-augmented aggregate supply curve, labelled *EAS*.

The expectations-augmented aggregate supply curve shows how the profit-maximizing and utility-maximizing quantity of output supplied varies as the price level varies — when the expected price level is fixed. Notice that the expectations-augmented aggregate supply curve (*EAS*) cuts the aggregate supply curve (*AS*) at the point at which the actual price level is equal to the expected price level. In the example in frame (c), this is at the price level P_0. This is not a coincidence. It happens because only when expectations turn out to be correct do we get the same aggregate supply as we would if everyone always had complete information.

This new aggregate supply analysis will be combined with the theory of aggregate demand in Chapter 20 to re-examine the effects of a change in aggregate demand on the level of output and prices.

Summary

A. Incomplete Information and the Labour Market

Because it is costly for workers to find suitable jobs and because it is costly for firms to find suitable employees, labour is not traded as if in a continuous auction market. Rather, contracts are entered into that run for a year or more. Because contracts last for a sizeable length of time and because it is expensive to write complicated contracts with detailed contingency clauses, it is typically the case that firms and households fix the price at which they will buy and sell labour in money units — that is, they fix a money wage. However, because their decisions to buy and sell labour are influenced by the real wage, it is necessary for both households and firms to form an expectation about the price level that will prevail over a wage contract period.

Firms and households can do a better job of forming a reliable expectation about the prices in their own sector of the economy than they can about prices in general. Firms typically sell a small number of commodities and have a large amount of information about the markets in which they operate. In contrast, households buy a very large range of commodities and are not typically well informed about future prices in those markets. As a first approximation, everyone knows the prices at which they will be selling their output over the future wage contract period; however, no one knows *all* the prices that they will be facing when buying, so it is necessary to form an expectation of those prices based on incomplete information.

B. Wrong Expectations and the Labour Market

For a given expectation of prices, a rise in the money wage will be read by households as a rise in the real wage and they will increase their supply of labour. A cut in the money wage will be read as a cut in the real wage, and they will decrease their supply of labour. However, each firm, knowing the prices of its own limited range of commodities will not be misinformed about the real wage it is paying and the demand for labour will depend on the *actual* real wage. The higher the actual price level relative to the expected price level, the lower is the real wage, the greater is the amount of labour that firms hire, the higher is the expected real wage, and the greater is the amount of labour that households supply. There are many equilibrium levels of the real wage and employment. The only equilibrium that corresponds to that in the classical labour market is the equilibrium in which the expected price level is equal to the actual price level. This occurs when everyone's expectation is correct.

C. *Definition of the Expectations-Augmented Aggregate Supply Curve*

The expectations-augmented aggregate supply curve traces out the quantities of aggregate output that firms will be willing to supply as the price level varies, at a given expected price level.

D. *Derivation of the Expectations-Augmented Aggregate Supply Curve*

The derivation is done in Figure 18.3. You should review Figure 18.3 as many times as necessary until you are thoroughly familiar with the derivation of the expectations-augmented aggregate supply curve.

Review Questions

1. What are the key assumptions of the new classical theory of the labour market?
2. What is the asymmetry in the labour market on which the new classical theory of aggregate supply is based? Does it imply that workers are more ignorant than their employers about prices?
3. What are the ways in which firms can vary the wage rate, independently of negotiating a new contract?
4. Why does the new classical theory of the aggregate demand for labour depend on the *actual* real wage? How can it do so when, by the new classical assumptions, no one knows the actual real wage?
5. Why, despite the fact there is never any involuntary unemployment in the new classical labour market, might there be concern about unemployment even in the context of that theory?
6. What markets are in equilibrium along the new classical *EAS* curve? Is there any involuntary unemployment?

7. What determines the slope of the new classical expectations-augmented aggregate supply curve? Show how the slope of the *EAS* curve changes as the supply of the labour curve becomes more elastic.

19

The New Keynesian Theory of Aggregate Supply

There has recently emerged a new Keynesian theory of aggregate supply that differs in subtle but important ways from the new classical theory. The principal architects of the new Keynesian theory are Stanley Fischer of the Massachusetts Institute of Technology, Edmund Phelps of Columbia University, and John Taylor of Princeton University.[1] The approach had its origins, however, in an interesting paper dealing not with the theory of aggregate supply but with a related matter that will be dealt with in Chapter 35, the linking of wages to the cost of living, by Jo Anna Gray.[2] The treatment of the new Keynesian theory that will be presented in this chapter is in some respects closer to that of Jo Anna Gray than to those of Fischer, Phelps, and Taylor. The work of these three scholars, in fact, have some interesting differences among themselves some of which will be noted later.

The point of departure of the new Keynesian theory is the description of the institutional arrangements in the labour market presented in the

---

1 The main contributions to the new Keynesian theory of aggregate supply are Stanley Fischer, 'Long-Term Contracts, Rational Expectations and the Optimal Money Supply Rule', *Journal of Political Economy*, 85 (February 1977) pp.191–206; Edmund S. Phelps and John B. Taylor, 'Stabilizing Powers of Monetary Policy under Rational Expectations', *Journal of Political Economy*, 85 (February 1977) pp.163–90; and John B. Taylor, 'Staggered Wage Setting in a Macro Model', *The American Economic Review, Papers and Proceedings* (May 1979) pp.108–13. The first two papers cited deal with a much broader range of issues than this chapter and extend into the policy questions that are dealt with in Chapters 31 and 32.
2 Jo Anna Gray, 'Wage Indexation: A Macroeconomic Approach', *Journal of Monetary Economics*, Vol. 2, No. 2 (April 1976) pp.221–35.

first section of the previous chapter. A key aspect of that institutional description is the general prevalence in labour markets of contracts that specify an agreed and, for a predetermined period, fixed money wage rate. The new classical theory assumes that there remains sufficient flexibility in the labour market for the average money wage to be in a state of continuous adjustment so as to achieve continuous labour market clearing. It is this assumption of the new classical theory that the new Keynesian theory replaces.

The new Keynesian theory regards the contractual fixing of money wages as being such a crucial feature of the labour market that it must figure prominently in any theory of how the labour market works. According to the new Keynesian theory, labour markets do not act like markets that are in a state of continuous auction, with prices (wages) being frequently adjusted to achieve an ongoing equality between supply and demand. Rather, supply equals demand only on the average. At any particular moment in time, demand may exceed or fall short of supply. Taking explicit account of the institutional fact of contractually fixed money wages has important implications for the specification of the aggregate supply curve. This chapter explores these implications. By the time you have completed this chapter you will be able to:

(a) **State the key assumptions of the new Keynesian analysis.**
(b) **Describe how money wages are determined in the new Keynesian theory of aggregate supply.**
(c) **Show the implications of the new Keynesian theory of wage determination for the expectations-augmented aggregate supply curve.**
(d) **Describe the implications of overlapping labour market contracts.**

A. Assumptions of the New Keynesian Analysis

There are four key assumptions in the new Keynesian theory of aggregate supply. The first of these is that wages are set in money terms for a fixed contractual period before the quantity of labour supplied and demanded is known. Wages are not continuously adjusted so as to equate the *actual* supply of labour with the *actual* demand for labour. No explicit theory of maximizing behaviour on the part of labour suppliers and demanders is set out that rationalizes this, though the developers of the new Keynesian theories do have in mind some underlying optimization by individuals that involve trading off the costs of collecting information and negotiating changes in wages against the losses that arise when wages fail to adjust continuously to achieve market clearing. It is asserted that, for whatever reason, the real world so obviously is characterized by such arrangements in labour markets that it is inappropriate to develop an analysis of the labour market that ignores the contractual fixity of money wages.

The second key assumption of the new Keynesian analysis is that the actual quantity of labour traded is equal to the quantity demanded. After wages are set, the actual supply and demand conditions become known. Once those conditions are known, both suppliers and demanders in the labour market are tied into a labour contract. There has to be some rule for determining the quantity that will be traded. This rule could be that the short side of the market dominates. What this means is that if demand (D<S) is less than supply, the quantity traded is the quantity demanded, but (D>S) if demand exceeds supply, the quantity traded is the quantity supplied. However, this is *not* the assumption employed in the new Keynesian analysis. Instead, it is assumed that the demand side always dominates. The suppliers of labour are assumed to stand ready to supply whatever labour is demanded in exchange for the certainty of a fixed money wage over the duration of the existing contract.

The third assumption of the new Keynesian theory concerns the objectives that govern the setting of the money wage rate at the beginning of a contract. Here, the different scholars who have contributed to this approach each make their own special assumptions. Phelps and Taylor propose that wages of a given group of workers will be set at a level that takes account of:

(1) Any wage changes that have occurred among other groups in the period since the previous wage contract date.
(2) Any expected wage and price changes that are going to take place over the interval for which wages are now being agreed.
(3) The state of excess demand (or supply).

Wages will increase faster the faster the wages of other groups of workers have recently increased, the faster are the wages of the others, and prices, expected to rise over the term of the contract, and the greater is the state of excess demand for the particular group of labour in question.

Stanley Fischer makes a simpler assumption that ignores the effect of excess demand on the level of wages. He proposes wages will be set so as to achieve a *fixed* real wage rate. This assumption makes a great deal of sense for a world in which there are never any changes in technology that would shift the demand for labour curve and change the equilibrium real wage. If, however, technology does keep changing and equilibrium real wages change as a result, then any wage setting behaviour that seeks to fix the real wage will inject into the labour market a barrier that prevents the supply of labour from ever equalling the demand for labour, even on the average. It is very hard to see why people would want to be parties to contracts that had such a feature. Furthermore, we know from simple observation of the behaviour of real wages that, in fact, they do, from time to time, vary. This assumption then of Fischer's, although a useful one for his purposes, is too restrictive.

It seems more appropriate to adopt the Phelps and Taylor approach and assume that money wages not only respond to expectations of changes in the wages of others and prices but also respond to the state of supply and demand in the labour market. One way of allowing for the effects of supply and demand on wages that can be viewed as a special case of the Phelps and Taylor assumption is that money wages are set so as to achieve an equality between the expected supply and expected demand for labour over the duration of the labour contract. This assumption, in fact, is employed by Jo Anna Gray (referred to above) and it is the assumption that we will use in order to derive a new Keynesian theory of aggregate supply.

Before going on to do that, however, let us be sure that we understand exactly what this assumption is and how it relates to but also differs from the assumptions made by Phelps and Taylor and Fischer. We are going to assume that the money wage rate is set at the beginning of a contract and is held constant throughout the contract period so as to achieve an equality between the *expected supply* and *expected demand* for labour. It will be immediately clear that if there are no expected changes in supply and demand in the labour market then the expected real wage will be constant, and the money wage will be set so as to achieve this expected constant real wage. Thus, provided there are no expected labour market shocks, the assumption that we are making is equivalent to that made by Stanley Fischer. If, however, there are expected changes in supply and demand in the labour market, there will be an expected change in the real wage, and the money wage will be set to reflect that expectation. To this extent the assumption that we are making is more general than that made by Fischer.

Next compare our assumption with that of Phelps and Taylor. They propose that when there is an excess demand for labour, money wages will rise faster than they otherwise would do. Our assumption agrees with that. If there is an excess demand for labour (which is expected to continue into the future), then money wages will increase by more than they otherwise would have done but by a very specific amount — the amount that produces an expected equality between supply and demand for labour. Phelps and Taylor are not quite as precise as that: they simply say that if there is an excess demand, money wages will rise faster than they otherwise would do. They will not necessarily rise by an amount that will completely close the gap between supply and demand in a given contract period. To this extent the assumption that we are making is slightly more restrictive than that of Phelps and Taylor.

The fourth key assumption of the new Keynesian theory of aggregate supply is that labour market contracts last for a longer term than the frequency with which the economy is being bombarded by various kinds of random and policy shocks. This means that workers and their employers often become aware of the fact that the contractually agreed-upon wage, based on information that was available at the time the agreement was drawn up, may now be in some sense inappropriate for the new conditions. Nevertheless, being tied into an agreement, both sides of the market have to live with the pre-committed money wage until the next review date. Taken on its own, this would imply that any shocks occurring after a wage contract has been written will have effects that could persist to some future date on which the longest term existing contract is to be reviewed.

There is, however, a further consideration that generates even more persistence in the effects of shocks than that. It arises from the fact that not all labour market contracts are signed on the same day to run for the same duration. Rather, they are signed on different dates for different durations (although the differences in durations are not so important as the differences in the dates on which the contracts are signed). The fact that contracts overlap or are 'staggered' rather than bunched to the same date and time interval has important implications that will be discussed later in this chapter. The next two sections will not take account of the overlapping nature of labour market contracts, but for simplicity will proceed as if all contracts are signed on the same day and run for the same duration.

B. Determination of Money Wages

The process whereby the money wage rate is determined in the new Keynesian theory is illustrated in Figure 19.1; it is analogous to the diagram used in Figure 18.2. The level of employment is measured on the horizontal axis, and the money wage rate is measured on the vertical axis. The supply curve of labour $n^s(P^e = P_0)$ is drawn for a fixed expected price level equal to P_0. It is assumed that the labour market convenes and negotiations take place and that the money wage contract is signed prior to the commencement of the period for which the labour will be supplied and demanded. The price level at which the demanders of labour will sell their output is therefore unknown at the time that the labour market contract is signed.

The demand for labour that is relevant for the determination of the wage contract is that based on the expected price level. Such a demand function is drawn in Figure 19.1 as the curve labelled $n^d(P^e = P_0)$. This is the expected demand for labour curve, given the expected price level equal to P_0. Where the expected demand curve cuts the expected supply curve determines the expected labour market equlibrium. The level of employment n_0^e is the expected equilibrium level of employment, and the wage rate W_0 is the expected market-clearing money wage rate.

The contractually determined money wage rate will be set equal to this expected market-clearing money wage. Once the money wage is determined, nothing is allowed to change it until the next bargaining date at some time in the future. In the meantime, the actual level of employment will be determined at the contracted money wage by the *actual* demand for labour curve. Suppose that the actual price level turns out to be P_a,

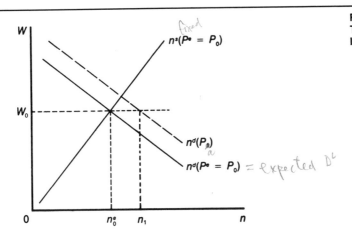

Figure 19.1
The new Keynesian labour market

The labour market meets and a money wage is set before the actual price level is known. That wage rate, W_0, is set to achieve an equilibrium in the labour market based on the expected price level (P_0). When the actual price level (P_a) is revealed, the quantity of labour traded is the quantity demanded (n_a).

so the actual demand for labour curve is $n^d(P_a)$. In this case, the quantity of labour employed is n_a, and the wage rate remains at W_0. The real wage falls because the price level P_a is higher than the expected price level P_0, on which the fixed money wage rate W_0 is based.

C. The New Keynesian Expectations-Augmented Aggregate Supply Curve

The new Keynesian theory of aggregate supply implied by the theory of wage determination just presented is very similar, in qualitative terms, to the new classical theory. The derivation of the new Keynesian expectations-augmented aggregate supply curve is presented in Figure 19.2. It will be recognized that this figure is almost identical to Figure 18.3, which was used to derive the new classical expectations-augmented aggregate supply curve.

The labour market analysis presented above in Figure 19.1 is repeated in frame (a). The production function appears in frame (b), and the aggregate supply curve is generated in frame (c). As described above, the money wage is determined at W_0, which is the money wage that achieves an expected equilibrium in the labour market. That is, it achieves an equality between the expected supply of labour and the expected demand for labour with the expected price level P_0. If the actual price level turned out to be P_1 so that the demand for labour curve was in fact $n^d(P_1)$ then the quantity of labour demanded would be n_1. The quantity of labour n_1 would, through the production function, generate a level of

**Figure 19.2
Derivation of the
expectations-
augmented
aggregate supply
curve in the new
Keynesian model**

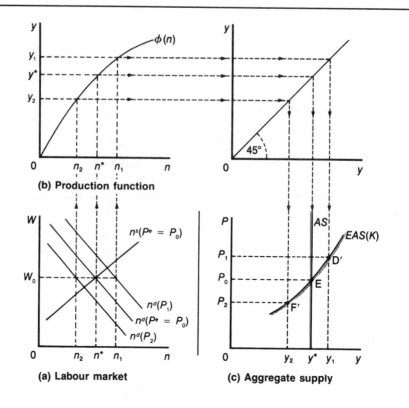

(b) Production function

(a) Labour market

(c) Aggregate supply

The development in this diagram parallels that of Figure 18.3. In frame (a), the labour market sets a money wage at W_0 based on the expected price level P_0. Full-employment equilibrium is at n^*. Different actual price levels (P_0, P_1, P_2) generate different demand curves. The quantity traded is read off from the demand curve (n_1 at price level P_1 and n_2 at price level P_2). The output produced by these different labour inputs are read off from the production function in frame (b). The resulting new Keynesian expectations-augmented aggregate supply curve is traced out as $F'ED'$. The aggregate supply curve based on correct information is that of the classical aggregate supply curve labelled AS.

output equal to y_1. Tracing the output level y_1 around through the 45° quadrant to the aggregate supply diagram in frame (c), gives the output level y_1 on the horizontal axis of frame (c). This output level y_1 is associated with the price level P_1 so that point D' is a point on the expectations-augmented aggregate supply curve of the new Keynesian analysis.

If, conversely, the price level was lower than P_0 at, say, P_2 so that the demand for labour curve dropped to the curve $n^d(P_2)$, then the quantity of labour demanded would be n_2 on the horizontal axis of frame (a). This level of employment generates an output level y_2 read off from the vertical axis of frame (b). Transferring the output level y_2 through the 45° quadrant to the aggregate supply diagram shows that the output level y_2 is associated with the price level P_2 at point F'.

If the price level turned out to be that which was expected, namely P_0, then the quantity of labour employed would, of course, be n^* and the output level would be y^*, generating a point on the aggregate supply curve, point E. Joining together points F', E, and D' and extrapolating beyond those points traces out the new Keynesian expectations-augmented aggregate supply curve, labelled *EAS(K)* in frame (c).

So that you can see clearly the relationship between the new Keynesian expectations-augmented aggregate supply curve and the new classical aggregate supply curve, Figure 19.3 superimposes the two analyses on top of each other.

You can easily verify that Figure 19.3 contains everything that is in

Figure 19.3
A comparison of the new Keynesian and new classical aggregate supply curves

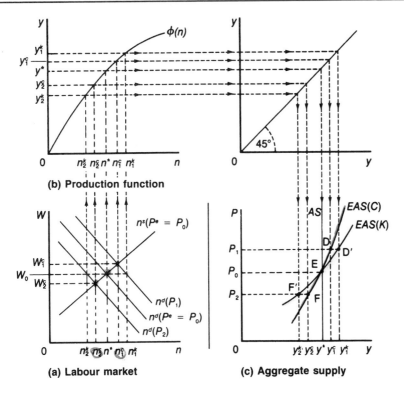

(b) Production function

(a) Labour market

(c) Aggregate supply

This diagram superimposes Figure 18.2 upon Figure 19.2. The key differences between the new Keynesian and new classical models are seen in frames (a) and (c). In the new Keynesian model, the money wage is fixed at W_0 so that as the price level varies between P_1 and P_2 the quantity of labour traded varies between n_1 and n_2 and output between y_1 and y_2. In the new classical analysis, as the price level varies between P_1 and P_2 shifting the demand curve between $n^d(P_1)$ and $n^d(P_2)$ so the money wage rate fluctuates between W_1^* and W_2^*. These fluctuations in the wage rate dampen off fluctuations in the quantity of labour demanded so that employment and output fluctuate between n_1^* and n_2^* and output fluctuates between y_1^* and y_2^*. The two expectations-augmented supply curves cut the classical aggregate supply curve at the expected price level, point E. The new classical curve is steeper than the new Keynesian curve.

Figure 19.2 that generates the curve *EAS(K)* (the new Keynesian aggregate supply curve) and also everything that is in Figure 18.3 that generates the new classical aggregate supply curve, the curve *EAS(C)*. Notice that the new Keynesian aggregate supply curve is flatter than the new classical curve. In a sense, this says that the new Keynesian analysis gives rise to more pessimistic predictions than the new classical analysis about the effects on the price level of a cut in aggregate demand, but it also gives more optimistic predictions concerning the inflationary consequences of stimulating aggregate demand.

Aside from the slopes of the two curves, the two theories as presented so far look very similar. There is, however, a crucial difference between the two that has not yet been revealed as fully as it needs to be, and that arises from the fact that the contractually determined wages are not all set on the same date but rather overlap each other. Let us now turn to an examination of the implications of this factor.

D. Overlapping Wage Contracts

The new Keynesian theory of aggregate supply developed above is based on the idea that at the beginning of each period of time, workers and employers sit down together, form an expectation of what the price level will be over the coming period (say a year), agree on a money wage rate that will achieve an expected equilibrium in the labour market, and then agree to trade at that wage for the coming year. The amount of labour that they trade will be determined by the actual demand for labour once the general price level is revealed.

The assumption that all contracts start and end at the same time as each other is obviously a fiction used purely to simplify the diagrammatic analysis. Let us now get rid of that assumption. Suppose, instead, that one half of the labour force sits down at the beginning of January each year and negotiates a wage that is to prevail, not for one year but for two years. The other half of the labour force will negotiate a wage on the alternate January, again for a period of two years. The analysis contained in Figures 19.1 and 19.2 still applies, but now it only applies to one half of the labour force. The other half of the labour force has already performed that same exercise one year earlier and will be performing it one year later. Thus, the actual wage rate that is observed at any one point in time in the economy will be an average of the wages that have been set at various dates in the past on contracts that are still current.

In the example, if one half of the labour force sets its wages in January of one year and the other one half in January of the alternate year, then the wage that prevails in any one year will be equal to one-half of the wage determined at the beginning of January of the year in question plus one half of the wage determined at the beginning of the preceding

January. This wage will be based on expectations of the general price level that were formed at two different dates in the past.

This being so, the expectations-augmented aggregate supply curve will depend not only on current expectations of the current price level but also on older (and perhaps by now known to be wrong) expectations of the current price level. Once agents are locked into a money wage decision based on an old, and perhaps falsified, expectation of the price level, there is, by the hypothesis embodied in the new Keynesian analysis, nothing they can do about it until the next wage review date comes along.

It would be incorrect, however, to jump to the conclusion that the effects of expectations are now known to be wrong would be eliminated once a new contract was written. The fact that contracts overlap means also that they influence each other in a persistent manner. To see this, consider a group of workers setting their wage in the current period. One of the things that they will want to do in determining the money wage is to take a view of the expected behaviour of the price level over their own contract period. Another thing that will influence them is the levels of wages that have already been set by other workers. To move their own wages too far out of line with those earlier wages could cause employers to find ways of substituting among different types of labour. Thus, the money wage being negotiated today is not going to be entirely independent of money wages that have been negotiated in the past. A forecasting error made by those who set wages in the previous period will influence the wages that are going to be set in the current period, and these effects will persist (although in diminishing form) into the indefinite future.

The fact that labour market contracts are long term and overlapping has very important implications for the analysis of economic policy as you will see in subsequent chapters in this book.

This new Keynesian analysis is a way of rationalizing 'sticky money wages'. Money wages are sticky not because of some mysterious downward rigidity as in Keynes's analysis, but because contractual commitments prevent people from adjusting money wages in the light of new information. In effect, workers and firms have said to each other, 'these are the terms on which we are willing to do business *come what may* until the next time we sit down two years from now'.

There is a lively debate in the current literature concerning the efficiency of the labour market contracts that the new Keynesian economists use in their theory of aggregate supply. New classical economists such as Robert Barro insist that such contracts are inefficient and cannot be rationalized as the kinds of contracts that rational profit-maximizing and utility-maximizing agents would enter into.[3] The new Keynesians agree that it is hard to think of convincing reasons why people would enter

3   Robert J. Barro, 'Long-Term Contracting, Sticky Prices, and Monetary Policy', *Journal of Monetary Economics*, 3 (July 1977) pp.305—16.

into contracts such as these. They insist, however, that we do observe such contracts as commonplace, and in the absence of a firm understanding as to why, they argue that we have no alternative but to incorporate them into our macroeconomic models.

The new Keynesian analysis can be viewed as having replaced the traditional Keynesian assumption of a fixed money wage with the assumption of a fixed timing structure for the changes in money wages, that arise in a rather rigid contractual setting.

Summary

A. Assumptions of the New Keynesian Analysis

There are four key assumptions of the new Keynesian analysis:

(1)   Money wages are set for an agreed period and do not continuously adjust.
(2)   The actual quantity of labour traded is determined by the quantity demanded.
(3)   Money wages are set so as to achieve equality between the expected supply and expected demand for labour.
(4)   Wage contracts last for a longer term than the frequency with which the economy is hit by shocks and overlap in time.

B. Determination of Money Wages

Money wages are determined in the new Keynesian theory of aggregate supply by equating the supply of labour that is expected on the basis of the expected price level with the demand for labour that is expected on the basis of the expected price level. Figure 19.1 illustrates this relationship and should be thoroughly understood.

C. The New Keynesian Expectations-Augmented Aggregate Supply Curve

The new Keynesian theory of wage determination implies that the expectations-augmented aggregate supply curve will have the same basic shape as the new classical expectations-augmented aggregate supply curve. The new Keynesian aggregate supply curve will, however, be flatter than the new classical curve. This arises because, when the demand for labour function shifts because of changes in the actual price level, there are no partially compensating adjustments in the money wage rate to dampen off some of the effects of the shift in demand function on the quantity demanded. The quantity of labour demanded adjusts fully to reflect shifts in the demand function at the fixed money wage rate, and the level of output therefore fluctuates by a larger amount than otherwise would be the case.

D. Overlapping Wage Contracts

The fact that not all labour market contracts are signed on the same date, but overlap each other, has fundamental implications for the aggregate supply curve. Instead of the position of the aggregate supply curve depending only on *current* expectations of the price level, it will also depend on previous expectations of the current period's price level. Expectations formed in the past and now known to be wrong will be embodied in the position of the Keynesian expectations augmented aggregate supply curve.

Review Questions

1. What are the four key assumptions of the new Keynesian theory of the labour market?
2. Why is the new Keynesian expectations-augmented aggregate supply curve flatter than the new classical curve?
3. Why do the new Keynesian, new classical, and classical aggregate supply curves all intersect at full-employment output and the expected price level?
4. The new Keynesian theory of the labour market assumes that households can be 'off' their supply curves. How might firms induce households to behave in such a way? Could households be induced to be permanently 'off' their supply curves?
5. What are the implications of overlapping labour market contracts?
6. An economy is described by the following equations: the marginal product of labour curve is described by the equation

$$MPL = 5 - 5n$$

The supply of labour is given by

$$n^s = W/P$$

(a) What is the equilibrium level of employment and the real wage, given complete information? That is, what is the full-employment equilibrium?

(b) If the production function is $y = 5n - 2.5n^2$, calculate and plot an equation for the new classical expectations-augmented aggregate supply curve, assuming that the expected price level remains constant at unity.

(c) Calculate and plot an equation for the new Keynesian expectations augmented aggregate supply curve assuming that the expected price level is fixed at unity. (*Hint:* try actual price levels of 1/2, 1, and 2 for the purpose of this exercise.)

20

Equilibrium with Fixed Expectations

You are now getting to the point at which you can pull together the various strands in the macroeconomic theory that you have been studying. In Chapters 8 to 16 you have studied the theory of aggregate demand. In the last three chapters you have studied three alternative approaches to the theory of aggregate supply. We are now going to take the next natural step and study macroeconomic equilibrium. In studying macroeconomic equilibrium we are going to work on the presumption that one of the two 'new' theories of aggregate supply is the relevant one. That is, we will study equilibrium in an economy in which the expected price level is not always equal to the actual price level so that the aggregate supply curve is of either the new classical or new Keynesian variety. We will also begin our analysis by considering a closed economy. Chapter 23 will extend the analysis to the open economy.

Specifically, this chapter employs the expectations-augmented aggregate supply curve and analyses what happens when aggregate demand in a closed economy changes but the expected price level is fixed. By the time you have completed this chapter you will be able to:

(a) Define *full-employment equilibrium*.
(b) Characterize the full-employment equilibrium in a simple diagram.
(c) Explain how output, employment, the real wage, the price level, and the money wage are affected by a rise or fall in aggregate demand when the expected price level is fixed.

(d) **Explain how output, employment, the real wage, the price level, and the money wage are affected by a rise or fall in the expected price level when aggregate demand is fixed.**

A. Full-Employment Equilibrium

Full-employment equilibrium is a situation in which the actual price level is equal to the expected price level. The full-employment equilibrium levels of output, employment, and the real wage are the levels of those variables that occur when the actual price level is equal to the expected price level.

Although the name *full-employment equilibrium* is used to describe a situation in which the price level is equal to the expected price level, it does not mean that there is no unemployment in full-employment equilibrium. This may seem like a contradiction of terms, but it really is nothing more than a convenient use of language. We will study in some detail, in Chapter 25, a variety of factors that can give rise to unemployment. Such things as minimum wages that raise the economy average real wage above the equilibrium real wage, or an economy-wide trade union that raises the real wage above the equilibrium wage, or the presence of generous unemployment benefits, or unusually large reallocations of labour across sectors or regions will be shown to be factors that could generate unemployment — and sizeable amounts of it. Such unemployment is sometimes called *natural unemployment*. At full-employment equilibrium, the unemployment rate is equal to the natural unemployment rate.

As a matter of definition, then, when the unemployment rate is equal to the natural unemployment rate, the term *full employment* is used to describe the condition of the labour market.

In what follows in the rest of this and the next two chapters, the analysis abstracts from the natural rate of unemployment. That does not mean that the natural rate of unemployment is ignored or assumed not to exist. Rather, the analysis will be thought of as determining the level of unemployment relative to the natural rate of unemployment. In the formal analysis, the natural rate of unemployment will be treated as if it was zero. That is only an analytical convenience. The reason for making this abstraction is that the natural unemployment rate itself is not affected by the factors that are being considered. Conversely, the natural unemployment rate does not affect the factors that will be considered. It is possible, therefore, to analyse fluctuations of unemployment around the natural rate independently of what the natural rate of unemployment is.

To summarize: full-employment equilibrium values of real income, employment, and the real wage occur when the price level is equal to its expected level. There will be some unemployment in that situation, determined by the real factors (that are discussed in Chapter 26) that determine the natural rate of unemployment.

B. A Simple Diagram to Characterize Full-Employment Equilibrium

It is important to characterize full-employment equilibrium before moving on to analysing the effects of a change in the money supply on the levels of output, employment, and the price level. Figure 20.1 illustrates a full-employment equilibrium, and the text in this section guides you through that figure.

Notice that the diagram is similar to Figures 17.6 and 18.3. Frame (a) shows the labour market with the money wage on the vertical axis and employment on the horizontal axis. Frame (b) shows the production function — the relationship between the maximum amount of output that can be supplied and the level of employment. Frame (c) shows the

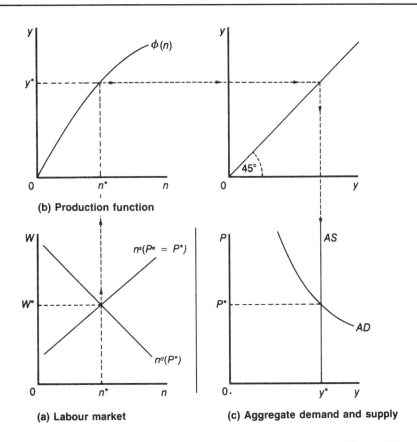

Figure 20.1
Full-employment equilibrium

(b) Production function

(a) Labour market

(c) Aggregate demand and supply

Where the aggregate demand curve cuts the classical aggregate supply curve [frame (c)] determines the full-employment equilibrium price level P^*. When the supply of labour and demand for labour curves are plotted in frame (a) against the money wage rate, but given an actual and expected price level fixed at P^*, they intersect at n^* and determine the money wage rate W^*.

aggregate goods market with aggregate demand and aggregate supply for goods plotted against the price level.

First, pretend that there are no curves in frame (a) at all. Instead of using frame (a), recall the diagram for the classical labour market (frame (a) of Figure 17.6). You will recall that in that frame, we plotted the level of employment against the *real* wage. Where the supply of labour curve cut the demand for labour curve, the equilibrium real wage and the level of employment were determined. Let us suppose that the level of employment determined in that frame is the value n^* plotted on the horizontal axis of frame (a) of Figure 20.1. That is, we have determined n^* from the classical labour market of Chapter 17.

You can now determine the level of output that will be produced with the level of employment n^*. Following the dotted line from frame (a) to frame (b), you see that the level of output associated with n^* is equal to y^*. Transferring that level of output (following the dotted line) to the aggregate supply and demand diagram [frame (c)] generates the classical aggregate supply curve AS.

From the closed economy theory of aggregate demand (recall Chapter 14), we may obtain the aggregate demand curve. This curve is shown in frame (c) as that labelled AD. Where the aggregate demand and aggregate supply curves intersect determines the equilibrium price level P^*.

Now that the equilibrium price level P^* has been determined, it is possible to work backwards and determine the money wage. This could not have been done before determining the equilibrium price level because you would not have known where in frame (a) to plot the labour supply and demand curves. Recall that although these curves are fixed when graphed against the real wage, they shift with the price level when plotted against the money wage. The demand for labour curve depends on the actual price level, and we can draw this curve as that labelled $n^d(P^*)$. This is the demand for labour curve plotted against the money wage rate when the price level is equal to the equilibrium price level P^*. The supply of labour curve is plotted against the expected price level.

Since the diagram is characterizing full-employment equilibrium, the supply of labour curve is drawn for an expected price level equal to the actual price level, which in turn is equal to P^*. The supply curve is shown as the curve labelled $n^s(P^e = P^*)$. This supply curve cuts the demand curve at the level of employment n^*. This follows directly from the fact that the demand and supply curves are fixed when plotted against the real wage and shift proportionately to each other as the price level varies when plotted against the money wage. It follows that if the supply and demand curves are plotted against the money wage, but for the same given price level, then these curves must cut at the full-employment level of employment n^*.

You can now read off, finally, the money wage that is associated with an equilibrium in the labour market at the given actual and expected price level P^*. This money wage is denoted in frame (a) as W^*.

This completes the characterization of full-employment equilibrium.

C. Effects of a Change in Aggregate Demand with a Fixed Expected Price Level

Suppose that the expected price level P^e is equal to P^* and is fixed at that value. Later (in the next chapter) we will inquire what determines the expected price level and how it might change. It will be clearer, however, if we proceed in steps, and the first step is to examine what happens to the levels of output, employment and unemployment, the real wage, and the price level when the economy experiences a change in aggregate demand but the expected price level does not change.

(i) The Expectations-Augmented Aggregate Supply Curve

The starting point for the analysis is the expectations-augmented aggregate supply curve discussed at length in the previous two chapters. Either the new Keynesian or new classical version of the *EAS* curve could be employed. The treatment here uses the new classical version. You may find it a useful exercise to carry out a parallel exercise using the new Keynesian version. Figure 20.2 summarizes the derivation of the new classical aggregate supply curve.

You will recall that the supply of labour curve shown in frame (a) depends on the expected price level. Since the expected price level is being held constant, the supply of labour curve is also held constant. You will also recall that the demand for labour curve depends on the *actual* value of the price level. The demand curve labelled $n^d(P^*)$ is drawn for a level of prices equal to P^*. Where that demand curve intersects the supply of labour curve determines the full-employment equilibrium money wage W^* and employment level n^*. The production function in frame (b) shows that the employment level n^* will produce a level of output equal to y^*. Following the dotted line from frame (b) to frame (c), you arrive at point A, which represents the full-employment equilibrium point where P^*, the actual price level, is equal to the expected price level.

If the price level being considered is at a higher value than P^*, say P_1, as shown on the vertical axis of frame (c), then you have to replot the demand for labour curve, showing it to have shifted upwards. This curve is shown as $n^d(P_1)$ in frame (a). This labour demand curve intersects the fixed labour supply curve to determine the higher money wage W_1 and employment level n_1 and, through frame (b), the higher level of output y_1. If this output level is transferred (following the dotted line) to frame (c), we see that at the price level P_1, the output level will be y_1 and the economy will operate at the point marked B.

**Figure 20.2
The expectations-
augmented
aggregate supply
curve**

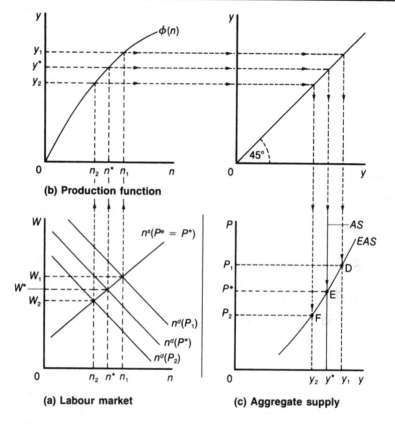

(b) Production function

(a) Labour market

(c) Aggregate supply

As the actual price level varies between P_1 and P_2 in frame (c), the demand for labour curve shifts between $n^d(P_1)$ and $n^d(P_2)$ in frame (a). With the expected price level fixed at P^*, the supply of labour curve does not shift. In frame (a) equilibrium employment and wages vary between n_1 and n_2 and W_1 and W_2, generating output fluctuations between y_1 and y_2. Thus, as the price level moves from P_1 to P_2, output moves from y_1 to y_2 along the curve EAS.

Now consider the price level as being less than P^*, say, at P_2, as marked on the vertical axis of frame (c). In this case, the labour demand curve has to be shifted downwards. This curve is shown as $n^d(P_2)$ in frame (a). This labour demand curve intersects the fixed labour supply curve to determine the lower money wage W_2 and employment levels n_2. At the employment level n_2, the economy will produce an output level of y_2. Transferring the output level y_2 (following the dotted line) to frame (c) shows us that the economy will produce at the point marked C, where the price level is P_2 and the output level is y_2. Joining up all the points C, A, and B generates the expectations-augmented aggregate supply curve marked EAS.

Now that your knowledge of the expectations-augmented aggregate supply curve has been reviewed, it is a very simple matter to see how changes in aggregate demand affect output, employment, the real wage, and the price level. First of all, the effects on prices and output will be considered and then subsequently the effects on the labour market.

(ii) The Effects of a Change in Aggregate Demand on the Levels of Output and Prices

Figure 20.3 summarizes the effects of a change in aggregate demand on the price level and output. The starting point, A, is a full-employment equilibrium. Here the price level, P^*, and output level, y^*, are determined by the intersection of the aggregate demand curve, AD^*, and the aggregate supply curve, AS, as well as by the intersection of the expectations-augmented aggregate supply curve, EAS. The point A is the full-employment equilibrium as defined above, in the sense that the actual price level P^* is equal to the expected price level that underlies the EAS curve.

Hold the expected price level constant at P^* and ask what happens if the level of aggregate demand changes. You can think of aggregate demand changing because the money supply rises, government spending rises, taxes are cut, or there is a shift in the demand for investment goods.

Depending on which of these shocks occur, the rate of interest, that is simultaneously determined with the variables being considered here, will either rise or fall. It is a fairly straightforward matter to work out the implications for the rate of interest by going back to the derivation of aggregate demand in Chapter 14.

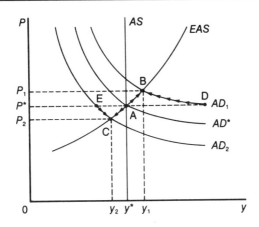

Figure 20.3
The effects of a change in aggregate demand with fixed price level expectations

If the expected price level is fixed at P^*, the EAS curve does not move. When aggregate demand is AD^*, the actual price level is P^*, and the economy is at full employment. If aggregate demand was AD_1, the equilibrium would be at point B with a higher price level and output (P_1, y_1). If aggregate demand fell to AD_2, then the price level and output would fall to P_2 and y_2, point C. Fluctuations in aggregate demand when the expected price level is constant produce procyclical movements in output and the price level.

Suppose that for whatever of the above reasons, the aggregate demand curve shifts from AD^* to AD_1. It is clear that with this new higher level of aggregate demand, there is only one point where the economy can come to an equilibrium, and that is the point marked B. At point B, output is y_1, and the price level is P_1.

How does this new equilibrium point B come about? Suppose the economy started out in the full-employment equilibrium at point A. Suppose then that aggregate demand suddenly increased from AD^* to AD_1. At the new higher level of aggregate demand, but with the price level remaining at P^*, there would be an excess demand for goods equivalent to the distance AD in Figure 20.3. This excess demand would generate rising prices, as people who sought to raise their expenditure would find it necessary to offer higher prices in order to acquire the goods that they were demanding. As the price level was forced upwards, the quantity of goods demanded would decline — as shown in Figure 20.3 by the arrows moving up the aggregate demand curve.

There would also be a response on the supply side of the economy. As the prices of some goods began to increase, firms, being well informed about the markets in which they operate and observing the rising price of their output, would start to increase their demand for labour. Their demand for labour curves would begin to shift upwards, as in frame (a) of Figure 20.2. This would produce a rise in the money wage but a fall in the real wage, and therefore, a rise in employment and a rise in the aggregate supply of goods. Households would be willing to supply additional labour in this situation because, although they see a rising money wage rate (and rising prices for the goods that are being sold by their own employers), they do not see the rise in the general price level and so continue to maintain given expectations about the general level of prices. As a result, they believe the real wage to have increased and willingly supply additional labour. There would, therefore, on the supply side, be a tendency for the economy to slide up its aggregate supply curve from A to B, as shown by the arrows in Figure 20.3. As the price level increased, the excess of demand over supply would be choked off, and the economy would come to rest at point B, with firms satisfied that they were supplying the profit-maximizing quantity and households satisfied that they were supplying the right quantity of labour and buying the right quantity of goods.

Next, consider what would happen if aggregate demand was to fall. Specifically, suppose aggregate demand fell from AD^* to AD_2. This aggregate demand curve cuts the expectations-augmented aggregate supply curve at C. This new equilibrium point is at the price level P_2 and output y_2. To see how this equilibrium comes about, perform a conceptual experiment similar to that which you have just performed in the case of a rise in aggregate demand.

Suppose that the price level is initially at P^* and there has just been a fall in aggregate demand to AD_2. In such a case, there will be a cutback in demand, and there will be an excess of supply over demand equal to the distance AE in Figure 20.3. This excess supply will cause prices to fall. As prices begin to fall, firms' demand for labour curves [frame (a) of Figure 20.2] will be shifting downwards. The supply of labour curve would not shift, however, because households continue to expect the price level to remain at its initial level. Thus, the amount of labour employed and the amount of output supplied will fall. The actual real wage will rise since, although the money wage rate falls, it does so by a smaller proportion than does the price level. The expected real wage rate, however, will fall since the money wage rate falls while the expected price level remains constant. As a result of these actions the economy travels down along its expectations-augmented aggregate supply curve from A to C, as shown by the arrows. Households will move along their demand curves, resulting in a movement along the aggregate demand curve from E to C. At point C there is a balance between the aggregate output supplied and demanded, and there is no further tendency for the price level or the level of output to change.

Although the analysis that has just been performed has been done explicitly within the framework of the new classical theory of aggregate supply, the same broad predictions would have been generated if the new Keynesian theory had been used. In that case, however, the output movements would have been greater and the price movements less than in the new classical case. You can easily verify this by checking back to the comparison of the new Keynesian and new classical expectations-augmented aggregate supply curves. Since the Keynesian curve is flatter than the classical curve, swings in aggregate demand have bigger output and smaller price effects in the Keynesian case than in the classical case.

(iii) Key Assumption of Equilibrium Analysis

We assume that the equilibrating processes just described that move the economy from position A to position B when aggregate demand rises and from position A to position C when aggregate demand falls occur quickly enough for points A, B, and C to be the only points observed.

(iv) Summary of Effects of a Change in Aggregate Demand on Output and Price Level

We can now summarize the effects of a rise or fall in aggregate demand on the level of output and prices:

1. If the expected price level is constant and aggregate demand rises, then output and the price level will both rise.
2. If the expected price level is constant and aggregate demand falls, then output and the price level will both fall.

(v) Effects of a Change in Aggregate Demand on Employment and Wages

The effects of a change in aggregate demand on the level of employment, money wages, and the real wage will now be analysed. Because of the way in which the aggregate demand experiment has been set up, these effects can immediately be read off by referring back to Figure 20.2.

First, consider the case of a rise in aggregate demand. This moves the economy, as you saw in Figure 20.3, to position B. Position B is also shown in Figure 20.2, so that you can easily see the effects on the labour market. At the price level P_1, which is the consequence of a rise in aggregate demand to AD_1, the demand for labour curve will shift to the right and be in the position shown as $n^d(P_1)$. This shift produces a higher money wage, W_1, and a higher employment level, n_1. It also produces a lower real wage. The real wage falls because the money wage rises by less than the rise in the price level. (Refer back to Chapter 18, Figure 18.1, and the associated discussion if you cannot see that this is true.) Indeed, it is the fall in the real wage that induces a higher level of employment. Firms, seeing that the real wage has fallen, find it profitable to hire additional workers. Households, on the other hand, having a fixed expectation of the price level, think that the real wage has increased and therefore are willing to supply more labour.

Next, consider the case of a cut in aggregate demand. If aggregate demand is cut to the curve AD_2, it will intersect the expectations-augmented aggregate supply curve at point C in Figure 20.3. Point C is also shown in frame (c) of Figure 20.2. You can see that at that price level, the demand for labour curve is shown as $n^d(P_2)$, and the equilibrium levels of wages and employment are W_2 and n_2. Thus a cut in aggregate demand leads to a cut in the money wage and in the level of employment. In this situation, *real wages* will have increased. This rise occurs because the price level will have fallen by more than the money wage has fallen. Firms, knowing this, will cut back on their demand for labour. Households will not resist this cutback in the demand for labour because, as far as they are concerned, the real wage that they have been offered has fallen. This arises because the money wage has fallen while the expected price level has remained constant.

Although the above effects have been stated in terms of the new classical theory, similar effects would occur in the new Keynesian case. The key difference between the two would be that in the new Keynesian case, households would be knocked off the supply of labour curve. When aggregate demand increased to AD_1, the money wage rate would remain constant, the price level would rise, and the real wage would fall. This fall in the real wage would induce an increase in the demand for labour that would not be matched by an increase in the supply of labour. Nevertheless, workers, because of the assumed nature of the contract they have with their employers, would be required to supply the extra labour even though this was in excess of their labour supply.

In the reverse case, when aggregate demand falls to AD_2, workers are knocked off their supply curves in the opposite direction. In this case, the price level falls, so that with a fixed money wage rate, the real wage rises, thereby lowering the demand for labour. Firms now hire less labour than would like to work. In this case, there will be unemployment over and above any natural unemployment in the economy, and it will have the appearance of being involuntary, in the sense that if they could have signed different contracts, workers would have done so.

(vi) Summary of the Effects of a Change in Aggregate Demand with a Constant Expected Price Level

To summarize, the effects of a rise in aggregate demand with a fixed expected price level are as follows:

(1) With a fixed expected price level, a rise in aggregate demand raises output, raises the price level, raises the level of employment, and lowers the real wage. Unemployment falls below the natural rate of unemployment.
(2) With a fixed expected price level, a cut in aggregate demand lowers the level of output, lowers the price level, lowers the level of employment, and raises real wages. It also creates unemployment in excess of the natural rate of unemployment.

This completes the formal analysis of the effects of a change in aggregate demand on the levels of output, employment, the real wage, and the price level — when price expectations are fixed.

Although positions B and C (Figure 20.3) in this economy are equilibrium positions, they differ from equilibrium A in a fundamental respect. Positions B and C cannot be sustained forever, whereas position A can. To see why they cannot be sustained forever takes us into a discussion of how expectations are formed and changed, which will be the subject of the next chapter. Before turning to that, however, let us deal with the final topic of this chapter.

D. Effects of a Change in the Expected Price Level with Constant Aggregate Demand

Although the title of this chapter is 'Equilibrium with Fixed Expectations', it will be useful if we analyse what happens if the expected price level changes. Let us start the economy out at full-employment equilibrium such as that depicted by P^* for the price level and y^* for real income, in Figure 20.4. These points lie at the intersection of the aggregate demand curve, AD, and the expectations-augmented aggregate supply curve, EAS, and are also on the aggregate supply curve, AS. The expected price level evidently will be P^*, the same as the actual price level.

**Figure 20.4
The effects of a
change in the
expected price level
when aggregate
demand is constant**

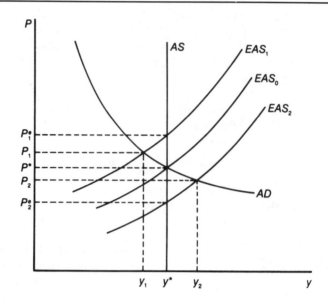

If aggregate demand is fixed, then the *AD* curve does not move. When the expected
price level rises to P_1^e, the *EAS* curve moves to EAS_1, so that the price level rises to P_1,
and output falls to y_1. If the expected price level falls to P_2^e, the actual price level falls to P_2,
and income rises to y_2. Changes in the expected price level with constant aggregate
demand lead to counter-cyclical movements in output and prices.

Hold the level of aggregate demand constant at *AD*, but now imagine
that the expected price level for some reason rises to P_1^e. What are the
effects of such a change? You already know that lying behind the *EAS*
curve is a supply of labour curve that itself depends on the expected price
level. A rise in the expected price level shifts the supply of labour curve
upwards and by the same percentage amount as the rise in the expected
price level. As a result the *EAS* curve shifts upwards to become the curve
labelled EAS_1 in Figure 20.4. We know that the *EAS* curve shifts by this
much because we know that the *EAS* curve cuts the *AS* curve at the
expected price level. The new *EAS* curve intersects the fixed *AD* curve
at the price level P_1 and the income level, y_1. This position is the equilibrium when the expected price level is P_1^e and aggregate demand is given
by the curve *AD*. In this situation, the economy is producing less than
its full-employment output level. The actual price level is below the
expected price level. Notice that this situation (P_1, y_1) in Figure 20.4 is
comparable to point C in Figure 20.3.

Returning to Figure 20.4, let us next suppose that the expected price
level was to fall from P^* to P_2^e. In this case, the *EAS* curve shifts downwards to become the curve labelled EAS_2. Again, the new *EAS* curve cuts
the *AS* curve at the expected price level. As before we will hold the level
of aggregate demand constant at *AD*. The new *EAS* curve cuts the *AD*

curve at the price level P_2 and income level y_2. In this situation the level of output is higher than if the full-employment level and the price level has fallen relative to P^* but is now above its expected level. This equilibrium (P_2, y_2 in Figure 20.4) is comparable to position B in Figure 20.3.

You will now be able to see some clear similarities in, but also some important differences between, the effects of a change in aggregate demand when the expected price level is constant and the effects of a change in the expected price level when aggregate demand is constant. The similarities are these: only when the expected price level and actual price level are equal to each other is the economy at full employment. If the actual price level is below the expected price level, then output is below its full-employment level. This outcome can result either because of a rise in the expected price level with constant aggregate demand or because of a drop in aggregate demand with a constant expected price level. In the opposite case, if the actual price level is greater than the expected price level, then output will be above its full-employment level. This result can arise either because of a rise in aggregate demand with a constant expected price level, or because of a fall in the expected price level with a constant level of aggregate demand.

The differences between the two experiments in the preceding section and this one are the following: a rise in aggregate demand with a fixed expected price level raises both output and the price level, and a fall in aggregate demand lowers both output and the price level, so that output and prices move in the same direction as each other. That is, movements in output and the price level are procyclical. A change in the expected price level with a constant level of aggregate demand leads to changes in output and in the price level that move in opposite directions to each other. That is, movements in output and the price level are counter-cyclical.

Aside from these differences in the directions of movement of output and the price level between the two cases, all other properties of the equilibria analysed are the same. The detailed story told concerning how the economy moves from one position to another in the previous section applies with equal force here.

The analysis of the effects of a change in inflation expectations on real wages and the labour market are easy to figure out. Anything that lowers output below its equilibrium level also lowers employment. Anything that lowers employment also raises the real wage. From this you can immediately figure out that a rise in the expected price level leads to a rise in the money wage that exceeds the rise in the price level, and a drop in the expected price level cuts the money wage rate by more than the cut in the price level.

However, if the labour market is to be in equilibrium (continuing to operate with the new classical model), then anything that lowers the equilibrium level of output and employment also lowers the expected real wage. Conversely, anything that raises output above its full-employment level raises the expected real wage. Thus, we can immediately figure out that a rise in the expected price level raises the money wage rate by more than it raises the actual price level, but by less than it raises the expected price level. The effect of this is to raise the actual real wage but lower the expected real wage. Conversely, a cut in the expected price level lowers the money wage by more than it lowers the price level, but by less than the amount by which the expected price level falls. In this case, the actual real wage falls, but the expected real wage rises.

You have now seen how changes in aggregate demand affect output and the price level when the expected price level is constant and, also, how changes in the expected price level affect the *actual* price level as well as the level of output. Evidently, expectations of the price level are of crucial importance in influencing the behaviour both of the actual price level and other real variables in the economy. In the next chapter we will investigate more thoroughly how expectations of the price level are themselves formed and what factors lead to changes in those expectations.

Summary

A. Full-Employment Equilibrium

Full-employment equilibrium values of output, employment, unemployment, and the real wage occur when the price level is equal to the expected price level. The unemployment present at full-employment equilibrium is called the *natural rate of unemployment*.

B. A Simple Diagram to Characterize Full-Employment Equilibrium

Figure 20.1 is a diagram of full-employment equilibrium, and you should be thoroughly familiar with it.

C. Effects of a Change in Aggregate Demand with a Fixed Expected Price Level

If the expected price level is fixed, a rise in aggregate demand raises the level of output, employment, and the price level. It also lowers the real wage and makes unemployment fall below its natural rate.

When the expected price level is fixed and aggregate demand falls, there is a fall in output, in employment, and in the price level. The real wage rises, and unemployment rises above its natural rate.

D. *Effects of a Change in the Expected Price Level with Constant Aggregate Demand*

If aggregate demand is fixed, a rise in the expected price level raises the actual price level but by less than the expected price level has increased, and it lowers output. Real wages and unemployment rise, and employment falls. Money wages rise by more than the price level but by less than the expected price level. When aggregate demand is fixed and the expected price level falls, the actual price level falls, and output rises. The fall in the actual price level is less than the fall in the expected price level. Real wages fall, but expected real wages rise. Unemployment also falls below its natural rate.

Review Questions

1. Define *full-employment equilibrium*.
2. Explain why there will be some unemployment at full-employment equilibrium.
3. Define the *natural unemployment rate*. Is the natural unemployment rate affected by the price level? Why or why not? Explain.
4. Characterize full-employment equilibrium in a set of diagrams like those shown in Figure 20.1.
5. Consider Figure 20.2. Suppose the expected price level was to rise to P_1. What would happen to the *EAS* curve? Draw a new curve to illustrate your answer.
6. Why does the *EAS* curve slope upwards?
7. What happens to the levels of: (a) output, (b) employment, (c) unemployment, (d) the money wage, (e) the real wage, and (f) the price level, if the money supply rises but the expected price level remains constant?
8. What happens to all the variables listed in (a) to (f) of Question 7 if the expected price level falls, while the money supply remains constant?
9. What happens to all the variables listed in (a) to (f) of Question 7 if both the expected price level and aggregate demand rise by the *same* percentage amount?
10. Review the following terms or concepts: *rational maximizing behaviour* and *full-employment equilibrium*.

21

Price Level Expectations

We saw, when we examined the connection between real and market interest rates, the importance of the *expected* rate of inflation. We have also seen, in the new theories of aggregate supply, that the expected price level plays a crucial role in influencing the behaviour of the economy. So far, however, we have made no attempt to explain where the expected price level, or the expected rate of inflation, comes from or what causes it to change. It is certain that both the expected price level and the expected rate of inflation do change and clear, therefore, that we need a theory of expectations.

Not only does the *expected* inflation rate or *expected* price level play an important role in our theories of macroeconomics, it also is featured in much of the more popular (if imprecise) discussions on inflation. We often hear, for example, that there is an 'inflation psychology' that is considered to be one of the major causes of inflation.

Thus, both in our theories and in popular discussion, the role played by expectations is central. The time has come to examine the determination of expectations more closely, and to move beyond the assumption that they are exogenous. The two central questions that this chapter deals with are, what determines the expected price level, and what factors lead to changes in the expected price level? You are going to discover that, paradoxical though it may seem, there is no rational basis for a view that inflation can be *caused* by an 'inflation psychology' − by inflation expectations. Rather, the very things which generate inflation also generate inflation expectations.

By the time you have completed this chapter you will be able to:

(a) **Explain the relationship between the expected price level and expected rate of inflation.**

366

(b) State the distinction between a subjective expectation and a conditional mathematical expectation.

(c) Explain why wrong expectations are costly.

(d) Explain the concept of a rational expectation.

(e) Explain the concept of the rational expectation of the price level.

(f) Describe how to work out the rational expectation of the price level.

A. The Expected Price Level and Expected Rate of Inflation

You are already familiar with the distinction between inflation and the price level. You know that inflation is the percentage rate of change in the price level. You also know that in the analysis that we are doing in this part of the book, we are abstracting from inflation. That is, we are conducting an analysis that presumes that the average rate of inflation is zero, which means that the price level is fluctuating around some constant value. Nevertheless, even though we are abstracting from inflation, it is important that you know the connection between the expected rate of inflation and the expected price level. That connection follows directly from the definition of actual inflation and its relation to the actual price level. Equation 21.1 defines the rate of inflation (π) at a particular point in time (t) as:

$$\pi_t = \left(\frac{P_t - P_{t-1}}{P_{t-1}}\right) \times 100 \tag{21.1}$$

Here, P_t is the price level at date t, and P_{t-1} is the price level at date $t - 1$. The rate of inflation at t is the change in prices from $t - 1$ to t, expressed at a percentage of the prices that prevailed at the previous point in time. For example, if the previous price level was 95 and the current price level is 100, the rate of inflation will be given by

$$\pi_t = \left(\frac{100 - 95}{95}\right) \times 100$$

$$= 5.2\%$$

The expected rate of inflation and the expected price level are related to each other by an equation similar to the above; that is,

$$\pi_t^e = \left(\frac{P_t^e - P_{t-1}}{P_{t-1}}\right) \times 100 \tag{21.2}$$

This says that the expected rate of inflation is equal to the expected price level minus the previous period's price level, expressed as a percentage of the previous period's price level. As before, suppose the previous period's price level was 95, but the expected price level is 99. Then,

$$\pi_t^e = \left(\frac{99 - 95}{95} \right) \times 100$$

$$= 4.2\%$$

Notice that the expected rate of inflation is the expected percentage change in the price level and not the percentage change in the expected price level. In fact, the change in the expected price level is not a very interesting concept. You could calculate the change in the expected price level if you wished. It would be this period's expected price level minus the previous period's expected price level, expressed as a percentage of that previous period's expected price level.

It is clear from the above that there is a close connection between the expected inflation rate and the expected price level. The key thing to note for current purposes is that in order to calculate the expected inflation rate, you need to calculate the expected price level. It is expectations about the price level that we shall focus on in the rest of this chapter. We are going to get to that, however, by a slightly roundabout route and shall not reach a good understanding of how the expected price level is determined until later in this chapter.

Let us now begin the first of three preliminary tasks that will lead us to an understanding of how price level expectations are formed.

B. The Distinction Between a Subjective Expectation and a Conditional Mathematical Expectation

(i) Subjective Expectation

The term *expectation* has two distinct meanings. In ordinary speech it is used to describe a more or less *vague feeling* about some future event. This is a subjective expectation. For example, we might be planning to travel by car along a congested highway and expect that it will take an hour to complete our journey; or we might be planning to travel by bus and expect the bus to be running 10 minutes behind schedule because of bad weather. Another example concerns the expectations of a skilled snooker player. Such a person might have an expectation as to what will happen when the cue is aligned in a particular direction and applied to the cue ball with a particular direction of spin and force. That expectation may be, for example, that the second ball is dispatched to the centre-right pocket and that the cue ball comes to rest lined up for an easy next shot.

Typically, we do not explicitly analyse the reasons why we hold the expectations that we do. We have subjective feelings which, on the average, seem to be right, and we do not consciously examine the sources of these feelings. The snooker player, for example, does not ask himself from where his expectation comes. He simply knows how to play the game and uses a well-developed instinct and skill to achieve the appropriate movements of the balls.

A subjective expectation, then, is simply a feeling that an individual has about the likely consequences of some particular action or as to the likely outcome of some particular event.

(ii) Conditional Mathematical Expectation

There is a more precise usage of the term expectation — a conditional mathematical expectation. A mathematical expectation is nothing other than an *average*. An example will make it easy to understand this. Suppose we have 3000 cards: 1000 of them are printed with the number 4 on one side, another 1000 with the number 5, and another 1000 with the number 6. These cards are put into a bag and are shaken up so that they are thoroughly mixed. Then, 300 cards are drawn from the bag at random. You are asked to predict what the average of the numbers drawn will be. You know that there are three kinds of cards in the bag, and that one-third of them have the number 4, one-third have the number 5, and one-third the number 6. Since the cards have been shuffled very thoroughly and they have been drawn at random, you will predict that, on the average, out of 300 cards drawn, 100 will have the number 4, 100 the number 5, and 100 the number 6. You calculate the average of this and you arrive at a prediction that the average of all the cards drawn will be 5. You have just calculated a mathematical expectation.

A conditional mathematical expectation is a mathematical expectation calculated when some information is already given. For example, suppose in the numbered card game described above, you were told that of the 300 cards drawn, 200 were numbered 6. (This would be an improbable, although possible, outcome.) You are now asked to predict the average value of all 300 cards drawn. You know that there are as many 4s as 5s in the bag, so you will expect that, of the remaining cards, 50 will be 4s and 50 will be 5s. The average which you will calculate from 200 6s, 50 4s, and 50 5s is

$$\left(\frac{200}{300}\right) \times 6 + \left(\frac{50}{300}\right) \times 4 + \left(\frac{50}{300}\right) \times 5 = 5.5$$

You have now calculated a conditional mathematical expectation, or more simply, a conditional expectation. You have calculated the expected average value (expected value) of the cards, *given* that 2/3 of them are 6s.

Let us go back to those earlier examples of subjective expectations and see whether we can think of a mathematical expectation interpretation of them.

Consider first of all your car journey along a congested highway. Many factors will determine the number of minutes that it will take for you to arrive at your destination. It will depend on the number of cars on the road ahead of you, whether there are any road works that have closed one or more of the lanes, whether or not there are any accidents blocking the road, and perhaps a thousand other things that are difficult to enumerate. Suppose, however, that you have travelled this particular part of this highway many times in the past. You have a stock of experience from those previous journeys concerning the length of time that it takes. If you had actually kept a written record of the number of minutes it took each time you went on this particular journey, then you could calculate the average journey time. That calculation would be a mathematical expectation.

You may, however, be able to do better than that. It may be that you know that in certain circumstances the journey is quicker than others. Perhaps you know that if you begin your journey between 8.00 a.m. and 9.00 a.m. or between 5.00 p.m. and 6.00 p.m. it takes longer than if you set out at other times of the day. You might also know that the journey typically takes less time on Tuesdays, Wednesdays, and Thursdays than it does on Mondays and Fridays or that it takes longer in rainy or icy weather than on a sunny day. Given all this extra information, you could calculate the average number of minutes it takes you to complete this particular journey at different times of the day, different days of the week, in different weather conditions and allowing for other factors that you have noticed affect the outcome. These averages would be conditional expectations. They would be conditional on the information concerning the time of day, day of the week, state of the weather, and so on.

We could tell an identical story concerning the number of minutes that you expect to have to wait for a bus.

In the case of the snooker player example, if the player could solve complicated geometrical problems in a very short span of time in his head and program himself to carry out the instructions implied by those solutions, he could make the cue ball follow exactly the trajectory and with exactly the force required to achieve his objective. This would be a rather complicated mathematical expectation calculation; it would be the calculation of a mathematical expectation of the paths of (at least) two balls. Of course, just as in the case of the numbered cards in the bag, there will be no certainty as to the outcome in any of these examples. Unless we were to pull all 3000 cards from the bag, we would not be able to predict for sure the average value of the cards drawn. Likewise, going back to the car journey example, unless we knew absolutely everything about the conditions of the road ahead of us, we would not be able to make an exact prediction concerning the time by which it would take to arrive at our destination. We would, nevertheless, be able to calculate a mathematical expectation. That is, we would be able to calculate the expected value of the relevant variable conditional on all the information available.

C. Why Wrong Expectations are Costly

Although expectations are sometimes formed purely for fun, so that wrong expectations have very little consequence other than generating mild displeasure or surprise, you will be able to think of many examples, especially those that impinge on economic behaviour, where forming a wrong expectation will lead an individual to incur costs that would be better avoided. The costs arising from wrong expectations come in a variety of sizes and forms.

Consider the examples that were introduced in the previous section when we looked at the distinction between subjective and mathematical expectations. Forming an inaccurate assessment of how long a particular journey would take could have a variety of consequences. Suppose that you expected a journey to take one hour, but in fact it turned out to take an hour and a half. It may be that this is of very little consequence, causing you perhaps simply to have a half an hour less time for shopping, sitting on the beach, or doing whatever it is that you are planning to do at the end of your journey. At the other extreme, it could be very costly indeed. It could cause you to miss the departure time of an airplane on which you have a non-refundable ticket, or to miss the beginning of a play or concert. Of course, the more serious the consequences of mis-estimating the length of the journey, the more time you are likely to allow yourself. Even that, however, is not costless. It might involve forcing yourself out of bed at an earlier hour than seems to you ideal, or missing out on some other pleasurable or profitable opportunity.

Next, consider the numbered card game example that we used in the previous section. This is a simplified version of many games that form the backbone of the economy of Las Vegas. Suppose that you are running a casino in that town, and that in the operation of your roulette wheel, you offer the same odds on red as on black. You do this because on most roulette wheels the number of red spots and number of black spots are equal, so that there is an equal chance that a ball will land in one colour or the other. Further suppose though that someone has tampered with your roulette wheel and, in fact, 55 per cent of the spots are black and 45 per cent are red. Let us further suppose that you did not bother to inspect the wheel too carefully, and are operating on the *expectation* that the wheel is a standard one with half the spots red and half the spots black. It will not be long before astute investors are putting money on the black spots, thereby making a nice profit and leaving you rushing for a lawyer and seeking to declare bankruptcy.

This is an example which illustrates rather nicely a further important distinction. It is the distinction between being wrong about an *individual event* and being wrong *on the average*. There is no way in which a casino operator can be right about every single event. Sometimes a client gets lucky and wins an enormous amount of money. Events that have a low probability do happen sometimes. It is possible, nevertheless, to avoid being wrong on the average. That is, it is possible to form expectations such that if we took the average of all our expectations over a period of time and compared them with the average of the events that occurred over that same period of time, although each individual event would not have been correctly predicted, on the average, the outcome and the prediction agree. In the case of the casino operator, on the average, black was coming up 55 per cent of the time and red was coming up 45 per cent of the time. The roulette wheel operator was working on the presumption that the two colours would come up 50 per cent of the time each, which meant he was wrong on the average.

There is nothing we can do about being wrong in the case of individual events. We simply have to take random things as they come. What we can do, however, is to try to avoid being wrong on the average. By so doing we shall minimize the errors that we make in particular cases. We will not eliminate the errors, but we will be reducing their consequences to the smallest possible level.

All the examples of costs that have been discussed above have been in areas other than those with which macroeconomics is centrally concerned. Let us now consider some macroeconomic examples. Expectations have arisen in our model because of their effects on the supply of labour. Suppose a household has formed an expectation of the price level and makes a labour supply decision on the basis of it, and then discovers that the expectation was wrong. If too high a price level was expected, then too low a real wage would have been calculated, and too little work will have been done. The household will wind up having consumed more leisure than is now regarded as ideal and will have a lower income to spend on consumption goods than is regarded as ideal. Conversely, if the expectation of the price level was too low, then the calculated real wage would be too high, and the household would wind up doing more work and having a larger income and more consumption goods but less leisure than seems, from the perspective of the individual, ideal.

More important economic examples in terms of costliness of errors arise in the area of capital investment decisions. Firms making multimillion- or even billion-dollar investment decisions have to form expectations about the future demand for particular products, the costs of labour and other inputs. Errors made in such expectations can have enormous costs.

Notice that in the labour supply example (and if we had developed it more fully, the same would apply to the capital investment examples) costs of wrong expectations are symmetric. Expecting a higher price than occurs is just as bad as expecting a lower one. Also notice that the economic example is like the casino example — one in which it is quite impossible for expectations to be always correct but one in which expectations could be correct on the average.

If wrong expectations inflict costs on individuals, it seems reasonable to suppose that they will try to avoid those costs. Of course, the bigger the costs, the harder people will try to avoid making mistakes. We could summarize this by saying they will try to form their expectations rationally.

Let us now go on to apply the ideas of a subjective expectation — a vague feeling about some likely event — and a mathematical expectation

— a precise calculation of the expectation of some outcome based on all the information that is relevant and available — and make more precise the concept of a rational expectation.

D. Rational Expectation

(i) Definition

The definition of a rational expectation is as follows.[1] An expectation is said to be rational when the subjective expectation coincides with the conditional mathematical expectation based on all available information. Notice that the definition says that when a mathematical and a subjective expectation coincide, *then* the expectation is rational. It does not say that a rational expectation is arrived at by performing all the complicated calculations which it would be necessary to perform in order to arrive at the appropriate conditional mathematical expectation. As in the example given above, an expectation about the length of time it would take to complete a particular journey would be rational if the expectation arrived at by instinct, intuition, or judgment, based on casual observation, turned out to coincide with the expectation based on a careful and systematic recording of previous experience and on the calculation of a conditional expectation from those data.

An alternative way of thinking about a rational expectation is to regard it as implying the absence of *systematic* error. If people formed expectations that repeatedly and systematically led them astray in an avoidable way, then those expectations would not be rational.

(ii) Some Further Intuition on the Meaning of Rational Expectations

In order to get a better feel for what a rational expectation is, it might be helpful to consider expectations of a particular variable in which man has always been interested, namely, the future state of the weather. There are many ways in which we can arrive at an expectation of the future state of the weather. One would be to turn on the appropriate TV channel and read the latest forecasts being put out by the meteorological office. Another would be to watch the squirrels and observe how many nuts they are stockpiling. Yet a further method would be to recall the various traditional sayings, such as the proposition about the number of days it

---

1 The concept of rational expectations presented here is that of John F. Muth, 'Rational Expectations and the Theory of Price Movements', *Econometrica*, 29 (July 1961) pp.315–35. This concept was first introduced into macroeconomics by Robert E. Lucas, Jr. in 'Some International Evidence on Output–Inflation Tradeoff', *American Economic Review*, 63 (September 1973) pp.326–34.

will rain or not rain following a rainy or a fine St Swithin's Day or the proposition about March beginning like a lion and ending like a lamb, or vice versa. All of these would be methods of forming a view about some future state of the weather.

At the present time and in the present state of knowledge, it is clear that the rational expectation of the future state of the weather is obtained by employing the first of these devices — the forecasts of the weather bureau. Expectations based on the other procedures, unless they are based on well-established empirical regularities, would not be rational. It may be that the squirrel actually does have some antennae that enable it to know what the likely future winter length is going to be and to react accordingly by stockpiling the appropriate quantity of nuts. In that event, it would be rational to base an expectation of the likely future winter length on the basis of that observed behaviour. This simply says that a rational expectation can be based on any information, provided that information can be demonstrated to be *relevant* to the forecasting of the future value of the variable of interest.

Although, in the current state of knowledge, forming a rational expectation of the weather involves the taking of meteorological observations followed by the use of meteorological theory to generate inferences concerning the implications of those observations for the future course of the weather, such predictions are not exact. This inexactness arises from the fact that meteorological information collection is far from total. It would cost an infinite or close to an infinite amount of resources to collect enough information to make predictions about the state and movement of every last molecule of air. Rather than do that, we invest a smaller amount of resources in sampling the atmosphere at various levels and in various places and make inferences concerning the behaviour between those points. Further, we do not evaluate intricate, complicated meteorological models involving millions and millions of differential equations. Rather, the meteorologists rely upon simpler theories, which, on the average, work out all right, although they do not work out in every case. So, in the area of the weather, a rational expectation is an expectation that is based on all the information that is available, even though that information is far from the total set of information that one could imagine being available. This means that a rational expectation will not always be right. It will only be right *on the average*.

Notice, that in this meteorological example, we do not require that each and every individual be an expert meteorologist and be able to work out the weather forecast for himself. All that is necessary is that there be a body of science, and a systematic observation process to inform that body of science, to enable the scientific community to make the relevant predictions. The rest of us can then consume the fruits of that scientific activity.

E. Rational Expectation of the Price Level

(i) The Concept of Rational Expectation Applied to the Price Level

A rational expectation of the price level follows very directly from the examples that have been introduced so far. The rational expectation of the price level is the price level that is predicted on the basis of *all* the available information at the time at which the expectation is formed. Such information might include all the past history of the key economic variables, such as the price level itself, output, the real wage, the money wage, the money supply, and many other economic variables.

Expectations (forecasts) concerning economic variables are typically made available to the general public by the economics profession in much the same way as weather forecasts are made available by the meteorological profession. Such newspapers and journals as *The Financial Times*, *The Economist* and the *National Institute Economic Review* bring together and appraise forecasts of diverse groups of economic analysts. Economic science is less settled than is meteorology. There are, as you were made aware of in Chapter 1, a variety of schools of thought concerning the way the economy works. In the present state of economic knowledge it is necessary, therefore, for each individual, in forming a rational expectation, to weigh the 'economic weather forecasts' that are put out by the economics profession against his or her own personal knowledge, information, and experience. Each individual's expectation will be arrived at using a large variety of inputs. That expectation will be a rational expectation if it coincides with the conditional expectation based on all the information that is available.

(ii) A More Precise Definition of the Rational Expectation of the Price Level

We can make the definition of the rational expectation of the price level (or the inflation rate) more precise in a way that utilizes the brilliant insights of John F. Muth.[2] The ideas advanced by Muth are fairly deep and apparently difficult to grasp. Let us proceed with some care. First, let us remind ourselves (and keep on reminding ourselves) that a rational expectation is just an average. Second, consider the question (which seems at first thought totally irrelevant to what we have just been discussing) 'what is theory?'. Theory is a set of propositions designed to make predictions about the behaviour of some variable or variables. A theory of the price level (or the inflation rate) for example, is designed to make predictions about prices. Now no theory, of course, is exact. The best that we

---

2 Ibid.

can expect of any theory is that it will be right on the average. Or more directly: all theories are designed to make predictions about the average behaviour of the phenomena that they address. Realizing that theories are designed to make predictions about averages, and also realizing that a rational expectation is nothing other than an average, led John Muth to a neat and powerful operational definition of a rational expectation. That definition states that a *rational expectation is the same thing as the prediction of the relevant theory*. Thus, the rational expectation of the price level is the same thing as the prediction of the relevant theory for determining the price level.

This statement does not say that the rational expectation of the price level is the prediction of *any* theory of the price level. Theories that are clearly wrong would not yield predictions that coincided with the rational expectation. Only a theory that is not wrong would do so.

In the current state of knowledge, we do not know, at least not with any certainty, what the relevant theory for predicting the price level is. We are still in that stage of scientific inquiry of advancing alternative hypotheses and determining which if any of these alternatives are compatible with the facts. Although we do not know for sure that any particular theory is the correct theory, each time we advance a theory we do so in the hope that it will turn out to be the right one. Where that theory contains as part of its structure people's expectations of magnitudes predicted by the theory, the only internally consistent assumption that we can make concerning the way in which those expectations are formed, is to postulate that they are formed in the same way as that particular theory says the variable is determined. In so doing, we have a very powerful technique for developing, testing, and usually though hopefully not always, rejecting a succession of alternative hypotheses concerning the determination of the macroeconomic variables.

You may be suspecting that to assume that people form their expectations in the same way that a particular theory says the variables in question are determined somehow stacks the cards in favour of the theory by making the predictions self-fulfilling. Nothing could in fact be further from the truth. A moment's reflection will convince you of the reason for this. Suppose that we allowed ourselves the freedom to propose any hypothesis we like about expectations formation. We could invent all kinds of *ad hoc* theories linking expectations of inflation to past values of actual inflation, to past values of the money supply, or to just about anything else that came to mind. We would then be able to assume that the expected rate of inflation had changed for no reason other than that we need this assumption in order to make a particular theory fit the facts. We can put this slightly differently by saying that we would be in a position of having one theory telling us how the inflation rate (or price level) evolved for a given expected rate of inflation and then another theory generating inflationary expectations. It is immediately obvious that if we develop theories in that way, we give ourselves sufficient 'degrees of freedom' to be able to make any theory fit any set of facts. In contrast if we restricted ourselves by insisting that the expectations of inflation not be allowed to change conveniently so as to 'fit the facts' but evolve to coincide with the predictions of the theory, then we would be giving ourselves no additional 'degrees of freedom' with which to explain the facts. By insisting that expectations be formed in such a way that they coincide with the predictions of the model places greater demands on the model and forces us to work harder to find the right one.

In the next section we will go on to employ these ideas to calculate the rational expectation of the price level. Specifically, we will use the theory developed in the previous three chapters that makes predictions about the price level, and we will assume that people's expectations of the price level coincide with the prediction of the theory.

F. How to Work Out the Rational Expectation of the Price Level

(i) The Boot-Laces Problem!

There is a preliminary problem which needs some discussion, arising from a key difference between the rational expectation of the price level and the rational expectation of something like how hot the summer will be or the amount of rain that is going to fall tomorrow. Tomorrow's weather is not going to be affected, at least as far as we know on the basis of existing information, by our expectations of what it will be.

From the work already done in Chapter 20, however, you know that this is *not* true of the price level. The price level next year, according to our theory, depends on our expectation of the price level next year. To see this more clearly, consider Figure 21.1.

The vertical axis of Figure 21.1 measures the price level, and the horizontal axis measures the level of output. The curve AD is the aggregate demand curve, and AS is the aggregate supply curve derived from the labour market equilibrium conditions and the production function. The curve EAS_0 is the expectations-augmented aggregate supply curve drawn for an expected price level equal to P_0^e. Notice that the curve EAS_0 cuts the aggregate supply curve AS at the price level P_0^e. If the expected price level is P_0^e, so that we are on EAS_0, and if aggregate demand is AD, then the intersection of EAS_0 and AD determines the actual price level as P_0 and the level of output as y_0. If, however, the expected price level was higher than P_0^e at, say, P_1^e, then the expectations-augmented aggregate supply curve would become the curve shown as EAS_1, which cuts the aggregate supply curve AS at P_1^e. In this case, with the aggregate demand curve held constant, the actual price level would be P_1 and the level of output y_1.

From this exercise you see that the actual price level is not independent

Figure 21.1
The effect of the
expected price level
on the actual price
level

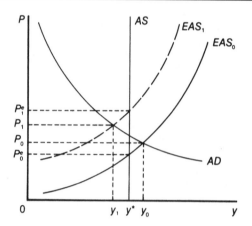

Aggregate demand is held constant at the curve *AD*. If the expected price level is P_0^e, then the expectations-augmented aggregate supply curve is EAS_0, and the actual price level is P_0 (and income y_0). If the expected price level was P_1^e, then the *EAS* curve would be EAS_1, and the actual price level would be P_1 (and income y_1). Thus holding everything else constant, the higher the expected price level, the higher the actual price level.

of the expected price level. All that has been done in Figure 21.1 is to consider two alternative expectations for the price level, with everything else the same. Reading off the equilibrium solutions shows that there is a direct relationship between the expected and actual price levels. The higher the expected price level, the higher is the actual price level, given constant aggregate demand.

How then can economic theory be used to determine the expected price level when the actual price level depends on the expected price level? It is rather like asking the question, 'how can we lift ourselves off the ground by pulling at our own boot laces'? We can pull as hard as we like, but no matter how hard we pull we will stay put on the ground and make no progress. It looks a little bit as if the same is true concerning the use of economic theory to generate a prediction about the expected price level. If the expectation of the price level is necessary for forecasting the actual price level, how can the predictions of economic theory be used to form an expectation about the price level? How can we get off the ground?

(ii) Working Out the Rational Expectation of the Price Level

It turns out that we can solve this problem. The way in which it is solved is illustrated in Figure 21.2. Remember that what we want to do is to form an expectation of the price level that will prevail in a *future* period, and we want that expectation to be the prediction of the theory of the actual price level that will prevail in that future period.

The starting point has to be to form an expectation of the position of

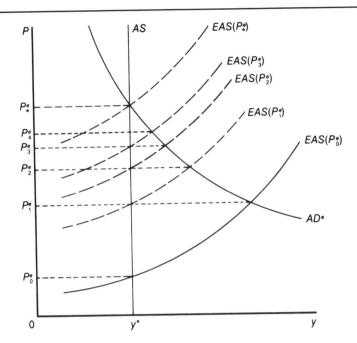

Figure 21.2
Calculating the
rational expectation
of the price level

The starting point for the calculation of the rational expectation of the price level is the formation of an expectation of aggregate demand. This requires that an expectation be formed of the values of the variables that determine aggregate demand as well as their influence upon demand. The curve AD^e denotes the expected aggregate demand curve. The rational expectation of the price level can be calculated by performing a conceptual experiment. Try P_0^e as the expected price level. This cannot be the rational expectation because the predicted price level P_1^e is different from that expected. The expected price level P_1^e, in turn, predicts P_2^e as the actual price level. The expected price P_2^e, in turn, predicts P_3^e, and so on. Only the expected price level P_*^e predicts an *actual* price level equal to P_*^e. This is the rational expectation of the price level. It is the price level at which the expected aggregate demand curve (AD^e) cuts the full-employment aggregate supply curve (AS).

the aggregate demand curve. Suppose that the aggregate demand curve that we expect in the following period is shown as AD^e. What this means is that we have formed an expectation of the value of the money supply, government expenditure, and taxes in the next period and have figured out what they imply for the position of the aggregate demand curve in the next period. Let us also put in the diagram the aggregate supply curve, the vertical line labelled AS, with the full-employment output level y^*.

Now let us perform a purely conceptual experiment. Let us suppose that we start out with an entirely arbitrary expectation of the price level for the next period equal to P_0^e, as shown on the vertical axis of Figure 21.2. We can now locate the expectations-augmented aggregate supply curve based on that expected price level – the curve shown as $EAS(P_0^e)$. If P_0^e is the expected price level, then we see, given our expectation aggregate demand for the next period, that we would be forecasting a price level which is higher than the expected price level P_0^e. In fact, we would be forecasting a price level equal to P_1^e. It is clear that we have a conflict. We started with a purely arbitrary expectation of P_0^e, and we see that if P_0^e is our expectation our theory does not lead to a prediction that the price level will in fact be the value that we are expecting. Therefore, the expectation P_0^e is not a rational expectation. It is not the conditional expectation of the price level that is generated by our theory.

Suppose, continuing to perform the conceptual experiment, we now try a different expected price level. In particular, let us try P_1^e as the expected price level. This is the price level predicted by the first experiment conducted. With this higher expected price level, we now have a different expectations-augmented aggregate supply curve, namely, $EAS(P_1^e)$. (Recall that EAS cuts AS at the expected price level.) This higher expected price level, P_1^e, generates, as we see, a forecast for the price level next period of P_2^e. That is the price level at which the expected aggregate demand curve cuts the expectations-augmented aggregate supply curve EAS_1. Again, we have a conflict. The forecast of our theory is different from the expectation P_1^e, which we arbitrarily assumed. Also, the prediction of the theory is higher than the assumed expectation.

Still continuing with the conceptual experiment, let us now try a yet higher expected price level, namely, P_2^e. With this expected price level, the expectations-augmented aggregate supply curve becomes $EAS(P_2^e)$. This curve cuts the expected aggregate demand curve at the price level P_3^e. Yet again there is a conflict.

You can now see what is happening. Each time we use a trial value for the expected price level, we generate a prediction for the actual price level that is higher than the expected price level. However, you will notice that the gap between the initially assumed expected price level and the conditional prediction of the price level is becoming smaller. Can we bring this process to an end? The answer is that we can, and we do this by expecting the price level generated by the intersection of the expected aggregate demand curve and the classical aggregate supply curve AS — P_*^e.

Suppose we started out with that expectation for the price level. The expectations-augmented aggregate supply curve that passes through the AS curve at that price level is $EAS(P_*^e)$. That is the expectations-augmented aggregate supply curve based on an expected price level of P_*^e. The theory now predicts that the price level in the next period will also be P_*^e. Notice that we are not saying that the price level next period will actually turn out to be P_*^e. Rather, we are saying that the prediction of our theory concerning the price level is that it will be P_*^e, given that our expectation is that the aggregate demand will be AD^e.

This leads to a very important proposition: the rational expectation of the price level is equal to its expected full-employment value. This expectation of the price level is the only one which is consistent with the prediction of our theory concerning what the price level will be. You should not confuse this proposition with the statement that 'everyone expects full employment always to prevail'. People know that random shocks hit the economy and that we may *never* have full employment. They do the best they can, however, before the event, to form an expectation about the price level that, should that expectation turn out to be correct, will ensure full employment.

You now know how to determine the rational expectation of the price level in the context of the new theories of aggregate supply and the theory of aggregate demand.

(iii) Individual Thought Experiments

The hypothesis about individual economic agents is that they behave on the basis of a subjective expectation of the price level that coincides with a conditional mathematical expectation of the price level, given the available information. That is, they behave on the basis of a rational expectation of the price level. That is not to say that everybody knows the same piece of economic theory that you know and that they are capable of calculating the rational expectation from this model or any other particular model. Rather, it is to say that people form their expectations of the price level in much the same way as the snooker player forms his expectation of the trajectories of the balls. Just as the snooker player follows instinctive and subjective calculations of the appropriate angles and forces and degrees of spin, so economic agents form their price expectations on the basis of ill-articulated thought processes. Not everyone is a good snooker player and not everyone is good at forming expectations of future levels of prices. Those who are good snooker players, however, typically play a lot and are paid for their skills. Likewise, those who are good at making price level expectations (and who approximate to making rational expectations) typically make the expectations upon which the rest of us base our behaviour. They also get paid for their special skills.

Summary

A. The Expected Price Level and Expected Rate of Inflation

The expected rate of inflation is equal to the expected price level minus the previous price level expressed as a percentage of the previous price level. It is not the percentage change in the expected price level but rather the expected percentage change in the price level.

B. *The Distinction between a Subjective Expectation and a Conditional Mathematical Expectation*

A subjective expectation is a vague intuitive feeling about the likely value or outcome of some future event. A conditional mathematical expectation is the true average value of the outcome of a future event conditional on (i.e. given) whatever are the known actual values of all the relevant variables.

C. *Why Wrong Expectations are Costly*

Actions are based on expectations, and wrong expectations lead to actions that may turn out to be inappropriate. If the price turns out to be higher than expected, real wages will be lower than expected, and people will have ended up doing more work and consuming less leisure than they would have like to have done had they known the correct real wage ahead of time. A symmetric cost applies to an error in the opposite direction. It is important to distinguish between being right every time (which in general is impossible) and being right on the average. The casino example in the text illustrates that distinction.

D. *Rational Expectation*

A rational expectation of a variable is a subjective expectation that *coincides* with the conditional mathematical expectation of that variable, given the available information.

E. *Rational Expectation of the Price Level*

The rational expectation of the price level is the prediction of the price level that is based on all the available information at the time at which the expectation is formed. This information includes the body of economic theory relevant for predicting the price level.

F. *How to Work Out the Rational Expectation of the Price Level*

The rational expectation of the price level is the price level at which the expected aggregate demand curve cuts the aggregate supply curve. (The conceptual experiment whereby this expectation is worked out is discussed in the section on rational expectations and illustrated in Figure 21.2 and should be thoroughly understood.)

Review Questions

1. What is the connection between the expected price level and expected rate of inflation?
2. Define a *subjective expectation*.
3. Define a *conditional mathematical expectation*.
4. Give some examples of the costs of wrong expectations.
5. Give the definition of a *rational expectation* and explain the relationship between a rational, a conditional mathematical, and a subjective expectation.
6. What are the key distinguishing features of a rational expectation?
7. What basic postulate concerning economic behaviour suggests that individuals would form expectations rationally?
8. Give some examples of economic agents (firms, individuals, etc.) who are 'in the business' of providing forecasts and selling other informational services. How do individuals benefit from these services?
9. What factors govern the degree to which the expectation of the price level affects aggregate supply? Under what circumstances will an increase, for example, in the expected price level have the greatest effect on aggregate supply?
10. What factors would you expect to determine the expected price level? How responsive might the expected price level be to observations on past prices?
11. Illustrate diagrammatically the derivation of the expected price level.
12. What relationship does the rational expectation of the price level bear to the full-employment price level?

Appendix: The Signal Extraction Problem

In Chapter 18 when we derived the new classical expectations-augmented aggregate supply curve, we supposed that people formed expectations about the average price level, ignoring the knowledge that is readily available to them concerning the price of the output of their own industry. In this chapter, we have calculated the rational expectation of the price level using only an expectation of the level of aggregate demand. We have again ignored any current information that might be available concerning the prices of some limited range of goods and services.

This Appendix extends those analyses to the case in which people do use currently available information concerning the price in their own sector of the economy.[3] The level of analysis in this Appendix is more demand-

---

3 The analysis presented in this Appendix is a simplified version of that developed by Robert E. Lucas Jr. in 'Some International Evidence on the Output–Inflation Tradeoff', *American Economic Review*, 63 (September 1973) pp.326–34.

ing than that in the text. To follow everything in this Appendix you need to know a small amount of statistics and calculus. You will probably, however, be able to obtain a good feel for what is going on even if you do not have that background.

The starting point is to imagine that the economy comprises many 'islands' of information. Individuals (firms and their employees) know the prices on their own island, but do not know the prices on any other. Imagine that the individual firms and workers on a given island that we will call island i observe their price to be P_i. Then let us suppose that everyone knows that the price on island i deviates from the economy average price, P, by a random amount, R_i, which itself is not observed. In other words, everyone knows that

$$P_i = P + R_i \tag{21A.1}$$

The price P_i on the left-hand side of Equation (21A.1) is observed, but the general price level, P, and the deviation of the individual price from the general price, R_i, are not observed.

Rational people would like to use the information that they have on P_i to make the best inference possible concerning P and R_i. Let us suppose that people know that on the average $R_i = 0$. Let us also suppose that people know that the relative price on island i deviates from the average price by a random amount that is drawn from a normal distribution that has a fixed amount of dispersion, which we will measure by its 'variance'. Let us denote the variance of the distribution of R_i as τ^2. A small value of τ^2 would mean that the relative price deviated very little from the economy average price (such as the curve labelled B in Figure 21A.1.)

Next, let us suppose that people have formed an expectation of the economy average price just prior to observing the price on their own island. Call that expectation P_0^e. You can imagine that P_0^e has been calculated in exactly the same way as was done in the body of this chapter.

Suppose that everyone knows from past experience that the actual economy average price deviates from the prior expectation by some random amount that we will call U (for unexpected price fluctuations), so that the actual price level is equal to the sum of the expected price level and the unanticipated component. That is

$$P = P_0^e + U \tag{21A.2}$$

This equation contains no variables that people observe, although P_0^e is known to them because it is their prior expectation. Let us suppose that U, the unexpected portion of prices, has an average value of zero, but it too is drawn from a normal distribution and that it has a dispersion measured by its variance which we will call σ^2.

An economy that has little variability of prices will have a small variance to the unexpected component of prices and will look like the distribution labelled A in Figure 21A.1. An economy that has very volatile or noisy

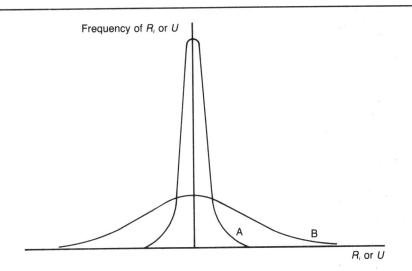

An economy that has low variability of prices will have a small variance to the unexpected component of prices (like the distribution labelled A) and an economy that has very volatile or noisy prices will have a large variance to the unexpected component of prices (like the distribution labelled B).

prices will be one in which people's expectations frequently deviate substantially from the actual level, so that the distribution of U will be like that labelled B in Figure 21A.1.

Now it is possible to combine Equations (21A.1) and (21A.2) by noticing that we can replace P in Equation (21A.1) with the right-hand side of Equation (21A.2). That gives

$$P_i = P_0^e + U + R_i \qquad (21A.3)$$

If we subtract P_0^e from both sides of Equation (21A.3), we obtain

$$P_i - P_0^e = U + R_i \qquad (21A.4)$$

Notice that what is on the left-hand side of this equation is something that is known to everyone on island i. It is the difference between the price that they have just observed on their own island and the price level that, prior to that observation, they expected would prevail on the average in the economy as a whole. They also know that $P_i - P_0^e$ is equal to the sum of two random variables — their error in forecasting correctly the economy-wide price level, U, and the random price on their own island relative to the economy average price, R_i.

Their task is to decompose the observed sum of these two variables into their separate components so that a better expectation of the economy-wide average price level may be calculated. It is important to notice that prior to observing the price on their own island, they expected that both U and R_i would be zero. Now that they know the sum of these two random variables, unless that sum happens to be zero (which is a possibility, although not a very likely one), they will now want to revise their estimate of the values of these variables.

We could say the same thing slightly differently. That is, the people on island i had a prior expectation about the economy-wide price level, P_0^e; they have now observed a new piece of information, the price on their own island; and they now want to use the new information to revise their expectation about the economy average price.

To make this revision they can use the so-called *Law of Recursive Projection*. The law is easily stated and intuitively appealing. In order to state the law, we need one small piece of notation. Let us agree that the expectation of a random variable (x) given the piece of information (I) will be called $E(x \mid I)$. We can use this notation to express the expectation of the price level that the people on island i originally had before observing the price on that island as

$$P_0^e = E(P \mid I_0)$$

Here, I_0 stands for all the information originally available before observing the price. What the people on island i are going to calculate is the expectation of the price level in the economy as a whole, given that initial information, I_0, and the observation of the price on island i. That is, they are going to calculate

$$E(P \mid I_0, P_i)$$

To perform that calculation, they are going to use the law of recursive projection, which is as follows:

$$E(P \mid I_0, P_i) = E(P \mid I_0) + E([P - E(P \mid I_0)] \mid [P_i - E(P_i \mid I_0)]) \quad (21A.5)$$

This looks much more formidable than it is. The left-hand side is simply the expectation that the agents want, namely their expectation of the economy average price level, given all the information that they now have available to them. The starting point for the calculation is given by the first term on the right-hand side of Equation (21A.5) and is nothing other than their original expectation. The second term on the right-hand side is the adjustment that is going to be made to the original expectation. It too is an expectation. It is the expectation of the error made in originally predicting the general price level,

$$P - E(P \mid I_0)$$

That expectation itself is going to be calculated, given the information

$$P_i - E(P_i \mid I_0)$$

What is this information? Evidently it is the difference between the actual price observed on island i and the expectation of what that price would be given the initial information. In other words, it is the error in forecasting the price on island i.

You can now interpret Equation (21A.5) in the following way. It says that the expectation of the general price level, given the original information and the new information about island i's price, will be equal to the original expectation made prior to knowing island i's price plus the expectation of the error made in forecasting the general price level, given knowledge of the error that has been made in forecasting the island's own price. If you inspect Equation (21A.2), you will see that

$$P - E(P|I_0) = U$$

Therefore, we can replace $P - E(P|I_0)$ with U in Equation (21A.5). Also, by examining Equation (21A.3), you will see that the expectation of the price on island i prior to observing that price must have been that it would be the same as the price in the economy as a whole, P_0^e, since the expectation of the random variables U and R_i are both zero. Thus, the difference between P_i now observed and its prior expectation must be the sum of the two random variables, $U + R_i$. We can use that sum therefore to replace $P_i - E(P_i)$ in Equation (21A.5). Making these adjustments gives

$$E(P|I_0, P_i) = P_0^e + E(U|U + R_i) \qquad (21A.6)$$

What the people on island i need to do then, according to Equation (21A.6), is to figure out as best they can the likely value of U, given that they know $U + R_i$.

A natural way to proceed is to imagine that some fraction of the sum of U and R_i is to be treated as being generated by U and one minus that fraction by R_i. Of course, if a particular fraction of $U + R_i$ is assigned to U, in general, an error will be made. Call the fraction in question a. Then the following equation can be defined to be true

$$U = a(U + R_i) + Error \qquad (21A.7)$$

What this says is that the random variable U that people would like to observe but have not observed is equal to some fraction a of the random variable $U + R_i$ that they have observed plus some error. Equivalently, we could say that the error that they will make in estimating the value of U as a fraction a of $U + R_i$ is given by

$$Error = U - a(U + R_i)$$

How can a value for a be chosen to make this into an operational estimation procedure? Clearly, the *expected* error is equal to zero since the expectation of U and R_i is equal to zero. Any value of a would deliver an expected error of zero. What people care about presumably is not just having an expected error of zero but in some sense making the least possible errors. Since positive errors and negative errors will cancel out, a useful way of giving weight to the errors is to consider the square of the error made. Taking the square of the error made renders all the errors positive and gives symmetric weights to both positive and negative errors. Let us square the error and see what we get. Evidently, squaring the error gives

$$Error^2 = U^2 + a^2(U^2 + R_i^2) - 2aU^2 - 2aUR_i$$

No one knows the actual error made at any point in time. It is possible, nevertheless, to calculate the *expected* squared error. Calculating the expectation of the squared error gives

$$E(Error^2) = E(U^2) + a^2E(U^2 + R_i^2) - 2aE(U^2) - 2aE(UR_i)$$

The expectation of $E(U^2)$ is the variance of the distribution of U which we are calling σ^2, and the expectation of $E(R_i^2)$ is simply the variance of the distribution of R_i that we are calling τ^2. The expectation of the product of U and R_i is, by assumption, zero. That is, we are supposing that the random shocks hitting the individual island's relative price are independent of the random shocks that hit the economy average price level. With that assumption, it is evident that

$$E(Error^2) = \sigma^2 + a^2(\sigma^2 + \tau^2) - 2a\sigma^2 \tag{21A.8}$$

What the people on island i would like to do is find a value for a that minimizes this expected squared error. In so doing they will reduce to a minimum the costs of having wrong expectations. They can do this by differentiating Equation (21A.8) with respect to a and setting the result equal to zero, and then finding the value of a that satisfies that equation. Evidently, the required value for a is

$$a = \frac{\sigma^2}{\sigma^2 + \tau^2}$$

This value can now be used to calculate the expectation of U, given an observation of $U + R_i$. That expectation is

$$E(U|U + R_i) = a(U + R_i)$$

But, we know from Equation (21A.2) that $U = P - P_0^e$ and from Equation (21A.3) that

$$(U + R_i) = (P_i - P_0^e)$$

Using these two equations enables us to write the expectation of the economy-wide price level on island i as

$$E(P|I_0, P_i) = P_0^e + a(P_i - P_0^e)$$

or, equivalently,

$$E(P|I_0, P_i) = aP_i + (1 - a)P_0^e \tag{21A.9}$$

You can now perhaps see more clearly why the calculation just performed is called the law of recursive projection. A projection is made

$- P_0^e$; new information arrives $- P_i$; the old projection and the new information are then combined to arrive at a new projection. The weights attached to the original belief $(1 - a)$ and the new information a depend on the quality of the new information.

Let us try to make the notion of the 'quality of the new information' a bit more precise. You know that

$$a = \frac{\sigma^2}{\sigma^2 + \tau^2} \qquad (21A.10)$$

and therefore that

$$1 - a = \frac{\tau^2}{\sigma^2 + \tau^2}.$$

You can think of σ^2 as measuring the amount of aggregate noise in the economy. A large value of σ^2 signifies a very noisy economy, that is, an economy whose price level is very hard to forecast. You can think of a large value of τ^2 as indicating considerable randomness in relative prices; that is, an economy in which relative prices are hard to forecast. Evidently, the bigger the value of σ^2, the bigger the value of a; and the bigger the value of τ^2, the smaller the value of a. Since a is the weight that we attach to the new information, we could equivalently say that the noisier is the aggregate price level, the bigger the weight we attach to the new piece of information; and the noisier are relative prices, the smaller the weight we attach to the new piece of information. This seems to be natural enough.

If the economy is subject to very large random fluctuations in the general level of prices, then an observation on one price that is very different from what was previously expected will be interpreted as indicating that what was previously expected was wrong and is in need of major revision. Thus, the weight attached to the new piece of information will be large. Conversely, if relative prices are exceedingly random, then observing the price on an individual island is not going to be giving very much information concerning movements in the average price level. Hence, a small weight would attach to the current piece of information in that case. The precise way in which aggregate noise and relative price noise are combined is given by Equation (21A.10) that defines a.

So far we have only talked about one island, island i. Let us suppose that the economy is made up of many such islands. Furthermore, suppose that all the islands are similar in the sense that they all are bombarded by random shocks to their own relative price that come from the same distribution as the one that we have just analysed. Different islands get different values of the random shock, R_i, at each moment in time, but they all come from the same distribution with the same amount of dispersion τ^2 around a zero mean. In this case, the expectations of the economy-wide price level on each island are going to be determined by an equation like (21A.9).

We may aggregate these price expectations over all the islands to arrive at the economy average beliefs about the price level. Those economy average beliefs are given by

$$P_t^e = aP_t + (1 - a)P_0^e \qquad (21A.11)$$

We are calling P_t^e the economy-average expected price level at time t. It will be a weighted average of the actual price level, P_t, and the prior belief about the expected price level, P_0^e. The weights will be the same as the weights attaching to each individual island's price expectations. It is important to remind yourself that no individual knows the economy-wide average price, P_t, and no individual knows the economy average of the expectations of the price level, P_t^e. On each island there is a different expected price level as described by Equation (21A.9). Equation (21A.11) is something that the economist analysing this economy can construct, but it is not something that people in the economy observe at the time at which the events that we are analysing are occurring.

Let us now see how these considerations affect the labour market and the *EAS* curve. Figure 21A.2 is the vehicle for our analysis.

First identify, in Figure 21A.2, Figure 21.2. Notice that the upward-sloping curve $n^s(P^e = P_0, a = 0)$ is the same curve as that shown in Figure 15.2 and the three demand curves are the same as those in Figure 15.2. The supply curve is drawn for a value of a equal to zero. In other words, everyone ignores the information contained in their own price and sticks to their prior expectation of the economy-wide average price regardless of what they observe.

Let us go to the opposite extreme. Imagine that $a = 1$. We will examine below precisely what that would mean. For the moment simply assume that a is 1, which means that in observing their own island price level, P_i, people assume that the entire movement in their own price level reflects a movement in the economy average price, and they revise their expectations accordingly. Thus, if the economy average price was P_1, moving the demand curve for labour to n_1^d, and if everyone on seeing their own island's price revises their expectation in accordance with their observed own price, the average expectation in the economy as a whole would move in exactly the same way as the actual price level had moved.

You know from the analysis lying behind Figure 18.1 that a change in the actual price level that is fully expected will move the supply and demand curves for labour in exactly the same way. The supply of labour curve, instead of staying at $n^s(P^e = P_0, a = 0)$, would now move up parallel to itself to pass through the point marked A. Conversely, if the price level was to fall to P_2, so that the demand for labour curve fell to n_2^d, and again if everyone seeing their own prices inferred that the economy average price had changed in exactly the same way as their own price had, the supply curve of labour would shift down parallel to itself to pass through the point D. In effect, the locus AED represents the effective supply curve of labour when a weight of one is placed on current

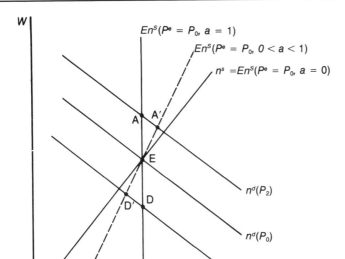

Figure 21A.2
Signal extraction and
the labour market

Consider what happens when the actual price level fluctuates between a low level of P_1 and an upper level of P_2. The demand for labour curve fluctuates between n_1^d and n_2^d. Individual prices fluctuate, and the amount of information extracted from those individual prices concerning the general price level affect the supply of labour. If individual prices fluctuate so widely around the average price level that they give no information, then the supply of labour curve remains fixed at $n^s(P^e = P_0, a = 0)$. If individual prices never deviated from the average price level, so that the observation of an individual price gives complete information about the aggregate price level, then the supply of labour curve becomes $n^s(P^e = P_0, a = 1)$. In general, observations of individual prices contain *some*, although incomplete information about the general price level. In this case, the labour supply curve is such as that labelled $n^s(P^e = P_0, 0 < a < 1)$. The more information that individual prices contain, the smaller are the fluctuations in employment and output, and the larger are the fluctuations in money wages and the price level.

---

price information that is observed. That vertical line is therefore labelled $n^s(P^e = P_0, a = 1)$. It is not really a labour supply curve, although it is the equilibrium supply locus that is obtained as a result of allowing price expectations to react to current actual prices with a coefficient of one.

It is easy to see that if a was something greater than zero but less than one, the labour supply curve would slope upwards and would lie somewhere between the original curve (for $a = 0$) and the vertical line (for $a = 1$). Passing through a point like A', there would be a supply of labour curve parallel to the curve $n^s(P^e = P_0, a = 0)$. That curve would have shifted upwards as a result of the revised price level expectations but not by as much as the actual price level had increased. Likewise, there would be a supply curve passing through the point D' that would represent a downward revision of price level expectations resulting from an actual price level of P_2.

You can see then that the slope of the effective labour supply curve depends on the extent to which people revise their current price level expectations in the light of their current observation of the particular price level in their own sector of the economy. The more those price expectations are revised, the closer is a to unity, and the steeper is the labour supply locus. The special case discussed in Chapter 18 is for $a = 0$.

Evidently, by tracing through the implications of this analysis in Figure 18.3, the slope of the EAS curve will also depend upon the value of a. The curve shown in Figure 18.3 is for $a = 0$. If $a = 1$, evidently the EAS curve would become the same curve as AS. It too would become vertical. For intermediate values of a, the EAS curve will lie somewhere between the AS and EAS curves in Figure 18.3 – being closer to the AS curve, the closer is a to one; and being closer to the EAS curve, the closer is a to zero.

We have seen that the value of a will in fact depend on how 'noisy' the economy is at the aggregate level and how big the relative price shocks are that hit the individual 'islands'. An economy that is subject to a large volume of aggregate noise, (large σ^2) will be one that has a high value of a. This means that such an economy will have a steep EAS curve compared with an economy that has a small amount of aggregate noise.

Relative price 'noise' works the other way. The bigger is the source of 'noise', (the larger is the value of τ^2), the smaller is a. Thus, an economy with highly variable relative prices will have a flat EAS curve compared with an economy that has a small amount of relative price noise.

The key conclusion of the analysis that we have just conducted is that the slope of the EAS curve is not independent of the amount and sources of noise in the economy.

22

Equilibrium in the Closed Economy

This chapter takes the next step in completing the rational expectations theory of the determination of the price level and real economic activity. From what you have learned so far you will almost be able to guess what this chapter has to deal with. You now know that the expected price level is determined by expected aggregate demand. You also know, from your analysis of the determination of output and prices with a fixed price level expectation, that the actual price level and output are determined where the actual demand curve cuts the expectations-augmented aggregate supply curve. All that now needs to be done, therefore, to complete our analysis is to explore the full implications of the distinction between expected (or anticipated) and unexpected (or unanticipated) changes in aggregate demand. By the time you have completed this chapter you will be able to:

(a) Explain the distinction between an anticipated and unanticipated change in aggregate demand.
(b) Explain how output, employment, unemployment, the real wage, money wage, and price level are affected by an *anticipated* change in aggregate demand.
(c) Explain how output, employment, unemployment, the real wage, money wage and the price level are affected by an *unanticipated* change in aggregate demand.

A. Anticipated and Unanticipated Changes in Aggregate Demand

(i) Definition of Anticipated and Unanticipated Changes in Aggregate Demand

The level of aggregate demand in any particular year (say, year t) may be thought of as being equal to aggregate demand in the previous year (year $t - 1$) plus the change in demand over the year (Δy_t^d). That is

$$y_t^d = y_{t-1} + \Delta y_t^d \tag{22.1}$$

Notice that since actual output is always equilibrium output, actual output at $t - 1$, y_{t-1}, is equal to y_{t-1}^d (aggregate demand at time $t - 1$). As soon as time $t - 1$ is past, the value of output at that date becomes known. (Actually it's a little bit strong to say that this becomes known *as soon as* the time is past. It takes a short while for the data to be accumulated.) The level of aggregate demand for time t, however, will not be known. Since rational economic agents need to form an expectation of the price level, and since the price level depends upon the level of aggregate demand, it is necessary, in order to form a rational expectation of the price level, to form a rational expectation of the level of aggregate demand. It is necessary, therefore, to forecast the change in aggregate demand so that its future value may be predicted.

The predicted component of the change in aggregate demand is referred to as the *anticipated change* in aggregate demand, and the unpredicted component is known as the *unanticipated change* in aggregate demand.

The actual change in aggregate demand is made up of these two components. That is

$$\Delta y_t^d = \Delta y_t^{de} + \Delta y_t^{du} \tag{22.2}$$

The superscript e denotes the expected or anticipated part of the change in aggregate demand, and the superscript u, the unanticipated or unexpected part. There is not, in general, any reason why the expected and unexpected components of the change in aggregate demand should be of the same sign. They may be, in which case they will each be a fraction of the actual change. It is possible, nevertheless, for the anticipated change to be greater than the actual change so that the unexpected change is negative.

Four examples give the range of possibilities. They are set out in Table 22.1. The first example is of a correctly anticipated change in aggregate demand. The actual change is 100, and the expected change is 100. The second example is one in which the change in aggregate demand is entirely unanticipated. The expected change is 0, but the actual change is 100. The third example is one in which the actual change in aggregate demand is divided between an anticipated and unanticipated component. This example may be thought of as the most likely case. In the particular example, the division is 50/50, although in general it may not be so evenly split. The fourth and final example is one in which the actual change is

Table 22.1 **Examples of divisions of the actual change in aggregate demand between anticipated and unanticipated changes**

Example	Δy_t^d	=	Δy_t^{de}	+	Δy_t^{du}
1	100	=	100	+	0
2	100	=	0	+	100
3	100	=	50	+	50
4	100	=	200	−	100

less than the anticipated change, so that there is a negative unexpected component. (These are all examples of a rise in aggregate demand. Aggregate demand could actually fall and be expected to fall.)

(ii) Measurement of the Anticipated and Unanticipated Changes in Aggregate Demand

In order actually to measure the anticipated and unanticipated changes in aggregate demand, it is necessary to divide the changes in the variables that determine aggregate demand into their anticipated and unanticipated components. One such variable is the change in the money supply.

What determines the division of the actual change in the money supply between its anticipated and unanticipated components? The answer to this question is not a settled matter. Robert Barro[1] of Harvard University and Cliff Attfield, D. Demery, and Nigel Duck[2] of the University of Bristol have conducted the pioneering studies on this question, using US and UK money supply data respectively. They have attempted to decompose the actual money supply growth into its anticipated and unanticipated components. However, this work is by no means uncontroversial, and matters are not yet settled.

The way in which this research has proceeded is to search for statistical regularities in the past history of money supply growth and then to suppose that rational agents would exploit those statistical regularities in forming a rational expectation of money supply growth. Specifically, Attfield, Demery and Duck discovered that the money supply growth rate tends to be faster:

1. The faster the money supply growth has been in the preceding year; and
2. The bigger is the real value of the central government borrowing requirement.

---

1 The most comprehensive account of Barro's work is Robert J. Barro and Mark Rush, 'Unanticipated Money and Economic Activity', Ch. 2 in Stanley Fischer, (ed.), *Rational Expectations and Economic Policy*, National Bureau of Economic Research Conference Report (Chicago and London: University of Chicago Press, 1980).
2 An account of the work on the United Kingdom may be found in C.L.F. Attfield, D. Demery and N.W. Duck, 'A Quarterly Model of Unanticipated Monetary Growth, Output and the Price Level in the UK: 1963–1978', *Journal of Monetary Economics* Vol. 8, No. 3 (November 1981) pp.331–50.

These findings are more than statistical patterns. They also make good intuitive sense. The proposition that money supply growth will be faster, the faster the previous two years' money supply growth has been, reflects the fact that the Bank of England exhibits some inertia in its decision making. It does not change course suddenly and rapidly in a zigzag fashion; rather, it changes course gradually. This means that the behaviour of the Bank can, on the average, be described by a version of the formula that says that tomorrow will be very much like today.

The proposition that money supply growth increases when central government borrowing requirement increases and decreases when central government borrowing requirement decreases is a natural consequence of the fact that money printing is a form of taxation. When there is a burst of government expenditure or a sharp drop in government expenditure, it is much easier to vary the rate at which money is printed than it is to vary such things as, for example, VAT, income tax, or capital gains tax. Hence, the efficient financing of government expenditure entails varying the growth rate of the money supply to cover unusually large changes in expenditure.

Attfield, Demery and Duck were unable to find any systematic responsiveness of the money supply to other variables such as, for example, the previous year's unemployment, output growth or inflation. This suggests that, despite widespread belief that governments can manipulate the economy by activist monetary policies, they have not, in the UK at least, done so. The Keynesian idea that stimulating demand in times of depression and holding demand back in times of boom will moderate the business cycle does not seem to have affected UK monetary policy action.

The propositions just discussed can be given a precise numerical form by the use of statistical techniques that lie outside the scope of this book. From those statistical exercises it is possible to make a forecast of what the money supply will be in the subsequent year (or in distant future years for that matter) conditional on information about the previous year's money supply growth, and the behaviour of the central government borrowing requirement. Such a forecast becomes the anticipated change in the money supply. A movement in the actual money supply which is different from the calculated anticipated change becomes the calculated value of the unanticipated change in the money supply.

The above discussion concerning the decomposition of changes in the money supply into anticipated and unanticipated components applies in principle to changes in government expenditure, taxes, or any other variables which influence aggregate demand.

Now that the distinction between anticipated and unanticipated changes in aggregate demand is understood, and we have seen how in practice it is possible to distinguish between them, it will be useful to go on to analyse the way in which these two components of the change in aggregate demand influence the key macroeconomic variables.

B. Effects of an Anticipated Change in the Aggregate Demand

The effects of an anticipated change in aggregate demand are analysed first. This is an extreme case, but it is the clearest and simplest case with which to begin.

Figure 22.1 illustrates the analysis. Suppose that you are looking at an economy at a particular time, called year 0. At that time the money supply is M_0, and aggregate demand is the curve labelled AD_0. Suppose that year 0 is one of full-employment equilibrium. This assumption simply gives us a convenient reference point. With full-employment equilibrium, the expectations-augmented aggregate supply curve, the aggregate supply curve, and the aggregate demand curve all intersect at the same point. Thus, the actual price level P_0 and the expected price level P_0^e are equal. (If you do not understand why this is so, review Chapter 18.)

Now imagine that you are looking forward to the next year, year 1, and are trying to form a view about the price level in that year. Suppose that you expect aggregate demand to rise, such that expected aggregate demand is the curve labelled AD_1. You can now calculate the rational expectation of the price level. It is P_1^e. (If you are not sure as to the reason for that, check back to Chapter 21, Figure 21.2.) The expected price level P_1^e is the only expected price level which is consistent with the prediction of this model, given that expected aggregate demand is AD_1^e. Thus, the

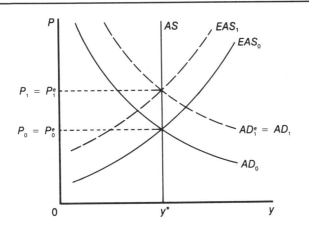

Figure 22.1
The effect of an anticipated change in aggregate demand on the price level and output

The economy is initially at full-employment equilibrium where AD_0 intersects EAS_0 at output y^* and price level P_0. Aggregate demand increases in an anticipated way from AD_0 to $AD_1(= AD_1^e)$. The expected price level rises to P_1^e so that the expectations-augmented aggregate supply curve shifts to become EAS_1. The actual price level is P_1 and output is y^*. An anticipated rise in aggregate demand raises the price level, but leaves output unaffected.

expectations-augmented aggregated supply curve for year 1 is the curve EAS_1.

Next, suppose that aggregate demand actually increases by exactly the amount expected, so that the aggregate demand change is anticipated. This means that the *actual* aggregate demand curve is the same as the *expected* aggregate demand curve. To remind you of this, the aggregate demand curve has been labelled twice as $AD_1 = AD_1^e$.

What is the new equilibrium output and price level in this economy? Recall that equilibrium occurs at the point at which the aggregate demand curve cuts the expectations-augmented aggregate supply curve. The expectations-augmented aggregate supply curve is EAS_1 — the aggregate supply curve when the expected price level is P_1^e, based on the expected aggregate demand curve AD_1^e. You can now read off the new equilibrium. The aggregate demand curve AD_1 cuts the expectations-augmented aggregate supply curve EAS_1 at full-employment output y^* and the price level P_1. Thus the price level rises, and output remains unchanged.

This is the first proposition concerning the effect of an anticipated change in aggregate demand. An anticipated rise in aggregate demand raises the price level and leaves output unchanged.

What happens to the remaining variables in the economy? Specifically, what happens to employment, unemployment, the real wage, and money wage?

You will recall that the diagram displayed in Figure 22.1 was derived originally (in Chapter 20) from an analysis of the labour market and the production function. It is convenient now to recall Figure 20.2. (Refresh your memory by turning back to it.) Starting from the fact that output has not changed, you can travel back (reversing the arrows in Figure 20.2) through the production function and immediately establish that the level of employment has not changed. If the level of employment has not changed, then firms must be willingly hiring the same quantity of labour as they were hiring before. This immediately implies that the real wage has not changed. Furthermore, if the level of employment has not changed, the level of unemployment is also unchanged — it remains at the natural unemployment rate. Finally, since the real wage has not changed, but the price level has risen, the money wage rate must also have risen and by the same percentage amount as the price level has risen.

It is now possible to summarize all the consequences of an anticipated change in the aggregate demand: an anticipated change in aggregate demand changes the price level and the money wage by the same percentage amount as each other. It has no effects on any of the real variables in the economy, i.e. on output, employment, unemployment and the real wage.

Let us now go on to analyse the opposite extreme.

C. Effects of an Unanticipated Change in Aggregate Demand

Figure 22.2 will be used to illustrate the effects on the price level and output of an unanticipated change in aggregate demand. Suppose that the economy is initially in exactly the same situation as that depicted in Figure 22.1 for year 0. That is, the aggregate demand curve is AD_0, and the expectations-augmented aggregate supply curve is EAS_0. These curves intersect at the price level P_0, which is also the expected price level P_0^e. Output is at the full-employment level, y^*.

Unlike the previous example, suppose that everyone expects that in year 1 aggregate demand will remain at AD_0. This aggregate demand curve is marked $AD_0 = AD_1^e$ to remind you that aggregate demand expected in year 1 is the same as actual aggregate demand in year 0. Thus, the rational expectation of the price level in year 1, P_1^e, remains at P_0^e. The expectations-augmented aggregate supply curve for year 1, marked EAS_1, is the same as EAS_0.

Now suppose that instead of remaining constant at AD_0, aggregate demand actually rises in year 1 to AD_1. You can read off the equilibrium output and price level in year 1, given that the expected price level P_1^e is constant but that actual aggregate demand has increased above that expected. Equilibrium is at the point at which the expectations-augmented

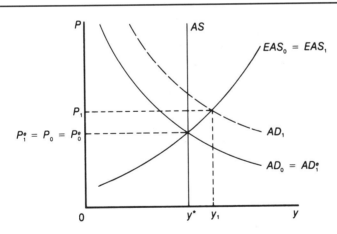

Figure 22.2
The effect of an unanticipated change in aggregate demand on the price level

An initial equilibrium at P_0 and y^* is disturbed by an unanticipated shift in aggregate demand to AD_1. The expectations-augmented aggregate supply curve remains fixed at EAS_0. The new equilibrium price level and output are where the new aggregate demand curve cuts the original EAS curve at P_1, y_1. An unanticipated rise in aggregate demand raises output and the price level, but the percentage rise in the price level is less than that in aggregate demand.

aggregate supply curve EAS_1 cuts the *actual* aggregate demand curve AD_1. The price level and output are P_1 and y_1 respectively.

Notice that in this experiment we have an *unanticipated rise* in aggregate demand. Anticipated aggregate demand remains constant, but actual aggregate demand rises, so the unanticipated rise in aggregate demand is exactly equal to the actual rise in aggregate demand.

The effects of this unanticipated rise in aggregate demand are as follows: the price level is above its expected level and output is above full-employment output. The percentage by which the price level rises above its expected level is less than the percentage unanticipated rise in aggregate demand because part of the unanticipated rise in aggregate demand raises real income, and part of it raises the price level. Any given percentage unanticipated rise in aggregate demand results in the combination of a rise in output and a rise in the price level, which, in percentage terms, sum to the percentage change in aggregate demand. How much of the unanticipated aggregate demand rise goes into output and how much into the price level depends on the steepness of the EAS curve. A very steep EAS curve will result in a large price level and small output rise. A flat EAS curve will produce the reverse allocation of the effects of the unanticipated demand increase with a large output rise and a small price rise.

What are the effects on the other variables in the economy? (Again recall Figure 20.2.) Since you know from Figure 22.2 that output has risen, you also know that employment has risen. How does this come about? For employment to have increased there must have been a rise in the demand for labour. You can easily verify that this indeed has happened. The unanticipated rise in the price level has produced an upward shift in the demand for labour curve, but since the expected price level is constant, there has been no rise in the position of the supply of labour curve. As a result, the money wage has increased. Its increase, however, is less than the percentage rise in prices, so that the real wage has fallen, and therefore firms are employing more labour. With a rise in the money wage but no change in the expected price level, the expected real wage has increased, and thus households slide along their labour supply curve and willingly supply the additional labour demanded.

It is now possible to summarize the effects of an unanticipated change in aggregate demand: An unanticipated rise in aggregate demand raises the price level, but by a smaller percentage amount than the unanticipated rise in aggregate demand. It also produces a rise in the money wage, but by an even smaller percentage than the percentage rise in the price level. It causes a fall in the real wage and a fall in unemployment below the natural rate. It also raises employment and output to above their full-employment levels. The above can be readily restated for an unanticipated fall in the money supply.

Summary

A. Anticipated and Unanticipated Changes in Aggregate Demand

The change in aggregate demand may be decomposed into its anticipated or expected component and its unanticipated or unexpected component. The anticipated change in aggregate demand may be greater or smaller than the 'actual change. When the anticipated change is exactly the same as the actual change we speak of an anticipated change in aggregate demand. The unanticipated change in aggregate demand is the difference between the actual and anticipated changes. Since the change in actual aggregate demand is determined by changes in the money supply, government spending, and taxes, decomposing the change in aggregate demand into its expected and unexpected components involves decomposing the changes in these determinants of aggregate demand into their anticipated and unanticipated components.

B. Effects of an Anticipated Change in Aggregate Demand

An anticipated change in aggregate demand has the effect of changing the price level and the money wage by exactly the same percentage amount as each other and by the same percentage as the rise in aggregate demand. It has no effects on any of the real variables. Specificically, it has no effect on output, employment, unemployment, or the real wage.

C. Effects of an Unanticipated Change in Aggregate Demand

An unanticipated change in aggregate demand has both real and nominal effects. It raises the price level, but by a smaller percentage amount than the unanticipated rise in aggregate demand, and it raises the money wage by an even smaller percentage amount than it raises the price level. Thus it lowers the real wage, raises employment, raises output, and lowers unemployment.

Review Questions

1. What is the distinction between anticipated and unanticipated changes in aggregate demand?
2. What factors determine anticipated changes in aggregate demand?

3. What factors determine unanticipated changes in aggregate demand?
4. In what ways do the effects of anticipated changes in the money supply differ from the effects of unanticipated changes in the money supply?
5. Illustrate diagrammatically the effects of:

    (a) an anticipated increase in the money stock;
    (b) an unanticipated increase in the money stock;
    (c) an increase in the money supply — part of which was anticipated and part of which was unanticipated;
    (d) an anticipated rise in the money stock which turns out to be the opposite of the actual change.

6. 'Whereas an unanticipated increase in the money supply lowers the real wage rate paid by firms, it increases the perceived real wage rate received by employees'. Is this statement true or false? Explain.
7. 'Only anticipated increases in the price level have output effects, since in order for producers to increase production during times of high prices, such increases must be anticipated'. Within the context of the model we have developed, explain what is wrong with this statement.

Appendix: The Algebra of Rational Expectations Equilibrium

This Appendix sets out the simple algebra of a rational expectations equilibrium model. It presents the simplest example of a rational expectations equilibrium so that you may see the connection between the solution to this model and the solution of the fixed price *IS–LM* model of aggregate demand. There is nothing of substance in this Appendix that does not appear in the preceding chapters. As with the other algebraic appendices, if you feel comfortable with this kind of treatment, you will probably find this a convenient, compact summary of the material presented in words and diagrams in the text of the chapter.

The starting point is the *IS–LM* theory of aggregate demand. Recall, or check back if necessary to Equation (14A.11) from the Appendix to Chapter 14, that the level of real income as determined in the *IS–LM* model is:

$$y = \frac{a + i_0 + g - bt + \dfrac{h}{l}\left(\dfrac{M}{P_0} - m_0\right)}{1 - b + kh/l} \tag{22A.1}$$

This is the level of real income (y) if the price level is *fixed* at P_0. You may think of Equation (22A.1) as determining *aggregate demand* by allowing the price level to *vary*. The level of real income at each price level (P) is the level of aggregate demand (y^d). To emphasize this, Equation (22A.1) is modified as follows:

$$y^d = \frac{a + i_0 + g - bt + \dfrac{h}{l}\left(\dfrac{M}{P} - m_0\right)}{1 - b + kh/l} \tag{22A.2}$$

Notice that the difference between Equations (22A.1) and (22A.2) is that Equation (22A.1) tells us the actual level of y for a given level of P (that, is P_0), whereas (22A.2) tells us what the level of aggregate demand (y^d) will be as the price level (P) varies.

We can rewrite Equation (22A.2) with a different emphasis as

$$y^d = \left[\frac{a + i_0 + g - bt - (h/l)m_0}{1 - b + kh/l}\right]$$

$$+ \left[\frac{(h/l)}{1 - b + kh/l}\right]\left(\frac{M}{P}\right) \tag{22A.3}$$

Calling m the logarithm of M and p the logarithm of P, we may write an approximation to the above as

$$y_t^d = \alpha_t + \beta(m_t - p_t), \qquad \beta > 0 \tag{22A.4}$$

In Equation (22A.4), α represents the first term in brackets in Equation (22A.3), and $\beta(m - p_t)$ is a logarithmic approximation to the second term. The subscript t is added to each variable in Equation (22A.4) to remind us that these magnitudes vary over time. Thus, t represents a given point in time. Evidently, α stands for all the things that cause aggregate demand to vary, other than the real money supply. It incorporates, therefore, government expenditure, taxes, and any shifts in the investment function or the demand for money function. The money supply (m) and the price level (p) are expressed as logarithms, so that $m - p$ is the same as $\log(M/P)$. (This formulation, which is linear in the logarithm of real money balances rather than the level of real money balances, makes the explicit calculation of expectations more straightforward.) The parameter β is the multiplier effect of a change in the logarithm of real money balances on aggregate demand.

We can represent the expectations-augmented aggregate supply curve in equation form as:

$$y_t^s = y^* + \gamma(p_t - p_t^e), \qquad \gamma > 0 \tag{22A.5}$$

where y^* represents full-employment output and p and p^e are the logarithms of the actual and expected price level, respectively. This is just a convenient translation into equation form of what you already know. To convince yourself of this, notice first that if the price level was equal to its expected value ($p = p^e$), then aggregate supply would be equal to full-employment aggregate supply y^*. As the actual price level exceeds the expected price level, so output rises above y^*. The positive parameter γ captures this. The only difference (in this simple treatment) between the new classical and new Keynesian approaches to the aggregate supply curve is that the value of γ would be different in the two theories — because the new Keynesian aggregate supply curve is flatter than the new classical curve, the new Keynesian would be represented by a larger γ.

Next, equilibrium prevails, in the sense that aggregate supply equals aggregate demand, and actual output y is also equal to demand and supply. We can write this as two equations. That is

$$y_t = y_t^d = y_t^s \tag{22A.6}$$

The first step in finding the rational expectations equilibrium is to calculate the expected values of output and prices, *given* the expected values of α and m. (A full treatment would also have an explicit theory for the determination of α and m. We will not make that extension here.) Calculating the expected values of y and p, given the expected values of α and m, simply involves taking the expectations of Equations (22A.4) and (22A.5) and using the fact that actual output is the same as aggregate demand and supply. Letting the superscript e stand for the expected value of a variable, you can immediately see that this implies

$$y_t^e = \alpha_t^e + \beta(m_t^e - p_t^e) \tag{22A.7}$$

and

$$y_t^e = y^* \tag{22A.8}$$

Equation (22A.7) follows directly from Equation (22A.4). If Equation (22A.4) describes what determines the actual level of aggregate output demanded and if demand equals actual output, then expected output must be equal to the expected value of α plus β times the expected value of real balances. That is all that Equation (22A.1) says.

Equation (22A.8) follows directly from Equation (22A.5). It says what you already know, namely, that expected output is equal to full-employment output since the expected price level is the rational expectation. That is, p_t^e is the same thing as the expectation of p_t, and so the second term in Equation (22A.5) is expected to be zero.

You can now solve Equations (22A.7) and (22A.8) for the price level. Substitute Equation (22A.8) into Equation (22A.7) and rearrange to give

$$p_t^e = m_t^e - \frac{1}{\beta}(y^* - \alpha_t^e) \tag{22A.9}$$

Recall that p and m are logarithms, so that this says that the expected price level is proportional to the expected money supply.

To calculate the actual output and price level, first of all, subtract Equation (22A.7) from (22A.4) and Equation (22A.9) from (22A.5). The results are

$$y_t^d - y^* = (\alpha_t - \alpha_t^e) + \beta(m_t - m_t^e) - \beta(p_t - p_t^e) \tag{22A.10}$$

$$y_t^s - y^* = \gamma(p_t - p_t^e) \tag{22A.11}$$

Equation (22A.10) says that aggregate demand deviates from its full-employment level by the amount that α deviates from its expected level, plus the amount that the money stock deviates from its expected level, multiplied by the parameter β, minus the amount by which the price level deviates from its expected level, multiplied by the same parameter β. It is, in terms of the concepts discussed in the chapter, the unexpected component of aggregate demand.

Equation (22A.11), in effect, is simply a rearrangement of Equation (22A.5). It says that deviations of aggregate supply from its full-employment level is proportional to deviations of the price level from its expectation.

We may now solve these two Equations (22A.10) and (22A.11) for the *actual* output and price level. Using Equations (22A.10) and (22A.11) with (22A.6), these solutions are

$$y_t = y^* + \frac{\gamma}{\gamma + \beta} [\alpha_t - \alpha_t^e + \beta(m_t - m_t^e)] \tag{22A.12}$$

and

$$p_t = m_t^e - \frac{1}{\beta} (y^* - \alpha_t^e) + \frac{1}{\gamma + \beta} [\alpha_t - \alpha_t^e + \beta(m_t - m_t^e)] \tag{22A.13}$$

The output equation says that output deviates from its full-employment level by an amount that depends on the unexpected components of α and the money supply. The price level deviates from its expected level — the first two terms in Equation (22A.13) — by an amount that depends on the deviations of α and the money supply from their expected levels.

Thus, you can see that it is only unanticipated shifts in aggregate demand that affect output, and it is both the anticipated and unanticipated shifts in aggregate demand that affect the price level. The multipliers of the *IS–LM* analysis tell us about the distance of the horizontal shift.of the aggregate demand curve. Equations (22A.12) and (22A.13) tell us that, to the extent that that horizontal shift is anticipated, it does nothing but raise the price level. To the extent that it is unanticipated, it raises both output and the price level and distributes its effects between output and prices in accordance with the parameter γ, the slope of the *EAS* curve. You can see, as a matter of interest, that if γ was infinitely big, the effect of an unanticipated shift in aggregate demand would be exactly the same as the *IS–LM* model says, and it would have no effect on prices. You can see this immediately for the price level in Equation (22A.13). For output, divide the top and bottom of $\gamma/(\gamma + \beta)$ by γ to give $1/[1 + (\beta/\gamma)]$. You can now see that as γ approaches ∞, so $1/[1 + (\beta/\gamma)]$ approaches 1, so that Equation (22A.12) becomes the *IS–LM* solution for income.

23

Equilibrium in the Open Economy

You are now ready to bring together the various components of the open economy and study equilibrium. You will study the determination of output, the price level, interest rates, the balance of payments and the foreign exchange rate and examine how these variables are affected by domestic and foreign shocks that are both anticipated and unanticipated.

We will tackle these problems in two stages much as we did when studying the closed economy. The first tasks in this chapter will take you through some analysis of the effects of expected or anticipated changes in variables so that we will be analysing an economy that remains at full employment. We will then go on to the more complicated analysis of the effects of unanticipated disturbances to the economy.

By the time you have completed this chapter you will be able to:

(a) Explain how aggregate demand 'surprises' affect output, the price level and the balance of payments with a fixed exchange rate regime.

(b) Explain how aggregate demand 'surprises' affect output, the price level and the exchange rate in a flexible exchange rate regime.

(c) Explain the effects of an unanticipated real exchange rate shock on output, the price level and the exchange rate in a flexible exchange rate regime.

A. Aggregate Demand Shocks with a Fixed Exchange Rate

The theory of aggregate demand under fixed exchange rates was generated in Chapter 16 and is summarized in Figure 16.8. This aggregate demand curve may be used in an analogous way to the closed economy aggregate demand analysis to determine the rational expectation of the price level and, therefore, the position of the expectations-augmented aggregate supply curve. Figure 23.1 illustrates the analysis.

In this figure, the aggregate supply curve is shown as AS at the output level y^*. The aggregate demand curve drawn for the expected values of the variables that determine its position, $AD^e(P^e_f, y^e_f, r^e_f, E^e, g^e, t^e)$, is the aggregate demand curve that is expected on the basis of expectations of the exogenous variables that influence aggregate demand and given that the economy is operating under fixed exchange rates. The rational expectation of price level P^e is determined where this expected aggregate demand curve intersects the AS curve. The expectations-augmented aggregate supply curve passes through that point and is the upward-sloping curve EAS. The EAS curve for the open economy is identical to that for the closed economy. You may think of this EAS curve as having been generated by the new classical theory of aggregate supply (Chapter 18) or the new Keynesian theory (Chapter 19).

If the actual aggregate demand curve is in exactly the same position

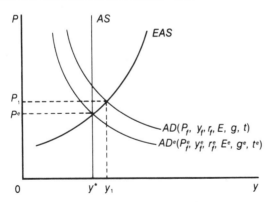

Figure 23.1
Equilibrium with a fixed exchange rate

With fixed exchange rates, the expected price level is determined where the expected aggregate demand curve cuts the aggregate supply curve. This equilibrium depends on the expected values of the foreign price level, real income and interest rates, and on the exchange rate and domestic fiscal policy variables. Actual output and prices are determined where the actual aggregate demand curve cuts the expectations-augmented aggregate supply curve. An anticipated change in any of the variables that determine aggregate demand will have price level effects only, and an unanticipated change will affect both output and prices.

as the expected aggregate demand curve, then output and prices will be determined at their full-employment and expected levels respectively. The balance of payments will be in equilibrium, with perfect capital mobility ensuring a capital account surplus that exactly matches whatever the current account deficit is (or capital account deficit matching the current account surplus).

If, however, the actual values of the variables that determine aggregate demand turn out to be different from their expected values, so that the actual aggregate demand curve is in a different position, say, at $AD(P_f, y_f, r_f, E, g, t)$, then actual output and the price level are determined where that actual demand curve cuts the expectations-augmented aggregate supply curve at (y_1, P_1). This equilibrium is exactly the same as in the closed economy except that the factors that shift the aggregate demand curve in this case are different from those responsible for shifts in the closed economy aggregate demand curve. Random fluctuations in actual demand around its expected value generate procyclical price level and output co-movements.

The balance of payments will be in equilibrium at the higher price and output levels, but the mix between the current account and capital account will be different from the full-employment mix. With a fixed exchange rate and fixed world price level, the higher domestic price level will mean that the real exchange rate will have fallen, so that imports will rise and exports will fall. The higher real income level will also raise imports. Thus, the current account of the balance of payments will move into a smaller surplus or larger deficit. This change in the current account will be matched by an equal, but opposite, change in the capital account.

That is all there is to the determination of output, the price level, and the balance of payments in a fixed exchange rate economy with perfect capital mobility. As in the closed economy case, anticipated changes in aggregate demand will have price level effects only, and unanticipated changes will have the effects traced out in Figure 23.2. Changes that are partly anticipated and partly not anticipated will have effects that combine the effects shown in Figure 23.2 with the pure price level adjustment that would occur in the anticipated case. Notice that the domestic economy is not immune from shocks occurring in the rest of the world. Other things being equal, an anticipated change in the foreign price level or an anticipated devaluation of the currency will raise the domestic price level by the same percentage amount. Fluctuations in world output, the price level, and interest rates will lead to fluctuations in domestic aggregate demand, and if they are not anticipated, will lead to fluctuations in output in the domestic economy that are procyclical with fluctuations in the world economy.

Let us now go on to consider the more difficult, but perhaps more interesting, case of flexible exchange rates.

B. Aggregate Demand Shocks with a Flexible Exchange Rate

We will proceed in a similar way in analysing the flexible exchange rate economy as we did with the fixed exchange rate. The first task is to determine the rational expectation of the price level and, therefore, the position of the expectations-augmented aggregate supply curve. This case is not as straightforward as that for a fixed exchange rate. The reason is that the exchange rate contains information that it will be rational for people to use in forming their expectation of the price level. There is a fundamental informational difference between a fixed exchange rate and flexible exchange rate economy. Under fixed exchange rates, it is the stock of foreign exchange reserves that adjusts on a daily basis to random shocks that hit the economy. These movements in the stock of foreign exchange reserves are not continuously reported and are unknown outside the central bank. In a flexible exchange rate economy, the exchange rate itself is constantly adjusting to reflect the random forces that influence the economy and is available for all to see at almost zero cost. There is, therefore, more widespread information available in a flexible exchange rate economy than in a fixed exchange rate economy, and that information may be used in order to make inferences about the shocks that are hitting the economy. Making complete sense of this will take a paragraph or two.

(i) Pre-trading Expectations

Let us begin by imagining that we are at the beginning of a trading period before any trading has begun. All the markets — labour, money, goods, and foreign exchange — are not yet open for business. We are standing at the beginning of the business 'day' and trying to form expectations about all the variables in the economy. Figure 23.2 will be used to analyse this situation.

Frames (a) and (b) of Figure 23.2 are exactly the same as frames (b) and (c) of Figure 23.1. The top left frame of Figure 23.2 is simply a device for turning the price level through 90° so as to read the same price level on the horizontal axis as we are reading on the vertical axis. Frame (c) is a device for determining the exchange rate. The way to read this is as follows: recall that the real exchange rate θ, is defined as

$$\theta = EP_f/P$$

Multiply both sides of this equation by P, so that you obtain

$$\theta P = EP_f$$

**Figure 23.2
Rational expectations
at the commence-
ment of trading**

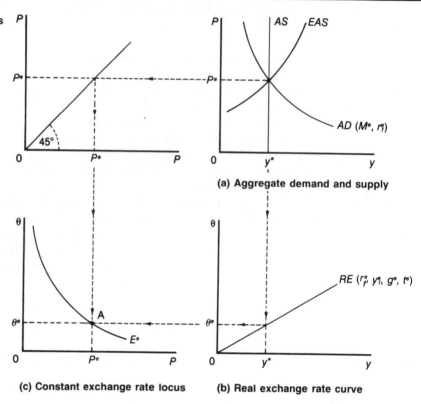

(a) Aggregate demand and supply

(c) Constant exchange rate locus   (b) Real exchange rate curve

Before any information is revealed, the rational expectation of the price level, the (nominal)
exchange rate and the real exchange rate can be calculated. Where the expected
aggregate demand curve (based on expected money supply and expected foreign interest rates) cuts the AS curve, determines the expected price level P^e. Expected income
is y^*, and the expected real exchange rate is θ^e. There will be one (nominal) exchange
rate only, E^e, that is compatible with the expected price level and the expected real
exchange rate. This exchange rate is shown by the value of the constant exchange
rate locus through at point A in frame (c).

Now the foreign price level P_f is being treated as fixed, and if we hold
the exchange rate constant, EP_f will be constant. This equation says that
θP (the real exchange rate multiplied by the domestic price level) is equal
to a constant, once we have determined the exchange rate.

   For a particular exchange rate, we could draw a rectangular hyperbola
in frame (c) that shows the relationship between θ and P. Thus, for some
particular exchange rate, as shown in the diagram as E^e, and for a given
world price level P_f, if the domestic price level rises, then the real
exchange rate θ must fall by an equal percentage amount. That is what
the curve E^e traces out.

   In principle, there is a whole family of such curves, all rectangular hyper-
bolas and all drawn for different values of the exchange rate. We don't

need the whole family of those curves for the moment (although we will need more than one subsequently). Now that you know how to read frame (c), the only slightly tricky part of the diagram, let us proceed to use the diagram to analyse the determination of the rational expectation of the price level and the exchange rate.

The starting point is in frame (a). The *AS* curve is the classical aggregate supply curve and is located at y^*. The curve $AD(M^e, r_f^e)$ is the expectation of the aggregate demand curve for a flexible exchange rate economy, based on the derivation in Figure 16.8. Its position depends only on the expected money stock and expected world rate of interest. The rational expectation of the price level is determined where that curve cuts the *AS* curve. The rational expectation of output is y^*.

Next, the expected real exchange rate is read off from the *RE* curve in frame (b) as the value of the real exchange rate consistent with expected output y^*. That value is θ^e. This same value may also be read off from the vertical axis of frame (c). To calculate the rational expectation of the nominal exchange rate, transfer the rational expectation of the price level from frame (a) through the 45° line to the horizontal axis of frame (c). Then join θ^e and P^e to give point A in frame (c). Point A lies on a rectangular hyperbola, the location of which determines the nominal exchange rate. There is a unique constant exchange rate locus, labelled E^e, that passes through point A. Any other nominal exchange rate would involve a different combination of the price level and the real exchange rate than what is implied by the rational expectations of these two variables.

Just prior to the commencement of business in this economy, the expectations of output, the price level, and the real and nominal exchange rates are those depicted in Figure 23.2. A higher expected money supply would result in a higher expected price level, no change in the real exchange rate, and a higher expected nominal exchange rate (a depreciated currency). You can easily work out this result for yourself by considering what happens in this diagram if we replace the expected *AD* curve with an equivalent curve located to the right of the existing curve. There will be no change in expected output or the expected real exchange rate. There would simply be a rise in the expected price level and a rise in the expected nominal exchange rate that would be proportional to each other.

(ii) Extracting Information from the Exchange Rate

Next, imagine that this economy has just started to do business. No one knows what the money supply is that underlies the actual aggregate demand curve, so no one can do any better, on the basis of information available about the economic aggregates, than continue to expect that the aggregate demand curve is in the position shown in frame (a) of Figure 23.2. But there is more information now than there was before trading began. In particular, everyone now knows the actual value of the nominal exchange rate as it is determined on a minute-by-minute basis in the foreign exchange market. In other words, as soon as trading begins, it is known whether or not the exchange rate expectation was correct. If the exchange rate expectation was incorrect, then it will be immediately clear to everyone that the initial expectation of the price level must also have been incorrect.

Let us think through the consequences of this new information, using Figure 23.3. The starting point is the initial expected values for prices,

Figure 23.3
The information content of the exchange rate influences the rational expectation of the price level

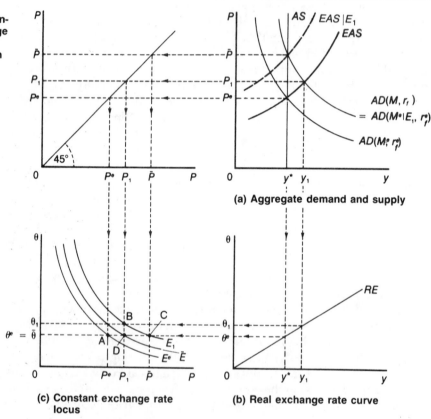

(a) Aggregate demand and supply

(c) Constant exchange rate locus

(b) Real exchange rate curve

Before trading begins, the expected aggregate demand is $AD(M^e, r_f^e)$. The expected terms of trade curve is RE. The expected equilibrium for the economy is a price level of P^e, real income of y^*, real exchange rate of θ^e and nominal exchange rate of E^e.

The economy is shocked: aggregate demand turns out to be higher than expected at $AD(M, r_f)$. The real exchange rate curve remains at RE. The expected price level of P^e, generates an actual price level of P_1, an actual real income of y_1, actual real exchange rate of θ_1 and an actual (nominal) exchange rate of E_1. Since the expected exchange rate, E^e, is different from the actual exchange rate E_1, and since the exchange rate is observed, people will know that their expectation of the price level was wrong. They will revise their expectation of the price level. Only if the expected price level is $\hat{P}$ will the expected exchange rate equal the actual exchange rate (at point C). In that case, the actual price level will also be $\hat{P}$, output y^* and the real exchange rate θ^e. (In this example, the equilibrium and initial exchange rates are the same — E_1. This is a special case and will not in general occur.)

the nominal exchange rate, and the real exchange rate, shown as P^e, E^e, and θ^e. Suppose that the actual aggregate demand curve turned out to be $AD(M, r_f)$ and not $AD(M^e, r_f^e)$ as shown in frame (a) of Figure 23.3. According to this theory, the actual output and the price level will be determined as y_1, P_1, where the actual aggregate demand curve cuts the expectations-augmented aggregate supply curve. Transferring this solution for output down to frame (b) gives us an actual real exchange rate of θ_1. Transferring the price level, P_1, from the vertical axis of frame (a) through the 45° line to the horizontal axis of frame (c) gives the point B in frame (c) as the real exchange rate-price level point. Point B lies on the constant (nominal) exchange rate locus E_1 and so determines the exchange rate at that value.

Now the actual price level and income, although determined by the analysis, are not known to the people in the economy. They only observe the prices of the small range of goods that they are currently engaged in trading, and do not know the general price level or any of the other aggregates. But everyone knows the nominal exchange rate. It is observed on a continuous basis and is therefore available for all to see. In the situation depicted in Figure 23.3, everyone knows that the exchange rate is E_1 and that it is different from E^e. The economy is not at point A in frame (c), but at point B. No one knows that, for no one knows the *real* exchange rate. It is not directly and instantly observed. But people know that the nominal exchange rate is different from what they had expected. That being so, everyone knows that a mistake was made in forming expectations about aggregate demand. Aggregate demand cannot be the curve $AD(M^e, r_f^e)$. If it was, the exchange rate would be E^e, and not E_1, which it has turned out to be. The price level P_1 and the income level y_1 cannot therefore be a rational expectations equilibrium.

If the exchange rate is higher than it was expected to be, then the aggregate demand curve must be higher than it was previously expected to be, and the expected price level needs to be revised upwards. By how much does the expected price level need to be revised upwards? To answer this question we need to see how a change in the expected price level affects both the expected exchange rate and the actual exchange rate. Only when the expected price level is such as to generate an expected exchange rate that is the same as the actual exchange rate will that price expectation be rational. That is, only in such a situation will all the information available have been incorporated into price level expectations.

We can examine how the rational expectation of the price level will be formed when information conveyed by the exchange rate is employed if we perform a conceptual experiment. Imagine that the expectation of the price level is increased from P^e to P_1 — in frame (a) of Figure 23.3. (Be clear that this story is not a description of the *process* that would go on in the world because P_1 is not observed and could not therefore be used to calculate an expected price level. This imagined experiment will simply help you find the *amount* by which the expected price level must rise and not the *process* whereby it does so.)

What we need to do is to examine the effects of the higher expected price level on both the actual and expected exchange rate. Consider first its effects on the expected exchange rate. With an expected price level of P_1, the EAS curve shifts up (not shown in the figure) to intersect the AS curve at P_1. The expected level of aggregate demand remains constant at y^*. In turn, the expected real exchange rate remains constant at θ^e. To see what this revised expectation of the price level implies for the (nominal) exchange rate, all we have to do is to trace through as we have done before to frame (c) of Figure 23.3. Tracing the price level P_1 and the real exchange rate at θ^e into frame (c) shows that they imply a nominal exchange rate equal to $\bar{E}$ (meeting at point D on the constant exchange rate locus $\bar{E}$). Thus, raising the expected price level raises the expected exchange rate. In fact, although not transparent from the diagram, there will be a one-to-one correspondence between the change in the expected price level and the change in the expected exchange rate. If the expected price level rises by x per cent, the expected exchange rate also rises by x per cent.

Next consider the effect of a change in the expected price level to P_1. It is clear that with an expected price level of P_1 but with the aggregate demand curve remaining in its position, $AD(M, r_f)$, the actual price level rises above P_1. Further, output will be above y^*, but it is below y_1. (These values have not been shown in the figure.) With output between y^* and y_1, the real exchange rate will lie between θ^e and θ_1. With the price level above P_1 and the real exchange rate below θ_1, it is evident that the actual value of the nominal exchange rate could rise or fall depending on whether the price level or the real exchange rate effect is larger. The rise in the price level tends to raise the nominal exchange rate, whereas the fall in the real exchange rate tends to lower it.

Although there is ambiguity as to the direction of movement of the exchange rate, there is no ambiguity about the fact that the actual exchange rate will have moved closer to the expected exchange rate. How do we know this? We know, first, that in the initial experiment the pre-trading expected exchange rate was E^e and the actual exchange E_1. Thus, the actual exchange rate was higher than the pre-trading expected exchange rate. We also know that a rise in the expected price level raises the expected exchange rate by the same percentage amount as the rise in the price level, but it raises the actual exchange rate by less than that and could even result in a fall in the actual exchange rate. Thus, raising the expected price level to P_1 closes the gap between the actual and the expected exchange rate. But, we can see that the expected price level P_1 cannot be the rational expectation of the price level because it does not generate an actual value of the exchange rate equal to itself. That is, with an expected price level of P_1, the real exchange rate lies between θ_1 and θ^e. The actual price level is above P_1 but below $\bar{P}$. (Verify that you indeed agree with the propositions just stated.)

With the real exchange rate between θ_1 and θ^e and the price level between P_1 and $\bar{P}$, it is evident that the actual (nominal) exchange rate locus must lie between E_1 and $\bar{E}$. Thus, the actual exchange rate implied by an expected price level of P_1 is higher than the expected exchange rate implied by this expected price level. It is evident that we could repeat the experiment just conducted with a higher price level (equal to the actual price level generated by the expected price level P_1). If we did perform such an experiment, we would discover that, with one exception, we repeatedly obtained the same type of result that we have just obtained.

There is just one price level that would give a different result and that is $\bar{P}$. The price level $\bar{P}$ occurs where the actual aggregate demand curve cuts the AS curve. Expected output remains at y^* and the expected real exchange rate remains at θ^e. With an expected price level of $\bar{P}$, this implies an expected exchange rate of E_1 — point C in frame (c) representing the expected equilibrium. With the actual aggregate demand curve intersecting the AS curve at $\bar{P}$, the actual price level is also determined at $\bar{P}$. Thus, the actual exchange rate is also E_1. Point C becomes not only the expected but also the actual equilibrium position of the economy.

To avoid having to shift the constant exchange rate locus too many times, we have used a special set of assumptions to ensure that the final equilibrium exchange rate and the initial exchange rate implied by the initial expectation and the aggregate demand shock are the same, E_1. There is, in general, no reason why the exchange rates would be the same. Indeed, for them to be the same the RE curve must be a straight line and the aggregate demand curve must be a rectangular hyperbola (have an elasticity of minus one).

In the setup in Figure 23.3, we have rigged things such that people are able to work out exactly what the actual aggregate demand curve is from the observation of the exchange rate. This outcome has arisen because, purely for the purpose of introducing you to the ideas involved, we have imagined that there is just a single source of random disturbance to the economy, namely, a random disturbance to aggregate demand. That being so, from observing the exchange rate it is possible to infer exactly what that random disturbance is and, as a result, to correct for it by adjusting the expectation of the price level conditioned on the knowledge of the exchange rate.

The expectations-augmented aggregate supply curve conditional on the actual exchange rate, $EAS|E_1$, moves to intersect the actual aggregate demand curve, which in turn becomes the expected aggregate demand curve conditional on the exchange rate $AD(M^e|E_1, r_f^e)$ at full-employment output. If there were additional sources of disturbance so that the aggregate demand being analysed here was just one of several random disturbances affecting the economy, then it would *not* be possible to make a direct inference from the exchange rate as to the position of the aggregate demand curve. Even though people might know they had made a mistake, in the sense that the exchange rate turned out to be different from what they had expected it to be, they would not know for sure the source of that mistake. That being so, they would not be able to identify correctly the actual values of the exogenous variables that are influencing the economy.

We can see this implication a little clearer if we consider a case in which there are two sources of shocks — shocks to the aggregate demand curve (coming from the money supply or the world rate of interest) and shocks to the *RE* curve (coming from world real income or fiscal policy). We will consider two experiments. Both of them are highly artificial. But despite this they are useful experiments for clarifying the concepts and propositions about the behaviour of a flexible exchange rate economy.

(iii)   An Unexpected Change in Aggregate Demand

The first experiment imagines that the economy has always had a completely predictable level of aggregate demand, so that expected aggregate demand and actual aggregate demand have always been one and the same. That is, this economy has never in the past experienced an aggregate demand shock. But this economy has often been subjected to real exchange rate shocks — shocks from world real income or from domestic fiscal policy. In fact, the normal state of affairs is for the real exchange rate curve to be constantly bombarded in a random fashion. Imagine that in a particular period this economy experiences an aggregate demand shock, but no real exchange rate shock occurs. This situation is very unusual for this hypothetical economy. It is in fact something that, by the hypothetical setup assumed, has never happened before. Naturally, the nominal exchange rate will respect to the shock. It will be rational in this situation for people to infer that there has been a real exchange rate shock. It will also be rational for them in infer that there has been no aggregate demand shock. They will be wrong, but they will not be irrational. To see what happens in this situation, let us use Figure 23.4.

The setup in Figure 23.4 is comparable to that of Figure 23.3. Before trading began, people formed expectations about aggregate demand and the real exchange rate and, as a result, formed their pretrading rational expectations of the price level, the real exchange rate, output, and the nominal exchange rate. These are shown in Figure 23.4 in the following way. The curve labelled AD^e in frame (a) is the expected aggregate demand curve. Where it intersects the AS curve determines the rational expectation of the price level, P^e. The expectations-augmented aggregate supply curve EAS passes through the point A′ where the expected aggregate demand curve cuts the aggregate supply curve. The real exchange rate curve, both actual and expected, is labelled $RE = RE^e$ in frame (b). At the expected full-employment output, the expected real exchange rate is θ^e on the vertical axis of frame (b). Transferring the expected price level through the 45° line to frame (c), and also transferring

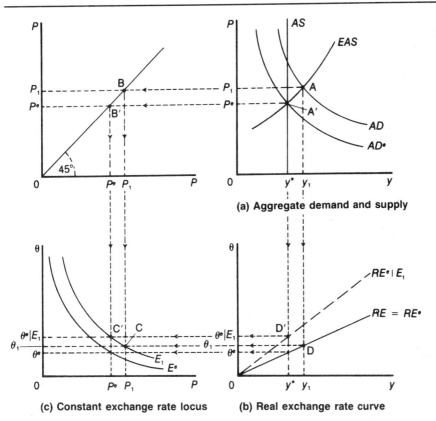

Figure 23.4
The effects of an
unanticipated
aggregate demand
shock

(a) Aggregate demand and supply

(c) Constant exchange rate locus

(b) Real exchange rate curve

The economy is initially at y^*, P^e, θ^e and E^e on the aggregate demand curve AD^e, the expectations-augmented aggregate supply curve EAS, the real exchange rate curve $RE = RE^e$ and the constant exchange rate locus E^e. There is then a completely unanticipated rise in aggregate demand to AD. This shock raises the price level to P_1 and real income to y_1. It also raises the real exchange rate to θ_1. At the price level P_1 and real exchange rate θ_1 the exchange rate becomes E_1. The higher nominal exchange rate is incorrectly interpreted as a rise in the real exchange rate to $\theta^e|E_1$. The corners of the square ABCD describe the actual situation, and the corners of the square A'B'C'D' describe the situation that agents rationally believe to be occurring. The effect of an unanticipated rise in aggregate demand is to raise the price level, output, the real exchange rate and the nominal exchange rate. The higher real exchange rate tells us that the nominal exchange rate rises by more than the price level does.

the expected real exchange rate across from frame (b) to frame (c), we arrive at a point in frame (c) that lies on a constant exchange rate locus that determines the expected nominal exchange rate (E^e). This set of expectations is the pretrading rational expectation for this economy.

The shock described above is an aggregate demand shock, but one that is completely misperceived. The actual aggregate demand curve that incorporates this shock is shown in frame (a) as the curve AD. Where the actual aggregate demand curve cuts the expectations-augmented aggregate supply curve (point A) is determined the actual price level P_1 and output y_1. At the output level y_1, reading from frame (b), we may determine the real exchange rate as θ_1. If the price level is P_1 and the real exchange rate θ_1, transferring these two magnitudes to frame (c) takes us to point C on a constant exchange rate locus E_1. Thus, the actual exchange rate is E_1, the price level P_1, income y_1, and the real exchange rate θ_1. People will see that the exchange rate is different from what they expected. But they do not see any reason to revise their expectations of the price level. As far as they are concerned, there must have been a change in the real exchange rate. Shocks are normally real exchange shocks. Aggregate demand shocks never occur, so there is no reason, based on observed regularities in the past, to revise the expectation of aggregate demand.

People are able to reconcile the currently observed exchange rate E_1 with the currently expected aggregate demand AD^e and the currently expected price level P^e, by adjusting their expectations of the real exchange rate to fall on the line labelled $RE^e|E_1$. To see how, notice that there is a square, the corners of which are A', B', C', D', that just touches the intersection of AD^e and EAS, the 45° line, the constant exchange rate locus E_1, and the expected real exchange rate curve $RE^e|E_1$. Thus, the expected price level P^e, and the expected real exchange rate $\theta^e|E_1$, and the actual (nominal) exchange rate E_1 are all compatible with each other and with an expectation that the economy is at full-employment output y^*. The other square, ABCD, represents the actual situation. That is, where the actual aggregate demand curve cuts the expectations-augmented aggregate supply curve, the economy is on the actual RE curve and again on the actual constant exchange rate locus. Both C and C' are on the same constant exchange rate locus. Thus, the actual exchange rate E_1 is compatible with the combined expectation of the price level and the real exchange rate.

In effect, people are making two offsetting mistakes. Aggregate demand is actually higher than they believe it to be, and the real exchange rate curve is actually lower than they believe it to be. In combination, these two mistakes generate the same expectation of the exchange rate as the actual exchange rate and therefore cannot be corrected simply by observing the exchange rate.

Before leaving this highly artificial economy that has frequently been bombarded with real exchange rate shocks, but never before with an aggregate demand shock, let us consider what would happen if there was no aggregate demand shock, but if the economy indeed did undergo a real exchange rate shock. Specifically, imagine that the aggregate demand curve had remained at AD^e, but that the real exchange rate had in fact changed, so that the actual real exchange rate was denoted by the line $RE^e|E_1$. If that shock had occurred, then the economy would have remained at full-employment output y^*, the price level would have remained at P^e, the nominal exchange rate would have moved to E_1, and the real exchange rate to $\theta^e|E_1$. The square A'B'C'D' would in fact describe the actual situation. Thus, by forming expectations on the basis of what usually happens, people would have correctly inferred the real exchange rate shock by using the information given to them by the exchange rate. In the previous experiment, where there was an unanticipated change in aggregate demand leading to a rise in the price level, output, the real exchange rate, and the (nominal) exchange rate, it was the unanticipated nature of the aggregate demand change that caused the problems.

Let us now briefly turn our attention to what is happening to the current account of the balance of payments during the period of the shock. The economy was subject to an unexpected aggregate demand shock, and there was a rise in the price level, output and the real exchange rate. The higher real exchange rate leads to a rise in world demand for domestic output (exports) and a drop in domestic demand for world output (imports). Other things being equal, this tends to raise the current account surplus (or lower the deficit). But other things are not equal. The higher real income raises imports, thereby contributing to a lowering of the current account surplus (or increasing the deficit). We do not, in general, know which of these two offsetting forces is the stronger and do not therefore know in which direction the current account balance changes. But, the overall balance of payments remains at zero as a result of the flexible exchange rate.

C. Real Exchange Rate Shocks

Let us now leave this highly artificial economy and go on to consider another equally highly artificial, but opposite extreme, situation. Imagine an economy that is always being bombarded by aggregate demand shocks, but which has never before known a change in its real exchange rate. Imagine that in some period the economy suffers a real exchange rate shock, but has no aggregate demand shock. Just as above, this event is. very unusual — something that has perhaps never happened before. The nominal exchange rate responds to the real exchange rate shock, but people rationally attribute the nominal exchange rate adjustment to an aggregate demand shock — to something that commonly occurs — and not to the real exchange rate shock — something that has never before been known. What happens to output, the price level, the exchange rate, and the real exchange rate in this case? Figure 23.5 analyses this situation.

(i) Pretrading Expectations

Let us first use Figure 23.5 to describe the pretrading rational expectations of the variables. The expected aggregate demand curve is AD^e in frame (a) and, where this curve intersects the AS curve determines the

Figure 23.5
The effects of a real
exchange rate shock

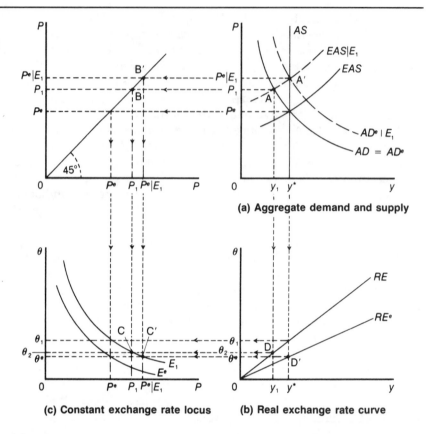

(a) Aggregate demand and supply

(c) Constant exchange rate locus   **(b) Real exchange rate curve**

The economy is initially at P^e, y^*, θ^e and E^e on the aggregate demand curve $AD = AD^e$, the expectations-augmented aggregate supply curve EAS, the real exchange rate curve RE^e and the constant exchange rate locus E^e. There is then an unanticipated rise in the real exchange rate to RE. With no change in income and the price level, this shock raises the exchange rate to E_1 (the exchange rate compatible with the price level P^e and the real exchange rate θ_1). Since the real exchange rate shock is unanticipated, the higher nominal exchange rate will be read incorrectly as an aggregate demand shock. The expected price level will be revised upwards to $P^e|E_1$, which shifts the expectations-augmented aggregate supply curve to $EAS|E_1$. Actual output, the price level and the real exchange rate are y_1, P_1 and θ_2. The price level P_1 and the real exchange rate θ_2 are consistent with the exchange rate E_1. The actual situation as described by the corners of the square ABCD and the expected situation by the corners of the square A'B'C'D'. The unanticipated rise in the real exchange rate raises the price level, lowers output and raises the nominal exchange rate. The nominal exchange rate rises by more than the price level does, therefore the real exchange rate rises.

rational expectation of the price level P^e and the location of the EAS curve. The expectation of the real exchange rate in frame (b) is the curve labelled RE^e, so the rational expectation of the real exchange rate is θ^e. Transferring the rational expectation of the price level through the 45° line to frame (c) and transferring the expected real exchange rate to frame

(c) gives a point on the constant exchange rate locus E^e. These expectations, then, are the initial pretrading rational expectation for the economy.

Imagine that there is now a real exchange rate shock and the actual real exchange rate becomes the line RE. If there was no change in the rational expectation of the price level, and if actual aggregate demand equals expected aggregate demand (as we will assume), output and the price level would remain constant at P^e and y^*, but the real exchange rate would rise to θ_1. At the price level P^e and the real exchange rate θ_1, the economy would be on a constant exchange rate locus E_1 shown in frame (c). Thus, the (nominal) exchange rate would be higher than expected.

(ii) Extracting Information from the Exchange Rate

Recall that this economy has never had a real exchange rate shock before, but often has aggregate demand shocks. Then people will read the higher (nominal) exchange rate as implying that there must have been an aggregate demand shock. As a result, they will revise their expectations of the price level upwards. Since they know that the exchange rate is E_1, and since they firmly expect the real exchange rate to remain at θ^e, they will believe the economy to be at the point C' on the constant exchange rate locus E_1. They will read off from that point on the locus E_1 the rational expectation of the price level, conditional on knowing that the exchange rate is E_1. This exchange rate is labelled $P_1^e|E_1$ in frame (c) . That is, given that people firmly believe that the real exchange rate has remained at θ^e, but that they know the (nominal) exchange rate to be E_1, they calculate a rational expectation of the price level that is compatible with these two facts.

Now transfer the rational expectation of the price level $P^e|E_1$ from frame (c) through the 45° line to frame (a). This takes us to the point A' in frame (a). Passing through the point A' is an expectations-augmented aggregate supply curve, given knowledge of the exchange rate as E_1. This curve is labelled $EAS|E_1$. Where this expectations-augmented aggregate supply curve intersects the actual aggregate demand curve (point A) determines output y_1 and the price level P_1. The actual real exchange rate is determined by the RE curve at the output y_1 and is θ_2. (The real exchange rate θ_1 would be associated with full-employment output y^*.)

Now transfer the price level P_1 through the 45° line to frame (c) and transfer the real exchange rate θ_2 across to frame (c). These meet at point C on the constant exchange rate locus E_1. Thus, the nominal exchange rate E_1 that gives rise to an expectation of the price level of $P^e|E_1$, and an expected real exchange rate of θ^e (point C') also gives rise to an actual price level P_1 and an actual real exchange rate θ_2 at point C. The actual equilibrium is described by the corners of the square ABCD, and the expected equilibrium by the corners of the square A′B′C′D′. The effects of this unanticipated rise in the real exchange rate curve have been to raise the domestic price level, raise the exchange rate (depreciate the currency), and lower output.[1]

(iii)   Aggregate Demand Shocks

Now consider what would have happened in this economy if it had actually been subjected to the shock that normally occurs, namely, an aggregate demand shock. Imagine that instead of having a real exchange rate shock, the real exchange rate remained at its normal level RE^e. Imagine further that there was a shock to aggregate demand that shifts the actual aggregate demand to the curve labelled $AD^e|E_1$. Such a shock would have raised the exchange rate, and the higher exchange rate would have been interpreted as evidence of a positive aggregate demand shock. People would have adjusted their expectations of the price level upwards, thereby building into their current expectations the information known from by the exchange rate. The only equilibrium to which this economy could have come would be the one described by the corners of the square A′B′C′D′. That is, the economy would have remained at full-employment output, the price level would actually have risen to $P^e|E_1$, and the exchange rate risen to E_1. The real exchange rate would have remained at θ^e.

This example emphasizes that the reason why the real exchange rate shock in this economy had an effect on output was because it was unanticipated. This reason is directly analogous to why the aggregate demand shock had output effects in the previous extreme example.

In this case of the economy that is normally subjected to aggregate demand shocks, but was unusually subjected to a real exchange rate shock, there is no ambiguity as to what happens to the current account balance. There is a fall in output and a rise in the real exchange rate. The combination of these two things unambiguously raises the current account surplus (or lower the deficit), since the lower real income lowers imports, whereas the higher real exchange rate lowers imports and stimulates exports.

More General Shocks   The experiments conducted and illustrated in Figures 23.4 and 23.5 are excessively simplified. In practice, *both* the real exchange

---

1   In order to keep the diagrammatic analysis clean, we have rigged this experiment to yield a rational expectations equilibrium in 'one iteration' by selecting convenient slopes for the *EAS* and *RE* curves. In general, although the characterization of equilibrium shown in Figure 23.5 is correct, a lengthier iterative process would have to be followed in order to establish what the equilibrium is. Its defining characteristics are the two squares: ABCD, which describes the actual situation, and A′B′C′D′, which describes the expected situation. The points C and C′ are on the same constant exchange rate locus.

rate and aggregate demand will be shocked simultaneously, and there will be difficulty in disentangling the extent to which each of these two have been shocked. Nevertheless, the conclusions that we have reached using the simplified analyses apply to the more general case. The propositions made above concerning the effects of unexpected changes in aggregate demand and the real exchange rate, taken by themselves, apply to cases where there is a mixture of both shocks. Shocks that reveal themselves through changes in the exchange rate will, in general, be misinterpreted not completely, as in the two extreme examples used above, but partly. The more common is a particular type of shock, the more inclined will people be to infer the presence of that shock when there is a previously unanticipated change in the exchange rate. The smaller will be the real effects, and the larger will be the price level effects of such a shock. Notice that it is not possible, given that people observe the exchange rate, for there to be unanticipated changes in one variable that are not offset by unanticipated changes in other variables. At least two mistakes must be made.

Fixed versus Flexible Exchange Rates   It is often said that flexible exchange rates give an economy insulation from foreign shocks. What can we conclude from the above analysis? Certainly we discovered when analysing the fixed exchange rate economy that an unanticipated change in the foreign price level, real income, or interest rates would produce a change in domestic output and prices. Does the same apply in the flexible exchange rate case? The answer is clearly yes.

Foreign interest rate shocks affect the position of the aggregate demand curve; foreign real income shocks affect the position of the real exchange rate curve; and foreign price level shocks affect the position of the constant exchange rate locus. Thus, each of these shocks will have an effect upon the exchange rate. Through their observed effect on the exchange rate they will lead to inferences about the positions of each of the aggregate demand and real exchange rate curves. If the only foreign shock that occurred was to the foreign price level and if it was known that that was the only shock that had occurred then it would be known that the change in the foreign exchange rate had arisen from that source alone and correct inferences would be made concerning the source of that shock. No variable other than the exchange rate would change and the domestic economy would be completely insulated from that foreign nominal shock.

If, in contrast, shocks occur to all three of these variables, movements in the foreign exchange rate will lead to inferences about the sources of shock that will, in general, be incorrect. Foreign shocks — even foreign price level shocks — will partly be misperceived as domestic demand shocks or as foreign real shocks (real interest rate or real income). To the extent that they are so misperceived, they will lead to output, employment, and price level effects in the domestic economy. Interestingly, a foreign shock that raises the expected price level will, other things being equal, produce a stagflation style of result comparable to that which we saw when analysing the effects of supply shocks in Chapter 17.

What the flexible exchange rate does offer is insulation from the effect of anticipated foreign shocks. Any such shocks will come out entirely in the exchange rate and leave the domestic price level and output undisturbed. Such shocks will be pretty hard to imagine occurring uncontaminated by unexpected components. Nevertheless, and importantly, flexible exchange rates *do* give insulation from ongoing, anticipated, trend changes in the rest of the world price level.

Summary

A. *Aggregate Demand Shocks with a Fixed Exchange Rate*

The expected values of fiscal variables and foreign variables determine the expected aggregate demand curve, which in turn determines the rational expectation of the price level. The actual aggregate demand curve intersecting the expectations-augmented aggregate supply curve determines actual output and the price level. Anticipated changes in fiscal policy or foreign variables have price level effects only; unanticipated changes affect both output and the price level. Fluctuations in the current account of the balance of payments are countercyclical. Domestic output is procyclical with world output. An anticipated foreign inflation or depreciation of the currency raises the price level proportionately.

B. *Aggregate Demand Shocks with a Flexible Exchange Rate*

With flexible exchange rates, the continuous information given by the exchange rate has to be used to form a rational expectation of the shocks influencing the economy. If there is one, and only one, source of shock, then knowledge of the exchange rate would enable a perfect inference to be made and would ensure that the economy is always at full-employment equilibrium.

If there is more than one source of shock — in this case an aggregate demand shock and a real exchange rate shock — then observation of the nominal exchange rate does not enable a complete inference to be made concerning the magnitudes of those shocks separately. As a result unanticipated fluctuations in aggregate demand lead to procyclical co-movements in output and prices as they do in the closed economy case.

C. *Real Exchange Rate Shocks*

An unexpected (and misperceived) rise in the real exchange rate leads to a rise in the nominal exchange rate. If this depreciation of the domestic currency is perceived as having arisen from a domestic aggregate demand shock it will lead to a rise in the expected price level, shifting the *EAS* curve upwards. The result will be a rise in prices and a drop in output—stagflation.

Review Questions

1. How is the rational expectation of the price level determined when the exchange rate is fixed and capital is perfectly mobile?
2. Work out the effects on the rational expectation of the price level (with fixed exchange rates and perfect capital mobility) of the following:
   (a) An anticipated rise in the world price level of 10 per cent.
   (b) An anticipated rise in world income.
   (c) An anticipated rise in domestic credit.
   (d) An unanticipated devaluation.
   (e) An anticipated devaluation of 10 per cent.
   (f) An unanticipated rise in domestic credit.
   (g) An unanticipated tax cut.
   (h) An anticipated rise in government spending.

3. Work out the effects on output, the price level, and the current account balance (with fixed exchange rates and perfect capital mobility) of the eight shocks listed in Question 2.
4. What is the fundamental difference between a fixed and a flexible exchange rate regime? Which generates the most information?
5. How is the rational expectation of the price level determined when the exchange rate is flexible and when capital is perfectly mobile:

   (a) Before the markets begin trading?
   (b) When trading is taking place?

6. How is the rational expectation of the price level affected by the eight shocks listed in Question 2, when the exchange rate is flexible and capital is perfectly mobile?
7. How are output, the price level, the exchange rate, and the current account balance affected by the eight shocks listed in Question 2, when the exchange rate is flexible and capital is perfectly mobile?
8. Do flexible exchange rates provide better insulation from foreign shocks than do fixed exchange rates?

24

Output Growth

We saw in Chapter 2 that the most dominant feature of the path of output is its long-term growth trend. Average output in the UK has grown at 1.7 per cent a year since 1900. Population has grown during that same time period at 0.4 per cent per annum, so that *per capita* income has grown at 1.3 per cent per annum. This growth rate is equivalent to a doubling of per capita income every 54 years. The theories that you have studied so far in this book have abstracted from these long-term trends in output growth. Understanding what determines the trend will be the subject of this chapter.

The subject of this chapter is an enormous one. To do full justice to it would require another book at least as long as this one. Economists have been interested in the questions concerning long-term growth for as long as there has been a subject of economics. The founder of economics as we know it today, Adam Smith, wrote at length on the subject in his famous *On the Nature and Causes of the Wealth of Nations* published in 1776. In the period since then, the topic has exercised the talents of the giants in our discipline such as Thomas Malthus and David Ricardo and, in more recent years, James Meade of Cambridge University, Trevor Swan of the Australian National University, Robert Solow of MIT, and James Tobin of Yale University.[1] These scholars have made their major contributions

---

1 Some of the seminal contributions to this topic are: James Meade, *A Neoclassical Theory of Economic Growth* (London: Allen & Unwin, 1960); Trevor Swan, 'Economic Growth and Capital Accumulation', *Economic Review*, 32, (November 1956), pp. 334–61; Robert M. Solow, 'A Contribution to the Theory of Economic Growth', *Quarterly Journal of Economics*, 70, (February 1956), pp. 65–94, and James Tobin, 'A Dynamic Aggregative Model', *Journal of Political Economy*, 63, (April 1955), pp. 103–15.

to the abstract analysis of the determinants of economic growth. In addition, many scholars have undertaken careful measurement and empirical investigation, the most notable of these being Edward F. Denison, of the US Department of Commerce and Brookings Institution.[2]

In view of the enormous volume of literature on the topic of economic growth,[3] this chapter cannot pretend to do any more than provide an account of the highlights of the subject and we will concentrate on matters of principle rather than on empirical issues.

By the time you will have completed this chapter you will be able to:

(a) **Explain the concept of the *per capita* production function.**
(b) **Represent *per capita* output and savings in a simple diagram.**
(c) **Explain the concept of the steady-state investment rate.**
(d) **Explain how to find the equilibrium values of *per capita* output, capital, consumption, savings and investment.**
(e) **Explain what determines the trend rate of growth of output.**

A. The Per Capita Production Function

You are already familiar with the concept of the production function. You met it in Chapter 17 when dealing with aggregate supply and the labour market. As you discovered there, a production function is simply a statement about the maximum output that can be produced with a given list of inputs and, more than that, a statement of how that maximum level of output will vary as the inputs themselves are varied. The maximum output of some particular good that can be produced will depend on the amount of capital employed, the state of technology, the amount of land resources used, and the number and skill of the workers employed. In Chapter 17, where we were concerned only with the short run, we supposed that all of the inputs into the production process, with the exception of the number of workers employed, were fixed. In this chapter, however, we want to focus on the process of growth itself and to allow for variations in inputs other than labour.

It will be a useful approximation to imagine that total land resources

---

2 Edward F. Dennison, *Accounting for the United States Economic Growth 1929–1969* (Washington, DC: Brookings Institution, 1974).
3 There are many excellent, although advanced, treatments of this topic that cover the subject in a comprehensive way. Perhaps the best introductory collection of readings of some of the major contributions to this topic is *The Modern Theory of Economic Growth* edited by Joseph E. Stiglitz and Hirofumi Uzawa (Cambridge, Mass.: MIT Press, 1969). In addition to presenting the original contributions on which this chapter is based by James Meade, Robert M. Solow and Trevor W. Swan, this book also contains a seminal contribution that integrates monetary and growth theory by James Tobin, as well as much other material. The level of difficulty of the essays in that work is, however, substantially higher than the presentation given in this chapter.

are fixed and that, over the long run, what may be varied in order to vary output are the amounts of labour and capital employed and the state of technology that is utilized. The larger the number of people employed or the larger the stock of capital equipment used, the greater will be the volume of output. As labour and capital inputs are increased, output increases, but by diminishing amounts — the law of diminishing returns applies to both labour and capital. However, with technological advances, the amount of output that is attainable from any given amount of labour and capital will increase over time.

Since the focus of our attention in this chapter is going to be on long-term trends in output, it is useful to consider the *per capita* (per head) production function rather than the aggregate production function. The previous paragraph has talked about the relationship between aggregate output and the amount of labour and capital employed in the production process. The per capita production function is a statement about how output per head varies as we vary both the inputs per head and the state of technology. It turns out to be extremely convenient to assume that output per head varies as capital per head is varied and does so similarly to the way in which total output varies as the capital input is changed. Thus, as capital per head is increased, output per head increases but in successively diminishing amounts — the law of diminishing returns again.

In general, it is possible that output per head depends on both capital per head and the number of people employed — the scale of output. By assuming that output per head depends *only* on capital per head, we are assuming that there are constant returns to scale. This assumption is an important, though probably not an unreasonable simplification. There is a great deal of evidence to the effect that the real-world production functions are characterized by constant returns to scale.

B.   Per Capita Output and Savings

The per capita production function can be represented in a diagram and it looks much like the short-run production function with which you are already familiar (Figure 17.2). Figure 24.1 illustrates this type of relationship but in per capita terms.

As you see, we measure the amount of capital per head (k/n) on the horizontal axis in Figure 24.1, whereas in Figure 17.2 we measured the number employed n. On the vertical axis in Figure 24.1 we measure output per head (y/n) whereas, in contrast, in Figure 17.2 we measured aggregate output (y). The production function is the line labelled $f(k/n, t)$. This line shows that, as capital per head is increased, so output per head increases. The curvature of the function shows that as capital per head is increased so output per head increases, but by decreasing amounts.

The curve is labelled $f(k/n, t)$ to remind you that there are two things that affect output per head. The first of these is capital per head. The effect

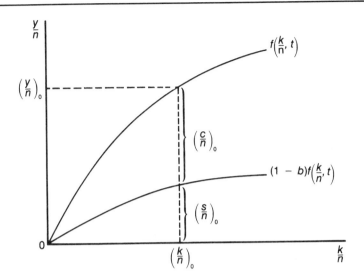

Figure 24.1
**Per capita produc-
tion and savings
functions**

Per capita output is an increasing function of the capital–labour ratio and is subject to diminishing marginal productivity of capital — the curve labelled $f(k/n, t)$. Per capita savings is a fraction of per capita output — the curve labelled $(1 - b)f(k/n, t)$. At the capital–labour ratio $(k/n)_0$, output per head is $(y/n)_0$, consumption per head is $(c/n)_0$ and savings per head is $(s/n)_0$.

increasing of capital per head on output per head is measured by a movement along the per capita production function. The second variable that affects output per head is the state of technology represented by the letter t. At any given point in time there is a given state of technology and a given per capita production function. As time progresses and technology changes, the per capita production function shifts upwards indicating that, at a given level of capital per head, output per head increases.

The term *capital per head* is a slightly clumsy one and is replaced by the equivalent term, the *capital–labour ratio*.

As you already know both from the discussion of flows and stocks in Chapter 3 and from our analysis of investment demand in Chapter 10, there are some important linkages between investment, savings and the capital stock. Capital stock changes as a result of investment activity. In our analysis of fluctuations of economic activity around its trend, we found it convenient to ignore the ongoing effects of investment on capital accumulation and proceeded on the simplifying assumption (although strictly untenable assumption) that the capital stock was constant. Now that we are analysing the determinants of the long-term trends in output, we need explicitly to focus on the effects of ongoing savings and investment on the rate of capital accumulation.

Think of the rate at which capital is being accumulated as the difference between the rate at which goods are being produced and consumed. You need to be careful to include in your definition of consumption the consumption of capital goods through their wear and tear and depreciation — what is called *capital consumption*. Provided that consumption is measured to include capital consumption it will be clear that the change in capital stock is identical to income minus consumption. You know, however, (ignoring government and international economic activity for simplicity) that income minus consumption is savings. In the long run, you also know that the proposition about savings being equal to some constant fraction of income is reasonable. Just as we did in Chapter 9, call the fraction of income consumed b, so that the fraction of income saved is $1 - b$.

We can represent the amount of income saved in the same diagram as the per capita production function (Figure 24.1). This savings function is the lower line labelled $(1 - b)f(k/n, t)$. It is simply the production function scaled down by the fraction $1-b$, so that it shows the amount of per capita income that is not consumed — in other words, that is saved — at each capital–labour ratio. For example, if the capital–labour ratio was $(k/n)_0$, then per capita income would be $(y/n)_0$, as indicated on the vertical axis of the figure, and that income would be divided between consumption of $(c/n)_0$ and capital accumulation — savings — of $(s/n)_0$.

Figure 24.1 now shows us the amounts of output per head and savings per head — capital accumulation per head — that will be achieved at each possible capital–labour ratio. The diagram has an interesting feature that has not been met before in this book — one of the variables that has been measured on the vertical axis represents the amount by which the variable on the horizontal axis is *changing*. That is, if we pick a particular capital–labour ratio again, say $(k/n)_0$, then a certain amount of output would be produced, a certain fraction of that output would be consumed and the rest would be added to the stock of capital. Thus, the stock of capital will be changing. If the labour force is also growing (f n is rising) then, the capital–labour ratio will either rise, fall or stay constant depending on whether the rise in the labour force exceeds, falls short of or equals the growth of the capital stock.

The next section analyses the process of determining the actual rate of savings, investment, and output.

C.   Steady-State Investment Rate

There is one, and only one, rate of investment that is compatible with the economy being in a steady state. By *steady state* we mean a situation in which the relevant variables are constant over time. The relevant variables for the present are per capita output and capital stock and the rates of consumption, savings and investment. To figure out what the steady-state rate of investment is we want to work out the rate of investment that maintains the capital–labour ratio at some given constant level.

Let us begin with the obvious proposition that the rate of savings is equal to the change in the stock of capital or investment; that is,

$$s = \Delta k \tag{24.1}$$

We can divide savings and the change in the capital stock by the population to give per capita savings that are equal to per capita capital accumulation; that is,

$$s/n = \Delta k \tag{24.2}$$

Let us now do something that may seem pointless, but which turns out to be very useful. That is, multiply and divide the right-hand side of Equation (24.2) by the capital stock. This multiplies the right-hand side of the equation by one leaving it unchanged, and gives us

$$s/n = (\Delta k/k)(k/n) \tag{24.3}$$

But Equation (22.3) is only a definition. It says that per capita savings are equal to the growth rate of the capital stock $(\Delta k/k)$ multiplied by the capital–labour ratio (k/n).

Now, for the economy to be in a steady state, the capital–labour ratio (k/n) must be a constant. That can only occur when the stock of capital is growing at the same rate as the labour force is growing. If, for example, neither was growing at all, then the capital–labour ratio would be constant. Equally, the capital–labour ratio would be constant provided each was growing at the same rate. Thus, the condition for the steady state is that

$$(\Delta k/k) = (\Delta n/n) \tag{24.4}$$

Equation (24.3) is simply a definition and Equation (24.4) is the condition that, if satisfied, gives rise to a steady state. We can combine these two propositions to give

$$(s/n) = (\Delta n/n)(k/n) \tag{24.5}$$

This equation says that in the steady state, per capita savings will be equal to the growth rate of the population multiplied by the capital–labour ratio. The growth rate of the population is treated as being exogenous — that is, it does not vary as a consequence of variations in any of the variables whose values we are determining in the analysis. (This assumption of neoclassical growth theory contrasts with that of the classical economists such as Malthus and Ricardo, who viewed the population growth rate as one of the factors that adjusted to the underlying economic conditions.)

We can represent the steady-state rate of capital accumulation in a simple diagram such as Figure 24.2. This figure, like Figure 24.1, measures the capital–labour ratio on the horizontal axis and measures the rate of savings (capital accumulation) per head on the vertical axis. The slope

Figure 24.2
Steady-state invest-
ment ray

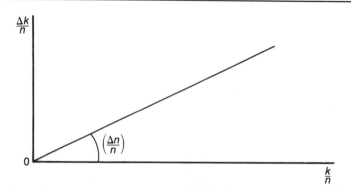

The rate of per capita capital accumulation that maintains a constant capital–labour ratio is shown as the ray having a slope equal to the growth rate of the population.

of the line, as is readily seen from Equation (24.5), is equal to the (exogenous) population growth rate, $\Delta n/n$.

Like Figure 24.1, Figure 24.2 has the interesting property that the value of the variable measured on the vertical axis is the change in the variable on the horizontal axis, for a given value of n. The line plotted in Figure 24.2 however, traces all those values of s/n that deliver a constant k/n. If the economy was above that line with s/n greater than the steady-state value, the capital stock would be growing faster than the population, and k/n would be rising. At points below the ray in Figure 24.2, the rate of capital accumulation would be less than the rate of population growth, and the capital–labour ratio would be falling. The points on the line are those at which the capital stock and labour force are growing at the same rate and therefore deliver a constant capital–labour ratio.

D.   Equilibrium Per Capita Output, Capital, Consumption, Savings and Investment

It is now a relatively simple matter to bring together the analyses of the two preceding sections and determine the equilibrium levels of per capita output, consumption, savings, investment and capital. Figure 24.3 illustrates these equilibrium levels.

Figure 24.3 is a combination of Figures 24.1 and 24.2. The curve labelled $f(k/n, t)$ is the per capita production function. That labelled $(1-b)f(k/n, t)$ is the savings rate as a function of the capital–labour ratio, and the ray having the slope $\Delta n/n$ is the steady-state investment ray.

To get a feel for how the figure works and how it determines the equilibrium, imagine initially that the economy has a capital–labour ratio of $(k/n)_0$ as marked on the horizontal axis. The level of output per head

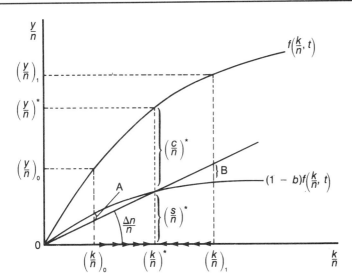

**Figure 24.3
Equilibrium per
capita output,
capital, investment
and savings**

The per capita production and savings functions are combined with the steady-state investment ray to determine the steady-state capital–labour ratio and output per head. At $(k/n)_0$, capital grows at a faster rate than the steady-state requirement so that the capital–labour ratio rises. At $(k/n)_1$ the capital stock grows at a slower rate than that required for the steady state so that the capital–labour ratio falls. At $(k/n)^*$, the savings rate equals the steady-state investment rate and the capital–labour ratio remains constant.

is immediately determined as $(y/n)_0$. How much capital accumulation is taking place in this situation? Is it more or less than that required to main-tain the capital–labour ratio at its constant $(k/n)_0$ level? You know that the amount of actual capital accumulation is that read off from the sav-ings line $(1 - b)f(k/n, t)$. You also know that the amount of capital accumulation required to maintain the capital–labour ratio at a constant is read off from the steady-state investment ray. At the capital–labour ratio of $(k/n)_0$, there is evidently a gap between these two amounts — labelled A in the figure. At the capital–labour ratio $(k/n)_0$, actual capital accumulation exceeds that required to maintain a constant capital–labour ratio by the amount A. Thus the capital–labour ratio will not remain con-stant at $(k/n)_0$. Instead it will be rising.

Next consider what will be happening if the economy had a capital–labour ratio $(k/n)_1$ on the horizontal axis of Figure 24.3. In this case, out-put per head would be $(y/n)_1$. Conducting exactly the same type of exercise as that above, you can now see that there is a gap between the amount of capital accumulated and the steady-state investment line equal to the amount labelled B in the diagram. This time, however, there is less capital being accumulated than that required to maintain a constant capital–labour ratio. That is, the steady-state investment line lies above the savings function. In this case the capital–labour ratio $(k/n)_1$ is not a steady state because if the economy started out in that position, capital would be growing at a slower rate than the labour force, so that the capital–labour ratio would be falling. You can now immediately see that there is one, and only one, capital–labour ratio that is consistent with a steady state, and that is $(k/n)^*$.

This capital–labour ratio generates an output rate of $(y/n)^*$ and a savings rate equal to the steady-state rate of capital accumulation. That is, at $(k/n)^*$, the savings function intersects the steady-state investment line. There is no gap between the rate at which capital is being accumulated and the rate at which it needs to be accumulated in order to maintain a constant capital–labour ratio. Thus, $(k/n)^*$ and $(y/n)^*$ represent the equilibrium capital–labour ratio and output per head in the economy. Output is divided between consumption and savings (capital accumulation) with $(c/n)^*$ being consumed and $(s/n)^*$ being saved and added to the stock of capital. In this economy, the long-term trend in output will have the same growth rate as that of the population $(\Delta n/n)$.

E.   Determinants of the Trend Rate of Growth of Output

In the analysis of the preceding section, you saw that the trend growth rate of output is equal to the population growth rate, since there is a built-in equilibrating mechanism that ensures that the capital–labour ratio approaches its steady-state rate, thereby producing a fixed output per head. The diagrams used in order to characterize the solution in the previous section use a per capita production function that itself does not move. If, however, as a result of technical change, the production function is continuously shifting upwards, then output per head will grow at a rate over and above the population growth rate. This growth rate, however, will depend only on the rate at which the production function is shifting upwards and will have to be added to the basic growth rate of output — the growth rate of the population.

The trend growth rate of output is determined by the trend growth rate in the population as well as the trend growth rate in output per head which is made possible by the trend in technology. Specifically, the growth rate of output does not depend upon the rate of saving. A change in the rate of saving would affect the level of output per head and the capital–labour ratio but would not affect the growth trend.

You can see this result very clearly by considering the analysis in Figure 24.4 which, again, abstracts from changing technology and analyses the situation for a given production function at a given moment in time. The initial equilibrium depicted in Figure 24.3 is reproduced as the equilibrium labelled $(k/n)_0^*$ and $(y/n)_0^*$. This equilibrium is associated with a given population growth rate $(\Delta n/n)$ and a savings rate equal to $(1 - b_0)$. Now imagine that the savings rate increased to $(1 - b_1)$. As a result the savings function shifts upward as shown in Figure 24.4. Starting out at

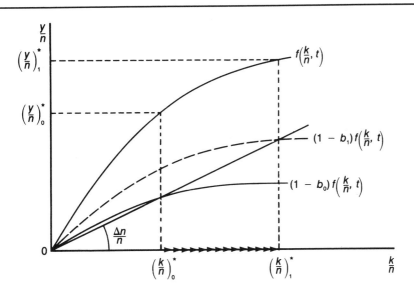

Figure 24.4
The effect of a
change in the sav-
ings rate

If the savings rate rises from $(1 - b_0)$ to $(1 - b_1)$ the savings function shifts upwards. At $(k/n)_0^*$, the rate of capital accumulation exceeds that necessary to maintain a constant capital–labour ratio. Thus, the capital–labour ratio rises and continues to do so up to $(k/n)_1^*$ when a new steady state is reached.

$(k/n)_0^*$, the savings rate is now be higher than that required to maintain a constant capital-labour ratio. As a consequence, the capital–labour ratio rises, and as it does so, output per head also rises. The higher the capital–labour ratio, the higher is the rate of saving needed to maintain a given constant capital–labour ratio (we move along the steady-state investment ray).

Eventually we reach the capital–labour ratio $(k/n)_1^*$, which produces the steady-state income level $(y/n)_1^*$. At this capital–labour ratio, the steady-state investment ray intersects the savings function, so that the capital–labour ratio remains constant. During the transition from the initial to the new steady-state capital–labour ratio, the growth rate of output will have exceeded the growth rate of the population — because the ratio (y/n) has increased, y must have been growing faster than n. However, once the new steady state is reached, the rate of growth of output is again equal the rate of population growth.

Thus, except for the process of adjustment from one steady state to another, the growth rate of output is independent of the savings rate. A different way of putting this result would be to say that the growth rate of output does not depend on the savings rate but does depend on *changes in* the savings rate.

Although the savings rate does not affect the growth rate of output, it does affect the level of output per head. You can see immediately from

Figure 24.4 that the higher the rate of savings, the greater will be the levels of capital and output per head.

Although the savings rate does not affect the growth rate of output, the population growth rate does. It also influences the level of output per head in a way that you can readily see. Figure 24.5 illustrates the analysis this time.

Again, the initial equilibrium as depicted in Figure 24.3 is reproduced in Figure 24.5 as $(k/n)_0^*$ with per capita output at $(y/n)_0^*$. This equilibrium is associated with the population growth rate of $(\Delta n/n)_0$. Now imagine that the population growth rate declines to $(\Delta n/n)_1$. As a result the steady-state investment ray rotates downwards as shown in Figure 24.5. At the initial capital–labour ratio $(k/n)_0^*$ there is now a level of savings and capital accumulation that exceeds the steady-state investment requirement. Thus the capital–labour ratio is rising. It will continue to rise until it reaches $(k/n)_1^*$, at which point the new steady-state investment line intersects the savings function. During the process, the capital–labour ratio will have increased from $(k/n)_0^*$ to $(k/n)_1^*$ and per capita output will have grown from $(y/n)_0^*$ to $(y/n)_1^*$. In the new steady-state, the growth rate of total output will have declined by exactly the same amount as the growth rate of the population. In the transition to the new steady state, output will have grown at a faster rate than the population growth rate.

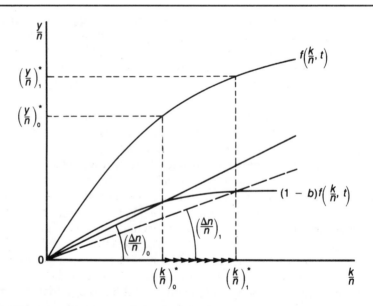

**Figure 24.5
The effects of a change in the population growth rate**

The population growth rate decreases from $(\Delta n/n)_0$ to $(\Delta n/n)_1$. At the initial equilibrium $(k/n)_0^*$ the savings rate is bigger than that required to maintain a constant capital–labour ratio. The capital–labour ratio, therefore, increases and continues to do so until it reaches $(k/n)_1^*$, its new steady state.

You have now seen that the *level* of output per head depends on both the population growth rate and the savings rate. The lower the population growth rate or the higher the savings rate, the higher is output per head, and the higher is the capital–labour ratio. The output growth rate however, except for transitions arising from changes in the savings rate or the population growth rate, depends only on the population growth rate and the rate of technical change.

We have focused on the effects of the population growth rate and the savings rate on per capita output and the capital–labour ratio. It is now of some interest to examine how the rate of per capita consumption is influenced by these factors. Let us examine the possible steady-state per capita consumption levels. Figure 24.6 shows these possibilities.

The figure contains the production function and the steady-state investment line. The gap between these two lines indicates the steady-state consumption possibilities. But in order to realize any one of these possibilities, the actual savings behaviour of the population would have to be appropriate.

Let us suspend consideration of what that savings behaviour needs to be for a moment and simply look at the amounts of consumption per capita that are available in different steady states. Visual inspection of

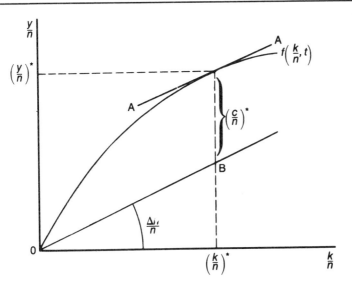

Figure 24.6
Per capita consumption and the golden rule

Possible steady-state values of consumption are shown by the vertical distance between the per capita production function $f(k/n, t)$ and the population growth rate $(\Delta n/n)$. Evidently consumption per capita is at a maximum at $(k/n)^*$. At that capital-labour ratio the marginal product of capital, which is the slope of the line AA, is equal to the population growth rate. That is the Golden Rule. If the savings function passes through B, then per capita consumption will in fact be maximized. Savings may be either too great or too small to maximize per capita consumption.

Figure 24.6 reveals that, as the capital–labour ratio increases from zero per capita consumption starts to increase. However, a point is reached at which per capita consumption is at a maximum. That is at the capital–labour ratio $(k/n)^*$ in Figure 24.6. At capital–labour ratios greater than $(k/n)^*$, consumption per capita declines as the capital–labour ratio increases. You can see, as a result of the line labelled AA in Figure 24.6, that the slope of the production function at the point of maximum per capita consumption is equal to the slope of the steady-state investment line. That slope you know to be the growth rate of population.

What does the slope of the per capita production function measure? A moment's reflection will convince you that it measures the marginal product of capital. Think of increasing capital per head by a small amount and ask how much extra output per head do we get; the answer is that it depends on the slope of the per capita production function. At very low capital–labour ratios, we get a large amount of extra output; whereas at very high capital–labour ratios we get very little. The slope of the per capita production function thus measures the (diminishing) marginal productivity of capital. The slope of the line AA measures the marginal product of capital at the point of maximum per capita consumption.

You have just discovered what is known as the 'golden rule'. The golden rule states that per capita consumption is maximized when the marginal product of capital is equal to the growth rate of population.

To achieve the golden rule it would be necessary that the fraction of income saved be such as to pass the savings function through the point marked B in Figure 24.6. Savings rates larger than that would imply a higher capital–labour ratio than $(k/n)^*$, a higher output level than $(y/n)^*$, but a smaller consumption rate than $(c/n)^*$. Savings rates lower than that necessary to pass the savings function through B would be associated with lower output per head, lower capital per head, and lower consumption per head.

You have now seen that the growth rate of output depends on the growth rate of population and on the rate of technical change. You have also seen that the level of output per head and the capital–labour ratio depend on both the population growth rate and the savings rate. in addition you have also seen that the ultimate objective of economic activity, consumption, at any given point in time in a given state of technology, has a well-defined maximum. Thus, there is a unique per capita consumption-maximizing rate of saving which, if achieved, would deliver not the maximum possible output per head and capital stock per head, but the optimum values of those variables.

Over time output per head and consumption per head will increase if technical change is shifting the production function upwards. But there is no 'free lunch' in this direction because more rapid technical change would require devoting more resources to research and development and less resources to consumption. Just as there is a per capita consumption-maximizing rate of saving, so there is also be an optimum rate at which to devote resources to research and development. Like all other economic activities, that too is subject to the laws of diminishing returns.

Summary

A. The Per Capita Production Function

The per capita production function shows the maximum amount of per capita production obtainable as the capital–labour ratio is increased. The per capita production function shifts over time as a result of technical change.

B. Per Capita Output and Savings

Per capita savings (which is the same thing as per capita capital accumulation) is some fraction of per capita output. Thus, the rate of per capita capital accumulation depends on the level of capital per head.

C. Steady-State Investment Rate

Because the per capita rate of capital accumulation depends on the capital–labour ratio, it follows that, in general, at any given capital–labour ratio, there will be a tendency for the capital–labour ratio to either rise or fall. The steady-state investment rate is that rate of investment (of capital accumulation) that maintains the capital–labour ratio constant. The investment rate that maintains the capital–labour ratio constant is the capital–labour ratio multiplied by the population growth rate.

D. Equilibrium Per Capita Output, Capital, Consumption, Savings and Investment

The equilibrium value of the capital–labour ratio is determined as that capital–labour ratio that generates a volume of savings per head equal to the steady-state rate of investment per head. When savings per head equal steady-state investment per head, the capital–labour ratio, output per head, consumption per head and savings per head are all constant.

E.   Determinants of the Trend Rate of Growth of Output

The trend rate of growth of output is determined by the population growth rate and the rate of technical change. It does not depend on the savings rate. But if the savings rate changes there is a transition from one level of output per head to another that involves a change in the growth rate. Specifically, a rise in the savings rate raises the capital–labour ratio and output per head. A fall in the population growth rate also has those same effects. Per capita consumption is maximized when the marginal product of capital equals the population growth rate. This situation is known as the 'golden rule'. There is a unique saving rate that will deliver the golden rule. Too much savings relative to the golden rule will produce a higher output per head but a lower consumption per head than the golden rule value.

Review Questions

1. What is a per capita production function? How does it differ from an ordinary aggregate production function? Does it still possess the property of diminishing returns?
2. What happens to the per capita production function if there is technical progress? Illustrate in a diagram.
3. How does savings per head vary as output per head varies?
4. You are given the following information:

k/n	0	1	2	3	4	5	6	7	8	9	10
y/n	0	2.0	3.7	5.0	6.2	7.2	8.0	8.6	9.1	9.5	9.8

   Plot the per capita production function. If the fraction of income consumed is 0.8, plot the relationship between capital per head and savings per head.

5. What is the meaning of the concept the steady-state rate of investment?
6. What determines the steady-state rate of investment?
7. Show in a diagram how the equilibrium values of output per head, consumption per head, savings per head, and investment per head are determined. Analyse the forces that would act on these variables if they were not at their equilibrium values.
8. Review what happens to the four variables referred to in the previous question if there is a rise in the production function generated by technical progress.

9. Analyse the effects on the four variables set out in Question 7 in the event of a rise in the growth rate of population.
10. Does capital accumulation cause a growth in the standard of living? If not, what does?

Part IV

UNDERSTANDING
THE FACTS

25

Unemployment

You are now approaching the most interesting part of your study of macroeconomics. You are familiar with the questions that macroeconomics seeks to answer; with the main facts about UK macroeconomic history; and with the key elements of the theory of macroeconomics — the theory of the determination of output, the price level, employment, unemployment, wages, interest rates, the balance of payments and the exchange rate.

This and the following two chapters will extend and apply the analysis that you have studied in the previous part of the book and show you how it is possible to make sense of the macroeconomic phenomena described in Chapter 2. Specifically, you will come to understand the reasons why unemployment, inflation, exchange rates, the balance of payments and real GNP fluctuate to create an ebb and flow in the overall level of economic activity known as the business cycle.

You are already aware that when aggregate demand is anticipated (or expected) the economy is at full-employment equilibrium. When aggregate demand deviates from its expected level then output, employment and unemployment, and the other macroeconomic variables depart from their full-employment equilibrium values. We are going to find it convenient in studying unemployment, inflation, and other macroeconomic phenomena first of all to focus exclusively on situations in which aggregate demand fluctuations are anticipated (or expected). By so doing we will be able to obtain a clear understanding of the sources of the major movements in unemployment, of trends in inflation, interest rates, the balance of payments and exchange rates and in output growth. When we have applied our theories and extended them to show how fluctuations and trends may be understood even in the absence of unanticipated demand shocks, we will then come back to the case in which such shocks are present and cause additional macroeconomic fluctuations.

For emphasis, and in order to be absolutely clear, you should note that initially we are going to narrow our vision and focus only on fluctuations that occur when aggregate demand is anticipated so that we can get some fundamental principles straight. We are not asserting that unanticipated aggregate demand shocks are unimportant. Once we have understood what happens in the absence of unanticipated shocks to aggregate demand we will be able to sharpen our focus on the source of aggregate fluctuations.

The central focus of this first chapter is unemployment. You do not need reminding that unemployment is an important problem in the UK today. In November 1980 the number unemployed exceeded 2 million for the first time since the years of the Great Depression. By February 1984 that number had passed the three million mark, and unemployment continued to rise to a peak of 3.2 million in 1986. Though it has been falling in recent years there remain more than 2 million unemployed at the beginning of 1988. The objective of this chapter is to help you to understand some of the reasons why unemployment exists, why it persists, and why it has increased so dramatically in the 1980s.

In keeping with the above remarks, the chapter will focus on fluctuations in unemployment that occur independently of unexpected shocks to aggregate demand. We will deal with the effects of such shocks in Chapter 27. The economy will be at full employment even though we are studying the factors that cause unemployment! This may sound paradoxical but a moment's reflection will tell you that it is not. You will recall that, by definition, the economy is at full employment if expectations are realized. There can be, and as you will see there often is, a sizable amount of unemployment in such a situation. Also its rate fluctuates as a result of the forces that we are going to analyse in this chapter.

The unemployment that exists at full employment is often called the 'natural rate of unemployment'. It is fluctuations in the natural rate of unemployment that we are going to study. Calling the full-employment rate of unemployment the 'natural rate of unemployment' often conjures up in people's minds a sense of approval or even inevitability of 'natural' unemployment. That is not the perspective adopted here. We use the term 'natural' rate of unemployment simply to distinguish between unemployment that results from real underlying forces in the labour market from unemployment resulting from unanticipated shocks to aggregate demand. By studying the forces that determine that natural rate of unemployment and cause variations in its rate we can hope to discover policies that will modify the natural rate of unemployment.

Because there has been such a high rate of unemployment for such a long period in the UK, the problem has been the subject of many books and articles. We cannot hope to summarize everything that has been said on the subject here, nor can we hope to offer you a perfect substitute for what has been written by others. We urge you to sample the large literature for yourself.[1]

The particular forces that we are going to study that effect unemployment are the following: the actions of trade unions; the effects of unemployment benefits; the effects of an uneven pace of technical change in different sectors of the economy leading to changes in the amount of labour being reallocated between sectors; and finally the effect of taxes. We will examine the importance of these factors in recent UK macroeconomic history. To help you to understand some of the reasons why unemployment arises and what leads to variations in its rate this chapter pursues five tasks, which are to:

(a) **Explain how trade unions can raise wages and create unemployment.** *3*
(b) **Explain how job search can cause unemployment.** */*
(c) **Explain how unemployment benefits schemes can create unemployment.** *2.*
(d) **Explain how taxes affect unemployment.** *4.*
(e) **Evaluate the importance of these influences on recent UK unemployment.**

A. Trade Unions and Unemployment

Trade unions are a dominant institution in the labour market. They act as an agent for households in the negotiation of employment and wage contracts. However, a much larger fraction of the labour force works on contracts negotiated by unions than are members of unions. In analysing the effects of unions on the macroeconomic variables we will pretend that there is a single economy-wide union — one that embraces the entire labour force.

The economy will be described using Figure 25.1. First, focus on the competitive equilibrium. The curves labelled n^d and n^s are the demand and supply of labour curves and the real wage $(W/P)^*$ and the employment level n^* are their competitive equilibrium values. Now suppose that

---

1 A useful comprehensive econometric study is provided by Richard Layard and S. Nickell in 'The Causes of British Unemployment', *National Institute Economic Review* (February 1985), pp. 62–85. For an excellent comprehensive treatment you should look at Patrick Minford, *Unemployment: Cause and Cure* (2nd edn), Oxford: Basil Blackwell, 1985. An important study of the effects of unemployment benefits, a topic that we will deal with later in the chapter, is by A.B. Atkinson and John Micklewright, *Unemployment Benefits and Unemployment Duration*, Suntory–Toyota International Centre for Economics and Related Disciplines, The London School of Economics and Political Science, London, 1985. A broader historical perspective has been provided by Mark Casson in *Economics of Unemployment: An Historical Perspective*, Oxford: Martin Robertson, 1983. A further excellent historical perspective (though not related to the UK at all) has been provided by Michael J. Poire in 'Historical Perspectives and the Interpretation of Unemployment', *Journal of Economic Literature* Vol. XXV (December 1987), pp. 1834–50.

**Figure 25.1
Labour market
equilibrium with an
economy-wide union**

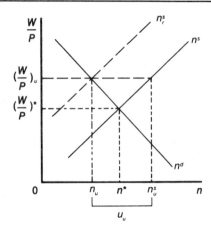

An economy-wide union would either restrict the supply of labour below the competitive supply n_f^s or would raise the wage rate to $(W/P)_U$ which is above the competitive equilibrium rate $(W/P)^*$. The effect is the same in either case. It lowers the quantity of employment from n^* to n_u but raises the quantity supplied from n^* to n_u^s. The gap between the quantity of labour supplied and quantity demanded is the amount of union-induced unemployment u_u.

all the workers in this economy join an economy-wide trade union which seeks to raise real wages.

There are two types of things that the trade union could do in order to raise the real wages of its members. One possibility would be to declare that no one may work for a réal wage of less than, say, $(W/P)_u$, and then to enforce this rule either by having some sort of legal protection or by using more indirect pressures. Alternatively, the union could restrict the supply of labour by, for example, defining minimum acceptable qualifications for particular jobs such that the number of people able to meet the minimum qualifications was less than the labour supply in the absence of the union. In that event, supply would be artificially restricted, and the supply curve would move to the left of the non-union supply curve.

Either way, the result would be a higher real wage and a lower level of employment. Figure 25.1 illustrates this analysis. In examining Figure 25.1, keep the competitive equilibrium firmly in mind as a reference point. We can illustrate what happens if the union declares a *minimum wage* below which no one may be employed by recording that wage, say, $(W/P)_u$, on the vertical axis of the figure. That wage will be above the competitive equilibrium real wage. Then, simply by reading off from the demand for labour curve, you can see that at the real wage (W/P_u), the level of employment becomes n_u. This employment level is less than the competitive employment level n^*. At the real wage set by the union, n_u^s people would like to have a job, and the difference between n_u^s and n_u represents the level of unemployment induced by this economy-wide trade union.

If, alternatively, the union enforced *minimum qualifications* that had the effect of shifting the labour supply curve to the left — to a position such as that shown as n_r^s — the effect would be increased real wages and lower employment. (The diagram is drawn so that the same effect arises from either of these policies. This has been done only to simplify the diagram. There is no presumption that both union strategies would have exactly the same effect.)

In this case, the people unemployed are unemployed because they do not meet the minimum qualification standards for the job. This situation can often be made to look semi-respectable, for example, by dressing up the restriction as 'protecting the consumer', and is therefore a much more common practice among trade unions than that of simply declaring that no one may work for less than a certain wage. It is especially widely practised by professional trade unions such as those in the legal and medical industries. It is also an easier restriction to enforce.

Either way, whether an economy-wide trade union sets a minimum real wage or restricts supply, it raises the real wage above its competitive equilibrium level, lowers the level of employment, raises the quantity of labour supplied, and generates unemployment. The greater the ability of the union to raise the real wage above the competitive equilibrium level, the bigger are these effects.

B. Job Search and Unemployment

People allocate their time to three major economic activities: work, leisure, and job search. Jobs cannot be found without search, and search is costly. Thus, it is useful to think of job search as being an investment. There is a cost and an expected return. The higher the cost, the smaller will be the amount of job search activity undertaken. The higher the expected return or payoff, the bigger will be the amount of job search activity undertaken.

Much job searching is done on a casual basis while the person is employed. Some job searchers, however, specialize in searching; that is, they cease to be workers and they spend all their non-leisure time in job search activities. These job searchers are interesting from a macroeconomic point of view for they are recorded as unemployed.

For a given cost of job search, it seems reasonable to suppose that the number of people engaged in full-time job search depends on two main factors. They are: the size of the labour force and the spread between the highest and the lowest wages that are available. First, consider the relationship between full-time job search and the size of the labour force. As you already know, the higher the real wage, the bigger the labour force. This might lead us to suppose that the supply of job search increases as the real wage increases. We need to be careful, however, before we accept that conclusion. Caution is needed because increases in the real wage also affect the costs and benefits of job search.

You can think of the wage as being part of the opportunity cost of job search. That is, over and above the direct costs involved (phone calls, travel, etc.), there is the cost of forgone earnings measured by the wage that would have been obtained from accepting the first job that comes along. The higher the average real wage, the higher is that portion of the opportunity cost of job-search activity. On the other side of the calculation, the real wage obtained from the best job that could be found after an appropriate search process is part of the benefit from job search. Again, the higher the average real wage, the higher is that benefit on the average. Thus, the higher the real wage, the higher is both the cost and the expected benefit from job search activity.

It will be assumed that these two forces working in opposite directions to each other approximately offset each other, so that, as real wages rise, the ratio of costs to benefits stay fairly constant, and the *fraction* of the labour force engaging in full-time job-search activity remains fairly constant. This implies that the *number* of people involved in job-search activity will rise as the labour force rises, which in turn means that the number of people engaged in job-search activity will rise as the real wage rises.

The supply of job search embodying the above considerations is shown in Figure 25.2. If the real wage rate was $(W/P)_0$, there would be J_0 full-time job searchers recorded as unemployed (equivalently shown as the distance AB).

Next consider the relationship between wage differentials and job search. Suppose that all jobs paid the same wage. In such a case, as people retire and as new people enter the labour force some job search activity would take place but it would not be search connected with finding a good wage. Rather it would be search for a job that had other desirable characteristics such as, for example, location, or compatibility with the individual's talents and abilities. But, it seems clear that as the spread

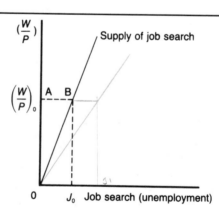

**Figure 25.2
The supply of job
search**

Job search is an alternative activity to working and taking leisure. The higher the economy average real wage, the more people will join the pool of job searchers. At the real wage $(W/P)_0$, J_0 workers will join the labour force and search for jobs.

between the highest wages available and the lowest wages on offer becomes larger, so it would pay more and more people to engage in the activity of searching out the more highly paid jobs. This idea is illustrated in Figure 25.3. The vertical axis in that figure measures not the level of wages but the gap between the highest wages (W_{max}) and the lowest wages (W_{min}) that are available. As that gap gets larger so the supply of job search increases. This is shown as the upward-sloping line labelled supply of job search. The line indicates that, even with no wage differential the amount of job search supplied would be J_T and this captures the notion that demographic change and labour turnover would produce some job search even if there was no wage differential. If the gap between the highest and lowest wages was the amount labelled D_0 on the vertical axis then the amount of job search activity would be J_0 or, equivalently, the distance marked AB.

Notice that the distance AB in Figure 25.3 is identical to the distance AB in Figure 25.3. You should not think of these curves as two different theories of the supply of job search. Rather each shows us one aspect of the forces determining the amount of job search. If the wage differential was D_0 in Figure 25.3, and if the average real wage was $(W/P)_0$ in Figure 25.3, then the amount of job search supplied would be J_0. If we vary the wage differential, but hold the average real wage constant, then we can think of what is happening as travelling up the curve in Figure 25.3 and shifting the curve in Figure 25.2. Conversely, if we hold the wage differential constant and raise the average real wage then we travel up the curve in Figure 25.2 and the curve in Figure 25.3 shifts to the right.

For the most part it will be convenient to work with the supply of job search as pictured in Figure 25.2. As the wage differential varies then the supply of job search curve shifts. A higher wage differential rotates the

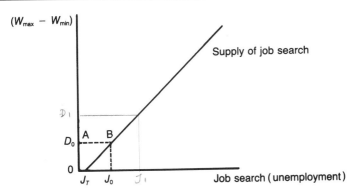

Figure 25.3
The supply of job
search and wage
differentials

The larger the gap between the highest and lowest wages available ($W_{max} - W_{min}$), the bigger the inducement to undertake job search in order to try to find one of the higher paying jobs. This is shown as the upward-sloping curve. At a wage differential of zero there will be some minimal job search (J_T). At the wage differential of D_0, job search will be AB (or J_0).

curve to the right and a lower wage differential rotates the curve to the left. Figure 25.4 illustrates the effect of the wage differential on the supply of job search. This figure shows three supply of job search curves:one for a high differential, one for an average differential and one for a low differential. At an average differential and at the real wage of $(W/P)_0$ the amount of job search is J_0 (the distance AB) as in Figure 25.2. At that same real wage but with a low difference between the highest and lowest wages the amount of job search would be J_s or the distance AC. With a high gap between the highest and lowest wages the amount of job search would be J_L or the distance AE.

Next, let us distinguish between the supply of labour and the labour force. The *labour force* is defined as the supply of labour plus the supply of job search. The supply of labour is defined as the number of people who, at a given real wage, are willing to supply their labour services to a full-time job immediately without further search.

Figure 25.5 shows how these magnitudes are related to the real wage. The curve n^s is the supply curve that was used above in Chapter 17. It shows the number of people immediately available for work without further search at each real wage. Adding horizontally to that curve the amount of job search that would be undertaken at each real wage gives the labour force (the curve ℓf). This curve shows the total number of people available for work right now at each real wage, plus the total number of people at each real wage who would still be searching for a job. The distance AB in Figure 25.5 is equivalent to the distance AB in Figure 25.3. Thus, the curve ℓf simply adds the supply of job search curve to the supply of labour curve. If the real wage was $(W/P)_0$, the amount of labour supplied would be n_0, and the labour force would be ℓ_0.

The vertical distances AC and BD are interesting economic magnitudes.

Figure 25.4
Job search, real wages and wage differentials

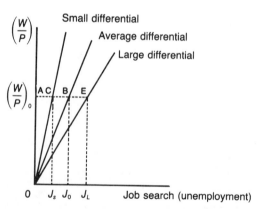

This figure is like Figure 25.2 except that it shows the supply of job search against the real wage for three different levels of wage differentials. On the average, at the wage rate $(W/P)_0$ job search is J_0. If wage differentials are unusually small, job search will decline to J_S and if wage differentials become larger than usual, job search would rise to J_L.

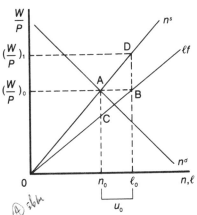

Figure 25.5
Equilibrium employ-ment, unemployment and real wage

If the supply of job search is added to the supply of labour n^s, the labour force curve *lf* is derived. (The distance AB is the same as the distance AB in Figure 25.2.) With the demand curve n^d, the equilibrium is at $(W/P)_0$ and n_0. The labour force at this equilibrium average real wage is l_0, and the number of unemployed (job searchers) is u_0. The distance AC measures the value placed on job search by the last person to be employed. The economy average real wage would have to drop by AC to induce that person to leave the labour force. The distance DB measures the value placed on job search by the last person to join the labour force. The economy average real wage would have to rise by BD to $(W/P)_1$ in order to induce that person to take a job.

The marginal person in employment is the last person to become employed at the employment level n_0. At the economy average real wage $(W/P)_0$ this person is on the margin of indifference between accepting a job and continuing to search for a job. If the real wage was marginally below $(W/P)_0$, that person would quit and start to search for a new job. The distance AC measures the value that this marginal worker places on job search.

There is another margin, that between being in the labour force and not being in the labour force. This individual is the last person to join the labour force of l_0. At a real wage $(W/P)_0$, such an individual feels that it is just worthwhile searching for a job. The value that this individual places on job search is the distance BD. A real wage equal to $(W/P)_1$ would be necessary to induce this marginal worker actually to accept a job instantaneously with no further search.

Given the demand curve n^d, the real wage $(W/P)_0$ is the competitive equilibrium real wage. The economy is in an equilibrium characterized by less than complete knowledge about job opportunities, so that there is always a certain number of people searching for jobs. The labour force is l_0, the employment level n_0, and there are u_0 unemployed job searchers.

It is important that you realize that the labour marked as depicted in Figure 25.5 is not in a static state, with a certain number of people being permanently employed and another group being permanently unemployed. Rather, there is a continuous turnover, with people leaving jobs to search for new ones, other people entering the labour force to search for jobs, others leaving the labour force, and still others being hired. Thus, the flows of hires and leavings will be matched, and the flows of people into and out of the labour force will be balanced, so that the individuals involved are continuously in a state of flux, although the economy, on the average, is in the position shown in Figure 25.5.

It is also important to realize that the labour market theory that we have just reviewed in no way predicts that the level of search and employment will be constant. That is going to depend on, among other things, the wage differential between the highest and lowest wages of the economy. In some periods of time the differential will be large and in others small. One of the key factors likely to produce movements in that differential is the uneven pace of technical change across different sectors of the economy. Let us pursue this idea a little bit more deeply.

Imagine, for simplicity, that the economy is divided into two sectors. The labour force is allocated between these two sectors and, initially, there are no wage differentials between the sectors. Figure 25.6 illustrates such an economy. Frames (a) and (b) represent the two sectors of the economy. The curves labelled n_0^d are the initial demand curves for each sector. The economy demand curve is the horizontal sum of the two individual sector demand curves. The aggregate employment level is n_0^* as shown in frame (c) and that is allocated across the two sectors in the amounts n_0^1 and n_0^2 as shown in frames (a) and (b). The real wage in each sector is $(W/P)_0$.

Now imagine that there is a technical advance in Sector 1 that leads to a rise in the marginal product of labour in this sector and thus shifts the demand for labour curve to n_1^d. There are no other shocks. This is the only thing that happens. How does the economy adjust in this new situation? It is helpful to begin by noticing that since the marginal product of labour curve is shifted in one sector it must have shifted for the economy as a whole. The curve n_1^d in frame (c) reflects that fact. These figures have been drawn on the presumption that initially Sectors 1 and 2 are of equal size so that the shift in frame (c) (which is drawn on one-half the scale of the other two frames) is equal to one-half of the shift in Sector 1. Now look at the new equilibrium for the economy as a whole, frame (c). The higher demand for labour produces a higher equilibrium real wage, $(W/P)_1$ and this encourages more people to join the labour force (n_1^*). Labour also reallocates between the two sectors. Employment in Sector 2, frame (b), declines from n_0^2 to n_1^2, while Sector 1 employment increases from n_0^1 to n_1^1, frame (a). This is the new equilibrium.

It does not mean however that this particular equilibrium is instantly reached. Rather, there could, quite reasonably, be an equilibrium path from the initial position to the final position. We can see this by looking at the state of the economy at the instant that the productivity shock hits.

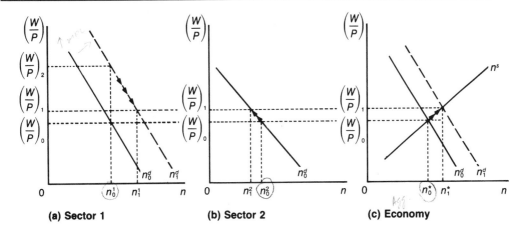

Figure 25.6
Sectoral reallocation and job search
The economy has two sectors initially of equal size shown as Sector 1 and Sector 2 in frames (a) and (b). The aggregate economy is shown in frame (c). The scale on the horizontal axis in frame (c) is half that in frames (a) and (b). The equilibrium is at $(W/P)_0$, n_0^*, n_0^1, n_0^2. Technical progress in Sector 1 raises the marginal productive of labour and raises the demand for labour to n_1^d in frame (a). It raises the aggregate demand for labour accordingly in frame (c). Initially wages are bid up in Sector 1 to $(W/P)_2$. This creates a wage differential between the two sectors and increases the economy average real wage. This wage differential and the rise in the average wage available induce job search activity. New workers enter the labour force and workers leave Sector 2 to find better jobs in Sector 1. The economy gradually moves to a new equilibrium where there is no wage differential and no further (unusual rise in) job search activity. The equilibrium is $(W/P)_1$, n_1^1, n_1^2, n_1^*. This single shock has produced a cycle in the natural rate of unemployment.

At this point in time there are n_0^1 workers in Sector 1. Firms in this sector will probably find it most natural, initially, to compete among themselves to attract workers already in this sector — or to prevent their own workers from leaving. The wages in Sector 1 will, therefore, be bid up to $(W/P)_2$. Thus there will be a large wage differential — a gap between the wages being paid in Sector 2 $(W/P)_0$ and those being paid in Sector 1 $(W/P)_2$. This gap will induce an increase in job search activity. Also, this high wage differential and the higher economy average real wage will attract new workers to join the labour force. A large number of people will withdraw themselves from work in Sector 2 in order to search for jobs in Sector 1 and also people who have not previously been in the labour force will begin to become full-time job searchers. As a consequence of this activity, people will gradually find jobs in the higher paying sector and wages in Sector 1 will decline — firms will move down their demand for labour curves. Also, as workers withdraw from Sector 2 both to search for jobs and to accept jobs in Sector 1, wages in Sector 2 will rise — firms will move up their demand for labour curves. The gradual changes that will take place are shown as the arrowed lines in

Figure 25.6. Lying behind these arrows are gradual processes through which individuals will have been temporarily full-time job searchers or, in other words, temporarily unemployed.

There will be times in economic history when the amount of technical change is slow and even across the sectors of the economy. Such will be times in which the supply of job search is low and, therefore, the natural rate of unemployment will be low. There will be other times when technical progress is either rapid or very different across the different sectors of the economy — indeed the world economy — thereby leading to massive amounts of job search activity.

Returning to Figure 25.5, you can imagine what is going on in the actual world as being described by the equilibrium adjusting as the demand for labour curve continuously shifts around. As the demand for labour curve shifts to the right and to the left, the equilibrium real wage and employment level rise and fall, as read off from the n^s curve. The labour force also rises and falls, as read off from the ℓf curve. In addition, the gap between the labour force and the employment level, as read off from the figure as the horizontal distance between the ℓf and n^s curves, widens and narrows thereby raising and lowering the equilibrium full-employment rate of unemployment.

One interesting implication of the foregoing is worth emphasizing. It is very likely that the forces that we have just described and analysed are very likely to lead to fluctuations in the rate of unemployment and output. Even the simplest theory of aggregate supply — the classical theory that ignores discrepancies between actual and expected prices and which is based on the notion that the aggregate supply curve is vertical — is capable of generating cyclical movements in the unemployment rate and level of output.

There is a further potentially important influence on the unemployment rate that we will now analyse.

C. Unemployment Benefits and Unemployment

Suppose the government introduces an unemployment benefits scheme which makes it possible for people, while searching for a new job, to receive an income from the government equal to some fraction of the wage that they had previously been earning while employed. What effects would this policy have?

It is immediately clear that such a policy lowers the cost of job search. Therefore, it makes job search activity, at the margin, more attractive. You have already seen that there are two relevant margins of job search. One is the margin between search and employment, the other is the margin between employment and complete leisure (withdrawal from the labour force). Improving unemployment benefits would alter both of these margins. There would be a tendency for people to search longer before accepting employment, thereby lowering the amount of work that people in aggregate would be willing to do at any given real wage. Thus, improving unemployment benefits would have the effect of rotating the labour supply curve n^s upwards, such as the movement from n_0^s to n_1^s in Figure 25.7. Additionally, people who previously were not in the labour force will now be induced to enter it and take a temporary job to qualify for unemployment benefits, and then later search for a more acceptable long-term job. Therefore, the labour force curve rotates in a rightward direction. Again Figure 25.5 shows this rotation as the movement from ℓf_0 to ℓf_1.

The curves n_0^s and ℓf_0 and the equilibrium $(W/P)_0$, n_0 represent the economy with no unemployment benefits scheme and are the same as those illustrated in Figure 25.5. The curves n_1^s and ℓf_1 represent the new labour force and the labour supply curves induced by an unemployment benefits scheme.

It is now possible to read off the effects of an unemployment benefits scheme on the variables. The labour market will be in equilibrium at the real wage $(W/P)_1$ and the employment level n_1. The labour force will rise to ℓ_1, and unemployment will be u_1 which is $\ell_1 - n_1$. Thus, an unemployment benefits scheme raises the real wage, lowers the level of employment, raises the size of the labour force, and increases the number unemployed.

The analysis that we have just conducted has ignored the question of who pays the taxes that provide the unemployment benefits. In the next

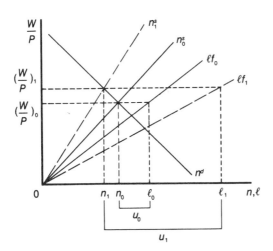

Figure 25.7
How unemployment
benefits increase
unemployment

Unemployment benefits lower the cost of job search and, therefore, make job search a more attractive activity relative to either working or consuming leisure. The supply of labour falls from n_0^s to n_1^s and raises the labour force supply curve from ℓf_0 to ℓf_1. The real wage rises, the employment level falls, the labour force rises and the number of workers unemployed rises.

section of this chapter we will analyse the effects of employment taxes and income taxes on the level of employment, unemployment and real wages. This analysis applies more generally than just to those taxes used to pay unemployment benefits, it applies to any taxes. The analysis just conducted may be augmented by the analysis of effects of taxes, to which we will now turn.

D.   Taxes and Unemployment

It will be convenient, in analysing the effects of taxes, to abstract from the considerations of job search that were the central feature of the analysis of the previous section. This is not to say that the above analysis is irrelevant when considering the effects of taxes. It is simply a convenient way of considering one thing at a time. Once you have thoroughly mastered the material in this and the preceding sections, it will be a straightforward matter for you to consider both effects simultaneously. There is no gain, however, from presenting them as a simultaneous analysis.

The questions that we want to address now are: first, what are the effects of income taxes — taxes on labour income — on real wages, employment and unemployment? Second, what are the effects of employment taxes — taxes on firms that vary with the number of workers they employ — on the level of employment, unemployment and real wages? And third, what are the effects of expenditure taxes — taxes on consumption — on the level of employment, unemployment and real wages?

As a starting point, let us begin with an economy that has no taxes and then consider what happens as we introduce these alternative taxes — first separately and secondly simultaneously. Figure 25.8 illustrates the analysis. The curves labelled n^s and n^d are the supply and demand curves for labour in a world in which there are no taxes. The competitive equilibrium in this economy is at point B, where the real wage is $(W/P)^*$ and the employment level is n^*. This position is exactly the same as the competitive equilibrium in Figure 25.1, with which we started this analysis of the labour market.

There is one additional thing which you can work out about the economy, to which attention has not previously been drawn but which is of some interest for the purpose of the present exercise — that is, the distribution of national income between labour and the owners of capital. Labour income is equal to the rectangle $0(W/P)^*Bn^*$. You can readily verify that this is so by noting that the number of workers is n^*, and the wage per worker is $(W/P)^*$ so that labour income, being the product of employment and wages, is given by the area of that rectangle.

The income accruing to the owners of capital is the triangle $(W/P)^*AB$. This proposition is a less obvious than the previous one. You may, however, verify that that triangle represents the part of total product not paid to labour. To do so, begin by recalling that the demand for labour curve measures the marginal product of labour. Thus, the first worker

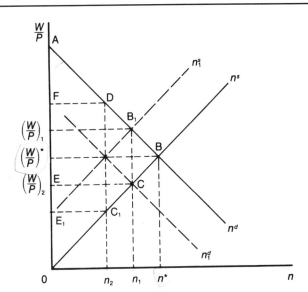

Figure 25.8
The effects of taxes
on the labour market

A competitive equilibrium is shown at the real wage $(W/P)^*$ and employment level n^*. This equilibrium is disturbed by the introduction of a tax on labour income or by a tax on consumption that shifts the labour supply curve to n_1^s. The real wage rises to $(W/P)_1$, and employment falls to n_1. The after-tax real wage falls. Alternatively, the equilibrium is disturbed by the introduction of an employment tax that shifts the labour demand curve down to n_1^d. Again the level of employment falls to n_1, and the real wage becomes $(W/P)_2$, equivalent to the after-tax wage level of E in the previous experiment. Both sets of taxes introduced together lower the level of employment to n_2. As taxes on employment are successively increased, labour's share of national income (defined to include the taxes) increases, while the share accruing to the owners of capital decreases.

hired would produce a marginal product of A (that is, where the demand curve hits the real wage axis). As more and more workers are hired, the marginal product declines until the final worker is hired at the equilibrium level of employment n^*, by which time the marginal product has fallen to B. For each extra worker hired, the extra output produced is equal to the marginal product, and the total product accruing to the producer is given by the entire area underneath the marginal product curve all the way up to the level of employment n^*. Total product in the economy, then, is the trapezium $0ABn^*$. That which is paid to labour is $0(W/P)^*Bn^*$, and that which is paid to the owners of capital is $(W/P)^*AB$. (In the economy shown in Figure 25.8, labour gets two-thirds and capital one-third of the economy's output.)

Now consider the introduction of an income tax. Instead of keeping all the wages they earn, workers now have to pay some fraction of their labour income to the government in the form of a tax. Thus the real wage received by workers is less than the real wage paid by employers. Assuming, as we are, that the supply of labour curve is not vertical so that a higher real wage always increases the quantity of labour supplied, this implies that for any given real wage paid by the employer, there will now be a smaller supply of labour. Thus a tax on income shifts the labour supply curve to the left. For simplicity, the figure has been drawn on the presumption that the labour supply curve shifts parallel, so that the new curve, after allowing for taxes, is the one labelled n_1^s. The way to read n_1^s is as follows: for any given level of employment, without taxes, the wage that would have to be paid is read off from the n^s curve; but with the taxes in place the wage that would have to be paid to call forth the same level of employment would be read off from the higher curve n_1^s. The vertical gap between n_1^s and n^s is the level of taxes.

To determine the equilibrium in this case, we have to find the point where the new effective labour supply curve n_1^s intersects the demand for labour curve n^d. Equilibrium occurs at point B_1, with a real wage $(W/P)_1$ and an employment level n_1. Thus, the introduction of a tax on labour income raises the real wage and lowers the employment level. The after-tax income of workers falls from a wage rate of $(W/P)^*$ to the real wage rate given by the position E on the vertical axis. In fact, total wages are $0ECn_1$. The tax receipts of the government are $E(W/P)_1B_1C$, and the income accruing to capital is the triangle $(W/P)_1AB_1$. The overall effects, then, of the imposition of a tax on labour income is a drop in after-tax real wages, a rise in pre-tax real wages, a fall in labour income, a rise in the government's income, and a fall in the income accruing to the owners of capital. There is also a fall in the level of employment.

The drop in employment from n^* to n_1 cannot, properly speaking, be regarded as unemployment. Although there are fewer people in employment in the situation n_1 as compared with n^*, the situation that prevails is a competitive equilibrium. Nevertheless, it may be the case that the workers who withdraw from the labour force as the after-tax wage rate falls from $(W/P)^*$ to E will be entitled to unemployment benefits and will, therefore, appear to swell the ranks of the unemployed job searchers — if not forever, at least for a period. In this limited sense, the raising of taxes on labour income can be said to 'create unemployment'.

Next consider the effects of imposing a tax on the other side of the labour market — on the employers. Imagine that firms have to pay a tax on each worker that they employ. Firms will no longer regard the marginal product of labour as being equivalent to the value of labour. Rather, they will regard labour as being worth its marginal product minus the tax that it has to pay on each worker employed. Thus the demand for labour curve will shift downwards. The curve n_1^d in Figure 25.8 illustrates such a demand curve.

What is the effect of this tax on employment, unemployment and wages? Let us first answer this question in the absence of income taxes. In that case, the new equilibrium will be where the curve n_1^d cuts the original supply curve n^s. The equilibrium occurs at the wage rate $(W/P)_2$ or E and at the employment level n_1.

Notice that this experiment has been set up so as to yield an identical amount of revenue for the government as the income tax did in the previous experiment. In principle, we could analyse cases where different amounts of revenue are raised. It does, however, seem to be more instructive to hold the government revenue constant for the purpose of comparing the effects of alternative taxes.

It is now possible to read off all the effects of this employment tax on the level of employment and wages. These effects are, evidently, exactly the same as in the previous case. Employment falls from n^* to n_1; labour's share of national income falls to the same level as before, namely, $0ECn_1$; and the government revenue is exactly the same as before, as is the share of income accruing to the owners of capital. The only difference between the two cases is that the wages paid by firms fall, and firms pay the taxes to the government. In the first experiment conducted, the wages paid by firms increased, but after workers had paid their taxes, the net of tax wage decreased. Workers had exactly the same net of tax income in the previous situation as they do in this one.

Next, consider what happens when taxes are imposed on the expenditure on consumer goods by workers. From the perspective of the analysis conducted here, this will have identical effects to the first tax analysed — a tax on labour income. The easiest way to see this is to consider the way in which income taxes and expenditure taxes both affect the relative price between labour and consumption. Equivalently, we may ask how income taxes and expenditure taxes affect the relative price of labour with respect to consumption goods. The wage rate that a worker receives is equal to the gross wage paid, scaled down by the income taxes levied by the government. Suppose that we call the income tax rate t_y. Then, the after-tax wage rate is $W(1 - t_y)$. When a worker purchases consumer goods, the price paid is equal to the price received by the producer, P, plus any taxes levied by the government. Call the rate of tax on expenditure t_c. Then the price paid by the consumer is $P(1 + t_c)$. Evidently, the ratio of the price received by the worker to the price paid for goods by the worker is equal to:

$$\frac{W(1 - t_y)}{P(1 + t_c)} \tag{25.1}$$

You may think of the expression $(1 - t_y)/(1 + t_c)$ as the wedge which taxes drive between the price that firms have to pay for their labour, W, and the price that they receive for their output, P. From the household's point of view, for any given real wage, W/P, the bigger the tax wedge, the smaller will be the supply of labour. Thus, you may think of the shift in the labour supply curve from n^s to n_1^s, analysed in the first experiment conducted above, as arising from either the imposition of an income tax or an expenditure tax having an equivalent total yield.

Finally, consider what happens when all of these tax measures are introduced simultaneously. In this case, the relevant supply curve is n_1^s, and the demand curve is n_1^d. The equilibrium employment level falls still further to n_2, but by the construction of the example, the real wage remains at the no tax equilibrium level of $(W/P)^*$. [To avoid having too many equilibrium positions on the one diagram, we have caused these two curves to intersect at the original real wage, $(W/P)^*$.] Worker's incomes will now be $0E_1C_1n_2$, the government's tax receipts will be E_1FDC_1, and the income accruing to capital owners will be FAD. Employment will have fallen from n^* to n_2.

It is worth highlighting what happens to the relative shares of labour and capital in national income as we move from the initial no-tax equilibrium to the after-tax equilibrium. The most convenient way of making this comparison is to use the accounting conventions employed in the national income accounts. In those accounts, labour income is defined to include the payments of employment taxes by firms to the government. The fiction is that this tax is really part of the wages of the workers that is being deducted at source and handed over to the government in much the same way as the workers' income taxes are also withheld by the employer and paid to the government.

Thus, in the no-tax situation, labour income is $0(W/P)^*Bn^*$ and in the after-tax situation (after all taxes), labour income is $0FDn_2$. Using this accounting convention, it is evident that, as taxes are increased, the share of national income accruing to labour increases —as you can see in Figure 25.8. In the initial situation, labour income was equal to two-thirds of total income, whereas in the after-tax situation, it is equal to six-sevenths. What happens as taxes are increased is that although the number of workers employed declines, the average wage per worker (defined in the gross terms as it is being defined here) increases. But total product declines in the experiment conducted here.

The experiments just reviewed started with an economy that had zero taxes and then introduced some positive taxes. The same results could have been generated, however, if we had started with an economy with a given level of taxes and then raised those taxes. Thus, if taxes on labour (whether paid by workers or employers) are increased, the prediction is that there will be a drop in the level of employment, a rise in labour's share in the national product, and, a temporary rise in the measured rate of unemployment.

E. UK Unemployment

We have now reviewed the forces that can influence unemployment, (abstracting from surprise changes in the level of aggregate demand), and are now ready to examine the extent to which these various forces have been at work in recent macroeconomic history of the UK. We will begin by examining unions; we will then look at unemployment benefits and taxes. After that we will examine some recently developed ideas about how sectoral reallocation of labour induced by differential rates of technical change move the rate of unemployment.

Union Strength

When we analysed the effects of unions on unemployment, in Section A of this chapter, we showed how unions can raise real wages but at the expense of employment. A first thought may be that we can look at real wages and unemployment to see whether unions have pushed real wages up and caused unemployment. But there have been many influences on real wages in recent years and it would not be helpful simply to examine the movements in that variable. No matter what we found we would not be able to attribute movements in real wages to any one particular source. What we can do, however, is to examine the strength of trade unions as measured by some other independent characteristic. A commonly employed measure of trade union strength is the percentage of the labour force that belongs to trade unions. It might be thought that the larger that percentage, the stronger the trade unions, and the more able are they to press *real* wage demands. In the UK setting, it is probably not unreasonable to proceed on the assumption that the economy is entirely unionized. While many workers do not belong to trade unions, very few of them are able to negotiate their employment terms independently of the terms negotiated by the unions. In other words, the fraction of workers whose wages and other employment conditions are determined by the outcome of a union — employer negotiation is very small. That being so, changes in the percentage of the labour force belonging to unions may well be a good indicator of the ability of what is, in effect, an economy-wide union to press for higher real wages.

What are the facts about union strength on this criterion? Figure 25.9 provides the answer. It shows the percentage of the total working population belonging to trade unions from 1965 to 1983. Evidently union strength increased sharply in the late 1960s, increasing by more than 4 per cent between 1969 and 1970 alone. Through the decade of the 1970s union strength continued to rise until, by 1979, it reached a peak at almost 50 per cent of the working population. Since that time there has been a dramatic fall, and by the mid-1980s union strength was back where it had been in the late 1960s.

While these facts, taken by themselves, prove nothing, they do indicate an increasingly strong trade union movement between 1969 and 1979. That increased strength may have been associated with increased bargaining power and increased union funds with which to subsidize strikes thereby strengthening the bargaining position of union negotiators. The decline in union strength since 1979, by this same measure, should have had the reverse effects. We will examine the relationship between these movements in union strength and other variables later in this section. Let us next turn to an examination of unemployment benefits.

Unemployment Benefits

There have been many minor and two major changes in the arrangements concerning unemployment benefits in the post-war years. The first major

Figure 25.9
Trade union member-
ship 1965–1983

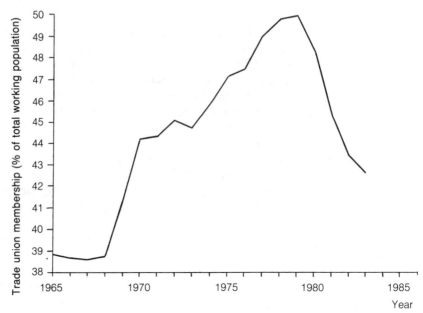

The fraction of the labour force in trade unions was around 39 per cent in the mid-1960s. That percentage grew rapidly in 1969–70. It then stabilized for a while and then grew strongly again until 1979. Since that time trade union membership has steadily declined. *Source: British Labour Statistics, Historical Abstract, 1886–1968*, HMSO, 1971, Tables 118, 119. *British Labour Statistics Year Book, 1969*, HMSO, 1971, Tables 45, 156. *Annual Abstract of Statistics*, HMSO, 1986, pp. 104 and 133.

change was the introduction, in 1966, of the earnings related supplement — an increase in benefits based on the unemployed person's prior earnings experience. Prior to that date unemployment benefits were paid at rates which were independent of the prior earnings of the unemployed person. Further, the benefits were fixed in money terms and increased from time to time by statute. In 1966 unemployment benefits consisted of two parts: one, unrelated to the person's previous earnings and the other, directly tied to the earnings of the person experiencing unemployment. This arrangement provided an automatic adjustment for unemployment benefits as earnings and prices increased at increasing rates throughout the 1970s. The second major change occurred in 1982 when the earnings related supplement was phased out.

The effects of the changes in the rules governing unemployment benefits can be summarized by calculating the amount of unemployment benefit that would be paid to an unemployed person, on the average, expressed a percentage of net of tax average earnings. This number is called the replacement ratio. Table 25.1 provides an outline of the main trends in this variable since 1951. What you see from inspecting the figures in that

Table 25.1   Unemployment income

Year	Benefits* as a percentage of net average earnings	Supplementary benefits as a percentage of net average earnings
Earnings		
1951	33.1	48.3
1961	42.1	53.6
1966	66.7	63.9
1971	69.6	57.2
1976	66.0	61.1
1977	65.8	61.8
1978	55.5	56.4
1979	51.0	56.0
1980	46.0	59.0
1981	43.0	62.0
1982	33.0	64.0
1983	33.0	62.0

Source: Social Trends 10, 1980, p. 139 and 15, 1985, p. 80 (London, HMSO).
* Including earnings related supplement from 1966 to 1981.

table is that unemployment benefits rose from being about one-third of net average earnings in 1951 to almost 70 per cent by 1971. Since that time, the replacement ratio has slipped to about two-thirds in 1976–7, down to 55 per cent by 1978, and gradually by the early 1980s to the same level as in 1951.

Though the unemployment benefit expressed a percentage of net average earnings in 1983 was almost the same as in 1951, an important change in social security makes the comparison of those two years on the basis of these data alone a misleading one. Basic social security in the UK has gradually improved since the Second World War and, at the present time, arrangements are in place to provide supplementary benefits to all low income families ensuring that they have adequate housing, heating, food, dental, medical and other benefits. By way of example, the scale of such benefits for a single person exceeds £40 a week and for a married couple with three children exceeds £100 a week. Since the unemployed, in the absence of an earnings related supplement, are among the lowest paid people in the country they, like low-paid workers, qualify for supplementary benefits under the social security system.

Professor Patrick Minford of the University of Liverpool has worked out the replacement ratios for different family types and income levels when supplementary benefit as well as unemployment benefit is taken into account. His calculations are set out in Table 25.2. As you can see from those data, married couples with children are better off unemployed than working, unless they can generate incomes in excess of about £120 a week. Minford believes that these very high replacement ratios are the major source of high and persistent unemployment.

Let us now turn to the third labour market variable that we analysed, the tax wedge.

Table 25.2   Replacement ratios for different family types

Gross Income (£p.week)	Single person (%)	Married man* (%)	Married man* +1 child (%)	Married man* +2 children (%)	Married man* +3 children (%)	Married man* +4 children (%)
50	102.7	116.3	95.9	99.6	99.4	104.5
60	94.2	108.6	96.5	99.9	99.4	102.9
70	86.8	102.6	96.8	100.2	99.7	103.0
80	80.4	96.7	96.9	100.4	99.8	103.1
90	74.4	91.1	103.3	100.6	99.9	103.1
100	68.1	85.8	98.1	109.4	99.9	103.2
110	61.9	80.8	93.0	104.4	110.5	120.2
120	56.8	75.2	87.8	99.9	105.5	115.1
130	52.5	69.9	81.9	93.7	99.7	109.2
140	48.8	65.2	76.8	88.1	94.1	103.4
150	45.5	61.1	72.3	83.2	89.1	98.2
160	42.7	57.5	68.2	78.8	84.6	93.4

Source: Patrick Minford, *Unemployment: Cause and Cure*, Oxford: Martin Robertson, 1983, Table B3.
* wife not working

The Tax Wedge

There have been literally hundreds of changes in tax regulations that may be expected to have effects on the supply of and the demand for labour in the UK in recent years. We have tried to condense and summarize those changes into a single number. In so doing we have necessarily had to make some simplifying assumptions. What we have done is to calculate the effects of taxes on employment by considering separately taxes on labour income and taxes on household expenditures. The taxes on expenditure are expressed as an equivalent tax on income, the idea being that from the point of view of workers and firms, it makes no difference whether the wedge between the real wage paid and the real wage received arises from taxes levied directly in the labour market or in the market for output. (This is a simplification, but one that should not do violence for the purpose at hand.)

The tax wedge calculated by us is set out in Figure 25.10.[2] Evidently the tax wedge has increased dramatically in the period since 1965. The direction of change has not been uniformly upward, however. There was a sharp rise in the second half of the 1960s reaching a peak in 1970. The tax wedge then fell through 1973. It then increased to a new peak in 1977, dipped slighly in 1978 and reached its all time maximum at 43 per cent in 1982. Since 1982 the tax wedge has remained high but has fallen slightly.

---

2   The precise sources of data and the method of calculation of the tax wage is set out in the Appendix to this chapter.

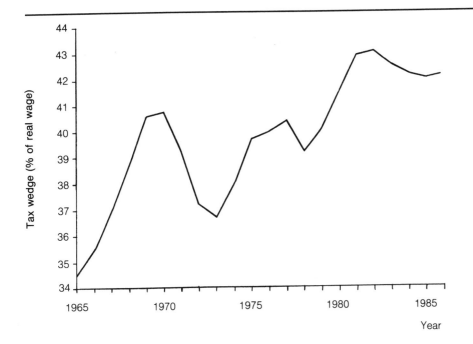

**Figure 25.10
The tax wedge
1965–1986**

The tax wedge, the difference between what firms pay for labour and what households receive expressed as a percentage of the total wage bill, has increased steadily from around 35 per cent in 1965 to 43 per cent today. Most of the increase took place in the late 1960s but there was then a fall in the early 1970s followed by a further sharp rise. *Source*: Note to this chapter.

Explaining Unemployment

How well do the developments in the labour market that we have just examined explain the movements in unemployment? Figure 25.11 provides a summary basis for providing a partial answer to this question. The movements in unemployment since 1965 are shown as the thick line that relentlessly snakes upwards throughout the period.

The various labour market shocks that we have examined are also shown in the figure. Union strength is the thin line that increases sharply between 1968 and 1970 then more gently to 1979 and thereafter declines. Evidently the relationship between unemployment and this measure of union strength is not very close. At the time when unemployment was increasing most strongly (after 1979) union strength was actually declining. It is true that union strength and unemployment both moved in the same direction from 1969 to 1979 but, in the light of the opposite movements in the 1980s, that common trend must be seen as a coincidence rather than cause and effect.

Consider next unemployment benefits which we summarized in Table 25.1. These benefits are shown in Figure 25.11 as the ten crosses. Since

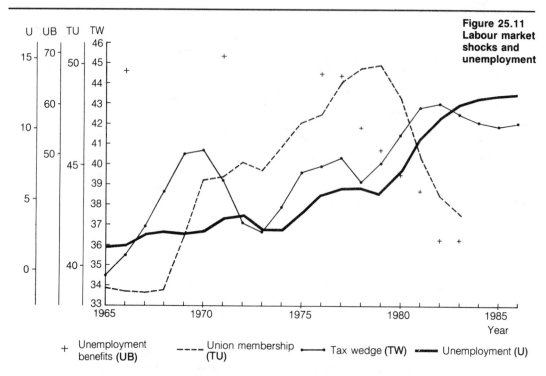

Figure 25.11 Labour market shocks and unemployment

| + | Unemployment benefits (UB) | – – – – | Union membership (TU) | •——• | Tax wedge (TW) | ▬▬ | Unemployment (U) |

Unemployment (thick line) is not closely related to unemployment benefits or trade union membership but does correspond closely with movements in the tax wedge.
Sources: Unemployment rate, Appendix to Chapter 2; tax wedge, see note at end of chapter; unemployment benefits, Table 25.1; trade union membership, see Figure 25.9.

unemployed families have their incomes topped up by supplementary benefits, we have shown here the maximum of unemployment benefits and supplementary benefits. As we noted above, the removal of earnings related unemployment benefits has made the supplementary benefits a much more important element of total unemployment income. Comparing unemployment benefits (and supplementary benefits) with unemployment reveals at best a loose connection between the variables. Further, between 1970 and 1979 benefits fell, while at the same time unemployment increased. The poor relationship in the aggregate time series data between unemployment benefits and the unemployment rate may be seriously misleading. What matters for an individual family is the marginal not the average benefit rate. Partick Minford has calculated (see Table 25.2) that the marginal benefit rate exceeds 100 per cent for many families, especially those with a larger number of children and lower earnings potential. But high marginal benefit rates are not a recent phenomenon. They have been in place for many years. So this factor alone cannot account for the strong rise in unemployment over the past twenty years.

Next consider the tax wedge. This appears as the dotted line in Figure 25.11. It is evident that in this case there is a much closer correspondence with unemployment than in the case of the two preceding variables. The tax wedge rises in line with rising unemployment right through the 1960s, 1970s and 1980s. There is a tendency for the tax wedge to rise faster than unemployment in the late 1960s, at about the same pace in the 1970s. In the 1980s the tax wedge has fallen slightly while unemployment has continued to rise. The divergence of the two series, however, is not a strong one.

Figure 25.12 illustrates the relationship between unemployment and the tax wedge in a slightly different way. In that figure the unemployment rate is plotted on the vertical axis and the tax wedge on the horizontal axis. Evidently, as the tax wedge rises from around 34 per cent to 40 per cent, as it did in the second half of the 1960s, not much happens to the unemployment rate. As the tax wedge continues to increase from 40 per cent to 44 per cent, as it did between 1975 and 1980, the unemployment rate rises sharply. This figure also reveals, however, that there are many independent cyclical movements in both the unemployment rate and the tax wedge that are not captured by any simple relationship between these two variables.

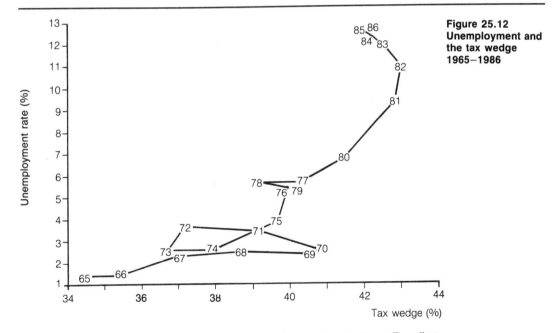

Figure 25.12 Unemployment and the tax wedge 1965–1986

The relationship between unemployment and the tax wedge is not a simple one. The effect of a rise in the tax wedge on unemployment appears to become larger as the tax wedge itself rises. There are, however, many independent cyclical movements in each of the two variables which are not closely related. *Sources*: Unemployment rate, Appendix to Chapter 2; tax wedge, see note at end of chapter.

In our analysis of labour market turnover we emphasized the possible importance of intersector turnover resulting from different rates of technical change in different parts of the economy. When one sector expands and another contracts labour has to leave the contracting sector and find work in the expanding sector. This process takes time and results in higher unemployment. We do not know of any systematic study of this phenomenon in the UK. There is, though, an ingenious study of the same phenomenon in the United States and in Canada both of which point to the potential importance of this source of unemployment. David Lillien[3] has proposed that it should be possible to measure variations in the amount of job search unemployment by calculating the gross flows of labour across the sectors of the economy. Specifically he proposed a measure that calculates the change in employment in an individual sector of the economy relative to the change in employment in the economy as a whole averaged across the economy. (The precise details of Lillien's method of calculation need not concern us here.) Applying his ideas to US data since 1947, Lillien showed that fluctuations in the amount of labour force reallocation and the average rate of unemployment were very highly correlated. Using techniques similar to Lillien's, but overcoming some of the shortcomings in his work, Lucie Sampson[4] has performed similar calculations for Canada and obtained similar findings.

It would be interesting to replicate the work of Lillien and Sampson using UK data.[5] There is one feature of the UK labour market that makes it possible that this type of phenomenon has become especially important in recent years. This is the potential for the interaction of high marginal unemployment and social security benefits rates combined with a high degree of labour market turnover. The massive changes that have confronted the UK economy in recent years, having not only a sectoral but also a regional dimension when combined with high marginal unemployment benefit rates, could lead to unusually large unemployment as those who are put out of work respond to the incentives that confront them by taking an unusually long period of time to find new employment and possibly an entirely new way of life in a new part of the country.

Those who have studied UK unemployment have not yet reached a clear agreement on its sources and on what has to be done to reduce its incidence. Major disagreement centres on the importance of unemployment compensation and social security arrangements. Patrick Minford

---

3   See David Lillien, 'Sector Shifts and Cyclical Unemployment', *Journal of Political Economy* (August 1982), pp. 777–93.
4   See Lucie Sampson, 'A Study of the Impact of Sectoral Shifts on Aggregate Unemployment in Canada', *Canadian Journal of Economics* (August 1985), pp. 518–30.
5   As a matter of fact Lucie Sampson's unpublished PhD dissertation (University of Western Ontario) does report some preliminary findings for the UK as well as several other countries, but since this work is of a preliminary nature and unpublished we do not describe it here.

places most of his emphasis on this source of unemployment. Others, whose work we cited earlier in this chapter, place less emphasis on this source of unemployment and argue for demand increases (sometimes across the board, sometimes selective) to address the problem. At the heart of the controversy is disagreement on the question of whether the natural rate of unemployment has increased, or whether unemployment has risen above its natural rate because of demand side considerations (not elaborated in this chapter).

Summary

A. *Trade Unions and Unemployment*

An economy-wide trade union, by pressing for a higher real wage or the raising of minimum qualifications, raises the real wage, lowers employment, increases the labour force and raises the level of unemployment.

B. *Job Search and Unemployment*

People allocate time to three activities: leisure, job search and work. The lower the cost of job search, the higher the average real wage, and the higher the gap between the highest and lowest wages available, the larger will be the equilibrium amount of job search activity. The factor influencing the gap between the highest and lowest wages available is the sectoral incidence of technical change. When technical change is rapid in some sectors relative to others, wage differentials will widen and induce increased job search activity as new workers enter the labour force and other workers switch from the lower to the higher paid sector.

C. *Unemployment Benefits and Unemployment*

The introduction of an unemployment benefits scheme lowers the cost of job search and makes job search more attractive than work and more attractive than leisure at the margin. Therefore, it raises the labour force and cuts the supply of labour; the equilibrium real wage rises, employment falls, the labour force rises, and unemployment rises.

D. *Taxes and Unemployment*

If the level of taxes is increased, there will be a fall in the level of employment and a rise in labour's share of national income. The fall in employment will manifest itself as measured unemployment if the workers who withdraw their labour supply remain in the labour force.

E. UK Unemployment

Trade union strength, as measured by the percentage of the labour force unionized, does not appear to be a major contributory factor in understanding movements in UK unemployment.Unemployment benefit rates (including earnings related supplements and sup-plementary benefits) are high, both on the average and at the margin. But these rates have been high for some time and cannot, on their own, account for the rise in unemployment. The tax wedge in the labour market has increased steadily over the years and it may be responsible for some part of the rise in unemployment. Increased shocks to the economy requiring labour reallocation (both sectoral-ly and regionally) in combination with high unemployment benefit rates may well have led to a high (and persistent) rate of unemployment.

Review Questions

1. Suppose the labour market in some particular industry is described in the following way. The demand for labour is

$$n^d = 100 - 5(W/P)$$

the supply of labour is

$$n^s = 5(W/P)$$

(a) Plot the demand curve and state in words what the demand equa-tion means.

(b) Plot the supply curve and state in words what the supply equa-tion means.

(c) Calculate (either algebraically or graphically) the equilibrium real wage and level of employment.

(d) How much unemployment is there in the equilibrium calculated in (c)?

(e) If the price level is 1.2, what is the equilibrium money wage?

(f) Suppose that all the workers in this industry became unionized, and the union sets its wage at £18. What is the real wage that is paid, and how many workers are now employed and how many cannot find work in this industry?

2. An economy consisting of 1000 firms has a labour demand given by

$$n^d = 4000 - 0.5(W/P)$$

and a labour supply given by

$$n^s = 3000(W/P) - 2000$$

(a) What is the equilibrium real wage?
(b) If the price level is 2, what is the money wage?
(c) If all the firms in this economy become 100 per cent unionized and the union sets the union wage at £5, how many workers are employed and unemployed?
(d) Assume that there is no unionization of labour but that the government introduces an unemployment benefits scheme which compensates any unemployed worker 75 per cent of the money wage paid to employed workers. Using a diagram, show the impact of this programme on the money wage paid, the number of workers employed, the number of workers unemployed, and the cost to the government of this scheme.

3. An economy with a competitive labour market has a demand curve given by

$$n^d = 1008 - 4(W/P)$$

and a labour supply given by

$$n^s = 960 + 2(W/P)$$

(a) What is the equilibrium real wage?
(b) Assume the price level to be 1, so that the equilibrium real wage is the equilibrium money wage. Now assume that the government imposes an employment tax of £1 per worker. Calculate the new equilibrium level of employment and the money wage.
(c) Calculate the level of real national income and the share of national income accruing to labour, the government, and the owners of capital.
(d) Now suppose that the government introduces a tax on labour income that shifts the labour supply curve to

$$n^s = 954 + 2(W/P)$$

What is the new equilibrium real wage, employment level, and share of national income accruing to labour, government, and owners of capital?

4. Why would we suppose that the wage differential (between highest and lowest wages) will influence the amount of job search activity?
5. Suppose that there is a rise in the marginal product of labour in one sector of the economy and no change in the marginal product in the other sector. Trace the events that follow such a shock. Pay attention to the amount of job search activity and unemployment. Is the unemployment generated by such a shock permanent or temporary?
6. Describe the main movements in unemployment benefit arrangements in the UK in the last twenty years.

7. Describe the relationship between the tax wedge and unemployment in the UK in recent years.
8. Why might a high degree of labour market turnover interact with constant unemployment benefits to produce a rise in the natural rate of unemployment.

Appendix: A Note on the Tax Wedge

The tax wedge was calculated in the following way: the money wage paid by firms is W and the price of output received by firms is P. Thus the real wage, ignoring taxes, is (W/P). Households pay taxes on their income at rate t_y and also, when households buy goods, they pay the price received by firms plus expenditure taxes at a rate t_c. Thus the net of tax real wage is $[W(1 - t_y)]/[P(1 + t_c)]$.

The tax wedge is the difference between the gross of tax real wage (W/P) and the net of tax real wage that we have just calculated, expressed as a percentage of the real wage. Thus the tax wedge is given by:

$$(t_c + t_y)/(1 + t_c)$$

The tax rates were calculated according to the following formulae:

$$t_y = \frac{\text{total personal income} - \text{personal disposable income}}{\text{total personal income}}$$

$$t_c = \frac{\text{expenditure taxes}}{\text{consumers' expenditure}}$$

The source for all these variables is *United Kingdom National Accounts*, 1987 edition, pp. 22–5.

26

Inflation, Balance of Payments and Exchange Rates

The focus of this chapter is inflation, the balance of payments and the exchange rate. The question of what causes inflation and what can be done to control it has occupied the minds of some of the best economists. Despite this fact, the question remains surrounded by a great deal of mythology as well as sheer nonsense. The material presented in this chapter is designed to help you to arrive at a clear understanding of what does and does not cause inflation and also to help you understand and avoid some of the principal errors that are made in popular discussion — in the popular press and by political commentators — on this topic.

The balance of payments and the exchange rate are also topics of major importance and the subject of much confusion. There was a time, not very many years ago, when the pound was regarded as some kind of sacred beast that must be protected at all cost. Even today when the pound falls sharply on the foreign exchange market a common reaction is to regard the nation's virility as being in question. This chapter is also designed to help you cut through the confusion and popular misunderstanding that surrounds these two international macroeconomic variables.

By the time you have completed this chapter you will be able to:

(a) State the distinction between a once-and-for-all rise in the price level and inflation.

(b) Explain how a once-and-for-all rise in the money stock or a once-and-for-all cut in aggregate supply raises the price level.

(c) Explain how continuing growth in the money supply leads to inflation and to a gap between the market and real rates of interest.

(d) Explain how a change in the growth rate of the money supply leads to a change in inflation and to more volatile inflation than money supply growth.

(e) Explain the 'law of one price': (i) purchasing power parity; (ii) interest rate parity.

(f) Explain how inflation and the balance of payments are determined at full employment when the exchange rate is fixed.

(g) Explain how inflation and the exchange rate are determined at full employment in a flexible exchange rate regime.

(h) Explain how inflation, the balance of payments and the exchange rate are linked at full employment in a managed floating regime.

(i) Examine the relationship between inflation, the balance of payments, the exchange rate and the money supply in recent UK macroeconomic history.

A.   Once-and-for-All Price Level Rises and Inflation

Inflation is an ongoing process whereby prices are rising persistently year after year. A once-and-for-all rise in the price level occurs when the economy experiences a price level that is generally stable but occasionally jumps to a new level. Recall Figure 5.1 in Chapter 5, illustrating two economies. One has a price level that increased from 100 to 200 over a period of 4 years. In the other economy, the price level suddenly rose from 100 to 200, and for the rest of the time the price level was stable. The first economy has experienced inflation. The second economy has experienced a once-and-for-all rise in the price level. This distinction is important in analysing the effects of various shocks on the price level.

We are going to study the forces that can generate once-and-for-all changes in the price level and those that can produce inflation. To keep things as clear as possible, we are first of all going to study these matters in the context of a closed economy. We'll then, later in the chapter, go on to study the determination of the price level and inflation in an open economy. Let's begin with once-and-for-all changes in the price level.

B.   Once-and-for-All Changes in the Price Level

Study the factors that produce once-and-for-all changes in the price level by applying the *IS–LM* analysis of aggregate demand of Chapter 14 with the full-employment theory of aggregate supply that you met in Chapter 17. (A reminder: we are not saying that the new theories of aggregate supply are irrelevant. We are abstracting from the effects of unanticipated shocks so as to get the clearest possible picture of the consequences of anticipated shocks.)

Figure 26.1 illustrates the determination of the price level. Notice that

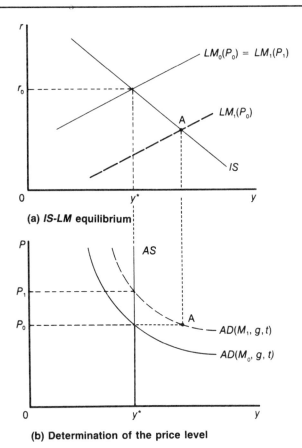

Figure 26.1
The effect of a once-and-for-all rise in the money supply on output and the price level

(a) *IS-LM* equilibrium

(b) Determination of the price level

At full employment a rise in the money supply produces a proportionate rise in the price level. An initial equilibrium (y^*, r_0, P_0) shown is the intersection of *IS* and *LM* in frame (a) and the intersection of *AD* and *AS* in frame (b). This equilibrium is disturbed by a rise in the money stock. If the price level stayed constant, the *LM* and *AD* curves would shift, and the economy would move to the position A. But at A the economy cannot be in equilibrium because output cannot exceed y^*. The price level has to rise to P_1 [frame (b)], and the *LM* curve shifts back to its original position [frame (a)].

frame (a) contains an $IS-LM$ analysis, and frame (b) contains an aggregate supply and demand analysis. The level of real income is measured on the horizontal axis of each diagram and refers to the same magnitude in each case.

Initially the full-employment equilibrium is at the price level P_0. Such an equilibrium is depicted in frame (a) as the intersection point of the curve $LM_0(P_0)$ and the IS curve. Equilibrium income is y^* and the interest rate is r_0. The same equilibrium is depicted in frame (b) as the point at which the aggregate demand curve labelled $AD(M_0, g, t)$ intersects the aggregate supply curve AS. The price level is P_0 and the output level is y^*.

Now imagine that the money supply rises from M_0 to some higher level, say, M_1. If the price level remained at P_0, the LM curve representing a money stock of M_1 and the price level of P_0 would be to the right of the original LM curve. Such an LM curve is shown in frame (a) as that labelled $LM_1(P_0)$. It intersects the IS curve at the point A. This higher money stock (M_1) shifts the aggregate demand curve in frame (b) so that it lies wholly to the right of the original aggregate demand curve. Such an aggregate demand curve is shown as that labelled $AD(M_1, g, t)$. Notice that the point on that aggregate demand curve marked A in frame (b) corresponds to the point A in frame (a) and is at the price level P_0, but is displaced horizontally to a higher level of real income. That level of real income corresponds to the intersection of the IS and $LM_1(P_0)$ curves.

It is evident that a position like A cannot be sustained. At point A there is an excess demand for goods. There is also an excess demand for labour. Such a situation would produce higher prices and higher wages. How much higher? The answer can be seen by looking in frame (b) at the point at which the new aggregate demand curve, $AD(M_1, g, t)$ (the line drawn for a money stock of M_1) cuts the aggregate supply curve. That point is at the price level P_1 in frame (b). It is a price level that is higher than P_0 by the same percentage amount that the money stock M_1 exceeds the money stock M_0. At that higher price level, the LM curve would not be the curve shown as $LM_1(P_0)$ but rather the curve $LM_1(P_1)$. This LM curve is identical to the curve $LM_0(P_0)$. (If you are not sure why, check back to Chapter 13, where the LM curve was derived and where the factors that cause the LM curve to shift were analysed.)

You have now analysed the effects of a once-and-for-all rise in the money stock at full employment. These effects are so simple and yet so important that they are worth emphasizing and highlighting. In frame (a) of Figure 26.1 the initial equilibrium is r_0 and y^* on the IS curve and on the LM curve labelled $LM_0(P_0)$. Now there is a one-shot rise in the money stock, from M_0 to M_1. If the price level remained constant, the LM curve would move to the dashed LM curve, $LM_1(P_0)$. But the price level will not remain constant at full employment. It will have to rise, and by an amount such that the LM curve shifts back (as indicated by the arrow) to the original position, so that it becomes the same curve as before, relabelled $LM_1(P_1)$.

What are the effects of this one-shot rise in the money stock? The answer is very clear from the diagram. There is no effect on the rate of interest and no effect on output: the price level rises proportionately to the one-shot rise in the money stock.

Let us now analyse a different once-and-for-all shock to the economy — a drop in aggregate supply. You are aware from your study of the determination of aggregate supply that shifts in the production function lead to shifts in the aggregate supply curve. Imagine that for some reason, such as a production function shock, the aggregate supply curve shifts to the right. What happens to output, interest rates and, more importantly, for present purposes, the price level? Figure 26.2 illustrates the analysis of this case. Imagine that the economy starts out in exactly the same situation as it did in Figure 26.1. There is a full-employment equilibrium with an output level y_0^*, an interest rate of r_0 and a price level of P_0. That is, the economy is at the point of intersection of the IS curve and LM curve labelled $LM_0(P_0)$ and at the point of intersection of the aggregate demand curve and the aggregate supply curve AS_0.

Now a shock to aggregate supply causes the aggregate supply curve to shift leftwards to the curve labelled AS_1. What happens? Clearly the economy cannot simply stay at the old price level P_0. If it did it would be at the point marked B in frame (b). Clearly this position is not sustainable for there is, at that point, an excess of demand over supply. That excess demand raises the price level and the price level will continue to rise until it reaches P_1. With a price level of P_1 the real money supply will have declined so the LM curve moves to the left. Such an LM curve is shown as that labelled $LM_0(P_1)$ in frame (a). The equilibrium rate of interest has risen from r_0 to r_1. The rate of interest rises because at a lower level of income less is saved. Since in a closed economy savings-plus-taxes must equal investment-plus-government spending, the level of investment will also have declined. Investment declines only if the interest rate rises and that is precisely what happens in equilibrium.

You can now see that the effects of a once-and-for-all drop in aggregate supply are entirely the same as the effects of a once-and-for-all rise in the supply of money. In the case of the monetary shock, the only thing that happens is that the price level rises by the same percentage amount as the rise in the money supply. The values of no real variables change. In the case of an aggregate supply shock, there are real effects. That is not surprising since the shock was a real shock. A drop in aggregate supply represents a real change — a change in the economy's real productive potential. The price level rise is similar in the two cases but there the similarity ends. In the case of the aggregate supply shock, output falls and the real rate of interest rises.

There are, within the framework of this model, two other types of shocks that we could analyse that would have the effects of changing the price level in a once-and-for-all fashion. We will not work through those in detail but leave them as exercises that you may find interesting to undertake in order to reinforce your understanding of the work that you have just done. One such shock would be to the IS curve. Suppose that there was, let us say, an anticipated rise in government spending or cut in taxes that shifted the IS curve to the right. You should be able to work out that its effects are a rise in the real rate of interest and a rise in the price level in a once-and-for-all fashion. Output remains constant.

The second kind of shock that you can analyse is one to the demand for money function. Suppose that the propensity to hold money changed in a predictable but sizeable way. Suppose the propensity to hold money

**Figure 26.2
The effect of a once-
and-for-all drop in
aggregate supply on
output and the price
level**

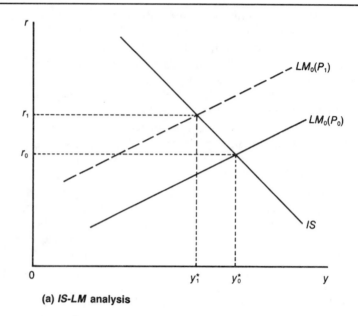

(a) *IS-LM* analysis

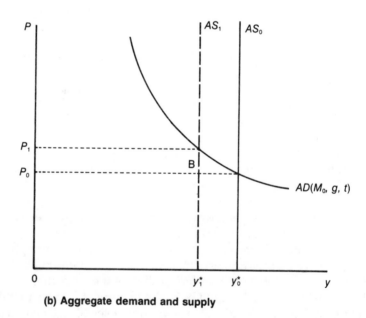

(b) Aggregate demand and supply

An initial equilibrium (y_0^*, r_0, P_0) is shown as the intersection of *IS* and $LM_0(P_0)$ in frame (a) and of the *AD* curve and AS_0 in frame (b). A production function shock lowers aggregate supply to AS_1. This fall in aggregate supply means that, at the old price level P_0 there is an excess demand. The price level rises to P_1. At P_1 the real money supply declines so that the *LM* curve becomes $LM_0(P_1)$. The interest rate rises to r_1. The drop in aggregate supply leads to a higher price level, a higher real interest rate and lower output.

declined. You should be able to work out that such a change would produce a rightward shift in the *LM* curve which in turn would lead to a
rise in the price level. In this case, like the case of a rise in the money
supply, the only thing that happens is that the price level changes. There
are no changes in the real variables.

You have now reviewed all the shocks that are capable of generating
a once-and-for-all change in the price level. (The analysis that we have
conducted looked at the case of a rise in the price level. You can reverse
the exercises to produce once-and-for-all drops in the price level.) It is
now time to move on to consider the perhaps more interesting case of
the factors that can produce a continuously rising price level — inflation.

C. How Inflation is Generated

We will discover how inflation is generated most effectively by taking
a slightly roundabout route. The starting point for our analysis is to recall
that the demand for money depends on the rate of interest that is available
on other financial assets. That is, the demand for money varies inversely
with the *market* rate of interest. The market rate of interest equals the real
rate of interest when there is no inflation. In an inflationary world as you
have already discovered, the market rate of interest is higher than the
real rate of interest by precisely the same amount as the expected rate
of inflation. That is,

$$r_m = r + \pi^e \qquad\qquad (26.1)$$

Since the demand for money depends on r_m and not on r, it is
necessary to be rather careful in figuring out how to determine equilibrium
at full employment when the expected inflation rate is not zero. Figure
26.3 will help you understand how to determine a full-employment
equilibrium with inflation that is not zero.

First of all, notice that the vertical axis of Figure 26.3 measures two rates
of interest, the real rate, r, and the market rate, r_m. The diagram also
shows the full-employment output level y^*. We are considering only
anticipated changes in the money supply so conduct the analysis entirely in terms of the economy being at that output level. Since the demand
for money depends on the market or nominal rate of interest, it is
necessary to plot the *LM* curve against the market rate of interest. You
should be careful to remember that the *LM* curve is indeed plotted against
the market rate of interest.

The position of the *LM* curve depends, as you know, on the real money
supply, M/P. We are going to analyse a situation in which both M and
P are rising. As a result, the *LM* curve will be continuously shifting unless
M and P are growing at the same rate. When M and P are growing at
the same rate, M/P will be constant, and as a result the *LM* curve will
be stationary.

Figure 26.3
The effect of a con-
tinously rising
money supply

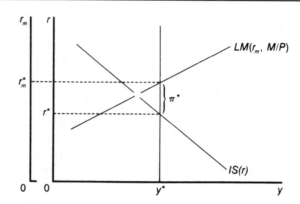

A continuously rising money supply drives a wedge between the real rate of interest and the market (or money) rate of interest. The *IS* curve is drawn against the real rate of interest *r*, and the *LM* curve is drawn against the money rate of interest r_m. The real interest rate r^* is determined where *IS* cuts the full-employment line, and the market rate of interest r_m^* is determined where *LM* cuts the full-employment line. The vertical distance between the *IS* and *LM* curves at full employment is the rate of inflation, π^*.

To remind you that the *LM* curve is plotted against the market rate of interest, r_m, and that it depends on the real money supply *M/P*, the *LM* curve has been labelled $LM(r_m, M/P)$.

The *IS* curve, defined as it is by the equality of investment-plus-government spending with savings-plus-taxes, depends on the real rate of interest. To remind you we have labelled the *IS* curve *IS(r)*. Notice that the *IS* and *LM* curves have been drawn with a break in them. The break coincides with the point at which those two curves would have intersected if they had been drawn continuously. This break is to remind you that the point at which those two curves cut in this diagram is irrelevant. (Strictly speaking, there is no point at which these two curves cut because one of them is plotted against the market rate of interest and the other against the real rate of interest. So, in effect, the two curves are not drawn in the same space at all.) You may perhaps find it helpful to think of there being two diagrams, one with an *IS* curve plotted against the real interest rate and another one with an *LM* curve plotted against the market rate of interest. Nevertheless, it is useful to draw the two curves in the same picture because we do know that there is a simple link between the two interest rates. This link is the expected rate of inflation. The market rate of interest is equal to the real rate of interest plus the *expected* rate of inflation.

Since we are assuming that there are no 'surprises' — no unexpected changes in the money supply — the expected rate of inflation and the actual rate of inflation are equal. That is, the gap between the market rate of interest and the real rate of interest also represents the actual rate of inflation. If we are at a given level of income (marked on the horizontal axis of Figure 26.3) and if we are on both the *IS* and *LM* curves, then we can think of the vertical gap between the two curves as measuring the (expected equals actual) rate of inflation. Such an inflation rate is shown as the distance π^* in the diagram, at the income level y^*.

Figure 26.3 now can be interpreted as characterizing a full-employment equilibrium with an expected and actual inflation rate of π^*. The real interest rate is r^*, and with an income level y^* the economy on the *IS* curve, so that there is equality between the expenditure and income flows in the goods market. The market interest rate is the real interest rate plus π^*, which equals r_m^*. This market rate of interest, along with an income level of y^*, puts the economy on the *LM* curve, so that there is an equality between the supply of and demand for money.

You have now reached the point at which you can almost see what is generating the ongoing inflation. If the price level is rising at a rate π^*, other things being equal, the *LM* curve would be moving leftwards. If the *LM* curve is not moving, it must be that something else is happening that is just offsetting the pressure of the rising price level to move the *LM* curve. It is rather clear that what is happening is that the money supply is continuously rising. Underlying the *LM* curve, when inflation is proceeding at the rate π^*, there is a rising money supply *and* rising price level. Each is rising by precisely the same percentage amount so that the real money supply is unchanged. That is, a continuously rising money supply (that is anticipated) generates an anticipated inflation and a gap between the market rate of interest and the real rate of interest.

The precise quantitative relationship between the growth rate of the money supply and inflation needs to be elaborated a little. In the example that we have just worked through we held output constant at y^*. In that particular case, the growth rate of the money supply and the rate of inflation are identical to each other. But what would happen if real income was, on the average, growing? We know that real income is trended upwards.

This question is obviously important and practical. You can answer it very directly by extending the analysis that we conducted in the previous section concerning the effects of a once-and-for-all drop in aggregate supply on the price level. There we discovered that a cut in aggregate supply increases the price level. By reversing that analysis a once-and-for-all rise in aggregate supply leads to a drop in the price level. It follows immediately from this line of reasoning that an ongoing rise in aggregate supply — a continuous and steady rightward drift in the aggregate supply schedule — leads to continuously falling prices (other things being equal). The precise quantitative amount by which prices decline depends on the income elasticity of demand for money. Let us see why. If the demand for money was unit elastic with respect to real income then an *x* per cent change in real income would lead to an *x* per cent change in the demand for money. To attain equilibrium if the money supply itself was constant, the real money supply would have to rise as a result of a fall in the price level. Real money supply needs to rise by x per cent and the price level would have to fall by x per cent — that same per cent rise in real income that we imagined as initiating this adjustment process.

If the demand for money is less than unit elastic — say has an elasticity of 1/2 — then a rise in real income of x per cent will lead to a rise in the demand for real money of less than x per cent — 1/2 of x per cent in the special case that we are assuming. If the money supply was constant, then real money would have to increase by 1/2 of x per cent and this would occur as a result of the price level falling by 1/2 of x per cent.

You can now see that a continuous rise in real income, other things being equal, leads to the price level continuously falling at a rate equal to the rate of growth of real income multiplied by the income elasticity of the demand for real balances.

You can now bring these two ideas together. You have seen that a continuously rising money supply, other things being equal, leads to a continuously rising price level with the rate of growth of the money supply equal to the rate of price level increase — the rate of inflation. You have also seen that a continuous rise in real income leads to a continuous decline in the price level equal to that real income growth rate multiplied by the income elasticity of demand for real money.

Bringing these two ideas together enables us to write what might be called the *fundamental steady-state inflation equation* which says

$$\pi = \mu - \alpha\rho \qquad (26.2)$$

where, as before, π is the rate of inflation, μ is the growth rate of the money supply, ρ is the growth rate of real income and α is the income elasticity of demand for real balances.

Shortly we are going to go on to analyse what happens to inflation if the growth rate of the money supply *changes*. Before we do that let us ask the question: is there anything else that can produce continuous inflation? We studied the things that can influence the price level in a once-and-for-all fashion. We examined the effects of a change in the money stock, a change in income, and, in less detail, the effects of a shift in the *IS* curve and in the propensity to hold money — shifts in the *LM* curve induced by things other than a change in the money stock. Could these same factors generate ongoing inflation? To put that question slightly differently, could the *IS* curve continuously shift or could the *LM* curve continuously shift even if the money stock was not growing?

It seems hard to imagine a situation in which the *IS* curve would continuously shift to the right thereby generating continuous upward pressure on the price level. There are natural limits to all the things that underlie the *IS* curve and, while it is imaginable that over prolonged periods sizeable rightward shifts could occur in the *IS* curve, movement in the *IS* curve does not appear to be a potential source for ongoing inflation. For example, a period during which government expenditure increases rapidly thereby leading to an ongoing rightward shift in the *IS* curve would produce a temporary period of perhaps quite serious inflation. But such a process would come to a natural end since there are limits to the volume of government expenditure and capacity to tax. This is not to say that there are not some important connections between fiscal policy and inflation. These connections will be explored in the policy chapters toward the end of this book.

Would continuing changes in the propensity to hold money generate an ongoing inflation? There seems to be more potential here. Improvements in the technology of the financial sector — the application of computers and mechanized record keeping methods — do seem to lead to ongoing reductions in the amount of real money demanded. Imagine, as a result of the greater use of credit cards and other devices, that people continuously reduce, year after year, their desired holdings of real balances; then, even if real income was constant, and even if the money supply was not growing, there would be inflation. There would be inflation because people would be trying to reduce the amount of real money they held and, with income and the nominal money supply constant the only way in which that could occur would be for prices to rise, thereby eroding the real value of money. In terms of Figure 26.3 the *LM* curve would be continuously shifting to the right if the price level was constant. Since this could not be an equilibrium the price level would have to be rising by exactly the correct amount to offset the tendency for the reduced demand for money to shift the *LM* curve.

In the light of these considerations we need to modify the fundamental inflation equation to read as follows:

$$\pi = \mu - \alpha\rho + \Delta v \tag{26.3}$$

where Δv stands for the rate of change in the velocity of circulation of money (the equivalent of the rate of decline in the propensity to hold money). You can think of the effects on inflation of ongoing real income growth and of ongoing changes in the demand for money (changes in the velocity of circulation) as being technologically driven and, in a fundamental sense, uncontrollable. But you can see from the fundamental inflation equation that the monetary authorities do have a weapon with which they can control the trend rate of inflation very precisely. That weapon is the trend growth rate in the money supply. Furthermore you can see that, even though there are some complexities in the link between real income growth and inflation, the link between money growth and inflation, on the average, is direct and one-for-one. If the monetary authority wishes to slow the inflation trend it has to deliver a lower trend growth rate for the money supply. In this sense, therefore, anti-inflation policy is trivially simple to design and execute. There are complexities that have to do with implementing a policy that delivers a very predictable money supply growth rate, and also with interactions between unanticipated changes in the money supply and the level of real economic activity, employment and unemployment. We will explore some of those linkages in subsequent chapters. But these complexities should not be allowed to cloud the main issue. That main issue is revealed with crystal clarity from the foregoing analysis and in the fundamental inflation equation set out above.

Let us now go on to consider one other complication in the link between money and inflation and analyse what happens to the inflation rate when the money supply growth rate is *changed*.

D.   What Happens to Inflation when the Growth Rate of the Money Supply is Increased?

You can think of the analysis that we have conducted in the preceding section as telling us about inflation and money supply growth in an economy in which the money supply growth rate is constant. You could think of the analysis also as being relevant to a comparison of two economies, one that has a high money supply growth rate and one that has a low money supply growth rate. But it does not tell us what happens when the growth rate of the money supply is changed — say increased. That is what we will now examine. What happens to the equilibrium depicted in Figure 26.3 if there is a rise in the growth rate of the money supply? The answer is illustrated in Figure 26.4.

The increasing rate of money supply growth, other things being equal, tends to make the *LM* curve move to the right. If the inflation rate stayed constant at π_0, then the market rate of interest and the real rate of interest fall and generate an excess demand for goods. The excess demand for goods puts pressure on the inflation rate, and the rising infla-

Figure 26.4
The effect of a rise in the growth rate of the money supply

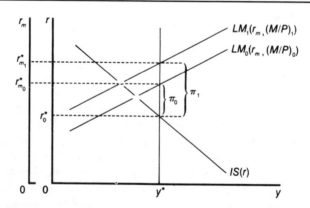

The initial equilibrium (subscripted 0) is disturbed by making the money supply grow at a faster rate. This produces a faster rate of inflation that is initially greater than the growth rate of the money supply. This lowers the stock of real balances and shifts the *LM* curve to the left. The new equilibrium, subscripted 1, is one in which the inflation rate (π_1) equals the new higher money supply growth rate.

tion rate offsets the rightward movement of the *LM* curve and starts the *LM* curve moving in the opposite direction. The only new equlibrium that is possible is the one that arises when the *LM* curve has shifted, not to the right at all, but to the left and by enough to have raised the market rate of interest above the real rate of interest by the amount of the new, higher rate of money growth and rate of inflation. By the time the economy settles down on the *LM* curve labelled $LM_1(r_{m_1}, (M/P)_1)$ such a situation will have arisen. In this situation, the real interest rate is unaffected, and the output level is unaffected; but the market rate of interest is higher, the inflation rate is higher, and the money supply growth rate is higher, all by the same amount as each other.

How does the economy get from the curve LM_0 to LM_1? The answer must be that the real money supply has fallen between these two situations. How could this fall have happened? The answer essentially is that, at the moment the money supply growth rate increases there are two forces working on the inflation rate: one of these forces is the higher money supply growth rate; the other is a fall in the demand for money. How does this fall in the demand for money come about? As you are aware, a rise in the money supply growth rate which raises the inflation rate also raises the nominal rate of interest. That means that the opportunity cost of holding money increases. The implication of that is that people will try to economize on their money holdings thereby reducing their demand for money. This drop in demand for money induced by higher nominal interest rates also puts additional excess demand pressure on the markets for goods and services and produces a yet higher price level. If everything works out smoothly and instantaneously this extra effect on the price level would occur at the point in time at which the money supply growth rate increased. The paths of the money supply and the price level would be as depicted in Figure 26.5.

The way to read Figure 26.5 is as follows. First, the vertical axis measures the logarithms of the price level and the money supply. The horizontal axis measures time. The change in the logarithm of a variable measures that variable's growth rate. Thus we can depict a continuous growth rate in the money supply or the price level as a straight line (sloping upwards) in this figure. Imagine that between period 0 and period z the money supply and the price level were growing at the same constant rate as depicted in the figure. Then imagine that at point z the money supply growth rate increases (doubles from say 5 per cent to 10 per cent). The dashed line shows what happens to the price level. At the point in time z the price level jumps. Immediately thereafter the price level continues to rise but at the same rate as the money supply is growing. If you like, there is a spike in the inflation rate for an instant and thereafter the inflation rate equals the money supply growth rate. This jump in the price level is what makes the level of real money balances decline and what makes the *LM* curve shift to the left from the curve labelled LM_0 to the curve LM_1.

Figure 26.5
The price level and
the money supply

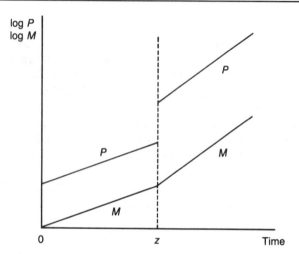

As the money supply growth rate is increased at time z there is a rise in the inflation rate. The higher inflation rate raises the market interest rate and lowers the demand for money. The drop in the demand for money adds additional excess demand pressure and this produces a once-and-for-all rise in the price level at time z.

The particular relationship between the price level and money supply shown in Figure 26.5 is not likely to be seen in any real world data. The hypothetical experiment that we have conducted to generate that change is very special. Strictly speaking, the experiment requires the following conditions. First, before the point in time z, everyone fully expected that the money supply growth rate would remain at its low level forever. At the moment z when the money supply growth rate increased people were caught by surprise but, immediately thereafter they came to believe, and correctly, that the money supply growth rate would now be at its new higher rate forever.

In any actual economy this experiment is not going to be conducted. Rather, when the money supply growth rate changes it will to some extent be regarded as a permanent change in the trend growth rate and to some extent it will be suspected as being temporary. This means that instead of a clean jump in the price level at the point in time at which the money supply growth rate changes there will be a tendency for the price level to rise but in a steady fashion and at a somewhat higher rate than the growth rate of the money supply. Figure 26.6 illustrates.

Figure 26.6 is identical to that presented above except that the effects, rather than being concentrated on the particular point z, are distributed over time. In more intuitive, if somewhat looser, terms we can describe the process illustrated in Figure 26.6 as follows. First, when the money supply growth rate is increased from 5 per cent to 10 per cent, people are not sure whether that increase is permanent or temporary. To the

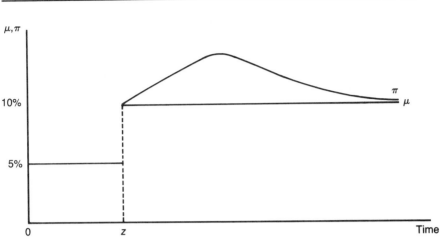

Figure 26.6
The overshooting proposition

If the money supply growth rate increases and if that increase is not initially expected to be permanent, interest rates will not rise by enough to cause an instantaneous jump in the price level. Instead, the inflation rate will rise by only the amount of the rise in the money supply growth rate. If the higher growth rate of money is maintained and people come to regard it as permanent, then expectations of inflation will be increased and so market interest rates will rise. The resulting drop in the demand for money causes the inflation rate to rise even higher, thus overshooting the growth rate of the money supply.

extent that they believe the increase to be temporary they do not revise their long-term inflationary expectations and market rates of interest do not increase. As a result the demand for money does not decline by very much and so not much additional pressure is placed on the inflation rate. Thus, at the point in time z, the only force working on the inflation rate is the growth rate of the money supply itself. The longer the new higher growth rate of the money supply is maintained, the more people come to realize that this higher growth rate is permanent. Therefore, they increase their long-term inflation expectations and these expectations get incorporated into higher nominal rates of interest. The higher interest rates induce further reductions in the demand for money and these falls in the demand for money are added to the increase in supply of money as inflationary forces. Thus, they force the inflation rate up even higher. The inflation rate follows the path marked π which overshoots the growth rate of the money supply but which approaches the money supply growth rate gradually.

You can now see that, although the appropriate policies for avoiding inflation are clear and straightforward, policies for lowering the inflation rate are not so straightforward. If you were to reverse the analysis that we have conducted here you would see that if the monetary authorities cut the growth rate of the money supply suddenly to achieve a lower rate of inflation, the inflation rate would fall but it would undershoot the new lower growth rate of the money supply. This policy could, if pursued vigorously enough, even produce a falling price level for a period. Therefore, the best way to slow down inflation requires some analysis of these various forces that we have studied here.

There is one very important implication of the analysis that we have just conducted. This implication is that it is not possible for the monetary authority permanently to lower the rate of interest by increasing the money supply. We have seen that a once-and-for-all rise in the money stock produces a once-and-for-all rise in the price level with no change in the rate of inflation and no change in the market rate of interest. We have also seen that an increase in the growth rate of the money supply produces a rise in the inflation rate and a rise in the market rate of interest in equilibrium. Initially, it is possible for the rise in the growth rate of the money supply to create a fall in the market rate of interest, but such a fall could only be temporary.

You now have a much richer understanding of the theory of inflation and of the inflation process in a closed economy. Let us now turn to the task of what determines the inflation rate, balance of payments and the exchange rate in an open economy.

E.   The 'Law of One Price'

A fundamental law of economics that is of great use in understanding the forces that determine inflation, the balance of payments and the exchange rate is the 'law of one price'.

The law of one price is a proposition concerning the effects of arbitrage. Arbitrage is the buying of a commodity at a low price and simultaneously contracting to sell it for a higher price, thereby making a profit in the process. If it is possible to buy a particular good for some price, say, p_b, and sell the good for a price p_s, then it is possible to make a profit at a rate given by:

$$\text{Arbitrage profit rate} = \frac{(P_s - P_b)}{P_b}$$

If such a situation exists, individuals who see the profit opportunity available will increase their demand for the good whose price is p_b. They also increase their supply of the good at the price p_s. This arbitrage activity of increasing demand at the price p_b and increasing supply at the price p_s will put upward pressure on the buying price — that is, p_b will rise — and downward pressure on the selling price — that is, p_s will fall. Arbitrage will continue to the point at which one price prevails, that is, $p_s = p_b$, or until there is no arbitrage profit to be made.

The law of one price says that arbitrage will compete away all price differences between identical commodities. Where there are transport costs between two locations, or where there are tariffs and impediments to trade imposed by government, or where there are costs of acquiring information about the the prices of alternative sources of supply, arbitrage will not compete price differentials all the way to zero. But, it will compete differentials down to the level such that the only remaining price difference reflects underlying real technological- or government-induced barriers to further price gap reductions.

The law of one price has two important implications that are useful for understanding the determination of balance of payments and exchange rates — namely, the purchasing power parity and interest rate parity theorems.

(i) Purchasing Power Parity

The purchasing power parity theorem (PPP) states that the price of a good in one country will be equal to the price of that same good in another country where the prices are expressed in units of local currency and converted at the current exchange rate. If there are any tariffs and transportation costs the purchasing power parity theorem is modified such that there is a gap between the two prices which just equals the tariff or transportation costs.

As an example, if a computer in the United States costs $US 500,000, that identical computer (trade barriers and transport costs absent) would, at an exchange rate of $2 US per £, cost £250,000 in the United Kingdom. Even allowing for transport costs and tariffs, if these factors were *constant*, then, although the *level* of prices in the United States might be different from the *level* of prices in the United Kingdom, the *rate of change of prices* in the two countries would be linked to each other by the relation:

> Percentage change in £ price
> *equals*   percentage change in $US price
> *plus*   the percentage rate of depreciation of the £ against the $US

To go back to the computer example, suppose that computer prices in the United States are falling by 5 per cent per annum. Then the computer that sells for £500,000 this year would sell for £475,000 next year. Further, suppose that the pound depreciates from $2 US per £ to $1.90 US per £ — a 5 per cent depreciation — then the purchasing power parity theorem states that in the United Kingdom the price of the computer next year will remain at £250,000. That is, computer prices in the United Kingdom will change by the percentage change of computer prices in the

United States, adjusted for the percentage change in the value of the pound in terms of US dollars.

(ii)   Interest Rate Parity

The interest rate parity theorem (IRP) is a close cousin of the purchasing power parity theorem. It arises from arbitrage activities in asset markets. The interest rate parity theorem states that (abstracting from political risk differences) the market (or nominal) rate of interest available in one country equals the market rate of interest available in another country adjusted for the expected rate of change of the exchange rate between the currencies of the two countries.

Thus suppose, for example, the market rate of interest in the United Kingdom is 10 per cent per annum, and the market rate in the United States is 8 per cent per annum. Then, if it is expected that the pound is going to depreciate by 2 per cent per annum, the rate of interest that would be obtained by an American investing in a UK security will be the 10 per cent interest rate on UK bonds minus the expected depreciation of the pound of 2 per cent, which would equal 8 per cent per annum the same as could be obtained by investing in a US security. Conversely, a UK resident investing in a US bond obtains the 8 per cent interest rate on the US security plus a 2 per cent gain from the appreciation of the $US *vis-à-vis* the pound, totalling 10 per cent per annum. This return is equivalent to what could be obtained by investing in a UK security.

As another example, if the rate of interest in the United Kingdom was greater than 10 per cent per annum, the rate of interest in the United States was 8 per cent per annum, and the expected rate of depreciation of the pound was 2 per cent per annum, there would be gains to be made from investing in the United Kingdom. As investors sought to exploit these gains, they would increase the demand for UK securities and lower the demand for US securities. This switch of demand from US to UK securities raises the price of and lowers the rate of interest on UK securities and lowers the price of, and raises the interest rate on US securities.

If exchange rates were flexible, the flow of funds into the UK would also lead to an immediate appreciation of the pound. This current appreciation of the pound means that its expected rate of future depreciation rises. The combination of a higher US interest rate, a lower UK interest rate, and a rise in the expected rate of depreciation of the pound *vis-à-vis* the US dollar restores the interest rate parity relation. That is, the interest rate in the United Kingdom equals the interest rate in the United States plus the expected rate of depreciation of the pound *vis-à-vis* the US dollar.

These two propositions may now be used to enable you to understand the basic forces that determine the balance of payments and the exchange rate at full employment.

F.   Inflation and the Balance of Payments at Full Employment Under a Fixed Exchange Rate Regime

The starting point for an analysis of inflation and the balance of payments[1] is the discussion in Section E of Chapter 15 concerning the links between the money supply and the level of foreign exchange reserves. Recall Equation (15.8). That equation states that

$$\Delta M = \Delta F + \Delta DC \tag{26.4}$$

The change in the stock of foreign reserves is the balance of payments and the change in domestic credit, ΔDC, is usually called *domestic credit expansion*.

It will be convenient to write this equation in terms of the growth rates of reserves, the money supply and domestic credit. To convert this equation into growth rates, first divide both sides of Equation (26.4) by M, which gives

$$\frac{\Delta M}{M} = \frac{\Delta F}{M} + \frac{\Delta DC}{M} \tag{26.5}$$

Terms like $\Delta F/M$ and $\Delta DC/M$ do not have immediately obvious meanings. They become much clearer if the first term is multiplied and divided by F and if the second term is multiplied and divided by DC. (Be sure that you understand how the equation below was obtained.)

$$\frac{\Delta M}{M} = \left(\frac{F}{M}\right)\frac{\Delta F}{F} + \left(\frac{DC}{M}\right)\frac{\Delta DC}{DC} \tag{26.6}$$

Equation (26.6) can be interpreted very easily. First notice that the first term $\Delta M/M$ is the growth rate of the money supply, which we have been calling μ. Next, define F/M to be ψ so that DC/M is $(1 - \psi)$. The symbol ψ (the Greek letter psi) is the fraction of the money supply that is held by the banking system in foreign exchange reserves, and $1-\psi$ is the fraction of the money supply held by the banking system in domestic assets. (Stop: Check that $F/M + DC/M = 1$, since $F + DC = M$.)

Also define $\Delta F/F$ as f and $\Delta DC/DC$ as dc. The letter f is the rate of change of foreign exchange reserves, and dc is the rate of change of domestic credit.

---

1   The origins of this theory, a theory that has not changed much in more than two hundred years, is David Hume, 'Of the Balance of Trade', *Essays: Moral, Political and Literary* (London: Oxford University Press, 1963) pp. 316–33; first published in 1741. An excellent modern restatement of Hume's theory, in slightly more general terms than that given in this chapter, is Harry G. Johnson, *Further Essays in Monetary Economics* (London: Allen & Unwin 1972), pp. 229–49.

The somewhat cumbersome Equation (26.6) may, with the new definitions, be written as the simpler equation

$$\mu = \psi f + (1 - \psi)dc \qquad (26.7)$$

This relationship between the rate of growth of the money supply, the rate of change of foreign exchange reserves, and the rate of growth of domestic credit is fundamental. It says that the growth rate of the money supply, μ, is a weighted average of the growth rate of the stock of foreign exchange reserves, f, and domestic credit, dc. The weights, which add up to one, are the fraction of the total money supply backed by holdings of foreign exchange reserves, ψ, and the fraction of the total money supply backed by domestic credit $(1 - \psi)$.

The rate of change of foreign exchange reserves, f, is the balance of payments (expressed as a proportion of the existing stock of reserves). The factors that determine f are therefore exactly the same as the factors that determine the balance of payments. It is tempting to rearrange the above equation so that the variable in which we are interested, f, appears on the left-hand side. If you divide the Equation (26.7) by ψ and then subtract $[(1 - \psi)/\psi]dc$ from both sides of the equation, you obtain

$$f = \frac{1}{\psi}\mu - \left(\frac{1 - \psi}{\psi}\right)dc \qquad (26.8)$$

This equation says that the percentage change in the stock of foreign exchange reserves — the balance of payments expressed in percentage terms — depends on the rate of growth of the money supply and the rate of growth of domestic credit. If it is possible to work out what determines these two factors, then we will have a theory that explains the balance of payments.

(i) Domestic Credit Expansion

Let us deal first with domestic credit expansion, dc. In an open economy with a fixed exchange rate, domestic credit is the variable that the monetary authorities can control by their monetary policy actions. If the Bank of England wants to see the growth of domestic credit increased, then all it has to do is buy bonds from individuals, thereby increasing its own stock of domestic securities. As the Bank of England buys more bonds it makes more reserves available to the commercial banks and encourages them to acquire more domestic securities. Conversely, if the Bank of England wants to reduce the growth of domestic credit, it can do so by selling government securities, thereby reducing its own holdings of those items. As the Bank of England sells some of its bonds the reserves available to the commercial banks fall and they also sell some of their securities.

Thus, *the Bank of England controls the growth rate of domestic credit*. This variable is exogenous. But under fixed exchange rates the the Bank of England cannot control the money supply. The very act of pegging the foreign exchange rate means that the Bank of England must always be willing to buy and sell foreign exchange. That is, the Bank of England must always be willing to raise or lower its own stock of foreign exchange in order to preserve the fixed value of its currency in terms of foreign currencies. Thus, although the Bank of England can decide how many domestic assets to buy and hold, it has no control over the gold and foreign exchange reserves that it holds. Therefore, the Bank of England cannot control the money supply since the money supply is the sum of domestic credit (which the Bank of England can control) and foreign exchange reserves (which it cannot control).

Now note that Equation (26.8) above tells us that the balance of payments depends *both* on the growth rate of the money supply and the growth rate of domestic credit. Although the growth of domestic credit may be treated as being under the control of the Bank of England, the money supply growth rate may not be regarded as being controlled by the Bank of England, so it is necessary to enquire what does determine its value.

(ii)   Growth Rate of Money Supply

When the Bank of England pegs the foreign exchange rate and is, as a result, unable to determine the supply of money, the quantity of money in existence is determined by the amount of money demanded. We have already discovered, in Chapter 12, what determines the demand for money — it depends upon the price level, real income, and the rate of interest. Therefore, the demand for money changes as the price level changes, as real income changes, and as the interest rate changes. In a steady state, when the rate of interest is constant and the income elasticity of the demand for real balances in one, the growth rate of the money supply equals the rate of inflation plus the rate of growth of output. That is,

$$\mu = \pi + \rho \tag{26.9}$$

Now recall from Chapter 24 that the rate of output growth depends on such things as demographic trends, capital accumulation, and technical progress — all of which are being treated as exogenous to and independent of the processes that are being analysed here. The rate of output growth, then, may be taken as given. Thus, in Equation (26.9) there are still two variables — the rate of inflation and the rate of money supply growth — which have to be determined.

The theory of inflation developed in Section C (which dealt only with a closed economy) used Equation (26.9) to determine the steady-state rate of inflation. In the closed economy the Bank of England can control the growth rate of the money supply (μ) and with a given output growth rate

Equation (26.9) determines the steady-state rate of inflation. But, in a fixed exchange rate open economy it is not possible for the Bank of England to decide what the money supply growth rate will be since it has no control over one of the components of the money supply, namely, the change in the foreign exchange reserves. Therefore, Equation (26.9) cannot be regarded as determining the rate of inflation. Rather, given the inflation rate and the growth rate of output, and given a fixed exchange rate this equation determines the growth rate of the money supply. Thus, the growth rate of the money supply is determined by the growth rate of the demand for money.

If the growth rate of the money supply is determined by the growth in the demand for money, what determines the rate of inflation in a fixed exchange rate economy? The answer is the law of one price.

(iii)   The Law of One Price

The next step in the story is to recall the law of one price and its implication — the purchasing power parity proposition. You will recall that the law of one price says that the rate of change of the price level in one country (where prices are expressed in the currency of that country) is equal to the rate of change of the price level in another country (where prices are expressed in units of currency of that other country) plus the rate of depreciation of the first country's currency against that of the second country. In other words, calling the rate of inflation in the rest of the world π_f and the rate of depreciation of the domestic currency, $\Delta\epsilon$, we have

$$\pi = \pi_f + \Delta\epsilon \tag{26.10}$$

This equation may be better understood with an example. Suppose that inflation in the rest of the world was running at 10 per cent per annum and that the domestic currency was depreciating at 2 per cent per annum. This equation tells us that the rate of inflation in the domestic economy would be 12 per cent per annum. Thus, there is a relationship between inflation rates in different countries and the exchange rate between those two national monies which arises from arbitrage operations in the markets for goods and services.

Now, recall that the analysis being conducted refers to an economy with a fixed exchange rate. If the exchange rate is fixed, then the rate of change of the exchange rate is zero. Thus, in a fixed exchange rate economy, the domestic rate of inflation, π, equals the inflation rate in the rest of the world, π_f. That is,

$$\pi = \pi_f \tag{26.11}$$

This proposition concerning the behaviour of the rate of inflation in an open economy operating under a fixed exchange rate is fundamental. It does not hold exactly because there are other real disturbances going on that change *relative* prices in the world. We will see how useful an approximation to reality it is later in this chapter.

You can think of the rate of inflation in the rest of the world as being independent of the behaviour of the domestic economy that we are analysing. You may think of the world inflation rate as being determined by world aggregate money supply growth in exactly the same way as it was in the closed economy in Section C above. It is as if the whole world has one money, since all monies can be converted into any money at a known fixed exchange rate. The relevant money supply, therefore, is not the national money supply, but the sum of all the national money supplies (converted into a common unit). It is the growth rate in the world money supply that determines world average inflation.

With domestic inflation being determined by world inflation, it is now clear that in a fixed exchange rate economy the fundamental inflation equation becomes an equation that tells us about the rate of growth of the money supply rather than about the rate of inflation itself. That is, the equation

$$\mu = \pi_f + \rho \tag{26.12}$$

determines μ. The rate of inflation π_f is determined in the rest of the world, and the rate of output growth ρ is determined by long-run forces that are exogenous. What this equation says is that in a fixed exchange rate open economy, the rate of growth of the money supply is equal to the rate of growth of the demand for money. More money is demanded if prices become higher, and more money is demanded if output increases. The growth in the demand for money is equal to $\pi_f + \rho$. Money is supplied to meet this demand automatically as a result of the central bank's operations in the foreign exchange market, which are designed to peg the value of the exchange rate. If the demand for money rises and the central bank does not supply the extra money needed, the currency would appreciate. To prevent the exchange rate appreciating the central bank would have to take in additional foreign exchange reserves and supply additional domestic money in exchange for the foreign money taken into its reserves.

(iv) The Balance of Payments

It is now possible to see what determines the balance of payments at full employment. The balance of payments (expressed as a proportion of the stock of reserves) is equal to

$$f = \frac{1}{\psi} \mu - \left(\frac{1 - \psi}{\psi} \right) dc$$

Also, the money supply growth rate is given by:

$$\mu = \pi_f + \rho$$

By combining these two propositions, we now have

$$f = \frac{1}{\psi}\,\pi_f + \frac{1}{\psi}\rho - \left(\frac{1-\psi}{\psi}\right)dc \qquad (26.13)$$

This equation is a fundamental proposition concerning the determination of the balance of payments at full employment under fixed exchange rates. It says that a country at full employment with a fixed exchange rate may have either a balance of payments surplus, deficit, or equilibrium, and it is a simple matter to achieve whatever outcome is desired.

The one policy variable that determines the balance of payments at full employment is the domestic credit expansion. By selling government securities from its portfolio and tightening reserves, which also encourages commercial banks to sell securities from their portfolios, the central bank can achieve a surplus on the balance of payments. By doing the opposite, that is buying domestic securities from the general public and giving the commercial banks enough reserves to increase their holdings of domestic securities, the central bank can generate a deficit on the balance of payments.

The balance of payments is fundamentally a monetary phenomenon caused by the monetary policies of the central bank. As a first approximation, the balance of payments is independent of the trade flows and capital flows that underlie it.

(v) Aggregate Demand and Supply

Since the money supply is endogenous and not subject to control, you may be wondering what has become of our theory of aggregate supply and aggregate demand in an open economy at full employment with a fixed exchange rate. Figure 26.7 illustrates what is going on and uses a standard aggregate supply–aggregate demand diagram.

If the rate of growth of output is zero, then y^*, full-employment output, is constant. Also, if the level of foreign prices is held constant, the inflation rate will be zero. Suppose the foreign price level is P_f, so that the domestic price level implied by that foreign price level is EP_f, the foreign price level converted into domestic currency at the exchange rate E. This domestic price level EP_f is marked on the vertical axis. Aggregate supply is the curve AS. Point A is the equilibrium point for the economy. Point A is the point on the aggregate supply curve at which the price level is EP_f.

But what if the aggregate demand curve does not pass through point A? The answer is that the aggregate demand curve cannot avoid passing through point A because the money supply, which determines the position of the aggregate demand curve, is determined by the demand for money. The demand for money at point A is an amount such that the

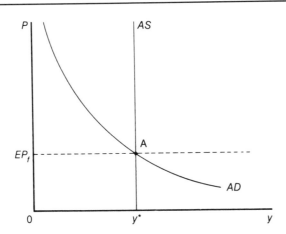

Figure 26.7
Output, the price level and aggregate demand in a fixed exchange rate open economy

The aggregate supply curve *AS* determines full-employment output, y^*. The foreign price level P_f, when converted to domestic prices at the exchange rate E, determines the domestic price level as EP_f. Position A denotes the equilibrium. Aggregate demand *AD* will automatically pass through this point because the supply of money that influences the position of the aggregate demand curve is determined by the demand for money and, therefore, by the price level and real income level at the point A (rather than being determined exogenously as in the case of the closed economy).

aggregate demand curve evaluated for that money supply passes exactly through A.

If you conduct a thought experiment, you can see that the economy can only be at point A. Such a thought experiment was conducted in 1741 by David Hume and is still relevant today.

> Suppose four-fifths of all the money in Great Britain is to be annihilated in one night, and the nation reduced to the same condition, with regard to specie [money supply] as in the reigns of the Harrys and Edwards, what would be the consequence? Must not the price of all labour and commodities sink in proportion, and every thing be sold as cheap as they were in those ages? What nation could then dispute with us in any foreign market, or pretend to navigate or to sell manufactures at the same price, which to us would afford sufficient profit? In how little time, therefore, must this bring back the money which we had lost, and raise us to the level of all the neighbouring nations? Where, after we have arrived, we immediately lose the advantage of the cheapness of labour and commodities and the farther flowing in of money is stopped by our fulness and repletion.
>
> Again, suppose that all the money of Great Britain were multiplied fivefold in a night, must not the contrary effect follow? Must not all labour and commodities rise to such an exorbitant height, that no neighbouring nations could afford to buy from us — while their commodities, on the other hand, became comparatively so cheap, that, in spite of all the laws which could be formed, they would be run in upon us, and our money flow out — till we fall to a level with foreigners, and lose that great superiority of riches, which had laid us under such disadvantages?

Now it is evident, that the same causes, which would correct these exorbitant inequalities, were they to happen miraculously must prevent their happening in the common course of nature, and must for ever, in all neighbouring nations, preserve money nearly proportionable to the art and industry of each nation. All water, wherever it communicates, remains always at a level. Ask naturalists the reason: they tell you, that, were it to be raised in any one place, the superior gravity of that part not being balanced, must depress it, till it meet a counterpoise; and that the same cause, which redresses the inequality when it happens, must for ever prevent, without some violent external operation.[2]

We have now completed our analysis of the trend in inflation and the balance of payments in a fixed exchange rate economy. Let us now go on to see how, with a flexible exchange rate regime, inflation and the exchange rate are determined.

G. Inflation and the Exchange Rate at Full Employment Under a Flexible Exchange Rate Regime

(i) Fundamental Inflation Equation Again

The starting point in understanding what determines the exchange rate at full employment is to recall the factors that determine trend movements in inflation in a closed economy. Provided the rate of money supply growth is steady and the income elasticity of the demand for real balances is one, the rate of inflation will settle down at a rate equal to the difference between the growth rate of the money supply and the growth rate of full-employment output. That is, the fundamental inflation equation is

$$\pi = \mu - \rho \tag{26.14}$$

Recall why this relationship holds. If the rate of money supply growth (less the growth rate of output) is higher than the rate of inflation, then real money balances will be increasing faster than the demand for money is increasing, and the aggregate demand of goods curve will shift outwards, thereby raising the rate at which the price level rises. If the rate of money supply growth (less the growth rate of output) is slower than the rate of inflation, then real money balances will be declining faster than the demand for real money balances is declining. As people attempt to restore their money balances to the desired level, the aggregate demand for goods falls, and this in turn slows the rate at which the price level rises. These forces always operate when the rate of inflation is different from the money supply growth rate (less the growth rate of output).

---

2 David Hume, 'Of the Balance of Trade', pp. 318–19.

(ii) What is True for One Country is True for Another

The fundamental inflation equation used above, Equation (26.14)

$$\pi = \mu - \rho$$

is not a proposition that is true for only one country. It is true for all countries. Consider some other country, called *f* for foreign. The fundamental inflation equation must also be true for the foreign country. That is,

$$\pi_f = \mu_f - \rho_f \tag{26.15}$$

This equation simply says that in the foreign country the rate of inflation is equal to its rate of money supply growth minus its rate of full-employment output growth.

(iii) Purchasing Power Parity Again

Next recall the important proposition that arbitrage in goods generates purchasing power parity. You will recall that although tariffs, transport costs, and other impediments to trade may drive a wedge between the level of prices in one country and the level in another, arbitrage will ensure that, for given levels of trade distortions, the rate of change of the price level in one country will be brought to equality with the rate of change of the price level in the other when adjusted for any change in the exchange rate. That is,

$$\pi = \pi_f + \Delta\epsilon \tag{26.10}$$

This equation says that the rate of inflation in the domestic economy (π) is equal to the rate of inflation in the foreign economy (π_f), plus the rate at which the currency of the domestic economy is depreciating against the currency of the foreign economy ($\Delta\epsilon$).

(iv) Movements in the Exchange Rate

The above propositions may now be brought together to work out what determines the foreign exchange rate at full employment. Combining the domestic forces that produce domestic inflation with the international arbitrage forces that ensure that purchasing power parity is, on the average, maintained, produces a theory of the trend movements in the exchange rate. To see this, first of all notice that the purchasing power parity relationship, Equation (26.10) may be rewritten using the two fundamental inflation Equations (26.14) and (26.15). Since the domestic inflation rate π is equal to the domestic money supply growth rate (μ) minus the rate of output growth (ρ), the left-hand side of the purchasing power parity Equation (26.10) — π — may be replaced with $\mu - \rho$. The same is true of π_f. Notice that π_f is equal to the rate at which money supply is growing in the foreign country (μ_f) minus the rate of output growth in that country (ρ_f). Let us therefore replace π_f on the right-hand side of Equation (26.10) by $\mu_f - \rho_f$. Making both of these substitutions result in:

$$\mu - \rho = \mu_f - \rho_f + \Delta\epsilon \tag{26.16}$$

This equation is nothing other than the purchasing power parity proposition (Equation (26.10)] combined with the fundamental inflation equation for each country [Equations (26.14) and (26.15)]. This equation may now be rearranged so that it provides an explicit statement as to what is happening to the exchange rate ($\Delta\epsilon$). That is,

$$\Delta\epsilon = (\mu - \mu_f) - (\rho - \rho_f) \tag{26.17}$$

This is the *fundamental exchange rate equation*. It says that

> The rate of change of the foreign exchange rate between the currencies of two countries

equals the difference between the money supply growth rates in the two countries

minus the difference between the output growth rates in the two countries

This equation also says that:

1. The faster the money supply growth rate in the domestic economy, the faster the domestic currency depreciates (the bigger $\Delta\epsilon$ will be).
2. The faster the money supply growth rate in the foreign country, the faster the domestic currency appreciate in terms of the foreign currency.
3. The faster the growth rate of output in the domestic economy, the stronger the domestic currency ($\Delta\epsilon$ will be smaller).
4. The faster the rate of growth of output in the foreign economy, the weaker the domestic currency in terms of the foreign currency.

(v) Supply and Demand Yet Again

The factors which determine the exchange rate in the above analysis are nothing other than the forces of supply and demand. The exchange rate is a price like any other price. It is the relative price of two national monies. The exchange rate is determined by the supply of and the demand for domestic money relative to the supply of and demand for foreign money. (Remember that money is a stock, not a flow.)

Look again at the fundamental exchange rate equation — Equation (26.17). The first part of that equation tells us about the growth rate of the relative supplies of two monies ($\mu - \mu_f$). If ($\mu - \mu_f$) is positive, the domestic money supply is growing at a faster rate than the foreign money supply because the domestic money supply is rising relative to the foreign money supply. The second part of the equation ($\rho - \rho_f$) tells us about the growth rate in the relative demands for the two monies. If the growth rate in output is greater in the domestic economy than in the foreign economy, then the demand for domestic money is growing at a faster rate than the demand for foreign money.

Now, if the growth in the relative supplies of money $(\mu - \mu_f)$ is just equal to the growth in the relative demands for money $(\rho - \rho_f)$, the exchange rate will not change. That is, $\Delta\epsilon$ is zero. Thus, there is a critical growth rate for the domestic money supply (let us call it μ^c) at which the exchange rate is steady. To find the growth rate μ^c, simply solve the fundamental exchange rate equation — Equation (26.17) — for the particular μ that is associated with $\Delta\epsilon$ being zero. That is,

$$\Delta\epsilon = (\mu - \mu_f) - (\rho - \rho_f) = 0 \tag{26.18}$$

so,

$$\mu^c = \mu_f + (\rho - \epsilon_f) \tag{26.19}$$

If the money supply grows at a faster rate than μ^c, the domestic currency depreciates ($\Delta\epsilon$ is positive); and if the money supply grows at a slower rate than μ^c, the domestic currency appreciates ($\Delta\epsilon$ is negative).

Therefore, the key thing that a country can control in order to influence its exchange rate is its money supply growth rate. Other things being equal, the faster the money supply grows, the faster will the currency depreciate (or the slower will it appreciate). The exchange rate will be steady only if the money supply grows at the critical rate that equals the foreign money supply growth rate plus the difference between the domestic and foreign output growth rates.

(vi) Does a Depreciating Currency Cause Inflation?

There is a popular view which says that inflation is caused by a depreciating currency and that a country can be trapped in a vicious circle of inflation and depreciation about which nothing can be done. You now know enough to know that this is not true. A depreciating exchange rate is a symptom of inflation and is caused by the same thing that causes inflation. You know from the fundamental inflation equation that, other things being equal, inflation is higher, the higher the money supply growth rate. You also know from the fundamental exchange rate equation that the exchange rate depreciates faster ($\Delta\epsilon$ is positive and increasing), the bigger the growth rate of money supply (μ). Thus both inflation and a weak currency are caused by too high a growth rate of the money supply.

If a country wants to maintain a steady exchange rate, it is necessary for that country to achieve a money supply growth rate relative to the money supply growth rate in the rest of the world that exactly offsets the difference in the growth in demands for domestic and foreign money arising from any differences in output growth rates. This being the case, with a steady exchange rate, the country must accept the inflation rate that is generated in the rest of the world. If, on the other hand, a country wants to achieve a zero inflation rate, it is necessary for the country to make its own money supply grow at the same rate as its own output growth. That is, set μ equal to ρ. But, this policy will not ensure a constant value for the exchange rate since the exchange rate depends on both domestic monetary policy and the monetary policy of the rest of the world. If the rest of the world is inflating, whereas the domestic economy is maintaining a stable price level, then the domestic currency will appreciate ($\Delta\epsilon$ will be negative). But if the foreign economy is deflating — its price level is falling — while the domestic economy is maintaining a steady price level, then the domestic currency will depreciate ($\Delta\epsilon$ will be positive).

(vii) Stable Exchange Rates versus Stable Prices

The above remarks serve to emphasize that a country cannot choose both its inflation rate and the behaviour of its exchange rate simultaneously. A country must make a choice as to whether it wants to achieve a stable price level, thereby allowing its exchange rate to adjust from time to time to reflect the difference between domestic and foreign inflation; or whether it wants to achieve a fixed exchange rate with the rest of the world, in which case it will have to allow the foreign inflation rate to be fully reflected in the domestic inflation rate.

You now have an understanding of the factors that determine the long-term movements in inflation and exchange rates. You see that there are no effects on the exchange rate in the long run arising from such things as import and export demands and the flow of goods and services across national boundaries. In the long run, the exchange rate is determined by monetary equilibrium. With a fixed exchange rate, the country abdicates control over its money supply and inflation. The automatic changes in the stock of foreign exchange reserves ensure that the growth rate of the money supply is exactly equal to the growth rate of the demand for money, the latter being equal to the world rate of inflation plus the domestic output growth rate. Domestic inflation is the same as world inflation. In the case of a flexible exchange rate, the domestic monetary authority controls the stock of foreign exchange reserves and the domestic money supply, thereby forcing the adjustment onto the exchange rate itself. It is movements in the exchange rate that ensure that the stock of money that has been determined by the Bank of England is willingly held by private economic agents. Domestic inflation equals the domestic money supply growth rate less the rate of growth of domestic output.

H. Inflation, the Balance of Payments and the Exchange Rate at Full Employment in a Managed Floating Regime

The theory of the determination of the exchange rate under a floating regime and of the balance of payments under a fixed exchange rate regime at full employment may be combined in a fairly natural and perhaps even obvious way to set out the fundamental constraints upon the actions of a central bank seeking to pursue a managed floating exchange rate policy. To see these constraints, we simply need to combine three bits of information that have already been examined in the previous sections of this chapter. The first is the relationship between the growth of the money supply, the growth of foreign exchange reserves, and the growth of domestic credit. That is, Equation (26.7) which says that

$$\mu = \psi_f + (1 - \psi)dc \qquad (26.7)$$

The second ingredient is the steady-state relation between money growth, inflation, and output growth, Equation (26.9), which says that

$$\mu = \pi + \rho \qquad (26.9)$$

The final ingredient is the purchasing-power parity proposition, Equation (26.10), which says that

$$\pi = \pi_f + \Delta\epsilon \qquad (26.10)$$

Combining these three propositions — substituting the inflation rate out of Equation (26.9), using Equation (26.10), and substituting the money supply growth rate out of Equation (26.7), using Equation (26.9) — gives

$$\pi_f + \Delta\epsilon + \rho = \psi f + (1 - \psi)dc$$

If you subtract π_f, ρ and ψf from both sides of this equation, you obtain

$$\Delta\epsilon - \psi f = (1 - \psi)dc - (\pi_f + \rho) \qquad (26.20)$$

The left-hand side of this equation contains the rate of change of the exchange rate ($\Delta\epsilon$) minus the rate of change of foreign exchange reserves (weighted by the fraction of the money stock backed by those reserves, ψ) that is ψf. Let us give a name to the left-hand side of Equation (26.20): *exchange market pressure*.[3] The right-hand side is simply the growth rate of domestic credit weighted by the fraction of the money supply backed by domestic credit $(1 - \psi)dc$ minus the foreign rate of inflation (π_f) and minus output growth (ρ).

Equation (26.20) says that for a given foreign rate of inflation, π_f, the greater the rate of domestic credit expansion and the lower the output growth, the stronger is the exchange market pressure. Exchange market pressure has to be reflected in either the exchange rate or the stock of reserves. Either the exchange rate will have to rise (the currency will have to depreciate) or reserves will have to fall. Some combination of these two things cannot be avoided. If the central bank wants to manage the

---

3 The term was first suggested by Lance Girton and Don Roper in 'A Monetary Model of Exchange Market Pressure Applied to the Postwar British Experience', *The American Economic Review*, 67 (December 1977), pp. 537–48.

exchange rate and keep the exchange rate from falling, then it will have no alternative but to accept a drop in its foreign exchange reserves — a balance of payments deficit.

The converse of all this is that the lower the domestic credit growth and the higher the output growth relative to the foreign rate of inflation, the less will be the exchange market pressure. This situation implies that the lower the growth rate of domestic credit, the more the foreign exchange reserves rise, and/or the stronger is the rate of appreciation of the currency ($\Delta\epsilon$ negative). In other words, a central bank wishing to pursue tight domestic credit policies (low dc) but at the same time prevent the exchange rate from appreciating (prevent a high negative value of $\Delta\epsilon$) would have to be willing to allow the foreign exchange reserves to rise — a balance of payments surplus. Equation (26.20) states the fundamental constraint on the freedom of the central bank to pursue a managed floating policy.

A fixed exchange rate is the special case of Equation (26.20) where the central bank manages the value of $\Delta\epsilon$ equal to zero, permitting all of the exchange market pressures to come out on the stock of foreign exchange reserves — on the balance of payments. A flexible exchange rate regime is the other extreme, where f is set equal to zero (reserve changes do not occur), and all exchange market pressures are felt by the exchange rate itself. A managed float is simply a linear combination of these two extremes determined by the political and other pressures that operate on the conduct of monetary policy.

What happens to inflation under a managed floating exchange rate depends on world inflation and on the extent to which the central bank permits the exchange rate to move. Equation 26.10 determines the domestic inflation rate in just the same way as it does under fixed exchange rates. The only difference is that with fixed exchange rates the change in the exchange rate is zero, while under managed floating the exchange rate changes by whatever is the amount chosen and or permitted by the monetary authority.

I. Money, Inflation and the Exchange Rate in Recent UK History

In examining the monetary shocks that have hit the UK economy, we need to distinguish between the fixed exchange rate period and the flexible exchange rate period. We have made the division in 1970 though fully flexible exchange rates were not established until 1972. Thus we will call the period up to 1970 fixed exchange rates and that starting in 1971 a period of flexible exchange rates. Under fixed exchange rates, the prediction is that UK inflation will be closely related to that in the rest of the world. Under floating exchange rates, there is no such prediction. Rather, in that case, UK inflation will be influenced by UK money growth.

Let us look first at the relationship between world inflation and UK inflation. Figure 26.8 provides a description of that relationship for the period between 1963 and 1970. The continuous line sloping upwards in the figure shows the line of equality between UK inflation and world inflation. The two broken lines show a range of 2 per cent around the equality between the inflation rates. In other words, any observation lying inside these two broken lines show that world inflation and UK inflation did not deviate by more than two percentage points. The inflation rates used in constructing Figure 26.8 are those for the GDP Deflators.

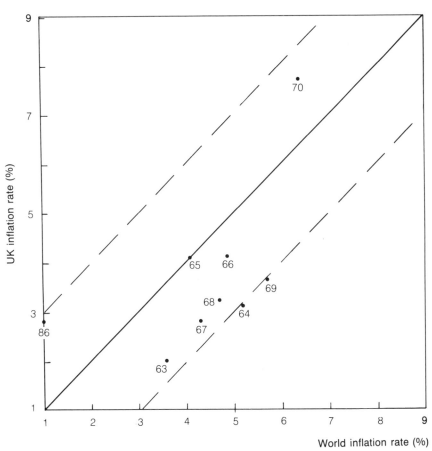

Figure 26.8
UK and world inflation under fixed exchange rates

Under fixed exchange rates UK inflation has been within 2 per cent of world inflation. But within that range there have been some important independent changes in UK inflation. For example, between 1969 and 1970 UK inflation more than doubled while world inflation hardly increased at all.
Sources: UK inflation rate, Appendix to Chapter 2; World inflation rate, *International Financial Statistics Yearbook*, 1987.

Evidently, there is a tendency for UK inflation to lie within a 2 per cent band of world inflation when exchange rates are fixed. However, though in broad terms the predictions of the theory of inflation under fixed exchange rates is borne out by Figure 26.8, the relationship is by no means precise. There is quite a lot of independent movement in UK inflation which is not accounted for by variations in the world inflation rate. Those movements are especially marked between 1969 and 1970 when UK inflation more than doubles while the world inflation rate hardly changes at all.

Next, let us turn to an examination of money supply growth in the UK. Figure 26.9 charts the growth rate of three monetary aggregates and their average. The aggregates are monetary base (M0), narrow money (M1), and broad money (M3). Perhaps the most noteworthy feature of the money supply figures shown in Figure 26.9 are their erratic nature and the lack of any tendency for the difference aggregates to move in unison with each other. A more careful examination of the figure does reveal, however, that the money supply growth rate, regardless of how it was measured, was higher in the 1970s than it had been in the 1960s. This observation is consistent with the tendency for inflation in the 1970s to exceed what it had been in the 1960s. The relationship between the rise in money supply growth and inflation, however, is far from precise. Furthermore, the different monetary aggregates behave in different ways and, therefore, there is considerable ambiguity as to which of the aggregates is the one that we ought to look at in order to explain movements in inflation.

Although not resolving the issue, rather than looking at each individual monetary aggregate taken on its own, we have chosen to calculate an average of the three money supply growth rates. Such an average has the advantage of removing the more erratic fluctuations in each of the individual series. Our constructed average of the three growth rates (M0, M1, and M3) reveals clearly the same pattern as the three underlying growth rates, concerning the rapid acceleration of money growth in the 1970s and its persistently high value through that decade compared with the 1960s. The average also shows that money supply growth declined in the early 1980s though it has tended to increase again since 1983.

To study the relationship between money growth and inflation, we have calculated a version of the money supply growth rate that smooths out fluctuations over time as well as differences across the different aggregates. Specifically, we have constructed a three-year moving average of the average money growth rate shown in frame (d) of Figure 26.9. That moving average growth rate is plotted in Figure 26.10 and shown alongside the inflation rate (of the GDP Deflator). It is evident from Figure 26.10 that there is a clear and strong positive relationship between inflation and money growth. But the relationship is not precise. Indeed the theory of inflation predicts that inflation rates will be more volatile than money supply growth rates. A change in the money supply growth rate will produce a change in the inflation rate in the same direction but by a bigger magnitude. That is, inflation will overshoot money growth changes. This prediction is strongly borne out in the data shown in Figure 26.10 both in the period of rising inflation and of falling inflation.

The time series relationship between inflation and money growth shown in Figure 26.10 cannot, of course, tell us in which direction causation runs. Indeed our theory tells us that during the period of fixed exchange rages (up to 1970–1) inflation is caused by world inflation and money supply growth responds to the inflation rate. In the period of floating exchange rates, inflation is generated by money supply growth and movements in the exchange rate accommodate differences between domestic and world inflation.

The relationship between domestic and world inflation and the exchange rate, however, does not fit any simple theory of exchange rate and inflation determination. To keep things as clear as possible, we focus here on the UK–US inflation differential and the pound–US dollar exchange rate. Figure 26.11 tracks three relevant variables during the period of floating exchange rates.

The difference between US and UK inflation is the thick continuous line. (This is measured as US inflation minus UK inflation.) As you can see, UK inflation was substantially higher than US inflation through the 1970s and particularly strongly so in 1975. Since 1981, the two inflation rates have been almost identical. The dashed line tracks the nominal exchange rate — the per cent change in the sterling value of the US dollar. When this number is positive, the pound is depreciating. When the number is negative, the pound is appreciating.

As you can see, the nominal exchange rate and the inflation differential are not at all closely related to each other. The departures are particularly marked after 1975. The pound depreciated strongly in 1976 even though the inflation differential narrowed. The pound continued to depreciate through 1977 even though the inflation differential narrowed yet again. Then, for the next three years the pound appreciated but much more than it should have done given the fact that UK inflation was still running ahead of US inflation. By the 1980s the inflation differential had virtually disappeared. Despite this fact there remained considerable movements in the pound–US dollar exchange rate.

The movements in the pound–dollar exchange rate were associated with enormous changes in the real exchange rate. This time series is also plotted in Figure 26.11 as the thin continuous line. As you can see the real exchange rate and the nominal exchange rate are almost the same series after 1976. This strong correlation between the real and nominal exchange rate and the lack of a correlation between the nominal exchange

**Figure 26.9
UK money supply
growth rates**

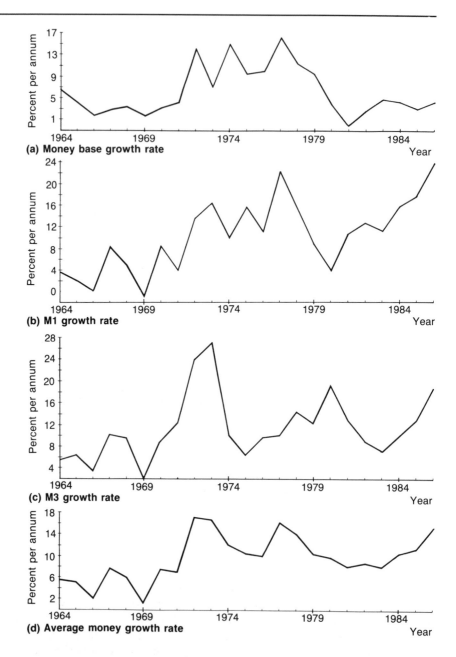

(a) Money base growth rate

(b) M1 growth rate

(c) M3 growth rate

(d) Average money growth rate

The growth rates of monetary base [frame (a)], M1 [frame (b)], and M3 [frame (c)] are shown from 1963 to 1986. The growth rates are volatile and each definition of the money supply seems to have a life of its own. The one striking feature that each has in common is that growth rates were higher in the 1970s than in the 1960s. Frame (d) shows the average of the three growth rates. This average growth rate shows more strongly the acceleration of money growth in the 1970s compared with the 1960s. It also shows that money supply growth rates fell in the early 1980s but have increased again.
Sources: Bank of England Quarterly Bulletin, various issues with the latest possible being used and earlier data rescaled to preserve growth rates in the face of changing coverage.

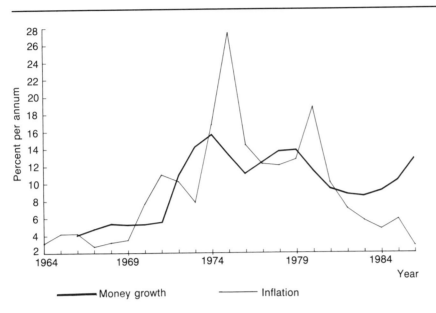

Figure 26.10
UK money growth
and inflation
1964—1986

A three-year moving average growth rate of the average of the three monetary aggregates (M0, M1, M3), lagged one year, is shown as the thick line. The inflation rate (of the GDP Deflator) is shown as the thin line. As predicted by the theory, inflation and money growth are strongly related to each other with inflation overshooting money growth. The overshooting is very strongly present in the mid-1970s when inflation was accelerating strongly. It is also present in the 1980s when inflation was decelerating.
Sources: Inflation rate, Appendix to Chapter 2; Money supply growth rate, same as Figure 26.9.

rate and the inflation differential is not predicted by the simple full-employment theory of inflation and the exchange rate. Either it is a phenomenon associated with the business cycle (which we will study in the next chapter) or it has some as yet unexplained origin.

Finally let us look at the balance of payments. The path of this variable is shown in Figure 26.12. According to the theory that we have studied, under the fixed exchange rates the balance of payments is determined by the difference between the change in the demand for money and the change in domestic credit. Under floating exchange rates the balance of payments is zero and adjustments in exchange market pressure come through as changes in the exchange rate. Under managed floating exchange rates, exchange market pressure will manifest itself partly in the balance of payments and partly in a change in the exchange rate.

As you can see from the figure during the period up to 1970, when the pound was operating on a fixed exchange rate there were sizeable movements in the balance of payments. There continued to be sizeable movements even through the 1970s after the exchange rate started to float. Evidently the float was strongly managed during the 1970s and particularly so during 1977 when a strong surplus in the balance of

**Figure 26.11
Exchange rate
overshooting**

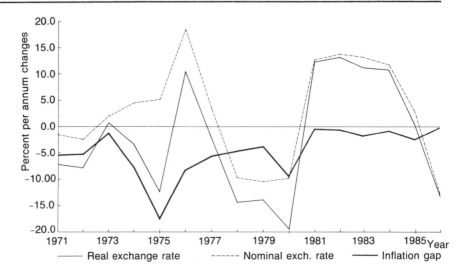

The UK–US inflation differential is plotted as the thick line. It is plotted as US inflation minus UK inflation. UK inflation has always exceeded US inflation but, since 1981, the two have been close. The dashed line is the rate of change of the pound–US dollar exchange rate. When that line is above zero the pound is depreciating. The thin continuous line shows the rate of change of the real exchange rate. There is almost no relation at all between movements in the exchange rate and the inflation differential. The real exchange rate tracks the nominal exchange rate very closely.
Sources: US inflation, Economic Report of the President, 1987; other variables Appendix to Chapter 2.

**Figure 26.12
The balance of
payments**

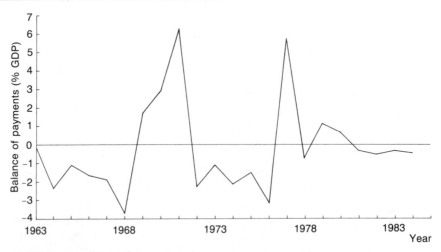

The UK balance of payments behaves as predicted by theory. When the exchange rate is fixed there are large movements in the balance of payments generated by differences in the growth rate of the demand for money and of domestic credit. During the 1970s, under floating exchange rates, the float was managed and the balance of payments was still permitted to fluctuate a great deal. Only in the late 1970s and 1980s has the balance of payments been close to zero as required by a freely fluctuating exchange rate.

payments was permitted. You will recall that in 1976 and 1977 there was a strong depreciation of the pound against the US dollar that was much larger than the UK–US inflation differential. In effect, what happened at that time was that the Bank of England permitted exchange market pressure to come out so strongly in the exchange rate that it ran a balance of payments surplus. Instead of permitting the exchange market pressure to divide itself between exchange rate and balance of payments pressure the exchange rate was overadjusted. In the period since 1980 the balance of payments has been very close to zero, reflecting an almost clean floating exchange rate regime. It is during this clean floating period that the most troublesome and puzzling overshooting of the exchange rate has occurred as seen earlier in Figure 26.11.

This completes our brief review some of the key facts about inflation, money supply growth, world inflation, the exchange rate, and the balance of payments. As you can see there remain as many puzzles as there are answers. But we have made some progress. The broad trends of inflation are well understood and well predicted. Under fixed exchange rates inflation is determined by world inflation and under floating exchange rates by domestic monetary policy. Inflation is more volatile than money supply growth but that is entirely in line with predictions of theory. The balance of payments behaves in a manner predicted by theory, with the largest fluctuations occurring when the exchange rate is fixed or on a managed float. The major puzzles and unresolved issues that remain concern the exchange rate, especially the real exchange rate and its high correlation with the nominal exchange rate. These matters will continue to attract research attention for some years to come.

Summary

A. *Once-and-for-All Price Level Rises and Inflation*

Inflation is an ongoing process of persistently rising prices. A once-and-for-all rise in the price level occurs when the price level moves from one steady-state level to another steady-state level.

B. *Once-and-for-All Changes in the Price Level*

A once-and-for-all rise in the money supply, a once-and-for-all cut in output, a once-and-for-all rightward shift in the IS curve, or a once-and-for-all drop in the propensity to hold money all will lead to a once-and-for-all rise in the price level.

C. *How Inflation is Generated*

Growing inflation will be generated by an ongoing increase in the money supply. A fundamental inflation equation states that the rate of inflation equals the rate of growth of the money supply minus the rate of growth of real income (multiplied by the income elasticity of demand for money) plus the rate of change in the propensity to hold money.

D. *What Happens to Inflation when the Growth Rate of the Money Supply is Increased?*

A change in the growth rate of the money supply will lead to a change in the rate of inflation. The inflation rate change will be greater than the change in the growth rate of the money supply. In other words, inflation will overshoot the money supply growth rate.

E. *The 'Law of One Price'*

The law of one price asserts that arbitrage will reduce price differentials to the minimum consistent with transport costs, tariffs, and other physical barriers and impediments to trade.

The purchasing power parity theorem states that the price of a particular good in one country will be the same as the price in another country (when the prices are converted at the current exchange rate). This proposition does not strictly apply to price levels, since tariffs and transportation costs drive a wedge between price levels. However, it does apply to price *changes* expressed in percentage terms. That is, the percentage change in the price of some commodity in the UK is equal to the percentage change of the price of the same commodity in the United States (say) plus the percentage rate of depreciation of the pound in terms of US dollars.

The interest rate parity theorem is an application of the law of one price to asset markets. It states that the UK interest rate is equal to the US interest rate plus the expected rate of depreciation of the pound.

F. *Inflation and the Balance of Payments at Full Employment Under a Fixed Exchange Rate Regime*

In an economy at full employment with a fixed exchange rate, domestic inflation is equal to the world inflation rate. The balance of payments (as a first approximation) is determined by the domestic credit policies of the central bank. If the central bank creates too much domestic credit, there will be a balance of payments deficit. If the central bank creates too little domestic credit, there will be a balance of payments surplus. The central bank can always achieve a zero balance by permitting exactly the right amount of domestic credit to be created.

G. *Inflation and the Exchange Rate at Full Employment Under a Flexible Exchange Rate Regime*

When the exchange rate is flexible and the economy is at full employment, the money supply and its growth rate are controllable by the central bank. Inflation is determined in exactly the same way as it is in the closed economy, by the growth rate of the money supply. The exchange rate is determined by differences in money supply growth rates and output growth rates between countries. Specifically, the exchange rate, being a price like any other price, is determined by supply and demand. Since the exchange rate is the relative price between two monies, it is determined by the relative supplies (stocks) of the two monies and the relative demands for them. There is a sense in which the exchange rate is unlike any other price in that its value depends directly on the relative monetary policies of the two countries.

H. *Inflation, the Balance of Payments and the Exchange Rate at Full Employment in a Managed Floating Regime*

For a given foreign rate of inflation, the faster the growth rate of domestic credit, the greater will be the amount of exchange market pressure. Exchange market pressure must come out either in a depreciation of the currency or a loss of foreign exchange reserves. The central bank can select a policy that favours smoothing exchange rate adjustments by permitting reserves to take the strain, or may select a policy which favours a steady stock of foreign reserves by permitting the foreign exchange rate to take the strain. The central bank cannot choose both the exchange rate and the stock of foreign exchange reserves. To the extent that it chooses the exchange rate the less control it has over the domestic money supply and consequently over domestic inflation.

I. *Money, Inflation and the Exchange Rate in Recent UK History*

Under fixed exchange rates UK inflation is closely linked to inflation in the rest of the world. Under floating exchange rates UK inflation depends on UK monetary policy. Fluctuations in the growth rate of the money supply are associated with subsequent fluctuations in the inflation rate. Inflation fluctuates by more than the money supply growth rate in line with the theory.

Fluctuations in the exchange rate are much more volatile than required by the inflation differential between the UK and the rest of the world. This fact is strongly borne out by the example used in the chapter — UK–US inflation differentials and the pound–dollar exchange rate. Movements in the nominal exchange rate are largely unconnected with movements in the inflation differential and produce massive changes in the real exchange rate.

The balance of payments behaves in a manner predicted by theory. When the exchange rate is fixed the balance of payments fluctuates strongly and is determined by the difference between the change in the demand for money and the change in domestic credit. When exchange rates are freely floating the balance of payments is close to zero.

Review Questions

1. From the following, label those that are a once-and-for-all rise in the price level and those that are inflation:
   (a) The price of beef this week rose by 10 per cent.
   (b) The Retail Price Index, after having been steady for one year, jumped 10 per cent at the beginning of last winter but has been steady ever since.
   (c) Over the past decade the Retail Price Index has gradually and consistently increased, so that today it is double what it was a decade ago.
   (d) Over the last decade the Retail Price Index doubled but this is the result of two big jumps, one in 1974 and one in 1979.
2. Imagine an economy that has been experiencing stable prices for as long as anyone can remember. Suddenly there is a doubling in the quantity of money. The money supply then remains constant at its new level. What happens in that economy to output, employment, real wages, and the price level? Why? Trace out all the effects and fully set our your reasoning.

3. Does the price level 'overshoot' the money supply in the situation described in Question 2? If so, why? If not, why not?

4. Imagine an economy that has experienced 10 per cent inflation for as long as anyone can remember. Output has been constant, and the money supply has grown at the same 10 per cent rate as inflation. Suddenly there is a doubling in the growth rate of the money supply, after which the new higher (20 per cent) growth rate is maintained. What happens in this economy to output, employment, real wages, and inflation?

5. Does the inflation rate 'overshoot' the money supply growth rate in the economy described in Question 4? If so, why? If not, why not?

6. Describe what would happen to interest rates in the event of monetary shocks such as those set out in Questions 2 and 4 above.

7. Analyse the effects on the price level of a rise in government spending, and a once-and-for-all drop in the demand for money.

8. Does the fact that output growth and ongoing changes in the demand for money affect the rate of inflation mean that the monetary authorities have no tools with which to manipulate the inflation rate?

9. Review the connection between the rate of inflation and the real and nominal rates of interest. What policy actions could the government take that would lower real rates of interest? What actions could they take that would lower nominal interest rates? Are there some policies that might raise real interest rates and lower nominal interest rates?

10. What would be the UK price of jelly beans if the US price was $US5 per kilogram and if there were no tariffs or taxes on jelly beans, and if the pound was worth $1.62 US? Suppose, one year later, that jelly beans cost $US5.50 per kilogram and the pound was worth $1.70 US. What is the percentage change in the UK price? What is the percentage change in the US price? What is the percentage change in the exchange rate? How do these variables relate to each other?

11. You have £10,000 to invest for one year. If you buy a UK government bond, it will give you a sure return after one year of 10 per cent. If you convert your £10,000 into US dollars, you can do so at an exchange rate of $1.50 US per £. You can buy a US government bond that will give a sure return after one year of 13 per cent.
    (a) What would the exchange rate between the pound and the US dollar have to be one year hence for it to be just worth buying the US bond?
    (b) If you firmly expected the US dollar to be cheaper than your answer to (a), what would you do?
    (c) If people generally shared your expectation, what would happen?

12 You are given the following information about two open economies:

Year	Money Supply Growth Rates (% p.a.)		Real Income Growth Rates	
	Country A	Country B	Country A	Country B
1990	10	5	8	3
1991	10	5	8	3
1992	10	5	8	3
1993	5	5	3	3
1994	5	5	3	3
1995	5	5	3	5
1996	15	5	3	5
1997	15	5	3	5
1998	15	5	3	5
1999	10	5	3	5
2000	10	5	3	5
2001	10	5	3	5

There is perfect capital mobility between the two economies. The exchange rate is flexible. All the changes in money supply and real income growth are fully anticipated. The income elasticity of the demand for money is one.

(a) Draw graphs of the money supply growth rates and real income growth rates for the two countries.

(b) Sketch the possible paths of inflation rates in the two countries.

(c) Sketch the possible path of the exchange rate.

(d) Sketch the nominal interest rates in each country.

13. Suppose that the two countries you analysed in Question 12 had a fixed exchange rate between 1990 and 2001. Also suppose that the real income growth rates were exactly the same as listed above. Further, suppose that country B had the same money supply growth rates as those listed.

(a) What would country A's money supply growth rate path have been? Set out the path and draw a graph of it.

(b) What would the inflation rate have been in country A?

(c) How would country A's interest rates have behaved?

(d) Would country A have had a balance of payments problem?

14. In April, 1988, it was possible to borrow Swiss francs in Zurich at an annual interest rate of 5 1/4 per cent. In that same month, pounds could be deposited in a bank in London at an annual interest rate of 8 1/2 per cent.

(a) Do these facts show that interest parity does not hold?

(b) If the exchange rate between Swiss francs and £ sterling at the beginning of April, 1988, was 2.6 Swiss frances = £1, what do you predict the exchange rate would be at the beginning of July, 1988? What did it turn out to be?

15. Work out the effects on the balance of payments when the exchange rate is fixed and the economy is at full employment, of the following:
    (a) A rise in the price level.
    (b) A rise in interest rates.
    (c) A rise in real income.
    (d) A rise in domestic credit.
16. Work out the effects on the exchange rate, in an economy at full employment with a flexible exchange rate, of the shocks listed in Question 15 above.
17. Why can't a country pursue any balance of payments *and* exchange rate objectives it chooses? Draw parallels between a country's exchange rate policy and the price and output policies of a monopolist.
18. Review the main facts about UK inflation, money growth, the balance of payments and the exchange rate. Which of these facts are well understood and explained by theory and which remain unresolved?

27

Business Cycles

In the last two chapters you studied the forces that influence unemployment, inflation, the exchange rate, and the balance of payments while
abstracting from unanticipated or 'surprise' changes in aggregate demand.
It is now time to focus on those 'surprises' and analyse how they modify
the behaviour of the economy as compared with what would have happened in their absence. You can think of what we are going to do here
as adding noise (with some persistence in the noise) to the trends and
other fluctuations in unemployment (in the natural rate of unemployment)
and to the trends in the price level and the exchange rate that we have
studied in the two previous chapters.
By the time you have completed this chapter you will be able to:

(a) Explain how unanticipated changes in aggregate demand generate
procyclical co-movements in the price level;
(b) Explain how a combination of unanticipated and anticipated
changes in aggregate demand generates surges in inflation that
are independent of output and also procyclical co-movements in
the price level;
(c) Describe how the rational expectations theories explain the
autocorrelation of output and employment;
(d) Explain the implications of the rational expectations theories for
interest rate behaviour;
(e) Explain how international shocks influence the domestic business
cycle;
(f) Explain how the rational expectations theories explain the
business cycle;
(g) Explain the nature of the hypothesis testing problem posed by
the rational expectations theories.

A. Procyclical Co-Movements in the Price Level

You saw in Chapters 22 and 23 how an anticipated change in aggregate demand affects only the nominal variables of the economy, and how an unanticipated change in aggregate demand has both nominal and real effects. It is now possible to use this analysis to understand how the swings in economic activity that are characterized by procyclical co-movements in the price level occur.

For illustrative purposes it is easiest to assume that expected aggregate demand curve does not change. Equivalently, this assumption implies that the expected values of all the variables that influence aggregate demand are constant. (It would be possible to assume that their expected rates of change were constant so that the expected level of aggregate demand is increasing by a constant percentage amount each period.) In that case there would be a trend rate of inflation. We would then analyse variations in aggregate demand around its rising trend position. Such an exercise, however, would complicate the analysis without adding any insights so we will suppose, here, that the expected aggregate demand curve is fixed and that the rational expectation of the price level is constant.

The particular factors that influence the position of the aggregate demand curve depend on the exchange rate regime. Under fixed exchange rates aggregate demand is determined by domestic fiscal policy and by world variables. Under flexible exchange rates aggregate demand is determined by domestic monetary and fiscal policy and by the world rate of interest. To keep things as concrete as possible we will suppose, here, that we are dealing with a flexible exchange rate economy. We will also focus on the domestic money supply as the central variable that generates fluctuations in aggregate demand. We have made this choice, however, purely for illustrative purposes and for simplicity. Any and every of the variables influencing the position of the aggregate demand curve could be regarded as the source of the fluctuations that we are about to analyse.

Specifically, suppose that the level of aggregate demand that actually occurs differs from that which is expected because the actual money supply is randomly fluctuating around its anticipated level. Sometimes it is above and sometimes it is below its anticipated level. Figures 27.1 and 27.2 illustrate what is going on.

Figure 27.1 shows a hypothetical random path for the money supply. (These illustrative numbers are random drawings from a normal distribution with a mean of 100 and a standard deviation of 2.) The average value of the money supply is 100; therefore, the rational expectation of the money supply is also 100. The maximum value of the money supply in this example, 104, occurs in period 5 and is marked A. The minimum value, 95.8, occurs in period 9 and is marked B.

Figure 27.2 shows the aggregate demand and aggregate supply curves. The curve $AD(M = 100)$ is the aggregate demand curve drawn for the expected value of the money supply. The expectations-augmented

Figure 27.1
Hypothetical money
supply path

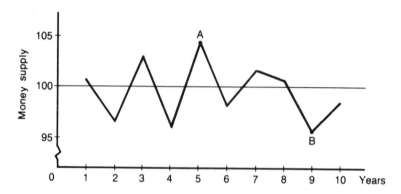

A hypothetical path for the money supply is generated by drawing random numbers from a normal distribution that has an average value of 100 and a standard deviation of 2. The path plotted was generated by taking ten drawings from such a distribution.

aggregate supply curve, EAS_0, is drawn for an expected price level equal to its rational expectation, P_0^e. The vertical curve, AS, is the full-employment aggregate supply curve.

If the money supply behaves as shown in Figure 27.1 then the economy will, on average, be at the price level P_0^e and, at full-employment output level y^*. But, there will be fluctuations around these levels. When the

Figure 27.2
The procyclical co-
movements of the
price level

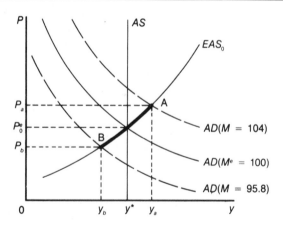

If the money supply was equal to its average value (and rationally expected value) of 100, the aggregate demand curve would be the solid line $AD(M^e = 100)$, output would be y^*, and the price level P_0^e. Actual movements in the money supply shift the aggregate demand curve as shown between the limits $AD(M = 104)$ and $AD(M = 95.8)$. With a constant expected price level, the expectations-augmented aggregate supply curve remains at EAS_0, and actual output and the price level are generated along the thick line AB. This thickened line traces out the generally procyclical co-movements of the price level.

money supply is at A, its maximum value in this example, the aggregate demand curve will be the curve shown as $AD(M = 104)$ and output will be y_a and the price level P_a. When the money supply is at B, its minimum value in this example, the aggregate demand curve will be at the position shown as $AD(M = 95.8)$. In this case, output will be y_b, and the price level will be P_b. For intermediate values of the money supply (periods 1 to 4, 6 to 8, and 10), output and the price level will be determined at points in between these two extremes and along the EAS_0 curve. The thickened portion of the curve traces out the range of values of y and P generated by this hypothetical money supply path.

Although random variations in the money supply about the anticipated level have been stylized as random variations around a *constant* anticipated money supply, as noted above it is not difficult to generalize this analysis. If the anticipated money supply was growing, then the expected aggregate demand curve and, therefore, the expectations-augmented aggregate supply curve would drift upwards. The actual variations in the money supply would then fluctuate around the rising trend, so that the actual aggregate demand curve would fluctuate around the expected curve. We would still generate procyclical co-movements of the price level, although the amplitude of the price movements would be accentuated, and those of the output movements would be smaller than those illustrated.

The predicted procyclical co-movements of the price level shown in Figure 27.2 can easily be translated into a predicted negative relationship between inflation and unemployment. When output is above its full-employment level, unemployment will be below its natural rate, and vice versa. When the price level is higher than expected, the inflation rate will also be higher than expected. Therefore, procyclical co-movements of the price level automatically imply a negative correlation between inflation and unemployment — the Phillips relation of Chapter 7.

You have now seen how unanticipated shocks to aggregate demand generate one aspect of the facts that need to be explained — the sometimes observed, systematic, procyclical co-movements of the price level. Let us now move on to review our understanding of the sources of independent movements (countercyclical movements) in output and the price· level.

B. Independent Movements in Output and the Price Level

To see how rational expectations theories are capable of accounting, in principle, for all the patterns that we observe in the co-movements of output and the price level, consider separately the effects of anticipated, unanticipated, and combined monetary shocks to the economy.

Suppose first, as described in detail in the previous section, that there is an unanticipated rise in aggregate demand. We know that such a change raises the price level (and the inflation rate) and raises output. Thus, from this source of shock the price level moves procyclically. Suppose, at the opposite extreme, that there is a rise in aggregate demand that is fully anticipated. This change leads to a rise in the price level (inflation rate) with no corresponding movement of output (recall Chapter 26). Now combine these two effects. There are two interesting cases. The first case is one in which aggregate demand increases by an amount that is partly anticipated and partly not. In this case, there is a rise in both output and the price level, but the rise in the price level is greater than if the rise in aggregate demand was unanticipated. Let us translate this result into a prediction about inflation and unemployment rather than about the price level and output.

In the experiment just reviewed, a higher output level is associated with a lower unemployment rate, and a higher price level is associated with a higher observed rate of inflation. Therefore, a rise in aggregate demand that was partly anticipated and partly not would generate a rise in inflation and a drop in unemployment. The amount by which the price level rises depends on the anticipated and unanticipated components of the rise in the money supply. The amount by which unemployment falls depends only on the unanticipated change in aggregate demand. This example implies that the slope of the Phillips relation of Chapter 7 is not constant and does, in general, depend on the decomposition of the change in aggregate demand between its anticipated and unanticipated components.

The second more extreme case is one in which aggregate demand is anticipated to grow at a high rate but that it actually increases at a slow rate. In this situation there is a rise in anticipated aggregate demand but unanticipated aggregate demand is negative. In such a situation, output falls, and unemployment rises. The inflation rate may either rise or fall, depending on the strength of the two offsetting effects on it. The effect of a high anticipated growth of aggregate demand will be to keep inflation high, whereas the effect of a negative unanticipated change in aggregate demand will be to lower inflation. We cannot say, *a priori*, which of these two effects will dominate. It is possible for the first to dominate, thereby producing a higher rate of inflation with a higher unemployment rate and an output rate that is below trend. This case corresponds to that observed on several occasions in the 1970s when there was a tendency for both inflation and unemployment to rise together. The continued rise in the UK unemployment in the late 1970s and early 1980s, with the tendency for output to fall below its trend value, while at the same time the inflation rate, although moderating in 1981, remained persistently high, may potentially be accounted for by this line of reasoning.

The crucial thing to emphasize and reiterate is that the way in which a change in aggregate demand is divided between a change in output and a change in the price level depends on the extent to which that change in aggregate demand is anticipated. On the average, output and the price level will move in the same direction as each other, since swings in actual aggregate demand are likely to have greater amplitude than swings in expected aggregate demand. But, from time to time there may be large shifts in anticipated aggregate demand, usually less than, but occasionally greater than, the change in actual aggregate demand. These occasional strong changes in expected aggregate demand will produce co-movements that are opposite to those normally observed, and when they occur, they will be associated with the appearance of badly deteriorating (or, although it did not happen in the 1970s, of miraculously improving) macroeconomic performance.

The discussion in this section and in the preceding one has focused on the way in which co-movements of the price level and output might be understood. But, there is one further feature of the behaviour of output which we have not yet discussed and to which we now turn.

C. Autocorrelation of Output and Employment

There are two distinct, although not mutually exclusive, explanations for autocorrelation of output and employment. One is based on costs of adjustment of labour and is employed in the new classical analysis. The other is based on overlapping contracts and is used in the new Keynesian theory. Let us look at each of them in turn.

(i) Adjustment Costs

The theory of profit-maximizing firms' demand for labour and supply of output, as developed in Chapter 17, which underlies all the theories of aggregate supply implicitly assumes that firms can vary their output and labour inputs instantly and without cost. This assumption is reasonable for the purpose of getting some theoretical principles straight. But, it is not a good assumption if we want to explain the facts as they appear in actual economies. It is costly for firms to hire and fire labour and it is costly for households to search out desirable employment opportunities. Therefore, in the event of a change in demand labour inputs and outputs will adjust only gradually to meet the new demand conditions. When the price level rises, instead of the demand for labour curve instantly shifting to reflect the new higher price level, it will move only gradually. Thus, if the economy experienced an unanticipated (say) rise in aggregate demand, then, although the response to that rise will be a higher price level and higher levels of output and employment, it will take firms some time to raise their output and employment levels by the amounts suggested by the theories developed in this book. Instead of the demand for labour curve suddenly shifting, it will gradually move to the right, thereby leading to a gradual change in employment and output rather than a sudden jump.

To make things clearer, suppose that after a period in which there had been an unanticipated rise in aggregate demand, there was a subsequent unanticipated fall. Firms will already have hired additional labour and be producing additional output, having moved some way toward satisfying the demand associated with the previously unanticipated rise in the money supply. Now that they are confronted with an unexpected fall in the money supply (and therefore an unexpected fall in the price level), they will not suddenly jump to the new lower employment and output position. Rather, they will, *starting from where they are*, gradually move toward the new lower output and employment position. This response of firms is not irrational nor are firms not maximizing profits. On the contrary, it is precisely because they are maximizing profits that their adjustments will be gradual. They have to take account not only of the cost of labour and capital and the price of output in their profit-maximizing decisions, but also of the costs of *changing* their output and employment. Thus, the costs of hiring and firing labour make the demand for labour curves move slowly, and this imparts gradual adjustment to output and employment.

Gradual adjustment may be described as *autocorrelation*. If output and employment adjust gradually, then where they will move to in the current period depends on where they started out from in the previous period, and where they will go to in the next period depends on where they are now. We can describe the path of output and employment by saying that the values of output and employment in period t depend in part on the values of those variables in period $t - 1$.

The explanation for autocorrelation just presented is the one that is incorporated in the new classical theory of aggregate supply. A second way in which autocorrelation of output and employment can arise is emphasized in the new Keynesian theory and comes from the fact that contracts in the labour market are long and overlapping. Let us now look more closely at this explanation of autocorrelation.

(ii) Overlapping Contracts

Not everyone negotiates a labour contract on the same day of each year for the coming year. Labour contracts are negotiated on different days. Also, some labour contracts run for less than a year, some for a year, some for more than a year. The fact that labour market contracts overlap has important implications for the amount by which wages will change.

These implications are most easily seen in a simplified framework in which we imagine that contracts run for two years and that one-half of them are renegotiated each year. Figure 27.3 illustrates this set-up.

There are two groups: group 1 negotiates contracts in odd-numbered years and group 2 in even numbered years. In 1988, group 2's wages were W_0 (fixed in 1987), and group 1 negotiated a wage of W_1 to run for 1988 and 1989. In 1989, group 1's wages were predetermined at W_1 and group 2 set its wages at W_2 to run for 1989 and 1990. The pattern repeats forever. Now when group 1 is deciding on the appropriate level of wages

**Figure 27.3
Overlapping
contracts**

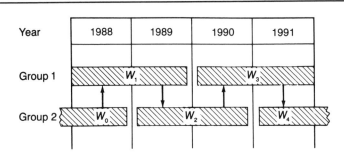

Wages set in 1988 (W_1) are influenced by wages already determined (W_0) and in turn influence wages that will be set in 1989 (W_2). The pattern repeats, so that wages set in 1991 (W_4) are indirectly influenced by all earlier set wages.

in 1988, it has to take some account of the wages that group 2 is receiving, W_0. How much influence group 2's wage will have on group 1's decision depends on how substitutable labour is between the two groups. If it is not very substitutable, then the wages of one group will not be a major factor influencing the wages of the other. If on the other hand, the two groups are very close substitutes for each other, then the wages of one will have a major influence on the wage level of the other. Why is this?

Recall that the basic assumption of the new Keynesian analysis is that money wages are set to achieve an expected equilibrium in the labour market. When just one group of workers are negotiating wages in their own sector, they have to take account of the fact that the demand for their services depends both on their own wages and on the wages of alternative substitute labour. There is also substitutability on the supply side. The higher the wages of one group relative to another, the more people will want to supply their services to the activities of that group. We see then, that the expected equilibrium wage for one group depends on the wage level of the other group. The closer substitutes that the two groups are for each other, the more sensitive will the equilibrium wage of one group be to the wage of the other group.

In terms of Figure 27.3, the wages set in 1988, W_1, will be influenced by the wages that already prevail in that year, (W_0). The arrow indicates the line of influence going from W_0 to W_1. Likewise, in 1989 when group 2 sets its wages, it will be influenced by the wages that have been set by W_1. Again, the arrow illustrates this line of influence. The same pattern repeats in 1990 and 1981 and so on. This overlapping pattern of wage contracts means that the wages that are being set at any particular date will be influenced directly by the wages that already prevail at that date, and will be influenced indirectly by all the wages that have been set at all previous dates. Thus, the wages at any particular point in time will be influenced by wages at all past points in time.

Wages will adjust more gradually as a result of overlapping contracts than they would if all contracts were renegotiated on the same day. Even though demand conditions might have changed, this gradual adjustment occurs because the movement of one wage too far out of line with other wages in competing activities would not be compatible with an expected full-employment equilibrium in the relevant labour market.

The fact that wages set at any particular point in time depend on the wages set at all previous points in time means that when setting a wage today, it is known by the parties agreeing to the wage that the decision being made will itself have an influence on decisions that are going to be made in the future.

Since future wages will be influenced in part by wages that are being fixed today, it is important in fixing today's wages to take account of likely future demand conditions. Rational wage setters in an economy in which contracts overlap will want to look as far into the future as they can in assessing the likely future course of aggregate demand and demand in their own particular sector. They will seek to form rational expectations not just about the immediate future period but about all future periods.

There is a second important implication of overlapping contracts. It is that contracts in existence in any particular year, having been negotiated at different dates in the past, will incorporate expectations that were formed in the past, and therefore based on old information — information available at the past dates on which wages currently enforced were set. Thus, what was unanticipated when one set of contracts was written, some time in the past, might already have occurred and therefore be part of the information on the basis of which some other, more recent contracts were written. Thus, an aggregate demand shock that occurs after a contract has been written, and which was unanticipated when the contract was written, will continue to have effects on output and employment until that particular contract is replaced with a new one. Furthermore, those effects will persist long beyond the date on which all existing contracts have been replaced with new ones.

To see why, you simply have to recall that wages currently being set are influenced by wages already in place. If the wages set last year (to run for two years) were set at a level that is now known to have been inappropriate in the light of changes that have occurred in aggregate demand, the fact that those wages are going to remain in place for another year means that wages being set this year, while taking some account of the new information about the change in aggregate demand, also have to be set such that they do not get so far away from the wages already set. The new contract does not want to create an excess supply or demand in the part of the market whose wages are currently being determined. Also, when the wages set last year are reset next year, they will be influenced by the wages that have been set this year. Therefore they too will not fully incorporate all the new knowledge about current demand conditions but will continue to be influenced in part at least by their own previous value.

Thus, random shocks that bombard the economy will have effects that persist from period to period over the indefinite future. Their effects will die away gradually but not instantly.

You will recognize fairly readily that the behaviour of wages in an economy with overlapping contracts may be described as displaying autocorrelation — that is, wages today depend on wages in some previous period. What we are seeking to understand, however, is not autocorrelated wages but autocorrelated output and employment. But it is only a short step from the behaviour of wages to the behaviour of employment and output. If wages are autocorrelated, so too are employment and output. To see why, you simply have to recall that the level of employment depends on the level of wages (real wages). The gradual adjustment of money wages takes account of the expected price level and is, in effect, an attempt gradually to adjust expected real wages. A gradual adjustment of real wages would automatically imply a gradual adjustment of the profit-maximizing level of employment and, therefore, of the level of output. Thus, overlapping labour market contracts lead not only to autocorrelated wages but also to autocorrelated output and employment.

An Analogy: The idea that costly labour input adjustments and overlapping long-term contracts can generate autocorrelation in output, employment, and the price level has a vivid physical analogy that perhaps will make things clearer. Suppose one was to hit a rocking horse at random.[1] The horse is sometimes hit frequently and sometimes infrequently, sometimes with a hard knock and sometimes with a gentle one. Within wide limits, the horse will rock in a very systematic and persistent fashion regardless of how hard or often it is hit. It will swing to and fro much more systematically than the shocks that are being imparted to it by the person who is rocking it. It is much the same with the economy. The adjustment costs in labour markets and the negotiation costs in setting up new contracts mean that when unexpected events occur, there is sufficient inertia in the economy to ensure that it does not radically alter its course as a result of the random shock. Rather, its course is much more systematic and smooth than the path of the shocks themselves.

D. Interest Rate Behaviour

Although in the presentation of the rational expectation equilibrium analysis in Chapters 22 and 23 we did not explicitly analyse the deter-

---

1 The rocking analogy was first suggested as long ago as 1907 by the brilliant Swedish economist, Knut Wicksell and was elaborated upon in 1933 by Ragnar Frisch: 'If you hit a wooden rocking horse with a club, the movement of the horse will be very different to that of the club'. Quoted from Ragnar Frisch, 'Propogation Problems and Impulse Problems in Dynamic Economics', *Economic Essays in Honour of Gustave Cassell* (New York: Augustus M. Kelley, 1967), p. 158; this was originally published in 1933.

mination of the rate of interest, there are strong implications for interest rate determination in the rational expectations theories. To explore those implications fully and completely would require more time and space than is available here and, in some respects, would take us into a level of analysis that is substantially more demanding than would be appropriate. Nevertheless, it is possible to obtain a good understanding of the general implications for interest rate determination in the rational expectations theories. This brief section will pursue that task.

You already know that the market rate of interest deviates from the real rate of interest because of expected inflation. Recall why this is so: people borrow and lend for future periods of different lengths. That being so, the real rate of return that they will obtain at the end of a loan term will be equal to the market rate of interest on the loan minus the actual rate of inflation that emerges over the term of the loan.

At the time at which a loan is contracted, that actual rate of inflation is unknown. The only substitute for the actual rate of inflation that both borrowers and lenders can use is their expectation of the inflation that will occur over the term of the loan. Lenders will demand a premium on the interest rate to compensate for their expectation of the inflation that is going to occur over the term of the loan, and borrowers will willingly pay a premium equal to their expectation of inflation. Since both borrowers and lenders occupy the same economic environment and form their expectations in the same rational manner, there should be a consensus as to what the expected rate of inflation is. That is, the market rate of interest that we observe is equal the equilibrium real rate of interest (itself a variable), plus the rational expectation of the rate of inflation *over the term of the loan in question*. Thus, for three-month loans, the anticipated three-month rate of inflation will be added to the real rate of interest; similarly, for 15–20-year loans, the rate of inflation expected over the long term, on the average, will be added to the real rate of interest.

The anticipated rate of inflation (the rational expectation of the future price level expressed as a percentage change over the current known price level and converted to an annual rate of change) is determined by the expectations of those things that determine the actual rate of inflation. Since the actual rate of inflation is determined by the growth rate of the money supply and the trend growth rate of output, the expected rate of inflation depends on the expected growth rate of the money supply and expected output growth. In general, we would expect the actual growth rate of the money supply (and the actual growth rate of aggregate demand) to be more volatile than movements in the expected growth rate of the money supply and expected growth of aggregate demand. This is precisely the consideration that led to the prediction of procyclical co-movements in the price level as discussed above.

Further, in general, we would expect fluctuations in the expected long-term average growth rate of the money supply to be much smaller than fluctuations in expectations of, say, the next three-months' growth rate of the money supply or the next twelve months' growth rate. Recall that the rate at which prices change depends on *both* the anticipated and unanticipated changes in the money supply. But, movements in the interest rate depend only on the anticipated inflation rate and therefore only on the anticipated movements of the money supply. Thus, fluctuations in the price level (inflation) will have greater amplitude and be more erratic than fluctuations in interest rates. Further, because fluctuations in the expected long-term average money supply growth rate will be smaller than fluctuations in the expected money supply growth rate over the short term, fluctuations in short-term interest rates will have greater amplitude than fluctuations in long-term interest rates.

It is an implication of the rational expectations theories that, like the price level, interest rates will display procyclical co-movements. But, interest rate fluctuations will have smaller amplitude than those of the price level, and the longer the term of the interest rate, the smaller will be the amplitude of the fluctuation. You will recognize these predictions as being in accord with the facts concerning UK interest rates, presented in Chapters 2 and 7 of this book.

E. International Transmission

So far, in our discussion of the business cycle, we have abstracted from international factors. Such factors are, however, of major importance. Let us consider such factors both under fixed and flexible exchange rates.

Under fixed exchange rates aggregate demand can be influenced by fluctuations in world income and interest rates. An unexpected rise in economic activity in the rest of the world will produce a surprise increase in domestic aggregate demand and the effects of this increase on domestic output will be similar to the effects of a domestic shock. Also, to the extent that world prices rise there will also be a rise in domestic prices.

There are also international transmission forces at work under flexible exchange rates. A surprise change in world macroeconomic activity that changes the world rate of interest will shift the domestic aggregate demand curve and produce changes in domestic output and prices and the real exchange rate along the lines that we analysed in Chapter 23.

F. The Business Cycle

This section does little more than bring together and consolidate what has already been said above.[2] The first feature of the business cycle that was identified in Chapter 7 was the description of the movements of real

---

2 For a much fuller treatment of this topic and more — indeed with the entire subject matter of this book — you will want to read two brilliant papers by Robert E. Lucas, Jr., 'Understanding Business Cycles', *Journal of Monetary Economics*, Vol. 5, supp. 1977, Carnegie–Rochester Conference Series on Public Policy; and 'Methods and Problems in Business Cycle Theory', *Journal of Money, Credit and Banking*, 12 Pt. 2, (November 1980), pp. 696–715. For a thoughtful critique, you will also want to read James Tobin's discussion paper of the second cited Lucas paper, on pp. 795–9 of the same journal.

economic activity (as measured by output) as a low-order stochastically disturbed difference equation. Specifically, we saw that it was possible to describe real GDP by an equation that says that deviations from trend in real GDP in year t is equal to 0.89 of its value in the previous year plus a random component. You can now see how the rational expectations theories explain that simple description of the evolution of real GDP. The autocorrelation component (the persistence effect) is rationalized either in terms of costly adjustment of inputs of labour or in terms of overlapping wage and employment contracts. The sources of randomness that hit the economy are identified as the unanticipated components of monetary and fiscal changes as well as, implicitly, randomness in decisions concerning private expenditure and money holding. A further and important source of random shocks is technological shocks to the production function described in Chapters 17 and 25.

The second feature of the business cycle described in Chapter 7 and identified as being present in the UK is the procyclical co-movement of the price level and interest rates. We have seen in this chapter how the normally observed procyclical co-movements of prices are to be explained as the consequence of fluctuations in actual aggregate demand having greater amplitude than the fluctuations in anticipated aggregate demand. We have also seen that the procyclical co-movements of interest rates, smaller in amplitude than the fluctuations in the price level and of even smaller amplitude in the case of long-term interest rates, are all explicable in these same terms. Basically, fluctuations in expected values of variables are (usually) less marked than fluctuations in actual values, and the longer the period over which an average expectation is being formed, the smaller will be the amplitude of the fluctuations in that expectation.

The key ingenuity of the rational expectations theories lies in their ability to account for the autocorrelated movements of output and the procyclical co-movements of the price level and interest rates, while at the same time being able to account for the infrequent but, when they occur, important independent movements of inflation and output. You have seen in this chapter how that explanation is achieved. Our final task is to set out a few problems that arise in the area of testing the explanation just advanced.

G. The Hypothesis Testing Problem Posed by the Rational Expectations Theories

This chapter has tried to show you how the rational expectations theories of income, employment, and the price level are capable, *in principle*, of explaining the facts. This exercise should not be confused with one of actually explaining the facts — a task that is much more difficult and requires careful, indeed, painstaking measurement and statistical inference.[3] Testing the explanations advanced in this chapter is something that is only in its infancy and is going to occupy a great deal of time and energy in the coming years.[4] This section merely reviews some of the highlights of the problems with testing the rational expectations explanations.

The first problem that has to be solved is that of finding a plausible, *a priori* defendable, and, ideally, non-controversial way of decomposing changes in money, government spending, taxes (and perhaps other exogenous variables) into their anticipated and unanticipated components. This involves studying the *processes* that describe the evolution of these variables and finding ways of forecasting them that mimic reasonably well the ways in which agents in the real world might go about that task. In the example of the money supply, referred to in Chapter 22, the money supply process was described as a low-order autoregression that reacts to unusually large fluctuations in government spending and to unemployment. This seems like a promising hypothesis for explaining how anticipations of monetary growth are formed.

The second major problem arises in discriminating between the new Keynesian and new classical theories. As you saw, these two theories are very similar, but they differ in three respects. First, they imply different slopes for the expectations-augmented aggregate supply curve, and second, one theory implies that households will always be 'on' their labour supply curve, whereas the other implies that they may at some stages be 'off' that curve. From an observational point of view it is very difficult to discriminate between these two differences, since we do not know, *a priori*, what the slope of the expectations-augmented aggregate supply curve is, nor would it be very easy, *a priori*, to identify whether or not individuals were 'on' or 'off' their labour supply curves.

The third source of difference does provide a potential way of discriminating, but it will not be easy to exploit. It is the difference between the two theories arising from the overlapping nature of labour market contracts emphasized by the new Keynesian theory. The difference in question is the way in which the random shocks combine to affect the current value of output, employment, and the price level. According to the new classical theory, the current random shock combined with the

3 A useful overview and survey of this topic may be found in Stanley Fischer, ed., *Rational Expectations and Economic Policy*, National Bureau of Economic Research Conference Report (Chicago and London: University of Chicago Press, 1980), esp. pp. 49–70.
4 Three good examples of such work, though much more demanding than the level of this book, are Robert J. Barro and Mark Rush, 'Unanticipated Money and Economic Activity', in Stanley Fischer, ed. (see note 4 above), pp. 23–54; Thomas J. Sargent, 'A Classical Macroeconomic Model for the United States', *Journal of Political Economy*, 84 (June 1976), pp. 207–37; and John B. Taylor, 'Estimation and Control of a Macroeconomic Model with Rational Expectations', *Econometrica*, 47 (September 1979), pp. 1267–86. The work of Barro and Sargent is 'new classical', and that of Taylor is new Keynesian.

previous actual value of output is all that is required to explain what is happening in the current period, whereas for the new Keynesian approach, the shocks from previous periods explicitly have to be combined with the current period shock to generate the current period output, employment, and price level.

There is a third problem known as 'observational equivalence'.[5] This problem arises from the fact that it is always possible to introduce *ad hoc* modifications to theories not based on rational behaviour such that the non-rational 'theory' makes the same 'predictions' as the rational theory. The words 'theory' and 'predictions' have been placed in quotation marks to raise alarm bells that the predictions that come from *ad hoc* modifications to a model do not provide a basis for testing that model. The ultimate test of any theory is its ability to predict the future, not the past!

Summary

A. *Procyclical Co-Movements in the Price Level*

Generally, the swings in the actual values of variables that determine aggregate demand (for example, the money supply) are bigger than the swings in the anticipated values of these variables. That is, the aggregate demand curve fluctuates with greater amplitude than does the expectations-augmented aggregate supply curve. As a consequence co-movements of the price level are in general procyclical.

B. *Independent Movements in Output and the Price Level*

Anticipated changes in aggregate demand move the price level but leave output undisturbed, whereas unanticipated changes in aggregate demand move both the price level and output. By combining anticipated and unanticipated movements in aggregate demand (generated by anticipated and unanticipated movements in monetary and fiscal policy variables), we are able, in principle, to account for the facts about output and the price level (or, equivalently, unemployment and inflation). As a general rule, the price level is procyclical (inflation and unemployment are negatively related) for the reasons summarized above. Occasionally there will be a surge in inflation that is independent of, or even sometimes goes in the

5. This problem is explained in Thomas J. Sargent, 'The Observational Equivalence of Natural and Unnatural Rate Theories of Macroeconomics', *Journal of Political Economy*, 84 (June 1976), pp. 631–40.

same direction as, the unemployment rate. These surges arise because the anticipated rise in the money supply is high, whereas the unanticipated change in the money supply is negative.

C. *Autocorrelation of Output and Employment*

Output is autocorrelated even though the shocks that hit the economy are purely random because the costs of changing labour inputs and overlapping labour contracts impart inertia into firms' adjustments of employment and output.

D. *Interest Rate Behaviour*

Money rates of interest exceed the real rate of interest by an amount equal to the anticipated rate of inflation. The term over which inflation has to be anticipated is the same as the term over which a loan is made. For 3-month loans, the relevant anticipated inflation rate is that over the next 3 months. For 20-year loans, the average anticipation of average inflation over the next 20 years is required. Anticipated inflation depends only on anticipated money growth, whereas actual inflation depends on both anticipated and unanticipated money growth. Interest rates generally fluctuate in a procyclical manner but with less amplitude than those of the price level because the anticipated money supply growth rate fluctuates with a smaller amplitude than the actual money supply growth rate. Fluctuations in long-term interest rates have an even smaller amplitude because fluctuations in the anticipated long-term average money supply growth rate have a smaller amplitude than those of short-term anticipations.

E. *International Transmission*

International variables that shift the aggregate demand curve will produce domestic fluctuations in a similar manner to those generated by domestic factors that shift aggregate demand. Those effects will operate in the same way as we worked out in Chapter 23.

F. *The Business Cycle*

The first feature of the business cycle, the autocorrelation of output, is explained by the costs of adjusting labour input and the costs of overlapping labour market contracts. The procyclical comovements of the price level and interest rates are explained by the tendency for the actual variables that generate aggregate demand (monetary and fiscal policy variables) to fluctuate with a bigger amplitude than the expected values. The non-universality of the pro-cyclical co-movements of the price level arises from the occasional jump in the anticipated money supply growth rate (sometimes in excess of that which actually occurs).

G.   The Hypothesis Testing Problem Posed by the Rational Expectations Theories

The major problem is that of finding a convincing and non-controversial way of decomposing changes in the actual values of exogenous variables into their anticipated and unanticipated com-ponents. Discriminating between the new Keynesian and new classical theories will be difficult because they are almost equivalent from an observational point of view. Further, discriminating the rational expectations theories from non-rational theory purely on the basis of the past will be difficult since it is always possible to patch up the traditional theory with *ad hoc* adjustments so that the theory yields identical predictions to the rational theories. The ultimate test of any theory will lie in its ability to predict the future rather than the past.

Review Questions

1. Explain how, in general, procyclical co-movements in prices and out-put are explained by the rational expectations theories.
2. Show how the rational expectations theories explain the fact that, on occasion, there is a strong rise in inflation accompanied by low out-put and high unemployment.
3. Do the new Keynesian and new classical theories differ as regards their explanation of the phenomenon described in Question 2? If so, how?
4. What is the explanation offered by the new classical theory of autocor-relation in output and employment?
5. What is the explanation offered by the new Keynesian theory of autocorrelation in output and employment?
6. What is the explanation given by the rational expectations theories of interest rate behaviour? Why do long-term interest rates fluctuate with smaller amplitude than short-term rates and why do short-term rates fluctuate with smaller amplitude than inflation?
7. Review the explanation offered by the rational expectations theories of the business cycle.
8. Assess the assertion that the rational expectations theories are non-scientific because they can never be falsified.

9. (Similar to Question 8!) Assess the assertion that since we can decompose the changes in monetary and fiscal variables into anticipated and unanticipated components so as to make the rational expectations theories fit the facts, any such theory will suffer from the ultimate weakness of being capable of explaining everything and predicting nothing.

10. State succinctly why the assertions in Questions 8 and 9 are wrong.

Part V

MACROECONOMIC POLICY

28

Introduction to Macroeconomic Policy

You have now completed your study of macroeconomic theory — the problem of explaining macroeconomic phenomenon — and are ready to examine the implications of that theory for the formation and conduct of macroeconomic policy. There has been a good deal of policy discussion implicit in the presentation of the theory itself, but it is now time to address the policy issues more directly and systematically. This brief introductory chapter will enable you to start on that process.

By the time you have completed this chapter you will be able to:

  (a) **State what macroeconomic policies seek to achieve.**
  (b) **State the highlights in the evolution of the policy debate.**
  (c) **Explain the idea that policy is a process and not an event.**
  (d) **Explain UK macroeconomic policy choices.**

A. What Macroeconomic Policies Seek to Achieve

There is little disagreement among economists concerning what ideal macroeconomic performance would look like. There might be some arguments of detail, but these are insignificant compared with the broad agreement on three matters. First, it would be ideal if unemployment, except for that associated with job searching and normal labour turnover, could be entirely eliminated. That is, it would be ideal if unemployment could be kept at its 'natural' rate. Equivalently, it would be ideal if output could be maintained at its full-employment equilibrium value on a continuous basis. Second, it would be ideal if inflation could be held at a steady, constant, low (perhaps, ideally, zero) rate. Associated with this would be the ideal that the market rate of interest would be equal to the real rate of interest. Third, it would be ideal if the balance of payments could be zero and if the foreign exchange rate was steady and predictable. Recognizing that perfection is impossible, the objective could be expressed slightly more generally as that of minimizing the deviations of: (1) unemployment from its natural rate, (2) output from its full-employment rate, (3) inflation from zero, (4) market interest rates from real interest rates, (5) the balance of payments from zero, and (6) the exchange rate from some fixed level.

It is worth emphasizing that the specification of the unemployment objective is that of keeping unemployment as close to its natural rate as possible and *not* that of lowering the natural rate to as low a level as possible. It is important to understand that too little unemployment can have serious consequences for the economic welfare of all, even those who are from time to time unemployed. Job search and job changing are productive activities. Further, even if it is judged that the natural rate of unemployment is, in fact, too high, then the only policy measures that can be taken to influence that rate are microeconomic (relative price) policies. It would be necessary to change the unemployment insurance arrangements, methods of taxing income from employment, or some other similar matter such as was discussed in Chapter 25. In other words, the natural rate of unemployment is not itself a variable that can be influenced by the macroeconomic policy instruments of aggregate government spending, taxes, or monetary growth.

The *objectives of macroeconomic policy*, then, are to minimize the variability of unemployment and output about their natural rates and to minimize the variability of inflation around some low, possibly zero, value.

B. Highlights in the Evolution of the Policy Debate

In the nineteenth and early twentieth centuries, the general feeling was that the fluctuations in economic activity that characterized the business cycle were natural phenomena that simply had to be put up with. They were in the same class as storms, floods, and tempests. They buffeted human societies in a serious and sometimes devastating way but simply had to be accepted as one of the harsh facts of life. The Keynesian revolution, which began in the mid-l930s, but didn't achieve its full influence until the 1950s and 1960s, radically changed that view. The business cycle was seen as being controllable. It was widely believed that monetary and fiscal policy could and should be used to manipulate aggregate demand to ensure the achievement of full employment and stable prices. Some believed that monetary and fiscal policies could achieve the objective of high employment and output but not that of price stability. They were nevertheless undaunted in their pursuit of both objectives and regarded the implementation of direct controls on wages and prices or, more euphemistically, 'incomes policies', as the appropriate additional instrument for achieving price stability.[1]

As we moved into the 1970s, it became increasingly apparent that macroeconomic policy was not delivering the promised stability. Inflation rates accelerated, and this despite the fact that unemployment rates were historically high and output growth sagging. Coinciding with this dismal macroeconomic policy performance, there emerged a radically new view of how economic fluctuatations are generated and what might be done to moderate them. The centrepiece of the new view is the hypothesis that expectations are formed rationally.[2] This hypothesis not only leads to a radical transformation in the explanation of the phenomenon of the business cycle, but also leads to a radically different view of policy.

The business cycle is viewed as the outcome of shocks to the economy that are either not correctly foreseen or not fully perceived. Policy influences the cycle in that the *unanticipated* variations in policy instruments lead to variations in output and prices. According to this view, policy is a process that has to be decomposed into an anticipated and unanticipated component. By minimizing the unanticipated variations in policy, the business cycle will be smoothed as much as is possible. There may be a case for having a pre-announced, countercyclical policy response, but there will never be a case for random, haphazard 'discretionary' policy intervention. The cycle will not go away, and it may sometimes be quite severe. But *ad hoc*, previously unexpected attempts to intervene and boost aggregate demand can only be more destabilizing on the average than doing nothing other than pursuing a previously announced policy strategy.

It is this new view of policy that you will be introduced to in the remaining chapters of this part of the book. Before moving on to that, it will be worthwhile spending a moment or two on the two remaining topics of this chapter.

---

1 For a superb account of this view, see Franco Modigliani, 'The Monetarist Controversy, or, Should We Forsake Stabilization Policies?' *American Economic Review*, 67 (March 1977), pp. 1–19.
2 A very good presentation of this view which does not explicitly introduce the rationality of expectations, but which is clearly groping in that direction, is Milton Friedman, 'The Role of Monetary Policy', *American Economic Review*, 58 (March 1968) pp. 1–17. The best discussion in the context of an explicit rational expectations framework is Thomas J. Sargent and Neil Wallace, 'Rational Expectations and the Theory of Economic Policy', *Journal of Monetary Economics*, 2 (April 1976), pp. 169–84.

C. The Idea that Policy is a Process and not an Event

The old-fashioned way of analysing macroeconomic policy was to ask questions like, what will happen if the level of government spending is raised by 10 per cent or if the money supply growth rate is cut from 7 per cent to 4 per cent? What will happen if taxes and spending are cut by the same amount? Questions of this kind are questions that treat policy as an *event*, in the sense that a certain well-defined policy action occurs. The idea, then, is to trace out the effects of this policy shock on output, the price level, interest rates, employment, etc. You now understand that accepting the hypothesis that expectations are formed rationally implies that such exercises are meaningless.

It is simply not possible to analyse the effect of a single-event policy change without knowing whether or not that change was anticipated or unanticipated. Once that is known, it is possible to analyse the effects on output, the price level, and the other variables in the economy. *But it is not possible to know whether or not a particular policy event was anticipated or unanticipated by considering that event in isolation.* It is necessary to have a model of the evolution of the policy instruments that enables the policy instruments at any particular time to be decomposed into their anticipated and unanticipated components.

It is unavoidable that the entire policy process be analysed so that a particular policy event may be identified as anticipated, unanticipated, or partly one and partly the other. It is also necessary to examine the broader institutional and political settings within which policies are being made, for it is the entire policy process that influences the quality of macroeconomic performance. Work of this kind is only in its infancy. It will, however, become a major part of the next generation of research in understanding and improving macroeconomic policy.

D. UK Macroeconomic Policy Choices

The macroeconomic policy choices which face the UK fundamentally boil down to choosing an exchange rate or money supply growth rate. That is, at the extremes, we could have rigid monetary targeting (cause the money supply to grow at a known, pre-determined rate) and have a flexible exchange rate determined on the foreign exchange market, or we could peg the foreign exchange rate (to the US dollar, any other individual currency, or a basket of currencies) and let the domestic money supply and price level be determined by the rest of the world. Some combination of these two extremes could be achieved by some pre-determined mechanism for a managed float of the pound. None of these policies avoids world shocks to the UK economy. You have seen why this is so in Chapter 23.

It is commonly believed that monetarists advocate fixing the money supply growth rate and floating the exchange rate, and that to advocate a fixed exchange rate is the ultimate in interventionism and, therefore, an extreme form of Keynesianism. Nothing, in fact, could be further from the truth. A fixed exchange rate policy is a monetary policy and often is the best monetary policy. The open economy version of monetarism says that for big countries there is really no alternative but to control the growth rate of the money supply, but for smaller countries there always is the alternative of pegging the value of domestic money against the value of some other money. In selecting a currency against which to peg, it is of some importance to pay attention to the monetary policies that will govern the value of that currency in terms of goods. Fixing the value of the pound against, say, the Deutsch Mark, would produce a very different behaviour for the UK price level than would fixing it against the US dollar.

The lesson that we learn from economic theory is that it seems to be very hard to insulate against real fluctuations (fluctuations in output growth). They are shared more or less uniformly by all countries regardless of the policies they have pursued. They are shared by countries with high inflation and by countries with low inflation, by countries whose currencies have been strong and those whose currencies have been weak, by countries with high interest rates and countries with low interest rates. The other lesson that is clear from theory and the facts is that it is possible to insulate a country from inflation arising in the rest of the world. By pursuing firm-enough domestic monetary policies (which also are credible and engender a rational expectation of future firm monetary policies), low inflation, low interest rates and a strong currency can be achieved. Furthermore, they can be achieved even in the face of massive relative price changes such as occurred in the price of energy in the mid-1970s. Yet further low inflation does not seem to require low growth.

In order to achieve low inflation and low interest rates, it is necessary to float the exchange rate and permit an appreciation of the value of the currency against those of countries whose inflation rates are higher than that being attained domestically. Whether or not that worsens macroeconomic fluctuations of real variables, such as output and unemployment, it is not possible to say in the current state of knowledge. Certainly, we know that aggregate demand is insulated from foreign shocks (provided capital is perfectly mobile) in the flexible exchange rate case. We also know, however, that rational expectations of the price level will be influenced by observations of the exchange rate, which will in turn be influenced by shocks arising in the rest of the world. On the basis of what we now know we cannot say whether these shocks will produce domestic output and employment movements that have bigger amplitude than those that would arise under a fixed exchange rate. But, for the time being the gains to be had on the inflation front from pursuing a flexible exchange rate would seem to be so worthwhile as to push us very strongly in the direction of choosing the money supply rule, flexible exchange rate extreme.

The next chapter examines the links between monetary and fiscal policy.

This will show you that when viewing the entire monetary and fiscal policy processes, these two sets of policies are inextricably linked together. Then, we will examine the way in which the Bank of England conducts its policies for achieving a particular path for the money supply. After these two preliminary chapters we will move to the substance of the policy debate and analyse the key reasons for the differences in policy views that were set out in Chapter 1 of this book.

Summary

A. *What Macroeconomic Policies Seek to Achieve*

Macroeconomic policies seek to minimize fluctuations of unemployment and output about their natural rates and to minimize the variability of inflation around some low, possibly zero, value. Other objectives, such as lowering the natural rate of unemployment, are not, strictly speaking, *macroeconomic* policies. They involve *microeconomic* intervention to change relative prices.

B. *Highlights in the Evolution of the Policy Debate*

The pre-Keynesian view of macroeconomic policy was that nothing could be done. Fluctuations simply had to be lived with in the same way as other natural disorders. The Keynesian revolution led to the optimistic view that by manipulating monetary and fiscal policy, aggregate demand could be controlled in such a way as to achieve full employment and price stability. The new view is that because expectations are formed rationally, the best that policy can do is to avoid injecting uncertainty into the economy. Fully predictable policy is therefore required. It may be possible to achieve the best outcome with a pre-announced policy-feedback rule, but it will not be possible to do better with *ad hoc* discretionary intervention.

C. *The Idea that Policy is a Process and not an Event*

If expectations are formed rationally, analysing the implications of a policy change requires that it be decomposed into its anticipated and unanticipated components. Only by analysing the entire process of policy is it possible to say whether a particular event was anticipated or unanticipated.

D. *UK Macroeconomic Policy Choices*

At the extreme, the UK may choose a flexible exchange rate with monetary targeting or a fixed exchange rate with the money supply and inflation being determined by the country (or countries) against whom the exchange rate is fixed. In the present state of knowledge we cannot say definitively that one of the extremes is better than the other. But, it is possible to say that world inflation may be avoided by firm domestic monetary policies that are pursued with long-term credibility. Such a policy requires that the exchange rate be flexible.

Review Questions

1. What are the objectives of macroeconomic policy?
2. Review your understanding of the three main stages in the evolution of ideas on the proper role of macroeconomic policy.
3. What does it mean to say that 'policy is a process and not an event'?

29

The Constraints on Monetary and Fiscal Policy

Although governments are sovereign (within the limits of the constitution) even they must obey certain economic laws. The most fundamental of these laws, to which even governments are subject, is the law of opportunity cost or, equivalently, the principle that 'there is no such thing as a free lunch.'

A government cannot command use over real resources without taking them from private individuals and firms. Like private individuals and firms, the government has a budget that must be balanced, in the sense that, in the short run, the government must either tax or borrow to cover its spending. In the long run, its loans have to be repaid, so that in some fundamental sense, the government must raise taxes in an amount sufficient to cover its expenditure. This places some important limitations on the conduct of fiscal and monetary policy and introduces some important linkages between these two areas of policy.

When you have completed this chapter you will be able to:

(a) Explain the nature of the government budget constraint.
(b) Explain the implications of the government budget constraint for the conduct of monetary and fiscal policy.
(c) Explain the balance of payments constraint and its implications along with the government budget constraint for the conduct of fiscal, monetary and exchange rate policy.
(d) Explain the implications of the government budget and balance of payment constraints for the formation of rational expectations.

A. Government Budget Constraint

Let us begin by examining the main items in the government's budget. Table 29.1 summarizes the government's payments and receipts. The first payment listed is government expenditure on goods and services. This variable appears in the national income accounts as one of the aggregate expenditure items; it also features prominently in the theory of aggregate demand. The second item is transfer payments. These payments are made by the government directly to households and firms under various income-support programmes. The third item is the interest that the government has to pay on outstanding debt. These three items added together constitute the total payments made by the government. They must be matched by government receipts.

The first item listed under receipts is legislated taxes. The prefix 'legislated' is there to alert you to the idea that there are some receipts by the government that are in the nature of taxes but are not explicitly legislated (more about these receipts in a moment.) The legislated taxes are those on incomes, expenditure, wealth, foreign trade, and a variety of specific activities. The second receipt item is net issues of debt. Like any large organization, the government is constantly borrowing and repaying debt previously contracted. The net issue of debt constitutes the excess of newly issued debt over loans repaid. The final receipt is the net issue of coin. In a sense, this item is not really a receipt. In effect, the government mints new coins simply by stamping the appropriate images on the appropriate bits of metal. Nevertheless, in terms of the government's accounts, the minting of new coins has to be reckoned as a receipt, since, from the point of view of the government, it is one of the things that government can use to cover its expenditures.

The debt issued by the government is not all bought by the general public. Some of it is bought by the Bank of England. Although the Bank is an independent agency, its profits, nevertheless, are paid to the government. This being so, it is of some importance to consider separately what

Table 29.1 The government's payments and receipts

	Item
	Payments:
	Government expenditure on goods and services
plus	Transfer payments
plus	Debt interest payments
equals	Total payments
	Receipts:
	Legislated taxes
plus	Net issues of debt
plus	Net issue of coin
equals	Total receipts

happens in the Bank of England when new debt issues of the government are purchased by the Bank rather than by the general public. Equally
important is to examine what happens inside the Bank when it buys
existing debt from the public. We can examine these Bank of England
transactions very straightforwardly by considering the changes in the
Bank's balance sheet that occur in any period of time. Table 29.2 summarizes these changes.

Table 29.2 is very closely related to Table 4.2, which you studied in
Chapter 4. In effect, it is the change in any given period in the items in
the fourth column (the Bank's balance sheet) shown in that table. The
first item is the change in the Bank's holdings of gold and foreign exchange
reserves. The second item is the change in government security holdings
by the Bank. These represent the changes in the Bank's assets. The next
two items — change in commercial bank deposits with the Bank of
England, and net issue of new bank notes — constitute changes in the
Bank's liabilities. The difference between the change in its assets and
liabilities constitutes the Bank's profit, or the change in the Bank's net
worth. You can see by checking back to the fourth column of Table 4.2
(Chapter 4) that these balance sheet changes agree with the balance sheet
levels set out in that table. The importance of changes in the Bank's
holding of government securities (minus Bank profits) is that they are
equivalent to changes in the two components of the economy's monetary
base — commercial bank deposits with the Bank and bank notes
outstanding.

We gain useful insights if we consolidate the government's receipts and
payments with the changes in the Bank of England's balance sheet. Let's
do this consolidation in Table 29.3. The first two items in Table 29.3 are
exactly the same as in Table 29.1 — government expenditure on goods
and services, and transfer payments. The next two items appeared in
Table 29.1 as a single item. Debt interest paid by the government has now
been divided into two items, that paid to the public and that paid to the
Bank of England. Total payments, then, in Table 29.3 are exactly the same
as those in Table 29.1, but with debt interest payments separated into
those paid to the Bank and those paid to the general public.

The receipts shown in Table 29.3 are more detailed than those in Table
29.1. The first item, legislated taxes, is exactly the same as before. The
next item shown in Table 29.1 has been split into two parts: net issue
of debt to the public and net issue of debt to the Bank of England. The

Table 29.2   Changes in the Bank of England's balance sheet

	Change in gold and foreign exchange reserves
add	Change in government securities
less	Change in commercial bank deposits with the Bank of England
less	Net issue of new bank notes
equals	Bank of England's profit

Table 29.3   Consolidation of government and the Bank of England

	Payments:	
	Government expenditure on goods and services	G
plus	Transfer payments	TR
plus	Debt interest paid to public	DI
plus	Debt interest paid to the Bank of England	
equals	Total payments	
	Receipts:	
	Legislated taxes	TAX
plus	Net issue of debt to the public	ΔD
plus	Profits of the Bank of England	
plus	Change in commercial bank deposits with the Bank	
plus	Net issue of bank notes	ΔDC_c
less	Change in gold and foreign exchange reserves	
plus	Net issue of coin	
equals	Total receipts	

first of these appears as the second receipt in Table 29.3. The net issue of debt to the Bank of England may be expressed more conveniently by using Table 29.2. Notice that the net issue of debt to the Bank (called 'change in government securities' in Table 29.2) is equal to the Bank's profit, plus the change in commercial bank deposits with the Bank of England plus the net issue of new bank notes minus the change in gold and foreign exchange reserves. These four items appear in Table 29.3 to represent the net issue of government debt to the Bank. The next item, net issue of coin, is exactly the same as that in Table 29.1.

Now focus on the column on the right-hand side of Table 29.3. It provides a summary of the payments and receipts by the consolidated government–central bank sector. Government expenditure is called G, transfer payments TR, and debt interest paid to the public DI. Debt interest paid to the Bank is not given a symbolic name, nor are profits received from the Bank. Assuming that the Bank's operating costs are small relative to the total interest payments received by the Bank, these two items may be regarded as approximately offsetting each other because one is a receipt, the other is a payment, and they are of approximate equal magnitude.

On the receipts side of the account, legislated taxes are labelled TAX, and the net issue of debt to the public is labelled ΔD. The final four items — the change in commercial bank deposits with the Bank, the net issue of bank notes, and net issue of coin, and the negative of the change in gold and foreign exchange reserves — are lumped together as a single item. You will recognize that item (referring back if necessary to Chapter 4 and to Chapter 15) as the change in the monetary base, ΔMB, less the change in reserves ΔF or, more simply, the change in central bank domestic credit, ΔDC_c. In what follows, we will suppose that we are studying an economy whose exchange rate is flexible and whose reserve changes are zero (or negligible) so we will use ΔMB and ΔDC_c interchangeably.

The sum of the receipts by the government must exactly equal the sum of the payments made by the government. Thus the government budget constraint is:

$$G + DI + TR - TAX - \Delta D - \Delta MB = 0 \qquad (29.1)$$

This constraint says that the government must raise taxes or borrow or create money on a scale exactly equal to the volume of its purchases of goods and services and its payments of debt interest and transfer payments. Let us now move on to consider some of the implications of this government budget constraint.

B. Government Budget Constraint and the Conduct of Monetary and Fiscal Policy

The government's budget constraint with which we ended the last section may be rewritten in the following form:

$$\Delta MB + \Delta D = G + DI + TR - TAX \qquad (29.2)$$

This way of writing the constraint emphasizes that the expansion of the stock of monetary base and of government debt is necessarily equal to the difference between the government's total spending and its legislated tax receipts. This constraint immediately links monetary policy and fiscal policy. You can think of monetary policy as the rate at which the money stock grows. You can think of fiscal policy as the scale of government spending and the scale of taxes. The government budget constraint says that there is a connection between these two. It also says, however, that so long as the government is able or willing to issue debt (ΔD) and pay interest on it (DI), there is no hard-and-fast link between the two branches of macroeconomic policy. In any given short-term period (a year or two, or perhaps even five years or so), the government may issue debt to loosen the link between monetary and fiscal policy. You are now going to discover, however, that on the average and in the long run, this loosening of the link between monetary and fiscal policy cannot be so.

To get an idea why, imagine what would happen if you spent more than your income. For the first year you could perhaps go to the bank and get a loan to cover the deficit. You might even be able to do that for two years, or if you had a very indulgent bank manager, perhaps for a third year. At some stage, however, the day of reckoning would arrive. It would be necessary to tighten your belt, lower consumption, and start to pay off the loans that you have accumulated. Although the details differ, exactly the same constraints necessarily apply to the government. To see why it is necessary to understand that when the government issues debt, it is doing nothing other than deferring taxes.

The government issues all kinds of debt. Some of it is long-term debt, with 25 or more years to run to the date at which the government will redeem it. Some debt is medium term, with 10–15 years to run to the redemption date; and some is short-term debt, with up to five years to run to the redemption date. In addition, the government issues very short-term debt in the form of three-month Treasury bills. Further, some government debt is non-marketable and takes the form of savings bonds. This type of debt is redeemable on demand, but at a penalty to the holder.

Although the government issues many different kinds of debt, it is sensible to think of government debt as if it was a *perpetuity*. A perpetuity is a bond that will never be redeemed by the issuer. The government issued such bonds in the eighteenth and nineteenth centuries. They are called *consols*. Although the government does not issue such bonds today, it is nevertheless sensible to think of all government debt as perpetual debt. The reason is that although the particular bonds issued by the government will be redeemed, when they are redeemed they will be replaced by new bonds. Thus, the debt is continuously turned over, with new bonds being issued to replace the old bonds that are retired. We can, therefore, think of government debt as perpetual debt rather than as debt that will be repaid.

A perpetuity is a bond that promises to pay a certain sum of money each year forever. Call that amount £c. The bond will never be redeemed, so that it has no redemption price. However, it can be sold to someone else, and the new owner will receive the £c per annum while in possession of the bond. How much would a person be willing to pay for a bond that promised to pay £c per annum in perpetuity? Let us call the price that a person would be willing to pay £V. If you invested £V in the best alternative asset, say a corporate bond or some physical capital or a private business, you would make a rate of return of, let us say, r per cent per annum. Clearly, you would not be interested in buying a government bond that promised to pay £c per annum unless the rate of return on that bond was at least as great as the r per cent per annum that you could obtain from some other activity.

Expressed as an equation — with the price of the bond £V and the payment by the government £c per annum — the rate of return on the bond is as follows:

$$\text{rate of return} = (£c/£V) \times 100$$

If $\quad (£c/£V) \times 100 > r \text{ per cent}$

then you would be interested in buying government bonds. But if

$$(£c/£V) \times 100 < r \text{ per cent}$$

then you would want to sell government bonds. Indeed, anyone holding a government bond in such a situation would want to sell it. In the first situation everyone would be wanting to buy government bonds and in the second situation everyone would be wanting to sell them. With everyone buying government bonds their price would rise and with everyone selling government bonds their price would fall. Thus, the equilibrium price of the government bond will be such that

$$(£c/£V) \times 100 = r \text{ per cent}$$

Or, the price of the government bond will be

$$£V = (£c/r \text{ per cent}) \times 100$$

For example, if a bond promised to pay £5 per annum, and if the rate of interest was 5 per cent per annum, then the price of the bond would be £100. The price of a government bond could be written equivalently as

$$£V = £c/r$$

where r is the rate of interest expressed as a proportion of 1 (i.e. r per cent ÷ 100).

Now suppose the government issues a bond and receives £V. So that you can see the value of this bond sale to the government, let us isolate the bond sale and subsequent interest payments on the bond from the other receipts and expenditure of the government. That is, we must assume that the government is not going to change its expenditure on goods and services or transfers, nor change the taxes that it legislates, nor create any new money. It is simply going to issue its bond and allow the bond to be completely self-financing. That is, when the government receives the proceeds from its bond sale, £V, it has to set aside a fund that will generate sufficient interest income to enable it to meet the interest payments on the bond of £c per annum in perpetuity.

Let us suppose, then, that the government sells a bond for £V (which is equal to £c/r, where £c is the number of pounds per annum that the government will pay out on the bond). How much must the government set aside to be able to meet these interest payments? At the end of the first year the government will need £c from its fund. If it sets aside a sum of money $£a_1$ such that $£a_1$ plus the interest received on $£a_1$, namely $r£a_1$, equals $£c_1$, then it will have enough money to pay out £c at the end of the first year. For example, if the rate of interest is 5 per cent and the government is committed to paying £5 on the bond at the end of one year, it needs to set aside approximately £4.76 at the beginning of the year. The £4.76 invested at 5 per cent would yield a 24p interest income which, when added to the £4.76 investment, would give the government the £5 that it needs to meet its interest payment at the end of one year.

To meet its interest payment in two years time, it needs to set aside a sum of money such that the interest on that sum plus the interest on the first year's interest would add up to a sufficient sum to pay the bond interest. Call this sum of money $£a_2$. It would be a sum such that $£a_2(1 + r)^2 = £c$. In general, then, in order to meet *all* its interest payments out into the future, the government would need to set aside the sums of money as shown in Table 29.4.

Table 29.4 The funds needed to pay interest on a perpetuity

To pay £c in 1 year you need	£a_1 now such that £$a_1(1+r) = $ £c
To pay £c in 2 years you need	£a_2 now such that £$a_2(1+r)^2 = $ £c
To pay £c in 3 years you need	£a_3 now such that £$a(1+r)^3 = $ £c
To pay £c in i years you need	£a_i now such that £$a_i(1+r)^i = $ £c

If the government is going to have enough funds to meet the interest payments on its bond over the infinite life of the bond, it will need a fund equal to £a_1 + £a_2 + £a_3 + ... + £a_i .... (The dots '...' stand for all the terms not written explicitly.) We can work out the value of each £a_i from Table 29.4: If you divide £c by $(1 + r)$, then you get £a_1; if you divide £c by $(1 + r)^2$, then you get £a_2; if you divide £c by $(1 + r)^i$, then you get £a_i. Thus, the amount that the government will have to set aside (S) to meet *all* the future interest payments on its bonds is

$$S = \frac{£c}{(1+r)} + \frac{£c}{(1+r)^2} + \ldots + \frac{£c}{(1+r)^i} + \ldots$$

or, equivalently,

$$S = \left[\frac{1}{(1+r)} + \frac{1}{(1+r)^2} + \ldots + \frac{1}{(1+r)^i} + \ldots\right]£c \qquad (29.3)$$

To work out how much this sum is, we need to add up the infinite sum inside the brackets in Equation (29.3) above. Multiply both sides of Equation (29.3) by $1/(1+r)$, which gives

$$\frac{1}{(1+r)}S = \left[\frac{1}{(1+r)^2} + \ldots + \frac{1}{(1+r)^i} + \ldots\right]£c \qquad (29.4)$$

All the missing terms in Equation (29.3) represented by the dots are identical to the missing terms in Equation (29.4), except for the last term in Equation (29.4). That last term in Equation (29.4) equals the last term in Equation (29.3) multiplied by $1/(1 + r)$. However, as you go further and further into the future, the terms $1/(1 + r)^i$ become very very small and can be ignored. So, ignoring the last term in Equation (29.4), you can subtract Equation (29.4) from Equation (29.3) to obtain

$$S - \frac{1}{(1+r)}S = \frac{1}{(1+r)}£c \qquad (29.5)$$

Then multiply both sides of Equation (29.5) by $(1 + r)$ to give

$$S(1+r) - S = £c \qquad (29.6)$$

or

$$S + rS - S = £c \qquad (29.7)$$

or, more simply,

$$S = \pounds c/r \tag{29.8}$$

So, S, the sum that the government needs to set aside in order to meet the interest payments on its bond, is equal to $\pounds c/r$. But this sum is exactly what the government receives when it sells the bond. *It would be necessary, therefore, if the government is to make its bond self-financing, to set aside all the receipts from the bond sale to meet future interest payments.* Thus, when proper accounting is made for the future interest payments that a bond will generate, the government gets precisely nothing when it sells a bond. You can think of selling a bond as simply putting off the evil day of raising taxes — or cutting spending. It is possible for the government to increase its revenue in any one year by selling more bonds, but it cannot increase its revenue indefinitely by selling bonds, since it immediately commits itself to an interest stream that exactly offsets the receipts that it obtains from its bond sales. The implication of this equality for the government's budget constraint is very important. It means that *the government cannot regard bond financing as anything other than deferred taxes.*

It may have occurred to you that there is the possibility of the government avoiding eventually having to raise taxes to pay for its current bond financing by always selling bonds to pay the future interest commitment on its current bonds. In effect, the government could put off the evil day forever by always borrowing more. A moment's reflection will lead you to the conclusion that if the government did pursue this course, and if — aside from borrowing to cover debt interest — the government had a balanced budget, the stock of government bonds outstanding would grow at a rate equal to the rate of interest on bonds.

You can see why by considering a situation in which the government initially had a stock of bonds outstanding of, say, £100, and in which the rate of interest was, say, 10 per cent per annum. The next year, in year two, the government would sell £10 worth of bonds to pay the interest on the initial £100 worth. Its outstanding stock of bonds would then be £110. In the next year, year three, the government would issue £11 worth of bonds to pay the £10 interest on the original £100 worth plus the £1 interest on the £10 bond issued in year two. This process would continue forever with the stock of bonds outstanding growing at 10 per cent per annum. Of course, since the rate of interest on bonds represents in part the real rate of interest and in part an inflation component, the real stock of government bonds outstanding would not be growing at that same rate of interest. The real stock would in fact grow at a rate equal to the real rate of interest. Provided the economy is growing — the population, the stock of capital equipment and wealth in general are growing — the government can get away with this device of always borrowing to pay interest on its debt, but only to the extent that it permits its stock of bonds outstanding to grow at the same rate as the economy as a whole.

Now consider what would happen if the government tried to issue new bonds to pay interest on its old bonds, but at a rate that involved the stock of government bonds growing faster than the growth rate of total wealth in the economy. In such a situation the fraction of government bonds held in the portfolios of households and firms would be continuously rising. There would come a point at which the total amount of private sector assets consisted of nothing other than government bonds. There would be no space in people's balance sheets to hold physical capital and corporate debt. Government debt would be the only debt in existence.

Real capital generates a real rate of return and is itself the source of economic growth. In contrast, government debt does not generate any real return for the economy as a whole. The interest payments on government debt simply constitute a transfer of wealth from taxpayers to bondholders. Thus, an economy in which the government attempts to increase its outstanding debt to pay interest on old debt at too fast a rate would be one in which the stock of capital declines and general economic decline sets in.

It is clear from these considerations that the maximum long-run sustainable growth rate of government debt equals the growth rate of the overall stock of real wealth in the economy. In what follows we shall abstract from such long-term growth considerations. You should be careful to note, therefore, that the analysis that follows would need to be modified slightly to allow for the case where the economy was growing at some positive steady rate. In effect, you would need to add to the government's revenue sources the possibility of obtaining revenue in perpetuity by allowing the stock of its bonds outstanding to grow at the same rate as the economy as a whole. Let us now return to the case where there is no ongoing growth and the government cannot regard its bond financing as a permanent source of revenue but rather as deferred taxes.

We can use the result that we obtained above to condense the government budget constraint into a more fundamental statement. First, let us consolidate taxes, *TAX*, and transfers, *TR*, into a single item — *NET TAX* which is *TAX* less *TR*. Second, since the receipts from bond sales exactly equal the present value of the future debt interest that will be paid on the outstanding bonds let us count the receipt from bond sales as the present value of future taxes that will have to be levied. To avoid double counting, though, let us subtract from the current sale of bonds current period interest payments. Combining these items with *NET TAX* we obtain a single tax revenue term, $\bar{T}$ equal to *NET TAX* plus ΔD less *DI*. Be careful to notice that this definition of taxes is unconventional. It includes all *current* taxes minus all *current* transfers plus the *future* taxes that are implied by the *current* difference between bond sales and interest payments.

The government budget constraint may now be collapsed into the simpler statement, namely,

$$G - \bar{T} = \Delta MB \qquad (29.9)$$

In the next chapter, the connection between the monetary base and the money supply itself will be explored. For the rest of this chapter, let us agree to take on trust the proposition that, on the average, the growth rate of the monetary base and the growth rate of the money supply will be the same. Equivalently, we could say that the change in the monetary base will be some fraction of the change in the money supply. Let us call that fraction q. In this case,

$$\Delta MB = q\Delta M \tag{29.10}$$

We could now use Equation (29.10) to replace the change in monetary base with the fraction q of the change in the total money supply to obtain

$$G - \bar{T} = q\Delta M \tag{29.11}$$

However, it may be more instructive to view this government budget constraint in *real terms* — the real government budget constraint. Let us divide the budget constraint by the price level, the GDP Deflator P to obtain

$$(G/P) - (\bar{T}/P) = (q\Delta M/P)$$

Defining $G/P = g$ and $\bar{T}/P = \bar{t}$, this equation can be written as

$$g - \bar{t} = q(\Delta M/P) \tag{29.12}$$

Next multiply and divide the right-hand side of this equation by M. That is,

$$q(\Delta M/P) = q(\Delta M/P)\,(M/M)$$

By changing the order of the variables, you can now see that

$$q(\Delta M/P) = q(\Delta M/M)\,(M/P)$$

Also, you will recall that $(\Delta M/M)$ is μ, the growth rate of the money supply. Therefore,

$$q(\Delta M/P) = q\mu(M/P)$$

Using this equation to replace the right-hand side of Equation (29.12) gives

$$g - \bar{t} = q\mu(M/P) \tag{29.13}$$

This equation is the *fundamental government budget constraint* and this constraint cannot be violated. It tells us that, whenever the government changes its expenditure, it must change at least one other variable. It must change either taxes or the growth rate of the money supply.

Another instructive way of looking at the fundamental government budget constraint is one that emphasizes the nature of money creation as a tax. When the government creates new money (increases the monetary base) it is able to use that money to acquire goods and services or make transfer payments in exactly the same way as it does when it spends the revenue collected in legislated taxes. Thus, money creation

is like a tax. Part of the money creation tax is available purely as a consequence of real economic growth. As real incomes grow, so also the
demand for money grows and the government can obtain resources by
spending the new money that is created merely to meet the growing demand for money. This part of the tax from money creation is known as
the *growth tax*.

If the government creates money at a rate in excess of that needed to
meet the demands of a growing economy it is still able to use that additional money to acquire goods and services. Inflation, however, will
ensue. The part of the tax from money creation over and above that needed to meet the demands of a growing economy is called the *inflation tax*.

The rate of economic growth tends to be rather constant so the growth
tax is not highly variable. Thus, variations in the tax from money creation are primarily reflected in variations in the inflation tax. To summarize:
the government must raise taxes to cover its spending. There are two
sources of taxes — legislated taxes, $\bar{t}$, and the money creation tax $q\mu(M/P)$.
The latter comprises the growth tax (which does not vary much) and the
inflation tax. There is no restriction on the government as to the extent
to which it uses either of these sources of revenue. The restriction is that
it must raise enough from both of these taxes, taken together, to cover
its expenditure.

C. Balance of Payments Constraint

The balance of payments constraint was introduced and explained in
Chapter 23 when we discussed the constraints upon a managed floating
exchange rate. We noticed that if the government fixes the exchange rate,
then the balance of payments is determined by the growth rate of domestic
credit, the world inflation rate and the growth rate of output. More
generally, we were able to show from Equation (23.11) that, if domestic
credit expansion was too fast in relation to world inflation and output
growth, then either the foreign exchange value of domestic money would
have to fall, or the balance of payments would have to go into deficit,
or some combination of those two things would have to occur. It will
perhaps be helpful to recall Equation (23.11) which is reproduced here as:

$$\Delta\epsilon - \psi f = (1 - \psi)dc - \pi_f - \rho \tag{29.14}$$

If you have forgotten how to interpret this equation it will be worthwhile
returning to Chapter 23 and refreshing your memory before attempting
to go further. This equation says that exchange market pressure — the
depreciation of the currency (positive values of $\Delta\epsilon$) minus the rate of
reserve loss (negative values of f, weighted by the fraction of the money
stock represented by foreign exchange reserves ψ) — will be greater, the
greater the domestic credit expansion (dc) and the lower world inflation
(π_f) and output growth (ρ). This equation, like the government budget

constraint, has to be satisfied on the average. Unlike the budget constraint, Equation (29.14) incorporates a behavioural proposition and is not a pure budget constraint. The behavioural proposition is that there exists a well-defined, stable and predictable demand for money function.

For the purposes of what follows it will be most convenient to concentrate, not on the general case of managed floating exchange rates, but on the two purer cases of fixed exchange rates and freely floating exchange rates. If the exchange rate is freely floating, then the authorities may determine the quantity of foreign exchange reserves that they hold and the rate at which those reserves grow, allowing the foreign exchange value of their currency to take on whatever value the market determines. To see what the value is, simply add ψf to both sides of Equation (29.14) to give

$$\Delta \epsilon = (1 - \psi)dc + \psi f - \pi_f - \rho \tag{29.15}$$

and notice (refreshing your memory with Chapter 23 if necessary) that, since the first two terms on the right-hand side of Equation (29.15) add up to the growth rate of the money supply (μ), we may express this equation equivalently as

$$\Delta \epsilon = \mu - \pi_f - \rho \tag{29.16}$$

This equation simply says that the rate at which the currency depreciates (positive values of $\Delta \epsilon$) is equal to the growth rate of the money supply minus the world inflation rate minus the rate of growth of output. In this case, the growth rate of the money supply is the outcome of the policy choice of the government or the central bank. In the case where the exchange rate is fixed, $\Delta \epsilon$ is maintained at zero and, in the process of pegging the exchange rate, the monetary authorities must stand ready to allow their stock of foreign exchange reserves to rise or fall according to demand. Thus, in that case, the growth rate of the money supply is determined by the demand for money and evidently will be

$$\mu = \pi_f + \rho \tag{29.17}$$

Putting this equation into words, under fixed exchange rates the growth rate of the money supply will be equal to the world rate of inflation, plus the rate of growth of output. In this case, the growth rate of the money supply will not be a variable chosen by the government or the central bank. It will be determined by market processes and will equal the growth rate of the demand for money.

Let us now explore the implications of the balance of payments constraint when combined with the government's budget constraint. First, consider the case of fixed exchange rates. You have seen in Equation (29.17) above that this implies that the growth rate of the money supply is equal to the world inflation rate plus the rate of growth of output. Substituting Equation (29.17) into Equation (29.13) gives

$$g - \bar{t} = q(M/P)(\pi_f + \rho) \qquad\qquad (29.18)$$

What this equation says is that the excess of government spending over taxes must, on the average, be financed by the inflation tax. This is exactly what Equation (29.13) above said. But you can see from Equation (29.18) that, under fixed exchange rates, the government really has no degrees of freedom left with which to manoeuvre, on the average. The inflation tax rate is determined entirely by world inflation and by the trend growth rate of output. The inflation tax base which is the quantity of high powered money, $q(M/P)$, is determined by the demand for money and so, once the government has determined the level of spending on goods and services, g, it is also constrained, on the average, to a particular value for taxes. There is, in effect, on the average, no scope for the pursuit of independent monetary and fiscal policy.

In contrast, under flexible exchange rates, the money supply growth rate is directly under the control of the central monetary authority and Equation (29.13) becomes the constraint on policy even after allowing for the implications of the balance of payments constraint.

To summarize, under fixed exchange rates there is no scope for independent monetary policy. Once the government's spending level has been selected, that implies a tax level which, on the average, must also be achieved. Under flexible exchange rates the balance of payments does not impose a constraint on the relationship between monetary and fiscal policy. A constraint on those policy combinations exists as a consequence of the government's budget constraint, but there is no additional constraint arising from balance of payments considerations.

An analogy may be helpful in making the preceding discussion clearer. Let us contrast the constraints on government spending at the level of local government with those of central government. A local government authority does not have the power to vary the exchange rate of the money used in its jurisdiction against the monies used in other local jurisdictions. In principle, we could imagine there being a Scottish pound, a Welsh pound, a Northern Irish pound, an English pound and even smaller subdivisions such as the Yorkshire pound and the Cornish pound. Given that we have a unified state with a single unified monetary system, the exchange rates between these imaginable pounds are all fixed and, from a practical point of view, irrevocably so at unity. That being the case, if a given local authority chooses to expand its spending programme it must, of necessity, plan to raise taxes at some date either now or in the future to cover that additional spending. Thus, the fixed exchange rate constraint Equation (29.18) applies to such a level of government. But, central government with control over its own central bank and with a monopoly on the issues of money within its area of jurisdiction is free to allow the value of its own money to vary against the value of the monies issued by other governments or central banks. It is therefore constrained by the flexible exchange rate constraint, Equation (29.13). Even if such a government decided for a period to maintain a fixed exchange rate, that fixed exchange rate would not be a constraint upon the government's behaviour. If ever the fixed exchange rate became inconvenient it could be abandoned.

Let us now turn to a consideration of the implications of the foregoing discussion for the formation of rational expectations.

D. Government Budget and Balance of Payments Constraints and Rational Expectations

The government budget and balance of payments constraints have dramatic implications for the formation of rational expectations. First, consider the case of a fixed exchange rate economy. We know from the above discussion that, on the average, in such an economy Equation (29.18) must be satisfied. That is, the excess of government spending over taxes must equal some number that is determined outside the control of the government. What would happen if the government was running a deficit, spending more than it was collecting in current taxes?

In forming expectations about future government spending, taxes and money growth, people will rationally use the knowledge that, on the average, such a deficit cannot persist. They will know that at some stage in the future either government spending must be cut, taxes increased, or the fixed exchange rate system must be abandoned and the growth rate of the money supply increased. The longer government spending exceeds current tax receipts by more than it can do, on the average, in the long run, the stronger will be the expectation that next period some changes in that direction will occur. Conversely, if the government was running too small a deficit and reducing its outstanding debt, it would be rational to expect that at some time in the future, either government spending will rise, taxes fall, or again, the fixed exchange rate system be abandoned and this time the currency allowed to appreciate.

In general, it would be rational to expect that the fixed exchange rate regime will not be permanent but will, at some time in the future, be abandoned. The bigger the accumulated change in the stock of government debt, the greater the probability that the fixed exchange rate system will be abandoned. It will always be rational to assign some non-zero probability to such an event. The magnitude of that probability may be trivial or sizeable. That will depend upon the history of the country in question. A country (or more generally jurisdiction) which has a long history of repeatedly taking serious fiscal policy steps to defend the value of its currency by raising taxes or cutting spending as appropriate, will be one to which a small probability of future exchange rate changes will be attached. At the other extreme, a country that has a long history of repeatedly abandoning fixed exchange rate regimes and permitting the currency to appreciate or depreciate in order to accommodate a persistent fiscal surplus or deficit, will be one to which a high probability of future exchange rate variability will be attached.

Consider next a country which is not currently pursuing a fixed exchange rate and is therefore not constrained by Equation (29.18), but is constrained by Equation (29.13). In this case, we know that it is possible for the level of *current* taxes to fall short of or to exceed current spending and for the gap to be made up by *future* taxes, that is by borrowing or reducing outstanding debt. But, we also know that in the long run borrowing makes no net contribution to government revenues. It will not be rational to expect a monetary and fiscal policy that violates the government's budget constraint. To expect a violation of this constraint is to expect something that cannot happen. Such an expectation would not be rational.

For example, if at some time the government is running a large current deficit and issuing a larger quantity of bonds, then the rational expectation will be that at some future date government expenditure will be cut, or legislated taxes will be increased, or the rate of money printing, and therefore inflation, will increase. Based on the best analysis available of the constraints operating on the government and its likely course in the future, individuals will rationally assign weights to these alternative future changes in government actions.

A government, or more generally, a political system that has a long-run track record of repeatedly inflating its way out of short-run financial problems will rationally be expected to pursue such policies again in the future. A government that has heavily constrained itself from using the inflation tax by, for example, setting up a highly independent central bank with extensive powers to control the growth rate of the money supply independently of the short-term wishes of the government will be one that will rationally be expected to correct any short-term deficit by either raising legislated taxes or cutting spending rather than by increasing the inflation tax. There will no hard-and-fast, simple-to-state rule that will enable individuals to make the correct inferences concerning future monetary and fiscal policy. The hard fact of the government budget constraint must, however, be taken into account in forming a rational expectation as to likely future changes in the direction of policy. Only if the government is currently running a deficit that is being financed by its current rate of money printing is it pursuing a policy that can be pursued on the average over the long term. The pursuit of such a policy will simplify the task faced by individuals in forming rational expectations, but it will by no means eliminate the problem.

Summary

A. *Government Budget Constraint*

The government budget constraint states that total government expenditure on goods and services, transfers to individuals, and debt interest must equal receipts from legislated taxes, the sales of new debt, and the creation of new money.

B. *Government Budget Constraint and the Conduct of Monetary and Fiscal Policy*

Although the government can issue debt, thereby weakening the link between monetary and fiscal policy in the short run, on the average over the long term, debt interest has to be paid that exactly offsets the receipts from debt sales. By issuing debt the government is, in effect, deferring taxes. The long-term average government budget constraint does not give the government the option of raising debt. There is, therefore, on the average, a fundamental connection between fiscal policy and monetary policy. Conventionally, legislated taxes together with the creation of new money must raise sufficient funds to cover the government's expenditure. Monetary policy and fiscal policy, on the average, are interdependent.

C. *Balance of Payments Constraint*

If the government permits the exchange rate to be flexible, then it is possible to set the growth of the money supply at any chosen rate. But, if the exchange rate is pegged, then the growth rate of the money supply is determined by the growth rate of the demand for money which, in turn, depends on the growth rate of output and world inflation.

The combination of the balance of payments and government budget constraint under fixed exchange rates implies no degrees of freedom, on the average, for the conduct of fiscal and monetary policy. The government can choose the scale of government spending, but it must raise sufficient taxes to cover that spending. Under flexible exchange rates, the balance of payments does not impose any additional constraints upon the government than those implied by the government budget constraint. In such a case, the government must cover its spending either by the inflation tax or other taxes. But, it may choose the extent to which it uses each of these sources of financing.

D. *Government Budget and Balance of Payments Constraints and Rational Expectations*

In general, it will not be rational to form an expectation of long-term money growth and inflation that is based on the maintenance, in perpetuity, of a fixed exchange rate. Under flexible exchange rates, or under fixed exchange rates which are not expected to be permanent, it will not be rational to form an expectation of long-term money growth and inflation that is based on a violation of the government's budget constraint. In a situation in which the government is running a deficit or surplus, issuing or retiring large volumes of debt, individuals will have to form a rational expectation concerning which of the variables in the government's budget constraint will be varied in order to satisfy the long-term average constraint. In situations in which the government has, in the past, satisfied its budget constraint by varying the rate of inflation, it will be rational to expect such action in the future. In other situations, where the government has taken steps to adjust its spending or other taxes in order to maintain a steady (or zero) rate of inflation, then it would be rational to expect a repeat of such actions in the future.

Review Questions

1. Review the items that appear in the government's budget constraint.
2. Sort the following items into the three items in the government's budget constraint (i.e. expenditure on goods and services, taxes, and money creation):
   (a) Welfare payments.
   (b) The purchase of a typewriter financed by printing £100.
   (c) The purchase of a foreign security (be careful here).
   (d) Social insurance payments and receipts.
   (e) National defence expenditure.
3. Why are 'legislated' taxes so-called?
4. Explain why transfer payments may (as a first approximation) be treated as negative taxes.
5. Review the links between the government and central bank and explain how the 'change in the monetary base' gets into the government's budget constraint?
6. What is the relationship between the price that someone will pay for a bond and the stream of interest payments on that bond?
7. Calculate the equilibrium market price of a perpetuity that promises to pay £1 per annum, given that interest rates on alternative available assets are currently 8 per cent.

8. 'The present value of a bond is always zero'. Explain.

9. If the price for which a bond can be sold is exactly the same as the present value of the future stream of interest payments, why would anyone issue bonds?

10. Explain why bond sales are deferred taxes.

11. If the government can issue money on which it does not have to pay interest, why do you suppose we observe governments issuing debt on which they do have to pay interest?

12. Explain why, on the average, the government that has adopted a flexible exchange rate must finance its expenditure with either legislated taxes or the inflation tax.

13. Explain why, on the average, the government which has adopted a fixed exchange rate cannot use the inflation tax to balance its budget.

14. Review your understanding of why it would be irrational to expect the government to be able to issue debt on an increasing scale indefinitely.

15. Looking at the government's monetary and fiscal policy in the 1980s, what conclusions do you reach concerning a rational expectation about future UK monetary and fiscal policy changes?

30

Control of the Money Supply

The quantity of money in existence — the money supply — features prominently in macroeconomic theory as a major influence on aggregate demand and the price level. The anticipated level and growth rate of money are the single most important factor determining the price level and the rate of inflation. Unanticipated changes in the money supply are a major source of fluctuations in output and employment.

The final thing that we need to do before getting on with the substance of analysing macroeconomic stabilization policy is to examine how the money supply is determined and controlled. In the last chapter we asked you to take on trust the proposition that, on the average, the monetary base and the total money supply stand in some constant relationship to each other. This chapter will explain why this proposition is reasonable. It will look at the detailed linkages between the money supply and the monetary base, and at the way in which the Bank of England has, in the past, conducted monetary policy with a view to achieving a target growth path for the monetary aggregate M3. But, the chapter will *not* present a comprehensive description of the Bank's operations.

By the time you have completed this chapter you will be able to:

(a) **Explain the links between the monetary base and the money supply.**

(b) **Explain how the Bank of England has operated to achieve a target growth path for the broad money supply.**

A. The Links between the Monetary Base and the Money Supply

The starting point for understanding the links between the monetary base and the money supply is two definitions. Both definitions are implied in the economy balance sheet structure that you studied in Chapter 4. The first is the definition of the money supply. It is convenient when analysing the determinants of the money supply to decompose it into two parts — the monetary base held by the public and the bank deposits held by the public. (Which bank deposits we would count would depend on which monetary aggregate we were dealing with. We are going to deal with M3 in this chapter, although we will use the symbol M to denote this aggregate.) Let us write the definition of the money supply as follows:

$$M = MB_p + D \tag{30.1}$$

In this definition, M stands for the money supply, MB_p for the notes and coins held by the public, and D for bank deposits.

The next definition concerns the monetary base itself. The monetary base consists of the notes and coins held by the public (MB_p), which is already in the above definition, and the notes and coins together with deposits at the Bank held by the commercial banks, which we will call MB_b. The monetary base, then, is allocated across the two holders — the public and the banks — so that

$$MB = MB_p + MB_b \tag{30.2}$$

These two equations are just definitions and they don't tell us anything about what determines either the money supply or the monetary base.

The first behavioural hypothesis that we need is one concerning the general public's allocation of money between notes and coins and deposits. The general idea is that in conducting our everyday transactions, there is a fairly stable fraction of those transactions that we would customarily undertake with notes and coins. Therefore, we would want to hold a fairly stable fraction of our total money holdings in the form of currency. Let us call that fraction v, which means that we could say that

$$MB_p = vM, \quad 0 < v < 1 \tag{30.3}$$

This equation simply says that v is some fraction, and the amount of monetary base (notes and coins) that people hold on the average is equal to that fraction v of their total money holdings. There is an equivalent proposition, which is that bank deposits are equal to one minus the fraction v times total money. That is,

$$D = (1 - v)M \tag{30.4}$$

Although this proposition is pretty mechanical about how people allocate their money between currency and bank deposits, provided the bank deposits are non-interest bearing, it seems to be a reasonable hypothesis and one that adequately describes the facts.

The next thing that we need to consider is how the banks decide how much monetary base to hold. That is, what is the demand for monetary base by the banks? This question is a lot like the question, what determines the demand for money by households and firms? Why do the banks hold monetary base? That is, why do they hold notes and coin and deposits with the Bank of England? The answer is that they hold notes and coin in order to be able to meet demands for currency on the part of their customers. They also hold deposits at the Bank of England so that they can make payments to other banks. They need to do this when the total value of all the cheques paid by their customers in any one trading period exceeds the value of cheques paid to their customers during that same period. As a general rule, the bigger the volume of bank deposits that a bank has accepted, the bigger is the size of currency reserves and Bank of England deposits the bank needs to keep on hand. The volume of bank deposits, then, is the first determinant of the demand for monetary base by the commercial banks.

When studying the demand for money by individuals, we discovered that, at high rates of interest (and high rates of inflation), there is a bigger incentive for people to try to economize on their holdings of money than when interest rates (and inflation) are low. The market rate of interest was seen as the opportunity cost of holding money. Similar considerations apply to the decision by a commercial bank on how much of its deposits to hold in the form of monetary base reserves. Deposits placed with a bank can be used by that bank for two kinds of purposes. One is to hold monetary base. The other is to acquire interest-earning assets of various kinds, including making loans to households and firms. Clearly, the bank earns no interest on its holdings of monetary base. Banks make a profit by making loans and buying interest-earning securities. Just as households economize on their holdings at high interest rates, so also will banks. The higher the rate of interest on loans and securities, the more will banks economize on their holdings of monetary base, and the smaller will be the fraction of their deposits held as reserves and the larger will be the fraction that is lent.

There are two factors, then, that determine the bank's demand for monetary base. One is the total volume of deposits that the bank has accepted. The larger is the volume of deposits, the bigger the amount of monetary base required. The other is the level of interest rates. The higher the interest rate, the more will banks seek to economize on their holdings of monetary base, and therefore the lower will be its holdings of monetary base.

We can summarize the banks' demand for monetary base in a very simple equation that looks a lot like the demand for money function of households and firms. This equation is

$$MB_b = zD + mb_0 - l_b r_m, \quad 0 < z < 1; \ mb_0, \ l_b > 0 \qquad (30.5)$$

What this equation says is that, for a given market rate of interest, the higher the level of bank deposits, the more monetary base banks will hold.

For a £1 million rise in deposits, they would hold a fraction z of £1 million in extra monetary base.

The fraction of total deposits z that the banks will want to hold in the form of monetary base represents two kinds of influences: one imposed on the bank, and the other part of its voluntary behaviour. Imposed on the bank is a minimum required reserve holding below which the bank is not permitted to let its monetary base holdings fall. Over and above this amount banks will find it prudent to hold, on the average, a certain level of reserves in excess of the required reserves. The fraction z represents the sum of both of these influences.

In addition to the effect of deposits on monetary base holdings of the bank, there is the influence of interest rates. Let us suppose that the term $mb_0 - l_b r_m$, on the average, is equal to zero. That is, if interest rates are at their long-run average level, the demand for monetary base by the banks would be completely described by the fraction z of total deposits. But, if interest rates go above their average level, then the banks will seek to economize on monetary base holdings; and if interest rates go below their average level, then the banks will be less eager to make loans and economize on monetary base. This effect of the variation in interest rates is what the second two terms in the above equation are saying.

In order to derive the supply of money in the economy, all that is necessary is to examine the equilibrium in the market for monetary base itself. The supply of money function is not like an ordinary supply function. Like the aggregate supply and aggregate demand functions, it is an equilibrium locus. The market that is in equilibrium on the money supply function is the market for monetary base. By setting the supply of monetary base equal to the demand for base, we can find the quantity of money that will be supplied. Let us begin by using the following equation:

$$MB = vM + z(1 - v)M + mb_0 - l_b r_m \tag{30.6}$$

The left-hand side of this equation is the supply of monetary base. The right-hand side is the demand for monetary base by the public and by the banks. The term (vM) is the demand for monetary base by the public (fraction v of the total money supply). The remaining terms represent the demand for monetary base by the banks. The first of these terms is z times bank deposits. Bank deposits are represented as $(1 - v)M$ — from Equation (30.4) above. The final two terms represent the interest-sensitive component of the demand for monetary base by the banks, which, on the average, we are taking to be zero. You can now collect together the first two terms that multiply M and obtain

$$MB = [v + z(1 - v)]M + mb_0 - l_b r_m$$

Then divide both sides of this equation by $[v + z(1 - v)]$, to give

$$M = \frac{1}{v + z(1 - v)} [MB - mb_0 + l_b r_m] \tag{30.7}$$

What this equation says is that the money supply will be some multiple of the monetary base — (the multiple being $1/[v + z(1 - v)]$ on the average — but it will deviate from that in the same direction as variations in the interest rate. The higher the market rate of interest, other things given, the higher would be the money supply.

You are now in a position to summarize the links between the monetary base and the money supply. When the demand for monetary base equals the supply of monetary base, there is a direct relationship between the supply of money and the supply of monetary base. Other things being equal, a £1 million rise in the monetary base will produce a rise in the money supply of $1/[v + z(1 - v)]$ million dollars. For a given monetary base, the higher the market rate of interest, the greater will be the money supply. This increase in the money supply arises because banks will seek to economize on their use of monetary base as interest rates rise above their average level.

We can link the above discussion with that in the previous chapter by noting that, on the average, the money supply and money base will be linked by the simpler relation

$$M = \frac{1}{v + z(1 - v)} MB \qquad (30.8)$$

or, more compactly, definining $v + z(1 - v)$ to be q, we have

$$M = (1/q) MB \qquad (30.9)$$

The fraction q in this equation is exactly the same fraction as q introduced in the previous chapter.

The link that we have established between the monetary base, interest rates, and the money supply is not to be confused for a statement that says the money supply is determined by the monetary base and the rate of interest. It could well be that the monetary base itself responds to interest rates and the money supply in such a way that the actual path of the money supply is determined by some exogenous policy decision, and the monetary base and interest rates are the variables that do the adjusting to make that path possible. To emphasize this possibility, consider the above relationship between the money supply and the monetary base written in the following way:

$$MB = qM \qquad (30.10)$$

If the money supply itself was determined by the factors that influence the demand for money, then the monetary base would be indirectly determined by the demand for money. Thus,

$$MB = qM^d$$

This alternative way of looking at the link between the money supply and the monetary base is, in fact, one that better describes the way in which the money supply and monetary base have been determined by the policy actions of the Bank of England. Let us now look at how the Bank of England controls the money supply.

B.   The Bank of England's Control of the Money Supply

If the relationship between the monetary base and the money supply which we have just examined was very precise, it would be possible for the Bank of England to exploit the relationship in order to achieve the desired path for the money supply. The Bank would simply have to manipulate the monetary base from day to day in whatever way was required in order to make the money supply grow at the desired growth rate. But, the Bank of England believes that the relationship between the monetary base and the money supply is not very precise and, in fact, is insufficiently precise to give predictable control over the money supply. Whether or not the Bank is correct in that belief is a question of some controversy, and it would not be possible to settle the matter here. There has, in fact, been some movement in the debate in recent years and, in the summer of 1981, the Bank of England modified the procedures whereby it seeks to control the money supply in such a way as to make it easier for it to exploit the relationship between the monetary base and the total money supply.

The changes which the Bank of England made in 1981 in its technique of monetary control may be described as a 'halfway house' between controlling the aggregate money supply by controlling the monetary base and the bank's traditional techniques of control. It will be helpful therfore if we begin by describing what that traditional technique of control has been.

Instead of using the relationship between the monetary base and the money supply to achieve its monetary target, the Bank of England has operated in an indirect way seeking to manipulate the quantity of money by operating on the demand side of the market for money. You will recall that the demand for money (thought of as the demand for real money) depends on the level of income and the rate of interest — the opportunity cost of holding money. By manipulating interest rates the monetary authorities can cause the economy to slide up and down its demand for money function, thereby resulting in changes in the quantity of money outstanding. This is how the Bank of England has operated. Let us examine in a little more detail exactly what is involved with this technique of monetary control.

The technique starts out with a demand for real balances of the type described in Chapter 12. That is,

$$\frac{M^d}{P} = ky + m_0 - lr_m \tag{30.11}$$

In effect, the way the Bank proceeded was to estimate, using statistical techniques, the values of the parameters of the demand for money function (k, m_0, l). It then selected its target for the money supply — we will call that monetary target M*. It then forecasted the price level and the income level that it thought would prevail on the average over the coming months. Let us call the Bank's forecasted values of the price level and real income, respectively, P^f and y^f. The Bank then 'solved' the demand for money function for the market rate of interest that would be required in order to make the amount of money demanded equal the money supply *target*, given the forecast of prices and income. We can obtain that solution simply by rearranging the demand for money function in the following way. First of all, set the demand for money M^d equal to the target money supply M* and set the levels of income and prices equal to their forecasted values y^f and P^f. That is,

$$\frac{M^*}{P^f} = ky^f + m_0 - lr_m \tag{30.12}$$

Now rearrange this equation to 'solve' for the market rate of interest. That is,

$$r_m = \frac{1}{l}\left(ky^f + m_0 - \frac{M^*}{P^f}\right) \tag{30.13}$$

This equation tells us the market rate of interest which, if the Bank achieves it and if the Bank's forecasts of income and prices are correct, will on the average make the money supply equal to M*, the target money supply.

The way in which the Bank actually gets the interest rate to move up or down to the desired level is by tightening or loosening its hold over the monetary base. If the Bank wants to make interest rates rise, it sells government securities from its own portfolio to the general public. As people pay for these securities, so the monetary base falls, and the banks find themselves short of reserves. To replenish their reserves the banks start to sell their short-term securities, thereby putting further upward pressure on market rates of interest. The Bank would hold conditions tight in the credit markets until the market rate of interest has risen to the level the Bank wishes to achieve in accordance with the above equation, a level that it is hoped will achieve the monetary target. If the Bank wants to lower the rate of interest, then it would go into the marketplace and buy government securities, paying for them, in effect, with newly created monetary base. In this event, the banks would find themselves with surplus reserves, would seek to lend those reserves, and in the process, would put downward pressure on interest rates. Again, the Bank would keep credit market conditions loose until interest rates had fallen to the level that it felt appropriate for the achievement of its monetary target.

This technique of monetary control which was employed by the Bank of England is far from perfect. The Bank could be considerably wrong in its forecasts of prices and income and, to the extent that it is wrong, it will miss its money supply target. You can see this very easily if you perform the following exercise. Use the equation that we solved above for the Bank's chosen rate of interest and substitute that back into the demand for money function. You will then obtain the following equation:

$$\frac{M^d}{P} = ky + m_0 - \frac{l}{l}\left(ky^f + m_0 - \frac{M^*}{P^f}\right) \qquad (30.14)$$

Notice that this equation simplifies considerably to the following:

$$\frac{M^d}{P} = \frac{M^*}{P^f} + k(y - y^f)P \qquad (30.15)$$

which may be further rearranged by multiplying through by the price level to give

$$M^d = M^* \frac{P}{P^f} + k(y - y^f)P \qquad (30.16)$$

Let us pause and see what this equation is telling us. Given the technique of control of the money supply used by the Bank of England, it is the demand for money that will determine how much money is in existence. The left-hand side of the equation therefore tells us what the quantity of money will be. It will be the same as M^d. How will that relate to the Bank's target? The answer is that it will deviate from the target in general. In order to be bang on target, the Bank would have to forecast the price level correctly. That is, the actual price level (P) would have to equal the forecasted price level P^f. Furthermore, the forecast of income would have to be equal to actual income. If the actual price level turned out to be bigger than the forecasted price level, then, with a correct income forecast, the money supply would exceed the desired money supply by the same percentage as the price level exceeds the forecasted price level. If the level of income turned out to be higher than the forecasted level of income, then the money supply would exceed its target by an amount equal to the excess of actual income over forecasted income multiplied by the price level and by the parameter k.

These imperfections in this technique of monetary control have resulted in spectacular failures on the part of the Bank of England to achieve its money growth targets. It is these failures that are responsible for the tentative steps being taken in the direction of modifying the technique of monetary control. Let us now turn to a brief description of what these steps are.

A central feature of the old technique of monetary control was the Bank of England's manipulation of interest rates so as to influence the opportunity cost of holding money. The interest rates in question which the

Bank controlled were, by and large, rates on three-month securities such as Treasury bills and commercial bills of exchange. In order to achieve fine control over rates of interest on three-month securities, the Bank had to stand ready to buy or sell Treasury bills and/or commercial bills in whatever quantities were demanded by the banks and other financial institutions so as to prevent the price of these bills (and therefore their rate of interest) from varying by more than the Bank of England wanted to see. There is an analogy here with a fixed exchange rate. Just as a central bank that is committed to a fixed exchange rate cannot control the quantity of its foreign exchange reserves, so a central bank that is committed to a particular rate of interest cannot control the monetary base. It must buy and sell securites (raising or lowering the monetary base) on demand, and not at its discretion.

The change introduced in August 1981 was for the Bank of England to redirect its efforts at interest rate control away from three-month interest rates to rates on very short-term securities — bills that have between one and two weeks to run to maturity. In other words, under the technique of control introduced in 1981, the Bank of England seeks to control very short-term rates of interest permitting interest rates of securities that are still very short term, but not as short as a week or two, to find their own level in the marketplace. This technique of control remains an interest rate management technique. It is, however, a 'halfway house' between the old policy and a monetary base policy in the sense that, as the bank accumulates experience at controlling very short-term rates, permitting three-month rates and longer rates to be market determined, it puts itself in a position to be able to take a next step, a step of ceasing to control even the seven-day rate of interest and instead controlling the monetary base itself, permitting even those very short-term rates to be market determined.

Although the current policy may be thought of as an intermediate policy between monetary base control and interest rate control, it may in fact have none of the desirable features of either of these policies. The old techniques of control at least had the virtue that the Bank was manipulating an interest rate that had reasonably predictable effects upon the monetary aggregate whose growth path the Bank was seeking to influence. The direct control of the monetary base would have the virtue that is was exploiting a remarkably stable relationship between the monetary base and the aggregate money supply.[1] The new technique relies on little-known linkages between the seven-day rate of interest and the three-month rate of interest that seems to be the one that most directly influences the demand for money. Thus, the errors in achieving the money target that are set out and summarized in Equation (30.16) above

---

1   Between 1972 and 1979, the ratio of the monetary base to £M3 (now called M3) was never less than 17.2 per cent and never greater than 21.8 per cent (using end quarter figures). See David Savage, 'Some Issues of Monetary Policy', *National Institute Economic Review*, No. 91 (February 1981), pp. 78–85 and Table 2, p. 82.

need to be supplemented by an additional error, namely the error on achieving the correct level for the three-month rate of interest. If, in manipulating the seven-day interest rate, the bank allows three-month rates to stay too low or go too high then the discrepancy between the required and actual three-month interest rate, multiplied by the parameter l, would have to be added to the errors set out in that above equation. Thus, the recent change in Bank of England control techniques, while a potentially useful step in the direction of changing over to a monetary base control procedure may well turn out to be an unfortunate intermediate resting place.

The Bank of England's choice of M3 (originally Sterling M3) as its monetary target has been surrounded by other difficulties then those aris-ing from imperfections in the techinque of monetary control. As we saw in Chapter 12 the demand function for M3 is not at all well behaved. Fluc-tuations in that demand function which themselves are difficult to predict add a further source of randomness to the quantity of money over and above that arising from errors in forecasting income and prices accurately. The volatility in the behaviour of M3 led the Governor of the Bank of England to question publicly whether M3 targets were worth specifying[2] and resulted in the Bank deciding that it was not useful to establish an M3 target for 1987.[3]

The implications of the foregoing are that, although the Bank of England has not and still does not exercise precise control over the money supply, we may, nevertheless, regard the money supply as a potentially con-trollable instrument of macroeconomic policy.

In the following chapters we are going to go on to analyse the effects of macroeconomic stabilization policies on output and price level (and other variables). We will analyse the effects of monetary and fiscal policies. In our study of monetary policy we will presume that we are dealing with an economy in which the monetary authority is in fact controlling the money stock and pursuing a policy of flexible exchange rates. But, the analysis can be interpreted differently.

Instead of imagining that the monetary authorities are trying to achieve a particular level of aggregate demand and by manipulating money supply you could imagine them attempting to achieve the same objective by manipulating the foreign exchange rate. Thus, either of the two theories of aggregate demand developed in Chapter 16 could be regarded as rele-vant for the exercises that will be conducted. If the economy has a flexi-ble exchange rate with money stock targeting then it is policy changes

---

2 'Financial Change and Broad Money', the Loughborough University Banking Centre Lecture in Finance, delivered by the Governor of the Bank of England, 22 October, 1986, *Bank of England Quarterly Bulletin*, Vol. 26, No. 4 (December 1986), pp. 499–507.
3 'The Instruments of Monetary Policy', the Seventh Mais Lecture, delivered by the Gover-nor of the Bank of England , City University Business School, 13 May 1987, published in the *Bank of England Quarterly Bulletin* Vol. 27, No. 3 (August 1987), pp. 365–70.

in the money stock itself that are seen as the instruments through which aggregate demand is affected. If, in contrast, the exchange rate is being targeted then the fixed exchange rate theory of aggregate demand is the relevant one and policy induced changes in the exchange rate that would shift the aggregate demand curve are regarded as the monetary policy being analysed.

Sight should not be lost, however, of a central confusion that emerges from the material presented in this chapter and that contained in Chapter 26 where we studied the links between the exchange rate and the domestic monetary policy. The implication is that, if the monetary authority so chooses it does have sufficient instruments to control the money supply and to treat the money supply as a direct instrument of aggregate stabilization policy.

Summary

A. *The Links between the Monetary Base and the Money Supply*

The money supply function is, like the aggregate supply function, an equilibrium locus. The market that is in equilibrium along the money supply function is the market for monetary base. The demand for monetary base by the public (the demand for currency) may be presumed to be a fairly stable fraction of the demand for money in total. The demand for monetary base by banks depends partly on the level of deposits and partly on the market rate of interest. The greater the level of deposits, the larger is the monetary base demanded by banks; the higher the market rate of interest, the smaller is the monetary base demanded by banks.

Other things being equal, the higher the monetary base, the higher is the money supply; and the higher the market rate of interest, the higher is the money supply. On the average, the money supply will be a fairly stable multiple of the monetary base, though over shorter periods there will be independent fluctuations in the two variables associated with movements in market rates of interest.

B. *The Bank of England's Control of the Money Supply*

The Bank of England has recently modified its technique of monetary control. Until 1981, it sought to achieve a target growth path for the money supply M3 by operating on the demand side of the money market. The Bank 'solved' the demand for money function for that level of interest rates that would induce the amount of money demanded to equal the target value of the money supply, given the Bank's own forecasts of the price level and the level of real income.

That technique of control was imperfect. Deviations of the price level or income from their forecasted levels led to serious deviations of the money stock from its target.

In 1981, the Bank abandoned this particular control procedure. Instead of seeking to control those interest rates which influence the demand for M3, the Bank now seeks to control only the very short-term one- to two-week interest rates. Three-month interest rates (those which influence the demand for M3) are left to be determined by market forces (but are heavily influenced by the Bank's own operations in the shorter-term, one- to two-week markets). The Bank views this move as an exploratory move towards possibly controlling the money supply via control of the reserve base of the banking system exploiting the linkages described in Section A of this chapter.

It is quite likely that the current policies of the Bank of England represent an inferior alternative both to the technique that has been abandoned and to the procedure of controlling money by controlling the monetary base.

Review Questions

1. What is the monetary base? Who issues it (whose liability is it) and who holds it (whose asset is it)?
2. What determines the demand for currency by households and firms?
3. What determines the demand for monetary base by the commercial banks?
4. What is the money supply function?
5. What markets are in equilibrium when the economy is 'on' the money supply function?
6. What would lead to a shift in the money supply function?
7. Does the money supply function imply that the monetary base determines the money supply?
8. Until 1981, how did the Bank of England seek to control the money supply? Did it exploit the money supply function analysed in this chapter?
9. How did the Bank of England use the demand for money function in its old method of controlling the supply of money?
10. What are the main potential sources of error, or looseness, in the Bank's old method of monetary control?
11. What are the main potential sources of error, or looseness, in the Bank's current monetary control procedures?
12. How would you set about comparing the effectiveness of the Bank's old and new techniques of monetary control?

31

Monetary Policy I: Aggregate Demand Shocks

You already know that monetary policy is of central importance for influencing the rate of inflation. You saw, in Chapter 25 how an ongoing growth rate of the money supply generates ongoing price increases — inflation. You also saw that although there are many other factors that can influence the inflation rate, by setting an appropriate long-term growth trend to the money supply the monetary authority can offset those factors and achieve any desired trend rate of inflation. You did note, however, when we studied trends in the inflation rate that there are important interactions between unanticipated demand shocks and the price level that modifies the course of inflation. We also learned, when we studied macroeconomic equilibrium with rational expectations, that unanticipated shocks to aggregate demand will produce not only departures of the inflation rate from its steady-state path but also fluctuations in output and employment.

What we are now going to do in this chapter is to focus on a central macroeconomic policy question, namely, what can and should monetary policy do to offset cyclical aspects of macroeconomic performance — to control the business cycle? This is a controversial question. There are two broad views concerning its answer, and this chapter, along with the next, is designed to help you understand the nature of the controversy. The material presented in these two chapters will take you right to the frontiers of the current debate in economics.[1] However, nothing that will be dealt with in these chapters is inherently more difficult than the material that you have handled so far.

By the time you have completed this chapter, you will be able to:

(a) **State the key difference between the monetary policy advice given by monetarists and that given by Keynesians.**

(b) **Describe what aggregate demand shocks are and explain how they affect the aggregate demand curve.**

(c) **Explain the consequences of following monetarist monetary policy advice in the face of aggregate demand shocks.**

(d) **Explain the consequences of following Keynesian monetary policy advice in the face of aggregate demand shocks.**

(e) **Explain why monetarists and Keynesians offer conflicting monetary policy advice.**

A.   Monetarist and Keynesian Monetary Policy Advice

For present purposes, monetary policy will mean manipulating the money supply. The procedures whereby the Bank of England could achieve money stock control described in the previous chapter, are understood to be capable of delivering whatever supply of money the Bank chooses. This chapter will be concerned with the effects of the Bank achieving alternative targets for the money supply rather than with the ways in which those targets are achieved.

The monetary policy advice given by Keynesians is:

1. Raise the money supply to a higher level than it otherwise would have been if output is (or is forecast to be) below its full-employment level.

2. Lower the money supply below what it otherwise would have been if output is (or is forecast to be) above its full-employment level.

The precise amount by which the money supply should be moved in order to achieve the desired level of output is a technically complex matter, but one that Keynesians believe they can handle with the help of large-scale econometric models.

---

1   The leading articles on this topic are much more demanding than the simplified presentation given in this and the next two chapters. On the monetarist side, the leading pieces are: Thomas J. Sargent and Neil Wallace, 'Rational Expectations and the Theory of Economic Policy', *Journal of Monetary Economics*, 2 (April 1976), pp. 169–84; and Robert E. Lucas, Jr., 'Rules, Discretion and the Role of the Economic Advisor' in Stanley Fischer, ed., *Rational Expectations and Economic Policy*, National Bureau of Economic Research (Chicago and London: University of Chicago Press, 1980), pp. 199–210. On the Keynesian side, the best pieces are: Edmund Phelps and John B. Taylor, 'Stabilizing Powers of Monetary Policy Under Rational Expectations', *Journal of Political Economy*, 85 (February 1977), pp. 163–89; and Stanley Fischer, 'Long-term Contracts, Rational Expectations, and the Optimal Money Supply Rule', *Journal of Political Economy*, 85 (February 1977), pp. 191–206.

The monetarist policy advice contrasts very sharply with the Keynesian advice and is as follows:

If output is below its full-employment level so that there is a recession, monetarists advise holding the money supply on a steady course that is known and predictable, rather than raising the rate of growth of the money supply above that known and predictable path. Conversely, when the economy is in a boom, with output above its full-employment level, monetarist advice is again to hold the money supply growing at a steady and predictable rate rather than to reduce its growth rate.

Thus, Keynesian advice is to manipulate the money supply growth rate, raising it in a depression and lowering it in a boom; the monetarist policy advice is to keep the money supply growth rate steady, regardless of whether the economy is in a boom or a slump.

To see *why* each group of economists gives the advice that it does and to see precisely why there is a disagreement, it is necessary to analyse how the economy reacts to shocks that do not themselves stem from the actions of monetary policy. It is then necessary to ask how monetary policy can be used to counter the effects of these shocks. There are two broad sources of shocks — one on the aggregate demand side, and the other on the aggregate supply side of the economy. The aggregate demand shocks are considered in this chapter, and the aggregate supply shocks in the next one.

B. Aggregate Demand Shocks and the Aggregate Demand Curve

The closed economy theory of aggregate demand, developed in Chapter 14 and the open economy theory of Chapter 16 did not explicitly contain aggregate demand shocks. The theory was presented as if the level of aggregate demand would be determined *exactly* once the value of the money supply and the fiscal policy variables were set. This assumption was an oversimplification, and one that it is now necessary to relax. In this chapter, we relax this simplification on the demand side of the economy.

You will recall that the theory of aggregate demand was developed from a theory of consumption, investment, and the demand for money and international trade and capital flows. A moment's reflection will tell you that holding the money supply and fiscal policy variables constant, the position of the aggregate demand curve will be fixed and fully predictable only if the consumption function, investment function, demand for money function and the international flows of goods and capital are fixed and fully predictable. If a significant group of individuals decided in one particular year that they would manage with a smaller ratio of money balances to income than normal, then in that particular year there would be a surge of expenditures. As these individuals put into action their decisions to lower their money balances below their normal level in relation to their incomes. Conversely, if a significant group of individuals decided in a particular year that they wanted a higher ratio of money balances to income than normal, they would cut back on their expenditures as they put their decisions into effect.

There are many factors that could lead individuals to vary, over time, their consumption, investment, and demand for money and international transactions. On the average, such factors would cancel out and, for most of the time, when aggregated over all the individuals in the economy, would not be very important. From time to time, however, such factors could be important and might knock the economy significantly away from its *normal* equilibrium position.

Perhaps some examples will be helpful. Suppose it is widely believed that there is going to be a major drought. This might lead people to invest in a stockpile of food and to lower their average money holdings for a period. While this stockpiling was going on, there would be an increase in the level of aggregate demand as people attempted to put through their increased expenditure plans. In the opposite direction, suppose that it was widely believed that there was going to be a major technical innovation in, say, automobiles, such that the current year's model will be quickly superseded by a vastly superior technology. In such a case, the sales of cars in the year in question would be unusually low, and people would hold on to their money balances in readiness for a subsequent increase in expenditures. In this case, there would be a retiming of expenditures, with sales in one year being unusually low, and sales in some subsequent year, or years, being unusually high.

These are simply examples; you can probably think of many more. Most of the examples which you will think of will turn out to involve randomness in the timing of people's expenditures in acquiring either durable goods, capital goods, or other goods to store. Random fluctuations in the composition of people's assets — between money holdings on the one hand and real asset holdings on the other hand — lead to random fluctuations in aggregate demand.

You can think of the aggregate demand curve that we have been working with in the earlier parts of this book as being the level of the aggregate demand curve *on the average*. This curve is reproduced in Figure 31.1 as the solid line labelled $AD(M_0)$. It is labelled in this way to remind you that the position of the AD curve depends on, among other things, the money supply, M. The subscript on M is there to denote the initial value of the money supply, M_0. Later we will analyse what happens when we change M, holding everything else constant.

Now allow also for random shocks arising from the considerations just described to affect the position of the aggregate demand curve. Sometimes aggregate demand will be higher than its average value, and sometimes lower than its average value. We can capture such random shocks as an addition to or subtraction from the average position of the aggregate demand curve. Let us call the aggregate of all the random shocks to

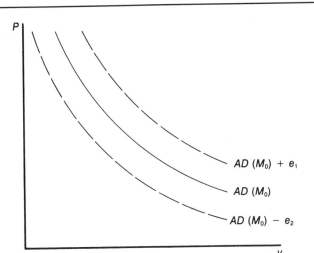

Figure 31.1
Aggregate demand
shocks

Random fluctuations in consumption, investment, and the demand for money summarized as the shock *e* shifts the aggregate demand curve around its average position, even though monetary and fiscal policy variables are fixed. On the average, the shocks will be zero. The shock e_1 is an example of a positive shock and minus e_2 is a negative shock.

demand *e*. On the average, *e* is equal to zero. It will, however, take on large positive or negative values. If *e* took on a positive value, say, e_1, then the aggregate demand curve would move to the right, such as the curve shown as the broken line $AD(M_0) + e_1$. If there was a negative random shock, say, *minus* e_2, then the aggregate demand curve would move to the left, such as that shown as the broken line labelled $AD(M_0) - e_2$. At any particular point in time the aggregate demand curve might lie anywhere inside the range of the two broken-line curves. On the average, the aggregate demand curve would be located in the middle of this range at $AD(M_0)$.

Thus, for any given level of the money supply you can think of there being a whole set of possible aggregate demand curves. The *actual* position of the aggregate demand curve depends on the size of the random shock, *e*, and on the money supply.

C. Consequences of Monetarist Policy

Let us now analyse what happens when there is an aggregate demand shock and when the monetary policy pursued is that advocated by monetarists. Figure 31.2 illustrates the analysis. Let us suppose that the anticipated money supply is M_0. Recall that the monetarist policy involves making the money supply follow a totally predictable path under all circumstances. Specifically, assume the actual money supply is held

**Figure 31.2
The consequences of
following monetarist
policy advice**

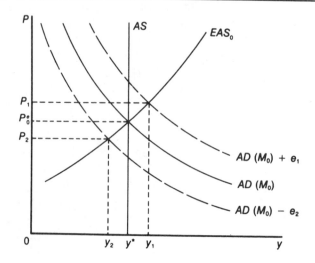

Monetarist policy holds the money stock constant. Expected aggregate demand will be
$AD(M_0)$, and the rationally expected price level P_0^e. Actual random fluctuations in
aggregate demand will generate fluctuations in output with procyclical co-movements in
the price level.

constant at M_0. It is now obvious that the actual money supply is equal
to the anticipated money supply. In other words, if the monetarist policy
rule is followed, there is no unanticipated change in the money supply.

Since, on the average, the aggregate demand shock e will be zero, it
will be rational to expect a zero aggregate demand shock. Thus the rational
expectation of the price level P_0^e is found where the expected aggregate
demand curve $AD(M_0)$ cuts the aggregate supply curve AS. This aggregate demand curve is the expected aggregate demand curve in the double
sense that it is drawn for an expected value of the aggregate demand shock
equal to zero and for the money supply equal to its anticipated level of
M_0. Passing through the point P_0^e and y^* is the relevant expectations-
augmented aggregate supply curve. This expectations-augmented aggregate supply curve is drawn for a rational expectation of the price level
of P_0^e.

Now suppose that there is a random increase in aggregate demand by
an amount e_1 such that the demand curve *actually* moves rightwards to
$AD(M_0) + e_1$. If the monetary policy advice of the monetarists is followed and the money supply is held at M_0, its anticipated level, the result
of this random shock to aggregate demand will be a rise in the price level
to P_1 and a rise in output to y_1.

Next consider the opposite case. Suppose there is a negative random
shock to aggregate demand — a random fall in aggregate demand — so
that the aggregate demand curve shifts leftwards to $AD(M_0) - e_2$. Again,
following the monetarist policy advice, the actual money supply is held

steady at its anticipated level M_0. There is therefore a drop in the price level to P_2 and a drop in output to y_2.

You can now see that the consequences of following the monetarist policy advice are that the economy will experience random deviations of output from its full-employment level and random deviations of the price level from its expected level as the economy is continuously 'bombarded' with random aggregate demand shocks. These shocks are not offset by changes in the money supply. There will also be fluctuations in employment, unemployment, the real wage, and the money wage. You can work out the directions in which these variables will move from Chapter 22. Further, for the reasons discussed in Chapter 27, there will only be a gradual return to full employment following a shock.

Let us now examine the consequences of following Keynesian policy advice.

D. Consequences of Keynesian Policy

Let us begin with exactly the same setup as before. In Figure 31.3 anticipated money supply is M_0 and the expected aggregate demand curve drawn for an expected zero aggregate demand shock is the curve $AD(M_0)$. (For the moment ignore the other labels on that curve in Figure 31.3.) The rational expectation of the price level is P_0^e and the relevant expectations-augmented aggregate supply curve is EAS_0.

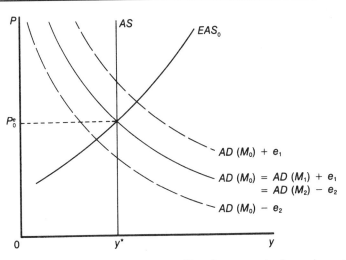

Figure 31.3
The consequences of following Keynesian monetary policy advice

If a random shock hits the economy, thereby shifting the aggregate demand curve (with the money stock constant), Keynesian policy would change the money stock so as to offset the random demand shift. The actual aggregate demand curve would remain constant as the continuous line in the figure. Output would be stabilized at full employment and the price level at its expected level.

Now suppose that there is a positive random shock to aggregate demand (e_1) taking the aggregate demand curve to the higher curve $AD(M_0) + e_1$. The Keynesian policy advice in this situation is to cut the money supply. If the money supply is cut by exactly the right amount, it is possible to offset the positive aggregate demand shock, thereby making the actual aggregate demand curve the same as the curve $AD(M_0)$. Suppose that the money supply that exactly achieves that effect is M_1. Then the aggregate demand curve would be the same as $AD(M_0)$. We have given that aggregate demand curve a second label, $AD(M_1) + e_1$. This label is to indicate to you that the same aggregate demand curve can arise from different combinations of the money supply and the random aggregate demand shock. If the aggregate demand shock was zero and the money supply was M_0, the aggregate demand curve would be the same as in a situation in which the money supply was M_1 (smaller than M_0) and the aggregate demand shock was e_1 (a positive value). Following this Keynesian policy rule of changing the money supply to offset the aggregate demand shock gives the prediction that the level of output will stay constant at y^* and the price level will stay at its rational expectation level P_0^e.

The same conclusion would arise if the consequences of a negative aggregate demand shock were examined. If aggregate demand fell by a random amount, e_2, with a fixed money supply M_0, the aggregate demand curve would move to $AD(M_0) - e_2$. If this random shock was offset by a rise in the money supply to (say) M_2 — a value big enough to raise the aggregate demand curve back to its original level — then the aggregate demand curve would again become the same as $AD(M_0)$. The curve $AD(M_0)$ has been labelled yet a third time as equal to $AD(M_2) - e_2$ to remind you that with a higher money supply (M_2) and a negative value of the aggregate demand shock (e_2), it is possible to place the aggregate demand curve in the same place as it would have been with a lower value for the money supply (M_0) and a zero random shock to aggregate demand.

Again, following Keynesian policy advice, the economy stays at the price level P_0^e and the full-employment output level y^* where the aggregate demand curve $AD(M_2) - e_2$ cuts the expectations-augmented aggregate supply curve EAS_0.

You see then that the consequences of following Keynesian stabilization policy are to remove all the fluctuations from output and to keep the price level at its rationally expected level.

E. Why Monetarists and Keynesians Offer Conflicting Advice

(i) Comparison: Keynesian Policy Seems to be Better than Monetarist Policy

From the above presentation of the effects of following a monetarist policy rule and Keynesian policy intervention, it is apparent that monetarist policy leaves the economy contaminated by the effects of random shocks to aggregate demand, whereas Keynesian policy completely insulates the economy from these shocks by exactly offsetting their effects. It would appear, then, that monetary policy can be used to keep the economy free from random fluctuations in output and the price level, and assuming that to be a desirable end, Keynesian monetary policy should so be used. Put more directly, it would appear that Keynesian policy is better than monetarist policy.

Naturally, since there is a debate about the matter, things are not quite as simple as they have been presented in the above two sections. Let us now try to find out why Keynesians and monetarists disagree with each other.

(ii)   *Informational Advantages*

In the two monetary policy experiments that we have conducted and compared in the preceding sections, we have not made the same assumptions concerning the information available to the Bank of England and to private economic agents.

When conducting the monetarist policy analysis, it was assumed implicitly — and it is now time to be explicit about the matter — that the Bank and private economic agents all had the same information. No one knew what value e would take in the coming time period. Everyone, including the Bank, expected that it would be zero.

When conducting the Keynesian policy analysis, however, it was assumed implicitly — and again it is now time to be explicit — that no private agent was able to forecast the value of the random shock e, but that the Bank knew the value of e exactly and was able to move the money supply so as to offset precisely its effects on aggregate demand. In other words, it was assumed that the Bank knew more than private economic agents concerning the position of the aggregate demand curve.

Instead of assuming that the Bank has such an informational advantage, let us analyse what would happen if the Bank had to operate a Keynesian policy with a time lag such that it could only change the money supply when it knew that there had been an aggregate demand shock that it had been able to observe. Also, however, let us recognize that what can be observed by the Bank can also be observed by anybody else. If the Bank knows that the economy is experiencing a positive (or negative) aggregate demand shock, then it seems reasonable to suppose that everyone else knows that too.

In order to make things as clear as possible, let us look at two periods of time (years). We will analyse what would happen if there was a positive aggregate demand shock (e_1) in the first period and then no aggregate demand shock in the second period. Suppose that the Bank reacts to an aggregate demand shock with a one-period lag. That is, if there has been a positive aggregate demand shock in period one, the Bank cuts back on the money supply in the second period in an attempt to offset the effects of the observed, first-period aggregate demand shock. Further, let us suppose that everyone knows as much as the Bank knows about the aggregate demand shock. Yet further, let us suppose that everyone knows that the Bank is pursuing a Keynesian policy and will react with a one-period lag by changing the money stock. Let us now work out what will happen as a result of this monetary policy response.

Figure 31.4 illustrates the analysis. The economy is initially expected to be on the demand curve $AD(M_0)$, at a price level P_0^e and an output level y^*. The relevant expectations-augmented aggregate supply curve is EAS_0. That is, the economy starts out at the price level P_0^e and full-employment output y^*.

In period one let there be a positive aggregate demand shock e_1. No one can predict the aggregate demand shock before it happens, and therefore, no one reacts to it until period two. However, the shock affects the actual behaviour of the economy in period one, and the price level and output level settle down at P_1 and y_1, respectively. These are the values of the price level and output at which the new aggregate demand curve $AD(M_0) + e_1$ cuts the expectations-augmented aggregate supply curve EAS_0.

Now, in the next period (period two), everyone has observed that there has been a positive aggregate demand shock. Furthermore, everyone can

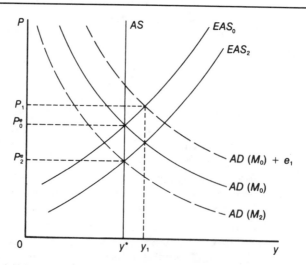

Figure 31.4
The consequences of following Keynesian monetary policy advice with an infor-mation lag

An economy initially at full-employment equilibrium (y^*, P_0^e) is disturbed by a random shock to aggregate demand (e_1). Output and the price level rise to y_1, P_1 the same as they would if the monetarist rule was being pursued. The higher output level induces a monetary contraction under the Keynesian rule, lowering the aggregate demand curve to $AD(M_2)$. Since everyone knows the government is using the Keynesian rule, the expected aggregate demand curve (in the absence of random shocks) will be the same as the expected curve. The economy will return to full employment but with a lower price level. Pursuing a Keynesian rule with a one-period lag leaves output on the same path as in the case of the monetarist rule but makes the price level more volatile.

work out the size of the shock from knowing what the actual price and output levels are. The Bank reacts to this aggregate demand shock by cutting the money supply in period two to a value of (say) M_2. Assuming that there is no aggregate demand shock in this second period, the new aggregate demand curve will be below the original curve $AD(M_0)$ since the money supply has been cut below M_0. In particular, the aggregate demand curve will be $AD(M_2)$. Private agents will expect the aggregate demand curve to be $AD(M_2)$ because they will expect the monetary authorities to cut the money stock as a reaction to the previous period's aggregate demand shock e_1. Private agents will form a rational expectation of the price level of P_2^e, and the expectations-augmented aggregate supply curve will become EAS_2. If (as we are assuming) there is no aggregate demand shock in period two, the economy will settle at its full-employment output level of y^* and the price level of P_2^e.

Thus, following a Keynesian policy rule, but with a one-period information lag, implying that the Bank of England has no better information than the private sector has, leads to a movement in output that is exactly the same as that which occurs when the monetarist policy rule is followed. However, there is a difference between the two policies in the behaviour of the price level. The price level fluctuates more when Keynesian policy advice is followed than it does with the monetarist rule. Output behaves exactly the same under either policy, but the price level is more variable with Keynesian than with monetarist policy.

We see, then, that following Keynesian policy advice, which has a one-period lag on information and with no informational advantage for the Bank, is exactly the same as following monetarist policy advice in its effect on output. However, it leads to bigger fluctuations in the price level than does monetarist policy.

(iii) The Essence of the Dispute Between Keynesians and Monetarists

The essence of the dispute between Keynesians and monetarists concerning the effects of monetary policy turns on the question of information and the use that may be made of new information. The monetarist asserts that the Bank of England has no informational advantage over private agents and that it can do nothing that private agents will not do for themselves. Any attempt by the Bank to fine tune or stabilize the economy by making the money supply react to previous shocks, known to everybody, will make the level of output behave no better than it otherwise would have done and will make the price level more variable.

Keynesians assert that there is an effective informational advantage to the Bank. They agree that individuals will form their expectations rationally, using all the information that is available to them. But they go on to assert that individuals get locked into contracts based on an expected price level that, after the fact of an aggregate demand shock, turns out to be wrong. The Bank of England acts after private agents have tied themselves into contractual arrangements based on a wrong price level expectation to compensate for and offset the effects of those random shocks. Figure 31.3 can be reinterpreted as showing what happens if the private sector is tied into contracts based on a wrong expected price level. In that case, if both the Bank of England and private agents *observe* an aggregate demand shock of (say) e_1, but if private agents are tied into contracts based on the expected price level P_0^e, *and if* the Bank can change the money supply quickly enough, then the Keynesian policy outcome shown in Figure 31.3 can be achieved.

The essence of the debate, then, concerns the flexibility of private sector responses *vis-à-vis* the flexibility of Bank's responses to random shocks that hit the economy. If everyone can act as quickly and as effortlessly as everyone else, there is no advantage from pursuing Keynesian policy, and indeed, there are disadvantages because the price level will be more variable. If, however, the Bank can act more quickly than the private sector, there may be a gain in the form of reduced variability of both output and the price level from pursuing Keynesian policy.

(iv)   An Unsettled Scientific Question

There is no easy way of deciding which of these two views better describes the world, and further scientific research is required before the matter will be settled.

One thing that can be said, however, is that because it is difficult to know exactly what random shocks are hitting the economy, attempts to pursue Keynesian policy will make the money supply more random and less predictable than would monetarist policy. You have seen (Chapters 23 and 27) that an unpredictable monetary policy gives rise to cycles in economic activity arising from the money supply movements themselves. Thus, Keynesian policy will necessarily impart some cyclical movements into the economy as a consequence of the fact that the money supply itself is less predictable under Keynesian policy than under a monetarist policy rule. Monetarist policy will (as far as possible) remove any fluctuations from aggregate demand that arise from the money supply itself. The only things that can lead to business cycles under a monetarist policy rule are the random fluctuations arising from private aggregate demand (or aggregate supply) shocks. The random shocks emanating from the behaviour of the Bank of England are eliminated.

Whether random shocks that arise from the private sector are the dominant shocks is another matter of dispute. But, there seems to be less room for disagreement. It is fairly well established that one of the major sources of fluctuations in economic activity in modern industrial economies is instability in monetary policy itself. Unanticipated variations in the money supply seem to account for much of the variation that we observe in the level of economic activity. However, they certainly do not account for all the observed fluctuations. To take an extreme, the Great Depression of 1929–34 has not yet been satisfactorily explained by *any* theory. We must therefore remain cautious and display a certain amount of humility. This does not, however, bode well for the Keynesian policy recommendation, which, in order that it may improve matters, must be based upon the presumption that we know rather a lot about the way in which the economy behaves.

The bottom line defence of the monetarist is that we are too ignorant about the workings of the economy to be able to do any better than to remove at least those sources of fluctuation in economic activity that we *can* control, namely, those that stem from instability in the money supply. If such fluctuations were removed, the economy would behave in a more stable manner than it has in the past. But, it would not be perfect. Perfection requires a great deal more information than we currently have available to us.

Summary

A. *Monetarist and Keynesian Monetary Policy Advice*

Monetarists recommend the adoption of a steady and predictable money supply growth rule. The money supply growth rate should be kept constant no matter what the current state of the economy.

Keynesians recommend the use of active variations in the money supply to offset aggregate demand shocks. They recommend raising the money supply when output is below its full-employment level and lowering the money supply when output is above its full-employment level.

B. *Aggregate Demand Shocks and the Aggregate Demand Curve*

Aggregate demand shocks are random variations in the level of aggregate demand that arise from random movements in the timing of expenditures and from random fluctuations in desired holdings of real assets and financial assets. If people try to hold more real assets and fewer financial assets, there will be a rise in the demand for goods — a rise in aggregate demand.

Aggregate demand shocks shift the aggregate demand curve. For any given price level, the level of aggregate demand will vary around its most likely value, depending on the size of the aggregate demand shock.

C. *Consequences of Monetarist Policy*

Adopting a monetarist policy permits fluctuations in output, employment, unemployment, the price level, the money wage, and the real wage. For example, in the case of a positive aggregate demand shock, output, employment, the price level, and the money wage will rise, and the real wage and unemployment will fall.

D. *Consequences of Keynesian Policy*

Keynesian policy is designed to isolate the economy from a random shock and eliminate fluctuations in output and the price level. In the case of a positive aggregate demand shock, Keynesian monetary policy advice is to lower the money supply so as to leave aggregate demand (and thus the position of the aggregate demand curve) unchanged. This policy would lead to no adjustment in the rational expectation of the price level, so that the level of output, employment, unemployment, the price level, the real wage and the money wage would remain constant.

E. *Why Monetarists and Keynesians Offer Conflicting Advice*

The dispute between monetarists and Keynesians rests on whether the Bank of England has an informational advantage over private agents in the economy. Monetarists argue that the Bank has no more information than do private agents. Any attempt by the Bank to off-set *previous* random aggregate demand shocks (now known to all agents in the economy) by varying the money supply will not reduce the fluctuations in output, whereas it will increase those in the price level.

Keynesians assert that the Bank has an *effective* informational advantage over private agents because private agents get locked in-to contracts that cannot be revised quickly as new information becomes available. Private agents are locked into contracts based on the wrong expected price level, whereas the Bank can respond quickly to the new information (the aggregate demand shock) and can change the money supply quickly enough so that output, employment, and the price level remain steady.

The successful application of Keynesian policy would require a large amount of information on the part of the Bank of England and government, and there is a presumption on the part of monetarists that, in the present state of knowledge, they do not have sufficient information. Monetarists assert that attempts at pursuing Keynesian policies will, in the current state of knowledge, generate larger fluctuations in both output and prices than would occur with the adoption of a monetarist rule.

Review Questions

1. Summarize and contrast the monetary policy positions of Keynesians and monetarists.
2. Give some examples of factors which might cause aggregate demand shocks.
3. Work out, using the appropriate diagrams, the consequences of pursuing monetarist policy in the face of random fluctuations in aggregate demand.
4. Explain the rationale that monetarists use for permitting random aggregate demand shocks to influence aggregate output and prices.
5. Work out, using the appropriate diagrams, the Keynesian monetary policy required to stabilize the economy in the face of a positive shock.
6. Work out, using the appropriate diagrams, the effects of pursuing Keynesian policy, but with the monetary authorities reacting with a one-period lag to aggregate demand shocks.
7. Set out the major differences in the predicted consequences of pursuing monetarist and Keynesian policies in the face of random aggregate demand shocks.
8. What is the primary source of disagreement between Keynesians and monetarists which causes each group of economists to give the advice that it does?

32

Monetary Policy II: Aggregate Supply Shocks

In September 1973, the members of the Oil-Producing Exporting Countries (OPEC) announced a fourfold increase in the price of crude oil. At the same time they announced an embargo on the shipment of oil to certain countries and a decision to cut back their production levels. In a single afternoon, the OPEC decision delivered a *supply shock* to the Western world which has only been matched by the events of major wars. The consequences of the OPEC oil price rise have been widespread and long drawn out. They also triggered a fierce debate as to what constituted the appropriate macroeconomic policy response.[1]

The supply shock administered by OPEC was an unusually large one. Supply shocks are not, however, unusual events. We saw, in Chapter 17, that supply shocks in the form of shifts in the aggregate production function arising from variations in the pace of technical change and capital accumulation as well as climatic factors can produce shifts in aggregate supply. This chapter is going to help you to evaluate alternative policy recommendations for dealing with supply shocks.

By the time you have completed this chapter you will be able to:

---

1 An excellent presentation of a Keynesian view on this is Robert M. Solow, 'What to Do (Macroeconomically) When OPEC Comes' in Stanley Fischer, ed., *Rational Expectations and Economic Policy*, National Bureau of Economic Research (Chicago and London: University of Chicago Press, 1980), pp. 249–64. Also see Neil Wallace's comment on Solow on pp. 264–7 of the same volume.

(a) Explain the distinction between the expectations-augmented aggregate supply curve and the expectation of the aggregate supply curve.

(b) Explain the consequences of following monetarist policy advice in the event of an aggregate supply shock.

(c) Explain the consequences of following Keynesian policy advice in the event of an aggregate supply shock.

(d) Explain the consequences of following a Keynesian policy with an information lag.

(e) Explain the essence of the dispute between Keynesians and monetarists concerning supply shock policies.

A. Expectations-Augmented Aggregate Supply Curve and the Expectation of the Aggregate Supply Curve

The point for your analysis of aggregate supply shocks is to recall the theory of aggregate supply presented in Chapter 17. In that chapter we analysed the way in which production function shocks can lead to shifts in the *AS* curve. If it is a little while since you have studied that material it will probably be worthwhile refreshing your memory before going further.

The next matter to which we have to attend is an important distinction concerning the use of the word 'expectation'. The word 'expectation' is going to be attached to the aggregate supply curve in two very different ways. First, there is the expectations-augmented aggregate supply curve (*EAS*). This curve is what it always has been, namely, a curve showing the level of aggregate supply for a given expected price level.

Second, the concept of the expectation of the aggregate supply curve will be used. This new concept has not been used before. The aggregate supply curve is the vertical aggregate supply curve *AS* — which shows the level of aggregate supply when the expected and actual price levels are equal to each other. If there are no aggregate supply shocks, the position of this curve is determined uniquely by the production function and the condition of equilibrium in the labour market. But, when random shocks affect the production function, they also affect the position of the aggregate supply function. The size and direction of random shocks to the production function cannot be known before they occur, though on the average, those shocks cancel out — are zero. Thus, the aggregate supply curve based on a zero aggregate supply shock — the expected or average aggregate supply shock — will be called the *expectation of the aggregate supply curve*.

Keeping this distinction clear, and as a prelude to analysing the effects of alternative policies towards aggregate supply shocks, let us see how each of these aggregate supply curves shifts in response to such a shock.

Figure 32.1 shows the effects of an aggregate supply shock on the

**Figure 32.1
An aggregate supply
shock and the
aggregate supply
curves**

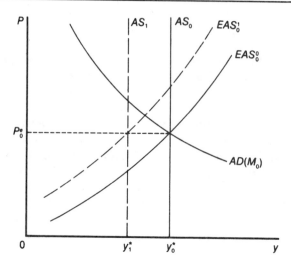

An unexpected aggregate supply shock shifts the aggregate supply curve for example from AS_0 to AS_1. The expectations-augmented aggregate supply curve is dragged along horizontally with the AS curve. EAS_0^0 is the expectations-augmented aggregate supply curve for the expected price level P_0^e (expected money stock M_0) and an expected aggregate supply curve of AS_0. The curve EAS_0^1 refers to the same expected price level and money stock but to the lower level of aggregate supply.

aggregate supply and expectations-augmented aggregate supply curves. Suppose that initially the economy was on the curve AS_0, and the aggregate demand curve $AD(M_0)$ at a full-employment equilibrium y_0^* and P_0^e. The expectations-augmented aggregate supply curve has both a superscript and a subscript. The subscript refers to the value of the money supply, and the superscript refers to the value of the aggregate supply curve. Thus, EAS_0^0 is at the point of intersection of AS_0 and $AD(M_0)$.

Now suppose that there is a random shock in aggregate supply that cuts the level of aggregate output supplied at each level of employment. As a result the aggregate supply curve shifts to the left by the amount of the drop in output that results from the aggregate supply shock to (say) AS_1. If the aggregate supply shock is unanticipated, then the expectation of the aggregate supply curve is that it remains at AS_0. Also suppose that the expected value of the money supply remains at M_0, so that the aggregate demand curve $AD(M_0)$ is expected to remain unchanged. In this case, the rational expectation of the price level remains at P_0^e.

What happens to the expectations-augmented aggregate supply curve? A moment's reflection will tell you that this curve must also shift horizontally by the same amount as the aggregate supply curve has shifted. The expectations-augmented aggregate supply curve always cuts the *actual* aggregate supply curve at the expected price level. Since the aggregate supply shock is (by assumption) unanticipated, there is no prior knowledge about it. The aggregate supply curve has shifted from its expected position AS_0 to an unexpected position AS_1. The expectations-augmented aggregate supply curve will have been dragged along with the aggregate supply curve so as to intersect it at the expected price level P_0^e. Given the aggregate supply shock, there will be a lower level of output available at all price levels. Nothing has happened to change the expected price level, which remains at P_0^e. That is, nothing has happened to yield new information to economic agents that would lead them to revise their price level expectation.

Thus, the effect on the aggregate supply curves of an aggregate supply shock is to shift both the aggregate supply curve and the expectations-augmented aggregate supply curve horizontally by the amount of the shock. The curve EAS_0^1 is the expectations-augmented aggregate supply curve when the expectation of aggregate demand is $AD(M_0)$ and when aggregate supply has unexpectedly dropped to AS_1.

You are now in a position to go on to compare the effects of alternative policies.

B. Consequences of Monetarist Policy

Figure 32.2 illustrates the consequences of following monetarist policy in the event of an aggregate supply shock. Suppose that there is a random drop in aggregate supply from AS_0 to AS_1 and that a monetarist policy rule of fixing the money stock at M_0 is followed, so that the

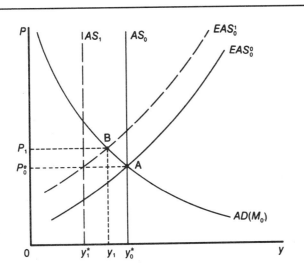

Figure 32.2
The consequences of following monetarist policy advice in the event of a supply shock — stagflation

An economy initially at full-employment equilibrium (y_0^*, P_0^e) is disturbed by a negative aggregate supply shock that unexpectedly takes the aggregate supply curve to AS_1, and the *EAS* curve to EAS_0^1. The impact equilibrium is at y_1, P_1. Prices rise and output falls: the economy experiences stagflation.

aggregate demand curve remains as $AD(M_0)$. The initial equilibrium in the economy is the point A, where output is y_0^* and the price level is P_0^e. When the supply shock occurs, the aggregate supply curve shifts to AS_1, and the expectations-augmented aggregate supply curve shifts with it to EAS_0^1. There is no monetary policy reaction, and the economy settles at point B, with a price level of P_1 and an output level of y_1.

If, in the next period, the aggregate supply shock disappears, so that the economy reverts to its normal position on the aggregate supply curve AS_0, with the expectations-augmented aggregate supply curve EAS_0^0, the economy returns to the full-employment point A from which it started. Thus, following monetarist policy in the face of an aggregate supply shock leads to a movement in output and the price level in opposite directions to each other. This phenomenon is sometimes called *stagflation*. That is, the economy stagnates and inflates at the same time. It is to avoid stagflation in the face of an aggregate supply shock that some economists advocate adjusting the money supply to accommodate the supply shock. Let us now see what would happen if we follow this Keynesian policy.

C. Consequences of Keynesian Policy

Figure 32.3 illustrates the analysis. Again, suppose the economy starts out at point A at the intersection of the aggregate demand curve $AD(M_0)$, the aggregate supply curve AS_0, and the expectations-augmented aggregate supply curve EAS_0^0. As before, let there be a shock to aggregate supply that moves the aggregate supply curve to AS_1, and the expectations-augmented aggregate supply curve to EAS_0^1. Keynesian policy would counter this drop in aggregate supply by stimulating the money supply. The Keynesian response would be to raise the money supply to (say) M_1, such that the aggregate demand curve shifts to the curve labelled $AD(M_1)$. The new equilibrium would then be at point C, with the output level at y_0^* as originally, but with the price level at P_1.

If, in the next period, the aggregate supply shock disappeared and the economy reverted to its normal aggregate supply curve AS_0, then one of *four* possibilities arises. First, if the money supply is returned to its original level M_0 and if everyone expects that to happen, the economy will return to the original position A. Second, if the money supply is kept at its higher level M_1 and, again, if everyone anticipates that that will happen, the economy will stay at point C, but the expectations-augmented aggregate supply curve EAS_0^1 will become EAS_1^0, being the expectations-augmented aggregate supply curve drawn for a value of the money stock equal to M_1 with the aggregate supply curve at AS_0. Third, and fourth, if there is confusion in the minds of economic agents as to whether the monetary authorities will revert to the original money supply or stay with the new money supply, then the expectations-augmented aggregate supply curve will be located somewhere in between positions A and C on the AS_0 curve, and the economy will experience an output boom if

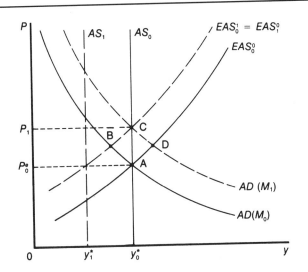

Figure 32.3
The consequences of
following Keynesian
monetary policy
advice in the event
of a supply shock —
avoiding stagflation

In the same situation as analysed in Figure 32.2, Keynesian advice is to raise the money supply, thereby raising aggregate demand from $AD(M_0)$ to $AD(M_1)$. This would move the economy to point C (full employment with a price level P_1). What happens in the next period depends on what the government does and what it is expected to do. An anticipated return of the money stock to its initial level will return the economy to its initial position A. An anticipated maintenance of the money stock of its new level will keep the economy at point C. If the money stock is expected to fall back to the original position but actually stays at the new position, the economy will go do D, and finally the money stock is lowered to its original level, but unexpectedly so, the economy will go to B.

the money supply stays at M_1, or an output slump if the money supply is returned to M_0. The price level will be between P_0^e and P_1. At the extremes, if the money supply was expected to revert to M_0, but in fact remained at M_1, the economy would move to point D; and if the money supply was expected to remain at M_1, but in fact reverted to M_0, the economy would move to point B.

Which of the above four possibilities would in fact arise depends on the monetary policy *process* being followed by the Bank of England. If the Bank had a history of responding to supply shocks with a one-period loosening of monetary policy and a subsequent reverting back to the original level of the money supply, then the first possibility analysed above would in fact arise. If the Bank had a history of expanding the money stock in response to a supply shock and then keeping the money supply at its new level, then the second possibility would arise. Possibilities three and four would only arise if the Bank had generated confusion in the minds of economic agents as a result of its own previous random behaviour.

We may now summarize the consequences of following a Keynesian policy in the face of an aggregate supply shock as follows: such a policy leads to inflation initially but with no drop in output and employment. In the next period, whether inflation falls and/or output falls, rises, or stays at its full-employment level depends on what the expected and actual money supplies are. Notice that the Keynesian policy of adjusting the money supply so as to accommodate the supply shock avoids the reduction in output generated by following the monetarist's policy, but only at the expense of higher inflation.

D. Consequences of Keynesian Policy with an Information Lag

Next, consider what would happen in the case of following Keynesian policy with an information lag. Suppose Keynesian policy is adopted with a one-period reaction lag to the aggregate supply shock. Figure 32.4 illustrates this analysis. Again, let the economy begin at position A on the aggregate demand curve $AD(M_0)$, the expectations-augmented aggregate supply curve EAS_0^0, and the aggregate supply curve AS_0. Then let there be an aggregate supply shock shifting the aggregate supply curve to AS_1 and the expectations-augmented aggregate supply curve to EAS_0^1. Since this random shock is not predictable, the economy moves to position B, with an output level of y_1 and a price level of P_2. *This outcome is exactly the same as that resulting from following the monetarist policy rule.*

Figure 32.4
The consequences of following Keynesian monetary policy advice in the event of a supply shock with an information lag

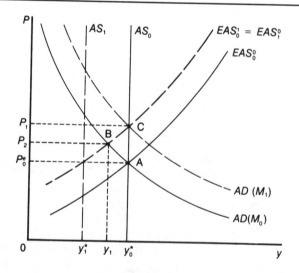

The economy is subjected to exactly the same shock as in the previous figures. Since there is a one-period policy response lag, in the first period of the shock the economy behaves in the same way as it would under a monetarist rule. It moves from A to B. If the monetary authority now stimulates demand, but people know that a Keynesian policy is being pursued and therefore expect this policy response, the price level will rise to P_1 and output returns to y_0^* in the next period. Thus, the behaviour of real output is identical in the Keynesian case to the monetarist case, but the price level is more variable under Keynesian policy.

Next, suppose that in the following period, the Bank reacts to this cut in aggregate output by raising the money supply to M_1. Provided that everyone correctly anticipates this monetary policy reaction, the economy returns to full-employment output, but at the higher price level P_1, at position C. To help you see more clearly what is going on at the equilibrium marked C, the expectations-augmented aggregate supply curve has been given a second label — EAS_1^0. These labels tell you that that particular EAS curve describes two situations: one in which the expected money supply is M_0 and the actual aggregate supply curve is AS_1; and a second situation in which the expected money supply is M_1 and the actual aggregate supply curve is at the position AS_0. Thus, with a one-period information lag, Keynesian stabilization policy in the face of an aggregate supply shock leads to exactly the same path for output as occurs under the monetarist policy, but the price level behaves differently. With the monetarist policy, the price level returns to its original level; but with the Keynesian policy, the price level rises to P_1.

E. The Essence of the Dispute between Keynesians and Monetarists

Exactly the same considerations are relevant in judging the appropriateness of Keynesian and monetarist policy responses to an aggregate supply shock as were relevant in the case of an aggregate demand shock. But, there is now an additional reason for suspecting that Keynesian policy will be difficult to carry out. You have already seen in the previous chapter that Keynesian policy requires a great deal of information. It requires information about the magnitude of the aggregate demand shocks. You now see that to pursue appropriate aggregate supply corrections, it is necessary to have good information about aggregate supply shocks as well. It will be apparent that if *both* of these types of shocks occur simultaneously, it is necessary for the monetary authorities to have the ability to disentangle the separate shocks that are affecting the economy and to offset both of them in the appropriate way and with greater speed than the private sector can react to them.[2]

Further, if the private sector learns that the public sector is going to react to aggregate supply shocks and if the private sector has as much information as the Bank of England does concerning those shocks, then the Bank's reaction will always be built into the private sector's expectations, and the Bank's actions themselves will result exclusively in price level variability.

---

2 A thorough (though demanding) analysis of precisely this topic is presented by Gary C. Fethke and Andrew J. Policano in 'Co-operative Responses by Public and Private Agents to Aggregate Demand and Supply Disturbances', *Economica*, 48 (May 1981), pp. 155–72.

Thus, the monetarists' objection to Keynesian policy is that it does not improve the performance of the economy as regards the behaviour of output, and unambiguously makes the price level less stable and predictable than would a monetarist policy.

Summary

A. *Expectations-Augmented Aggregate Supply Curve and the Expectation of the Aggregate Supply Curve*

The expectations-augmented aggregate supply curve traces the amount of aggregate supply as the price level varies for a given expected price level. The expectation of the aggregate supply curve refers to the vertical aggregate supply curve, which traces the quantity that will be supplied at each price level when that price level is fully expected. The expectation of that vertical aggregate supply curve refers to its position in normal or usual periods, when aggregate supply shocks are zero.

B. *Consequences of Monetarist Policy*

A random negative shock to aggregate supply with a fixed money supply will lower the level of output and raise the price level in the period in which the aggregate supply shock occurs. The level of employment will fall. The economy will experience stagflation.

C. *Consequences of Keynesian Policy*

Keynesian policy in the face of a negative aggregate supply shock would be to stimulate demand by raising the money supply. Perfectly conducted, Keynesian policy would have the effect of leaving output and employment unchanged, but raising the price level.

D. *Consequences of Keynesian Policy with an Information Lag*

If a Keynesian policy is followed but with a one-period lag in the receipt of information concerning the aggregate supply shock, the economy would respond in exactly the same way under a Keynesian policy as it would have done under a monetarist policy in the period in which the shock occurs. If, using a Keynesian policy, the monetary authorities stimulate demand with a one-period lag and if everyone correctly anticipates this response, there will be a rise in the price level but no output effect in the second period.

E. *The Essence of the Dispute between Keynesians and Monetarists*

The essence of the dispute between Keynesians and monetarists concerning the appropriate response to aggregate supply shocks is exactly the same as that discussed in the previous chapter concerning aggregate demand shocks. The issue turns on who gets information fastest and who can react fastest to new information. If the Bank of England has no superior information, then the use of Keynesian policy to correct aggregate supply shocks will leave the behaviour of output unaffected and will produce a greater degree of price level variability than will the pursuit of monetarist policy.

Review Questions

1. What is the distinction between the expectations-augmented aggregate supply curve and the expectation of the aggregate supply curve?
2. How does the expectations-augmented aggregate supply curve shift in the event of a negative aggregate supply shock?
3. Work out, using the appropriate diagrams, the effects of pursuing a monetarist policy in the face of a temporary (one period only), but unpredictable, drop in aggregate supply.
4. For the same shock as in Question 3, work out the effects of pursuing a Keynesian policy.
5. Contrast the paths of output and the price level in your answers to Questions 3 and 4.
6. If there was a previously unpredictable but, once occurred, known to be *permanent* shock to aggregate supply, what would happen to output and the price level:
   (a) With a monetarist policy?
   (b) With a Keynesian policy?
7. If a negative aggregate supply shock was always responded to with a rise in the money supply, and a positive aggregate supply shock was responded to with an unchanged money supply, what would the path of the inflation rate be like? (This question is tougher than the others.)

33

Fiscal Policy

This chapter examines how fiscal policy affects the level of output, employment, unemployment, the real wage, the money wage, the price level and the rate of interest. You will be aware that there is a great deal of popular discussion concerning the desirability of alternative government spending and tax policy changes. The chapter is designed to help you to understand and evaluate this discussion.

By the time you have completed this chapter you will be able to:

(a) **Explain the key differences between the Keynesian and monetarist policy recommendations concerning fiscal policy.**

(b) **Explain the distinction between anticipated and unanticipated fiscal policy.**

(c) **Explain how output, employment, unemployment, the real wage, money wage, and price level are affected by an anticipated change in government expenditure.**

(d) **Explain how output, employment, unemployment, the real wage, money wage and price level are affected by an unanticipated change in government expenditure.**

A. Keynesian and Monetarist Fiscal Policy Advice

The Keynesian and monetarist disagreement concerning the appropriate use of fiscal policy is much like their disagreement over monetary policy.

(i) Keynesian Fiscal Policy Advice

Keynesians recommend that:

1. When output is *below* its full-employment level, either
   (a) raise government expenditure, or
   (b) cut taxes, or
   (c) raise government expenditure and cut taxes together.
2. When output is *above* its full-employment level, either
   (a) cut government expenditure, or
   (b) raise taxes, or
   (c) cut government expenditure and raise taxes together.

Keynesians also tend to favour a political constitution that gives central-ized fiscal control so as to facilitate active fiscal policy changes.

(ii) Monetarist Fiscal Policy Advice

Monetarists disagree profoundly with the Keynesian fiscal policy advice. They say that government expenditure should be set at a level that is determined with reference to the requirements of economic efficiency rather than with reference to macroeconomic stability.

(a) Government expenditure Monetarists recommend that government expenditure be set at a level such that the marginal utility derived from public expenditure per pound spent is equal to the marginal utility derived from private expenditure per pound spent. (Recall your microeconomic analysis of the optimum allocation of a consumer's budget. Monetarists assert that the same considerations that apply to an individual's budget allocation are relevant for the allocation of resources between the public and private sector.) If the marginal utility per pound spent on private goods is less than the marginal utility per pound spent on government goods, then government expenditure is too low and private expenditure is too high, and there is a need to reallocate resources away from the private sector and towards the government sector — to increase public expenditure. Conversely, if the marginal utility per pound spent on private expenditure is greater than the marginal utility per pound spent by the government, then the government sector is too big, and there is a need to reduce government spending so that private spending may be increased.

Monetarists would therefore begin by looking at the marginal utility per pound spent on such items as national defence, law and order, educa-tion, health services, and all the other things purchased directly by govern-ment and would compare these with the marginal utility per pound of private expenditure. Monetarists assert that government expenditure should be set with reference to this economic efficiency criterion only.

Monetarists — or at least some of them — go on to argue that there is a problem arising from an imperfection in the political marketplace. They suggest that there appears to be a tendency for the interaction of politicians, the bureaucracy, and the electorate to generate a level of government expenditure that exceeds the efficient level. That is, there is a tendency for government expenditure to rise, relative to private expenditure, to a level such that the marginal utility per pound spent on goods bought by the government is below that in the private sector. They therefore advocate constitutional limitations on the fraction of aggregate output which may be spent by the government.

Further, monetarists tend to favour political constitutions that have decentralized federal and local fiscal authorities, so that those who levy and spend taxes on public consumption are not too distant from the people who they represent, and also so as to encourage competition between jurisdictions.

To summarize: monetarists advocate setting the level of government expenditure on considerations of economic efficiency and independently of the state of the aggregate level of output, employment, unemployment, or the price level. There is a presumption that government expenditure should be held to a steady fraction of aggregate output.

(b)   Taxes   Monetarists recommend that taxes be set at a level which enables the government to buy the utility-maximizing volume of public goods and services and maintain a constant money supply growth rate.

This policy recommendation follows directly from the monetarist view about the appropriate government spending policy and money supply policy. Recall that the government is constrained by the budget equation:

$$g - \bar{t} = qu(M/P)$$

Also recall from Chapter 31 that the monetarists' advice on the money supply growth rate, μ, is that it be set at a constant and steady value. One possible value would be zero, but usually monetarists recommend that μ be set equal to the rate of growth of output, so that the price level (recalling the fundamental inflation equation) is constant. Since monetarists recommend that government expenditure be set equal to its utility-maximizing level (independently of the state of the macroeconomy) and that the money supply should grow at a steady rate (independently of the state of the macroeconomy), it follows that they want to see the level of legislated taxes set such that these other two objectives may be met.

In other words, for monetarists, taxes and government expenditure go together. Both need to be set at levels such that an efficient allocation of resources between the government and private sector is achieved and, further, so that the money supply growth rate stays at a constant zero-inflation rate.

You see, then, as in the case of monetary policy, that Keynesians advocate that fiscal policy be used in an active manner to raise output if it is below its full-employment level and to lower it if it is above its full-employment level, whereas monetarists recommend that policy be set steady, independently of fluctuations in the level of output and the other macroeconomic variables.

B. Anticipated and Unanticipated Fiscal Policy

The distinction between anticipated and unanticipated fiscal policy is directly analogous to the distinction between anticipated and unanticipated changes in the money supply. The level of government expenditures, g_t, in any year t is equal to the value in the previous year g_{t-1}, plus the change between the previous year and the current year Δg. That is,

$$g_t = g_{t-1} + \Delta g$$

The change in government expenditure Δg can be decomposed into the change that was anticipated Δg^a and the component that was unanticipated Δg^u. That is,

$$\Delta g = \Delta g^a + \Delta g^u$$

The same distinction applies to taxes as well.

C. Effects of Anticipated Change in Government Expenditure

(i) The Effects on Output and the Price Level

The effects of an anticipated change in government expenditure will be analysed by working out, first of all, its effects on output and the price level. After that, the implications of these effects for changes in the labour market variables (employment, unemployment, the real and money wages and the rate of interest) will be worked out. Figure 33.1 will be used to illustrate the analysis.

Suppose that the economy is initially at full-employment equilibrium and that the money supply is fixed at M_0, the level of government expenditure is g_0 and taxes is t_0. Then the aggregate demand curve is the solid curve labelled $AD(M_0, g_0, t_0)$. Since expected aggregate demand is also $AD(M_0, g_0, t_0)$ the rational expectation of the price level is P_0^e. This price level is where the expected aggregate demand curve cuts the aggregate supply curve. The expectations-augmented aggregate supply curve EAS_0 cuts the aggregate supply curve at the same point. The actual price level is equal to the expected price level P_0^e, and the actual level of output is y^*.

Figure 33.1
The effects of an
anticipated change in
government
expenditure and
taxes on output and
the price level

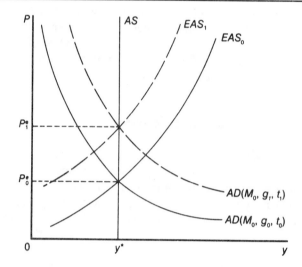

An anticipated rise in government spending and taxes with a constant money stock raises the expected and actual aggregate demand to $AD(M_0, g_1, t_1)$, raises the actual and expected price level to P_1^e, but leaves output undisturbed.

Now suppose there is an anticipated rise in government expenditure. Further, suppose that there is a matching anticipated rise in taxes, so that there is a balanced budget multiplier shift of the aggregate demand curve. (If you are not sure about this, check back to Chapter 14.) If government spending was to rise without a rise in taxes, then it would be necessary to raise the rate of money supply growth, which would generate inflation. (It would not be impossible to analyse this case, but the balanced budget fiscal policy is easier to analyse.)

Suppose that the balanced budget increase in government expenditure and taxes is such as to shift the aggregate demand curve to the broken line labelled $AD(M_0, g_1, t_1)$. With the money supply being held constant at M_0, but with government expenditure and taxes raised to g_1 and t_1 respectively, the aggregate demand curve has shifted rightwards.

Also, recall that the rise in government expenditure to g_1 is assumed to be anticipated. That is all economic agents will be aware that government expenditure has increased to g_1. Therefore, everyone will be aware that the price level is going to rise because the new aggregate demand curve is to the right of the original one. The new rational expectation of the price level will be P_1^e. This price level is where the new expected aggregate demand curve cuts the aggregate supply curve. A new expectations-augmented aggregate supply curve (the broken line labelled EAS_1) goes through the point where the new expected aggregate demand curve cuts the aggregate supply curve.

You can now read off directly the effects of an anticipated rise in government expenditure on output and the price level. If the level of government expenditure and taxes *actually* rises to g_1 and t_1, so that the actual aggregate supply curve becomes the same broken curve $AD(M_0, g_1, t_1)$, then the price level equals the rational expectation of the price level, namely, P_1^e and output remains at its full-employment level y^*.

You can see then that an anticipated rise in government expenditure (matched by an anticipated rise in taxes) raises the price level and leaves the level of output unchanged.

(ii) *The Effects on the Labour Market*

It is not difficult matter to work out the effects of an anticipated rise in government spending (matched by a tax rise) on the labour market variables. Since output has not changed, neither has employment, unemployment, nor the real wage changed. Since the price level has gone up, so must the money wage rate have risen. The money wage rate has risen by the same percentage amount as the rise in the price level, thereby leaving the real wage unchanged. The effects of an anticipated rise in government expenditure is a rise in the price level and a rise in the money wage rate.

But, there is a very important caveat. You should be aware that the analysis that has just been performed is based on the assumption that the extra taxes raised in the experiment are non-distorting. That is, that they are of a form that do not affect the supply of, or demand for, labour. If there were changes in such taxes as income or payroll taxes, there would be further important effects on employment and on the real wage to take into account. These in turn would lead to a different response of output to that worked out above. In fact, if higher taxes shifted the labour supply curve to the left, the levels of output and employment would *fall*, and the price level would rise by even more than that shown in Figure 33.1. This analysis is the essence of the supply-side analysis of some of the economists and other supporters of the Thatcher economic policies. They argue that by *cutting* highest marginal taxes and government spending, in a predictable, that is an anticipated, way the supply of labour will rise, output and employment will rise, and the inflation rate (the price level in the analysis here) will fall. You will be taken through an analysis of this view in the next chapter.

(iii) *The Effects on Interest Rates*

You can work out the effects of an anticipated rise in government spending and taxes on interest rates by using the analysis developed in Chapters 11 and 14. From that analysis you know that a balanced budget rise in government spending (rise in spending matched by tax rise) shifts the IS curve to the right by the amount of the spending rise. As a result, at full-employment, the rate of interest increases. You will recall that interest rates rise as part of the equilibrating mechanism whereby room is made for the extra government spending as a result of private investment decisions being cut back. This phenomenon is sometimes stated as the rise in government spending 'crowding out' private spending.

(iv)   Random Shocks and Policy Responses

If there was a random shock to aggregate demand or to aggregate supply such as those discussed in Chapters 31 and 32, it would not be possible to offset those random shocks with an anticipated change in government expenditure. Any anticipated fiscal policy action would be allowed for by private economic agents in forming their own rational expectations and would leave the level of output undisturbed. Therefore, anticipated fiscal policy changes cannot be used to stabilize the level of output, employment, and unemployment in the face of random shocks. They only have price level effects.

Let us now go on to analyse the effects of an unanticipated change in government expenditure.

D.   Effects of Unanticipated Change in Government Expenditure

(i)   The Effects on Output and the Price Level

To analyse the effects of an unanticipated change in government expenditure, let us again begin by working out its effects on output and the price level. Figure 33.2 illustrates the analysis. The economy initially has a money supply M_0 and government spending level g_0 and taxes t_0, so that the aggregate demand curve is the continuous line $AD(M_0, g_0, t_0)$. The aggregate supply curve is AS. Equilibrium is at the full-employment output level y^* and the actual and rationally expected price level of P_0^e.

Figure 33.2
The effects of an unanticipated change in government expenditure and taxes on output and the price level

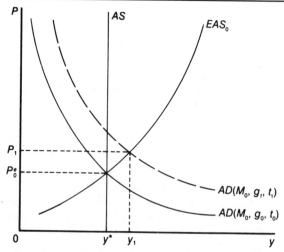

An unanticipated rise in government spending and taxes with a constant money supply shifts the aggregate demand to $AD(M_0, g_1, t_1)$. This raises output to y_1 and the price level to P_1.

Suppose that all economic agents anticipate that government expenditure, taxes and the money supply will be maintained at their initial levels of g_0, t_0, and M_0 respectively. But, suppose that the government unexpectedly increased its expenditure and taxes by equal amounts to g_1 and t_1 respectively. With equal unexpected rises in government expenditure and taxes, the Bank of England will maintain the money supply constant at the initial level of M_0. The unanticipated rise in government expenditure and the equal unanticipated rise in taxes shift the aggregate demand curve outwards to the curve $AD(M_0, g_1, t_1)$. Since this shift is unanticipated, the expectations-augmented aggregate supply curve remains the curve EAS_0. The new equilibrium is obtained at the point at which the new aggregate demand curve $AD(M_0, g_1, t_1)$ cuts the expectations-augmented aggregate supply curve EAS_0. You can read off this new solution as the price level P_1 and the output level y_1 in Figure 33.2.

You can now easily see the effects of an unanticipated rise in government expenditure (matched by an equal tax rise). An unanticipated rise in government expenditure (matched by an unanticipated tax rise to maintain a balanced budget) raises output and raises the price level.

We could easily reverse the above experiment and consider an unanticipated cut in government expenditure (matched by a tax cut to maintain a balanced budget), and this would lead to a fall in both output and the price level.

(ii)   The Effects on the Labour Market

It is now possible to work out the effects of these unanticipated changes in government expenditure on the labour market variables. Let us consider for illustrative purposes an unanticipated *rise* in government expenditure. (You can work out the effects of an unanticipated *fall* for yourself.)

Since an unanticipated rise in government spending raises output, it follows immediately that it must also raise the level of employment. You can read this off by considering Figure 20.2 in Chapter 20. Further, since the level of employment rises, the level of unemployment falls below its natural level. In order to induce a rise in employment, firms must willingly hire the additional labour and still be maximizing profits, which implies that the real wage must fall. But, the real wage falls only if the money wage rises by less than the rise in the price level. Therefore a further implication of the analysis concerning the effects of an unanticipated change in government spending is that money wages rise by less than the rise in the price level.

To summarize the effects of an unanticipated rise in government spending on the labour market variables: an unanticipated rise in government expenditure (matched by an unanticipated tax rise) raises the level of employment, lowers the level of unemployment, lowers the real wage, and leads to a rise in the money wage, but by a smaller percentage amount than the rise in the price level.

(iii)   Random Shocks and Policy Responses

You see, then, that an unanticipated change in government expenditure is capable of moving the level of aggregate output and employment around. It is possible to stimulate demand and raise output with an unanticipated rise in government spending and to cut back on output with an unanticipated cut in government spending.

It follows, therefore, that an unanticipated change in fiscal policy could be used to offset a random shock to either aggregate demand or aggregate supply. However, exactly the same considerations that were discussed in Chapters 31 and 32 concerning monetary policy apply here. If the government can change its expenditure (and taxes) quickly enough to offset shocks that private agents know have occurred, but which they are contractually unable to respond to, then it would be possible to use fiscal policy along the lines suggested by Keynesians to reduce the amount of variability in economic activity. However, if government expenditure and tax changes can only be engineered slowly and no more quickly than private contracts can be renegotiated, then there is no scope for government expenditure and tax variations to do anything other than lead to price level variability. Because of the legislative and bureaucratic lags in the enactment and implementation of fiscal policy changes, many Keynesians are now coming to the view that fiscal policy is not a useful stabilization weapon and are placing more emphasis on active variations in the money supply as the appropriate way of stabilizing the economy.

(iv)   Fiscal Policy and Inflation

There is a further reason for concern over the use of fiscal policy as a stabilizing device. This concern is about the inflationary consequences. Throughout the exercises conducted in this chapter, it has been supposed that the inflation rate was being held at zero, with the money supply growth rate held at the output growth rate (in the case of this model, both zero). If, starting from an initial situation of zero inflation, there was to be a permanent rise in government expenditure, with a permanent commitment not to change taxes, then we know that the money supply would eventually have to start growing at a faster rate. That is, the aggregate demand curve would begin to shift upwards continuously. Also, the expectations-augmented aggregate supply curve would shift upwards continuously as rational agents continuously revise their price level expectations upwards. Provided the money supply growth was anticipated, these two curves would move up at the same pace as each other, with inflation ensuing. With inflation anticipated the economy would stay at full employment.

But, it is unlikely that the money supply growth rate would be precisely anticipated. The money supply growth rate could be either above or below its anticipated level. As a result, there could be either an output boom or an output slump (stagflation) as the inflation rate increased. Either of these effects is possible, depending on whether the money supply growth accompanying a fiscal policy change is under- or over-anticipated.

Summary

A. *Keynesian and Monetarist Fiscal Policy Advice*

Keynesians recommend the active use of variations in government spending and taxes to raise demand when output is below its full-employment level and to lower demand when output is above its full-employment level.

Monetarists urge the maintaining of a steady fiscal policy that is dictated by resource-allocation considerations between the public and private sector, and not by economic stabilization considerations. They advocate a level of government spending consistent with an optimal division of resources between the government and private sector, and a level of taxes such that the money supply growth target that they advocate may be achieved.

B. *Anticipated and Unanticipated Fiscal Policy*

Just as in the case of monetary policy, a change in government expenditure or taxes may be decomposed into the part that was anticipated and the part that was unanticipated. The unanticipated change in government spending and taxes is simply the actual change minus the change that was anticipated. When there is no unanticipated change, fiscal policy is anticipated.

C. *Effects of Anticipated Change in Government Expenditure*

An anticipated rise in government expenditure matched by an equal anticipated tax rise raises the price level and raises the money wage by the same percentage amount as each other. It leaves the level of output, employment, unemployment, and the real wage unchanged. These predictions assume *neutral* tax changes.

D. *Effects of Unanticipated Change in Government Expenditure*

An unanticipated rise in government expenditure matched by an equal unanticipated tax rise raises output and the price level. It also raises employment and the money wage. But, the money wage does not rise by as much as the price level, and the real wage falls. There is also a fall in the unemployment rate.

Exactly the same considerations apply to evaluating the appropriateness of alternative fiscal policies as were discussed in Chapters 31 and 32 concerning monetary policies. That material should be studied carefully and its relevance to the fiscal policy debate understood.

Review Questions

1. Outline the key disagreements between Keynesians and monetarists regarding fiscal policy.
2. What criterion does the monetarist use for determining whether or not additional government spending is recommended? What criterion does the typical Keynesian policy adviser use?
3. Why is it that some monetarists feel there should be a constitutional limitation on the fraction of GDP which may be spent by the government?
4. What are the implications, in terms of the government's budget deficit, of following a monetarist rule of setting the rate of growth of the money supply equal to the rate of growth of real output?
5. Suppose there is a random shock to aggregate demand. Work out, using the appropriate diagrams:
   (a) The consequences for real income, the price level, employment, unemployment, and the real wage of monetarist fiscal policy.
   (b) The consequences for real income, the price level, employment, unemployment, and the real wage of Keynesian fiscal policy.
   (c) The consequences for real income, the price level, employment, unemployment, and the real wage of Keynesian policy with a one-period lag in changing government spending and/or taxes.
6. Suppose there is an anticipated rise in government expenditure not matched by a tax rise. Suppose further that initially the inflation rate was zero. Trace out the future time path of the inflation rate following this policy change.
7. Suppose there is a rise in government expenditure, not matched by a tax rise, that at first is unanticipated, but then is maintained and subsequently becomes anticipated. Trace out the time path of the rate of inflation, output, and unemployment.

34

The 'Supply Side'

In recent years, and especially in the period since Margaret Thatcher became Prime Minister and since Ronald Reagan became President of the United States, a great deal has been heard about 'supply-side' macroeconomics. Its proponents present 'supply-side' policies as some 'new' magic that, in contrast to the old Keynesian policies, can cure all our ills of inflation, unemployment, and sagging productivity. As a matter of fact, the economic analysis that provides the basis for the propositions of the 'supply-siders', as they are known, is not new at all. It is *pre*-Keynesian. That does not mean that it is wrong. But it does mean that the way in which it is presented, especially by the media, is misleading. This chapter is designed to help you evaluate the claims of the supply-siders.

By the time you have completed this chapter you will be able to:

(a) **Explain why governments are productive.**
(b) **Explain how productive government activity affects the production function and the demand for labour.**
(c) **Explain how paying for government (taxation) affects the supply of labour.**
(d) **Explain how efficient government raises output and employment.**
(e) **Explain how overgrown government lowers output and employment.**
(f) **Describe the effects of supply-side policies on the price level.**
(g) **Explain how the supply-side analysis can be extended to apply to savings and capital accumulation.**
(h) **Explain the predictions of supply-side policies.**

A.   Why Governments are Productive

The easiest way to convince yourself that governments are productive is to conduct a thought experiment. Imagine a world in which there is no government. What are the most basic services provided by government that such a world would lack?

Perhaps the most fundamental service provided by government is the establishment of property rights and the enforcement of contracts. Thus government can be thought of as an economic agent that has a monopoly in the legitimate use of coercion. Governments use that monopoly power to require the rest of us to behave in certain well-defined ways. If we enter into contracts with each other, then we are required to fulfil our part of the bargain. Failure to do so may result in the injured party seeking a satisfactory settlement by appealing to the courts. Our persons and our physical property are also protected by criminal laws that automatically come into action if those rights are violated. The punishment of those convicted of crimes is the governments' way of imposing a price or penalty that is designed to deter such criminal activity. The provision of national defence can be thought of as a natural extension of such activity whereby the government seeks to guard the personal and physical property of its citizens against damage or theft by foreigners.

Try to imagine a world in which these services are not provided by monopoly government. How are they provided? The answer is that individuals and groups will seek to provide for their own security by carrying arms themselves or hiring others to protect them. More of human history has been characterized by such arrangements than by those with which we are familiar in the modern world. In such a world, a large volume of human and physical resources would be devoted to the provision of personal and collective security. These resources, if released from such activities, could be put to another productive use. But, in the absence of a government, private individuals are not going to see it as being in their interest to divert resources from the provision of personal security to the production of other goods and services. They will use their scarce resources in the most productive way and that will involve protecting what they have acquired rather than producing additional goods and services.

The emergence of a government with a monopoly in the use of coercion that uses that monopoly to establish and enforce property rights by operating a criminal and civil legal system, confronts rational individuals with a different set of constraints. Instead of seeing it as being in their best interests to protect what they have, individuals will benefit from the collective (or shared) provision of such protection services and will enjoy a greater measure of freedom that may be employed in other productive activities.

A second activity which would not be present in a world without government is the provision of public health services. By *public* health services we mean such things as the provision of clean drinking water, sewage services, innoculation programmes against easily communicated diseases, and the like. Public health services should be distinguished from *private* health services, which deal with the prevention and treatment of conditions specific to a given individual. It is the nature of public health services (but not private health services) that their fruits may be consumed by all regardless of individual contributions. It is likely therefore that unless the government directly organizes and provides public health services, no one will see it as being in their own interest to expend such resources to provide an appropriate level of such a service. As a consequence, disease will reduce the effective productivity of the population.

Governments provide many things other than a basic legal system and public health services. Some of these are productive, although it is a controversial matter as to whether they may be more productively provided by government than the private sector. Still other activities of government are not productive at all. They involve, in effect, the replacement of private violations of property rights with public violation.

Examples of the former activities are the provision of a road system, schools and universities, and various kinds of insurance. There is no easy way of knowing whether the government provision of these activities is more or less efficient than private provision of the same services. Certainly there are large variations across jurisdictions in this regard. Some countries (for example Switzerland) seek to provide almost everything they can privately, whereas others (for example the Soviet Union) have sought to shrink the private sector to provide only a narrow range of consumer goods. Although it is controversial and impossible to settle in any definitive way whether private or public provision other than in the area of a basic legal and security system and the provision of public health is the more productive, it does seem reasonable to suppose that the more things government provides, the more likely it is that it will start encroaching on areas where it is less able to produce efficiently than the private sector would be.

Examples of activities indulged in by modern governments that appear to have no productivity at all involve the massive income and wealth redistributions that take place. Macroeconomics is not the part of economics that deals in detail with this topic. But, we may note that if it is desired to redistribute income and wealth in an efficient way, there exist well-defined so-called negative income tax schemes that could achieve this redistribution with vast reductions in the amount of bureaucracy required as compared with the schemes that most modern governments, including that in the UK, pursue at the present time. It is also transparently obvious that most of the transfers that take place do not go from the rich to the poor, but go from the rich and the poor to the politically powerful middle. Thus, the political process itself may be seen as, to some degree, performing the same function as is performed by a less formal system and indeed more primitive system of property expropriations.

It is easy to summarize the above: some things that governments do they do better than any other agent conceivably could. A monopoly provider of law and order and national security together with public health is almost certainly the most efficient such provider. A government monopoly in most other activities is probably about equally efficient with private provision. But, as an agent that transfers wealth among individuals, government is fairly definitely inefficient.

B. How Productive Government Activity Affects the Production Function and the Demand for Labour

In order to go beyond the description of government activity in the previous section and develop an analysis of how government affects aggregate economic activity, it is necessary to see how productive government activity affects the aggregate supply curve that we studied in Chapter 17.

The first effect that we will identify is perhaps the obvious one — this is the influence of productive government activity on the short-run production function and on the demand for labour. Figure 34.1. illustrates the analysis.

Frame (a) shows the production function for two economies. One economy has no government provision of productive services such as those described above, and its production function is the one labelled $\phi(n, g_0)$. The other is an economy in which the government is providing a level of activity that supports a legal system, national defence and public health services that raise the productive efficiency of the population and enables them at each level of employment to produce more output than they could in the absence of those government services. The production function that relates to that economy is the one labelled $\phi(n, g^*)$, as representing the maximum output that can be achieved no matter what services the government provides. In other words, think of g^* as a level of government activity that maximizes the economy's productive potential.

We do not need to become bogged down here in the controversies as to precisely what government services are involved in that production function. Certainly included are the provision of law and order, defence and public health, in addition to some other activities provided by modern governments.

Just as the provision of productive goods and services by the government shifts the production function, so it also shifts the labour demand curve. Recall from the discussion in Chapter 17 that the demand for labour curve is nothing other than the marginal product of labour curve. In the no-government economy of frame (a), the marginal product of labour is very low. Thus, the demand for labour curve in such an economy would be a curve such as that shown in frame (b) and labelled $n^d(g_0)$. In con-

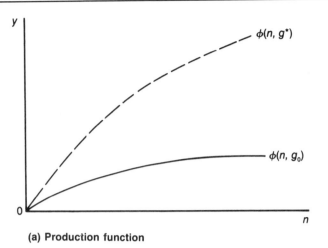

Figure 34.1
How productive
government affects
the production func-
tion and demand for
labour

(a) Production function

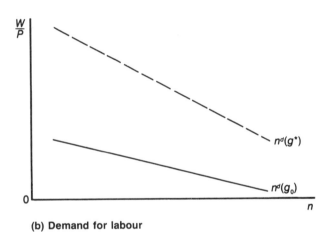

(b) Demand for labour

An economy with no government has a production function $\phi(n, g_0)$ in frame (a) and a demand for labour curve, $n^d(g_0)$ in frame (b). If the government provides productive ser- vices that enable individuals to pay less attention to the needs of their own security and also provides for basic public health, the production function and labour demand function shift upwards to become the curves labelled $\phi(n, g^*)$ and $n^d(g^*)$.

trast, in the economy that has a government providing the output-maximizing volume of public goods and services, the marginal product of labour is much higher — as depicted in frame (b) by the curve $n^d(g^*)$.

Recall that the slope of the production function measures the marginal product of labour. The slope of the production function with no government is much lower than that of the production function with productive government activity. These differences in the slopes of the production function are reflected in the levels of the demand for labour curves.

C. How Taxes Affect the Supply of Labour

Government services are paid for by taxes. Governments levy taxes on all kinds of activities, but to keep the analysis simple, we will suppose that all taxes are levied on labour income. What do taxes on labour income do to the supply of labour? Although there are qualifications to any answer (which you will probably study in a course on public finance), the basic answer is that taxes lower the supply of labour. Figure 34.2 illustrates why this is so. In this figure the curve labelled $n^s(t_0)$ is the labour supply curve in an economy that has no taxes. Thus, if the wage rate was the amount labelled 'after-tax (W/P)', then the quantity of labour supplied would be the amount labelled n^*.

Suppose now that the government was to levy a tax of an amount labelled t^*. Ask the question, How much would have to be offered in order to induce n^* workers to work in this new situation? The answer presumably is that the after-tax wage would have to be the same as the wage in the no-tax situation, which could only be achieved if the before-tax wage was the amount labelled on the vertical axis as 'before-tax (W/P)'. Thus, to induce the quantity of labour supplied to be n^*, the real wage would have to be t^* higher, if taxes were t^*, than they would have to be in a no-tax situation. The same would be true of any level of employment and so the entire labour supply schedule would be shifted to the left of $n^s(t_0)$ to become the supply curve labelled $n^s(t^*)$. Clearly the higher the taxes, the further will the supply curve shift to the left.

Figure 34.2
How taxes affect the supply of labour

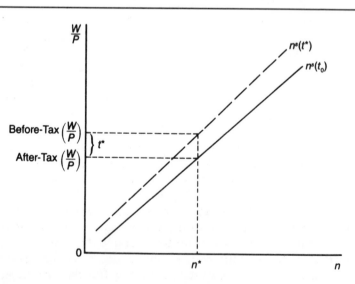

The quantity of labour supplied depends on after-tax real wages — higher after-tax real wages induce a larger quantity of labour supplied. The higher the taxes, the higher before-tax real wages have to be to induce any given quantity of labour to be supplied. Thus a tax of t^* at an employment level n^* shifts the supply of labour curve from $n^s(t_0)$ to $n^s(t^*)$.

D. How Efficient Government Raises Output and Employment

It is now possible to bring together the analysis of the two preceding sections and see how efficient government leads to a rise in both output and employment and also to a rise in real wages. There are two offsetting effects to be considered. First, the provision of government productive activities shifts the production function and the demand for labour curve upwards. Second, the payment for these government activities through taxes has the effect of lowering the supply of labour. There is a strong presumption that the former expansionary activity strongly dominates the latter contractionary activity. Figure 34.3 shows how things work out.

The figure contains two frames just like Figure 34.1 did and frame (a) is identical to that in Figure 34.1. Frame (b) of Figure 34.3 brings together the demand for labour from frame (b) of Figure 34.1 with the supply of labour from Figure 34.2. First, let us consider an economy with no government. This economy has a production function $\phi(n, g_0)$ and a demand for labour $n^d(g_0)$. With no government there are no taxes and the labour supply curve would be that labelled $n^s(t_0)$. Equilibrium in the labour market in this economy would occur at the employment level n_0 with the real wage $(W/P)_0$. The level of output in this economy would be read off from the production function in frame (a) as the amount y_0.

Contrast this economy with one in which there is a government that provides a level of services that makes it possible to raise output for each level of labour input, as depicted by the production function $\phi(n, g^*)$. In this case, the demand for labour would be $n^d(g^*)$. Assume that the government pays for its productive activities with the minimum possible taxes and that that level of taxes is t^* per worker. This tax would shift the supply of labour curve to $n^s(t^*)$. The equilibrium in this case occurs where the tax-distorted labour supply curve cuts the government productivity-enhanced demand for labour curve at n^* and the real wage rate $(W/P)^*$. The level of output in this economy is that read off from the higher production function $\phi(n, g^*)$ at y^*. Thus, in this economy, government has the effect of raising employment from n_0 to n^*, raising output from y_0 to y^*, and raising real wages from $(W/P)_0$ to $(W/P)^*$. The government has to be paid for with taxes, and the tax per worker of t^* multiplied by the number of workers n^* gives a total tax bill as indicated by the shaded area in frame (b). After-tax wages are $(W/P) - t^*$.

In terms of real world events, in the no-government economy a large amount of productive labour over and above n_0 will be expended on self-protection and property-protection, but only a small amount of goods and services (y_0) will be produced. People will be in a general state of belligerence and will not be very productive. In the economy with an efficient government, the government will be maintaining law and order (presumably with some equilibrium amount of violation taking place), and people will be freed from the need for self-protection and able to engage in productive work.

Figure 34.3
Efficient government

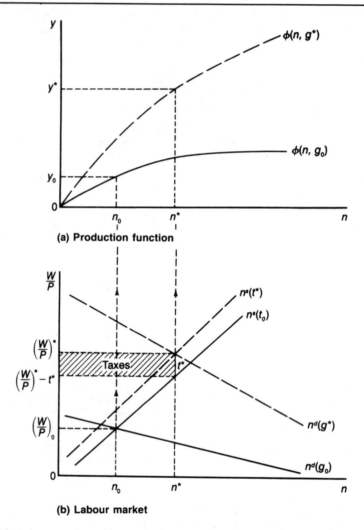

(a) Production function

(b) Labour market

An efficient government provides productive services that shift the production function up from $\phi(n, g_0)$ to $\phi(n, g^*)$ in frame (a), with an associated upward shift in the demand for labour curve in frame (b). This government activity will be paid for by the minimum possible level of taxes, which will have a modest distorting effect in the labour market shifting the labour supply curve from $n^s(t_0)$ to $n^s(t^*)$. The resulting equilibrium will be one that has higher employment (n^*), output (y^*) and after-tax real wages $(W/P) - t^*$ than in the no-government case.

E. How Overgrown Government Lowers Output and Employment

It will by now be pretty obvious to you that a government that grows too big will actually lower output. As government gets bigger and bigger, it contributes nothing extra to the productive capacity of the economy but it has a negative effect on production as a result of the fact that higher taxes lower the labour supply. Figure 34.4 illustrates an economy with an overgrown government. The equilibrium labelled y^*, n^*, $(W/P)^*$ is that for the economy with an efficient government as shown in Figure 34.3. The equilibrium marked y_0, n_0, $(W/P)_0$ is that for an economy with no government and exactly like that in Figure 34.3. Suppose that government grows bigger than the efficient size shown in Figure 34.3. Specifically, suppose the government raises taxes substantially above

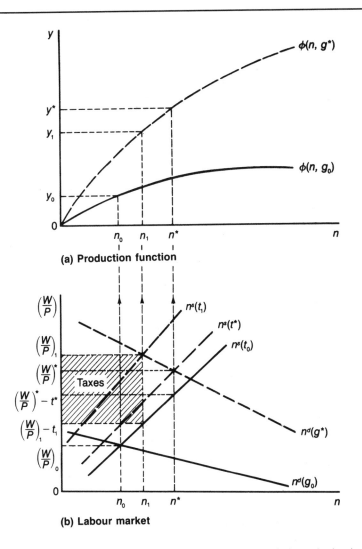

Figure 34.4
Overgrown
government

(a) Production function

(b) Labour market

A government that grows too big is one that raises taxes over and above the levels necessary to pay for the efficient scale of government, i.e. the tax rises from t^* to t_1. As this happens, the distorting effect of taxes shifts the supply of labour curve to the left from $n^s(t^*)$ to $n^s(t_1)$, thereby raising before-tax wages from $(W/P)^*$ to $(W/P)_1$ and lowering output (y^* to y_1) and employment from n^* to n_1. After-tax real wages fall from $(W/P)^* - t^*$ to $(W/P)_1 - t_1$.

those levels necessary to provide a volume of government services that maximize the productive potential of the economy.

It doesn't much matter what the government does with those taxes. The legislators may squander them on self-aggrandizement, they may be given to the poor, or they may be used to provide goods and services that would otherwise have been provided privately. The point is that the taxes are not spent on any activity that can enhance the productive capacity of the economy. Thus, the production function that is relevant remains that labelled $\phi(n, g^*)$.

The higher taxes shift the supply of labour curve to the left to a position such as that labelled $n^s(t_1)$. The demand for labour remains at $n^d(g^*)$. Equilibrium occurs at the employment level n_1 and the real wage $(W/P)_1$. The output level associated with that employment level n_1 is y_1. Clearly, by raising taxes above the minimum level necessary to provide the output-maximizing volume of government services, the government has introduced a distortion in the labour market that reduces overall work effort and output. Real wages exceed $(W/P)^*$ — those that occur in the economy with an efficient government (Figure 34.3). After-tax wages are lower in the economy with the overgrown government because the government takes a bigger tax bite — as shown by the shaded area in frame (b).

Figure 34.4 provides the essence of the supply-side argument. By lowering taxes and lowering the volume of unproductive government services provided with those taxes, it would be possible to raise output, raise employment and raise after-tax real wages. You can see this directly by comparing the equilibrium y_1, n_1, $(W/P)_1 - t_1$ with the equilibrium y^*, n^*, $(W/P)^* - t^*$. Clearly, if the overgrown government was to reduce its size to the efficient size, output, employment and after-tax wages would all rise.

In any actual real world situation there is disagreement and room for genuine doubt as to which government activities are productive and which unproductive. To a large degree disagreements between supply-siders and others turn not on the analysis contained in Figure 34.4 but on the empirical judgment concerning the productivity of government services. If reducing taxes involves reducing the provision of productive government services, then as taxes fall the production function would also fall and the demand for labour curve would shift downwards. Whether or not such a reduction in government would raise or lower output and employment depends on which of the two effects is stronger. If, at the margin, government activity is very unproductive and the distorting effects of taxes on labour supply are very severe, then a reduction in government would raise output and employment. If, in contrast, the marginal government activities are slightly productive and the disincentive effects of taxes on labour supply only slight, then a reduction in government activity could lower output and employment. There is little agreement on which of these two effects dominate and not much in the way of solid empirical evidence that can readily settle the issue.

In the above comparison of an economy with an efficient government and an economy with an overgrown government, we have stumbled onto a concept often used in discussion of supply-side matters — the so-called Laffer curve.[1]

Figure 34.5 illustrates a Laffer curve. It is a curve that measures the tax rate on the vertical axis and the amount of taxes paid on the horizontal axis. The curve has the shape shown for a reason that, if not immediately obvious will be obvious in a moment. If the tax rate was zero, fairly clearly no taxes would be paid. Thus, the Laffer curve starts at the origin of the diagram. If the tax rate was a 100 per cent then presumably nobody would do any work (or indulge in whatever other activity that tax is based on). Thus again, no revenue would be generated by the government and no taxes paid. The Laffer curve therefore bends back on itself starting at the origin when the tax rate is zero and returning to zero taxes raised when the tax rate is a 100 per cent.

For intermediate tax rates there is a range over which, as the tax rate rises, tax revenues also rise. This portion of the curve is labelled ODBC. As tax rates are increased above that marked t_m revenues fall because the activity that is being taxed will decline at a faster percentage rate than the tax rate itself increases. Figure 34.5 has been drawn such that the revenue-maximizing tax rate is 50 per cent. But, there is no presumption that 50 per cent will be the revenue-maximizing rate. Such a rate would vary and depend upon the slopes of the supply of and demand for labour curves. The economy with an efficient government shown in Figure 34.3 might be thought of as being at a point such as D on the Laffer curve. The economy with an overgrown government might be in a position such as that depicted by B on the Laffer curve.

A government that was interested in raising taxes to the maximum possible level, presumably to further the interests of bureaucrats and legislators, would levy taxes at the revenue-maximizing rate. It has sometimes been suggested that, prior to the cuts in the top tax rates that occurred in the early 1980s, UK taxes were so high that the economy was in a position like that shown as A on the Laffer curve. A moment's reflection will suggest that, though this is a possibility it is unlikely. If the government had raised taxes to such a high level that their revenues were the same as they would be with a much lower rate of taxes, then the government would be denying itself some revenue and at the same time would be inflicting costs on the rest of the economy over and above those that would be inflicted at a maximum revenue situation. In other words, at position A on the Laffer curve, the economy would generate an output level much below that being generated at position B on the Laffer curve.[2]

---

1 The Laffer curve is so-named because it was popularized by Professor Arthur B. Laffer of the University of Southern California.
2 Professor James Buchanan and Dwight Lee have an ingenious argument that suggests that perhaps it would be possible for a government to get to a position like A as a result of taking too myopic a view of the consequences of increasing tax rates. See James M. Buchanan and Dwight Lee, 'Politics, Time and the Laffer Curve', *Journal of Political Economy*, 90 (August 1982), pp. 816–19.

Figure 34.5
The Laffer curve

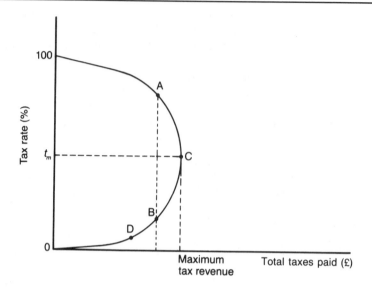

The Laffer curve shows the relationship between taxes paid and the rate of tax. At a zero tax rate no taxes are paid, and at a 100 per cent tax rate no one will have any incentive to work (or do whatever other activities are being taxed), and so again no taxes will be paid. The general shape of the curve is that shown, so that at some tax rate (t_m), tax revenues are at a maximum.

A key point to note is that it is unlikely that the economy is in a position like A and much more likely that it is in a position like B. If the economy is in a position like A, then it clearly pays to go to B, since that would involve the same tax revenues but more output and employment. However, if the economy is in a position like B, whether it would be desirable to move to a position like D depends on empirical judgments concerning the strength of supply-side effects.

F.   The Effect of Supply-Side Policies on the Price Level

Not much needs to be added to the analysis that you have already conducted in Chapter 8, Section B. There we analysed the effects of various labour market shocks on the price level, showing that anything that lowered the level of aggregate supply would raise the price level. Exactly the same considerations apply to the supply-side analysis. Any tax change which raises output will in effect shift the aggregate supply curve rightwards, thereby lowering the price level. This effect on the price level is why supply-siders believe that their policy recommendations will have advantageous effects on the inflation rate. But, it is important to notice that even if supply-side policies were successful, they would only have a once-and-for-all effect on the price level and no effect on the trend rate of inflation. That effect, as always, will be determined by the rate of growth of the money supply.

G. Extension of Supply-Side Analysis to Saving and Capital Accumulation

The entire analysis that has been conducted in terms of a short-run production function could also be extended to apply to longer-term savings and capital accumulation. Over time, the economy's productive potential grows as a result of technical progress and capital accumulation. The amount of this activity undertaken is determined by an equilibrium process much like that that determines the level of employment. Other things being equal, the more capital the economy has, the lower will be the marginal product of that capital. The higher the marginal product of capital, the more will people seek to save and acquire capital. Taxes on the income from capital will lower the incentive to save and lower the incentive to accumulate capital. These taxes will, therefore, act in exactly the same way as taxes on labour. They will reduce the amount of economic activity that is taking place and lower the output of the economy.

H. Predictions of Supply-Side Policies

This final section briefly examines the main predictions of a supply-side policy. But, it does not go into any great detail. It will simply help you to predict the outcome of such a policy.

Supply-side programmes usually have four key features. They are:

(1) The maintenance of a strong national defence system.
(2) Reductions in government expenditure on social programmes.
(3) Cuts in marginal tax rates.
(4) Deregulation and privatization.

(i) Supposed Effects (Claims by Supply-Siders)

What are the likely effects of a supply-side programme? Let us examine this question not in the journalistic terms with which you are probably familiar but in terms of the analysis that we have conducted in the previous sections of this chapter.

First, a rise in defence expenditure may be thought of as a provision of a larger volume of productive government activity. How much would be contributed by additional defence expenditure depends on the marginal productivity of the additional defence services provided. Presumably, the idea of the supply-siders is that, by providing more national defence the government is providing a greater measure of security than would otherwise be available, and that this added security is either desirable for its own sake (security is a good that people value) or because it will enable (and perhaps induce) a greater measure of confidence in the medium- to long-term future, thereby encouraging a greater volume of savings and investment.

The reduction in domestic programmes is presumably viewed as a reduction in either low-productivity or unproductive government activity. Taken together, the rise in defence spending and the cut in other programmes are viewed by supply-siders as releasing resources for productive use, thereby shifting the aggregate production function upwards.

The cuts in marginal tax rates are seen as increasing both the supply of labour and the supply of savings, thereby increasing the equilibrium amounts of employment and capital accumulation.

The deregulation and privatized aspects of a supply-side programme were not explicitly analysed in the previous sections of this chapter. You may, however, conveniently think of these policies as being equivalent to the reduction of taxes and the reduction of (unproductive?) government expenditure. If the government imposes a regulation on a private individual or firm, the effect of that regulation is to require that individual agent to undertake actions which would otherwise not be pursued. Thus the individual diverts resources from voluntary to involuntary uses. This aspect of regulation is exactly like the imposition of a tax that also diverts resources from voluntary to involuntary uses — from voluntary consumption and saving activity to the involuntary payment of taxes.

The other aspect of regulation is that it requires government itself to employ large numbers of professional and clerical labour simply to monitor the activities of those being regulated and enforce the regulations. Thus, regulation imposes additional government expenditure and additional diversions of private resources from voluntary uses. The reduction of regulation seen in these terms would involve a reduction in both taxes and government spending. Its effects, therefore, would be exactly the same as the effects of reducing taxes and reducing government spending on unproductive activities that we have analysed in earlier sections of this chapter.

In overall terms, a supply-side programme adds up to a net decrease in government spending and a net decrease in taxes — compared with their previous trend levels. But what are the effects of supply-side policies on the government's budget deficit. Supporters of supply-side policies argue that tax cuts, while temporarily raising the deficit, will eventually bring the deficit under control. They predict that the incentive effects of supply-side policies will be so strong as to raise income by enough to increase the overall tax revenues of the government in the medium and longer term.

These then, are the claims of the supply-siders. Are they justified?

(ii) Likely Effects of Supply-Side Programmes

In evaluating the effects of supply-side programmes it is vital to distinguish between long-run and short-run effects. It seems likely (and is apparently confirmed by most empirical investigations) that, in the short run, the responsiveness of labour supply and the supply of savings to changes in taxes will be small. The key reason why is that it is costly for people to change their behaviour. They will be inclined to change their behaviour only gradually in response to new conditions which call forth a different pattern of activity. Further, if there is some uncertainty as to the permanence of a change in policy, there will be even more reluctance to commit oneself to a change in behaviour. In terms of the diagrams that we have used in this chapter, you can think of this as saying that in the short run, the supply of labour curve (and the supply of savings curve) is very steep. That is, although a tax cut would indeed shift the labour supply curve (and the supply of savings curve) to the right, the amount of that rightward shift would be very small in the short run. In addition, the effects of changes in government activity on the overall productivity of the economy is likely to be slight in the short run. These two things taken together imply that the immediate and short-run effects of a supply-side policy are likely to be very small in terms of what they do to the level of employment and output.

There is an additional short-run consequence of supply-side policies. It is the essence of a supply-side policy that labour (and other) resources be *reallocated*. In other words, certain activities will be decreased and others will be expanded. For example, less urban renewal and more defence would involve a shifting of resources away from building and civil engineering activities and into electronics and high-technology metals. These are just examples of many millions of reallocations of labour and other resources. But labour is not reallocated costlessly. Workers leaving one type of job to find another job usually face a period of job search such as that analysed in Chapter 25. When policies are pursued that increase the amount of reallocation going on in the economy, they also increase the amount of job search activity. Thus unemployment rises.

We have already seen that the advocates of supply-side policies recognize that those policies will have the effect of increasing the government's budget deficit in the short run. The analysis that we have just conducted concerning short-run effects agrees with this prediction but would suggest adding an additional burden to the government's budget deficit, namely the increased expenditure on unemployment compensation that is a necessary accompaniment of the increased amount of resource and labour reallocation taking place.

The long-run effects of consistently pursuing lower taxes and lower levels of unproductive government activity will certainly, in qualitative terms, be the same as those claimed by the supply-siders. Output, employment and savings will all rise. How important this would be in *quantitative* terms is virtually impossible to say on the basis of what we currently know. Some believe that the effects would be slight; others that they would be enormous. What can be said with reasonable confidence, however, is that the long run may in fact be a very long way off. Notions of short run and long run in economic analysis are not clear statements about how long things take to happen in calendar time. Indeed, if properly understood 'short run' and 'long run' are not things that happen after a specified period of time at all. Rather, they are things that happen after certain adjustments have been made. By 'short run' we usually mean a situation in which adjustments have taken place in response to a given shock while holding constant all the stocks of the various capital assets (including human capital) in the economy. By 'long run' we mean the adjustment that will have taken place when all the capital stocks (physical and human) have adjusted to a given shock. Clearly, adjusting the stock of human capital takes at least as long as the length of time that it takes to replace a generation. Individuals typically acquire their human capital in specific form and just once in a lifetime. Long-run adjustments, therefore, can be presumed to take a very large amount of calendar time. In the intervening period the effects that will be felt will be those that pertain to the short run.

We have already seen that in the short run, supply-side policies are predicted not to make a direct contribution to the reduction in the government deficit. If a government deficit persists for a substantial amount of time, then it will place inflationary burdens on the economy. You know that this is the outcome from the analysis that we conducted, in Chapter 29, of the linkages between fiscal and monetary policy. This inflationary effect can be avoided if careful attention is paid to ensure that overall government receipts move toward covering total spending. By combining supply-side adjustments in taxes and other incentives with overall fiscal restraint the government is able to lend maximum support to an anti-inflationary monetary policy.

Summary

A.   *Why Governments are Productive*

Governments are productive because, by using their monopoly in coercion, they are able to reduce the resources involved in the protection of persons and property and are able to enforce public health standards that raise the productivity of labour. Governments do many other things that are productive, but there is controversy and imprecise knowledge concerning the productivity of those additional government activities as compared with the productivity of equivalent privately provided services. In addition, governments indulge in many activities that have either low or perhaps even negative productivity.

B. *How Productive Government Activity Affects the Production Function and the Demand for Labour*

Productive government activity can be viewed as shifting the production function upwards, so that higher output levels are attainable at each level of labour input. Similarly, the slope of the production function is increased or, equivalently, the marginal product of labour rises and so the demand for labour curve shifts upwards.

C. *How Taxes Affect the Supply of Labour*

The higher the taxes, the lower the supply of labour. The quantity of labour supplied depends on the after-tax real wage. In general, the higher is the after-tax real wage, the more labour that is supplied. Thus, a rise in taxes that lowers the after-tax wage rate causes the labour supply curve to shift to the left.

D. *How Efficient Government Raises Output and Employment*

Efficient government raises output, employment and real wages as a result of the operation of two offsetting forces, one of which clearly dominates. The dominant force is the rise in the production function and the rise in the demand for labour that results from the provision of productive government activity. To some degree offsetting this productive activity of government, although only partially so, is the effect of the taxes levied to pay for the government services. These taxes lower the supply of labour. Nevertheless, the two effects together result in higher output, higher employment and higher real wages.

E. *How Overgrown Government Lowers Output and Employment*

Government can grow too big in the sense that taxes continue to be increased and be spent on activities that do not raise the production function and the marginal product of labour. When that happens, all the effects of increased government size are negative, and the supply of labour curve shifts to the left, thereby producing a lower level of employment, lower output and a lower after-tax real wage.

F. *The Effect of Supply-Side Policies on the Price Level*

Any action that shifts the aggregate supply curve, other things given, changes the price level in the opposite direction. Thus, a rise in output resulting from supply-side policies, shifts aggregate supply to the right and lowers the price level. Supply-side policies in and of themselves have no effect on the rate of inflation, which is determined by the growth rate of the money supply.

G. *Extension of Supply-Side Analysis to Saving and Capital Accumulation*

The supply-side analysis applied in this chapter to the labour market could be equally well applied to the market for capital goods and the supply of savings. Just as higher taxes on labour income are a disincentive to work, so higher taxes on capital income are a disincentive to save. Lower savings result in lower capital accumulation and lower output. As an empirical matter, the importance of these effects is in dispute and is badly in need of detailed numerical measurement.

H. *Predictions of Supply-Side Policies*

The supply-side policies usually involve maintaining defence spending, cutting spending on social and welfare policies (relative to trend), cutting marginal tax rates, and by deregulation and privatization. In terms of the analysis of this chapter, these policies could be thought of as *attempting* to redirect government spending toward the more productive activities and improving private incentives to encourage both an increased supply of labour and savings. The hoped-for effects of these policies are higher output and employment levels, higher investment and a higher growth rate. It is recognized that these effects will occur in the long term and that in the short term it is necessary to take other actions to bring the government's budget into balance. Only by pursuing a mixture of supply-side incentive policies with overall fiscal restraint can the government hope to stimulate sustainable real economic activity and keep inflation in check.

Review Questions

1. What productive services does the government provide? List five government activities that you regard as definitely productive (*productive* meaning that the government can provide the services more efficiently than could the private sector); five activities that you think are neutral (meaning that you think that the private sector could provide them about as effectively as the government can); and finally, five activities that you think are definitely wasteful (meaning that you think that the activities either should not be pursued at all or that, if they are to be pursued, should be pursued by the private sector).
2. How do productive government activities affect the production function?
3. Show the effects of a rise in the provision of some productive government service on the demand for labour.

4. What happens to the supply of labour if taxes increase? Is it always the case that the supply of labour curve shifts in the way presented in this chapter?
5. (This question should be done only by students who have studied the appropriate microeconomic theory of public finance). Analyse the effects of a change in taxes on the supply of labour and on the demand for consumption using indifference curve analysis. What do you have to assume about the 'income effect' in order to ensure that a rise in taxes lowers the supply of labour?
6. Show in a diagram how a balanced budget cut in taxes and a cut in totally unproductive government spending affects the levels of output, employment and real wage.
7. Analyse the effects of the experiment described in the previous question on the price level.
8. Suppose that a tax cut induced an additional amount of savings. What would be the effect of the increased savings rate on the economy? (This is a more difficult question, and a full answer requires that you refer back to Chapter 24, which analysed long-term growth).

35

Prices and Incomes Policies

The emergence of rapid inflation combined with politically unacceptable unemployment rates has led, in the post-war years, to a search for new anti-inflation policies.

You already know from your understanding of the new theories of output and the price level that it is possible to reduce the rate of inflation by reducing the growth rate of the money supply. You also know that, provided the reduction in the growth rate of the money supply is anticipated, inflation will fall without causing a recession — without causing a drop in output and a rise in unemployment. However, it is practically impossible for the Bank of England to engineer a cut in the money supply growth rate that is anticipated. Simply to announce a cut is not sufficient. People have to see before they believe. The Bank of England has to convince people of its intention to lower the money supply growth rate and while it is doing so there will be a tendency for the actual money supply growth rate to be below the anticipated growth rate. In other words, the money supply will be below its anticipated level. As you know, the consequence of an unanticipated cut in the money supply is that the actual price level will be below the expected price level, and the actual level of output below the full-employment level.

It is to avoid this problem that new policies have been sought. The major alternative 'new' policy that has been widely advocated and used throughout the post-war years is that of prices and incomes policies — sometimes alternatively and more precisely called wage and price controls.

The UK and other Western European countries were among the first to embark upon such policies after the Second World War. In the UK there have been 11 episodes of wage and price controls. The US has had three such policies in the post-war years — the Kennedy 'guideposts', the Nixon controls, and the Carter 'price and pay standards'.

Although viewed by their supporters as sophisticated 'new' weapons, wage and price controls are perhaps better described as blunt old instruments.

One of the earliest recorded episodes of wage and price controls was in 301 AD, when the Roman emperor Diocletian, in his famous Edict, sought to control the prices of 900 commodities, 130 different classes of labour, and a large number of freight rates. Penalities for the violation of Diocletian's controls ran all the way to death. Controls have been used on and off ever since that time (and possibly in earlier times as well).

It is clear, then, that the controls are certainly an old and not a new idea. The view that they are a blunt instrument rather than a sophisticated weapon will take the rest of this chapter to develop. However, as a prelude to that and so as to leave you in no doubt about our view of controls, let us summarize our view in the following way:

> [T]he so-called 'new' policies are the oldest and crudest, best likened to medieval medicine based on ignorance and misunderstanding of the fundamental processes at work and more likely to kill the patient than to cure him.
>
> It was not until relatively recently in the long sweep of human history, in the seventeenth and eighteenth centuries, that the principles governing the determination of the general level of prices were made clear. The insights of Bodin and Hume and the refinements which have followed through the work and writings of Irving Fisher, Wicksell, Keynes and modern monetary theorists, such as Milton Friedman, are critical for understanding and influencing the monetary forces which determine the general level of prices [and] the rate of inflation.[1]

The new policies for controlling inflation, then, are monetary policies. There has been no essential technical advance in this field since the eighteenth century. There have been some refinements, but the fundamental ideas developed by Bodin and Hume remain the theoretical underpinnings of any successful anti-inflationary policy. The rest of this chapter is designed to help you understand and appreciate this.

By the time you have completed this chapter you will be able to:

(a) **Describe the main features of the content of a prices and incomes policy.**
(b) **Explain the distinction between a posted price and an actual price.**
(c) **Explain why wage and price controls do not affect the expected price level.**
(d) **Explain why wage and price controls do not affect the actual price level.**
(e) **Explain why wage and price controls can only make matters worse.**

---

1 From Michael Parkin, *The Illusion of Wage and Price Controls* (Vancouver: The Fraser Institute, 1976), pp. 101–2.

A.   Content of a Prices and Incomes Policy

A prices and incomes policy typically has three sets of features:

1. A set of rules about wages, prices, and, sometimes, profits.
2. A set of penalties for a violation of the rules.
3. A monitoring agency.

(i)   Rules

The rules concerning wages centre on the specification of a maximum normally allowable rate of increase of wages. Thus, for example, the policy may specify that the maximum rate of increase in wages will not normally exceed some given percentage amount over a given specified period. There are almost always exceptions clauses built into such rules. Often, these permit higher than 'normal' increases in the cases of the lowest paid workers.

The price rule sometimes takes a similar form to the wage rule. That is, a maximum allowed rate of price increase over a particular period is specified. More often, however, the price rule is couched in terms of a restriction allowing prices to rise only by an amount sufficient to cover the increased costs that arise from labour cost increases allowable under the wage rule.

Profit rules are more complex, both to state and to adminster, and often are absent. When explicit profit rules are used, they are typically couched in terms of some maximum percentage of a previous period's average profits.

(ii)   Penalties

Penalties for violation of the rules vary enormously. In the case of Diocletian's controls, the penalties ran all the way to death. In modern times they typically involve fines and *roll-backs* — a requirement that the wage or price be rolled back to the level that it would have been at had the rules been obeyed.

(iii)   Monitoring Agency

Monitoring agencies also vary enormously. Sometimes a special monitoring agency is set up. In other cases, existing government departments are used to provide the policing and monitoring, and the ordinary courts are used to carry out enforcement.

B.   Posted Price and Actual Price

There are many dimensions to a transaction. These can be conveniently summarized under three headings: (1) a price dimension, (2) a quantity dimension, and (3) a quality dimension.

When you decide to buy something, you are buying a certain quantity of a commodity of a presumed quality for a certain price. This is true not only for commodities; but it also applies to labour services. For example, you might hire a certain quality of plumber for a certain number of hours for a certain price (i.e. wage).

A prices and incomes policy seeks to control directly one dimension of a transaction, namely the price. In principle, what it is trying to control is the price at which a specific quantity and quality of product or labour service is traded. But, it is extremely difficult to monitor quantity and quality. Some examples will perhaps help to make this clear.

Suppose that the price dimension of a transaction is policed completely effectively. A good example would be the policing of the price of a university professor working for a British university. Suppose the wage of the university professor is controlled by an incomes policy and is effectively controlled to be below the market equilibrium wage. What will the professor do in that situation? It is clear that he or she will seek to maximize utility by changing either the quality or the quantity of the labour supplied. If the wage rate being offered is below the market equilibrium wage rate, then he will lower the quantity and/or quality of work below the market equilibrium quantity/quality. Specifically, he will either take more leisure or indulge in more non-teaching, non-research, income-earning activities. The effective price of a unit of professorial services will have have been controlled. The posted price will have been controlled fully, but the actual price — the price for a specific quality and quantity — will have risen in exactly the same way as it would have done in the absence of the controls.

As another example, suppose that to perform some industrial job a certain grade of electrician is required (call it a grade 3 electrician). Suppose that although a grade 3 electrician is required to do this particular job, the wages of grade 3 electricians have been controlled below the equilibrium wage, and a particular firm cannot hire enough of this type of labour. Clearly, what the firm will do is to hire the next, more expensive grade of electrician (call it grade 2), and, if necessary, upgrade people to that grade in order to get the job done and maximize profits. Again, the posted price — the price of a grade 3 electrician — will have been effectively controlled. However, the actual price paid to a particular individual supplier of effort will not have been controlled. People who otherwise would have been grade 3 electricians now become grade 2 electricians, and their wages rise in exactly the same way as they would have done in the absence of controls.

Consider a commodity market. The sticker price of a car is a posted price. But, as you know, the actual price at which a car gets traded is typically different from the sticker price, and includes a discount. Precisely what discount is offered is very hard to monitor and police. It is true that a discount is a reduction of the actual price below the posted price. However, if the posted price was controlled below its equilibrium level, then by reducing the size of the discount, the actual price could increase to achieve and maintain market equilibrium. Thus, when posted prices are controlled, the gap between posted prices and actual prices — if actual prices are at a discount — will narrow.

The distinction between posted and actual prices should now be clear from the above examples. The posted price is the visible price but not necessarily the price at which trade actually takes place. The posted price is the actual price and it is the average of all actual prices that constitutes the general price level and not the fictitious numbers that are stuck on car windshields or attached to jobs of specific grades.

Let us now move on to examine the effects of wage and price controls on actual prices. But, as a prelude it is necessary to analyse the effects of controls on *expected* prices.

C.   Wage and Price Controls and the Expected Price Level

The most sophisticated advocates of wage and price controls base their belief in the potency of these measures on a view that controls can effectively lower inflationary expectations and, as a result, lower the actual rate of inflation without generating a recession. You already know that if inflationary expectations indeed can be lowered, then it is possible to lower the inflation rate and even have an output boom while the inflation rate is falling. (Go back to Chapter 20 and study the analysis shown in Figure 20.4. If the expectations-augmented aggregate supply curve can be lowered while the aggregate demand curve is held constant, then you see that the equilibrium price level falls and equilibrium output rises.)

Let us begin our analysis of the effects of wage and price controls, then, by working out what their effects on the expected price level are. *Do wage and price controls lower the expected price level and lower the expectations-augmented aggregate supply curve?*

Figure 35.1 illustrates the analysis. The curve $AD(M_0, g_0, t_0)$ is the aggregate demand curve. To focus our attention exclusively on controls, let us hold the level of the money supply, government expenditure and taxes constant at the levels M_0, g_0, and t_0 and, furthermore, let us suppose that they are anticipated. You will recall that this assumption implies that the actual position of the aggregate demand curve and its expected position are one and the same. This assumption enables us to isolate the effects of the controls.

The curve AS is the aggregate supply curve generated from equilibrium in the labour market. The expected price level P_0^e is determined by the intersection of the aggregate demand curve and the aggregate supply curve. Through this same point at which the aggregate demand curve cuts the AS curve passes the expectations-augmented aggregate supply curve EAS_0. This aggregate supply curve is drawn for an expected price level of P_0^e which, in turn, is the rational expectation given a money supply of M_0 and a government spending level of g_0. Let us suppose

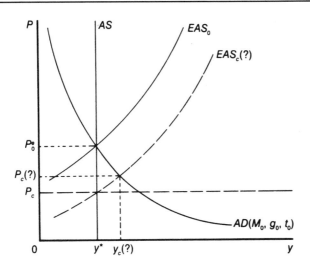

Figure 35.1
Why controls do not lower the expected price level

If the full-employment equilibrium is y^*, P_0^e, and a wage and price control programme seeks to maintain the price level at no higher than P_c, the expected price level will remain at P_0^e. If the controlled price level was the expected price level the *EAS* curve would be $EAS_c(?)$. But, in this case the price level would be $P_c(?)$. The only expected price level that is rational (that predicts itself) is P_0^e. Thus controls do not lower the expected price level.

that the economy is in equilibrium, with the actual price level at P_0^e and the output level at full employment, y^*.

Now suppose the government introduces price and wage controls. Mark on the vertical axis of Figure 35.1 the price level P_c that the government is seeking to achieve with its controls. It is the price level that would emerge if the rules that specify the allowable behaviour of wages and prices in the economy were effectively enforced. Thus the horizontal line at P_c represents the ceiling that the government would like to enforce on the price level.

It is important to recognize that there is a major difference between the government attempting to impose a price ceiling on the general price level and the imposition of a price ceiling on some specific commodity such as, say, flat or house rents. It is imaginable that sufficient resources could be devoted to monitoring and enforcing rent control regulations. But, enforcing rent controls is a far cry from being able to control the general price level. There are literally trillions of individual prices that make up a modern economy. To monitor, police and effectively control the *actual* prices — the actual as opposed to the *posted* prices — on all the trillions of different kinds of commodities and factor services would require more resources than the entire gross domestic product.

Private individuals, maximizing their utilities and profits, will do the best they can for themselves, subject to the constraints which they face. If, by adjusting the quality dimension of transactions, they can evade without detection the effects of a control on posted prices, then they will find it profitable to do so and, indeed, will do so. There is no presumption, therefore, that the actual price level in the economy will be equal to the price level that would emerge if all the rules that specified the allowable behaviour of wages and prices were followed. Such rules will not be followed, and the price level will be different from the level implied by the exact adherence to those rules.

With this in mind, we now want to return to the question, what will be the effects of controls on the expected price level? Specifically, will the target price level P_c become the expected price level? Let us conduct a conceptual experiment exactly like the one we conducted in Chapter 21 when discussing the determination of the rational expectation of the price level.

Let us first suppose that the expected price level is indeed the controlled price level P_c. Would this be a rational expectation? If P_c was the expected price level, then the expectations-augmented aggregate supply curve would become the curve $EAS_c(?)$. We have put a (?) after that expectations-augmented aggregate supply curve to remind you that we are conducting a conceptual experiment and we are asking the question, Could this be the relevant expectations-augmented aggregate supply curve once controls are imposed? You can see immediately that if the expectations-augmented aggregate supply curve is $EAS_c(?)$, and if the aggregate demand curve remains unchanged (which by assumption it does), then output and the price level will be determined at $y_c(?)$ and $P_c(?)$. Again, we have put a (?) after these quantities to remind you that they are conceptual experimental values that we are considering and not necessarily actual values that the economy will achieve.

Now, recall the concept of a rational expectation. It is the prediction implied by the relevant theory, conditional on all the information available at the time the prediction is made. If the prediction of the theory is that the price level will be $P_c(?)$, it is clear that we cannot have P_c as the rational expectation of the price level. Further, therefore, $EAS_c(?)$ cannot be the relevant expectations-augmented aggregate supply curve. If you follow through the analysis in Section F of Chapter 21 on the determination of the rational expectation of the price level, and apply that analysis to this case, you will see that there is only one price level that will be rationally expected. That price level is P_0^e. In other words, only the expected price level leads to the prediction that the actual price level will be equal to the expected price level; and hence, only the price level P_0^e is the rational expectation. It follows, therefore, that the expectations-augmented aggregate supply curve will not move as a consequence of introducing controls and will remain at EAS_0.

Another way of thinking about the above analysis is as follows. Rational economic agents will expect the price level to be determined by the forces that in fact determine the price level, namely, aggregate supply and aggregate demand. Wage and price controls (as a first approximation, to be modified in the final section) will not be expected to have much effect on aggregate supply. Further (again as a first approximation to be modified in the final section), controls will not affect the money supply or the level of government expenditure and taxes, so aggregate demand will be unaffected. Holding all these things constant, nothing that the controls have introduced would lead any rational person to expect that the actual price level would change as a result of the imposition of the controls. Hence, the rational person will expect the price level to be exactly the same with controls in place as without them.

The above remarks are to be interpreted as applying only if there is indeed no expectation that either aggregate supply AS, the money supply, government spending or taxes are going to be changed *as a consequence* of the introduction of controls. The possible effects of controls on these variables will be analysed in the final section of this chapter.

D. Wage and Price Controls and the Actual Price Level

You have now seen that the theory of output and the price level predicts that the introduction of wage and price controls will have no effect on the expected price level and no effect on the position of the expectations-augmented aggregate supply curve. It is now a simple matter to analyse the effects of controls on the *actual* price level.

Figure 35.2 illustrates the analysis. The curves AS, $AD(M_0, g_0, t_0)$, and EAS_0 are the relevant aggregate supply, aggregate demand, and

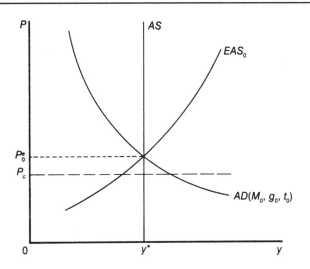

Figure 35.2
Why controls do not lower the price level (or the inflation rate)

The imposition of controls does not affect either the *EAS* curve or the *AD* curve. The equilibrium price level is determined at the intersection of those curves and therefore will be independent of the control price level.

expectations-augmented aggregate supply curve in the immediate pre-control situation. The economy is at full-employment output y^*, with the actual and expected price level at P_0^e. Now suppose that wage and price controls are imposed, which would imply, if they were fully observed, a price level of P_c, as shown on the vertical axis of Figure 35.2. What happens to the actual price level in this situation?

Recall that the actual price level is determined at the point of intersection of the expectations-augmented aggregate supply curve and the aggregate demand curve. By the analysis of the preceding section, the controls will not change the expected price level and will not, therefore, move the expectations-augmented aggregate supply curve. The expectations-augmented aggregate supply curve remains at EAS_0.

Wage and price controls are neither monetary policy nor fiscal policy. As a first approximation, there will be no change in the money supply and no change in government expenditure and taxes when the controls are imposed. Therefore, nothing happens to the aggregate demand curve when we impose controls.

Since nothing happens to the expectations-augmented aggregate supply curve, or to the aggregate demand curve, it is clear that the point at which these curves intersect remains unchanged. The price level remains at P_0^e and output remains at y^*. Thus, as a first approximation, controls have no effect on the actual price level. They may well control posted prices, and an index of posted prices may not rise by as much as actual prices. Indeed, an index of posted prices may well approximate to P_c for a period. But, the actual price level in the economy will be unaffected, and if the price index is constructed from accurate price sampling, the recorded overall price index will show a price level of P_0^e rather than the controlled price level of P_c.

It is often suggested that the use of wage and price controls in conjunction with appropriate monetary and fiscal policies (aggregate demand) can lower inflation at a more acceptable price than by pursuing demand policies on their own. The analysis that you have just been through explains to you why that line of reasoning is incorrect. You know from your analysis of the effects of monetary and fiscal policy in the three preceding chapters that a reduction in aggregate demand will have both output and price level effects. The closer the demand change comes to being anticipated, the greater those effects will be on the price level and the less on output. An ideal anti-inflation policy, therefore, would be one which lowered the rate of growth of aggregate demand in an anticipated way.

You have further seen in the analysis in this chapter that introducing wage and price controls does nothing *over and above* what is being achieved by aggregate demand policy to influence the expected price level. It follows that what is required in order to make anti-inflation policies more successful and less painful is not wage and price controls but greater credibility concerning the on-going pursuit of anti-inflationary aggregate demand policies. There are, unfortunately, good reasons for supposing that wage and price controls will actually work against the achievement of such credibility for they introduce additional problems of their own. Let us now examine these.

E. Wage and Price Controls Make Matters Worse

The conclusion of the preceding section is that wage and price controls have no effect. However, there are many reasons for supposing that they will have some effect upon the economy. It is best to regard the conclusion of the previous section as a first approximation rather than as the whole story. Let us now examine some of the possible effects.

First of all, controls divert real resources from other productive activities. The army of bureaucrats, accountants, lawyers (and even economists!) hired directly and indirectly by the wage—price monitoring agency could be employed in other productive activities. To the extent that there is a diversion of labour resources from producing goods and services (from producing y), there will be a shift in the aggregate supply available for private and government consumption. You can think of this shift in the aggregate supply curve (in Figure 35.3) as from AS_0 to AS_1. In asserting that the aggregate supply curve shifts to the left, we are asserting that the value of the output of the army of bureaucrats, accountants, lawyers, and economists employed in administering the control programme is zero.

Just as the price level may very well be incorrectly measured during a period of wage and price controls, so may the value of national income. The national income statisticians would certainly impute a value of output to those employed in administering the wage and price control programme equal to the factor incomes paid to them. In suggesting that income would fall in the event of the diversion of real resources away from productive activities to administering the programme, we are saying that the national income accounts are incorrectly calculated and that the wages of those employed in administering the programme should be regarded as a transfer payment from productive people to those who are unproductive. In this respect, it is no different from other forms of government transfer payments (although the remarks made here arise in connection with a discussion of wage and price controls, you may reflect on their more general applicability!)

Second, a wage and price control programme typically involves additional government expenditure, both on the bureaucratic side and on professional labour hired on a short-term contract basis. Such a rise in government expenditure and taxes needed to pay for this expenditure would lead to a shift in the aggregate demand curve, as illustrated in Figure 35.3, from $AD(M_0, g_0, t_0)$ to $AD(M_0, g_1, t_1)$.

It is clear that the combination of diverting resources from private activities, which lowers aggregate supply, and raising government expenditure and taxes, which raises aggregate demand curve, exerts separate but reinforcing effects on the price level. The rightward shift of the aggregate demand curve and the leftward shift of the aggregate supply curve both tend to make the price level higher than it otherwise would have been (and the inflation rate higher than it otherwise would have been). Also, output is lower than it otherwise would have been.

It would be wrong to suggest that these effects are likely to be of a large magnitude. However, they are certainly going to be present in the *directions* indicated in Figure 35.3, and there have been episodes in history when such effects may have been large.

There is a third possible factor to be taken into account. This is the effect of wage and price controls on monetary policy. With a wage and price control programme in place to control the inflation rate, it is possible that the Bank of England and government will become less concerned with maintaining anti-inflationary monetary policy. There also may be a temptation to use monetary policy in an attempt to stimulate aggregate demand, while using wage and price controls to keep inflation in check. If the money supply rises more quickly while the controls are in place, there will be a tendency for the inflation rate to rise even further than it would have done had there been no control programme.

A fourth and major consideration concerning the effects of the controls arises from the fact that some prices are in fact controlled effectively, whereas others are not. The overall average effect of controls on the general price level of zero can be seen as hiding some effective control in some particular areas, with a tendency for demand to spill over into

**Figure 35.3
Why controls can
only make things
worse**

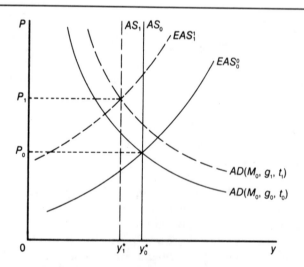

Controls divert resources from productive activity, thereby lowering aggregate supply from AS_0 to AS_1. They also involve additional government expenditure and taxes to administer the control programme. This raises the aggregate demand curve from $AD(M_0, g_0, t_0)$ to $AD(M_0, g_1, t_1)$. The consequence is a higher price level P_1 and lower output y_1. These effects are probably not large, but they are certainly in the wrong direction.

less controlled areas, where prices will rise to even higher levels than they would have in the absence of controls. If this happens (and there is good reason to suppose that it does because of the excessive attention paid by the wage and price monitoring board to specific sensitive sectors), then there will be some further serious economic losses inflicted.

Figure 35.4 illustrates the market for some particular good. It could be steel plate or any other highly visible commodity that the monitoring agency can effectively and fully control. The price on the vertical axis is the *relative* price of the good in question — the money price of the good P_i divided by the price level P. That is, the relative price $p = P_i/P$. The horizontal axis in Figure 35.4 measures the quantity of the good. The curves d_i and s_i are the demand and supply curves (which you develop in your microeconomic theory course), and p_i^* and q_i^* are the competitive equilibrium price and quantity, respectively.

Now suppose that an *effective* price control of p_c is imposed on this particular commodity. Assume that effective policing of quantity and quality ensures that p_c is the actual price and not just the posted price. It is clear that the quantity supplied will be reduced from q_i to q_c as the firms that produce this commodity seek to avoid the heavy losses that would be incurred if they maintained their output at q_i^*. The consumer places a value on the marginal quantity consumed of v_c. That is, the marginal utility of the last unit consumed exceeds the price by the distance $v_c - p_c$. The shaded triangle represents the total loss that results from the imposition of an effective price control of p_c. You can think of the shaded triangle as measuring the total difference between the value placed

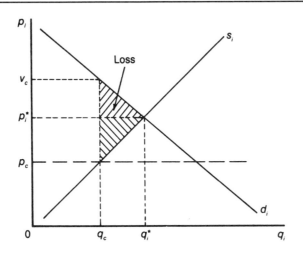

Figure 35.4
How an effective
price control causes
a loss of welfare

If a price control on some particular commodity (or group of commodities) is effective in holding the price of that good below the equilibrium level, the value placed on the commodity at the margin by the consumer (v_c) exceeds the cost of production (p_c). A loss of producer and consumer surplus (the shaded area) results.

on consumption of this commodity and the marginal cost of producing it as we move from the competitive equilibrium position of q_i^* to the controlled position of q_c. There will, in general, be a large number of losses of this kind arising from the unevenness with which wage and price controls are imposed on the economy.

Overall, then, the effects of wage and price controls that we can detect are all in the direction of either raising the price level or lowering output, or lowering economic welfare.

Summary

A. Content of a Prices and Incomes Policy

A wage and price control programme has three features:

1. Rules about wages, prices, and profits.
2. Sanctions and penalties.
3. A monitoring agency.

B. Posted Price and Actual Price

A posted price is the published or announced price; an actual price is the price at which a trade actually takes place for a given quantity and quality of product (or factor service).

C. Wage and Price Controls and the Expected Price Level

Since wage and price controls do not (as a first approximation) affect the level of the money supply or the level of government spending, they do not affect aggregate demand. Also, as a first approximation, they do not affect aggregate supply. Since they do not affect anything which determines the actual price level, it would be irrational to expect the actual price level to be affected by controls.

D. Wage and Price Controls and the Actual Price Level

The actual price level is determined at the intersection of the aggregate demand and expectations-augmented aggregate supply curves. Wage and price controls do not shift either of these curves and do not therefore affect the actual price level.

E. Wage and Price Controls Make Matters Worse

To the extent that wage and price controls divert resources from the private sector, they lower output and raise the price level. To the extent that they generate a bigger government spending level to finance the programme, they raise the price level. To the extent that they encourage slack monetary policies, they raise the inflation rate. To the extent that wage and price controls are applied unevenly and made to stick in some sectors, they generate relative distortions and produce losses of economic welfare from a misallocation of resources.

Review Questions

1. What are the three features of a wage and price control programme? Give an example of each of these features.
2. Distinguish between the actual price and the posted price in terms of the three dimensions of a trade outlined in this chapter.
3. Explain why wage and price controls may be used to control posted prices, but not actual prices.
4. List some products and the way in which each product's actual price can be adjusted in response to controls on its posted price.
5. Explain why wage and price controls cannot influence the rational expectation of the price level.
6. Work out, using the appropriate diagrams, the effects of expansionary monetary policy during a period of price controls.
7. Explain what is meant by the statement that 'wage and price controls can only make matters worse'.
8. In terms of ordinary demand and supply curves, illustrate the welfare loss associated with price controls.
9. Who benefits from wage and price controls? Why do you think they are so popular?

36

UK Macroeconomic Policy

We have now completed our examination of the theory of macroeconomic policy. The previous chapters in this part of the book have taken you through an analysis of what happens to aggregate output and the price level when alternative policy strategies are pursued. This final chapter is going to examine the macroeconomic policies that have been pursued in the UK in the post-war years. There exist many useful surveys of this topic. Most of them do not, however, examine policy from the perspective suggested by the analysis that you have just completed. The analytical viewpoint adopted by most available surveys of UK macroeconomic policy is that of the $IS-LM-BP$ model. Consequently, policy actions are descri-bed, and the likely effects of each policy change are calculated, using the types of policy multipliers that you studied in Chapters 14, 15 and 16.[1] There are a few surveys that do adopt the same analytical perspective as this book. We do not provide a detailed description of those surveys, nor do we provide a blow by blow account where we agree with or differ

---

1 The most comprehensive such surveys are J.C.R. Dow, *The Management of the British Economy, 1945−1960* (Cambridge: Cambridge University Press, 1964); F.T. Blackaby (ed.) et al., *British Economic Policy, 1960−1974*, (Cambridge: Cambridge University Press, 1978); Richard E. Caves et al., *Britain's Economic Prospects*, (Washington DC and London: Allen & Unwin, 1968), The Brookings Institution; and Richard E. Caves and Lawrence B. Krause (eds), *Britain's Economic Performance*, (Washington DC: 1980), The Brookings Institution. A useful study which adopts a narrower focus is Robert Bacon and Walter Eltis, *Britain's Economic Problem: Too Few Producers* (London: Macmillan, 1976). Two studies which fill in the political background (and which are more journalistic in style than those previously cited) are Michael Stewart, *Politics and Economic Policy in the UK Since 1964* (Oxford: Pergamon, 1978) and William Keegan and Rupert Pennant-Rae, *Who Runs the Economy* (London: Maurice Temple Smith, 1979).

from their interpretations. You should consult those surveys for yourself.[2]

You will probably find it helpful to read this chapter in conjunction with Chapter 2, as well as Chapters 25 to 27. Chapter 2 will help you to refresh your memory of the historical context in which the post-war years are placed. Chapters 25 to 27 will enable you to review your understanding of the determination of the key macroeconomic variables — unemployment, inflation, the exchange rate and the balance of payments, and interest rates — and the way in which they evolve over time to give rise to trends and cycles in aggregate economic activity. The present chapter provides you with yet a further opportunity to look at all the issues raised and discussed in those earlier ones but viewed from a very specific perspective, that of UK macroeconomic policy.

The theories of macroeconomics that you have studied in this book predict that the effects of policies depend, in part, on whether those policies are anticipated or not. This approach to macroeconomics requires that we take a broad view of the policy process in order to evaluate policy and understand the role that it might have played in influencing the economy. Since the theories that we have looked at are relatively new it is not possible to give a detailed, definitive, fully researched account of how policy has influenced the economy. Much more basic research has to be done before that is possible.[3] What we will do here is to take a broad look at the monetary and fiscal policy processes that have been at work in the UK in the post-war years, and form a tentative picture of what the major changes in direction of policy have been. We attempt to reach some tentative judgments as to whether or not the major changes in the thrust policy were anticipated or not. On the basis of our assessment we reach some tentative conclusions concerning the influence of policy on output, unemployment and inflation.

Some specific questions are suggested by the analysis that has been conducted in the previous chapters. For example, has UK macroeconomic policy been Keynesian or monetarist in nature? Yet more specifically, did

---

2 The surveys in question are Willem H. Buiter and Marcus H. Miller, 'The Thatcher Experiment: The First Two Years', *Brookings Papers on Economic Activity*, 2 (1981), pp. 315–80; Alan A. Walters, 'The United Kingdom: Political Economy and Macroeconomics', Carnegie–Rochester Conference Series on Public Policy 21 (1984) pp. 259–80; Kent Matthews and Patrick Minford, 'Mrs Thatcher's Economic Policies 1979–87' *Economic Policy*, October (1987) pp. 59–92. The papers by Walters and by Matthews and Minford give a sympathetic account of Mrs Thatcher's policies. One of us provided a critical appraisal of Walters evaluation: Michael Parkin, 'The United Kingdom: Political Economy and Macroeconomics, A Comment on the Walters Paper', Carnegie–Rochester Conference Series on Public Policy 21 (1984), pp. 281–94. Appraisals of the Matthews and Minford paper have been provided by Stephen Nickell and Elhanan Helpman in the same issue of *Economic Policy* as the original paper, pp. 93–100.
3 The survey by Matthews and Minford (see fn. 2) provides one view of the decomposition of shocks between policy and non-policy and anticipated and unanticipated focusing on the period since 1979.

UK macroeconomic policy become monetarist in the summer of 1979 following the election of the government headed by Mrs Thatcher?

This final chapter will address these questions, focusing on the period since 1950. By the time you have completed this chapter you will be able to:

(a) **Describe the content of fiscal policy.**

(b) **Describe the content of monetary policy.**

(c) **Describe the main patterns in monetary and fiscal policy and explain how those policies have influenced output, unemployment, interest rates and inflation.**

(d) **Assess the policies pursued since 1979 by the Thatcher governments.**

A. Fiscal Policy

We may summarize fiscal policy in the UK in the post-war years by using the accounting relations established in Chapter 33. That is, we may examine the course of government expenditure on goods and services, transfer payments, debt interest payments, tax receipts, receipts from the sale of new debt and the issue of new money. We know that the first three items (the expenditures) must exactly equal the second three (the receipts). The Appendix to this chapter provides a detailed listing of these data covering the period 1950–86. It is instructive to focus on the values of these variables expressed as a percentage of GDP. Three of the variables — total expenditure, total receipts, and expenditure on goods and services are graphed in Figure 36.1. Let us study that figure and see what we can learn from it about fiscal policy since 1950.

Some rather remarkable long-term patterns in the data are very apparent. Focus first on government expenditures on goods and services (g/y). After an initial expansion in 1951–2, there was a six-year downward trend in this variable that ended in 1958. For the next decade (1958–68) it followed a steady, persistent, upward trend. That trend was halted in 1968 and followed by four years in which the fraction of GDP spent by government was virtually constant. The mid-1970s saw a strong bulge in government expenditure which reached a peak in 1975. At the end of the 1970s the share of GDP being spent on goods and services by the government had returned to its mid-1960s level. In 1980 there was a sharp rise of 2 percentage points in government spending on goods and services. That rise seems to have been a permanent one. The government expenditure on goods and services has remained at close to 28 per cent of GDP throughout the 1980s.

Transfer payments by government follow a very similar pattern to spending on goods and services. This variable is visible in the figure as the vertical distance between the total government spending line and the

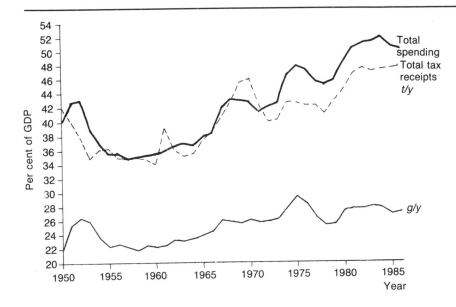

**Figure 36.1
Fiscal policy
1950–1986**

Expressed as a fraction of real GDP, government spending and taxes fell steadily from 1951 to 1958. Both then began to rise, at first gradually, but then in the late 1960s, very strongly. There was a short period (1969–72) of renewed tightening of fiscal policy, followed by a further burst of growth in spending and taxes. In the second half of the 1970s spending and taxes turned down again slightly. There was a further strong upsurge though in the early 1980s, after which spending and taxes stabilized.

Government spending on goods and services is shown separately in the figure. As you can see, its magnitude is increased but not nearly so strongly as total government spending. It has also fluctuated in sympathy with fluctuations in total spending.
Source: Appendix A to this chapter, Table 1(c).

line that measures spending on goods and services. It is clear that total spending (spending on goods and services and transfers as well as debt interest) has followed the same general pattern as spending on goods and services, but has been more volatile. The down-trend in 1952–8 is stronger, and the up-trend to 1968 is much stronger — especially so in 1967–8. When spending on goods and services was constant around 1970, transfer spending was declining somewhat. For the most part, however, the two variables have followed similar paths. The tendency for total spending (and for transfers and debt interest) to be more volatile than spending on goods and services is particularly strong in the 1980s. From 1979 to 1984, when it reached its peak, total government spending as a fraction of GDP increased by 7 percentage points. Since 1984 there has been a tendency for total government spending to fall back slightly but it remained in excess of 50 per cent of GDP in 1986.

Total tax revenue (*t/y*) has followed a course that has departed from that of total spending in some important and interesting ways. At the beginning of the 1950s, taxes fell short of spending by a sizeable amount. By 1955, however, the gap had been closed and, for the most part, during the second half of the 1950s the government sector had a modest surplus. A deficit arose briefly in 1956 and again in 1960. In 1961 there was a sudden and sharp rise in the fraction of GDP taken in taxes and that rise resulted in a substantial budget surplus. In the following year, however, taxes were cut (but not quite as dramatically as they had been increased in the previous year). Taxes continued to be cut in 1963 and a deficit re-emerged in that year. The deficit persisted until 1966 when taxes rose again fairly sharply.

Between 1969 and 1971 the government ran a very tight fiscal policy, with taxes increasing in the first of those two years and spending being cut in both of the years. As a result, a sizeable surplus emerged which persisted until 1972. In that year, however, at the same time as spending was beginning its mid-1970s bulge, a further tax cut turned the government's accounts into a deficit. Taxes rose slightly in 1974, but remained at a rather constant fraction of GDP throughout the balance of the 1970s, so that the bulge in spending that we have already examined came through as a bulge in the governments deficit. The deficit persisted through the rest of the decade of the 1970s and the 1980s. Indeed, for the entire period since 1973, there has been no trend in the government's overall budget deficit. That deficit has fluctuated between 2.5 and 5 per cent of GDP and has averaged 3.4 per cent.

The deficit is financed either by issuing debt or by creating monetary base. Money base creation has never accounted for a very large fraction of the deficit in the UK. On two occasions, in 1972 and 1974 money creation exceeded 1 per cent of GDP. For the most part, however, money creation has been a tiny fraction of 1 per cent of GDP. Thus, the bulk of the deficit is covered by issuing debt. Debt issue between 1950 and 1986 is shown in Figure 36.2. As you can see the patterns in debt issue follow closely the patterns in the deficit as measured by the gap between total government spending and total receipts seen in Figure 36.1.

Before attempting to account for these patterns in fiscal policy and also to analyse their likely effects upon the economy, let us turn to a brief description of monetary policy.

B. Monetary Policy

As you know from the analyses of Chapters 15, 16, 23, and 26, monetary policy is significantly affected by the exchange rate regime. Under a fixed exchange rate regime there is little scope for the pursuit of an independent monetary policy. In such a case, the money supply is determined by the demand for money rather than by the policy actions of the monetary authorities. Under the flexible exchange rate regime, of course, these constraints no longer operate and the money supply is the outcome

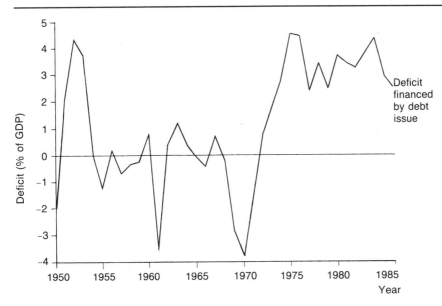

Figure 36.2
Debt issue
1950–1986

Deficit financed by debt issue

The bulk of the government's deficit — the balance of expenditure over taxes — is financed by issuing debt. This figure shows the scale of debt issue, as a percentage of GDP, between 1950 and 1986. The deficit, and debt issue, has fluctuated considerably. Surpluses were recorded in the 1950s and early 1960s and again in 1968–71. A large deficit emerged in the mid-1970s which has persisted through the balance of that decade and the entire 1980s to date.
Source: Appendix A to this chapter, Table 1(c).

of the policy actions of the monetary authority. As you also already know, the UK pursued a policy of rigidly adhering to a fixed exchange rate for the pound from 1949, when its value was first pegged at 2.80 US dollars, up to 1972 when the exchange rate was allowed to float. There was, of course, a devaluation to 2.40 US dollars in 1967 but, following that devaluation, a renewed commitment was made to pegging the exchange rate at the new value. Further adjustments in the exchange rate followed in the early 1970s and, by the middle of 1972, a fixed exchange rate for the pound was abandoned and flexible exchange rates formally adopted.

Bearing this in mind, let us now turn to an examination of Figure 36.3 which summarizes monetary policy in the shape of growth rates for three monetary aggregates, the monetary base, M1 and M3. Evidently, the change in exchange rate regime in 1972 brought with it a dramatic shift in the average growth rate of the money supply. Although money growth had been fairly volatile in the fixed exchange rate period, its volatility and average value very clearly became higher in the period after 1972. There was some tendency to increased volatility and increased average money growth in 1970–1, but the really dramatic rise occurred in 1972. Even under fixed exchange rates, it is evident that there was a slight tendency for money growth to be higher in the 1960s than it had been in the 1950s.

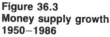

Figure 36.3
Money supply growth
1950–1986

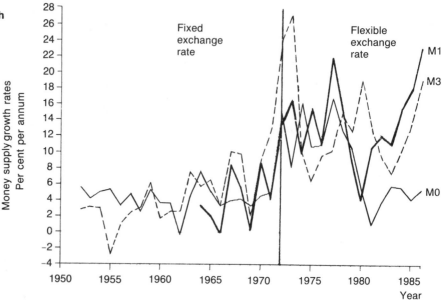

Up to 1982 the exchange rate of the pound was fixed so that fluctuations in the money supply were determined by fluctuations in the demand for money rather than by monetary policy actions. Since 1972 the pound has been flexible and money supply growth has been determined by the actions of the Bank of England. Clearly, after the pound floated, money supply growth became higher than previously and much more volatile. A strong burst of money growth in 1972–3 helped to generate the strong inflation in the UK in the mid-1970s. The tightening of monetary policy after 1978, as measured by M1 and the monetary base, is probably in part responsible for the contraction of economic activity that took place at the beginning of the 1980s. The further increase in money supply growth in the 1980s helped, in part, to increase output again.
Source: Appendix B to this chapter, Table 2.

This tendency, however, is not a reflection on the monetary policy of the UK authorities. It is a reflection of the fact that world inflation was higher in the 1960s than it had been in the 1950s and, with a fixed exchange rate, the 'law of one price' ensured that UK inflation and UK money growth increased to keep pace with the increase in world inflation.

Interpreting UK monetary policy in the flexible exchange rate period is made difficult because the different monetary aggregates have grown at very unequal rates. The picture obtained by following the growth rate of M3 is different from that shown by M1. The monetary base falls somewhere in between these two, but is somewhat closer to M1 in its overall pattern. Judged from the growth rate of M3, monetary policy became highly inflationary in the years immediately following the adoption of flexible exchange rates, then tightened substantially in 1974–5 and has been on a rising growth path since then. M1 became highly expansionary in 1972, but slowed more quickly than did M3. The acceleration of M3 growth after 1976 was matched by M1 through 1977 but, since then,

M1 growth has been falling. The growth rate of the monetary base did not rise as much as the broad aggregate in 1972–3 but continued to accelerate until 1977. Since that time monetary base growth has fallen very strongly. There was a slight upturn in the monetary base growth rate in 1982 and 1983, but there has been no further upward trend and the rate seems to have settled down at around 5 per cent a year. The other two aggregates, however, have grown at increasingly rapid rates in the mid-1980s and have followed each other closely, departing from the more stable behaviour of the monetary base.

Although there is ambiguity, it seems to us that a reasonable judgment is that monetary policy was expansionary in 1972–3. Much of the appearance of tight policy in 1973 in the M1 growth figure arises from a substitution out of non interest-bearing forms of money and into interest-bearing deposits. To some extent that was reversed in 1974. Policy became tight again in 1974–5. There was a loosening of policy through 1977–8 and, after 1978, policy became tight again. In interpreting monetary policy in this way, we are clearly putting more weight on M1 and the monetary base than on M3. This seems to us to be the correct place to put the weight, in view of the fact that the narrower aggregates more nearly correspond to the theoretical concept of money, while M3 includes term deposits and certificates of deposit which more closely resemble three-month bills of exchange than money. There is also ambiguity about the stance of monetary policy in the 1980s. Our interpretation is that monetary policy was particularly tight in 1980 and 1981, and then loosened somewhat and has remained neutral since 1982.

A feature of UK money supply growth rates both under fixed and flexible exchange rates, to which it is worth paying some attention, is their exceeding volatility. It is clearly extremely difficult to predict what the growth rate of any of these monetary aggregates is going to be one or more years into the future on the basis of the erratic way in which they have grown in the past. This is of some importance in understanding what has been happening to the UK economy.

Let us now turn our attention away from describing monetary and fiscal policy towards an attempt to discern patterns in those policies and identify some of their effects.

C. Policy Patterns and Effects

We will begin by considering briefly the political background to macroeconomic policy.

(i) The Political Background

(a) Churchill conservatism In 1951 a Conservative government led by Winston Churchill was elected to replace the Labour government of Clement Attlee. The previous Labour government had been active in

socializing much of the economy (nationalizing the coal, gas, electricity, transport and steel industries) and had been content to keep a good deal of central control over the private sector of the economy by retaining control measures introduced during the war. The newly elected Conservative government was, from a philosophical point of view, very close to the government of Margaret Thatcher and Ronald Reagan. Between 1952 and 1958, pursuing their conservative goals, the Churchill government reduced the fraction of GDP spent by the government from 43 per cent to 35 per cent. At the same time, and initially running ahead of the spending cuts, taxes were reduced from 40 per cent to 35 per cent of GDP. Thus, the Churchill government cut taxes and cut spending and eliminated a budget deficit of some 3 per cent of GDP. During this period the exchange rate was pegged and enthusiastically so. Thus, there was no independent monetary policy. World money growth and world inflation were moderate and so were UK money growth and inflation.

(b) Macmillan conservatism Following the military activities in Suez, Anthony Eden (Churchill's brief successor) was replaced as Prime Minister by Harold Macmillan, who was what might be described (depending on your preferences) as a progressive or socialistically-inclined Conservative. This more radical form of conservatism guided the formation of macroeconomic policy from 1958 to 1963. It was during that period that the long, steady trend rise in government spending both on goods and services and transfers began. By 1961, however, the pursuit of steadily increasing spending, combined with slightly falling taxes, gave rise to a deficit on the government's budget. A balance of payments deficit also emerged in that year. Remaining fully committed to a fixed exchange rate, the government had no alternative (as you know from the discussion of the government's budget constraint discussed in Chapter 29) but to make some policy changes. The particular change adopted in 1961 was a massive rise in taxes. The tax rise turned the government's budget position around and restored a surplus in the balance of payments. This gave the Macmillan government the breathing space that it needed to launch a major 'dash for growth' in 1962–3. During those two years, taxes were cut, spending increased and the government budget surplus of 1961 turned into a modest but nevertheless significant deficit by 1963. This renewed expansion of government spending and cut in taxes was not consistent with a balance of payments equilibrium and, accordingly, the balance of payments went into deficit again in 1963–4. This deficit was inherited by a new Labour government in the autumn of 1964.

(c) Wilson's first Labour government The Labour government headed by Harold Wilson, elected in the autumn of 1964, inherited from the previous Conservative government a growing balance of payments deficit. The new government was as dedicated as ever to both of the objectives that had been pursued by its predecessor — maintaining the exchange rate at 2.80

US dollars and expanding social and other government spending programmes. Further, like its predecessor, the new government was reluc-
tant to raise taxes too sharply. Accordingly, from 1964 to 1967 the Wilson
government increased public spending and also increased taxes, but the
latter not sufficiently to restore a surplus to the balance of payments. Increasing deficits and increasing difficulties in covering those deficits led
ultimately, in November 1967, to a devaluation of the pound. In the process of defending the pound, however, and in the process of further
defending it from subsequent devaluations, massive foreign borrowing
was undertaken both from the International Monetary Fund (IMF) and
other central banks. The result of this was much the same as what happens when an individual finds that debts have piled up to an uncomfor-
tably high degree: the bank manager steps in and starts ordering some
economies. That is precisely what happened to the UK. The IMF placed
severe restrictions on UK government room for manoeuvre. In the final
two years of its term of office the Wilson government, under restraints
from the rest of the world monitored by the IMF, cut government spending and raised taxes to open up a large overall surplus on the government account and, in so doing, turned the UK balance of payments
around to a massive surplus by 1970.

In many ways 1969 was a replay of 1961. During the late 1950s, the Macmillan government had tried to spend more than it raised in taxes and
more than was consistent with achieving balance on the balance of
payments. In 1961 its day of reckoning came. Similarly, the Labour
government had to face the fundamental budget constraint when it
realized that there was no other way of maintaining external balance at
the fixed exchange rate.

(d) Heath conservatism When the Wilson Labour government took office
in 1964 it inherited an economy that was suffering from a government
budget deficit and a balance of payments deficit. When the Heath Conservative government succeeded Wilson's Labour administration, exactly
the reverse situation prevailed. The last years of the Wilson government
had been spent in pursuing very tight policies which had generated a
strong balance of payments and government budget surplus. The Conservative government of Edward Heath, like the earlier Macmillan government, shared most of the social objectives of the Labour Party. Unlike
the Labour Party and the previous Conservative governments, Heath and
his followers were much more pragmatic on the issue of the exchange
rate. Indeed, they saw the fixed exchange rate as an impediment to the
pursuit of desirable growth policies. In this, they made a fundamental
error. The exchange rate, being a monetary phenomenon, is (and some
would argue ought to be) an impediment to pursuing *inflationary* policies
and not an impediment to pursuing policies of rapid technological progress and real economic growth. Nevertheless, with this philosophical
approach to macroeconomic policy, the Heath government embarked

upon a programme of massive economic stimulation. Taxes were cut dramatically and, though spending was held steady for one year (1971–2), it began to expand strongly in 1973–4. The large surplus inherited from the Labour government was quickly eroded and a deficit of almost unprecedented peacetime proportions emerged. When the balance of payments began to move into deficit (as it did by 1972) the remedy was simple — abandon the fixed exchange rate and keep the boom going. Money supply growth was accelerated at the same time as taxes were being cut and government spending on goods and services and transfers was being accelerated. By 1974 a strong inflationary situation had clearly developed.

(e)   Labour under Wilson and Callaghan   From 1974 to 1979 a Labour government was back in power, initially led by Harold Wilson but subsequently by James Callaghan. For the second time in post-war history a Labour government inherited a badly overheated economy from its Conservative predecessor. Although dedicated to the same social goals as its predecessor, the Labour government began first to hold the line on spending growth and then subsequently to cut government expenditures from their peak 1974 levels. At the same time it permitted tax revenues to decline slightly (as a fraction of GDP) and a deficit of between 3 and 4 per cent persisted. Money growth was highly erratic, but, on the average, slowed down, especially during 1978–9.

(f)   Thatcher conservatism   In May 1979 Margaret Thatcher was elected Prime Minister and inherited an economy that had been experiencing double-digit inflation and a large government budget deficit for close on half a decade. The philosophical leaning of Mrs Thatcher represented, in effect, a return to the approach embodied in the government of Churchill in the early 1950s. Smaller government and an enhanced role for personal responsibility and freedom were emphasized. In macroeconomic policy terms this amounted to a desire to cut government spending and taxes. On the monetary policy front the new government adopted, by self-proclamation, a policy described as monetarism. It even invoked the name of, and was visibly consulting with, such intellectual leaders of the monetarist school as Milton Friedman and Karl Brunner. During the balance of 1979 and 1980 the Thatcher government continued to pursue a tightening of monetary policy, held the line on government expenditures, and increased taxes. The government deficit was reduced slightly but remained close to 3 per cent of GDP. There is a remarkable contrast between the rhetoric of the government of Mrs Thatcher and its actions. The cry for small government and lower taxes has translated itself into a stable level of government, taking just over 50 per cent of GDP for its own expenditure and holding taxes constant at about 47 per cent of GDP.

(ii)   What has Triggered the Major Switches of Policy?

The political narrative of the preceding section serves to account to some extent for the broader trends in macroeconomic policy-making over the post-war years. It does not, however, in and of itself explain why there were, from time to time, sharp movements in the setting of policy instruments. What has triggered the main shifts of direction of policy? For the fixed exchange rate period up to 1972, the answer to this question is undoubtedly found in the commitment to the exchange rate with the need to achieve an external balance (or surplus). The sharp rise in taxes in 1961 and the tax rise and simultaneous spending cut in 1969–70 were clearly triggered by balance of payments problems. Further, the cut in taxes and the attempt to generate a strong output boom in 1962–3 and 1971–2 were triggered by the presence of a healthy payments balance. This strong balance of payments position was judged as allowing the more vigorous pursuit of social objectives, which has been present on a continuous basis between the Macmillan and Callaghan years, to take place.

Of course, the major policy shock in the UK in the post-war period was the abandonment of the fixed exchange rate in 1972. This policy change can be seen, however, as a natural consequence of the continuous and repeated attempt to run a fiscal policy characterized by high and growing government expenditures on goods and services and transfers, combined with a reluctance to see taxes growing at the required rate to finance those expenditures.

(iii)   What was Predictable and What was Not?

A careful, historical study which isolates what was known and not known, anticipated and not aniticipated about UK macroeconomic policy over this post-war period would be an undertaking with a very high rate of return. No one has yet provided such a study and, in its absence, all that we can do is draw some of the more obvious conclusions from the broad patterns in the evolution of policy.

First, it seems evident that the commitment to a fixed exchange rate during the 1950s and 1960s was a strong one and one that reflected a wide and deep consensus. That being so, policy expectations were almost certainly formed (at least until the mid-1960s) on the presumption that fiscal policy would be adjusted to fit in with the requirements of the fixed exchange rate. Further, the balance of payments position was a readily observable and widely known variable so that, as the balance of payments weakened, more and more people would come to anticipate a tightening of fiscal policy. That being so, it may be presumed that most of the fiscal policy actions during the fixed exchange rate period were reasonably well anticipated. Their precise magnitudes and their precise timing may not have been anticipated, but the broad direction and approximate timing almost certainly were.

During the 1960s the consensus on the exchange rate was beginning to break down. Increasingly, professional economists and others, including politicians, were expressing scepticism about the value of maintaining a fixed exchange rate. The devaluation of 1967, and the subsequent abandonment of fixed exchange rates in 1972, did not, therefore, come as a bolt from the blue. These things had to some degree been anticipated. What had almost certainly not been anticipated, however, at least not to the extent that it occurred, was the use to which a Conservative government would put the new found freedom from the exchange rate peg. When, in 1973, the government permitted money supply growth to rise to the mid-twenties per cent per annum and permitted the budget deficit to soar, this must, to a large degree, have taken people by surprise. Thus, in 1973 there was almost certainly a large positive random shock to aggregate demand generated by macroeconomic policy. Thus, a positive shock was followed by a sizeable negative shock. The rebound of money growth up to 1978 was probably not regarded as surprising, but the firm tightening of money growth after 1978 must, at least at first, have taken people by surprise especially as regards severity.

There was a further element of confusion injected into policy in the last years of the 1970s and the 1980s as a result of the continuation of a high government deficit in combination with tight monetary policies. As you know from our discussion in Chapter 29, such a state of affairs cannot continue indefinitely. Either the deficit has to be removed, or money growth will at some stage rebound as the inflation tax is used to replace the transitory and, from the long-run point of view of the government, worthless borrowing. How people will resolve this confusion is not something on which we can make firm propositions. It does, however, seem likely that people will regard a government deficit that has been in place for 14 years as being a more permanent feature of the scene than a money growth rate that seems to bounce around all over the place. Thus, with a high government deficit persisting, it is likely that the deceleration of money growth that occurred after 1978 was, to a large degree, unexpected. It is almost certain that the savage cut in money base growth from 10 per cent in 1979 to 5 per cent in 1980 and to 1 per cent in 1981 was almost entirely unexpected and the source of a massive negative shock to aggregate demand. The rebound of the money growth rate in 1982 and 1983 was probably fairly well anticipated and in line with long-term expectations. Nevertheless, if a deficit of between 2 and 3 per cent of GDP persists into the long term, it seems unlikely that money growth will be maintained at a rate consistent with low inflation.

(iv) Policy and the Economy

How do these tentative propositions about the decomposition of policy into expected and unexpected components fit the facts? Let's begin by focusing on deviations of real GDP around its trend and the random shocks that generate those deviations. We will then look at unemployment and finally at interest rates and inflation.

(a) Fluctuations of GDP around trend In Chapter 7 we described the business cycle in terms of the deviations of real GDP around its trend. We identified those deviations as being generated by a first-order difference equation disturbed by a random shock. We estimated those random shocks.

Figure 36.4 reproduces some of the data that you saw earlier in Figure 7.6. Here we concentrate only on the period since 1950. Frame (a) of the figure shows the actual deviations of GDP from trend. Frames (b) and (c) break those deviations into two parts — random shocks [in frame (c)] and the inertia representing the effects of the accumulation of all the previous shocks [in frame (b)].

The random shocks themselves may be interpreted as arising from a whole variety of sources such as foreign prices and income, long-term expectations about profit opportunities influencing investment spending, as well as unanticipated monetary and fiscal policy shocks. We have suggested that, prior to the floating of the pound, there probably wasn't very much unanticipated policy movement in the UK. Most of the shocks hitting the UK economy came from the rest of the world. During the floating exchange rate regime which began in the early 1970s, however, we suspect that there have been some major unexpected policy shifts. According to our estimates the biggest shock hitting the economy in the 1970s was a large positive one (almost 6 per cent of GDP) in 1973. This shock seems to coincide well with our supposition that both fiscal and monetary policy became unexpectedly expansionary during 1972–3. Further, according to our estimates, sizeable negative shocks occurred in both 1974 and 1975. These shocks are consistent with our notion that monetary policy was unexpectedly tight at that time.

The next negative shocks occurred in 1980 and 1981. These were the largest negative shocks experienced in the post-war period. According to our analysis in the previous section, these shocks too were generated in part by unanticipated policy, the rapid deceleration of monetary growth during 1980 and 1981 being responsible for them.[4]

Of course, the exercise that we have just conducted is not based on hard data about which policy changes were anticipated and which were not. We could equally well have started our exercise by looking at the shocks and then work backwards to figure out what the unexpected policy must have been! As a matter of fact that is *not* how we proceeded. But such an ungenerous interpretation could be placed upon it. What is now

---

4 Matthews and Minford interpret this episode differently from us, placing major emphasis on foreign shocks. They are correct in pointing out that massive deflation occurred in the United States and that UK monetary policy was not the sole source of the negative shock.

**Figure 36.4
Business cycle
fluctuations
1950–1986**

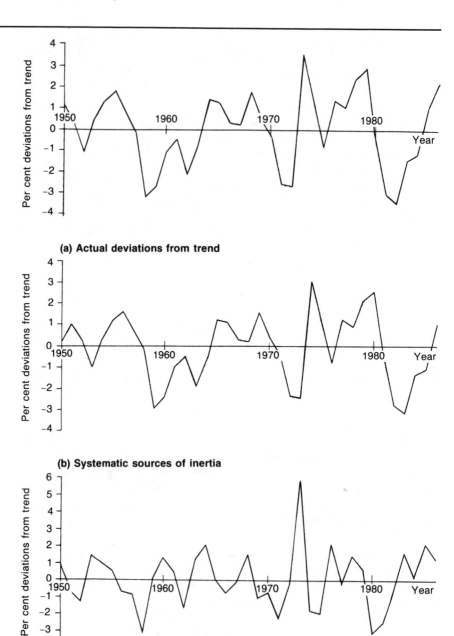

(a) Actual deviations from trend

(b) Systematic sources of inertia

(c) Purely random shocks

Business cycle fluctuations are described in frame (a). They are broken down into inertia
[frame (b)] and random shocks [frame (c)]. The random shocks arise from foreign as well
as domestic sources and non-policy and policy events. During the fixed exchange rate
era (before 1972) policy played a small role in generating these shocks. In the 1970s and
1980s, however, policy has played a major role. The two strongest shocks (a positive one
in 1973 and a negative one in 1980–1) are almost certainly associated with sharp
changes in the direction of monetary policy that were not anticipated.
Source: See Figure 7.6.

needed to provide a definitive analysis of these issues is a careful, serious, independent establishment of what was known and not known, expected and not expected, based on a detailed historical investigation. Nevertheless, we believe that the more limited exercise conducted here is an interesting one that gives insights into what might have been going on in the 1970s and 1980s in the UK.

(b) Unemployment An *unexpected* policy-induced *rise* in aggregate demand will lower unemployment below its natural rate. An *unexpected* policy-induced *fall* in aggregate demand will raise unemployment above its natural rate. How do fluctuations in unemployment line up with fluctuations in real GDP? We have already studied this relationship both in Chapter 7 (Figure 7.8) and in Chapter 25, and to help refresh your memory and focus on the salient features of unemployment relevant for the present exercise, the time series of unemployment since 1950 is reproduced in Figure 36.5.

As you can see, comparing the fluctuations of GDP from trend [Figure 36.4(a)] with the fluctuations in unemployment (Figure 36.5) there is no immediately apparent strong connection between the two variables. The dominant feature of unemployment is its upward trend, a feature which,

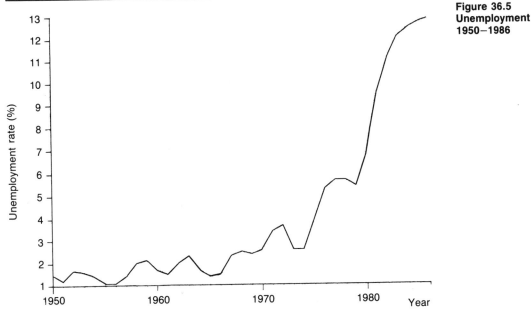

Figure 36.5 Unemployment 1950–1986

Fluctuations in unemployment have mirrored those in deviations of GDP from trend but, over and above that, have been dominated by the upward trend in unemployment itself. That upward trend is not accounted for by the random shocks to aggregate demand that we have analysed in this chapter. Rather they represent an increase in the natural rate of unemployment associated with the forces analysed in Chapter 25.
Source: See Appendix to Chapter 2.

by definition, cannot be seen in the graph of deviations of GDP from trend. Nevertheless, as we saw in Figure 7.8 (which you might like to flip back to to refresh your memory) there is a tendency for unemployment fluctuations to line up with fluctuations in real GDP. For example there are peaks in the unemployment rate in 1952, 1959, 1963 and 1972 that clearly coincide with troughs in the deviations of real GDP from trend. Also there are troughs in unemployment in 1955, 1961, 1965, 1973 and 1979 that clearly coincide with peaks in the deviations of real GDP from trend.

But the fact remains that the massive rise in unemployment, especially that occurring after 1980, is in no way connected with the types of policy shocks that we have identified earlier in this chapter. It seems clear that, though much of the rise in unemployment in 1980 and 1981 was associated with the massive unexpected monetary policy contraction of that time, the general persistent upward movement of unemployment that began in the mid-1960s and its strong continuation beyond 1982 cannot in any reasonable way be attributed to aggregate demand management policies. That rise in unemployment seems to be associated with rise in the 'natural rate' of unemployment and with the underlying forces operating upon that natural rate that we identified and elaborated upon in Chapter 25.

(c)   Interest rates and inflation   Anticipated changes in the growth rate of aggregate demand influence interest rates and inflation. Unanticipated changes in aggregate demand also influence interest rates and inflation but not by the same magnitude of anticipated changes.

Figure 36.6 focuses on the course of interest rates and inflation since 1950. We have already identified, in Chapter 26, the main influences on the trends in these variables as being trends in world inflation (up to the early 1970s) and trends in domestic monetary policy (in the 1970s and 1980s). We can also see the effects of the unanticipated policy actions (that we have identified earlier in this chapter) on these variables. Further we can see very clearly when the principal source of a shock was a shift in aggregate supply rather than aggregate demand.

The 1950s is a decade in which most of the shocks were unanticipated aggregate demand shocks. For the most part they came from the rest of the world rather than domestic policy. These shocks produced fluctuations in inflation and interest rates that coincide quite closely with the fluctuations from trend in real GDP. There is a similar pattern in the 1960s, though at somewhat higher average inflation and interest rates than had prevailed in the 1950s.

The 1970s are dominated by the supply shock that occurred in 1974 and that was reinforced by a policy-induced demand shock. The 1980s, to date, have been dominated by the massive negative demand shocks that we have already identified which not only took real GDP below trend and raised unemployment above its natural rate, but also brought inflation

**Figure 36.6
Interest rates and
inflation 1950–1986**

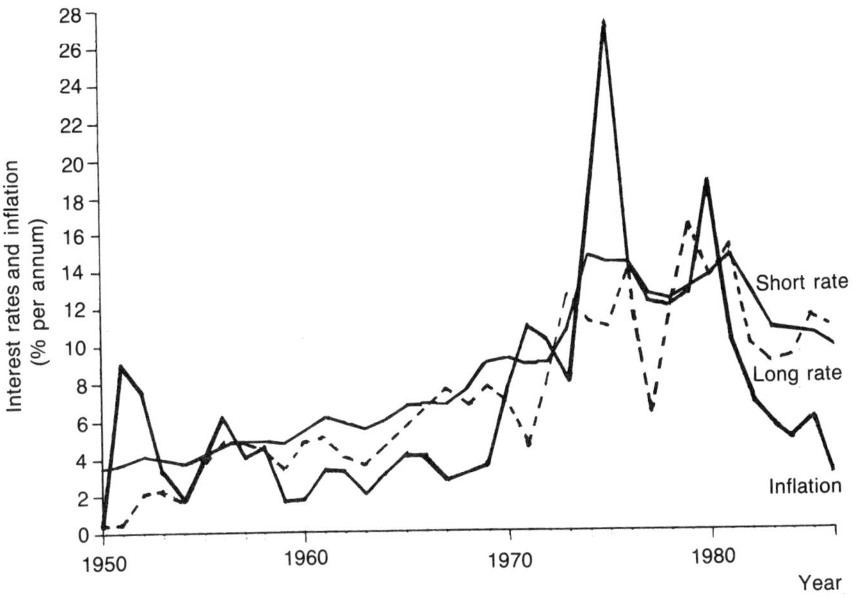

The trends in interest rates and inflation are accounted for primarily by trends in money
supply growth described in Chapter 26. Fluctuations around those trends are associated
with unanticipated fluctuations in aggregate demand and line up well with the business
cycle fluctuations of Figure 36.4.
Source: See Appendix to Chapter 2.

down dramatically from its two-digit levels of the 1970s to near price
stability by 1986.

It is noteworthy that interest rates did not fall as quickly as inflation
did during the 1980s. While we do not know for sure the reasons for this
phenomenon, a good bet is that the continuing high deficit, not only in
the UK but also in the United States, is keeping longer term inflation
expectations high, despite the return to lower inflation at the present time.

Let us now turn our attention from a long-term look at post-war UK
macroeconomic policy to its most recent episode — the period initiated
in 1979 with the election of Margaret Thatcher as Prime Minister.

D. Mrs Thatcher's Macroeconomic Policies

It is useful to consider the macroeconomic policies pursued by the Thatcher government under two broad headings: supply-side and demand-
side policies.

(i)   *Supply Side Policies*

The major supply-side policy of the Thatcher government is the restructuring of income taxes. The detailed analysis of such matters is the subject of a public finance course and a public finance text. We have already provided a brief analysis of the effects of taxes in our earlier study of supply-side policies in Chapter 34.

Mrs Thatcher's supply-side adjustment of taxes was undertaken with a constant overall level of taxes. The highest marginal rates of income taxation were reduced and the revenue lost from this operation was replaced by an increase primarily in Value Added Tax (VAT). The main predicted effect of a tax change such as that implemented, in line with the analysis of Chapter 34, is to shift the supply of labour curve to the right. As a consequence real GDP and employment are predicted to increase. However more rapid growth usually is accompanied by an increased dispersion of growth rates across sectors and regions and so calls forth an increased amount of resource reallocation resulting in a temporary, but perhaps prolonged, period of high unemployment.

The facts about real income, earnings and employment growth in recent years suggest that the economy is embarked upon a more encouraging path. Real GDP has increased by close to 3 per cent per annum, on the average, since 1980. Real wages have grown by almost 5 per cent per annum. However, the massive adjustments undertaken by the UK economy have created a heavy toll of unemployment that only in late 1987 and 1988 began to show some signs of returning to its more normal historical levels. If the predictions of Chapter 34 are correct, and if our analysis of the forces generating unemployment, reviewed in Chapter 25, are correct, UK unemployment will remain relatively high but not nearly as high as it has been through this period of massive resource reallocation associated with the Thatcher supply-side incentive changes.

(ii)   *Demand Policies*

Margaret Thatcher is a self-advertised monetarist. Is the Thatcher government monetarist? It seems to us that such a description would be inaccurate. It is certainly not accurate if the term 'monetarism' is to be used in the way in which we have used it in this book. In Chapter 1 we defined monetarism as the use of fixed rules for a limited number of macroeconomic policy instruments. Specifically, as elaborated in Chapters 31 and 32, a monetarist policy would set the money supply growing at a constant rate and hold the money stock growth rate fixed indefinitely regardless of the state of the economy. Further, as elaborated in Chapter 33, such a policy would involve placing the government's budget into a deficit that was small enough to be sustained in the long run while the money supply growth rate was maintained at its preannounced target rate.

There is no sense in which the Thatcher government could be said to have embarked upon a course such as that that characterizes monetarism. As we saw in Chapter 30, the Bank of England has not even adopted a technique of monetary control capable of delivering a growth rate of the money supply that is predictable in advance. Furthermore, as recently as 1987, the Governor of the Bank of England reverted to elevating short-term interest rates as the major instruments of monetary policy arguing that, in essence, there are no other instruments.[5] Indeed that lecture is so full of confusion that one wonders whether the Bank of England has learned anything from the experience of the past 20 years and the advances in macroeconomics that have taken place in that time and that are reviewed in this book. As we identified in Chapter 30, the instrument of monetary policy is the monetary base. The only thing that the Bank of England can control with any certainty is the scale of its own liabilities. The Governor of the Bank of England, in the lecture to which we have just referred, recognizes that the bank cannot, in fact, even control interest rates, unless its view about their appropriate levels are in line with those of the market.

Against this pessimistic and negative assessment of the Bank of England's recent pronouncements, its performance, at least as far as the control of the growth rate of the monetary base is concerned, has been encouraging. If we pay attention to what the Bank of England has done, rather than to what its Governor has said, we form the impression that perhaps the bank has been pursuing policies similar to those advocated by monetarists, at least since 1982. The target money stock, however, appears to be the monetary base itself, rather than any of the broader aggregates that include bank deposits. There is, nevertheless, one further aspect of government policy which suggests that monetarism has not been fully embraced. This feature is the behaviour of the deficit.

As we have seen earlier in this chapter, the Thatcher government has not taken steps to cut government spending and/or raise taxes by amounts sufficient to achieve a budget deficit that is compatible with long-run, steady, money growth objectives.

There is another fundamental sense in which the Thatcher government is not pursuing monetarist policies. This arises from the lack of consensus concerning monetarism, not only amongst the political parties but even within the Conservative Party. To pursue monetarist policies a course must be set which is held steady not just for a year or two, but for decades. To pursue such a policy requires a broadly based political consensus, so that people may form their expectations rationally on the presumption that the policy will be adhered to in all circumstances. In the British

---

5 'The Instruments of Monetary Policy', the seventh Mais Lecture delivered at the City University in May 1987, *Bank of England Quarterly Bulletin*, Vol. 27, No. 3, pp. 363–70, August (1987).

political system, either a change of Prime Minister and Chancellor of the Exchequer within a given political party, or a change in the political party in power, is capable of producing policy switches that are triggered by developments in the economy, thus abandoning any previously announced rules. The (unwritten) British constitution which assigns absolute power to Parliament and lacks restraints on parliamentary power and legal mechanisms for enforcing those restraints mitigates against monetarism being employed in the UK. This line of reasoning, although going well beyond the technical analysis that has been the concern of this book, suggests that the UK macroeconomy is in deep trouble and will not recover easily or quickly from its present painful state. For recovery to occur, a new consensus has to be forged, and that consensus then has to be embodied in statutes and institutions. Until that is done, we can predict (with some confidence) a continued erratic performance with a continuation of high and even possibly accelerating inflation over the longer run. Stopping that course will be a difficult task, but one that will at least not be made any harder as a result of having as thorough an understanding of macroeconomic processes as the current state of knowledge permits. We hope that this book has helped you towards such an understanding.

Summary

A. Fiscal Policy

Patterns in UK fiscal policy since 1950 are shown in Figures 36.1 and 36.2. Spending and taxes as a fraction of GDP tended to fall up to 1958. They rose from 1958 to 1968, then dipped briefly to 1972, rose again to 1975 and fell slightly in the final years of the 1970s. The deficit has fluctuated, and swung into surplus briefly in 1961 and more strongly in 1969–71. A persistent deficit emerged in 1973 and has remained firmly in place in the 1980s.

B. Monetary Policy

Up to 1972, the exchange rate of the pound was fixed so that there was, in effect, no independent domestic monetary policy. Money supply growth rates were volatile, but reflected fluctuations in world macroeconomic developments. After the pound had been floated in 1972, UK money supply growth became volatile and rapid. Money supply growth rates accelerated strongly in the 1970s and remained high until the end of that decade. In the 1980s money growth was cut back sharply, though in recent years the broader aggregates have begun to grow again at a quicker pace (Figure 36.3 illustrates).

C. Policy Patterns and Effects

The Conservative government of the early 1950s aimed at reducing the scale of government spending and taxes and succeeded in doing so. After 1958, regardless of whether the government was Conservative or Labour, the goals and objectives were the same — to expand social welfare and other government programmes and to raise government spending as appropriate. Taxes were increased more reluctantly so that, from time to time, budget and balance of payments deficits emerged. With a fixed exchange rate constraint, taxes were always increased eventually to cover the budget and restore balance of payments equilibrium. With the abandonment of a fixed exchange rate in 1972, a more sustained expansionary fiscal and monetary policy was undertaken.

Policy was probably fairly well anticipated during the fixed exchange rate period but, after the adoption of flexible exchange rates, the strength of expansion in 1972–3 was probably underestimated, and the degree of policy tightness in 1974–5 was also probably underestimated. Further, and perhaps more seriously, tight monetary policies, combined with a large and persistent deficit, are probably best interpreted as implying unexpectedly tight monetary policy. The pattern of shocks estimated (and shown in Figure 36.4) after 1972 is broadly consistent with this interpretation.

D. Mrs Thatcher's Macroeconomic Policies

Margaret Thatcher's Conservative governments have pursued supply- and demand-side policies. The main supply-side policy was a cut in the highest marginal rates of income taxation and the replacement of lost revenues by increases in other taxes, especially VAT. These policies are predicted to increase aggregate supply, but at the same time create unemployment during the process of transition. Real income growth and real earnings growth on a rapid scale in the 1980s are a sign that these policies are having their desired effects. Unemployment remained very high throughout the decade, but began to fall in 1987. The demand-side policies of the Thatcher government are self-declared monetarism. However, on the definition of monetarism employed in this book, it is evident that the Thatcher government is not a monetarist government at all. Indeed, it is difficult to visualize how there could be monetarist policy in the absence of a broad consensus embodied in appropriate statutory and institutional arrangements.

Review Questions

1. Review the main trends in fiscal policy since 1950:
   (a) during which periods was government expenditure on goods and services expanding (contracting) as a percentage of GDP?
   (b) during which periods did current tax revenues exceed (fall short of) expenditures?

2. Compare and contrast the fiscal policy patterns (the scale and directions of change in spending, revenue, and deficits) in the three decades since 1950.

3. Using the latest data available to you (which you will find in *Economic Trends*) update the figures given in Tables 1(a), 1(b), and 1(c) of the Appendix to this chapter to include 1980 (and when possible subsequent years). Is there any sign that government spending, taxes and deficit have changed markedly during the years of the Thatcher government?

4. Review the main patterns in money supply growth since 1950. During which periods was money supply growth rising? During which was it falling? During which periods is there ambiguity (because of divergences in growth rates of different aggregates)?

5. Compare and contrast money growth in the UK under fixed exchange rates with that under flexible exchange rates.

6. Has post-war macroeconomic policy in the UK been more like that described in this book as Keynesian or monetarist?

7. Examine the monetary and fiscal policies of the self-proclaimed monetarist government of Mrs Thatcher. Are those policies 'monetarist' in the sense in which that term is used by macroeconomists and as used in this book?

8. Is it possible to account for the rise in UK unemployment in 1981 to more than 3 million with existing macroeconomic models? What, according to those models, has been the role of policy in creating this unemployment? What can policy do to create a situation in which more people have jobs?

9. What have been the major influences on inflation in the UK in the period since 1950? How could policy have been modified to prevent the strong outburst of inflation in the 1970s?

10. Review the supply side policies of Mrs Thatcher's government and analyse their predicted effects on output, employment, real wages and the unemployment rate.

Appendix A: Fiscal Policy

Table 1(a) Government receipts and expenditures in current £s
(£ million)

Year	Government expenditure on goods and services	Transfer payments	Debt interest	Total outlays and receipts	Taxes	Debt issues	Money creation
1950	2 509	1 570	510	4 589	4 784	−236	41
1951	3 239	1 697	527	5 463	5 119	278	66
1952	3 693	1 739	575	6 007	5 320	582	105
1953	3 897	1 401	604	5 902	5 235	583	84
1954	3 748	1 499	602	5 849	5 703	43	103
1955	3 826	1 593	653	6 072	6 108	−152	116
1956	4 192	1 693	668	6 553	6 403	74	76
1957	4 363	1 784	666	6 813	6 832	−134	115
1958	4 454	2 014	716	7 184	7 306	−186	64
1959	4 825	2 077	688	7 590	7 606	−153	137
1960	5 091	2 236	774	8 101	7 855	147	99
1961	5 507	2 503	784	8 794	9 589	−882	87
1962	5 952	2 716	693	9 361	9 359	5	−3
1963	6 290	2 942	809	10 041	9 615	293	133
1964	6 911	3 071	807	10 789	10 366	193	230
1965	7 543	3 519	850	11 912	11 684	60	168
1966	8 206	3 753	879	12 838	12 832	−109	115
1967	9 185	4 590	948	14 723	14 312	271	140
1968	9 844	5 447	1 083	16 374	16 155	65	154
1969	10 283	5 798	1 120	17 201	18 182	−1 108	127
1970	11 465	6 187	1 126	18 778	20 289	−1 693	182
1971	12 863	6 836	1 059	20 758	21 544	−992	206
1972	14 452	8 028	1 115	23 595	22 791	155	649
1973	17 089	9 200	1 364	27 653	25 656	1 593	404
1974	21 059	12 293	1 832	35 184	32 019	2 295	870
1975	28 138	15 549	2 184	45 871	40 959	4 238	674
1976	32 262	18 450	3 031	53 743	47 584	5 402	757
1977	34 144	21 039	3 663	58 846	54 207	3 349	1 290
1978	37 675	25 266	4 308	67 249	60 276	5 813	1 160
1979	43 555	29 249	5 497	78 301	72 074	5 176	1 051
1980	54 577	35 084	7 050	96 711	88 852	7 252	607
1981	59 956	41 514	8 329	109 799	103 356	6 322	121
1982	64 884	46 974	8 728	120 586	113 884	6 256	446
1983	72 013	51 503	9 111	132 627	122 419	9 479	729
1984	76 335	56 432	10 641	143 408	131 036	11 619	753
1985	81 253	60 591	11 204	153 048	142 937	9 533	578
1986	86 823	62 362	11 106	160 291	150 328	9 187	776

Table 1(b) Government receipts and expenditures in current £s
(£ millions)

Year	Government expenditure on goods and services	Transfer payments	Debt interest	Total outlays and receipts	Taxes	Debt issues	Money creation
1950	20 962	13 117	4 261	38 340	39 970	−1 972	343
1951	24 794	12 990	4 034	41 818	39 185	2 128	505

Year	Government expenditure on goods and services	Transfer payments	Debt interest	Total outlays and receipts	Taxes	Debt issues	Money creation
1952	26 269	12 370	4 090	42 729	37 842	4 140	747
1953	26 841	9 649	4 160	40 650	36 056	4 015	579
1954	25 363	10 144	4 074	39 581	38 593	291	697
1955	24 930	10 380	4 255	39 565	39 800	−990	756
1956	25 738	10 395	4 101	40 234	39 313	454	467
1957	25 741	10 525	3 929	40 196	40 308	−791	678
1958	25 113	11 355	4 037	40 505	41 193	−1 049	361
1959	26 740	11 511	3 813	42 064	42 153	−848	759
1960	27 725	12 177	4 215	44 117	42 777	801	539
1961	29 032	13 195	4 133	46 360	50 551	−4 650	459
1962	30 403	13 874	3 540	47 817	47 806	26	−15
1963	31 497	14 732	4 051	50 281	48 147	1 467	666
1964	33 551	14 909	3 918	52 378	50 324	937	1 117
1965	35 193	16 419	3 966	55 578	54 514	280	784
1966	36 779	16 821	3 940	57 539	57 512	−489	515
1967	40 061	20 020	4 135	64 215	62 423	1 182	611
1968	41 606	23 022	4 577	69 206	68 280	275	651
1969	41 963	23 661	4 571	70 194	74 198	−4 522	518
1970	43 442	23 443	4 266	71 151	76 876	−6 415	690
1971	43 894	23 327	3 614	70 835	73 517	−3 385	703
1972	44 759	24 864	3 453	73 076	70 586	480	2 010
1973	49 053	26 408	3 915	79 376	73 644	4 573	1 160
1974	51 775	30 223	4 504	86 503	78 721	5 642	2 139
1975	54 285	29 998	4 213	88 496	79 020	8 176	1 300
1976	54 400	31 110	5 111	90 621	80 235	9 109	1 276
1977	51 271	31 593	5 500	88 364	81 398	5 029	1 937
1978	50 461	33 841	5 770	90 072	80 733	7 786	1 554
1979	51 728	34 738	6 529	92 994	85 599	6 147	1 248
1980	54 577	35 084	7 050	96 711	88 852	7 252	607
1981	54 453	37 704	7 565	99 722	93 870	5 742	100
1982	55 047	39 853	7 405	102 304	96 619	5 308	378
1983	57 801	41 338	7 313	106 452	98 258	7 608	585
1984	58 442	43 204	8 147	109 793	100 321	8 896	576
1985	58 747	43 808	8 101	110 655	103 344	6 892	418
1986	61 081	43 873	7 813	112 767	105 758	6 463	546

Table 1(c) Government receipts and expenditures in current £s

Year	Government expenditure on goods and services	Transfer payments	Debt interest	Total outlays and receipts	Taxes	Debt issues	Money creation
1950	21.87	13.69	4.45	49.00	41.70	−2.06	0.36
1951	25.35	13.28	4.12	42.76	40.06	2.18	0.52
1952	26.48	12.47	4.12	43.06	38.14	4.17	0.75
1953	25.89	9.31	4.01	39.21	34.77	3.87	0.56
1954	23.56	9.42	3.78	36.77	35.85	0.27	0.65
1955	22.42	9.33	3.83	35.58	35.79	−0.89	0.68
1956	22.71	9.17	3.62	35.49	34.68	0.40	0.41
1957	22.29	9.11	3.40	34.81	34.90	−0.68	0.59
1958	21.80	9.86	3.50	35.17	35.76	−0.91	0.31

Year	Government expenditure on goods and services	Transfer payments	Debt interest	Total outlays and receipts	Taxes	Debt issues	Money creation
1959	22.44	9.66	3.20	35.31	35.38	−0.71	0.64
1960	22.25	9.77	3.38	35.41	34.34	0.64	0.43
1961	22.51	10.23	3.20	35.94	39.19	−3.61	0.36
1962	23.30	10.63	2.71	36.64	36.63	0.02	−0.01
1963	23.13	10.82	2.98	36.93	35.36	1.08	0.49
1964	23.44	10.42	2.74	35.59	35.16	0.65	0.78
1965	23.94	11.17	2.70	37.80	37.08	0.19	0.53
1966	24.54	11.22	2.63	38.39	38.37	−0.33	0.34
1967	26.00	12.99	2.68	41.67	40.51	0.77	0.40
1968	25.85	14.30	2.84	42.99	42.42	0.17	0.40
1969	25.66	14.47	2.80	42.93	45.37	−2.77	0.32
1970	26.03	14.05	2.56	42.63	46.06	−3.84	0.41
1971	25.65	13.63	2.11	41.39	42.96	−1.98	0.41
1972	25.79	14.33	1.99	42.11	40.68	0.28	1.16
1973	26.19	14.10	2.09	42.38	39.32	2.44	0.62
1974	27.83	16.25	2.42	46.50	42.32	3.03	1.15
1975	29.36	16.22	2.28	47.86	42.74	4.42	0.70
1976	28.35	16.21	2.66	47.23	41.82	4.75	0.67
1977	26.42	16.28	2.83	45.54	41.95	2.59	1.00
1978	25.27	16.95	2.89	45.11	40.43	3.90	0.78
1979	25.40	17.06	3.21	45.67	42.04	3.02	0.61
1980	27.34	17.57	3.53	48.44	44.50	3.63	0.30
1981	27.54	19.07	3.83	50.42	47.47	2.90	0.06
1982	27.54	19.94	3.70	51.19	48.34	2.66	0.19
1983	27.93	19.97	3.53	51.43	47.48	3.68	0.28
1984	27.74	20.51	3.87	52.12	47.63	4.22	0.27
1985	26.87	20.03	3.70	50.61	47.26	3.15	0.19
1986	27.21	19.54	3.48	50.23	47.11	2.88	0.24

Sources for Table 1(a) 1950−1955:

Government expenditure on goods and services is the sum of the expenditures on goods and services by the central government and local authorities on the current account and the capital account.

Transfer payments is the sum of subsidies and grants made by the central government and local authorities on the current account and grants made by central government and local authorities on the capital account, less grants from abroad and transfers from abroad.

Debt interest is the sum of the central government's and local authorities' debt interest, less interest and dividends, etc. made by the central government and local authorities.

Total outlays and *receipts* is the sum of government expenditure on goods and services, transfer payments and debt interest.

Taxes is the sum of taxes on income, taxes on expenditure collected by central government and local authorities, gross trading income of the central government and local authorities, gross rental income of the central government and local authorities, and taxes on capital.

Debt issues is total outlays and receipts, less money creation.

Money creation is the change in monetary base.

1950   *National Income and Expenditure 1960,* Table 43, pp. 40–1.
1951–2 *National Income and Expenditure 1962,* Table 42, pp. 44–5.
1953–4 *National Income and Expenditure 1964,* Table 43, pp. 48–9.
1955   *National Income and Expenditure 1966,* Table 48, pp. 58–9.

Sources for Table 1(a) 1956–1986:

Government expenditure on goods and services is the sum of current expenditure on goods and services, non-trading capital consumption, gross domestic fixed capital formation and increase in value of stock.

Transfer payments is the sum of subsidies, current grants to personal sector, current grants paid abroad (net), and grants and other transfers.

Debt interest is the sum of the central government's and local authorities' debt interest, less interest and dividends, etc. made by the central government and local authorities.

Total outlays and *receipts* is the sum of government expenditure on goods and services, transfer payments and debt interest.

Taxes is the sum of taxes on income, taxes on expenditure collected by central government and local authorities, gross trading income of central government and local authorities, gross rental income of the central government and local authorities, and taxes on capital.

Money creation is the change in monetary base.

1956–8   *National Income and Expenditure 1967,* Table 47, pp. 56–7.
1959–65 *National Income and Expenditure 1970,* Table 43, pp. 50–1.
1966   *National Income and Expenditure 1966–76,* Table 9.1, p. 61.
1967   *National Income and Expenditure 1967–77,* Table 9.1, p. 65
1968   *National Income and Expenditure 1979 edition,* Table 9.1, p. 63.
1969–79 *National Income and Expenditure 1980 edition,* Table 9.1, p. 59.
1980–6   *National Income and Expenditure 1987 edition,* Table 9.1, p. 59.

Source for Table 1(b): Government receipts and expenditure in constant 1980 pounds are government receipts and expenditure in current pounds deflated by the GDP Deflator which has the value of 100 in 1980. The Appendix to Chapter 2 gives the GDP Deflator.

Source for Table 1(c): Government receipts and expenditure in constant 1975 pounds as a percentage of real GDP are calculated by dividing government receipts and expenditure in constant 1980 pounds by real GDP and multiplying by 100. The Appendix to Chapter 2 gives real GDP.

Appendix B: Monetary Policy

Year	MB	MB growth rate	M1	M1 growth rate	£M3	£M3 growth rate
1951	1 869	—	—	—	8 841	—
1952	1 974	5.62	—	—	9 094	2.86
1953	2 058	4.26	—	—	9 381	3.16
1954	2 161	5.00	—	—	9 670	3.08
1955	2 277	5.37	—	—	9 403	-2.76
1956	2 353	3.34	—	—	9 490	0.93
1957	2 468	4.89	—	—	9 735	2.59
1958	2 532	2.59	—	—	10 030	3.03
1959	2 669	5.41	—	—	10 652	6.20
1960	2 768	3.71	—	—	10 848	1.84
1961	2 869	3.65	—	—	11 130	2.60
1962	2 862	-0.24	—	—	11 426	2.66
1963	2 995	4.65	7 824	—	12 294	7.59
1964	3 225	7.68	8 084	3.33	13 007	5.80
1965	3 393	5.21	8 258	2.15	13 862	6.58
1966	3 508	3.39	8 247	-0.13	14 323	3.32
1967	3 648	3.99	8 952	8.55	15 771	10.11
1968	3 802	4.22	9 456	5.62	17 324	9.85
1969	3 929	3.34	9 478	0.23	17 693	2.13
1970	4 111	4.63	10 309	8.78	19 348	9.36
1971	4 317	5.01	10 758	4.35	21 842	12.89
1972	4 966	15.03	12 240	13.78	27 111	24.12
1973	5 370	8.14	14 291	16.76	34 492	27.22
1974	6 240	16.20	15 705	9.89	38 023	10.24
1975	6 914	10.80	18 135	15.47	40 480	6.46
1976	7 671	10.95	20 165	11.19	44 384	9.65
1977	8 961	16.82	24 627	22.13	48 935	10.25
1978	10 121	12.94	28 536	15.88	56 251	14.95
1979	11 178	10.44	31 129	9.08	63 390	12.69
1980	11 785	5.43	32 393	4.06	75 509	19.12
1981	11 906	1.03	35 877	10.76	85 500	13.23
1982	12 352	3.75	40 290	12.30	93 850	9.77
1983	13 081	5.90	44 820	11.24	100 791	7.40
1984	13 834	5.76	51 800	15.57	111 123	10.25
1985	14 412	4.18	61 110	17.97	126 221	13.59
1986	15 188	5.38	75 244	23.13	150 422	19.17

Source for Table B: Bank of England Quarterly Bulletin, latest available figures, earlier data rescaled to preserve growth rates in the face of changing definitions.

Index